If one thing is synonymous with the [illegible] [illegible] of [illegible], it is his passion for worship. Those who experienced firsthand the way he conducted
worship in Tenth Presbyterian Church, as much as those who only saw it
from a distance through his writings and tapes, could not fail to be struck
by this dominant concern. Its impact was both God-exalting and soul-up-
lifting. That is worship at its best, and this volume is a fitting exposition of
what it entails in its richest essence.

— Mark G. Johnston

The church needs this book! A Reformed view of the various nuances of
worship—its place in the Bible, the elements that give it legitimacy, the
personal and affective aspects of worshiping God, as well as its place in
the history of the church—has been lacking in the literature. This has finally been rectified with a volume that will stimulate discussion and inform the church.

— Iain D. Campbell

A worthy tribute of love and honor to the memory of James Montgomery
Boice. In it a galaxy of his colleagues and friends address the theme that
was the heartbeat of his life and ministry. The contributors offer important
instruction, insight, and challenge on the grand theme of worship.

— Sinclair B. Ferguson

Any book dedicated to the memory of James Boice would have to be marked
by sanctified scholarship, solid biblical content, and warm pastoral application. These essays from the pens of his friends and fellow soldiers in the
cause of the gospel meet that standard. Reading this material I found my
mind being stretched and my heart stirred.

— Alistair Begg

A significant contribution. As a theologian, I believe that worship must
be at the heart and center of all that we are, all that we do, and all that
we write. This volume helps us to focus on this fundamental priority
while also reminding us that God is concerned with the form and content of our worship.

— A. T. B. McGowan

GIVE PRAISE
TO GOD

GIVE PRAISE TO GOD

A VISION FOR REFORMING WORSHIP

CELEBRATING THE LEGACY OF

JAMES MONTGOMERY BOICE

EDITED BY
PHILIP GRAHAM RYKEN
DEREK W. H. THOMAS
J. LIGON DUNCAN III

P&R
PUBLISHING
P.O. BOX 817 • PHILLIPSBURG • NEW JERSEY 08865-0817

Unless otherwise indicated, Scripture quotations in chapters 1, 2, 5, 7, 11, 12, and 13 are from the New American Standard Bible®. Copyright © 1960, 1962, 1963, 1968, 1971, 1972, 1973, 1975, 1977, 1995 by The Lockman Foundation. Used by permission.

Unless otherwise indicated, Scripture quotations in the introduction and chapters 6, 8, 9, 10, 14, 15, and 18 are from the HOLY BIBLE, NEW INTERNATIONAL VERSION®. NIV®. Copyright © 1973, 1978, 1984 by International Bible Society. Used by permission of Zondervan Publishing House. All rights reserved.

Unless otherwise indicated, Scripture quotations in chapter 4 are from The Holy Bible, English Standard Version, copyright © 2001 by Crossway Bibles, a division of Good News Publishers. Used by permission. All rights reserved.

Unless otherwise indicated, Scripture quotations in chapter 17 are from the Revised Standard Version. Copyright © 1946, 1952, 1971 by the Division of Christian Education of the National Council of the Churches of Christ in the United States of America. Published by Zondervan Publishing House.

Page design by Lakeside Design Plus
Typesetting by Andrew MacBride

Printed in the United States of America

The Library of Congress has cataloged the hardcover edition as follows:

Give praise to God : a vision for reforming worship : celebrating the legacy of James Montgomery Boice / edited by Philip Graham Ryken, Derek W.H. Thomas, J. Ligon Duncan III.
    p. cm.
Includes bibliographical references and index.
ISBN 0-87552-553-9 (cloth)
    1. Public Worship—Reformed Church. 2. Reformed Church—Liturgy. 3. Reformed Church—Doctrines. I. Boice, James Montgomery, 1938– II. Ryken, Philip Graham, 1966– III. Thomas, Derek, 1953– IV. Duncan, J. Ligon, 1960–

BX9427.G59 2003
264'.042—dc22

    2003059661

Paperback ISBN: 978-1-59638-392-0

CONTENTS

To worship God we must know who God is, but we cannot know who God is unless God first chooses to reveal himself to us. God has done this in the Bible, which is why the Bible and the teaching of the Bible need to be central in our worship.

—James Montgomery Boice

FOREWORD

R. C. SPROUL

One of the great ironies of church history occurred in the sixteenth century in Paris. The very day that magisterial Reformer John Calvin completed his academic work at the university—the day of his departure from that place—was the same day that a young man arrived on campus dressed in the garb of a beggar, who then enrolled as a student. The young man was Ignatius Loyola, destined to become the founder of the Society of Jesus, known more commonly as the Jesuits. For the rest of the sixteenth century and into the future, the followers of Calvin and those of Loyola would be locked in fierce theological conflict as doctrinal and ecclesiastical adversaries.

James Montgomery Boice and I were hardly theological adversaries. But we did share a common twist of geographical proximity as experienced by Calvin and Loyola. We grew up about five miles from each other in the outskirts of Pittsburgh, Pennsylvania, but to either of our recollections we did not meet until we discovered each other in Philadelphia when we were both in our early thirties, functioning as theological "Young Turks."

Jim lived in McKeesport, Pennsylvania, a steel-mill town on the banks of the Monongahela River. McKeesport was directly across the river from Clairton, another mill-town in the Steel Valley, a town featured in the Hollywood movie *The Deerhunter*. I went to Clairton High School, where our Clairton Bears were the archrivals of the McKeesport High School Tigers. The athletic contests between these figurative carnivores were the stuff that fueled pep rallies, bonfires, and cheerleading squads.

I visited McKeesport many times to engage in contests of football, basketball, and baseball. My leg was broken on the goal line in McKeesport. I "ate leather" when I was stuffed in the lane by a McKeesport player who was 6'7". Our hopes of a national baseball championship died in Renzie Park where we lost to McKeesport by the score of 1–0. In a word, my memories of McKeesport are grim—so grim that I frequently wondered, "Can any good thing come out of McKeesport?"

But that was before I met Jim Boice, and before I realized that he had no part in the ignominy of my many defeats at the hands of the hated Tigers. Jim went away to high school in Stony Brook, New York, where he played his high school football.

If it is true that men are simply grown-up boys and that the man never sheds the boy inside, then it would seem to follow that what is in the boy will give a glimpse into what the man will be. The position a lad plays on a football team gives a clue to his personality and character. Given this axiom it would seem that Jim Boice must have been a quarterback or a deft halfback. Not so. Jim Boice played fullback. He was the player called on when it was third and short and the team desperately needed a first down. It was Boice up the middle; Boice with head down and legs churning to produce three yards and a cloud of dust.

In the model of the fullback, we see a person who must have courage, perseverance, tenacity, and character. These attributes were manifested with a vengeance in the life of James Montgomery Boice. He became a scholar, preacher, statesman, reformer, author, conference speaker, editor, and the voice of "The Bible Study Hour." To accomplish these many and varied tasks he had to be gifted with an uncommon, nay uncanny, measure of discipline. But whatever the task, whatever the obstacle, Jim Boice lowered his head and went without fear into the middle of the line.

When I reflect on Jim Boice's ministry, four things stand out to me—four accents—four passions that gripped his soul. The four may be distinguished one from the other, but they are all inseparably related and never functioned in isolation from each other. The four passions of Jim Boice's

Christian life and ministry were (1) the inspiration and authority of the Bible, (2) the doctrines of grace, (3) preaching via the exposition of the word, and (4) godly worship in the life of the church.

The first Festschrift I ever read was dedicated to my graduate-school mentor G. C. Berkouwer of the Free University of Amsterdam. Since Berkouwer sought zealously to build his theology on a biblical foundation, his Festschrift was entitled *Ex auditu verbi* (Out of the hearing of the word).

Surely Jim Boice was one who had an acute sense of hearing the word. Of course, he did far more than listen to it. He expounded it. He taught it. He preached it. He defended it. He lived it. As a follower of the sixteenth-century Reformers, Jim, like Luther before him, had a conscience that was held captive by the word of God. The captivity of his conscience by Scripture could be seen with facility in even a casual observation of the man. He wrote many commentaries on various books of the Bible. He preached through much of the Bible in his thirty-plus years in the pulpit of Tenth Presbyterian Church in Philadelphia.

Dr. Boice's firm commitment to sacred Scripture may be seen in the service he rendered to the International Council on Biblical Inerrancy. Jim was chairman of the council through its ten-year mission to restore the church's confidence in the divine origin, inspiration, and authority of the Bible. The council included such Christian leaders as Francis Schaeffer, J. I. Packer, Edmund Clowney, Roger Nicole, John Gerstner, and Norman Geisler. The highlight of this endeavor was the Chicago Summit that involved over two hundred scholars and leaders who drafted and adopted the Chicago Statement on Biblical Inerrancy.

The second passion that grew out of the first was Dr. Boice's passion for the doctrines of grace that are central to Reformed theology. He saw in these doctrines, abbreviated by the *solas* of the Reformation, the crystallized essence of biblical theology. It was his love and passion for these doctrines that prodded him to launch the Philadelphia Conference on Reformed Theology, which expanded far beyond the confines of the City of Brotherly Love to be held annually at sites all across America.

One of my great memories of time shared with Jim Boice is in sharing the pulpit in many of these conferences, as well as in other conference events of like format. I remember one week-long conference where Jim and I were co-lecturers. We were lecturing on the classic five points of Calvinism to an audience that was almost monolithically Arminian in their theological orientation. The experience for me was somewhat like antiphonal singing. I would give a lecture with some bold passion. Then Jim would rise to give his lecture with even greater boldness. His passion ignited me so that my next lecture was even more fiery. And so it went. If no one else in attendance was moved by what we were saying, we knew for certain that we were moving each other.

It was also his passion for the doctrines of grace that provoked Jim to found the Alliance of Confessing Evangelicals. The mission of the alliance is to call the church away from worldliness and back to its confessional roots. The Alliance of Confessing Evangelicals held a major conference in Cambridge, Massachusetts, in the shadow of Jim's alma mater, Harvard University. This convocation produced the Cambridge Declaration, with its reaffirmation of the *solas* of the Reformation.

The third passion of Dr. Boice's life and ministry was expository preaching. This was his trademark as a pastor. Jim had no time for using the pulpit to entertain people or to offer pop psychology for their felt needs. As the Old Testament priests were called upon to weep between the porch and the altar, so Jim Boice saw it as his duty to tremble between the study and the pulpit. He understood that what the people needed to hear was not the latest Christian fad or the private opinions of the pastor. They needed to hear a word from God—an unvarnished, unembellished, undiluted, accurate, and faithful exposition of God's very word. It was the word of God preached that stirred Jim Boice's juices and fueled his viscera. Of course, Dr. Boice loved the sacraments. But he always saw the sacraments as tied to the word, as the sign and seal of its teaching.

The fourth passion of Dr. Boice was his passion for godly worship. If he shared Luther's zeal for the doctrine of justification by faith alone (*sola fide*), so he also shared Calvin's zeal for the reform of worship (*soli deo gloria*).

Worship for Dr. Boice meant honoring God in spirit and in truth. It required giving the sacrifice of praise in a godly manner. He was deeply concerned about the encroachment of the world's methods into the sanctuary—methods used to entertain and justified by a misguided sense of evangelism. Just as word and sacrament belong together, so Jim Boice saw a necessary marriage between word and worship.

O how I loved to stand next to him on the chancel floor as we sang the great hymns of the church. Jim would put his right hand in the right rear pocket of his suit pants as he sang. He would rise and fall on his toes as he lifted his voice in exuberant praise. He was remarkable in his memory of all the verses of the classic hymns. I loved joining him without the use of the hymnal as we sang the strains of "A Mighty Fortress" or "Holy, Holy, Holy." But after those two hymns I had to resort to peeking. When I fled to the hymnal to remember the words to great hymns Jim would look at me with a mischievous glint in his eye that instantly reminded me of my dereliction in failing to master all the verses.

Jim's love of hymnody based on Scripture was not exhausted by the singing of traditional hymns. It also led to another contribution he gave to the church—the hymns that came from his pen. Those hymns celebrate the grand themes of the Bible and set forth in majestic language the doctrines of grace.

This book serves as a Festschrift in memory of James Montgomery Boice. As a "written celebration" it is designed not only to serve as a memorial to Jim's ministry but also to provide a platform for continuing reflection on the great issues that absorbed his energy during his life and ministry. Were he still with us in this world, the contents of this book would yield a warm smile and radiant look, signifying his delight and pleasure with its themes.

James Montgomery Boice and the Huguenot Fellowship

WILLIAM EDGAR

Royalties for the present volume will be awarded to the Huguenot Fellowship's special fund for the James Montgomery Boice Chair of Practical Theology at the Reformed Seminary in Aix-en-Provence, France. The principle of a professor's chair, following the practice of many academic institutions, is to endow an individual faculty position with sufficient capital so that the salary, benefits, and employer tax obligations can be funded from the income.

Naming this chair after Jim Boice is a most meaningful way not only to honor his memory, but to recognize one of his great priorities. A founding member and the vice president of the Huguenot Fellowship, Jim had a special love for church work in French-speaking Europe. He spoke the language well, and he and his family visited France and Switzerland regularly. He was one of the major leaders in the formation of an evangelical congregation in Suisse Romande. A number of his books are translated into French and are much appreciated by readers from Europe to Africa.

But the connection between Jim's work and the seminary at Aix goes back even further. The property on which the seminary stands was purchased in the 1940s with funding provided by Donald Grey Barnhouse, the remarkable pastor of the Tenth Presbyterian Church in Philadelphia, and

Jim's predecessor. Barnhouse was a Francophile and spent much of his free time in France, preaching in the local Reformed churches.

When Edmund P. Clowney, then president of Westminster Theological Seminary, founded the Huguenot Fellowship in 1978, he immediately called on Jim to be on the executive committee of the trustees. Meetings were held at Tenth Presbyterian Church. To this day, the Huguenot Fellowship exists to support the seminary at Aix-en-Provence and all works connected to it.

The seminary restructured in 1974, becoming a confessionally based institution at the service of several churches and committed to the task of planting new churches throughout the French-speaking world. The board and professors there believe that a large part of the Protestant church today has lost touch with its Reformation roots. There is considerable theological confusion in the historic denominations, and the seminary responds by staying resolutely evangelical and Reformed. No more than Luther and Calvin in their day, the seminary does not want to stop the clock at a particular moment of history. The Reformation sought to reshape the church in the image of biblical doctrine, which had become obscured in the Middle Ages. Likewise, the Reformed Seminary at Aix seeks to renew the church by shining the light of biblical truth on its life.

The seal of the seminary shows the burning bush from Exodus 3, a traditional symbol of the persecuted church in France. The tetragramaton, yhwh, the name of the Lord, appears in the flame. Under it are the words *mon nom pour l'eternité* (my name forever, from Ex. 3:15). Indeed, the Lord has guided the French church through many times of affliction. This bush has remained inviolate down through the centuries. Similarly, in spite of many hindrances, the work of the seminary in Aix carries on, reflecting God's own light, shining like a bright fire in a dark world. This academy features a full theological curriculum, including instruction in Old and New Testaments, apologetics, systematic theology, church history, and practical theology. All of these are crucial, and we could hope for a day when each faculty position in each of these disciplines would be fully endowed.

Why begin with practical theology? First, because it is a *final* discipline, summing up all the others and applying them to the needs of the ministry. Second, because the practical theology department at Aix has already proven itself particularly effective. Through the leadership, most notably, of Pierre Courthial and Harold Kallemeyn, the practical theology department provides numerous ways for students to train for hands-on ministry. According to Kallemeyn, practical theology is a bridge from seminary into the real world of the church and the mission field. It seeks to move from foundational instruction to practical instruction. From preaching to counseling, catechism, missions, church-planting, and diaconal outreach, the preparation received at Aix is both thorough and effective.

A third reason is that practical theology captured Jim Boice's heart in a special way. We do not know all of the reasons. But as Richard A. Muller puts it: "Inasmuch as practical theology is *theology* and a category for the gathering together of several theological subdisciplines, it brings with it both the theoretical considerations characteristic of its separate disciplines and the theological *praxis*, the orientation toward the goal of salvation that is characteristic of all the theological disciplines."[1] Like many American Christians, Jim had a particular burden for the practical outworking of theological training. Because of this, we believe this cause will strike a responsive chord in the hearts of many of the readers of this book.

In addition to the purchase of the present volume, gifts may be made directly to the Huguenot Fellowship. We are a charitable, nonprofit foundation, type 501(c)(3), and all gifts are tax deductible. They may be earmarked for the general budget, most of which goes to special projects of the Reformed Seminary, or to the James Montgomery Boice Chair of Practical Theology. Simply send them to The Huguenot Fellowship, P.O. Box 877, Glenside, PA 19038. *Soli deo gloria!*

INTRODUCTION

PHILIP GRAHAM RYKEN

James Boice loved to worship. One of the remarkable things about his public ministry was the obvious and intense pleasure he took in giving praise to God. Dr. Boice brought a special exuberance to the celebrations at Christmas and Easter, as well as to the many Bible conferences where he was a featured speaker. Then there was the Philadelphia Conference on Reformed Theology, for him the high point of the worship year. Those who attended will recall how he used to sing without his hymnal, rocking forward and backward to the music and grinning at the triumphant close of Luther's great hymn, "A Mighty Fortress."

His enthusiasm was not for show. James Boice always approached the weekly worship service at Tenth Presbyterian Church with the same joyous dignity, expecting God to gain glory for himself through the praises of his people. Worship—majestic, historic, logocentric, theocentric, christocentric worship—was one of his consuming passions.

A Life of Worship

In a Festschrift it is customary to give some account of the life of the person whose work is celebrated. This is not the place for a full biography. That would be somewhat unnecessary, since many of Dr. Boice's experiences and accomplishments are described in a special memorial magazine entitled *The Life of Dr. James Montgomery Boice, 1938–2000*.[1] This *is* the place, however, to trace his life of worship in the church.

Some of James Boice's earliest experiences of public worship took place in Philadelphia's historic Tenth Presbyterian Church. Not long after his first birthday, his parents moved to Philadelphia, where his father, Newton, was to study medicine at the University of Pennsylvania. Newton's mother, Nettie, was an avid listener to "The Bible Study Hour," featuring Donald Grey Barnhouse, and she urged the family to attend Barnhouse's famous church in Center City.

The Boices ended up worshiping at Tenth Presbyterian Church for about two years. It was there that young Jimmy learned his first Bible verses, which are still preserved in a family album. It was also there that a famous encounter took place. One night shortly before Christmas, Newton dropped his wife, Jean, and son at the door of the church and went to look for parking. Once inside, they were met by the imposing figure of Dr. Barnhouse, who said, "What, may I ask, are you doing here tonight?"

Jean responded, "Isn't this the night for the Christmas party for the children?"

"No, it's next Sunday—you come back next Sunday."

"Suddenly," Jean remembers, "he picked Jim up, put his hand on Jim's head, and prayed silently. I didn't hear the prayer, but I always felt that the Lord used that prayer in a special way in Jim's life."[2]

Dr. G. Newton Boice eventually took up his medical practice in McKeesport, Pennsylvania, where the family made many lifelong friends at the First Evangelical Free Church. The minister there, Philip Hanson, preached clear, biblical sermons, and the Boice children were nourished by the church's Bible-based Sunday school curriculum. The family's oldest son was about twelve years old when he had his first opportunity to preach. His sermon received an encouraging response from the senior men in the congregation, and the boy was given his first confirmation that God was calling him to the gospel ministry.

James Boice left McKeesport not long afterward, shortly before starting the eighth grade. Dr. Barnhouse often traveled to western Pennsylvania on preaching tours in those days, and he was a frequent visitor to the Boice home. One evening in late summer 1951 he spoke with the Boices about sending their son to Stony Brook, a Christian prep school on Long Island. The younger Boice later recounted the conversation for an alumni magazine:

> We had been talking about Stony Brook as we sat around the dinner table one Friday evening. As it turned out, this was the Friday on which the fall term at Stony Brook was beginning. In the course of the conversation he [Barnhouse] asked, "Jimmy, would you like to go to Stony Brook this year?" I said, "Yes." So he answered, "All right." And he got up from the dinner table—we were between the main course and dessert—went to the telephone and called Dr. Frank E. Gaebelein, who was the headmaster at the time. I was admitted by phone, and two days later on Sunday I was on Long Island.[3]

Stony Brook was a rich experience, not only for its academic, athletic, and dramatic challenges, but also for its godly role models and keen sense of Christian purpose.

From Stony Brook, James Boice went on to Harvard University. While there was no question about that school's academic excellence, there had been some concern about its spiritual atmosphere. Yet Boice was active in the Inter-Varsity Christian Fellowship and attended the historic Park Street Church, where he sat under the expository preaching of Harold John Ockenga.

In the fall of 1960 James Boice began his graduate studies in divinity at Princeton Theological Seminary. Shortly after matriculating, he received word that Donald Grey Barnhouse had died suddenly from a brain tumor. Barnhouse had a profound personal influence on his eventual successor, and his death led Boice to recommit himself to God's service. Remembering the request that Elisha made when Elijah was taken up into heaven (2 Kings 2:1–14), Boice asked for a double portion of God's Spirit.

At Princeton, James Boice was confronted by the neo-orthodox doctrine of Scripture, with its tendency to undermine biblical authority. His recollections of the struggle to clarify his own convictions are worth quoting in full:

> I wrestled with the inerrancy of the Bible during my seminary years. It is not that I questioned it. My problem was that my teachers did not believe this, and much of what I was hearing in the classroom was meant to reveal the Bible's errors so that students would not depend on it too deeply. What was

a student to do? The professors seemed to have all the facts. How were professors to be challenged when they argued that recent scholarship has shown that the old, simplistic views about the Bible being inerrant are no longer valid and that therefore we should admit that the Bible is filled with errors?

As I worked on this I discovered some interesting things. First, the problems imagined to be in the Bible were hardly new problems. For the most part those problems were known centuries ago, even by such ancient theologians as Augustine and Jerome, who discussed apparent contradictions in their substantial correspondence.

I also discovered that the results of sound scholarship have *not* tended to uncover more and more problems, as my professors were suggesting, still less disclose more and more "errors." Rather they have tended to *resolve* problems and to show that what were once thought to be errors are not errors at all.[4]

Resolving these issues was crucial for Boice's future ministry, which was based on the exposition of the Bible as God's authoritative word. Many years later, on the occasion of his twenty-fifth anniversary at Tenth Presbyterian Church, he summarized his doctrine of Scripture: "We believe the Bible to be the Word of God, the only infallible rule of faith and practice . . . and . . . we believe the Bible must be the treasure most valued and attended to in the church's life."[5]

James Boice's commitment to the Bible compelled him to pursue further studies in the New Testament. By this time he had married Linda McNamara, and the couple traveled to Basel, Switzerland, where Boice studied for his doctorate with Professor Bo Reicke. The most obvious benefits of this time of preparation were academic: He received a first-rate education in biblical exegesis. But there was also time for significant involvement in Christian ministry. Sensing a greater need for worship and Bible teaching, a Filipino couple proposed beginning a worship service for English-speaking internationals. Soon a church began to meet in the Boice living room. Some friends rented a piano to accompany hymns, family members shipped thirty copies of the Inter-Varsity hymnbook, and Boice preached weekly from his own studies in the New Testament. Eventually the Basel Community Church, as it was called, also hosted a Monday night prayer meeting, a midweek Bible study for business people, and occasional congregational dinners.

James Boice later credited that small fellowship with teaching him what was essential for a true church. The participants in a weekly Bible study were the ones who asked, "Couldn't we meet for worship together, and for you to teach us, Jim?" The times of fellowship came from a recognized need for Christian community. Similarly, the weekly prayer meeting was established, not because of tradition, but because of the evident need for prayer. Later the church outgrew the Boice apartment and began to meet in a building owned by the Moravians. With the added space came the opportunity to start a children's Sunday school class. The church was small, but complete, with Bible teaching, prayer, worship, and fellowship. Furthermore, its international membership gave witness to the worldwide communion of the saints.

The story of this congregation in Switzerland makes this a logical place to mention Dr. Boice's lifelong interest in promoting Reformed theology among the Protestant churches of French-speaking Europe. Until the time of his death he served as vice president of the Huguenot Fellowship, which for many years met in his office at Tenth Presbyterian Church. In his honor, the fellowship has established the James Montgomery Boice Chair of Practical Theology at the Reformed Seminary in Aix-en-Provence. The editors of and contributors to the present volume are pleased to donate their royalties to help fund this new academic post.

Upon his return from Switzerland, Dr. Boice served as an assistant editor for *Christianity Today*, where he served under Carl F. H. Henry, the evangelical stalwart and champion of biblical orthodoxy. Yet Boice had not abandoned his aspiration to serve as a minister of the gospel. He often preached on weekends, especially at McLean Presbyterian Church in Virginia. He also completed his requirements for ordination, which took place in April 1967 and was arranged by Robert Lamont, minister of First Presbyterian Church in Pittsburgh. Henry preached the sermon, closing with these memorable words: "James Boice, you bear the name of a brother of our Lord. You cherish the message of all the apostles. May you share the momentum of the apostle to the Gentiles in matching the myths of our age with the timeless truth of the revelation of God's word."

The following spring, through a providential series of circumstances, James Montgomery Boice was called to become minister of Tenth Presbyterian Church. There he would have the opportunity to apply everything he had learned about Bible-based, God-glorifying worship in the context of a local church.

The Worshiping Church

James Boice often taught on the subject of worship—from the pulpit, over the airwaves, and in print. Usually he began by emphasizing the priority of worship. This is what human beings were made for: to give praise to God. In the words that he loved to quote from the Westminster Shorter Catechism: "Man's chief end is to glorify God, and to enjoy him forever" (Q. 1). Dr. Boice also quoted from John Stott: "Christians believe that true worship is the highest and noblest activity of which man, by the grace of God, is capable."[6]

What is worship? From his study of English literature from Chaucer to Shakespeare, James Boice knew that the word *worship* is derived from "worth-ship." To worship God, therefore, is to assign him his supreme worth, acknowledging him to be the Creator and Redeemer revealed in the holy Scriptures. Similarly, the word *glory* (*doxa*) in the Greek New Testament means to have a good or right opinion of some illustrious individual. To worship God, then, is to have the correct opinion about him, properly recognizing his holy sovereignty.

God is to be worshiped "in spirit and in truth" (John 4:24). Dr. Boice often quoted these words of Jesus to the woman at the well, and they came to have a significant influence on his teaching about worship. Some of his comments are worth quoting at length:

> Many people worship with the body. This means that they consider themselves to have worshiped if they have been in the right place doing the right things at the right time. In Christ's day the woman (at Sychar) thought this meant being either in Jerusalem, at the temple there, or on Mount Gerizim at the Samaritans' temple. In our day this would refer to people who think they have worshiped God simply because they have occupied a seat in a church on Sunday morning, or sung a hymn, or lit a candle, or crossed themselves, or knelt in the aisle. Jesus says this is not worship. These customs may be vehicles for worship. In some cases they may also hinder it. But they are not worship in themselves. Therefore, we must not confuse worship with the particular things we do on Sunday morning.
>
> In addition, however, we must not confuse worship with feeling, for worship does not originate with the soul any more than it originates with the body. The soul is the seat of our emotions. It may be the case, and often is, that the emo-

tions are stirred in real worship. At times tears fill the eyes or joy floods the heart. But, unfortunately, it is possible for these things to happen and still no worship to be there. It is possible to be moved by a song or by oratory and yet not come to a genuine awareness of God and a fuller praise of His ways and nature.

True worship occurs only when that part of man, his spirit, which is akin to the divine nature (for God is spirit), actually meets with God and finds itself praising Him for His love, wisdom, beauty, truth, holiness, compassion, mercy, grace, power, and all His other attributes.[7]

Given the priority that he placed on honoring God in our worship, Dr. Boice understandably was troubled by the shift from God-centered to human-centered worship in the contemporary church. Particularly in the last years of his ministry, he believed that many (if not most) Christians had forgotten the meaning of true worship. In seeking to explain this unfortunate phenomenon, Dr. Boice observed the following connections between contemporary culture and the evangelical church: (1) Ours is a trivial age, and the church has been deeply affected by this pervasive triviality; (2) ours is a self-absorbed, human-centered age, and the church has become, sadly, even treasonably self-centered; and (3) our age is oblivious to God, and the church is barely better, to judge from its so-called worship services.[8]

In Dr. Boice's view, the result of God's dramatic disappearance from Christian worship could only be a catastrophic loss of divine transcendence, not only in our worship, but in every aspect of the Christian life. The Cambridge Declaration he helped to produce gave voice to his concern:

> Whenever in the church biblical authority has been lost, Christ has been displaced, the gospel has been distorted, or faith has been perverted, it has always been for one reason: our interests have displaced God's and we are doing his work in our way. The loss of God's centrality in the life of today's church is common and lamentable. It is this loss that allows us to transform worship into entertainment, gospel preaching into marketing, believing into technique, being good into feeling good about ourselves, and faithfulness into being successful. As a result, God, Christ and the Bible have come to mean too little to us and rest too inconsequentially upon us.[9]

The only way to recover is to honor God in our worship. To that end, James Boice was a strong advocate of the order of service used at Tenth Presbyterian Church, an order that has remained largely unchanged for a century or more and is still in use today.

The service begins with the call to worship. Dr. Boice often chose a text related to the theme of the sermon, but these verses from Isaiah 55, with their emphasis on the ministry of God's word, were a special favorite:

> As the rain and the snow
>   come down from heaven,
> and do not return to it
>   without watering the earth
> and making it bud and flourish,
>   so that it yields seed for the sower and bread for the eater,
> so is my word that goes out from my mouth:
>   It will not return to me empty,
> but will accomplish what I desire
>   and achieve the purpose for which I sent it. (Isa. 55:10–11)

The call to worship is followed by the doxology, the invocation, and an opening hymn of praise. Then comes a responsive reading from the Psalms. From week to week the congregation reads consecutively through the Psalter; upon the completion of Psalm 150, the cycle begins again with Psalm 1. Next the congregation stands to sing the *Gloria patri* as a response to the psalm and also to confess its faith using the words of the Apostles' Creed. These ancient liturgical elements serve to connect God's people with the communion of saints across time and space.

The service continues with the pastoral prayer—usually a long one. Dr. Boice abhorred perfunctory prayers and believed that public worship should include a comprehensive prayer of adoration, confession, thanksgiving, and supplication. At Tenth Presbyterian Church the pastoral prayer covers a wide range of personal, congregational, national, and international concerns.

Tenth Presbyterian Church has also revived the Puritan practice of including a regular Scripture reading in the service, preceded by five or so minutes of exposition. Although by Puritan standards the preliminary comments are brief, visitors sometimes mistakenly assume that they have already heard the sermon! The readings themselves are taken from consecutive passages in the New Testament. Late in Dr. Boice's pastorate, a segment called "Living Church" was added at this point in the order of service. Living Church is used for baptism, public reception of new members, ordination, installation, commissioning, missionary and other ministry reports, and public testimonies of God's work in the church.

Following the Living Church and prior to the sermon is another hymn and an offertory. Here perhaps something more should be said about music in worship. In keeping with his commitment to total excellence, Dr. Boice worked with a series of talented musicians to expand the music ministries of Tenth Presbyterian Church. His top priority was vigorous congregational singing of the great hymns of the faith. He loved to point out that among the major world religions, Christianity alone gave its followers something to sing about: eternal life through the death and resurrection of Jesus Christ. Dr. Boice also recognized the important role that instrumentalists, choirs, and soloists can play in moving God's people to prayer and praise and also in proclaiming God's word.

The high point of the service is the sermon. Indeed, everything else in worship builds to this point: the clear, careful exposition of God's word. Dr. Boice's vibrant yet serious demeanor when leading worship produced a strong sense of expectancy and gravity to what was about to happen when he entered the pulpit to preach. His commitment to systematic expository preaching is well known and is amply documented in his many books and commentaries. He often observed that the minister's primary purpose is simply to teach the Bible, and his ministry was characterized by serious Bible teaching. Over the course of his thirty-two-year ministry he sought to preach the whole counsel of God, working his way—passage by passage—through whole books of Scripture. His substantial preaching legacy includes many of the New Testament epistles, the gospels of Matthew and John, Genesis, the Minor Prophets, Psalms, and his famous sermons on Romans, as well as shorter series on books like Joshua and Nehemiah.

Six times each year, morning worship culminates in the reverent celebration of the Lord's Supper. The service always concludes with a hymn and a benediction. Here again, Dr. Boice often correlated the text to his theme, but he had a special fondness for the end of Romans 11:

> Oh, the depth of the riches of the wisdom and knowledge of
> God!
> How unsearchable his judgments,
> and his paths beyond tracing out!

> "Who has know the mind of the Lord?
>   Or who has been his counselor?"
> "Who has ever given to God,
>   that God should repay him?"
> For from him and through him and to him are all things.
>   To him be the glory forever! Amen. (Rom. 11:33–36)

James Boice's commitment to a traditional order and style of worship is widely known. What is perhaps less widely known is his commitment to the participation of children in worship. He did not believe in lowering the content or quality of worship for their sake—"dumbing down," as he called it. On the contrary, he believed in helping children grow into spiritual maturity by teaching them how to give praise to God. "The goal we should have with our children," he wrote, "is to bring them up to the level of the adults— that is, to enable them to begin to function on an adult level in their relationships to God. . . . Even if they cannot follow what goes on at first, our task is to teach them so they both can and will."[10]

Especially in the last years of Dr. Boice's ministry, a concerted effort was made to help the children of Tenth Presbyterian Church glorify and enjoy God in their worship. A special children's bulletin clarifies difficult words in the creed or hymns and provides questions to help the children understand the sermon. First and second graders are dismissed before the sermon to receive additional instruction in worship. The children sing hymns, study the Apostles' Creed, and learn the sermon passage. But Dr. Boice himself introduced the most significant change. During the opening exercises of the children's Bible school, he began to give a five-minute summary of the main points of his sermon. This enables the children to listen with understanding during worship; it also strengthens their relationship with their pastor.

Dr. Boice's passion for worship never diminished. If anything, the last years of his ministry were characterized by a growing zeal for God and his glory. Perhaps this was fueled in part by his preaching through the Psalms from 1989 to 1997. These sermons were later published, and in the preface to the third and final volume, Dr. Boice notes:

What is particularly striking about these last psalms is that in one way or another they all deal with worship. All the psalms are intended for worship and have been used in worship throughout the ages, but these final psalms in particular teach us what true worship is, who should worship, and when and how we should praise God. I can think of few points of Bible teaching that are of greater importance for today's church, when worship of God in so many of our churches is at a low ebb.[11]

Like the close of the Psalter, Dr. Boice's ministry ended with a crescendo of praise. His final series of sermons came from Revelation. The sermons were memorable, and few in the congregation will ever forget their pastor's preaching on the worship of heaven. Speaking of the importance of confessing our faith by singing God's praise, he asked, "Can anything be more joyful and uplifting than that? Nothing at all, until we do it perfectly in the presence of our Savior and God." God was preparing Dr. Boice—and his church—for his entrance into glory.

Something else important happened during that last year in ministry. For the first time in his life James Boice was writing hymns—twelve of them in all, plus two songs for children. This too was part of his preparation for glory. It was also his last gift to the church. Dr. Boice had often expressed concern about contemporary Christian worship. His concern was not limited to the style of the music, but focused more specifically on the content of its lyrics, which he considered theologically shallow and biblically uninformed. But rather than merely complaining, he decided to do something constructive for the cause of a modern Reformation. The theme of his new hymns is perhaps best summarized in the first verse of the opening hymn:

> Give praise to God who reigns above
> For perfect knowledge, wisdom, love;
> His judgments are divine, devout,
> His paths beyond all tracing out.
> Come, lift your voice to heaven's high throne,
> And glory give to God alone![12]

About This Book

Give praise to God—that is both the theme and the purpose of this collection of essays. The book's title comes from Dr. Boice's first hymn. It expresses one of the Reformation slogans he loved to quote: *soli deo gloria* (to God alone be the glory). That Latin phrase and *sola scriptura* (Scripture alone) capture the essence of James Montgomery Boice's view of worship. The Bible is our only ultimate authority for worship, as it is for everything else. Scripture alone determines how we are to please God in our worship. *Sola scriptura*. All of our worship is dedicated to the greater glory of God, who alone is the chief end of all our praise. *Soli deo gloria!*

The first section of the book is called "The Bible and Worship." What is the Bible's own theology of worship? This section answers with a robust defense of what theologians call the regulative principle of worship. Stated briefly, this is the principle that human beings should offer to God only such worship as he has expressly commanded in his word. Although Dr. Boice did not often speak of the regulative principle, he agreed with its essential principle, namely, that our worship must be according to the Bible.

The second section of the book is also the longest: "Elements of Biblical Worship." Here the contributors address the standard elements of a worship service. Priority is given to expository preaching, because that was the heart of Dr. Boice's own ministry, yet without neglecting the other important aspects of public worship.

The third section of the book — "Preparing for Biblical Worship" — sets worship within the wider context of the whole Christian life, all of which is dedicated to the glory of God.

The fourth and final section of the book — "Worship, History, and Culture" — attempts to place Christian worship in its historical and ecclesiastical context. Dr. Boice was a keen student of church history and treasured the rich legacy we inherited from the fathers and Reformers of our faith. It was partly for this reason that he placed such a high priority on corporate worship and also sought its reformation in our day.

This book is for everyone who loves to worship God. Our hope is that it will help ministers who lead their congregations in worship, musicians who seek a deeper understanding of the spiritual purpose of their work, seminary students who are clarifying their commitment to biblical worship, and everyone else who sincerely desires to give praise to God.

All of the contributors have some connection to James Montgomery Boice. Most are his friends. Some were his colleagues in ministry at Tenth Presbyterian Church. Others worked with him in the Alliance of Confessing Evangelicals. Still others looked to his example from a greater distance. But all of us owe Dr. Boice a debt of gratitude for his encouragement in the worship of God—an immeasurable debt only partly satisfied by contributing to this book in his honor.

Worship can be a controversial subject. It is not surprising, then, that not all the contributors are in complete agreement about all matters pertaining to the worship of God. For one thing, not all of us are Presbyterians (which Dr. Boice would appreciate, given his tireless efforts to promote the Alliance of Confessing Evangelicals). Nor would Dr. Boice necessarily have endorsed everything in these pages. Perhaps this point should be emphasized. We have not attempted to write the book that he might have written, although all the chapters bear the mark of his influence and imbibe the spirit of his attitude to God in worship. His own views on the subject are widely available and are generally consonant with the approach taken in these pages. We do not presume to speak for him, however, and have tried instead to write a useful book on worship—the kind that Dr. Boice might have enjoyed reading.

There was some debate among the editors as to whether this volume could be described as a Festschrift. According to proper German usage, a Festschrift is a collection of essays celebrating a significant scholarly achievement, such as a promotion to a distinguished professorship. Ordinarily the term would not be used to honor someone who is deceased. However, the term has come to enjoy a wider use, especially in America, and can now safely be applied to any commemorative anthology. According to the *Oxford Encyclopedic English Dictionary*, a Festschrift is "a collection of writings published in honour of a scholar."

The term seems especially appropriate here. Although James Boice never accepted an academic appointment, he was a true scholar who set the highest intellectual standards for gospel ministry. Since he was not a professor, he never received an academic promotion. Instead, from the beginning of his ministry he served the church in the highest office it has to offer: pastor. Now, however, he can truly be said to have received his last and best promotion. He is in the presence of Christ, having been elevated from worship in this life, with all of its limitations and distractions, to the eternal worship of heaven. This collection of essays—this Festschrift—is presented in the memory of James Montgomery Boice upon the occasion of his promotion to glory.

One Saturday night, not long after Dr. Boice's death, I went into the sanctuary of Tenth Presbyterian Church to pray and also to lament the loss of my late mentor and friend. When I was finished I went upstairs to my of-fice, where I found a framed print propped up against the door. It had been left for me by Linda Boice, who had recovered it from her husband's office.

The print was a copy of a popular sign from colonial Williamsburg in Virginia. The small figure at the top, who was wearing a three-cornered hat, seemed weighed down by the cares of life. Apparently he was a shopkeeper, for the sign read: "Notice to all Patrons! I have been obliged by the sheer Weight of Fatigue to quit my Post, & repair to My Dwelling-house, until I have fully recovered My Usual Composure. All Patrons will find Me of a cheerful Demeanor, and in Readiness for Business or Consultation, upon a return." Printed in red at the bottom was the name of the owner and pro-prietor: James Montgomery Boice.

The sign captures the present situation perfectly: By the sheer weight of mortal fatigue, Dr. Boice has left his ministerial post and retired to his heav-enly home, there to regain his customary composure. When we see him again we will find him of cheerful disposition, employed in the serious and joyous business of heaven, which is giving glory to the triune God. Then there is the pleasing ambiguity of the sign's final phrase: "upon a return." Who will return to whom? James Montgomery Boice will not return to us, but one day soon we will join him in giving praise to God, who reigns above. "For from him and through him and to him are all things. / To him be the glory forever! Amen" (Rom. 11:36).

Part 1

THE BIBLE AND WORSHIP

*I*t seems almost an unnecessary question to ask, but we ask it nevertheless: Does the Bible tell us *how* we ought to worship God? Yes, the Bible tells us that we *should* worship God, that we were created *in order* to worship God. Worship, in one sense, is the natural response of our created nature: one way or another we respond to the Creator's self-revelation in worship. That we are fallen sinners means, as Calvin put it in his *Institutes of the Christian Religion,* that our hearts by nature are "factories of idols" rather than reservoirs of thanksgiving and praise to God. But, worship—whether true or false—is the natural instinct of the human heart.

A question then arises: Is there an acceptable way of worship? The answer is more complicated than at first appears. On one level, the answer is simple enough: *Yes,* of course the Bible tells us how we should worship! We are not free to worship God any way we please! There are ways that are acceptable and ways that are not. Just think of the elaborate way in which, under the old covenant, the sacrificial system was carefully laid out. It provided a regulative principle as to *how* God should be worshiped.

Another question then arises: Does this principle change when we move from the old covenant to the new covenant? Is New Testament worship devoid of a regulative principle? And still another question arises on the heels of the latter: Does the principle apply *only* to corporate worship rather than to private (personal) or family worship? Or does the principle apply to *all* worship, only *differently*.

These are the issues taken up in this section. Ligon Duncan seeks to address the fundamental questions: Does the Bible have a theology of worship? Is there such a thing as a regulative principle in the Scriptures and, if so, how is it formulated? Is the historic formulation of it outmoded for the church of today?

Derek Thomas takes this issue a step further, attempting to answer the criticisms of the regulative principle that have arisen in recent years, focusing particularly on those criticisms that arise from *within* the orbit of those who otherwise are committed to the historic understanding of worship.

Edmund Clowney, whose writings on worship and the church have been influential on several generations of Christians, addresses the importance of corporate worship as a means of grace. God designed corporate worship for Christians as *growing* ordinances. By reading the Bible, praying the Bible, expounding the Bible, and singing the Bible, God's people, Christ's bride on earth, grow into a "dwelling place for God by the Spirit" (Eph. 2:22 English Standard Version).

1

DOES GOD CARE HOW
WE WORSHIP?

J. LIGON DUNCAN III

James Montgomery Boice was, perhaps, the dean of North American evangelical/Reformed pastor-theologians for the last two decades of his life. No one could have been more worthy of a Festschrift in recognition of his ministry, though no one would have been quicker to deflect all praise to his gracious, sovereign God. This gift could not be given him during his life because of the wise but inscrutable providence of God. And so it is our desire to give praise to God in thanks for him and for his wisdom and ministry to us.

The subject of the volume is uniquely appropriate. This is so, first, because Dr. Boice had a passion for the corporate worship of the church—worship that was majestic and reverent, rooted in Scripture and history, God-intoxicated and Christ-exalting. Dr. Boice thought a great deal about corporate worship. It was a significant theme in both his teaching and writing ministry. We will not presume to speak for him, but it is our desire to speak in consonance with his voice on this vital issue. Second, this is an important issue to tackle in its own right. Indeed, it is a subject crying to be addressed. Confusion on basic issues is evident in both the theory and practice of the modern evangelical church. To be sure, many of us are helped by the research and writing of folks like Hughes Oliphant Old and Terry Johnson. These pastor-scholars lead us to a more intelligent appreciation of the biblical treasure bequeathed to us in the legacy of Reformed worship. They enlighten us to the guiding principles that for nearly four hundred years influenced in various ways the corporate worship of Congregational, independent, low-church Anglican, Baptist, Presbyterian, and Reformed churches.

But this central Reformed Protestant practice of worship is facing new pressures and questions. It is time to hear the basic biblical principles again. Furthermore, there are significant cultural issues to consider. David Wells, Ken Myers, Gene Edward Veith, Marva Dawn, and many others help us greatly in approaching these matters Christianly and ecclesially. Still, a distinctively Reformed, full-orbed, biblically rooted, historically savvy, twenty-first century entry on this discussion awaits. We aim to begin that conversation. In doing so, we are simply following in the footsteps of James Montgomery Boice, who offered both diagnosis of and prescription for the corporate worship of the contemporary evangelical church and wrote, not long before his death:

In recent years, I have noticed the decreasing presence, and in some cases the total absence, of service elements that have always been associated with God's worship.

Prayer. It is almost inconceivable to me that something called worship can be held without any significant prayer, but that is precisely what is happening. There is usually a short prayer at the beginning of the service, though even that is fading away. It is being replaced with a chummy greeting to make people feel welcome and at ease. Sometimes people are encouraged to turn around and shake hands with those who are next to them in the pews. Another prayer that is generally retained is the prayer for the offering. We can understand that, since we know that it takes the intervention of Almighty God to get self-centered people to give enough money to keep the church running. But longer prayers—pastoral prayers—are vanishing. Whatever happened to the *ACTS* acrostic in which *A* stands for adoration, *C* for confession of sin, *T* for thanksgiving, and *S* for supplication? There is no rehearsal of God's attributes or confession of sin against the shining, glorious background of God's holiness.

And what happens when Mary Jones is going to have an operation and the people know it and think she should be prayed for? Quite often prayers for people like that are tacked onto the offering prayer, because there is no other spot for them in the service. How can we say we are worshiping when we do not even pray?

The reading of the word. The reading of any substantial portion of the Bible is also vanishing. In the Puritan age ministers regularly read one chapter of the Old Testament and one of the New. Bible students profit from Matthew Henry's six-volume commentary on the Bible. But we should not forget that the commentary was the product of Henry's Scripture readings, not his sermons. His congregation received those extensive comments on the Bible readings *in addition to* the sermon. But our Scripture readings are getting shorter and shorter, sometimes only two or three verses, if the Bible is even read at all. In many churches there is not even a text for the sermon. When I was growing up in an evangelical church I was taught that in the Bible God speaks to us and in prayer we speak to God. So what is going on in our churches if we neither pray nor read the Bible? Whatever it is, it is not worship.

The exposition of the word. We have very little serious teaching of the Bible today, not to mention careful expositions. Instead, preachers try to be personable, to relate funny stories, to smile, above all to stay away from topics that might cause people to become unhappy with the preacher's church and leave it. One extremely popular television preacher will not mention sin, on the grounds that doing so makes people feel bad. He says that people feel badly enough about themselves already. Preachers speak to felt needs, not real needs, and this generally means telling people only what they most want to hear. Preachers want to be liked, popular, or entertaining. And, of course, successful!

Is success a proper, biblical goal for Christ's ministers? For servants of the one who instructed us to deny ourselves, take up our cross daily, and follow him (Luke 9:23)?

Confession of sin. Who confesses sin today—anywhere, not to mention in church as God's humble, repentant people bow before God and acknowledge that they have done those things they ought not to have done and have left undone those things that they ought to have done, and that there is no health in them? That used to be a necessary element in any genuinely Christian service. But it is not happening today because there is so little awareness of God. Instead of coming to church to admit our transgressions and seek forgiveness, we come to church to be told that we are really pretty nice people who do not need forgiveness. We are such busy people, in fact, that God

19

should actually be pleased that we have taken time out of our busy schedules to come to church at all.

Hymns. One of the saddest features of contemporary worship is that the great hymns of the church are on the way out. They are not gone entirely, but they are going. And in their place have come trite jingles that have more in common with contemporary advertising ditties than with the psalms. The problem here is not so much the style of the music, though trite words fit best with trite tunes and harmonies. Rather the problem is with the content of the songs. The old hymns expressed the theology of the church in profound and perceptive ways and with winsome, memorable language. They lifted the worshiper's thoughts to God and gave him striking words by which to remember God's attributes. Today's songs reflect our shallow or nonexistent theology and do almost nothing to elevate one's thoughts about God.

Worst of all are songs that merely repeat a trite idea, word, or phrase over and over again. Songs like this are not worship, though they may give the churchgoer a religious feeling. They are mantras, which belong more in a gathering of New Agers than among God's worshiping people.[1]

The contributors to this volume share Dr. Boice's burden for the reformation of worship in the various evangelical churches today. And whatever differences we may have, we are united in the desire to see biblical worship restored and flourishing in the Bible-believing, Christ-exalting, gospel-preaching churches of today. This book is no less than an outline of a biblical program for the renewal of Christian worship in our time.

The Bible as the Key to Reforming Worship

If such a renewal is to be undertaken, on what principle will it be founded? If we are to live and worship together *soli deo gloria,* then what shall be the basis and pattern? The only answer for the evangelical Christian is *sola scriptura.* God's word itself must supply the principles and patterns and content of Christian worship. True Christian worship is by the book. It is according to Scripture. The Bible alone ultimately directs the form and content of Christian worship.

This is a Reformational emphasis, which came to fruition especially in the Reformed branch of the great Protestant Reformation of the sixteenth century (in contrast to the Lutheran and Radical Reformation traditions and in direct contradiction of the Roman Catholic tradition). It is found in Calvin and other first-generation Reformed theologians. It is found in John Knox and the Scottish tradition. It is found in the Puritan tradition of the Church of England, from the days of Elizabeth I to the Commonwealth and thereafter in English Nonconformity. It is firmly established in the Baptist confessions and in the Congregational creeds.

This strong and special emphasis on the corporate worship of God being founded positively on the directions of Scripture came to be known as the regulative principle. It is an extension of the Reformational axiom of *sola scriptura*. As the Bible is the final authority in faith and life, so it is also the final authority in how we corporately worship—but in a distinct and special way. Whereas all of life is to be lived in accordance with Scripture, Scripture does not speak discreetly to every specific component of our lives. There are many situations in which we must rely upon general biblical principles and then attempt to think Christianly without specific guidance in various circumstances.

The Reformers thought the matter of corporate worship was just a little bit different than this. They taught that God had given full attention to this matter in his word because it is one of central significance in the Christian life and in his eternal purposes. Therefore, we are to exercise a special kind of care when it comes to this activity—a care distinct from that which we employ anywhere else in the Christian life. He told us what to do and how to do it, in such a way that the prime aspects of worship are a matter of following divine direction; and thus the decisions that remain to be made by us—thinking in accordance with the general principles of Scripture and sanctified common sense, in the absence of positive scriptural warrant—are relatively minor. It is not difficult to find this axiom being articulated, in various ways, from the earliest days of the Reformed tradition to our own time—and in all the representative branches of the Reformed community.

For instance, Calvin said: "God disapproves of all modes of worship not expressly sanctioned by His Word."[2] The Continental Reformed tradition, reflected in the Belgic Confession (article 32) and the Heidelberg Catechism (Q. 96), asserts the same. The Second London Baptist Confession of 1689 and the Philadelphia (Baptist) Confession of 1742 both say: "The acceptable way of worshiping the true God, is instituted by himself, and so limited by his own revealed will, that he may not be worshiped according

21

to the imagination and devices of men, nor the suggestions of Satan, under any visible representations, or any other way not prescribed in the Holy Scriptures" (22.1). They also assert that "the whole counsel of God concerning all things necessary for his own glory, man's salvation, faith and life, is either expressly set down or necessarily contained in the Holy Scripture: unto which nothing at any time is to be added, whether by new revelation of the Spirit, or traditions of men. Nevertheless, we acknowledge . . . that there are some circumstances concerning the worship of God . . . common to human actions and societies, which are to be ordered by the light of nature and Christian prudence, according to the general rules of the word, which are always to be observed" (1.6). The Savoy Declaration of Faith and Order (1658), the Congregationalist emendation of the Westminster Confession (1647), affirms the same principles.

More recently, Anglican David Peterson defines worship as "an engagement with [God] *on the terms that he proposes* and in the way that he alone makes possible."[3] Even more specifically, Hughes Old, who does not employ the term *regulative principle,* nevertheless offers a description of this fundamental Reformed corporate worship principle that would have satisfied the Westminster Assembly:

> Most things we do in worship we do because God has commanded us to do them. It is because of this that we preach the gospel, we praise God in psalms and hymns, we serve God in prayer, we baptize in the name of Christ. Some things we do in worship not so much because they are specifically taught in Scripture but because they are in accordance with Scripture. What is meant by that is that some of the things we do in worship we do because they are demanded by scriptural principles. For example we baptize in the name of the Father, the Son, and the Holy Spirit because this is specifically directed by Scripture. It is on the basis of scriptural principles that before the baptism we offer the Baptismal Invocation asking the Holy Spirit to fulfill inwardly what is promised in the outward sign. The basic acts of worship we perform because they are clearly commanded in Scripture. The ways and means of doing them we try to order according to scriptural principles. When something is not specifically commanded, prescribed, or directed or when there is no scriptural example to guide us in how we are to perform some particular aspect of worship we should try nevertheless to be guided by scriptural principles.[4]

What is being argued here is that there must be scriptural warrant for all we do. That warrant may come in the form of explicit directives, implicit requirements, the general principles of Scripture, positive commands, examples, and things derived from good and necessary consequences. These formulations of the Reformed approach to worship also acknowledge that lesser things about corporate worship may be decided in the absence of a specific biblical command but in accordance with faithful biblical Christian thinking under the influence of scriptural principles and sanctified reason and general revelation (e.g., whether to use bulletins, what time the services are to begin, how long they are to last, where to meet, what the ministers and congregation will wear, whether to use hymnals, how the singing is to be led, and the like). But the first things—the central elements, the principle parts, the essentials—have a positive warrant. The incidentals and accidentals will be guided by scriptural principles.

In order to sharpen this principle and make it more perspicuous and useful, Reformed theologians speak about the substance of corporate worship (the content of its prescribed parts or elements), the elements of worship (its components or specific parts), the forms of worship (the way in which these elements of worship are carried out), and the circumstances of worship (incidental matters that of necessity demand a decision but that are not specifically commanded in the word). Reformed theologians argue that the whole substance of worship must be biblical. Not that only words from the Bible can be used, but that all that is done and said in worship is in accordance with sound biblical theology. The content of each component must convey God's truth as revealed in his word. They also assert that God specifically commanded the elements he desired in worship (reading the word, preaching the word, singing, prayer, administration of the sacraments, oaths and vows, etc.). To and from these, we may neither add nor take away. As for the form of the elements, there will be some variations: different prayers will be prayed, different songs sung, different Scriptures read and preached, the components of worship rearranged from time to time, the occasional elements (like the sacraments, oaths, and vows) performed at various chosen times, and the like. There will be, of necessity, some human discretion exercised in these matters. So here, Christian common sense under the direction of general scriptural principles, patterns, and proportions must make a determination. Finally, as to circumstances—whether we sit or stand, have pews or chairs, meet in a church building or storefront, sing from a hymnal or from memory, what time on the Lord's Day services are to be held, and more—these things must be decided upon in the absence of specific biblical direction, and hence they must be done (as with the case of the forms above) in accordance with "the light of nature and Christian prudence, according to the general rules of the word" (Westminster Confession of Faith 1.6; Baptist Confession of Faith 1.6).

Through the faithful implementation of this regulative principle, the various Reformed churches effected a renovation of Christianity, established a discipleship program unparalleled in Christian history, created a culture that survives to this day (albeit in a diminished scope and quality), and rejuvenated the apostolic norms of corporate worship. This chapter is a call for its deliberate reinstitution in the evangelical church as an indispensable axiom for and prerequisite to corporate worship as God intends it to be. This is a call issued by Dr. Boice himself when he said: "We must worship on the basis of the biblical revelation . . . [and] according to the doctrines of the Bible."[5] The key benefit of the regulative principle is that it helps to assure that God—not man—is the supreme authority for how corporate worship is to be conducted, by assuring that the Bible, God's own special revelation (and not our own opinions, tastes, likes, and theories), is the prime factor in our conduct of and approach to corporate worship.

Is the Regulative Principle Outmoded?

The regulative principle, however, strikes many evangelicals as outmoded. They see it as one historical expression of worship, but are not convinced that it is necessary or even applicable today. Of the more intelligent critics of this historic Reformed view of worship, some view it as a solely Puritan principle: characteristic of north European culture, invented by seventeenth-century scholastic theologians, narrower than Calvin's approach, and not embraced elsewhere in the best of catholic Christianity.[6] We will have an opportunity to respond to some of these objections in this and the next two chapters. But I want to suggest that the main reason why many evangelicals have a hard time embracing the regulative principle is that they do not believe that God tells us (or tells us much about) how to worship corporately in his word.

Evangelicals have for a century or more been the most minimal of all the Protestants in what they think the Bible teaches us about the church

24

in general and in their estimation of the relative importance of ecclesiology (the doctrine of the church). They do not generally believe that church government is established positively in the word; they often do not see the local church as essential to the fulfillment of the Great Commission or to the task of Christian discipleship; they are suspicious of order as restrictive of freedom; and they generally juxtapose the priesthood of believers and local church autonomy over against the didactic authority of established church norms, confessional theology, and the testimony of the *communio sanctorum* through the ages (under Scripture). Consequently, since the doctrine of worship is a part of what the Bible teaches about the doctrine of the church, they are not predisposed in general to expect much in the way of important, definitive teaching about the conduct of corporate worship.

So, to say it again differently, the single greatest obstacle to the reform of worship in the evangelical church today is evangelicalism's general belief that New Testament Christians have few or no particular directions about how we are to worship God corporately: what elements belong in worship, what elements must always be present in well-ordered worship, what things do not belong in worship. To be even more specific, when we recall from our study of Christian ethics that every ethical action has a standard (a norm), dynamic (that which enables or empowers someone to do the action contemplated in the norm), motivation (that which impels someone to do the action), and goal (the final object[s] or purpose[s] of the action), we may say that evangelicals emphasize the dynamic of Christian worship (the grace of the Holy Spirit) and its motivation (gratitude for grace, a passion for God), but de-emphasize the standard (the Bible) and goal (the prime *telos* of glorifying and enjoying God).

Evangelicals do think that worship matters, but they also often view worship as a means to some other end than that of the glorification and enjoyment of God: some view worship as evangelism (thus misunderstanding its goal); some think that a person's heart, intentions, motives, and sincerity are the only things important in how we worship (thus downplaying the Bible's standards, principles, and rules for worship); and some view the emotional product of the worship experience as the prime factor in "good" worship (thus overstressing the subjective and often unwittingly imposing particular cultural opinions about emotional expression on all worshipers). Evangelicals believe these things about worship, but they do not think that

25

there are many biblical principles about how to worship or what we are to do and not to do in worship.

In part, this may be the result of an understandable misunderstanding of the precise nature of the discontinuity between the worship of the people of God in the old covenant and the new covenant. Evangelicals have, by and large, gotten the point of Hebrews and the rest of the New Testament on the coming of Christ as the end of the types and shadows of the elaborate ceremonial worship of the old covenant. Thus they have, again rightly, rejected the approach of high-church traditions (whether Roman Catholic, Eastern Orthodox, or Anglo-Catholic) that attempt to reimpose and reapply a christological version of the priestly ceremonialism of old-covenant worship or draw on the liturgical symbolism of Revelation (itself based on the worship practices of the old covenant) as normative for the church militant of the new covenant. Evangelicals know that this approach is not only confused, it is wrong and unbiblical.

Consequently, though evangelicals know that the Old Testament has instructions on what Israel was to do in worship, they tend to think that there are few if any abiding principles to be gained for Christian worship from the Old Testament, or they think that the New Testament emphases on the heart, the activity of the Holy Spirit, and worship-in-all-of-life displace these Old Testament principles, or they think that the New Testament has correspondingly little or nothing to say about the how of corporate worship, and some even think that the category of corporate worship disappears altogether in the new-covenant expression of the economy of God. But these assumptions are as wrong in one direction as high-church approaches are in the other. And, not surprisingly, these assumptions help an evangelicalism enveloped in a culture of individualism, relativism, and situationalism remain, in its approach to the gathered worship of God's people, strong on the individual, weak on the corporate; strong on the subjective, weak on the objective; strong on the heart, weak on the principles.

God's Pervasive Concern for How He Is Worshiped

God makes it amply clear, however, throughout the Bible that he does indeed care very much about how we worship. The Bible's answer to this query—does God care about the how of worship?—is an emphatic yes, not only in the Old Testament but also in the New Testament. Where does the Bible teach this? Obviously one place is in the detailed provisions for tabernacle worship found in Exodus 25–31, 35–40, as well as in Leviticus. Exodus 25, for instance, in the middle of its divine instructions for the sanctuary and its furnishings, insists upon at least three aspects of the way that God's people are to worship (thus touching the standard, motivation, and goal of worship and indirectly the dynamic). First, Israel's worship was to be willing worship. It is to be "every man whose heart moves him" (25:2) who contributes to the sanctuary (note the contrast to this in the golden-calf incident in 32:2). If worship does not spring from gratitude for God's grace, if it is not the heartfelt response to who God is and what he has done, then it is hollow. Second, true worship (like the goal of the covenant itself) has in view spiritual communion with the living God. God orders construction of the tabernacle that he "may dwell among" his people (25:8). That is God's purpose in the old-covenant ordinances for worship, and so the people were to bear that goal in mind as they themselves built and came to the tabernacle. "I will be your God and you will be my people" is the heart and aim of the covenant—and the heart and the aim of worship. If worship aims for anything less than this, it is not worship at all but a vacuous substitute. Third, God's worship is to be carefully ordered according to his instructions. God's initiative is prime in the design of the tabernacle (again, in contrast to the golden-calf incident). God demanded that the tabernacle and all its furnishings be made "after the pattern . . . shown to you on the mountain" (25:40). God's plan, not the people's creativity, nor even that of the artisans who would build it, was to be determinative in the making of the place where his people would meet him (and indeed, in all the actions of the priests who would serve in this worship). This is, in essence, what the Reformers saw as a fundamental principle for Christian worship (an approach that came to be known as the regulative principle). This principle, in short, states that worship in its content, motivation, and aim is to be determined by God alone. He teaches us how to think about him and how to approach him. The further we get away, then, from his directions the less we actually worship.

But many fine evangelical theologians object at this point and say: "Yes, this principle was true for tabernacle worship, but not for new-covenant worship." The idea behind this objection is that because of its unique typological significance, Old Testament tabernacle worship was guarded by unique requirements that God did not apply elsewhere in the Old Testament or in the New Testament to the corporate worship of his people. So, they say, though our worship should be guided by biblical principles (in the same way as is the rest of life), it is not restricted to that which is positively warranted by the word (as was tabernacle worship).[7]

However, the Bible, the whole Bible, contradicts this position. The emphasis on God's concern for the how of worship (in its standard, motivation, dynamic, and goal) is pervasive, not only in the ceremonial code, but also in the moral law, not only in the Pentateuch but also in the Prophets, not only in the Old Testament but also in the New, not only in Paul but also in Jesus' teaching. Consider the following.

The Account of Cain and Abel

At the very beginnings of special revelation, integral to the postfall story of the seed of the woman and the seed of the serpent, is found the account of Cain and Abel (Gen. 4:3–8). Abel offers "the firstlings of his flock and of their fat portions" and Cain offers "the fruit of the ground," but the Lord "had regard for Abel and for his offering; but for Cain and for his offering He had no regard." Why? Well, the narrative is sparse but suggestive of the answer. The Lord's rebuke ("if you do well, will not *your countenance* be lifted up?") coupled with the stated contrast between the brothers' respective offerings indicates that Cain's offering was either deficient according the standard of God's requirements (and what they were is not spelled out for us, unless Moses expects his readers to think proleptically) or that his heart attitude/motivation in making the offering was deficient. In other words, Cain failed to worship in either spirit or truth or both. The how of worship was lacking in either its standard or motivation, and so God rejected his worship. Thus, at the outset of revelation, in a section of Genesis replete with emphases about the beginnings of worship and its importance, God sets forth a warning to every reader and hearer that he is very particular about how his people approach him in worship. It is before the moral law is expounded at Sinai. It is in no way connected to the tabernacle worship of Exodus or to the levitical system. It tells us before those things are ever announced that God cares about the how of worship.

The Story of the Exodus

Grounded in the great redemptive story of the exodus is another principle that shows the exceeding importance that God attaches to corporate worship and thus moves us to a concern for the how of worship. For instance, the whole exodus account, especially from Exodus 3:12 on, stresses that God's people are redeemed in order that they might worship him. Moses' very call emphasizes that God sends Moses to Egypt to deliver his people that they might worship him. Listen to the reiterated emphases of these passages: "When you have brought the people out of Egypt, you shall worship" (Ex. 3:12); "let us go a three days' journey into the wilderness, that we may sacrifice to the Lord our God" (3:18); "let My son go that he may serve [or worship] Me" (4:23); "let My people go that they may celebrate a feast to Me in the wilderness" (5:1); "let us go a three days' journey into the wilderness that we may sacrifice to the Lord our God" (5:3). Do not underestimate this repeated language. This is not merely a ruse to get Pharaoh to temporarily release the children of Israel. It is the primary reason why God sets his people free: to worship him. The primacy of worship in a believer's life is, thus, set forth. We are saved to worship! These passages, of course, reflect an interest in both worship in all of life and the specific activity of corporate worship. However, the highlighting of the specific activity of corporate worship in Moses' language and teaching about worship in the era of pretabernacle worship in Exodus (i.e., in his differentiation of the two types of worship [gathered praise and life service], in his description of the specific content of that gathered worship, in his interest in the initial location of that gathered worship [the mountain that God had shown], in the inclusion of stipulations on corporate worship in the moral law, in his heavily emphasized accounts of the subsequent abuse of corporate worship in the rebellion of the golden calf, and more) teaches us to be circumspect in our approach to corporate worship.

The First and Second Commandments

Grounded in the moral law itself and revealed in the first and second commandments (Ex. 20:2–6) is a fundamental indication that God is concerned not only with the whom of corporate worship, but also the how of corporate worship. No matter how these commands are numbered, the text still makes both points!

I am the Lord your God, who brought you out of the land of Egypt, out of the house of slavery. You shall have no other gods before Me. You shall not make for yourself an idol, or any likeness of what is in heaven above or on the earth beneath or in the water under the earth. You shall not worship them or serve them; for I, the Lord your God, am a jealous God, visiting the iniquity of the fathers on the children, on the third and the fourth generations of those who hate Me, but showing lovingkindness to thousands, to those who love Me and keep My commandments.

God indicates here not only that he alone is to be worshiped, but also that he is not to be worshiped via images. Additionally, he stresses his extreme sensitivity about these matters. The very mention of the use of images anchors this passage in a concern for corporate worship (although, of course, it has implications for worship in all of life). This text, expressing the eternal and abiding moral law and not merely the ceremonial system of the tabernacle is the very foundation of the Reformed concern for "carefulness in worship." Because God indicates that he is jealous about the whom and the how of worship, we are to be exceeding careful about the whom and the how of worship, and the best way to do that is to follow the regulative principle.

The ten words themselves are a disclosure of God's own nature and not merely a revelation of temporary social, religious, and moral norms. The first command shows us a Lord who alone is God. The second witnesses to a God who is sovereign even in the way we relate to him (since there he teaches us that we may neither think about him nor worship him according to our own human categories and designs, but must rather know him and glorify him on his own terms and by his own revelation). Because these commands teach us first and foremost about what God is like, they also provide for us permanent direction on how we are to think of God, how we are to worship God, and that God cares greatly about how we think of and worship him.

Three points arise from a careful consideration of the second command.

God's word must govern our knowledge of God, and thus its governance of worship is vital. Divine revelation must control our idea of God, but since worship contributes to our idea of God, the only way that God's revelation can remain foremost in our thinking about God is if God's revelation also controls our worship of God. God's self-disclosure, his self-revelation, is to dominate our conception of him, and therefore God's people are not to make images of God or the gods: "You shall not make for yourself an idol, or any likeness of what is in heaven above or on the earth beneath or in the water under the earth." An idol or graven image or carved image refers, literally, to something hacked or chiseled into a likeness. Thus the command demands that there is to be no image representation of God in Israel. The phraseology of Exodus 20:4 indicates that there is to be no image-making of God or gods for any reason. This prohibition clearly extends to images of other gods, as well as to images of the one true God. Deuteronomy 4:15–18 says:

> So watch yourselves carefully, *since you did not see any form on the day the LORD spoke to you* at Horeb from the midst of the fire, so that you do not act corruptly and make a graven image for yourselves in the form of any figure, the likeness of male or female, the likeness of any animal that is on the earth, the likeness of any winged bird that flies in the sky, the likeness of anything that creeps on the ground, the likeness of any fish that is in the water below the earth. (emphasis added)

This moral law expressly teaches us that the Bible is to be our rule for how we corporately worship and even think about God. The Bible (God's own self-disclosure and revelation) — not our own innovations, imaginations, experiences, opinions, and representations — is to be the source of our idea of God. By the way, this is why Protestant houses of worship have historically been plain, bereft of overt religious symbolism and certainly without representations of deity. The Bible is to be central in forming our image of God and informing our worship of him. And since the how of corporate worship contributes to our image of God, it is exceedingly important that we worship in accordance with the Bible. Jewish commentator Nahum Sarna expresses the force of the second command this way:

> The forms of worship are now regulated. The revolutionary Israelite concept of God entails His being wholly separate from the world of His creation and wholly other than what the human mind can conceive or the human imagination depict. Therefore, any material representation of divinity is prohibited, a proscription elaborated in Deuteronomy 4:12, 15–19, where it is explained that the people heard "the sound of words" at Sinai "but perceived no shape — nothing but a voice." In the Israelite view any [humanly initiated] symbolic representation of God must necessarily be both inadequate and a distortion, for an image becomes identified with what it represents and is

soon looked upon as the place and presence of the Deity. In the end the image itself will become the locus of reverence and an object of worship, all of which constitutes the complete nullification of the singular essence of Israelite monotheism.[8]

But there is even more to be said about the underlying rationale of the second commandment. Again we ask, Why is there to be no image-making in Israel? Marshall McLuhan's famous dictum that "the medium is the message" sparks this interesting observation by Neil Postman:

The clearest way to see through a culture is to attend to its tools for conversation. I might add that my interest in this point of view was first stirred by a prophet far more formidable than McLuhan, more ancient than Plato. In studying the Bible as a young man, I found intimations of the idea that forms of media favor particular kinds of content and therefore are capable of taking command of a culture. I refer specifically to the Decalogue, the Second Commandment of which prohibits the Israelites from making concrete images of anything [as a representation of God]. "Thou shalt not make unto thee any graven image, any likeness of any thing that is in heaven above, or that is in the earth beneath, or that is in the water beneath the earth." I wondered then, as so many others have, as to why the God of these people would have included instructions on how they were to symbolize, or not symbolize, their experience [of him]. It is a strange injunction to include as part of an ethical system unless its author assumed a connection between forms of human communication and the quality of a culture. We may hazard a guess that a people who are being asked to embrace an abstract, universal deity would be rendered unfit to do so by the habit of drawing pictures or making statues or depicting their ideas [of him] in any concrete, iconographic forms. The God of the Jews was to exist in the Word and through the Word, an unprecedented conception requiring the highest order of abstract thinking. Iconography thus became blasphemy so that a new kind of God could enter a culture. People like ourselves who are in the process of converting their culture from word-centered to image-centered might profit by reflecting on this Mosaic injunction.[9]

Thus, because Israel's view of God, its understanding of God was to be controlled by his self-revelation and by not human imagination or representation, therefore its worship was to be aniconic—without images and visible representation of deity—because the how of worship contributes significant components to our conception of God. That means, of course, that Christian worship, too, is to be aniconic. We expand on this thought in a second point of consideration.

God's own character and word must govern our worship of God. God's nature and revelation are to control our worship of him, and therefore God's people are not to worship images of other gods or worship the true God through images: "You shall not worship them or serve them" (Ex. 20:5a). This phrase further specifies that graven images are to be neither worshiped or served. Yes, of course, false gods are not to be served/ worshiped (which is obviously entailed in the first command), but even more to the point—the one true God is not to be served/worshiped through the use of images. This very point is driven home in the stories of the golden calf (Ex. 32:1–5) and the idolatry of Jeroboam (1 Kings 12:28). This command is obviously directly relevant to the use of images in worship and devotion in Roman Catholicism and Eastern Orthodoxy and even in branches of Protestantism (we must now sadly say). Still, we may venture that the greatest violations of this in our time are nonvisual, but rather mental and volitional. When people say things like, "Well, I know the Bible says that, but I like to think of God as . . ." they are no less idolatrous in their thinking, and thus worshiping, than was Israel at the foot of Sinai on that fateful day of spiritual adultery with the calf. In contrast to all human creativity and initiative, the Bible is to be our rule for how we worship God, because the Bible is our rule for how we are to think about God—and how we worship in turn impacts our concept of God. Put another way: how we worship determines whom we worship. That is why both the medium and the message, both the means and the object, must be attended to in true worship. So, the Bible (God's own revelation regarding himself and his worship)—and not our own innovations, imaginations, experiences, opinions, and representations—is to determine how we worship God. This reminds us that there are two ways to commit idolatry: worship something other than the true God or worship the true God in the wrong way. And the second word of the moral law speaks to them both. In fact, the second commandment disallows three things: making images of either false gods or the true God; using humanly initiated (un-

33

Read

warranted) images in worship; and, by extension, using means or media other than those by which God has appointed us to worship. Our Puritan ancestors called these innovations in corporate worship "will-worship." Not surprisingly, then, the second commandment is one of the biblical sources of what the Reformers called the regulative principle. Terry Johnson puts it this way: "In prohibiting worship through images, God declares that He alone determines how He is to be worshiped. Though their use be ever so sincere and sensible (as aids to worship) images are not pleasing to Him, and by implication, *neither is anything else that He has not sanctioned*."[10]

God's seriousness about worship is displayed in his threats against deviation from his word. The importance of the manner and purity of our worship is seen from God's nature, warnings, and promises as expressed in the second command, and so God's people are to refrain from this because of who God is and because of what he warns and promises. Exodus 20:5b–6 reads: "For I, the Lord your God, am a jealous God, visiting the iniquity of the fathers on the children, on the third and the fourth generations of those who hate Me, but showing lovingkindness to thousands, to those who love Me and keep My commandments." The character of God is presented here in a way shocking to our tolerance-drenched culture. He is jealous. He refuses to share his glory or his worship with anything or anyone else. The expression itself is an anthropopathism (an ascription of human emotional qualities to God), but it is linguistically or philologically an anthropomorphism (an ascription of human physical qualities to God): the older meaning of the word behind the term *jealous* or *impassioned* is that God is "to become red."[11] Alan Cole helps us appreciate the force of this kind of idiom in forming our understanding of the character of God:

> Like "love" and "hate" in the Old Testament (Mal. 1:2, 3), "jealousy" does not refer to an emotion so much as to an activity, in this case an activity of violence and vehemence, that springs from the rupture of a personal bond as exclusive as that of the marriage bond. This is not therefore to be seen as intolerance but exclusiveness, and it springs both from the uniqueness of God (who is not one among many) and the uniqueness of His relationship to Israel. No husband who truly loved his wife could endure to share her with another man: no more will God share Israel with a rival.[12]

The idiom, the expression, is obvious. God is calling to our minds the righteous jealousy of a husband wronged. Sarna puts it just right: "a jealous God" is "a rendering that understands the marriage bond to be the implied metaphor for the covenant between God and His people. . . . It underscores the vigorous, intensive, and punitive nature of the divine response to apostasy and to modes of worship unacceptable to Himself."[13] In other words, God is saying in this warning: "My people, if you commit spiritual adultery in your worship, I will righteously respond like the most fearsome wronged husband you have ever known." The discontinuities between divine and human behavior are assumed and implicit in the idiom, but the point is crystal clear. Betray God by idolatry, which is spiritual adultery, and he will deal with you like a red-eyed, jilted spouse.

Here again, then, we see further grounds for the Reformed doctrine of carefulness in worship. The strictness of his justice mentioned here, that he punishes sin indefatigably, only adds to that concern for carefulness. It is fascinating to note the language: those who are idolatrous hate God and that those who worship according to his commands love him. The respective meanings of "hate" (to disobey) and "love" (to obey) need to be appreciated here. This all adds up to stress that the way we worship or, more specifically, the way in which we follow his commands for worship is a reflection of our knowledge of God and how seriously we take him. One reason that "Sing the Bible, pray the Bible, read the Bible, preach the Bible" is a motto for worship in my own congregation is out of respect for this command. We strive to be sure that all that we sing is scriptural, that our prayers are saturated with Scripture, that much of the word of God is read in each public service, and that the preaching is based on the Bible—in order that we might honor the one true God and not some idol of our own invention. The Bible supplies the substance of and direction for our worship and thus provides the surest way to know who God is and what he is like.

The Story of the Golden Calf

Grounded in the trauma of the incident with the golden calf (Ex. 32–34) is yet another testimony to the sheer importance of the how of worship. If there is any lesson here at all, it is that we cannot take the worship of God into our own hands, for Israel's rebellion against the moral law's commands regarding worship is presented here as a breaking of the covenant and a rejection of God. It is vital to remember that this is not a defection from the ceremonial law or the worship of the tabernacle—the people had not yet received these. Moses presents the actions of Israel as a contradiction of moral law. Hence, this story has special abiding significance. Several huge themes are operating at once in this section of Exodus. Among others, this whole section highlights the doctrine of sin. It is a "fall story"—the story of Israel's covenant-breaking. We find a summary of this defection in Exodus 32:1–6:

> Now when the people saw that Moses delayed to come down from the mountain, the people assembled about Aaron and said to him, "Come, make us a god who will go before us; as for this Moses, the man who brought us up from the land of Egypt, we do not know what has become of him." Aaron said to them, "Tear off the gold rings which are in the ears of your wives, your sons, and your daughters, and bring *them* to me." Then all the people tore off the gold rings which were in their ears and brought *them* to Aaron. He took *this* from their hand, and fashioned it with a graving tool and made it into a molten calf; and they said, "This is your god, O Israel, who brought you up from the land of Egypt." Now when Aaron saw *this*, he built an altar before it; and Aaron made a proclamation and said, "Tomorrow *shall be* a feast to the Lord." So the next day they rose early and offered burnt offerings, and brought peace offerings; and the people sat down to eat and to drink, and rose up to play.

Israel, impatient at Moses' long delay comes to Aaron not only looking for a visible representation of deity or of the divine presence, but essentially looking for a new mediator (there is a sense in which the golden calf and Aaron serve as their chosen replacements for Moses). The people's request seems to be not a request for a different god, a god other than Yahweh, but rather a representation of him (or of the mediator). The people also speak disrespectfully and dismissively of Moses, God's handpicked mediator. Ironically, without him and his subsequent intercession, they would have all perished here! Their demand of Aaron, to make a graven image (whatever interpretation is put on it with regard to its violation of the first or second commandments), is astonishing. Aaron facilitates their requests. Why he does so, we are not told, but he does not come out of this narrative favorably. Some of the spoils of the Egyptians are used to create the idol, and the rebellion was widespread ("all the people"). Aaron makes a golden young bull or ox idol (was it a shadowing of Apis or the Canaanite deities or a proleptic foreshadowing of the idolatry of Jeroboam?) and identifies it with or as the God who brought them up from Egypt. Some commentators suggest that the young bull was the pedestal on which the invisible God of Israel was standing, while others argue that it was a representation of deity. Either way, it is a violation of the second command! In some ways, the suggestion that the idol is a representation of the mediator even further strengthens the traditional Reformed interpretation of this passage and the second command.

Now that a "do-it-yourself god" or representation of him or material mediatorial object of his presence has been made, Aaron proceeds to make a do-it-yourself altar/sanctuary/place of worship and encounter. He still insists, however, that this is the worship of the Lord, that is, the true God, which suggests that Moses is highlighting a defection from the second command in this story. The feast day comes, the people worship their self-derived god in their self-derived way, and gross immorality results. Idolatry leads to immorality. This is the chain of connection in false worship: wrong worship, which is impiety, leads to immorality. Cole says: "This is not a casual incident: it is an organized cult, with a statue, altar, priest and festival."[14] One even wonders if this could have been a deliberate reaction against the aniconic worship announced in the ten words by those who had become accustomed to iconic worship through years in Egypt. Syncretism or pluralism or both was a part of what was going on in the camp of Israel. It was syncretism in that some in Israel wanted to worship the God of Israel in a pagan way (in this case, through visible representation), though God's command made clear that Israel's worship was to be exclusively aniconic. If there was pluralism at work in the incident, it involved worshiping someone or something alongside of or in addition to Yahweh, which is also idolatry.

Whatever the case, the whole passage points up (again) that how we worship is very important to God. Several applications flow from this principle and its violation in the golden-calf event: (1) impatience with God's timing is an enemy of faith; (2) we cannot choose our own mediator; (3) we cannot picture the true God as we wish or will; (4) we cannot worship the true God and something else; (5) we cannot worship the true God except in the way he commands; and (6) false worship leads to false living and immorality. Cole perceptively notes: "It is because Israel is so like us in every way that the stories of Israel have such exemplary value (1 Cor. 10)."[15] Terence Fretheim offers striking insights on the whole incident of the golden calf:

At every key point the people's building project contrasts with the tabernacle that God has just announced. This gives to the account a heavy ironic cast. (1) The people seek to create what God has already provided; (2) they, rather than God, take the initiative; (3) offerings are demanded rather than willingly presented; (4) the elaborate preparations are missing altogether; (5) the painstaking length of time needed for building becomes an overnight rush job; (6) the careful provision for guarding the presence of the Holy One turns into an open-air object of immediate accessibility; (7) the invisible, intangible God becomes a visible, tangible image; and (8) the personal, active God becomes an impersonal object that cannot see or speak or act. The ironic effect is that the people forfeit the very divine presence they had hoped to bind more closely to themselves. At the heart of the matter, the most important of the commandments had been violated.[16]

God's verdict in Exodus 32:7–10 only reinforces this:

> Then the Lord spoke to Moses, "Go down at once, for your people, whom you brought up from the land of Egypt, have corrupted *themselves*. They have quickly turned aside from the way which I commanded them. They have made for themselves a molten calf, and have worshiped it and have sacrificed to it and said, 'This is your god, O Israel, who brought you up from the land of Egypt!' " The Lord said to Moses, "I have seen this people, and behold, they are an obstinate people. Now then let Me alone, that My anger may burn against them and that I may destroy them; and I will make of you a great nation."

God knows what is going on even though Moses does not, so he tells Moses to go see for himself. God uses the language of disownment here— "whom *you* brought up." It is also ironic in light of the people's disowning words about Moses in verse 1. God nails them in their crime accurately and specifically: They have (1) quickly (through impatience) (2) turned aside from the way (i.e., forsaken their covenant obligations of living in the Lord's way of life), (3) which he commanded them (i.e., they have broken the covenant directives); (4) more specifically, they have done this by making and worshiping an idol (in contradiction of the first and second commands) (5) and by claiming it to be the saving God of Israel (thus demeaning the one true God). It is important to note that, in his accusatory language ("they have quickly turned aside from *the way which I commanded them*"), God charges Israel not with departing from him, but from his way, his commands about worship (which consequently means a departure from God himself). Sarna notes: "Significantly, the text does not say 'from Me'; they have adopted pagan modes of worship, but in worship of the God of Israel."[17] This whole indictment emphasizes the importance of the how of worship. Violation of God's commands on worship is viewed as breaking the covenant and is cataclysmic in its consequences. Israel deserved to be disowned and cut off. That is why "before the Hebrews were allowed to erect the sanctuary and to worship in it, they had to repent of their sin and undergo a covenant renewal."[18]

We have now seen four old-covenant examples of the Bible's concern about the how of corporate worship. None of them are tied to the ceremonial code or to tabernacle worship. But Christians may be anxious to know if the New Testament really has testimony to this concern, and so we hasten on, leaving behind dozens of Old Testament passages that corroborate our claims, among them the following:

1. The story of Nadab and Abihu (Lev. 10), who offer up "strange fire" to the Lord, that is, making an offering in a manner "which He had not commanded them" (10:1), and God strikes them dead (10:2). Moses records a thundering axiom in God's verdict: "By those who come near Me I will be treated as holy" (10:3).
2. The warnings of Deuteronomy (4:2; 12:32) that stress God's demand that whatever he commands, especially in worship, "you shall be careful to do; you shall not add to nor take away from it."
3. God's rejection of Saul's unprescribed worship (1 Sam. 15:22): when Saul offered a sacrifice out of accord with God's instructions, he was rebuked with "to obey is better than sacrifice."
4. The story of David and Uzzah and the ark, which explicitly indicates that David knew he had violated the regulative principle of worship (2 Sam. 6, especially vv. 3, 13).
5. God's rejection of pagan rites in Jeremiah's day "which I never commanded or spoke of, nor did it *ever* enter My mind" (Jer. 19:5; 32:35).

Jesus' Rejection of Pharisaic Worship

Grounded in Jesus' rejection of Pharisaic worship (Matt. 15:1–14), we find a dominical, new-covenant reassertion of the importance of the way in which we worship. Jesus cares about the how of worship. This passage is easily and often misunderstood, precisely because we live in an antitraditional age (where "new" generally means "good"). We tend to view the Pharisees as being overly scrupulous in their study and application of God's law. Jesus, however, never makes that charge against them. His critique is always in another direction. It is their laxity about God's law and their tenuous casuistry that undermined the prime force of moral law and drew his ire. Matthew's text is a picture of the human-made ritual of the religion of the Pharisees:

Then some Pharisees and scribes came to Jesus from Jerusalem and said, "Why do Your disciples break the tradition of the elders? For they do not wash their hands when they eat bread." And He answered and said to them, "Why do you yourselves transgress the commandment of God for the sake of your tradition? For God said, 'Honor your father and mother,' and, 'He who speaks evil of father or mother is to be put to death.' But you say, 'Whoever says to *his* father or mother, "Whatever I have that would help you has been given *to God*," he is not to honor his father or his mother.' And *by this* you invalidated the word of God for the sake of your tradition. You hypocrites, rightly did Isaiah prophesy of you:

> 'This people honors Me with their lips,
> But their heart is far away from Me.
> But in vain do they worship Me,
> Teaching as doctrines the precepts of men.' "

After Jesus called the crowd to Him, He said to them, "Hear and understand. *It is* not what enters into the mouth *that* defiles the man, but what proceeds out of the mouth, this defiles the man."

Then the disciples came and said to Him, "Do You know that the Pharisees were offended when they heard this statement?" But He answered and said, "Every plant which My heavenly Father did not plant shall be uprooted. Let them alone; they are blind guides of the blind. And if a blind man guides a blind man, both will fall into a pit."

In this passage, the Pharisees bring a charge against Jesus that he allowed his disciples to break the "tradition of the elders" regarding ritual hand-washing. This hand-washing was not hygienic, but religious. Note that it is Jesus who particularly applies the issue to the matter of the act of worship.

Tradition in the New Testament can be either positive (2 Thess. 2:15; 3:6) or negative (Mark 7:3, 9, 13; Col. 2:8; 1 Peter 1:18), depending on the context. Here it refers to the traditions of the elders, which involved (1) very high estimation of the specific interpretations and applications of the Torah by the elders, even approaching the point of these views and deductions being considered to be equally binding as the law of God itself; (2) not only applications of the law of God that went beyond what the law of itself taught, but often went beyond it in the wrong direction; and (3) interpretations and applications of the law that failed to do justice to certain central moral requirements of the law (focusing, rather, on the ceremonial/ritual). This exchange on the issue of the tradition gives Jesus the opportunity to discuss the important matter of ceremonial versus moral defilement and, ultimately, that of worship.

Jesus, using a phrase that precisely parallels the charge of the Pharisees, responds by charging them with breaking God's commandment. He then juxtaposes God's commandment with a practice that they have invented or endorsed: the rule of *korban*. Jesus' charge against them is that they have undercut the authority of God's word in preference for human-made rules. They have taken away from the word by adding to it. Their teaching is "subtraction by addition." Jesus illustrates that the Pharisees have a fundamental misunderstanding and foster a misuse of the ceremonial code in relation to the moral law (Matt. 15:3–6); and his verdict is that this misunderstanding/misuse stems from a hypocritical heart (15:7–9).

It is important to note that Jesus does not critique the Pharisees for being too tied to old-fashioned practices, caring about what the Torah says too much, or being too nitpicky about God's law. He charges them with ignoring God's law and attacking God's law by adding to it! Indeed, Jesus says that the words of Isaiah are perfectly suited to describe the Pharisees' worship: (1) it is lip service rather than God-honoring, in which their hearts are far away from him, rather than truly loving him; (2) it is empty worship, mere form; and (3) it is human-made, not based on the prescriptions of the word. Note then that Jesus' critique is internal and external: it pertains to both the heart and to the outward obedience of God's word. It has definite application to "all-of-life worship," but also to corporate worship. Indeed, the parallel account in Mark 7 makes explicit what is implicit in Matthew. Jesus' teaching here has enormous significance for Christian corporate worship in relation to the ceremonial law. Mark 7:19 tells us that Jesus' words meant the abolition of the ceremonial code's food laws for all new-covenant believers. The Book of Hebrews, based upon the underlying rationale of the abolition of the food laws (which was the dominical fulfillment of the totality of the ceremonial system), applies this same principle to show that we are no longer to worship corporately via the ceremonial/sacrificial forms of old-covenant corporate worship. Back to our immediate point though, Jesus makes it amply clear here that he cares about the how of worship, about the heart and obedience to the word, not only in worship in all of life, but in the corporate praise we bring.

Jesus' Words to the Woman at the Well

We find in Jesus' words to the Samaritan woman (John 4:20–26) an indication of the importance of the how of worship for new-covenant believers. In this deeply moving account of Jesus' encounter with the woman at the well, after his uncovering of her hidden sin and shame, she asks him about a worship matter of long dispute between Jews and Samaritans and of great importance to them both:

> "Our fathers worshiped in this mountain, and you *people* say that in Jerusalem is the place where men ought to worship." Jesus said to her, "Woman, believe Me, an hour is coming when neither in this mountain nor in Jerusalem will you worship the Father. You worship what you do not know; we worship what we know, for salvation is from the Jews. But an hour is coming, and now is, when the true worshipers will worship the Father in spirit and truth; for such people the Father seeks to be His worshipers. God is spirit, and those who worship Him must worship in spirit and truth." The woman said to Him, "I know that Messiah is coming (He who is called Christ); when that One comes, He will declare all things to us." Jesus said to her, "I who speak to you am *He*."

Jesus' answer thunders with points of significance regarding the momentous redemptive-historical transition that he was effecting in his own life, ministry, death, and resurrection; but it also speaks specifically to numerous principles of corporate worship that remain essential for Christians today. We point to but three of them here.

Jesus indicates a redemptive historical shift regarding the place of worship. For hundreds of years, the divinely appointed site for sacrificial worship had been in Jerusalem. This was the only place where the acts of worship, originally authorized in the giving of the tabernacle structure and ordinances in Exodus, were to be done. It was the focal point of the manifestation of the presence of God with Israel. In response, however, to the woman's query whether to worship in this mountain or in Jerusalem, Jesus begins by stressing that "an hour is coming when neither in this mountain nor in Jerusalem will you worship the Father." In other words, in a sentence Jesus indicates a time not far in the future in which the old-covenant place for tabernacle/temple/ceremonial/sacrificial worship would no longer have relevance for the true believer. In that hour, which came through his resurrection and ascension and pentecostal affusion of the Spirit, the place of worship is no longer geographical but ecclesial. Wherever believers gather in his name will be the place of worship: "For where two or three have gathered together in My name, I am there in their midst" (Matt. 18:20). The house in which his presence is known is the house of his people, whatever physical structure they may find themselves in. This is one reason the Reformers shut and locked their church doors (outside of corporate worship times): to stress that no place or building held peculiar spiritual significance and value. This is a new-covenant principle of worship—it is not tied to any specific location. The Westminster Confession expresses this teaching of Jesus this way:

> Neither prayer, nor any other part of religious worship, is now, under the gospel, either tied unto, or made more acceptable by any place in which it is performed, or towards which it is directed: but God is to be worshiped everywhere, in spirit and truth; as in private families daily, and in secret each one by himself, so more solemnly in the public assemblies, which are not carelessly or willfully to be neglected or forsaken when God, by his word or providence, calls thereunto. (21.6)

Jesus stresses that worship is response to revelation and thus must be according to revelation. Jesus' answer "neither in this mountain nor in Jerusalem" was not all he had to say in response to what was, in effect, a query about the legitimacy of Samaritan worship. He went on to say, "You worship what you do not know; we worship what we know, for salvation is from the Jews." In other words, the Samaritans were wrong to worship in their own self-chosen place. And because their worship was not in accord with God's revelation, they were also confused about whom they were wor-

43

shiping. Jesus' words here are a confirmation that the Old Testament's teaching on the central significance of the tabernacle/temple worship had been rightly understood by Israel and that any departure from it (precisely because it would entail a departure from the commands of God's revelation) would lead worshipers, no matter how sincere, into confusion about God. Israel knew its God because it worshiped him according to his revelation; but because the Samaritans did not worship according to revelation, they did not know their God. This is a new-covenant example of the maxim "how you worship determines what you become." This is why Jesus later says that worship must be "in truth." True worship is impossible for the Samaritans (and for us) as long as they devise their own worship.

Jesus reemphasizes the importance of worship in the new-covenant era. He says: "An hour is coming, and now is, when the true worshipers will worship the Father in spirit and truth; for such people the Father seeks to be His worshipers." To glorify and enjoy God, to meet with God and engage with him, is so important to him that he himself is *seeking* us to become his worshipers. No higher commendation of the colossal importance of the activity of worship for new-covenant believers is imaginable. The plural *worshipers* indicates not only the scope of the future kingdom but also the corporate, congregational nature of the worship that God seeks. More, much more, could be said, but this suffices to show that far from being unconcerned about the how of worship in the new covenant, Jesus himself labored to stress the vital importance of how we go about worshiping God.

Paul's Rejection of the Colossian Heresy

Grounded in Paul's rejection of the Colossian heresy (Col. 2:16–19) is yet another reminder that in the new-covenant era the how of worship still matters very much. Without even considering his strong rejection of the ethical teaching of the errorists, it is obvious that Paul was responding to false teaching on worship in Colossae: "Therefore no one is to act as your judge in regard to food or drink or in respect to a festival or a new moon or a Sabbath day—things which are a *mere* shadow of what is to come; but the substance belongs to Christ." Paul here emphatically calls on Christians not to allow people to judge them according to or influence them into following human-made or abrogated old-covenant rituals, even the old-covenant seventh-day Sabbath. Nothing he says here denigrates the new-covenant Lord's Day in any way; the religious activities he mentions in 2:16 are all parts of old-covenant worship, no longer binding on the new-covenant Christian. Paul is simply reminding Christians that they are not under the ceremonial law. And he sees that as vital for right corporate worship among new covenant Christians. His words still speak today to those who long for the elaborate liturgical and symbolical worship of the old covenant. Do not pass by the substance to return to the shadows, he says. So this response of Paul has to do with understanding the discontinuities of redemptive history.

Then Paul takes on angel worship and the false humility that accompanies it: "Let no one keep defrauding you of your prize by delighting in self-abasement and the worship of the angels, taking his stand on *visions* he has seen, inflated without cause by his fleshly mind, and not holding fast to the head, from whom the entire body, being supplied and held together by the joints and ligaments, grows with a growth which is from God." His critique is a rejection of the visions on which such worship is based and a condemnation of the insufficient view of Christ inherently entailed in such an activity. The criticism also clearly pertains to corporate worship, at least in part. It is hard to imagine such a thing as "angel worship in all of life" no matter what one does with the notoriously difficult phrase *the worship of angels!*[19] Furthermore, the wrongheadedness of this worship has to do not merely with the internal and the subjective, but the external and the objective. Yes, Paul hints at heart insincerity in his comments about self-abasement juxtaposed with self-inflation, but his main points are that (1) the worship is not God-commanded but human-originated and (2) the worship does not do justice to the person and exaltation of Christ or our union with him. It is from this passage that the wise old Puritan divines got their phrase *will-worship*. Worshiping according to our ideas, however sincere, is an act of self-worship and specifically the worship of our own wills and wants. Here, once again, we find the New Testament far from unconcerned about the how of worship. For Paul it was vital, a fact even more apparent (if that is possible) in the next passage.

Paul's Directives for Corinth

Grounded in Paul's phenomenal directives for genuine charismatic worship in Corinth (1 Cor. 14) is an unparalleled expression of the new-covenant importance of the way in which we worship. Paul is perfectly willing to regulate the form and content of charismatic worship founded in the real and powerful working of the third person of the Trinity, God the Holy Spirit! Whatever we believe about the continuation of revelation, tongues, prophecy, and the like, this passage (in spite of its extreme interpretive challenges) yields crystal-clear teaching on numerous points relating to corporate worship, which are applicable to all Christians in all ages.

Paul places a premium on corporate worship that is understandable and mutually edifying. Hence, he values prophecy above uninterpreted tongues precisely because prophecy edifies the church:

> For one who speaks in a tongue does not speak to men but to God. . . . But one who prophesies speaks to men for edification and exhortation and consolation. One who speaks in a[n uninterpreted] tongue edifies himself; but one who prophesies edifies the church. Now I wish that you all spoke in tongues, but *even* more that you would prophesy; and greater is one who prophesies than one who speaks in tongues, unless he interprets, so that the church may receive edifying. (1 Cor. 14:2–5)

The edification that Paul contemplates is rooted in the mind, the understanding, and mature thinking. The vocabulary for this is apparent throughout. So edification, comprehensibility, the centrality of preaching, and the purpose in preaching to address the understanding and conscience, far from being cultural preferences derived from post-Renaissance, north-European rationalism, are instead apostolic principles or characteristics of new-covenant worship that trump even extraordinary activities enabled by God the Holy Spirit.

Paul describes apostolic-era corporate worship. Simply using Paul's vocabulary and phrases, we can build a description of the components and character of charismatic, apostolic-era corporate worship:

- ✧ spiritual gifts (1)
- ✧ prophecy (6)
- ✧ tongues (5 and elsewhere)
- ✧ edification, exhortation, and consolation (3)
- ✧ interpretation (26)

46

✧ revelation, knowledge, and teaching (6)
✧ meaning (10)
✧ prayer and singing with the mind (15)
✧ knowing what you are saying (16)
✧ instruction (19)
✧ mature thinking (20)
✧ conviction (24)
✧ calling to account (24)
✧ the secrets of the heart disclosed (25)
✧ falling on the face and worshiping God (25)
✧ God among you (25)
✧ psalm (26)
✧ silence (28)
✧ learning (31)
✧ not a God of confusion but of peace (33)
✧ as in all the churches (33)
✧ the Lord's commandment (37)
✧ all things done properly and in an orderly manner (40)

These words and phrases point up central elements in corporate worship (preaching, singing, praying) in common with the people of God in all ages, key motivations and objectives in corporate worship (congregational edification, engagement with God, the by-product of witness to unbelievers), the heart aspects of true worship (consolation, conviction, disclosure, subjection), and concern for form and order (silence, subjection, propriety). But the overwhelming impression made by a review of this service is the cognitive stress of Paul: he wants people to understand what they sing and pray and what others say and preach; he wants instruction, teaching, learning, knowledge, and mature thinking. For those who parody the supposedly overcerebral corporate worship of the Reformed tradition, there will be utterly no comfort found for them in the description of the charismatic worship of 1 Corinthians 14![20]

Paul regulates the number and order of people allowed to exercise extraordinary gifts vested in them by the Holy Spirit during corporate worship! One cannot conceive of such a restriction on "worship in all of life." Here are his rules: "If anyone speaks in a tongue, *it should be* by two or at the most three, and *each* in turn, and one must interpret; but if there is no interpreter, he must keep silent in the church" (1 Cor. 14:27–28). "Let two or three prophets speak, and let the others pass judgment. But if a revelation is made to another who is seated, the first one must keep silent. For you can all prophesy one by one, so that all may learn and all may be exhorted; and the spirits of prophets are subject to prophets" (14:29–32). Did you catch that? He said that no more than three shall speak in tongues or prophesy in a given service, and then only one at a time, even if God himself has granted one a prophetic revelation. There is no more astounding example of the sheer investment of dominical plenipotentiary authority in the apostles of the church in all of the holy Scriptures than we find here in this passage. If I could reverently suggest an imaginary dialogue. "But Paul, I have just received a prophetic revelation of God and I am constrained to disclose it." "One at a time," says Paul. "But Paul, God the Holy Spirit has given this word to me." "I understand—let me repeat, it's one at a time and if three have already spoken, remain silent," replies Paul. "Paul, how can you? I am a prophet of the Lord!" "Because, my dear brother, what I speak is the Lord's command for all the churches," says Paul. Here we have the revelational regulation of corporate worship extending even to activity generated and enabled by the third person of the Trinity. The idea that order, or a concern for it, is inimical to the work of the Spirit and our response to it is dashed against the rocks by this new-covenant passage. The suggestion that applying the rule and order of Scripture will somehow quench the Spirit in corporate worship looks fairly ludicrous in light of this passage. Because God the Spirit who wrote the Lord's command is the same Spirit who enables true worship, there can be no ultimate conflict between form and freedom, between the rules of Scripture and the heartfelt expression of praise, between the precepts of worship and unfettered engagement with God.

Paul puts restrictions on those who may preach the word in the corporate worship of the churches. He says: "The women are to keep silent in the churches; for they are not permitted to speak, but are to subject themselves, just as the Law also says. If they desire to learn anything, let them ask their own husbands at home; for it is improper for a woman to speak in church" (1 Cor. 14:34–35). Paul grounds this injunction not on some temporary cultural problem in Corinth but in the written word of God ("just as the

Law also says"). There is no more easily observable example of the wide-spread rejection of the authority of Scripture in the worship of the church than in the ever-growing number of female preachers (however sincere, dedicated, talented, and otherwise orthodox they may be), even in ostensibly evangelical circles. Paul's directive, however, is unmistakable. God's word alone determines who may or may not preach in public worship.

Paul views his commands as requisite for the corporate worship in all churches, and not simply for Corinth. He says: "If anyone thinks he is a prophet or spiritual, let him recognize that the things which I write to you are the Lord's commandment. But if anyone does not recognize *this,* he is not recognized" (1 Cor. 14:37–38). This comes in the wake of Paul's declaring his rules on the ordering of tongues, interpretation, prophecy, preaching, and singing, as well as his prohibition of the teaching of women. Why must it be this way? Because, Paul says earlier, "God is not *a God* of confusion but of peace, as in all the churches of the saints" (14:33). God is not a God of bedlam, and since the same God is God of all his churches the same norms obtain: "All things must be done properly and in an orderly manner" (14:40). Once again we see that the major thrust of this whole passage is that God cares very much how we worship; he cares not just about our attitudes and motives, but about our actions and order. It is beyond debate that in the new-covenant era God continues to be concerned about how we worship, even though the specifics of the how of worship change from those of the old-covenant ceremonial system.

It is also apparent, even from this abstract of New Testament teaching pertaining to worship (without the benefit of exploring key texts like 1 Cor. 11), that the New Testament has a distinctive category of corporate worship and that it has a special concern about worship that is uniquely and distinguishably corporate. This is important to say because serious voices in the worship debate question whether a distinct category of corporate worship can be found in the new-covenant era. Some suggest that we need to rethink altogether why the church gathers in the first place. For worship? They argue: No, that is not the New Testament answer. The New Testament does not apply the corporate-worship language and terms of the Old Testament to the gathered activity of the local church, but rather to all of life. Therefore, the prime reason we come together is to fellowship, study the Bible, hear preaching, pray together, and the like, but not to worship

God—that is what we do in our homes, communities, and vocations.[21] So, in this view, the New Testament fulfillment of Old Testament corporate worship is worship in all of life. This is a creative approach, to say the least, and it rightly stresses the New Testament's emphasis on worship in all of life (which is, of course, not without precedent in the Old Testament) and provides enough exegetical grounds and theological critique to prove fatal to any and all prescriptive high-church liturgical approaches to worship, but its word-study method does not do justice to the obvious continuities between the elements of Old and New Testament gathered worship (Bible reading, Bible exposition, singing, prayer, and sacraments). No matter what semantic designation is given in the New Testament for the general activity of the gathered people of God when it is engaged in reading, praying, preaching, and singing the word, it is clear that this constitutes corporate worship and that such a thing does exist even and especially in the new covenant. Only our modern tendencies toward individualism and reticence about distinctions blind us to this fact.

But the Bible does more than show us that there is such a thing as corporate worship and that God cares about how it is done. The Bible testifies, in both New Testament and Old, in its teaching about God and his enduring moral norms, by precept and example, that corporate worship is to be conducted in careful response to divine revelation. And thus we can say that the Bible itself provides us with what the Reformed tradition sometimes labels the regulative principle of worship. Much of what we have already learned substantiates this assertion, but in order to establish this point beyond the shadow of a doubt we will consider in the next chapter, not simply individual passages, but some of the broader theological themes of Scripture that provide the grounds for this distinctive approach to the form and content of biblical corporate worship.

2

FOUNDATIONS FOR BIBLICALLY DIRECTED WORSHIP

J. LIGON DUNCAN III

The Bible provides us with God's directions for the form and content of Christian worship. When we say that "the acceptable way of worshiping the true God is instituted by himself, and so limited by his own revealed will, that he may not be worshiped according to the imaginations and devices of men, or the suggestions of Satan, under any visible representation, or any other way not prescribed in the holy Scripture" (Westminster Confession of Faith 21.1), we anchor that assertion in a number of ways. Our affirmation is grounded not only in the exegesis of specific texts (like Ex. 20:4–6; Deut. 4:15–19; 12:32; Matt. 4:9–10; 15:9; Acts 17:24–25; 1 Cor. 11:23–30; 14:1–40; and Col. 2:16–23) and not only in the transcanonical refrain that God does not desire humanly devised worship. We build also and especially on a set of even broader biblical theological realities: the doctrine of God, the Creator-creature distinction, the idea of revelation, the unchanging character of the moral law, the nature of faith, the doctrine of carefulness, the derivative nature of the church's authority, the doctrine of Christian freedom, the true nature of biblical piety, and the reality of the fallen human nature's tendency to idolatry. Each of these key foundations for the Reformed view of the biblical doctrine of worship is worth consideration. We will explore each one briefly, concluding with a look at the testimony of church history to the Bible's teaching on worship.

Foundational Realities

The Nature of God

God's own nature—who God is—determines the way we should worship him. This is a primary principle of worship in both old and new covenants. In Deuteronomy 4:15–19, the second commandment's prohibition against images in worship is explicitly grounded in Israel's not having seen an image of God, which is, of course, in turn grounded in the nature of God's being. Again, this is precisely what Jesus told the Samaritan woman in John 4:24: "God is spirit, and those who worship Him must worship in spirit and truth." Whatever it means to worship in spirit and truth, Jesus unmistakably bases the requirement of it on the notion that "God is spirit," that is, he grounds it in the nature of God, in theology proper. So, in one sense, our doctrine of worship is an implication of our doctrine of God. This means that the how of new-covenant worship is not ultimately derived from temporary, transitional, positive law or even new-covenant norms, but is based rather upon the character of God himself. As R. C. Sproul often reminds us, the distinctive of the Reformed doctrine of God is that theology proper controls every aspect of our theology, including our worship. Correspondingly, corporate worship as the *locus* of God's prime means of grace is the instrument that God has chosen to grow and edify his church in the knowledge of himself, as well as the vehicle of our special earthly communion with him (Matt. 18). So, the regulative principle is grounded in God's character and not merely in some peculiarity of the Sinai covenant.

The parallel truth to the above point (that God's nature determines the nature of his worship) is that corporate worship informs our understanding of God and therefore must be superintended by him if his self-revelation is to be the prime factor in our knowing him. This is one of the underlying rationales of Exodus 20:4–6. If you worship God via the usage of images, it changes your view of God. Form impacts content. The means of worship influences the worshipers' apprehension of God. So, Christian corporate worship both requires and shapes our understanding of the Bible's teaching about God. The doctrine of God informs our corporate worship, and, in turn, our corporate worship refines our practical comprehension and embrace of the doctrine of God. It is true, of course, that worship in all of life impacts our corporate worship. Those who do not "present [their] bodies a living and holy sacrifice" are both unprepared to enter into the fullness of corporate worship as it is envisioned in the word and are not expressing one of its principal intended ethical effects. In fact, the person in whom there is an experiential dissonance between activity in gathered worship and worship in the rest of life is in danger of creating a parallel but juxtaposed life, the breeding ground of a fatal spiritual hypocrisy. Nevertheless, it is especially in the local church under the means of grace appointed by God for the edification of the church in corporate worship — that is, through the word (reading, preaching, singing the Bible), prayer (pleading the promises of the Bible, adoring and thanking the God of the Bible, confessing sin, interceding for the saints), and the sacraments (the divinely appointed tangible confirmatory signs of Bible promises) — that we come to know God. This context provides for both the revelational and relational aspects of Christian discipleship necessary for growth in the knowledge of God. Consequently, the how of worship is vital to our growth in grace and in the knowledge of the one true God because it contributes to our grasp of the one true God. Often we hear, and agree with, the dictum that "we become like *what* we worship," but the Reformed understanding of worship teaches us that it is also true that "we become like *how* we worship."

The Creator-Creature Distinction

The Bible's inviolable Creator-creature distinction influences the way we worship and makes necessary the regulative principle. The Bible celebrates that distinction from beginning to end. Genesis 1 emphasizes that God made the world and rules over the world and is not a part of or contained within the creation. Over and over we are reminded that he is God and we are not: "Know that the Lord Himself is God; / It is He who has made us, and not we ourselves; / *We are* His people" (Ps. 100:3, see also Ezek. 28:2). Repeatedly we are taught his incommunicable attributes and the irreversible discontinuities between his being and ours: "God is not a man, that He should lie, / Nor a son of man, that He should repent; / Has He said, and will He not do it? / Or has He spoken, and will He not make it good?" (Num. 23:19). Emphatically we are pointed not only to his moral but to his majestic holiness: "I saw the Lord sitting on a throne, lofty and exalted, with the train of His robe filling the temple. Seraphim stood above Him, each having six wings: with two he covered his face, and with two he covered his feet, and with two he flew. And one called out to another and said, 'Holy, Holy, Holy, is the Lord of hosts, The whole earth is full of His glory' " (Isa. 6:1–3). All of these highlight God's transcendence and the inability of our finite minds to fathom him. So if worship is going to be in accordance with his nature, and his nature is transcendent, infinite, and incomprehensible, then how else can we worship other than by the direction of his word? Once again, our doctrine of God impinges upon our doctrine of worship. Given the distance between Creator and creature (a point of emphasis in Calvin, the Scholastics, Westminster, Van Til, and even Barth!), given the undeniable biblical reality that God's ways and thoughts are as high above ours as the heavens are above the earth (Isa. 55:8–9), what makes us think we can possibly fathom what would please God, apart from his telling us what to do in his word?[1] The Westminster Assembly stated this argument more than 350 years ago: "The distance between God and the creature is so great that although reasonable creatures do owe obedience unto him as their Creator, yet they could never have any fruition of him as their blessedness and reward but by some voluntary condescension on God's part" (7.1).

The Nature of Revelation and Knowledge

The biblical idea of revelation and knowledge requires revelation-directed worship. Biblical worship inherently entails a response to revelation. As in the covenants, in which God sought out the patriarchs and took initiative in promise and blessing, to which they responded in faith and thanksgiving, so also God takes the initiative in worship. This is necessary now, not only because his nature determines worship and because his nature is infinite, but also because of the blinding impediment of sin: "Although the light of nature, and the works of creation and providence, do so far manifest the goodness, wisdom, and power of God, as to leave men unexcusable; yet are they not sufficient to give that knowledge of God, and of his will, which is necessary unto salvation" (Westminster Confession of Faith 1.1, based on Rom. 1:18–20; 1 Cor. 1:21; 2:12–14). It is also necessary for right worship, because of our sin: "Therefore it pleased the Lord, at sundry times, and in divers manners, to reveal himself, and to declare that his will unto his church" (Westminster Confession of Faith 1.1, based on Heb. 1:1), especially regarding the central issue of worship. As revelation is the divine foundation of human knowledge of salvation, so also is revelation the divine foundation of our worship of God, which is itself, when properly understood, a response to revelation. And if worship is to be a right response

54

to revelation, then it must be revelationally directed. Hence, we see the dialogical aspect in worship of God's call and our response. God takes initiative in worship through revelation, promise, and blessing. His people respond in worship through hearing, believing, and praise/adoration/confession/thanksgiving. This divine, covenantal pattern is reflected in the true worship of every biblical age, whatever the peculiar distinctives, and yields the irreducible core of reading, preaching (God's initiative in revelation), singing, and praying (our response to revelation) in accordance with divine revelation. R. P. Martin puts it this way:

> The distinctive genius of corporate worship is the two-beat rhythm of revelation and response. God speaks; we answer. God acts; we accept and give. God gives; we receive. As a corollary to this picture, worship implies a code word for man's offering to God: *sacrifice*. The worshiper is not a passive, motionless recipient, but an active participant, called upon to "make an offering."[2]

The Second Commandment

The enduring moral norm of the second commandment necessitates that true worship conform to the regulative principle. We have already seen in our study of the second commandment that it forbids not only the making of idols, not only the use of images in the worship of the one true God, not only the introduction of things forbidden into the worship of God, but also of anything not commanded or warranted. The abiding validity of this command is seen in its placement in the moral, not the ceremonial law; in its reflection of the character of God and not of changing moral norms; in the constant repetition of its core principle throughout Scripture; and in Paul's characterization of obedience to it as the essence of Christianity ("you turned to God from idols to serve a living and true God"; 1 Thess. 1:9). This is, by the way, why Robert Dabney calls the New Testament "a Book intended to subvert idolatry."[3] Indeed, the New Testament, precisely because of the abiding validity of the second commandment as an unchanging moral norm, even extends the Old Testament critique of idolatry further. Since there is a double essence to the idolatry prohibited in the second command (worshiping something other than the one true God or worshiping the one true God in a way he has not commanded), we must rely on the regulative principle to assist us in avoiding idolatrous worship. Thus the *elements* of worship must be instituted by God himself, the *forms* in which those elements are performed must not be inimical to the nature or content of the element or draw attention away from the substance and goal of worship, and the *circumstances* of worship must never overshadow or detract from the elements, but rather discreetly foster the work of the means of grace.

The Nature of Faith

Related to the biblical teaching regarding revelation and knowledge is another important building block of the Reformed approach to worship. It is called "the argument from faith" (and John Owen, for instance, states it convincingly). Since faith is essential to true worship, the conditions of worship must accord with the exercise of true faith. Faith is, in essence, a believing response to God's revelation, especially his revelation of covenant and promise. As the Westminster Confession says, by faith "a Christian believes to be true whatsoever is revealed in the word, for the authority of God himself speaking therein; and acts differently upon that which each particular passage thereof contains; yielding obedience to the commands, trembling at the threatenings, and embracing the promises of God for this life, and that which is to come" (14.2). Where God has not revealed himself, there can be no faithful response to his revelation, by virtue of the very nature of faith. Since "without faith it is impossible to please [God]" (Heb. 11:6) and since "whatever is not from faith is sin" (Rom. 14:23), God cannot be pleased by worship that is not an obedient response to his revelation, because it is by definition "un-faith-full" worship. Hence, once again we see that worship must be positively based upon the word of God.

The Doctrine of Carefulness

The Bible makes it exceedingly clear that we ought to be careful in worship. Our God is a consuming fire and not to be trifled with. The severity of the punishments inflicted upon those who from time to time offered to God, apparently in good faith, unprescribed worship catches our attention: the stories of Nadab and Abihu and their "strange fire" (Lev. 10:1–2) and of Uzzah and David and the ark (2 Sam. 6). But biblical doctrine of carefulness in worship is built on an even broader foundation than these breathtaking warning passages. It is supported by at least the following scriptural truths. (1) We were created to worship God, and hence the fulfillment of our very purpose behooves us to take care in how we worship. (2) Corporate worship dictates the quality of our worship in all of life and compels our carefulness. (3) That God himself is seeking worshipers who will worship him in spirit and in truth constrains all who would be those worshipers to acquaint themselves with care as to just how one goes about worshiping in spirit and truth. (4) God is dangerous to those who are careless in worship, however sincere. Thus the Reformed tradition has always understood that, especially in worship, the road to destruction is paved with good intentions. Intentions are not enough; we must submit ourselves to the authority of the word, be mindful to learn and obey the word, and neglect no part of the word. The way of carefulness is the way of the word and so corroborates the regulative principle.

The Church's Derivative Authority

The Bible's teaching on the derivative nature of the church's authority limits its discretionary powers in worship and enjoins its observance of the regulative principle. Jesus is the sole king of and lawmaker for the church (Matt. 28:18–20). All of the authority of the church derives from him. The ordinary officers of the church, as gifts of Christ for its upbuilding (Eph. 4:11–13), have no authority to instate their own laws and norms; their job is to administer his rule and law, revealed in the word. This is one reason that Presbyterians refer to their church councils and assemblies as "courts" (not legislatures). Their job is to administer the king's law, not to make it. Thus all church power is "ministerial and declarative." That is, it serves the word and declares the will of the king of the church. James Bannerman makes this argument in *The Church of Christ*: "The Church is an institution; instituted by the positive command of the risen Christ, and authorized by Him to require obedience to His commands and participation in His ordinances. The Church is given no authority to require obedience to its own commands, and is given no authority to require participation in ordinances of its own making."[4] If this is the case, then it is not surprising that Christ has not left the church with discretionary authority in the matter of the substance and elements of worship. It is the church's business simply to administer his rule for worship, as set forth in the word. So, this regulative principle of church government lies behind and necessitates the regulative principle of worship.

The Doctrine of Christian Freedom

The biblical doctrine of Christian freedom is vital to our doctrine of worship and can be protected only by the regulative principle. The Westminster Confession makes the bold declaration that "God alone is Lord of the conscience, and has left it free from the doctrines and commandments of men which are in any thing contrary to his word, or beside it in matters of faith or worship. So that to believe such doctrines, or to obey such commands out of conscience, is to betray true liberty of conscience; and the requiring of an implicit faith, and an absolute and blind obedience, is to destroy liberty of conscience, and reason also" (20.2). This manifesto of Christian freedom is based on Pauline principles found in Romans 14:1–4, Galatians 4:8–11, and Colossians 2:16–23. The regulative principle is designed to secure the believer's freedom from the dominion of human opinion in worship. But some people view the regulative principle as legalistic and constraining. They rightly note that it forbids a variety of activities and restrains others; but this is simply to say that it helps enforce biblical norms that are, upon reflection, freeing! Freedom from human opinions can be found only in the rule of God's good and gracious and wise law. If humans can dictate how we may worship, apart from the word or in addition to the word, then we are captive to their command. The only way we can really experience one of the key blessings of Christian freedom in the context of corporate worship—freedom from human doctrines and commandments—is if corporate worship is directed only according to the word of God, and that means following the regulative principle. Furthermore "God requires us to worship Him only as He has revealed. Therefore, to require a person, in corporate worship, to do something that God has not required, forces the person to sin against his/her conscience, by making them do what they do not believe God has called them to do."[5]

The Nature of True Piety

God repeatedly expresses his pleasure with and delight in those who do exactly what he says. In Isaiah 66:1–4 true religion ("the life of God in the soul of man") is characterized by one "who is humble and contrite of spirit, and who trembles at My word" in contrast to these who choose their own way. Deuteronomy 12:29–32 explicitly warns against establishing worship practices based upon prevailing cultural norms; true godliness is manifested in those who obey God's dictum: "Whatever I command you, you shall be careful to do; you shall not add to nor take away from it." In the Saul stories a dominant theme is that "to obey is better than sacrifice" (1 Sam. 15:3–22), a thought that puts a premium on strict obedience to God's word

58

in corporate worship. True piety manifests itself in humble obedience to God's word in our expression of worship and thus urges us to worship that is wholly in accord with Scripture.

Our Tendency to Idolatry

The biblical teaching on our fallen human tendency to idolatry affects our approach to the worship of God and moves us to embrace the regulative principle. Calvin called our minds "perpetual idol factories." Experience confirms his less-than-flattering estimation. Indeed, idolatry, not theoretical atheism, is the basic problem of the human heart. Luther said that "we are inclined to it by nature; and coming to us by inheritance, it seems pleasant." Humanity, having been created in God's image, and with a sense of deity indelibly written on its heart, is inescapably religious. However, since the fall, our tendency is to attempt to create God in our own image and thus worship ourselves rather than the one in whose image we were made. This is precisely Paul's argument in Romans 1:19–25:

> That which is known about God is evident within them; for God made it evident to them. For since the creation of the world His invisible attributes, His eternal power and divine nature, have been clearly seen, being understood through what has been made, so that they are without excuse. For even though they knew God, they did not honor Him as God or give thanks, but they became futile in their speculations, and their foolish heart was darkened. Professing to be wise, they became fools, and exchanged the glory of the incorruptible God for an image in the form of corruptible man and of birds and four-footed animals and crawling creatures.
>
> Therefore God gave them over in the lusts of their hearts to impurity, so that their bodies would be dishonored among them. For they exchanged the truth of God for a lie, and worshiped and served the creature rather than the Creator.

This indictment charges that though God's general revelation of himself is evident in and to the natural person, as well as in the larger creation, thus leaving us without defense against God's charges of rebellion, nevertheless this knowledge does not lead to worship and thanksgiving but to idolatry. It is part of Paul's accusation against the whole of humanity — Jew and Gentile. This is why even John Wesley could say that in his natural state, every man born into the world is a rank idolater. Now if this is true of us apart from God's saving grace, then a proper understanding of the ongoing depravity of the Christian life, the reality of indwelling sin, a knowledge of how master-sins work, an appreciation of the gradual and partial work of progressive sanctification, and an appropriate humility and self-knowledge ought to move us to avoid human invention and be careful of human creativity in worship. We are all recovering idolaters. Extreme caution is needed when it comes to how we worship. In the final analysis the world is divided into iconoclasts and iconodules. You must decide on which side you will stand.

The Testimony of Church History

The testimony (both positive and negative) of church history to the Bible's teaching on worship educates our worship and commends to us worship according to Scripture. Church history does not supply a normative authority for Christian worship, but it does supply a didactic authority that we would be foolish to ignore. As Hughes Old says: "In the last analysis we are not as much concerned about what the tradition tells us about worship as we are concerned with what tradition tells us about what Scripture has to say about worship."[6] What does Christian history teach us? Several things. (1) Simple but powerful biblical worship always characterizes the worship of the church in its best ages. The testimony of the healthiest Christianity is to Bible-filled, Bible-directed worship, worship in which the Scriptures are read, preached, sung, and prayed and the sacraments, as visible words, are administered in accordance with the word written—this is precisely what the regulative principle seeks to foster in the church today. (2) There is every evidence in both biblical and postbiblical church history that declension in corporate worship is tied to declension in religion. (3) Following on this, church history shows that even Christians, left to their own devices, inevitably produce worship that is unbiblical and impious. The Reformation was a gigantic protest against exactly this. (4) History is not normative, but it helps us understand Scripture, and it gives us perspective on the peculiar tendencies and temptations of our own age. The sweep of Christian history provides an opportunity to sit at the feet of the *sanctorum communio* and learn wisdom, to have our priorities weighed and measured and our practices compared and contrasted, in ways that they could not be otherwise. Both the accomplishments and the mistakes of the past bring didactic and diagnostic help to us as we attempt to faithfully worship according to the Scripture in our own time and cultural situation. (5) Finally, the best of Christian history instructs and inspires us for our worship today. Not that our worship can ever be a mere photocopy of the past; but an appreciation of the devotional treasures of the ages bequeathed to us in the legacy of the historic worship of the church helps us resist the rampant chronological snobbery of our own age.

Knowing That, What, Whom, When, Where, Why, and How

The foundational realities described above are connected and compounding and serve to corroborate the legitimacy and importance of the regulative principle—the axiom that we ought to worship God in accordance with the positive warrant of Scripture. This axiom applied, in turn, helps us with the whole scope of worship. Thus historic Reformed worship appreciates God's concern for the that, what, whom, when, where, why, and how of corporate worship.

It is important *that* we worship corporately, for God made us for his worship and for community with other worshipers. Worship is the one thing he "seeks" (John 4:23).

What corporate worship is matters to God too. It is not evangelism, nor is it even mutually edifying fellowship. It is a family meeting with God, it is the covenant community engaging with God, gathering with his people to seek the face of God, to glorify and enjoy him, to hear his word, to revel in the glory of union and communion with him, to respond to his word, to render praise back to him, to give unto him the glory due his name. John Piper puts it this way:

> The authenticating, inner essence of worship is being satisfied with Christ, prizing Christ, cherishing Christ, treasuring Christ. . . . [This] is tremendously relevant for understanding what worship services should be about. They are about "going hard after God."
>
> When we say that what we do on Sunday mornings is to "go hard after God," what we mean is that we are going hard after satisfaction in God, and going hard after God as our prize, and going hard after God as our treasure, our soul-food, our heart-delight, our spirit's pleasure. Or to put Christ in His

rightful place—it means that we are going hard after all that God is for us in Jesus Christ, crucified and risen.[7]

Worship is both active and passive: we come to bless and to receive God's blessing (Ps. 134). Christian corporate worship is Father-focused, Christ-centered, and Spirit-enabled (Eph. 1:3–14) and "offered up in the context of the body of believers, who strive to align all the forms of their devout ascription of all worth to God with the panoply of new covenant mandates and examples that bring to fulfillment the glories of antecedent revelation and anticipated the consummation."[8]

The *whom* of worship is, of course, central to true worship (John 4:22, 24). It is what the first commandment is all about. We aim to worship the God of the Bible, God as he reveals himself, for we cannot worship him as we ought unless we know him as he is—and we cannot know him as he is except insofar as he has revealed himself to us in his word. There is a god we want and the God who is, and the two are not the same.[9] The only way to be sure that we have the whom of worship right is to worship according to God's written self-revelation.

The *when* of corporate worship remains important in the new-covenant era. In the days of the old covenant, worship was to be rendered on the seventh day because of God's creational rest and on the various feast days that foreshadowed new-covenant realities. Now, in the end of the ages, corporate worship is to be done on the first day of the week, the Lord's Day. Even for those who do not embrace the Reformed view of the Christian Sabbath, four tremendous realities establish the importance of Lord's Day corporate worship: (1) the resurrection of Christ, which is foundational to the re-creative work of Christ in making a people for himself (Mark 16:1–8; cf. v. 9; 2 Cor. 5:14–17; Gal. 6:15–16; Col. 1:15–22); (2) the eternal rest fore-shadowed in the Lord's Day (Heb. 4:9); (3) the Lord's Day language and observance of the New Testament church (Rev. 1:10; cf. Matt. 28:1; Luke 24:1; John 20:1, 19–23; Acts 20:7; 1 Cor. 16:2); and (4) the New Testament command to the saints to gather, Christ's promise of presence with us when we do, the faithful example of the gathering of New Testament Christians, and Jesus' express command that we disciple new converts in the context of the local church (Heb. 10:24–25; Matt. 18:20; 28:18–20; Acts 1:4).

The *where* of new-covenant worship is important too, though it has also changed from the old-covenant era. Whereas once the answer to where was "the tabernacle" or "the temple" or "Jerusalem," the answer now is "wherever the Lord's house (i.e., his people) is gathered." Jesus stresses this to the Samaritan woman (John 4:21) and to his disciples in addressing congregational discipline (Matt. 18:20)—surely a solemn component of the life of the gathered church. The place of new-covenant worship is no longer inextricably tied to a geographical location and a physical structure but to a gathered people. This is why in the old Scottish tradition, as the people gathered to enter a church building, it would be said that "the kirk goes in" rather than, as we often say, "we are going to church." The new covenant *locus* of the special presence of God with the church militant is in the gathered body, wherever it might be—whether the catacombs or a storefront or beautiful colonial church building.

The *why* of corporate worship is vital to God as well, and there is more than one right biblical answer. Surely at the top of the list is "for his own glory" (1 Cor. 10:31; Ps. 29:1–2). There is no higher answer to "why do we worship?" than because the glory of God is more important than anything else in all creation. The chief end of the church is to glorify and enjoy God together forever, because the chief thing in all the world is God's glory (Phil. 2:9–11). John Piper communicates this as effectively as anyone in our generation. There are other answers as well: because God said to worship, because God created us to worship, because God saved us to worship, because it is our natural duty as creatures and joyful duty as Christians to worship, because our worship is a response of gratitude for saving grace, because those with new hearts long to hear his word and express their devotion, because God wants to bless us with himself, because God has chosen us for his own inheritance and seeks to commune with us in his ordinances, and more.

The *how* of corporate worship is the business of the second commandment, but as we have seen, it is a central concern for the New Testament church as well (John 4; 1 Cor. 11, 14; Col. 2). This is where the regulative principle is manifest most clearly. It is concerned to assure that corporate worship in all its aspects—standard, dynamic, motivation, and goal—is biblical. For the standard to be biblical means that the substance and elements and corporateness of worship are positively in accord with Scripture. For the dynamic to be biblical means that worship is Spirit-gathered, Spirit-dependent, Spirit-engendered, and Spirit-empowered, in accordance with the teaching of Scripture. For the motivation to be biblical means that worship is simultaneously a communal response of gratitude for grace, an expression of passion for God, the fulfillment of what we were made and re-deemed for, a joyful engagement in a delightful obedience, and a corpo-rate Christ-provided encounter with the triune God, again in accord with the Bible's teaching. For the goal to biblical means that all true corporate worship aims for and is an expression of God's own glory and contemplates the consummation of the eternal covenant in the church triumphant's ever-lasting union and communion with God.

The regulative principle aims to aid the church is ensuring that the ele-ments of worship are unequivocally and positively grounded in Scripture and that the forms and circumstances of worship are in accord with Scrip-ture. The Reformed tradition has not been concerned with forms and cir-cumstances so much for their own sake as much as for the sake of the elements and substance of worship and for the sake of the object and aim of worship. The Reformers also understood two things often lost on mod-erns. First, they understood that the liturgy, media, instruments, and vehi-cles of worship are never neutral, and so exceeding care must be given to the "law of unintended consequences." Often the medium overwhelms and changes the message. Second, they knew that the how of worship exists for the what, whom, and why of worship. The purpose of the elements and forms and circumstances of corporate worship is to assure that you are ac-tually doing worship as defined by the God of Scripture, that you are wor-shiping the God of Scripture, and that your aim in worshiping him is the aim set forth in Scripture. So the Reformers cared about the how of wor-ship not because they thought liturgy was mystical or sacramental, but pre-cisely so that the liturgy could get out of the way of the gathered church's communion with the living God. Its function was not to draw attention to itself but to aid the soul's communion with God in the gathered company of the saints by serving to convey the word of God to and from God, from and to his people. This is why the great Baptist preacher Geoffrey Thomas has said that in true worship men have little thought of the means of wor-ship because their thoughts are on God; true worship is characterized by self-effacement without self-consciousness. That is, in biblical worship we so focus upon God himself and are so intent to acknowledge his inherent and unique worthiness that we are transfixed by him, and thus worship is not about what we want or like (nor do his appointed means divert our eyes from him), but rather it is about meeting with God and delighting in his delights. Praise decentralizes self.

We should also note another thing about the Reformers' approach to worship. They did not have the same interest in cultural accommodation as many modern evangelical worship theorists do. They were against culture-derived worship and were more concerned to implement principles of Scripture in their specific cultures (and even to emulate the best of the Bible-inspired cultures of Scripture) than they were to reclaim current cultural forms for Christian use. This is precisely one of the areas productive of the greatest controversy in our own age.

The Form and Content of Worship

So far we have outlined a case for the historic Reformed approach to worship, often called the regulative principle. The regulative principle helps assure that our corporate worship is Bible-filled and Bible-directed, that the substance and structure are biblical, that the content and order are biblical. To put it slightly differently, Reformed corporate worship is by the book in two ways: both its marrow and means are supplied by the book. What then does a worship service look like that is done according to the regulative principle? The Westminster Confession outlines the components this way:

> The reading of the Scriptures with godly fear; the sound preaching; and conscionable hearing of the word, in obedience unto God with understanding, faith, and reverence; singing of psalms[10] with grace in the heart; as, also, the due administration and worthy receiving of the sacraments instituted by Christ; are all parts of the ordinary religious worship of God: beside religious oaths, vows, solemn fastings, and thanksgivings upon special occasions; which are, in their several times and seasons, to be used in an holy and religious manner. (21.5)

What is striking about the Reformed approach to worship is that it requires the substance of corporate worship to be suffused with Scripture and scriptural theology. An apt motto for those who embrace the regulative principle then might be, "Read the Bible, preach the Bible, pray the Bible, sing the Bible, and see the Bible."[11]

We are to read the Bible in public worship. Paul told Timothy to "give attention to the *public* reading *of Scripture*" (1 Tim. 4:13), and so a worship service influenced by the regulative principle will contain a substantial reading of Scripture (and not just from the sermon text). The public reading of the Bible has been at the heart of the worship of God since Old Testament times. In the reading of God's word, he speaks most directly to his people. It is one of the sad indictments of evangelical worship today that it has so little Scripture in it. By contrast, the Westminster Assembly's Directory for the Public Worship of God commends the reading of whole chapters!

We are to preach the Bible. Preaching is God's prime appointed instrument to build up his church. As Paul says, "Faith *comes* from hearing" (Rom. 10:14, 17). Faithful biblical preaching is to explain and apply Scripture to the gathered company, believer and unbeliever alike. James Durham puts it this way: "This is the great design of all preaching, to bring them within the covenant who are without, and to make those who are within the covenant to walk suitably to it. And as these are never separated on the Lord's side, so should they never be separated on our side."[12] This means expository and evangelistic preaching, squarely based in the text of the word of God. This is why our favorite Anglican bishop, J. C. Ryle, can say:

> I charge my readers to remember this. Stand fast on old principles. Do not forsake the old paths. Let nothing tempt you to believe that multiplication of forms and ceremonies, constant reading of liturgical services, or frequent communions, will ever do so much good to souls as the powerful, fiery, fervent preaching of God's Word. Daily services without sermons may gratify and edify a few handfuls of believers, but they will never reach, draw, attract, or arrest the great mass of mankind. If men want to do good to the multitude, if they want to reach their hearts and consciences, they must walk in the steps of Wycliffe, Latimer, Luther, Chrysostom, and St. Paul. They must attack them through their ears; they must blow the trumpet of the everlasting Gospel loud and long; they must preach the Word.[13]

People who hold to the regulative principle will have a high view of preaching and little time for the personality-driven, theologically void, superficially practical monologues that pass for preaching today. "From the very beginning the sermon was supposed to be an explanation of the Scripture reading," says Old; it "is not just a lecture on some religious subject, it is rather an explanation of a passage of Scripture."[14] "Preach the word," Paul tells Timothy (2 Tim. 4:2). "Expository, sequential, verse by verse, book by book, preaching through the whole Bible, the 'whole counsel of God' (Acts 20:27), was the practice of many of the church fathers (e.g., Chrysostom, Augustine), all the Reformers and the best of their heirs ever since. The preached word is the central feature of Reformed worship."[15]

We are to pray the Bible. We must restore the pastoral prayer to its former place of dignity. Our prayers ought to be permeated with the language and thought of Scripture. Perhaps the single most obvious departure from the regulative principle in the Reformed churches of today is precisely this absence of substantive prayer. And yet the Father's house "is a house of prayer," said Jesus (Matt. 21:13). Terry Johnson makes the case thusly:

> The pulpit prayers of Reformed churches should be rich in Biblical and theological content. Do we not learn the language of Christian devotion from the Bible? Do we not learn the language of confession and penitence from the Bible? Do we not learn the promises of God to believe and claim in prayer from the Bible? Don't we learn the will of God, the commands of God, and the desires of God for His people, for which we are to plead in prayer, from the Bible? Since these things are so, public prayers should repeat and echo the language of the Bible throughout. This was once widely understood. Matthew Henry and Isaac Watts produced prayer manuals that trained Protestant pastors for generations to pray in the language of Scripture, and are still used today. Hughes Old has produced a similar work in recent years.[16]

The call here is not for written and read prayer, but studied free prayer. Ministers ought to spend time plundering the language of Scripture in preparation for leading in public worship.

We are to sing the Bible (Ps. 98:1; Neh. 12:27, 46; Matt. 26:30; Acts 16:25; Eph. 5:19; Col. 3:16; Rev. 5:9). This does not mean that we can sing only psalms or sing only the language of Scripture, though this tremendous doxological resource of the church should not be overlooked. What we mean by "sing the Bible" is that our singing ought to be biblical, shot through with the language, categories, and theology of the Bible. It ought to reflect the themes and proportion of the Bible, as well as its substance and weightiness. Johnson provides this counsel:

> Our songs should be rich with Biblical and theological content. The current divisions over music are at the heart of our worship wars. Yet some principles

should be easy enough to identify. First, what does a Christian worship song look like? Answer, it looks like a Psalm. Reformed Protestants have sometimes exclusively sung Psalms. But even if that is not one's conviction, one should still acknowledge that the Psalms themselves should be sung and that the Psalms provide the model for Christian hymnody. If the songs we sing in worship look like Psalms, they will develop themes over many lines with minimal repetition. They will be rich in theological and experiential content. They will tell us much about God, man, sin, salvation, and the Christian life. They will express the whole range of human experience and emotion. Second, what does a Christian worship song *sound* like? Many are quick to point out that God has not given us a book of tunes. No, but He has given us a book of lyrics (the Psalms) and their form will do much to determine the kinds of tunes that will be used. Put simply, the tunes will be suited to the words. They will be sophisticated enough to carry substantial content over several lines and stanzas. They will use minimal repetition. They will be appropriate to the emotional mood of the Psalm or Bible-based Christian hymn. Sing the Bible.[17]

We are to see the Bible. We say "see" the Bible because God's sacraments are "visible words" (Augustine's phrase). The sacraments (baptism and the Lord's Supper) are the only two commanded dramas of Christian worship (Matt. 28:19; Acts 2:38–39; Col. 2:11–12; Luke 22:14–20; 1 Cor. 11:23–26). In them we see the promise of God. But we could also say that in the sacraments we see, smell, touch, and taste the word. In the other means of grace, God addresses our mind and conscience through the hearing. In the sacraments, he uniquely addresses our mind and conscience through the other senses. In, through, and to the senses, God's promise is made tangible. A sacrament is a covenant sign and seal, which means that it reminds us and assures us of a promise. That is, it points to and confirms a gracious promise of God to his people. Another way of saying it is that a sacrament is an action designed by God to sign and seal a covenantal reality, accomplished by the power and grace of God, the significance of which is communicated by the word of God and the reality of which is received or entered into by faith. Hence, the weakness, the frailty of human faith welcomes this gracious act of reassurance. And so these visible symbols of gospel truths are to be done as part of our corporate worship. They will be occasional, no matter how frequent, and so we are reminded that they are not essential to every service. This is not to denigrate them in the least. After all, they are by nature supplemental to and confirmatory of the promises held out in the word, and the grace conveyed in them is the same grace held out via the means of preaching.

There it is. There in a nutshell is the Reformed program for worship. It is simple, biblical, transferable, flexible, and reverent.

It is simple. Reformed worship is simple in that it requires no elaborate ritual, no prescribed book of common prayer, but is merely based on the un-adorned and unpretentious principles and order found in the Bible, by pre-cept and example, which supply the substance of new-covenant worship. There is, of course, a small but intelligent and literate movement advocat-ing formal liturgical renewal in Reformed evangelicalism. Usually empha-sizing the contributions of the early church and the early Reformed liturgies of Strasbourg and Geneva and unwittingly adopting a late-nineteenth-century Scoto-Catholic interpretation of their significance, this movement, open to a more Lutheran view of the sacraments (via the Mercersburg theology) and generally scathing in its estimation of the Westminster Directory and Puritan worship, is working to "liturgicalize" Reformed and evangelical corporate worship.[18] This group propounds what Old calls "Liturgical Romanticism"—the view that, if we could just get back to Bucer's liturgy all would be put right in the church today! This reform effort seems to have captured the imagination of many fine young conservative Reformed ordi-nands and shares a kinship with "the great tradition" movement evident in broader evangelicalism. This is not our call however. Our call is to some-thing both simpler and more profound. We are not harkening the church to fixed forms from the past, however elegant or even consonant with Re-formed worship they may be. We are, instead, calling the church to the Bible—to its simple principles and patterns.

It is biblical. We have argued this case over and over and so we shall not repeat or even summarize it here. We will, however, note two things. (1) While many present-day worship theorists spend much time seeking to adapt the forms of corporate worship, and especially musical forms, to cultural currencies and see such cultural adaptation as key to reaching the culture, the Reformers were not nearly so interested in that as they were in being biblical. (2) There is a recent common criticism of the kind of worship pro-moted by the regulative principle that goes like this: Much of what is called historic Reformed worship is derived from northern European culture and binds the church too closely to a past culture. What can be said to this in reply? Is what is called historic Reformed Protestant worship really just an imposition of north European culture on the practice of church? No. Do the principles and elements of historic Protestant worship derive from north European culture? The emphatic answer is *no!* They are biblically derived, though perhaps more fully implemented in the Reformation and post-Reformation Protestant tradition than anywhere else, and are manifest in churches today on every continent. The argument that historic Protestant worship is north European in essence is no more persuasive than the now-popular assertion that the doctrine of justification by grace alone through faith alone is sixteenth-century European in origin, or the tired old canard than nineteenth-century Americans at Princeton invented the doctrine of biblical inerrancy. It is ironic that some of the very people who make this dismissive assertion are themselves working hard to accommodate Christian worship to a tiny subculture. The historic worship norms reclaimed in Europe five centuries ago are not European in origin. They are Jewish! That is not to say that European culture (if we can even speak of such a thing in that time) made no impingement upon what we now identify as "historic worship," but that the Reformers and their successors were not as interested in accommodating their culture (or redeeming it through the forms of worship) as they were in having their worship according to the word of God.

It is transferable. Reformed worship has worked and is working in every situation and culture where there is a historic Protestant church committed to scriptural principles of worship. It is also more culturally transportable for the work of missions than the more elaborate high-church forms or the more electronic and entertainment-oriented forms of contemporary worship. It is easy to provide examples of how this principle is applied globally. You can find it in the following kinds of diverse settings. Alonzo Ramirez's little congregation in Cajamarca, Peru, up in the Peruvian Andes, gathers in a building they made with their own hands. Sometimes they sing straight out of the text of the Psalms in their Spanish Bibles, sometimes they use Peruvian tunes, sometimes American and British tunes. Here in a nominally Roman Catholic, economically impoverished setting, historic Reformed worship is gathering a congregation. It is evident in the famous Tenth Presbyterian Church in Philadelphia, where over a thousand gather on a Sunday morning in an enormous nineteenth-century building with architectural allusions to an ancient church in Ravenna, to engage in historic, Reformed,

Protestant worship—majestic, simple, and reverent praise of God, using a set order that has been in place since who knows when, with lengthy Scripture readings, traditional hymns, and weighty expository preaching by the able Phil Ryken. Or go across town to West Philadelphia and visit Lance Lewis at Christ Liberation Fellowship, and you will find a faithful African American pastor, deliberately committed to historic Reformed worship. You will also see it in any of the many congregations planted by Khen Tombing in India. In the simplest of structures, often in dangerous conditions, people wracked by poverty and terrorism gather every Lord's Day to hear the doctrines of grace proclaimed. Their worship? Read the Bible, preach the Bible, sing the Bible, and pray the Bible. True there are variations in custom and order, but the worship is recognizable, and Khen deliberately follows in the expository tradition of the great Robert G. Rayburn, feeding his people on the meat of the word. It is displayed in St. Peter's Free Church in Dundee, Scotland, where David Robertson now ministers. Once the pulpit of Robert Murray M'Cheyne, this venerable old building houses a young, growing, postmodern, psalm-singing congregation that features people from the widest conceivable cultural backgrounds. A dozen or so languages can be heard on their grounds, and they are reaching out to inner-city Dundee and fostering a church-planting movement across Scotland. Their worship is, of course, read the Bible, preach the Bible, sing the Bible, and pray the Bible. You will find it in the Los Olivos congregation in the slums of Lima, where the faithful William Castro labors. Street children abound, poverty is rife and this faithful local church is reading, preaching, praying, and singing the Bible. The new Peruvian psalter, it should be said, features tunes from Peru, America, Scotland, Wales, England, France, Germany, Switzerland, Italy, Egypt, and medieval Jewish origins. Then there is Capitol Hill Baptist Church in Washington, D.C., where Cambridge-educated Mark Dever gathers a congregation. Some of their musical forms might be identified as contemporary, but they are substantive, challenging, and reverent, and their service order changes weekly, by pastoral conviction. The sermon is usually an hour or more, and how would I characterize their worship? Read the Bible, preach the Bible, sing the Bible, and pray the Bible. Go across the Atlantic to Grove Chapel, Camberwell, in London, England, where Mark Johnston faithfully proclaims the word. What do you find there? Historic, simple, reverent, Reformed, Protestant worship. Move south, deep into sub-Saharan Africa into the cool green of Malawi. What do Augustine

71

Mfune's congregations of thousands do as they gather on Sunday mornings? They read, hear preached, sing, and pray the Bible. Then there is St. Helen Bishopsgate, back in London (where Dick Lucas ministered), and I have not spoken of the Independent Presbyterian Church in Savannah, with its Genevan-inspired order of service, or Rowland Ward's congregation (Knox Presbyterian Church of Eastern Australia) in Melbourne, Australia, or Reformed churches I know of in Japan and Israel. Do not let anyone tell you that historic Reformed worship will not transfer or that it cannot work outside of Anglo-American culture or in the context of a postmodern generation.

It is flexible. Reformed worship does not produce a cookie-cutter pattern. Following the Westminster Directory of Public Worship's guidelines does not eliminate diversity or different cultural expressions in the forms and circumstances of corporate worship (though it does mean that these are emphatically not the "first things" of the how of worship). Consider again the churches mentioned just above, representing Baptist, Presbyterian, Congregational, and low-church Anglican traditions, on six continents, first world and two-thirds world, ministering to every conceivable class of society—they are following in the train of historic Reformed Protestant worship. Their respective liturgies have strengths and weaknesses; the musical forms vary, with some using more contemporary material, others less; there are noticeable differences in the emphases of their worship orders and considerable diversity among them, but in all of them one would find it hard to forget that the Christian church has been worshiping this way for twenty centuries (and that is far more than can be said in many North American and European evangelical churches today). Worship with them and you will find no triteness or trendiness, no "more relevant than thou" antics, just meat and potatoes—simple, spiritual, passionate, biblical, reverent worship. And these congregations are finding historic Reformed worship more conducive to the service of God, to the cultivation of Christian discipleship, and even more culturally adaptable than the approaches of the fad-chasing churches around them (and those churches are everywhere, having been exported by North Americans).

It is reverent. If worship is meeting with God, how could it be otherwise? It is precisely the reverence and awe of the greatness of God that characterizes Reformed worship at its best. All of the ministers and congregations mentioned above would agree with Old: "The greatest single contribution which the Reformed liturgical heritage can make to contemporary . . . Protestantism is its sense of the majesty and sovereignty of God, its sense of reverence, of simple dignity, its conviction that worship must above all serve the praise of God."[19]

This then is our corporate worship manifesto, our call for the doxological reformation of the church: *sola scriptura* and *soli deo gloria*.

3

THE REGULATIVE PRINCIPLE: RESPONDING TO RECENT CRITICISM

DEREK W. H. THOMAS

"The wonder of Christian worship is that when we come to God in the way he has established, we find him to be inexhaustible and discover that our desire to know and worship him further is increased." So wrote James Montgomery Boice in 1996, just a few years before his death.[1] It was characteristic of him that his chief concern was both theological and doxological. Knowledge of God cultivates a desire to worship him; worship fosters a deeper knowledge of God. Knowing and glorifying God is our chief end, as the Shorter Catechism puts it so wonderfully. The knowledge of God and of ourselves, John Calvin (echoing Augustine) insists, makes us wise.[2] To that end, James Montgomery Boice was a very wise man, and his sagacity was learned at the feet of his Savior, whom he adored and spent a lifetime exalting.

It is, from one point of view, sad that Christians who share a common theological adherence should be divided over the practice of corporate worship. As someone who teaches a seminary course on worship, I invariably begin by saying something like, "This is the most important course you will ever take!" What could be more important than a course designed to teach the intricacies of our worship of almighty God? Worship is what we were made for and saved for, and knowing the *telos* of worship helps shape the mode of worship.

That brings us to the issue of this chapter. The biblical case for the regulative principle of worship has already been made by Ligon Duncan in the previous chapters. Stating the principle is one thing; defending it against criticism is another. And the regulative principle has seen a fair share of criticism both from those who are largely sympathetic to Reformed doctrine and practice and also from those whose agenda is much larger. Obviously, in attempting to answer these criticisms, I open myself up as the "bad guy" (to use an Americanism), but I will attempt to do so in a way that is in keeping with the tenor of this book.

Stated succinctly, the regulative principle of worship, as historically understood, can be defined this way: Nothing must be required as essential to public worship except that which is commanded by the word of God. Criticisms of the regulative principle of worship come from many different quarters. Some are knee-jerk cultural expressions of postmodernity. Others are thoughtful, if sometimes incoherent attempts at continuing reformation: *semper reformanda reformata est.* Sometimes, one suspects that a theological veneer is being given to baptize a particular practice. And sometimes no theological justification is given at all. It is a disturbing fact that our culture can affect our manner and style of worship more drastically than we give credit. Marva Dawn, who writes extensively on this issue,[3] applies to worship what David Wells trumpets more generally: that culture affects us in deep and serious ways and we had better wake up to it or find ourselves at culture's mercy.[4] The call for the church to be truly countercultural (to borrow John Stott's phrase),[5] an "alternative society" as Dawn labels it,[6] has never been more urgent than it is now, and nowhere is this seen more poignantly than at 11:00 a.m. on a Sunday morning. Public worship ought to be different from the routine of daily life, but in what way? It would be relatively easy to present a case for what some would regard as highbrow culture (I prefer Bach to the Back Street Boys)—and such a case needs to be done (and *can* be made) on grounds other than mere prejudice. But the point here is that what makes worship *different* is that its cultural ethos is determined by scriptural commands and principles rather than by personal or collective tastes and mores.

A casual glance at the worship bulletins of Tenth Presbyterian Church during Jim Boice's tenure reveals a deep concern for the elements and order of worship. John Piper is correct whenever he insists that the chief end of the church is not missions, but *worship*.[7] Though Boice was not a combative spirit, his evaluation of much contemporary worship was scathing. After citing Stott's comment that "true worship is the highest and noblest activity of which man, by the grace of God, is capable," he adds, "For large segments of the evangelical church, perhaps the majority, true worship is almost non-existent."[8] The need of the hour, as Boice saw it, was reformation in worship. To that extent, his vision was remarkably similar to that of the Genevan Reformer. In response to the urgings of Martin Bucer in 1544, Calvin drafted reasons why the reformation of the church was necessary:

> If it be inquired, then, by what things chiefly the Christian religion has a standing existence amongst us and maintains its truth, it will be found that the following two not only occupy the principle place, but comprehend under them all the other parts, and consequently the whole substance of Christianity, viz., a knowledge, *first*, of the mode in which God is duly worshiped; and, *secondly* of the source from which salvation is to be obtained.[9]

For Calvin, the primary need for the Reformation had to do with worship practices. In *The Necessity of Reforming the Church*, he writes:

> I know how difficult it is to persuade the world that God disapproves of all modes of worship not expressly sanctioned by His Word. The opposite persuasion which cleaves to them, being seated, as it were, in their bones and marrow, is, that whatever they do has in itself a sufficient sanction, provided it exhibits some kind of zeal for the honour of God. But since God not only regards as fruitless, but also plainly abominates, whatever we undertake from zeal to His worship, if at variance with His command, what do we gain by a contrary course?[10]

But that was the sixteenth century! Why did Boice conclude that true worship was almost nonexistent in the evangelical church? Though Boice himself did not personally engage in the often acrimonious exchanges of the "worship wars," he nevertheless agreed that the issues involved were more than a tempest in a tea cup. After all, we are confronted by the issue every Lord's Day. Is Elmer Towns correct, then, when he makes the assessment that "worship is like a car to get us from where we are to where God wants us to be. Transportation and communication is imperative; the mode or vehicle is not imperative"?[11] I think Boice would exclaim, "*Sola scriptura!*"[12] Analyzing current public worship practices, Boice complains of the absence of "service elements that have always been associated with the worship of God."[13]

Those who knew Jim Boice well know that this did not represent the hard-edged negativity of Calvinism turned mean, nor the diehard attachment to a bygone era. Rather, it was his concern for two things: on the one hand, a commitment to Scripture and its right to govern and oversee everything that we do, particularly the *way* that we worship God corporately, and, on the other hand, a respect for Calvinistic and Reformed tradition that confronts the arrogance of modernity and its distaste for the past. As for the first, the question has to be asked: Does Scripture tell us *how* we should worship God publicly? Are principles laid down in the word of God that shape the pattern of acceptable worship? Do elements of worship, some of which may be necessary and some occasional, constitute acceptable worship? Is there such a thing as a regulative principle of worship?

As for the second, various factors may be cited to explain the current antipathy to the regulative principle. Antipathy there is—one writer suggests that "it may be fair to state that, in practice today, there is no widely received formative or regulating principle of worship among evangelical Presbyterians."[14] Whether that assessment is overdone may be debated at length, but it cannot be denied that evangelical Presbyterianism (to confine ourselves to this grouping for a moment) is moving away from its creedal moorings as it disassociates itself more and more from its tradition regarding public worship. Part of the reason for that lies in both the modern disdain for history and the ignorance of it. "Chronological snobbery," to use C. S. Lewis's phrase, applies to those who suggest that we have nothing to learn from the two millennia since the resurrection of Jesus Christ and that worship is purely a matter of taste.[15] In this issue, as in so many others, a healthy respect for evangelical and Reformed tradition— a respect that in no way contravenes our adherence to the absolute authority of Scripture in all matters of faith and practice—would keep us on the road of

77

sanity. Every single week, as the people of God gather for worship in various lo-
cations, the question arises: Is this the right way to worship God? For our Reformed ancestors, the answer to this question lay by way of a consideration of
what Melanchthon, to cite but one example, called the formal principle of the
Reformation: *sola scriptura*. By it, the conscience is kept free from the legalism
that would impose human-originated rules in place of divine law in both individual and corporate life. The issue, at root, was one of conscience.[16]

For the Puritan mindset, and here their thought was exquisitely biblical,
the chief concern of biblical practice was the issue (the safety) of conscience.
As Edmund Clowney rightly points out: "For Calvin and for the Westminster divines, liberty of conscience was the issue. Any communal activity requires direction and corporate public worship is no exception."[17]

The regulative principle is important for two reasons. First, the church
has no power to impose on worshipers what they can and cannot do; it can
only insist that every Christian must be subject to the ordering of Scripture
on any given issue. The regulative principle, to cite the title of Martin
Luther's book written in 1520, is about the *freedom of the Christian*. It alone
can defend true Christian liberty in worship. The church's tendency to
tyranny needs to be constantly guarded against. This is of fundamental importance. Second is the fallen propensity to idolatry. Calvin captured Scripture's testimony well whenever he suggested that the human mind "is a
perpetual factory of idols."[18] In worship this becomes the crucial issue. The
imposition of unsanctioned features in worship is, according to Scripture
and Reformed tradition, idolatry, a violation of the second commandment—
however harsh that may sound. Idolatry is humankind's gravest sin, and
Scripture is stern in its condemnation (1 Cor. 10:14; 1 John 5:19–21).

It is time, then, for us to consider the arguments against the application
of the regulative principle. The order in which we will consider them does
not necessarily indicate the order of their merit (or demerit!).

"Calvin versus the Puritans"

That the regulative principle was neither peripheral for the Puritans nor
an invention on their part may be seen in a statement in the very first chapter of the Westminster Confession of Faith entitled "Of the Holy Scripture":

The whole counsel of God, concerning all things necessary for his own glory, man's salvation, faith, and life, is either expressly set down in Scripture, or by good and necessary consequence may be deduced from Scripture: unto which nothing at any time is to be added, whether by new revelations of the Spirit, or traditions of men. (1.6)

This section goes on to affirm "that there are some circumstances concerning the worship of God . . . which are to be ordered by the light of nature and Christian prudence, according to the general rules of the word." This gives rise to the classic distinction between elements, circumstances, and forms. According to this view, all public worship must be based directly on Scripture or on an inference from Scripture.

This statement in the Westminster Confession reflects general Puritan sentiments of the period. Writing in 1646, John Geree summed up the quintessential Puritan mindset this way: "The Old English Puritane was such an one that honoured God above all, and under God gave every one his due. His first care was to serve God, and therein he did not what was good in his own, but in God's sight, *making the word of God the rule of his worship.*"[19]

Clearest expression of the principle is to be found in the opening section of the Westminster Confession of Faith 21.1:

The light of nature shows that there is a God, who has lordship and sovereignty over all; is good, and does good unto all, and is therefore to be feared, loved, praised, called upon, trusted in, and served with all the heart, and with all the soul, and with all the might. But the acceptable way of worshiping the true God is instituted by himself, and so limited by his own revealed will, that he may not be worshiped according to the imaginations and devices of men, or the suggestions of Satan, under any visible representations or any other way not prescribed in the holy Scripture.

According to this view, acceptable worship is instituted by God in accordance with his own will and for the purposes of advancing his own glory. For the seventeenth-century Puritans, the medium is the message, and the mode of worship can in no way be considered secondary. The way we worship reflects our theological prejudice one way or another, for good or ill, and, more important, reflects on the very character of God.

But what does "making the word of God the rule of his worship" mean? James Bannerman, professor of apologetics and pastoral theology at New College, Edinburgh, following the Disruption of 1843, summarizes it this way:

> The doctrine of the Westminster Standards and of our church is, that what-soever is not expressly appointed in the Word, or appointed by necessary in-ference from the Word, it is not lawful for the Church to exercise of its own authority to enjoin; the restriction upon that authority being, that it shall an-nounce and enforce nothing in the public worship of God, except what God himself has in explicit terms or by implication instituted.[20]

This brings to the surface a burning issue that has marked theological dis-cussion of the Reformation and its relationship to the seventeenth century (i.e., the Westminster Assembly) for half a century. Is this expression of the regulative principle something that the seventeenth century invented? Is it an example of how theologians in one tradition have taken something to the Nth extreme? Does it highlight precisely what is wrong with Puri-tanism—a tendency to absolutize in instances when others, and the Scrip-tures in particular, do not?

This criticism has been made in a fairly mild form by two of the most well-known exponents of Puritanism, J. I. Packer and Horton Davies. They argue that the Puritan expression of the regulative principle actually de-parted from Calvin and Knox, though they may well have not realized it.[21] Much more vehemently, and with an altogether different agenda, it has been said that the seventeenth-century formulation of doctrine enshrined by the Westminster Confession out-Calvined Calvin. Whether it be the doc-trine of predestination (the issue of infralapsarianism or supralapsarianism), the role of the law (in sanctification, or Sabbath especially), assurance of salvation (Westminster's stress on law-keeping as a mark of sanctification made it more difficult to be assured of saving grace), or a host of other is-sues, the charge is made that a gulf exists between Calvin and Westmin-ster—and the sooner we get back to Calvin the better. This charge is also

80

made with respect to worship—witness the gulf erroneously envisioned by some of the Sabbath as *practiced* in Geneva and seventeenth-century Puritan England as a case in point (however infelicitously Calvin may have represented the theory).[22] But what is the evidence? Is it the case that the seventeenth century took the regulative principle in a direction that Calvin, for example, did not intend?

One such critic is R. J. Gore, who summarizes a lengthy discussion of the issue this way:

> Calvin's view of the regulation of worship may be formulated as "freedom to worship in any manner warranted by Scripture." In other words, whatever is consistent with covenantal life is allowed. Differing from Lutheranism, this principle does not allow everything that is not forbidden. Indeed, the Lutheran principle provides insufficient positive direction. Differing from Westminster's RPW [regulative principle of worship], this principle does not require a command or logical necessity to warrant a particular (form/element) of worship . . . Westminster's formula is too restrictive.[23]

Gore suggests that because Calvin argued for the inclusion of rites and ceremonies of worship under the rubric of *adiaphora* (things indifferent) Calvin wished to include certain elements other than those identified as such by the Puritan regulative principle.[24] Gore never once suggests what these might be, other than vague references that they might "at times" be "substantial parts or 'elements' of worship."

A more careful analysis of Calvin leads to the conclusion that what Calvin had in mind was the celebration of some special day (the Westminster Directory allows for this under the rubric of special days of thanksgiving) or perhaps some aspect of liturgy, like, for instance, the saying of the Lord's Prayer (something the divines regarded as a form rather than an element). It is true that the seventeenth-century divines found it difficult to agree on some of these issues, but nowhere was this a discussion of what was or was not an element of worship. It was, after all, the Scottish kirk that adopted the Westminster Confession and its directory, and it was the Scottish kirk that showed greater flexibility in forms of worship. There were certainly differences of opinion on just how liturgically complex a service could get and still maintain its adherence to a regulative principle of worship, but to suggest that the regulative principle itself is somehow to blame for this is going in the wrong direction.

Packer, too, thinks that the issue is felt most keenly whenever devotees of the regulative principle have within their sights Lutheranism and its ally on this score, Anglicanism. The charge is sometimes made, wrongly Packer insists, that the difference between Lutheran/Anglican worship and Calvinian/Puritan practice is one of commitment to the authority of Scripture: "The idea that direct biblical warrant, in the form of precept or precedent, is required to sanction every item included in the public worship of God was in fact a Puritan innovation, which crystallised out in the course of the prolonged debates that followed the Elizabethan settlement."[25] Packer goes on: "A truer way of stating the issue would be to say that the authority and sufficiency of Scripture in all matters of Christian and church life was common ground to both sides, but that they were not agreed as to how this principle should be applied."[26]

The difference between Lutheran (Anglican) and Puritan (Genevan-Calvin) approaches to worship is hermeneutical, Packer suggests, rather than dogmatic—a disagreement between friends rather than foes. Laudable as this aspiration might be, it is more than doubtful whether *Calvin* would have been so easily persuaded. To suggest as Packer does that the regulative principle is a "Puritan innovation" of the Elizabethan settlement is entirely false. Calvin wrote an attachment to his *Form for Administering Baptism* for the use of the church in Geneva:

> We know that elsewhere there are many other ceremonies which we deny not to be very ancient, but because they have been invented at pleasure, or at least on grounds which, be these what they may, must be trivial, since they have been devised without authority from the Word of God, and because, on the other hand, so many superstitions have sprung from them, we have felt no hesitation in abolishing them, in order that there might be nothing to prevent the people from going directly to Jesus Christ. First, whatever is not commanded we are not free to choose. Secondly, nothing which does not tend to edification ought to be received into the Church.[27]

Plainly, Calvin's language is more adversarial than ameliorating, but Packer's point is well made. He is right to insist on a breadth of perception in what this adherence means in practice. Thus, Calvin's liturgy at Strasbourg and Geneva would clearly have bothered John Owen (Owen's disdain for liturgy, including the formal saying of the Lord's Prayer makes for arresting reading),[28] just as the order of service at Tenth Presbyterian Church during Jim Boice's time would have bothered certain fellow Presbyterians in North America. More pertinently, Calvin's order of worship differed from that of his admirer John Knox, just as Owen would have differed from Matthew Henry. Adherence to the regulative principle, as we have already said, does not bring about uniformity of worship practice — it did not in the seventeenth century any more than it does today. That, in part, explains why the Westminster divines compiled a *directory* of worship, rather than a *manual*. Finally approved by parliament in 1645, the Directory for Public Worship was intended to produce a more uniform pattern in worship, but no more than that.[29] Its intention was never to legislate the order of worship in the way that, say, the 1662 Book of Common Prayer did for the Anglican communion.

This, in part, has been widely recognized and utilized, sometimes as a way of bridging the gulf between perceived sides in the current "worship wars." Things may not be as divided as they sometimes appear to be. Worship services with highly structured liturgy will look and sound very different to, say, the typical Westminster Directory service. But appearances can be deceptive, and there may well be a commitment to the regulative principle in both services. The issue has to be focused to ask the question: Is anything in the worship service that should not be there *and* are all the necessary elements of worship present?[30] They form, more or less, the framework of contemporary discussions regarding the propriety of the regulative principle of worship.

They lie, for example, behind two otherwise quite diverse publications on worship, one coming from the Founders Ministries (what was once called the Southern Baptist Founders Conference), jointly written by Ernest C. Reisinger and D. Matthew Allen.[31] From a different tradition entirely, Hughes Oliphant Old writes of what he calls the "baroque" and "mannerist" period where the regulative principle was taken "in ways that were very different from the Reformers."[32] Old's concern seems to be a desire to avoid what may appear to be an overly strict (precise, legalistic) definition of the regulative principle that is a quasi-attempt at uniformitarianism, thereby undoing the historical *breadth* introduced by the various ecclesiastical usages made of this principle over the past four hundred years. These are in-house attempts at ensuring that we are debating the same principle by the same rules. More serious objections have been leveled against the regulative principle, and it is to one such criticism that we now turn: the charge that the regulative principle represents the very worst kind of legalism, shackling the church in its expression of corporate adoration of God.

"Legalism of the Worst Sort"

Why is it that the regulative principle sounds so legalistic, as Anglican theologian and churchman Richard Hooker (ca. 1554–1600) insisted a half century before the framing of the Westminster Confession? Do the words *it is not lawful* and *worship* really belong in the same sentence? Is the regulative principle a Pharisaic invention to ensure conformity to a certain style of worship for prejudicial reasons? Why is it that the church reacts negatively to the idea that God regulated the way he is to be worshiped? The answers to these questions are many and diverse, some prejudicial and some principled.

But why should it be thought strange that God would regulate the way he is to be worshiped? It is, from one point of view, a corollary of the authority of Scripture. It is the authority of the Creator, the source of all that the Bible tells us. It is the authority of Jesus Christ, the Lord who reigns, to exercise his kingship through what the Bible tells us. It is the authority of the Holy Spirit, agent of the Father and the Son, to inspire, authenticate, interpret, and apply all that Scripture says.

Bucking authority shapes our postmodern society, as it does the confessing evangelical church. Antinomianism in all its guises abounds. What we see here, as knee-jerk antipathy to whoever or whatever seeks to control, regulate, or conform practices of public worship, is in fact just another display of our present difficulty with authority structures. Evangelicals respond to biblical authority (which they accept) by saying, "It all depends how you interpret Scripture." Interpretation is vital, of course, and submission to *sola scriptura* must in reality be a submission to Scripture *rightly understood*.[33]

But it is sometimes apparent that this response is not an objection based on principle, but on prejudice. Citing the hermeneutical caveat is useful in order to extradite oneself from anything that appears to some to be shackling and legalistic. One suspects that reformation in attitude to *sola scriptura* is needed before progress can be made in advancing the cause of biblical worship practice.

Other forms of antinomianism claim to be Spirit-centered, an evangelical consequence of living in post-Pentecost days. (In reality word and Spirit can never be in opposition.) Binding worship to certain regulations will inherently quench the Spirit's (and spirit's) promptings. On this platform, openness is the key that unlocks the door to a meaningful worship experience, and devotees of the regulative principle are seen as fuddy-duddies, chained to the past, and in need of liberation. As in ethics, so in liturgics, Scripture provides a rule of thumb for Christian behavior; but the situational reality, as Joseph Fletcher insists in his *Situation Ethics: The New Morality* (1966), is much more complex, requiring openness to the possibility that we must worship in a new way. The goal of worship has been turned on its head. Instead of seeking God, services seek seekers, attempting to make everything as appealing as possible. The Willow Creek model insists that the basic question is: Who do you expect to come to this service? There is no way, according to that principle, of avoiding total bondage to our present culture. The church can never become a place of refuge, for it is too reflective of our present society.

The truth is, if we are not at liberty to corporately worship God in ways other than that which he has revealed, we are heading for tyranny and bondage, for then we are at the mercy of someone's personal taste or newly discovered insight. But Scripture insists it is to be a matter of the will of God rather than our will (Col. 2:23). Indeed, for Calvin as well as the Westminster divines, it is an issue of the role of conscience. Having earlier stated the principle in its opening chapter, the Westminster Confession highlights the importance of this doctrine and its relation to worship in 20.2: "God alone is Lord of the conscience, and has left it free from the doctrines and commandments of men which are in any thing contrary to his word, or beside it in[34] matters of faith or worship. So that to believe such doctrines, or to obey such commands out of conscience, is to betray true liberty of conscience." William Cunningham goes further in attempting to identify the issue:

85

The direct object of the Confession in this passage [1.6] is no doubt to assert the right and extent of liberty of conscience; but along with that, it very distinctly enunciates the doctrine, that neither in regard to faith nor in regard to worship has the Church any authority beside or beyond what is laid down in the Bible; and that it has no right to decree and enforce new observances or institutions in the department of Scriptural worship, any more than to teach and indicate new truths in the department of Scriptural faith.[35]

For Cunningham, the issue was as much about keeping the rule of officers in check as it was about godly worship. Maintaining a good conscience toward God means conforming to the rule of law that God established and to that law *alone*. The alternative is tyranny. I recall being publicly scolded in a worship service in England for not participating in the required hand signals. Protestants may exercise a tyranny as fierce as Rome in the name of spirit-filled liberty! Only the regulative principle can maintain true Christian freedom. The regulative principle is not legalism for the simple reason that it is never legalism to obey what God has commanded out of a desire to please him and in response to the grace that he has shown.

But yet another criticism awaits. It comes from those who claim they accept the principle!

"I Believe in the Regulative Principle, I Just Understand It Differently"

Far and away the most important and certainly the most influential critique of the regulative principle to emerge in Reformed circles in recent years is that given by John Frame. His book *Worship in Spirit and Truth* was first published in 1996 and received much attention, some of it favorable, some of it vigorously critical.[36] The following year, Frame published a sequel, this time addressing the specific issue of contemporary worship music.[37]

What is it that Frame finds objectionable about the traditional formulation of the regulative principle? It is, to cite his most recent unpublished writings on this subject, that "the regulative principle for worship is the same as the regulative principle for the rest of life."[38] At the heart of Frame's argument lies the issue of whether it is fair to distinguish private and public worship. To insist that a certain calculus of necessary elements plays a role in public worship that it does not in private worship, or "the rest of life" is, according to this argument, misguided.

That such a calculus does indeed exist in Scripture is the page on which Reformed thinking about worship has historically been written. There are two ways of going about proving this. One would be to ask: Is there an activity that Christians are to perform worshipfully in "all of life" that would be wholly inappropriate in public worship? Clowney cites marital union. It is wholly appropriate within the privacy of the home but wholly inappropriate in a church service![39]

The point is that Scripture recognizes an event that we can label public worship in which it is appropriate to do certain things and refrain from others, even though those things from which we refrain are to be done to God's glory elsewhere. I may cook in the style of Emeril Lagasse and do it to the glory of God, but I am not permitted to do it in public worship nor bring any culinary dishes with me to a Sunday morning service (even though it is more than appropriate to do so for the after-service fellowship luncheon). No amount of theological hair-splitting over what may be termed broad and narrow worship can overcome the definable moment (signaled by a call to worship) when God's covenant people gather together and it is no longer permitted to do certain, otherwise legitimate, things. To cite Terry Johnson: "Whether or not I ought to dig ditches, fly kites, or bathe my children in the context of public worship is not the same question as whether or not God may be glorified by them."[40]

Nor is it sufficient to say that because all of life is to be regulated by Scripture, this proves the invalidity of the regulative principle as expounded by the Westminster Confession and subsequent tradition. The point is not, as Johnson so eloquently expresses, whether the regulative principle applies to the whole of life. It does! But it does so *in a different way*:

> For example, one would not be free to sacrifice a goat in family worship, or burn incense, whereas one should read the Bible, sing Psalms, and pray. In these instances the application is the same, public and private. On the other hand, one may not (as the Puritans would have argued) administer the sacraments in family worship. Why? At least at one level the answer is because the

regulative principle applies differently. What is permitted publically, at officially called and sanctioned services, is not permitted privately. All worship, then, is regulated by God's Word, *but the application is different in different contexts,* whether formal or informal, public or private.[41]

The slogan "Let's get back to the Bible" is both easy to make and appealing in form. Evangelical and Reformed Christians are drawn to the idea that criticizing canons of received doctrine is in the interest of *sola scriptura,* but this may be nothing more than Lewis's "chronological snobbery," which disdains the past in favor of the present.

"Jesus Attended Nonregulative Principle Services of Worship"

Another criticism of the regulative principle involves the existence of the synagogue. A vehement attack on the regulative principle comes from a series of articles written by Steve Schlissel, the first of which was entitled "All I Really Need to Know about Worship (I Don't Learn from the Regulative Principle)."[42]

Schlissel accuses the regulative principle of being "not biblical," that it is "an invention of men and therefore an imposition upon the consciences of those forced to accept it," that it is a "pattern of obfuscation," and that it "cannot survive when measured against Scripture." Schlissel suggests that the sixteenth and seventeenth centuries were far too close to Rome in their arguments on worship. The Reformers and Puritans desired the legalistic straitjacket of the regulative principle because, well, they were quasi-Romanists!

Two of Schlissel's arguments are worthy of consideration (though neither is unique to him). First is that advocates of the regulative principle cannot agree with each other. The principle leads some to a position of unaccompanied (*a cappella*) exclusive psalm singing, for example, a position not adopted in this volume. But what of it? The principle of *sola scriptura* also leads some to give canonical status to the Authorized (King James) Version of the Bible (1611). But that does not repudiate the principle for those who do not accept the validity of the Textus Receptus.

The form of worship at Tenth Presbyterian Church under the oversight of James Montgomery Boice was arranged with the regulative principle in mind. But the form of worship differed to some extent from week to week and from other churches equally committed to the regulative principle. What the regulative principle does is identify the various elements of worship and distinguish them from the form. These elements are preaching, prayer, singing, reading of Scripture (which includes what the Westminster Confession calls the "conscionable hearing of the word" [21.5]), sacraments (baptism and the Lord's Supper), and oaths, vows, solemn feasts, and thanksgivings. Identifying these elements (some of which are occasional elements — sacraments, for example) means that worship services whose liturgy may resemble John Calvin's Geneva in the mid-sixteenth century, or John Owen's Congregational church in Leadenhall Street according to the "congregational way" in the mid-seventeenth century, or Jonathan Edwards's congregation in Northampton in the eighteenth century, or Charles Haddon Spurgeon's Metropolitan Tabernacle congregation of the nineteenth century, or Tenth Presbyterian Church in the late twentieth century — all conform *in principle* to an adherence to the regulative principle. That, for this writer at least, is liberating and exciting. It provides breadth within a basic conformity.

The second major argument adopted by Schlissel against the regulative principle is the issue of synagogue worship. Put simply, Jesus worshiped in the synagogue and according to its liturgy, but nowhere does the Bible legislate for the existence or use of the synagogue. Schlissel is characteristically upbeat in putting forth his case:

> The very existence of the synagogue, however, undoes the regulativist's position! For he knows that synagogues existed. And he knows that Christ and the apostles *regularly* worshipped at synagogues without so much as a breath of suggestion that they were institutionally or liturgically illegitimate. And he knows that he cannot find so much as a sliver of a divine commandment concerning what ought to be done in the synagogue. And, according to his principle, if God commanded naught concerning what ought to done, then all was forbidden. And if all was forbidden then the whole of it — institution and liturgy — was a sinful abomination. But what brings him back to Christ's attending upon the service of God there and Christ's following its liturgy: did

he sin by participating in an entire order of worship that was without express divine warrant? The thought is blasphemy![43]

This argument appears with some frequency! Gore, for example, makes the point with considerable force in his Westminster Seminary dissertation.[44] Recent critics of the regulative principle on this point write as though our ancestors never thought of this issue. Were such Reformed scholars of ecclesiology and liturgy ignorant of the synagogue? Did men such as Samuel Miller or John Girardeau or Thomas E. Peck fail to inform American Presbyterians of this fly in the ointment? Did William Cunningham or James Bannerman or Douglas Bannerman omit any discussion of the synagogue for fear of undoing the Scottish kirk?[45] Did John Owen fail to inform the Congregationalists of a fatal flaw in their adherence to the Savoy Declaration? The truth is that this issue has been examined in detail and found to be a non sequitur.

The argument goes something like this: Jesus attended worship at the synagogue (an institution not sanctioned by direct Old Testament warrant) and temple feasts other than those prescribed by Old Testament law, for example, Channukah (John 10:22) and Purim (5:1). Arguments are also made with respect to the seder practices associated with Passover and based on the Jewish Mishnah, that is, rabbinic oral tradition dating from the third century b.c. The seder included, among other things, ceremonial handwashings. But there is no evidence that Jesus did any of the things associated with the seder ritual. Whether the feast in John 5:1 was Purim is a subject of considerable debate,[46] but assuming that this was indeed the case, what are the implications of Jesus' attending such feasts for our understanding of the regulative principle? Absolutely nothing at all that would cause even so much as a mild tremor.

The Westminster divines had already foreseen the argument, citing Purim (Esther 9:20–22) as a biblical example of "an occasional day of thanksgiving," adding, "It is lawful and necessary, upon special emergent occasions, to separate a day or days for public fasting and thanksgiving, as the several eminent and extraordinary dispensations of God's providence shall administer cause and opportunity to his people" (Directory for the Public Worship of God, Appendix "Touching Days and Places for Public Worship").

Some respond to this by saying that attendance at the synagogue was not a violation of the regulative principle because the synagogue was in fact warranted by the Old Testament itself! Some cite Leviticus 23:3 as proof that the Sabbath is "a day of sacred assembly."[47] Others cite Exodus 18:20.[48] From the earliest times, Jews gathered together for worship on the Sabbath.

Of interest to us here is to know whether synagogue worship contained anything in it that would be deemed contrary to the regulative principle. Did it contain an element of worship that was not warranted by the Old Testament? The answer is definitely in the negative. What did a typical synagogue worship service look like? Nothing that will give devotees of greater freedom any joy! The fact is that synagogue worship was remarkably predictable, containing a call to worship, a cycle of prayers, the singing of psalms, the recitation of portions of Scripture (the Shema in particular), reading of Scripture, and something that we would now call preaching or exposition, followed by a blessing.[49] It all sounds very similar to a traditional worship service!

"Consistency Will Make Us All Exclusive Psalm Singers"

There is one more issue to consider briefly: the charge that consistency will make us all either exclusive psalm singers or Reformed Baptists!

There is an argument (more precisely, a hermeneutical platform) that goes like this: unless the New Testament specifically warrants it, we are not at liberty to introduce it. In this form, two conclusions are sometimes drawn by those of a Reformed persuasion. One is the practice of unaccompanied, exclusive psalmody.[50] The other is the practice of exclusive believer's baptism.[51] I leave aside the issue of baptism, noting only the similarity of argument. What convinces the former group in their defense of their unaccompanied, exclusive psalmody is the silence of the New Testament, and it led to the view that exclusive and unaccompanied psalm singing is the only proper expression of corporate worship that is in accord with the regulative principle.[52]

The case for inclusive psalm singing (worship that uses both psalms and hymns) is made elsewhere in this volume by Terry Johnson. My concern here is merely to cite the argument as it is made by those whose intent is to disqualify the regulative principle. Thus, that we sing hymns to the accompaniment of instruments, so this argument suggests, is itself evidence of compromise. (I also leave aside the farcical argument that any instrument other than an organ is a denial of the regulative principle. It makes absolutely no sense since other musical instruments are mentioned in Scripture, the organ *not* being one of them!) The case needs, then, to be established and maintained that the regulative principle is an argument based on what is warranted by God in Scripture as a whole, and not merely in the New Testament church. In this instance, as regards the use of musical instruments and choral accompaniment, temple practice provides all the warrant that is needed.

And Finally

It would be reasonably easy to make the allegation that the regulative principle is narrow and restrictive. It hinders creativity. It drains motivation. It kills excitement. It encourages predictability. Easy it may be to make, but such allegations are of no consequence when faced with the alternative: being at the mercy of a worship leader with the Outback Steakhouse approach to Sunday morning worship—*no rules!* What prevents our adding a "Pet consecration moment" between the singing of "Jesus Is All the World to Me" and the offering? Or a section called "Getting in Touch with Feelings" led by Counselor Smith in place of the sermon? Or "Mrs. Beattie's Bread Board: Cooking with Jesus" as the closing facet of worship? The answer is "Nothing!" Only cultural mores and prejudice can keep worship sane if there is no distinction between the worship service and the rest of life.

In the same essay cited at the beginning of this chapter, Boice quoted approvingly some words of C. S. Lewis:

> As long as you notice, and have to count, the steps, you are not yet dancing but only learning to dance. A good shoe is a shoe you don't notice. Good reading becomes possible when you need not consciously think about eyes, or light, or print, or spelling. The perfect church service would be one we were almost unaware of; our attention would have been on God.[53]

In a sense, that is what the regulative principle achieves for us in worship —
a way of enabling us to be free from the whims of unwarranted structure so
that our attention can be given to God, a way of maintaining "decency and
order" in such a way that God approves and blesses.

Apart from it, we are at the mercy of tyranny and folly.

4

CORPORATE WORSHIP: A MEANS OF GRACE

EDMUND P. CLOWNEY

The topic of corporate worship belongs in a volume dedicated to the memory of James Montgomery Boice. Dr. Boice loved the worship of the people of God. He regularly rejoiced with the congregation of Tenth Presbyterian Church as they responded to the call of the word of God in preaching. Those of us who have worshiped with that congregation, even only occasionally, hold fond memories of the singing with the accompanying music and the teaching from the pulpit.

Regular worshipers in city churches — storefronts or cathedrals — may be puzzled by an essay defending public worship. Certainly everyone knows what it is and takes it for granted. We assume that every religion in our multicultural society has its own corporate worship. Our new awareness of Islam via television makes Muslim worship familiar. An imam speaks in the Washington Cathedral, and we assume that he is following the same familiar pattern that he knows from the mosque. Yet, some differences are obvious. We see the salaam in prayer, viewed from the rear, with the soles of bare feet in rows. Such worship would be entirely strange to the church in Corinth established by the Apostle Paul. There, the congregation gathered to hear the Scriptures, sing the praises of the Lord, and come to his table. The congregation responded to the word that was preached. Men of the congregation could ask questions. In song, the people addressed the Lord and also one another.

Fellowship was the key to worship at Corinth. Their fellowship was in the Spirit. In his letters Paul never provided a form for public worship. To bring more order to the observance of the Lord's Table, Paul does give an outline of its celebration, as the church received it from Christ (1 Cor. 11:23–34). He is concerned that the freedom of prophesying be maintained, but in an orderly way. Given the abundance of charismatic gifts at Corinth, there was good reason for his quite Presbyterian golden text, "Let all things be done decently and in order" (14:40 Authorized Version). For Paul, freedom from the law was freedom in the Spirit. This guided his teaching on worship.

Evangelical Christians often think of devotion as private. The favorite devotional hymn in many rest homes is "In the Garden." The preciousness of personal fellowship with the Lord makes the song dear to believers: "He walks with me, and he talks with me, and he tells me I am his own." But no one seems to cringe at the boast, "And the joy we share as we tarry there, none other has ever known."

Our daily devotions bring joy in our personal fellowship with the Lord. It is well that our prayers include petitions for others, by name, with thanksgiving. We need to remember that the grace that unites us to the Lord unites us to all who have been made members of his body.

Above all, we must prize the blessing of corporate worship. The church of the Lord, gathered for worship, marks the pinnacle of our fellowship with the Lord and with one another. The church is the people of God, the new humanity, the beginning of the new creation, a colony of heaven (Heb. 13:14). The threats of Islamic militants against Western society do not define the war of our time. The cosmic struggle is spiritual, and the weapons of our warfare are not hijacked planes or terrorist biological attacks. They are the weapons of divine love: the preaching of gospel and the showing of mercy in Christ's name.

In corporate worship we experience the meaning of union with Christ. We worship most fully when we together hear his words to us and encourage one another to grow in grace and in witness to the world.

The Lord is present among us in corporate worship. By the power of his Spirit he assures us that we are his and he is ours. In worship together, the Pentecost promise is renewed, not in visible flames, but in the presence of the Spirit who makes intercession for us as we pray. To be sure, the witness of the Spirit is also individual, bearing witness with our spirits that we are the Lord's. Yet the Spirit who makes individual believers into temples of the Spirit also makes the church his temple (1 Cor. 3:16; 6:19). Union with Christ is the secret of both.

By the presence of his Spirit, the Lord himself is present in his congregation as we worship. In the congregation, Jesus sings the Father's praise (Heb. 2:11–12), while Psalm 22:22 pictures the singing of God's praise in his house of worship when a thank offering is brought. God has answered — or surely will answer — the vow of the sufferer. This psalm has the form of the lament of the individual. In these psalms, after the prayer for deliverance, the vow of the sufferer is remembered and joined with thanksgiving. Doxology follows. In Psalm 66:13–15 we find a full statement of the place of the vow. The suppliant in trouble vows to praise God when God delivers. God does deliver, and now the suppliant will praise God, who has not rejected the prayer or withheld his love from his afflicted one. Jesus is the sufferer who cries out in his abandonment; he, too, is the victor who brings praise to the Father.

Jesus sang the psalms with his disciples in the upper room before he went out to Gethsemane and Calvary. Think of Simon Peter singing with Jesus! Our Lord sings with us now in the congregation of the redeemed. He is the sweet singer of Israel, the leader of heaven's praise.

In corporate worship we rise by faith to enter the heavenly assembly of the saints and angels. We join the praises of heaven, for we "have come to Mount Zion and to the city of the living God, the heavenly Jerusalem, and to innumerable angels in festal gathering, and to the assembly of the first-born who are enrolled in heaven, and to God, the judge of all, and to the spirits of the righteous made perfect, and to Jesus, the mediator of a new covenant, and to the sprinkled blood that speaks a better word than the blood of Abel" (Heb. 12:22–24).

In the Spirit, we worship in heaven in the great assembly where Jesus is. In the Spirit, Jesus worships on earth in the congregation where we are. In heaven and on earth, we are in the presence of Jesus. His presence in corporate worship assures us that our corporate worship is for us a means of grace. We taste grace in corporate worship, when, by the Spirit, we know the Lord is with us. That reality we perceive by faith.

Corporate worship is a means of grace in the singing of the church. In song we join in the praises of the Lord, call on his name for his saving power, and encourage one another. To remember God's mighty deeds of redemption draws our hearts to him. We praise him for his words as well as his deeds. The whole of Psalm 119 reflects the rich blessings of God's word.

We may bring together Paul's two passages about the singing of the church (Eph. 5:19; Col. 3:16). In these passages, we are taught that the richly indwelling word of Christ gives us wisdom of the Spirit to teach and admonish one another. We do this in psalms and hymns and spiritual songs, singing with grace in our hearts to the Lord and giving thanks in the name of Jesus to the Father.[1] Paul's reasoning in these passages makes it clear that he is not speaking of the canonical Book of Psalms, but of the songs of the new covenant in corporate worship. When Paul speaks of "spiritual songs" (Col. 3:16), we cannot limit this description to inspired songs. The term *spiritual* is used in Colossians 1:9 of "spiritual wisdom." This is the wisdom that finds utterance in song.

These spiritual songs are not verbally inspired by the Spirit. They do flow, however, from the wisdom that the Spirit gives as we reflect on both the word and the situation to which it applies.

Not only is the preaching of the word a means of grace in corporate worship, the singing of the people of God also ministers grace. Songs are addressed not only to the Lord in praise and petition, but also to one another as we instruct, warn, and encourage.[2] The preaching of the word in worship is accompanied and supported by the ministry of the saints to one another as they sing the new songs of Zion. Singing in unison long preceded the printing of music or of words. We now have hymnals with both words and music. *Trinity Hymnal,* published by the Orthodox Presbyterian Church and the Presbyterian Church in America, contains a treasure of hymnody. The *Psalter Hymnal* of the Christian Reformed Church has versification of all the psalms and many hymns.

The growth of more recent songs has established another category for congregational singing. Collections are being made, and new songs written. Many have their attraction from popular music, but lack the biblical teaching stressed in Paul's words. The teaching office of the church must again lead in instruction about hymnody. We remember Martin Luther, whose musical gifts supported his bold preaching.

We see, then, that God gives his grace in corporate worship through the presence and participation of the Son and the Spirit. Jesus sings in the congregation, and the Spirit leads in our songs.

Our assumptions about corporate worship are challenged by those who emphasize the change in new-covenant worship. The Book of Hebrews was written to dissuade those Christians who were tempted to return to Old Testament forms of worship. The Old Testament cultus has been done away; Jesus identified the true temple with his own body (John 2:19–21; 4:22–24). The sacraments of the new covenant are not the bloody rite of circumcision or the smeared blood of the Passover, for Christ has offered himself as the final sacrifice.

The conclusion is drawn that the New Testament says nothing about a corporate service of worship, at least until we come to the Book of Revelation. David Peterson presses this point in a long essay and contends that the New Testament contains no liturgy or cultus for public worship.[3] Only in the Book of Revelation is a heavenly liturgy described.

Yet there is always the danger of disregarding things that are not said in Scripture simply because they did not need to be. They were the things that the readers took for granted. The New Testament has its reason for speaking of the church as an *ekklēsia* and not a synagogue, but the synagogue was familiar to the readers of Paul's letters. Historians of early Christian worship distinguish two sources that came together in church gatherings. One was the synagogue, the other was the Lord's Supper.[4] The Lord's Supper seems to have been observed regularly in house-churches. Sabbath gatherings of the Jews in synagogues were regularly attended by our Lord in his ministry and by Paul in his missionary travels. When the Apostle Paul left the synagogue for the school of Tyrannus in Ephesus, he taught there. That may have been the meeting place for the church on the first day of the week. Two changes took place: from the synagogue to the church, and from the seventh day to the first. Paul waited until the first day of the week to meet with the church at Troas.

Corporate worship at Corinth was distinct from gatherings at homes. Paul rebukes them for evident divisions when they came together as a church. The language is definitive: "When you come together as a church [*en ekklēsia*]" (1 Cor. 11:18).[5] This is in distinction from being in their homes. Paul reminds them of the difference of eating meals at home and coming together at the table of the Lord in the fellowship of the church. Probably the *agapē*, the love feast, was eaten in connection with the supper. To regularize the observance of the Lord's Supper in the worship service, Paul rebuked disorder.

In the church of Corinth, prophets could be judged to be true or false (1 Cor. 14:29). In such settings, at least, Paul directs that husbands ask the questions in the service and instruct their wives at home (14:34–35). The authority of the teaching of the word does not rule out questions, however. The Spirit illumines the church in corporate worship, not only in the words of gifted teachers

In the church of the New Testament, corporate worship was a means of grace. We need not only recognize that it is, but seek to follow the example of the New Testament church. In our worship, we must recognize the central place of the word preached, but also increase the pace of our use of the word, addressing it to one another in song, in questions, in confession of faith. As we address the Lord in prayer, we also encourage one another and bring with united voice our praises, thanksgivings, and petitions.

The very word *ekklēsia* has its Old Testament background in the gathering of the people of God at Sinai to hear God's spoken word. The church is an assembly, called out of dwellings to stand together before the Lord. We may never suppose that small groups can replace the assembly of believers in a particular place: "The church of God that is in Corinth" (1 Cor. 1:2). To be sure, the definitive assembly for the church catholic is the assembly in the heavenly Zion (Heb. 12), but for that very reason those with access by faith to the festival assembly of heaven are "not neglecting to meet together, as is the habit of some" (10:25).

Paul's list of the spiritual gifts in 1 Corinthians 12 assumes the assembled gathering of the church. The gifts of the prophets have to be assessed. Are they true prophets? Others must judge. If prophets are interrupting one another, order must be restored in the assembly. Paul's letters are read to the church in assembly, and this is true of the other epistles in the New Testament.

As the assembled people of God, the body of Christ functioning in the presence of one another, and the fellowship created by the Holy Spirit, the church must gather in corporate worship. In the middle of fierce persecution, larger gatherings may be for a time impossible, but the calling of the Lord remains, and his saints yearn for the joy of standing together to bless his name.

The wonder of the gathering of the people of God and the mystery of worship can appear in house-churches. Paul sends greetings to the church in the house of Prisca and Aquila (Rom. 16:5) and in the same breath speaks of "all the churches of the Gentiles" (16:4). The Lord's people gather in smaller and larger assemblies, yet they do assemble. House-churches are not joined by the ties of family blood, but by the blood of Christ.

Corporate worship is a means of grace. It expresses the design of God's saving call, his gathering together from every tribe, tongue, and nation the people of God. In days when ethnic identity trumps all, the church gathered shows the true multiethnic identity of the nations brought to the Lord of all.

The word of God is the major means for the conversion of sinners and the nurture of saints. Therefore, the Lord calls preachers and teachers to proclaim that word to his people. The Apostle Paul emphasizes this in writing to the Romans: "But how are they to call on him in whom they have not believed? And how are they to believe in him of[6] whom they have never heard? And how are they to hear without someone preaching? And how are they to preach unless they are sent?" (Rom. 10:14–15).

In the Reformed churches, the word is always central, and the sacraments are never separated from the word. True enough, it is often supposed by evangelicals that any Christian can preach, but that ordination is necessary for those who baptize or celebrate the Lord's Supper. This view fails to see that it is God's word that gives authority, for in it the Lord himself addresses us.

Since prayer is included in the means of grace in the Larger Catechism, we may ask, "How does the Lord use prayer as a means of giving his grace to us?" If we understand that, we can apply the answer to the question of corporate worship, for worship enters the presence of God, and includes prayer.

Corporate worship is surely the fruit of God's grace. Because the Lord has called us, we call on him. He has revealed his saving name, and we lift up that name in devotion and praise. But does the Lord use our response also to give us grace? The basic question is easily answered when we remember the work of the Holy Spirit in our prayer and worship. We do not know how to pray as we should, but the Spirit is our teacher. He prays for us and in us, moving us to pray, opening the gates of heaven that we may enter the holy place. The Spirit confirms the presence of Christ our mediator and our heavenly priest.

Paul teaches this in the Book of Romans. He tells of three groanings: the groaning of the creation, waiting for its renewal; our groaning as Christians, yearning for the redemption of our bodies at the resurrection; and the groaning of the Holy Spirit who makes intercession for us (Rom. 8:19–27).

Surely the work of the Spirit in us is the major means by which the Spirit applies to us all the benefits of Christ. Charismatic worship is not alone in calling attention to our need for the work of the Spirit in our worship. Corporate worship in the Spirit is surely a means of grace, for the Spirit blesses it.

Part 2

ELEMENTS OF BIBLICAL WORSHIP

Among the central ideas informing historic Reformed worship is the conviction that worship must be "according to Scripture." The Westminster Confession of Faith puts it this way: "But the acceptable way of worshiping the true God is instituted by himself, and so limited by his own revealed will, that he may not be worshiped according to the imaginations and devices of men, or the suggestions of Satan, under any visible representation or any other way not prescribed in the holy Scripture" (21.1). Specifically, the confession notes certain fixed *elements,* some necessary, some occasional: "The reading of the Scriptures with godly fear; the sound preaching; and conscionable hearing of the word, in obedience unto God with understanding, faith, and reverence; singing of psalms with grace in the heart; as, also, the due administration and worthy receiving of the sacraments instituted by Christ; are all parts of the ordinary religious worship of God" (21.5). These are considered in this section.

Albert Mohler and Mark Dever write on two aspects of the preaching of the word. Mohler argues the case for *expository* preaching, boldly stating that "expository preaching is central, irreducible, and nonnegotiable to the Bible's mission of authentic worship that pleases God." Dever considers the important aspect of preaching that is both expositional (in terms of the text) *and* evangelistic (in terms of its audience). Arguing that it is the *content*—rather than method or intent—of the sermon that determines whether it is evangelistic, Dever insists that both Christians and non-Christians need to hear the gospel (*evangel*) preached.

If someone from a previous century should walk into one of our worship services, what would they notice that was different? Among many things, perhaps, the lack of Scripture reading and the poverty of pastoral prayer. Ligon Duncan and Terry Johnson address the oft-neglected matters of pulpit pastoral prayer and the public reading of Scripture. They argue for Scripture-infused corporate worship, especially in these elements.

The sacraments have been both undervalued and overvalued in the church's history. Getting the balance right on the purpose of their administration is tricky and requires some serious reflection on the theology of both baptism and the Lord's Supper. Carefully avoiding undue offense to one side or another with regard to the recipients of baptism, Marion Clark argues for making baptism significant as an event, recalling its administration at Tenth Presbyterian Church in the time of James Montgomery Boice. Richard Phillips deftly argues for a view of the Lord's Supper that is sensitive to biblical and historical debates, focusing on practical ways in which its administration can be improved so as to maximize the benefits it promises and proclaims.

Singing has become a focal point of discord in most discussions on worship, resolution often being accomplished by compromise rather than principle. Indeed, few people think that principle plays any part when music is the subject. After all, is not music merely a matter of taste and fashion? What, if anything, do we know of the music of biblical times? Paul Jones, organist and music director at Tenth Presbyterian Church, has thought long and hard on this issue, and his conclusions deserve serious consideration by all. He writes, in particular, on the use of hymnody in worship, arguing biblically, historically, and theologically. This was an issue close the heart of James Montgomery Boice, and some of the hymns that he composed are used to illustrate the principles that Jones (and Boice) would wish to see employed in the church today.

The singing of psalms is almost nonexistent in Reformed churches today, apart of course from those denominations committed to exclusive psalmody. Terry Johnson argues for *inclusive* psalmody, the singing of psalms (the hymnbook of the Bible) alongside hymns. No more powerful case has been made than this one, and readers are urged to consider its conclusions seriously. God-honoring worship is impossible without the use of the psalms.

5

EXPOSITORY PREACHING: CENTER OF CHRISTIAN WORSHIP

R. ALBERT MOHLER JR.

Most Christians are convinced that worship is central to the life of the church. A renaissance of interest in worship has spread throughout modern Christianity—all across the spectrum of Christian denominations and movements. Evangelical Christians have been especially attentive to worship in recent years. It seems that what A. W. Tozer once called the "missing jewel" of evangelical worship is being recovered.

Nevertheless, if most evangelicals would quickly agree that worship is central to the life of the church, there would be no consensus to an unavoidable question: What is central to Christian worship? Historically, the more liturgical churches argued that the sacraments form the heart of Christian worship. These churches argue that the elements of the Lord's Supper and the water of baptism most powerfully present the gospel.

Among evangelicals, some present a call for evangelism as the heart of worship. In many churches, every facet of the service of worship is planned with the evangelistic invitation in mind. Evangelism is the driving concern of songs, prayers, and the sermon. All other considerations fall in line behind the evangelistic imperative.

Though most evangelicals mention the preaching of the word as a necessary or customary part of worship, the prevailing model of worship in evangelical churches is increasingly defined by music, along with innovations such as drama and video presentations. When preaching retreats, a host of entertaining innovations will take its place.

Traditional norms of worship are now subordinated to a demand for relevance and creativity. A media-driven culture of images has replaced the word-centered culture that gave birth to the Reformation churches. In some sense, the image-driven culture of modern evangelicalism is an embrace of the very practices rejected by the Reformers in their quest for true biblical worship.

Music fills the space in most evangelical worship, and much of this music comes in the form of contemporary choruses marked by precious little theological content. Beyond the popularity of the chorus as a musical form, many evangelical churches seem intensely concerned to replicate studio-quality musical presentations. Baby boomers, whose tastes and expectations are shaped by acoustic sound and a constant rhythmic beat, are now the "old fogys" in many congregations. Younger worshipers expect even more radical musical forms and styles.

In terms of musical style, the more traditional churches feature large choirs—often with orchestras—and may even sing the established hymns of the faith. Choral contributions are often massive in scale and professional in quality. In any event, music fills the space and drives the energy of the worship service. Intense planning, financial investment, and preparation are invested in the musical dimensions of worship. Professional staff and an army of volunteers spend much of the week in rehearsals and practice sessions. An incredible attention to detail marks many of these services, with transitions and modulations carefully premeditated so that the worship experience moves smoothly from one segment to the next—just like on television.

All this is not lost on the congregation. Some Christians shop congregations in order to find the church that offers the worship style and experience that fits their expectation. In most communities, churches are known for their worship styles and musical programs. Those dissatisfied with what they find at one church can quickly move to another, sometimes using the language of self-expression to explain that the new church "meets our needs" or "allows us to worship."

A concern for true biblical worship was at the very heart of the Reformation. But even Martin Luther, who wrote hymns and required his preachers to be trained in song, would not recognize this modern preoccupation with music as legitimate or healthy. Why? Because the Reformers were convinced that the heart of true biblical worship was the preaching of the word of God.

Thanks be to God, evangelism does take place in Christian worship. Confronted by the presentation of the gospel and the preaching of the word, sinners are drawn to faith in Jesus Christ and the offer of salvation is presented to all who so respond. Likewise, the Lord's Supper and baptism are honored as ordinances by the Lord's own command, and each finds its place in true worship.

Furthermore, music is one of God's most precious gifts to his people, and it is a language by which we may worship God in spirit and in truth. The hymns of the faith convey rich confessional and theological content, and many modern choruses recover a sense of doxology formerly lost in many evangelical churches. But music is not the central act of Christian worship, nor is evangelism, nor even the ordinances. The heart of Christian worship is the authentic preaching of the word of God.

Expository Preaching as Worship

Expository preaching is central, irreducible, and nonnegotiable to the Bible's mission of authentic worship that pleases God. John Stott's simple declaration states the issue boldly: "Preaching is indispensable to Christianity."[1] More specifically, preaching is indispensable to Christian worship — and not only indispensable, but central.

The centrality of preaching is the theme of both testaments of Scripture. In Nehemiah 8 we find the people demanding that Ezra the scribe bring the book of the law to the assembly. Ezra and his colleagues stand on a raised platform and read from the book. When he opens the book to read, the assembly rose to its feet in honor of the word of God and their response to the reading was to answer, "Amen, Amen!"

Interestingly, the text explains that Ezra and those assisting him "read from the book, from the law of God, translating to give the sense so that they understood the reading" (Neh. 8:8). This remarkable text presents a portrait of expository preaching. Once the text was read, it was carefully explained to the congregation. Ezra did not stage an event or orchestrate a spectacle — he simply and carefully proclaimed the word of God.

This text is a sobering indictment of much contemporary Christianity. According to the text, a demand for biblical preaching erupted within the hearts of the people. They gathered as a congregation and summoned the preacher. This reflects an intense hunger and thirst for the preaching of the word of God. Where is this desire evident among today's evangelicals?

In far too many churches, the Bible is nearly silent. The public reading of Scripture has been dropped from many services, and the sermon has been sidelined, reduced to a brief devotional appended to the music. Many preachers accept this as a necessary concession to the age of entertainment. Some hope to put in a brief message of encouragement or exhortation before the conclusion of the service.

Michael Green describes the situation well: "The standard of preaching in the modern land is deplorable. There are few great preachers. Many clergy do not seem to believe in it any more as a powerful way in which to proclaim the gospel and change life. This is the age of the sermonette and sermonettes make Christianettes."[2]

But, if preaching is central to Christian worship, what kind of preaching are we talking about? Certainly not the sermonettes described by Green. The sheer weightlessness of much contemporary preaching is a severe indictment of our superficial Christianity. When the pulpit ministry lacks substance, the church is severed from the word of God, and its health and faithfulness are immediately diminished.

Many evangelicals are seduced by the proponents of topical and narrative preaching. The declarative force of Scripture is blunted by a demand for story, and the textual shape of the Bible is supplanted by topical considerations. In many pulpits, the Bible, if referenced at all, becomes merely a source for pithy aphorisms or convenient narratives.

The therapeutic concerns of the culture too often set the agenda for evangelical preaching. The issues of the self predominate, and the congregation expects to hear simple answers to complex problems. The essence of most therapeutic preaching comes down to an affirmation of the self and its importance.

Evangelicals, much like their secular neighbors, now represent the age of "psychological man" so well described by Philip Reiff.[3] The "triumph of the therapeutic" hits very close to home when evangelicals are honest about the preaching they want to hear and expect to receive.

Furthermore, postmodernism claims intellectual primacy in the culture,

110

and Americans are increasingly confused about the very existence of objective and absolute truth. They may not surrender entirely to moral relativism (at least not yet), but they allow and demand moral autonomy and a minimum of intellectual and moral requirements. Doctrinal preaching is by the art of suggestion, and the average congregant expects to make his or her own final decisions about all important issues of life, from worldview to lifestyle.

Church-marketing expert George Barna—no friend of traditional exposition—describes the modern congregation by explaining that "more and more of the audience members are also searching for preachers who come from the Bill Clinton school of preaching: empathetic public speaking ('I feel your pain')."[4] Such an audience will most likely be shocked by the directness of expository preaching.

Authentic Christian preaching carries a note of authority and a demand for decisions not found elsewhere in society. The solid truth of Christianity stands in stark contrast to the flimsy pretensions of postmodernity.

As theologian David F. Wells notes, "Sustaining orthodoxy and framing Christian belief in doctrinal terms requires habits of reflection and judgment that are simply out of place in our culture and increasingly are disappearing from evangelicalism as well."[5] The appetite for serious preaching has virtually disappeared among many Christians, who are content to have their fascinations with themselves encouraged from the pulpit—and are extremely resistant to any preaching that confronts or contradicts this self-absorption.

Modern Americans demand to be liberated from all external authorities and moral codes of obligation. All messages and messengers are judged by whether they champion what David Tracy calls the "emancipatory values" of modernity.[6] It goes without saying that this moral vocabulary has little or no space for a clear "you shall not."

The anemia of evangelical worship—all the music and energy aside—is directly attributed to the absence of genuine expository preaching. Such preaching would confront the congregation with nothing less than the living and active word of God. That confrontation will shape the congregation as the Holy Spirit accompanies the word, opens eyes, and applies that word to human hearts.

One symptom of our modern confusion is found in the response of some preachers and church consultants to the very concept of exposition. As a matter of fact, the concept of expository preaching demands a definition. We must define what we mean when we discuss authentic preaching as exposition. Many preachers claim to be expositors, but in many cases this means no more than that the preacher has a biblical text in mind or in reference, no matter how tenuous may be the actual relationship between the text and the sermon.

I offer the following definition of expository preaching as a framework for consideration:

> Expository preaching is that mode of Christian preaching that takes as its central purpose the presentation and application of the text of the Bible. All other issues and concerns are subordinated to the central task of presenting the biblical text. As the word of God, the text of Scripture has the right to establish both the substance and the structure of the sermon. Genuine exposition takes place when the preacher sets forth the meaning and message of the biblical text and makes clear how the word of God establishes the identity and worldview of the church as the people of God.

Expository preaching begins in the preacher's determination to present and explain the text of the Bible to his congregation. This simple starting point is a major issue of division in contemporary homiletics for, from Harry Emerson Fosdick onward, many preachers assume that they must begin with a human problem or question and then work backward to the biblical text. Expository preaching begins with the text and works from the text and its revealed truth to the application of that truth to the lives of believers. If this determination and commitment are not clear at the outset, something other than expository preaching will result.

The preacher comes to the text and to the preaching event with many concerns and priorities in mind. Many of their concerns are undeniably legitimate and important in their own right. Nevertheless, if genuine exposition of the word of God is to take place, those other concerns must be subordinate to the central and irreducible task of explaining and presenting the biblical text.

Application of biblical truth is a necessary task of expository preaching. But application must follow the diligent and disciplined task of explaining the text itself. T. H. L. Parker, commenting on Calvin's homiletic method, describes preaching like this: "Expository preaching consists in the explanation and application of a passage of Scripture. Without explanation it is not expository; without application it is not preaching."[7]

112

Expository preaching is inescapably bound to the serious work of exegesis. If the preacher is to explain the text, he must first study the text and devote the necessary hours of study and research necessary to understand the text. The pastor faces an immediate issue of priority when this is acknowledged. He must invest the largest portion of his energy and intellectual engagement (not to mention his time) to this task of "accurately handling the word of truth" (2 Tim. 2:15). There are no shortcuts to genuine exposition. The preacher must stand ready to present and proclaim the message of the Bible and bring the congregation into a direct confrontation with the biblical text. The expositor is not an explorer who returns to tell tales of the journey, but a guide who leads the people into the text and teaches the arts of Bible study and interpretation even as he demonstrates the same.

The shape of the sermon may differ from preacher to preacher and should differ from text to text. The Bible is the inerrant and infallible word of God. The affirmation of verbal inspiration reminds us that every word of the Bible is fully inspired. Therefore, the shape of the biblical text is also divinely directed.

God has spoken through the inspired human authors of Scripture, and the richness of the Bible is evident in the various genres of biblical literature. The Bible includes historical narrative, direct discourse, and apocalyptic symbolism. Each of these different forms of literary structure demands that the preacher give careful attention to the text and allow the text to shape the message. Far too many preachers come to the text with a sermonic shape in mind and a limited set of tools in hand. Genuine exposition demands that the text establish the shape as well as the substance of the sermon.

The preacher rises in the pulpit to accomplish one central purpose—to set forth the message and meaning of the biblical text. Using the most faithful and careful tools and practices of exegesis, the preacher sets forth the message of the text. This requires historical investigation, literary discernment, and the faithful employment of the *analogia fidei* to interpret Scripture by Scripture.

In so doing, the expositor must reject the modern conceit that what the text *meant* is not necessarily what it *means*. If the Bible is truly the enduring and eternal word of God, it means what it meant even as it is newly applied in every generation.

Once the meaning of the text is set forth, the preacher moves to appli-

113

cation. This stage is absolutely necessary, but fraught with danger. The first danger is the temptation to believe that the preacher can or should manipulate the human heart. The preacher is responsible for setting forth the external word of Scripture. Only the Holy Spirit can apply that word to human hearts or even open eyes to understand and receive the text.

Haddon Robinson describes the "heresy of application," warning that many preachers are faithful in the task of exegesis, but undermine the text at the point of application.[8] At the other extreme are preachers who never get to the task of application at all. Some argue that application is an attempt to do the work of the Holy Spirit. But the faithful preacher understands the difference between the external application of the text to life and the Spirit's internal application of the word to the heart.

True exposition demands a hearing from God's people and presents all hearers with a decision. As John MacArthur explains, "I believe the goal of preaching is to compel people to make a decision. I want people who listen to me to understand exactly what God's Word demands of them when I am through. Then they must say either, 'Yes, I will do what God says,' or 'No, I won't do what God says.' "[9]

As the word of God, the biblical text has the right to establish our identity as the people of God and to determine our worldview. The Bible tells us who we are, locates us under the lordship of Jesus Christ, and establishes a worldview framed by the glory and sovereignty of God. Put simply, the Bible determines reality for the church and stipulates a God-centered worldview for the redeemed.

In preaching the biblical text, the preacher explains how the Bible directs our thinking and living. This brings the task of expository preaching into direct confrontation with the postmodern worldview and the simple fact of human sinfulness. We do not want to be told how to think or how to live. Each of us desires to be the author of our own life script, the master of our own fate, our own judge and lawgiver and guide.

But the word of God lays a unique and privileged claim upon the church as the body of Christ. Every text demands a fundamental realignment of our basic worldview and way of life. Thus, the church is always mounting a counterrevolution to the spirit of the age, and preaching is the God-ordained means whereby the saints are armed and equipped for this battle and confrontation.

Every sermon presents the hearer with a forced decision. We will either obey or disobey the word of God. The sovereign authority of God operates through the preaching of his word to demand obedience from his people. Preaching is the essential instrumentality through which God shapes his people as the Holy Spirit accompanies the preaching of the word. As the Reformers remind us, it is through preaching that Christ is present among his people.

Authentic expository preaching is marked by three distinct marks or characteristics: authority, reverence, and centrality. Expository preaching is authoritative because it stands upon the very authority of the Bible as the word of God. Such preaching requires and reinforces a sense of reverent expectation on the part of God's people. Finally, expository preaching demands the central place in Christian worship and is respected as the event through which the living God speaks to his people.

Authority

A keen analysis of our contemporary age comes from sociologist Richard Sennett of New York University. Sennett notes that in times past a major anxiety of most persons was loss of governing authority. Now, the tables have been turned, and modern persons are anxious about any authority over them: "We have come to fear the influence of authority as a threat to our liberties, in the family and in society at large." If previous generations feared the absence of authority, today we see "a fear of authority when it exists."[10]

The Enlightenment culture that gave birth to modernity was subversive of every form of authority, though it has taken some centuries for this rebellion against authority to work its way throughout society. In the postmodern culture of the West, authority is under attack in every form, and a sense of personal autonomy is basic to contemporary ideals of human rights and freedom. We will have no king to rule over us; no parent to discipline us; no teacher to instruct us; and no truth to bind us. As two recent observers lament, "Americans have embraced freedom so tightly, they can see only one aspect of it, the side of autonomy."[11]

Some homileticians suggest that preachers should simply embrace this new worldview and surrender any claim to an authoritative message. Those who have lost confidence in the authority of the Bible as the word of God are left with little to say and no authority for their message. Fred Craddock, among the most influential figures in recent homiletic thought, famously describes today's preacher "as one without authority."[12] His portrait of the preacher's predicament is haunting: "The old thunderbolts rust in the attic while the minister tries to lead his people through the morass of relativities and proximate possibilities."[13] "No longer can the preacher presuppose the general recognition of his authority as a clergyman, or the authority of his institution, or the authority of Scripture," Craddock argues.[14] Summarizing the predicament of the postmodern preacher, he relates that the preacher "seriously asks himself whether he should continue to serve up a monologue in a dialogical world."[15]

The obvious question to pose to Craddock's analysis is this: If we have no authoritative message, why preach? Without authority, the preacher and the congregation are involved in a massive waste of precious time. The very idea that preaching can be transformed into a dialogue between the pulpit and the pew indicates the confusion of our era.

Contrasted to this is the note of authority found in all true expository preaching. As Martyn Lloyd-Jones notes: "Any study of church history, and particularly any study of the great periods of revival or reawakening, demonstrates above everything else just this one fact: that the Christian Church during all such periods has spoken with authority. The great characteristic of all revivals has been the authority of the preacher. There seemed to be something new, extra, and irresistible in what he declared on behalf of God."[16]

The preacher dares to speak on behalf of God. He stands in the pulpit as a steward "of the mysteries of God" (1 Cor. 4:1) and declares the truth of God's word, proclaims the power of that word, and applies the word to life. This is an admittedly audacious act. No one should even contemplate such an endeavor without absolute confidence in a divine call to preach and in the unblemished authority of the holy Scriptures.

The preaching ministry is not a profession to be joined, but a call to be answered. The church has no need of religious functionaries preaching up-to-date messages based on the latest therapeutic remedy or philosophical fad. Charles Spurgeon instructed his student preachers to pay heed to their call: "We must feel that woe is unto us if we preach not the gospel; the word of God must be unto us as fire in our bones, otherwise, if we undertake the ministry, we shall be unhappy in it, shall be unable to bear the self-denials incident to it, and shall be of little service to those among whom we minister."[17]

The call to preach is not merely an existential experience or perception embraced by an individual, but a call recognized and affirmed by the church. The teaching office is one of God's gifts to his people, not a career path for a "helping profession."

The authority of the preacher is rooted in this divine call to preach, and the church must respect the preaching office. But in the final analysis, the ultimate authority for preaching is the authority of the Bible as the word of God. Without this authority, the preacher stands naked and silent before the congregation and the watching world. If the Bible is not the word of God, the preacher is involved in an act of self-delusion or professional pretension.

Standing on the authority of Scripture, the preacher declares a truth received, not a message invented. The teaching office is not an advisory role based in religious expertise, but a prophetic function whereby God speaks to his people.

Martin Luther understood this responsibility very clearly, and as a pastor and theologian "never wanted to be anything else than an obedient hearer and student of the Scripture."[18] Paul Althaus expands on this comment:

> In this Luther was a perfect example of his own teachings concerning the authority of the Holy Scripture in the church. The Scripture is the record of the apostolic witness to Christ and is as such the decisive authority in the church. Since the apostles are the foundation of the church, their authority is basic. No other authority can be equal to theirs. Every other authority in the church is derived from following the teaching of the apostles and is validated only by its conformity to their teaching. This means that only Scripture can establish and substantiate articles of faith. The Scripture offers all that is necessary to salvation. Christians need no other truth for their salvation beyond that proclaimed in Scripture.[19]

Gardiner Spring, for more than sixty years pastor of the Brick Presbyterian Church in New York City, describes the preacher's authority in striking language: "The ministers of the Gospel are the appointed ambassadors of the Head and King of the church; he sends them on their great and responsible errand, and they possess authority to publish the Gospel in his name, which belongs exclusively to themselves. It is not an authority they usurp, nor an office which they themselves have sought, but one which has been imposed upon them."[20]

This means that imagination and inventiveness are not the central qualities of the preaching ministry. Instead, the true minister is he who seeks faithfully to teach, preach, and declare the message we have received in holy Scripture. As Spring describes true preachers: "Inspired men they are not, but sinning and fallible, like their fellows; yet do they utter his truth, not on their own responsibility, but God's; not in their own names, but his; not for themselves, but for him; not as men merely, but as accredited ministers of their divine Lord who sent them."[21]

The absence of authority in much contemporary preaching is directly attributable to the absence of confidence in the authority of the Bible. Once biblical authority is undermined and eroded, preaching becomes a pretense. The preacher stands to offer religious advice on the basis of the latest secular learning and the "spirituality" of the day. The dust of death covers thousands of pulpits across the land.

But when the Bible's authority is recognized and honored, the pulpit stands as a summons to hear and obey the word of God. True worship takes place when the authority of the Bible is rightly honored and the preaching of the word is understood to be the event whereby God speaks to his people through his word, by the human instrumentality of his servants—the preachers.

Reverence

The congregation that gathered before Ezra and the other preachers demonstrated a love and reverence for the word of God (Neh. 8). When the book was read, the people stood up. This act of standing reveals the heart of the people and their sense of expectancy as the word was read and preached.

Expository preaching requires an attitude of reverence on the part of the congregation. Preaching is not a dialogue, but it does involve at least two parties—the preacher and the congregation. The congregation's role in the preaching event is to hear, receive, and obey the word of God. In so doing, the church demonstrates reverence for the preaching and teaching of the Bible and understands that the sermon brings the word of Christ near to the congregation. This is true worship.

Lacking reverence for the word of God, many congregations are caught in a frantic quest for significance in worship. Worship is increasingly treated as an opportunity for entertainment mixed with the possibility of a numinous experience. Persons move from congregation to congregation looking for the worship experience that will meet their perceived spiritual needs. Worship is turned into just another consumer commodity.

This focus on the self and its perceived spiritual needs is another symptom of the basic narcissism at the heart of human sinfulness. Christians leave church services asking each other, "Did you get anything out of that?" Churches produce surveys to measure expectations for worship. Would you like more music? What kind? How about drama? Is our preacher sufficiently creative?

Expository preaching demands a very different set of questions. Will I obey the word of God? How must my thinking be realigned by Scripture? How must I change my behavior to be fully obedient to the word? These questions reveal submission to the authority of God and reverence for the Bible as his word.

The preacher must demonstrate his own reverence for God's word by dealing truthfully and responsibly with the text. He must not be flippant or casual, much less dismissive or disrespectful. Of this we can be certain— no congregation will revere the Bible more than the preacher does.

Calvin instructed his congregation about authentic worship by reminding them of the purpose of preaching: "We come together in the name of the Lord. It is not to hear merry songs, to be fed with wind, that is, with a vain and unprofitable curiosity, but to receive spiritual nourishment. For God will have nothing preached in his name but that which will profit and edify."[22]

Reverence is the only appropriate response to the acknowledgement that the Bible is the word of God and that preaching is the proclamation of that word to God's people. Luther continually pointed back to God as the divine author of the word: "Yes, I hear the sermon; but who is speaking? The minister? No indeed! You do not hear the minister. True, the voice is his; but my God is speaking the Word which he preaches or speaks. Therefore I should honor the Word of God that I may become a good pupil of the Word."[23]

Centrality

Worship properly directed to the honor and glory of God will find its center in the reading and preaching of the word of God. Expository preaching cannot be assigned a supporting role in the act of worship—it must be central.

In the course of the Reformation, Luther's driving purpose was to restore preaching to its proper place in Christian worship. Referring to the incident between Mary and Martha in Luke 10, Luther reminded his congregation and students that Jesus Christ declared that "*only* one thing is necessary"—the preaching of the word (Luke 10:42). Therefore, "for Luther the most important reform needed in the worship of the Church of his day was to reestablish the centrality of the reading and preaching of the Word in public worship."[24]

That same reformation is needed in American evangelicalism today. Expository preaching must once again be central to the life of the church and central to Christian worship. In the end, the church will not be judged by its Lord for the quality of its music but for the faithfulness of its preaching. In this judgment the preacher and the congregation will stand in mutual judgment. The preacher will be judged for his preaching and the congregation will be judged for its hearing—and for the preaching it has demanded and obeyed. Of course, as the Apostle James reminds us, the teacher will incur a stricter judgment (James 3:1).

Hughes Oliphant Old's monumental study of preaching throughout the history of the church starts with the preaching of the biblical period. Looking at the preaching of the Apostle Paul, Old gets to the heart of the matter:

The preaching and the hearing of the Word of God is in the last analysis worship, worship in its most profound sense. Preaching is not an auxiliary activity to worship, nor is it some kind of preparation for worship which one hopes will follow. To be sure, missionary preaching, catechetical preaching, and penitential preaching prepare the congregation for worship, but it is at the same time worship because it is a part of baptism. That is all quite true and elsewhere we have tried to make that point, but it is even more true that the proclaiming of the Word of God, simply in itself, is high service to God. The solemn reading and preaching of Scripture in the midst of the congregation is a cultic act, if we may use that term, in continuity with the sacrifices of the Old Testament. Even more it fulfills these ancient cultic acts. The Old Testament sacrifices were the type, the foreshadow, of something far greater, the proclamation of the gospel. The reading and preaching of

Scripture is worship of an even greater intensity, an even greater depth, and an even greater magnificence than were ever the sacrifices of the Temple.[25]

When today's evangelicals speak casually of the distinction between worship and preaching (meaning that the church will enjoy an offering of music before adding on a bit of preaching), they betray their misunderstanding of both worship and the act of preaching. Worship is not something we do before we settle down for the word of God, it is the act through which the people of God direct all their attentiveness to hearing the one true and living God speak to his people and receive their praises. God is most beautifully praised when his people hear his word, love his word, and obey his word. As Old reminds us, this is a privilege and a duty far greater than sacrifice.

As in the Reformation, the most important corrective to our corruption of worship (and defense against the consumerist demands of the day) is to return expository preaching and the public reading of God's word to their rightful primacy and centrality in worship. Only then will the "missing jewel" be truly rediscovered.

The ministry of James Montgomery Boice was a monument to expository preaching and a display of God's glory through the ministry of the word. "My ministry is based on regular, systematic Bible exposition," he explained.[26] The truth of that simple statement was demonstrated in the thousands of expository messages he preached from the pulpit of the Tenth Presbyterian Church in Philadelphia.

Few men exerted such a godly and faithful influence on their fellow ministers. He championed the inerrancy and full authority of Scripture and insisted that "the first and essential requirement [of expository preaching] is *a joyful and total commitment to the absolute authority of God's written revelation.*" He continued: "There has never been a great expository preacher who has not held this high conviction; there have been pulpiteers who have not, but never expositors."[27] This distinction is crucial. The nation and its airwaves are filled with pulpiteers, but true expositors are rare.

Those who love the Lord, love his word, and seek his glory in true worship must restore expository preaching to its rightful place—the center of worship.

6

EVANGELISTIC EXPOSITORY PREACHING

MARK E. DEVER

Much has been written on evangelistic preaching. And much has been written on expositional preaching. Often, though, we tend to think of the two as mutually exclusive, rather than as normally inseparable. We think that the converted need Bible teaching and the unconverted need evangelistic addresses. This chapter intends to question that conclusion. Instead, I want to suggest another way that we should think of our obligations in preaching to both Christians and non-Christians. We will proceed with the conviction that the converted and the unconverted need preaching in which the fullness of God's word is exposed and the atoning work of Christ explored.

That a Christian sermon should both expound God's word and declare his good news is not surprising. In fact, just in writing that sentence (without using the normal words *expositional* and *evangelistic*) it seems absurd to think otherwise. But many do. Perhaps we ourselves sometimes wonder how we can be better expositors, but we never consider our presentation of the gospel in our sermons. Or perhaps we want to be better evangelists, but we cannot see how that has anything to do with our preaching. It is the goal of this chapter to make plain how those two concerns are vitally connected. To be more specific still, in the previous chapter, we considered the nature of expositional preaching. In this chapter, we consider how such expositional preaching should particularly be evangelistic and how we can help it to be so.

A Biblical Pattern

The gospel is the story of the Bible. If we are committed to preaching the Bible, we will find ourselves preaching the gospel. Graeme Goldsworthy puts it forcefully: "All preaching, to be true to the biblical perspective, must in some sense be gospel preaching. . . . Expository, biblical preaching is always an exposition of the gospel and its implications."[1] Throughout the Old Testament, God's word is the fount and the focus of proclamation. In the New Testament, the fulfillment of his promises in Christ is at the center of the teaching.

The Lord Jesus' ministry centered on teaching the truth about his own identity and mission. In Mark 2, we see Jesus appropriating scriptural themes from the Old Testament, explaining that their true meaning was found in their pointing to him. So he presents himself as the bridegroom come for his bride, as the Son of Man, as the Lord of the Sabbath. All of these titles were connected closely with God himself in the Old Testament. Now, Jesus announced that they were fulfilled in him.

Throughout the New Testament, we find a close connection between exposing the meaning of Scripture and pointing to God's good news in Christ. In Luke 24, the risen Christ does an extraordinary Bible study with two of his disciples. We read in Luke 24:27: "And beginning with Moses and all the Prophets, he explained to them what was said in all the Scriptures concerning himself." A little later in the same chapter, Christ came to be with "the Eleven and those with them" (24:33) and said, " 'This is what I told you while I was still with you: Everything must be fulfilled that is written about me in the Law of Moses, the Prophets and the Psalms.' Then he opened their minds so they could understand the Scriptures. He told them, 'This is what is written: The Christ will suffer and rise from the dead on the third day, and repentance and forgiveness of sins will be preached in his name to all nations, beginning at Jerusalem' " (24:44–47).

The evangelistic sermons those disciples preached, recorded in the Book of Acts, follow this same pattern—they arise from the text and they point to Christ. So Peter at Pentecost begins by quoting a passage from the prophet

123

Joel and explaining it and current events in its light. Then he presses home the news about Jesus from various psalms.

Again in Acts 3, when Peter is presented with a crowd aware of a miraculous healing, he turns to the Lord's prediction through Moses in Deuteronomy 18 about God's raising up "a prophet like me" and announces that Jesus is that prophet. Peter then begins to make clear what their response to this should be. Throughout the Book of Acts this is the pattern we find: "As his custom was, Paul went into the synagogue, and on three Sabbath days he reasoned with them from the Scriptures, explaining and proving that the Christ had to suffer and rise from the dead. 'This Jesus I am proclaiming to you is the Christ,' he said. Some of the Jews were persuaded and joined Paul and Silas, as did a large number of God-fearing Greeks and not a few prominent women" (17:2).

Certainly, not every evangelistic address must be a straightforward exposition of one passage of Scripture. In Acts 17, in Athens, the center of Greek learning, Paul is drawn into a dispute with "a group of Epicurean and Stoic philosophers." Ten verses (17:22–31) record Paul's words—none of which cite any Old Testament passages—to the meeting of the Areopagus. Today, ministers of the gospel may have similar opportunities in series of evangelistic or apologetic talks outside the regular assembly of a Christian church, for example, on college campuses or in other meetings expressly for this purpose. We can certainly proclaim the gospel of Christ outside our regular expositional ministry.

Our regular preaching of God's word, however, should never fail to point to Christ. Whether we preach from the New Testament or the Old, the apostolic pattern is to declare God's word to God's people, always pointing to the fulfillment of his promises in Christ. This pattern is continued in the letters of the New Testament, a treasury of inspired Christian homilies. In his letters to the Galatian Christians and the Christians in Rome, Paul reasoned closely about the gospel from the Old Testament. His text of choice was often Genesis 15:6: "Abram believed the Lord, and he credited it to him as righteousness." From this passage, in Galatians 3 and Romans 4, Paul carefully reasoned and passionately declared the hope that we have in Christ. With believing eyes, the writer to the Hebrews leads us through the Old Testament stories and the practices of the temple. He does this with great care, and all to show us Christ. The biblical pattern is for a Christian preacher to proclaim and explain God's word to God's people. And the heart of that word is always Christ. So today, too, we need preaching that is both expositional and evangelistic. Let's consider those each briefly in turn.

The Need for All of God's Word: Expositional Preaching

Expositional preaching is all about giving God's people God's word. It is preaching in which the point of the biblical passage is the point of the preacher's message. This is what it means to preach expositionally—to expose God's word.

Christians are obviously to be fed with God's word. As our Lord said to the tempter: "Man does not live on bread alone, but on every word that comes from the mouth of God" (Matt. 4:4; Luke 4:4). Even in his answer, Jesus demonstrated his utter dependence upon God's word. He quoted Deuteronomy 8:3, where the Lord, through Moses, instructed his people at the end of their wilderness wanderings that his most important provision for them was not manna, but his word.

We saw in the previous chapter something of how expositional sermons are a normal part of God's feeding us his word. Non-Christians too, though, need God's word. Those who do not yet believe the gospel need to be told of their hopelessness apart from Christ. They need to have God's word presented to them; they need God's Spirit to convict them of their own sin and desperation. Being so liable to God's judgment, they need to hear of God's grace.

All this can happen through expositional preaching. Through such biblically faithful sermons, non-Christians can have Satan's lies exposed, God's truth revealed, their own hearts searched, and Christ's grace magnified to them.

In our day, we see evangelism as something usually brief and urgent, whereas the edification of believers is to be patiently and carefully done. In truth, real evangelism often needs to be every bit as patiently pursued and every bit as carefully done. It may be that the believers in your church need to be taught the truths in Genesis in order to understand more fully that the one who made them is holy, that this holy God is sovereign, or that they are to respond in repentance and faith to the mercies of God. But surely our non-Christian friends need this no less.

How often has God used the patient exposition of Genesis 1–3 or Mark's

125

Gospel or the early chapters of Romans to lead someone to himself? Non-Christians around us have been steeped in sin and Satan's deception for a lifetime; are we surprised if God normally takes longer than a couple of minutes to undermine Satan's lies and bring the sinner under conviction as he lays out his creation intent for marriage and sexuality, for work and supreme allegiance to him, for repentance and faith? We have all joined in Adam's rebellion heartily (not reluctantly) and completely (not partially). We may need to be made thoroughly aware of the responsibilities to our Creator that we have ignored and even denied.

Through expositional preaching, non-Christians need to be instructed in the truth and taught how God views his world—including them. They need to be challenged to rethink their priorities, their work, their family, and most of all their own lives. They need to be rediagnosed by God's word. Both Christians and non-Christians need to hear God's word expounded.

The Need for the Good News: Evangelistic Preaching

The need for evangelistic preaching is obvious, too. The Apostle Paul's riveting argument in Romans 10 is founded on the notion that "faith comes from hearing the message" (10:17). Those who have not yet heard the gospel of Jesus Christ need to do so. This is straightforward. There are, however, some important matters to consider about evangelistic preaching that are not so straightforward.

What Is an Evangelistic Sermon?

For one thing, some people have a mistaken notion of what constitutes an evangelistic address. Some think that evangelistic sermons must be histrionic. Others assume quite the opposite—that, in fact, your whole goal in commending the gospel to your visitor determines that the evangelistic sermon must be seeker sensitive. Still others think that any good evangelistic message will be packed with the latest apologetic arguments. But evangelistic preaching is not married to any certain style. Others feel that evangelistic sermons must be preached in the setting of a week-long mission, a revival, or a Sunday evening (as the tradition was in many evangelical churches in Britain in the twentieth century). But surely the setting does not determine what is truly an evangelistic sermon.

Still others feel that any sermon that is met with conversions must be an evangelistic sermon. And conversely, they may suggest, any that is not cannot have been truly evangelistic. But surely the results do not adequately evaluate whether we have been faithful. And still others may feel that if they intend a message to be evangelistic, then it must have been so. But, of course, messages are not truly evangelistic merely because the preacher's motive was that the sermons should be. Our intentions are not always realized in our sermons. Whether a sermon is truly evangelistic is determined not by our motives or the results afterward or by the setting or the style, the time or the place. One thing and one thing alone determines whether a sermon can properly be said to be evangelistic, and that is its content. Is the evangel—the good news—present? Even better, is it presented forcefully and with heart to sinners in need? This question of content is above all the question that determines whether a sermon is truly evangelistic.

Who Needs to Hear Evangelistic Sermons?

Another matter that confuses us in our evangelistic efforts is that it is not always obvious who the non-Christians are. Sometimes it is not obvious to them. Perhaps one person is fairly moral, even religious. Perhaps they are even a member of the church. The great Puritan preacher William Perkins said that generally churches have "both believers and unbelievers. This is the typical situation in our congregations."[2] Such unregenerate members may never see themselves as needing to hear the gospel declared and explained, and yet they may exist for years in the soundest of churches unconvicted of their sins and unconverted in their souls.

This confusion is compounded when even preachers of the word do not realize the people's state. While those who are called to preach God's word to God's people should be gifted with above average discernment, no pastor can look into the human heart as the Lord Jesus did. There may be those among the apparently committed in a congregation who are actually self-righteous or, as the Puritans used to name them, "gospel hypocrites." The famous example in Puritan literature was created by John Bunyan in a character called "Mr. Badman." Bunyan's fictitious hypocrite lived an apparently virtuous life, knowing some involvement with his church, and he even died with a clear conscience! As Bunyan said at the end of the first part of *Pilgrim's Progress*, "I saw that there was a way to hell, even from the gates of heaven, as well as from the City of Destruction!" Preachers need to be confident of this and so realize that the gospel is always in need of being proclaimed.

Sound evangelistic preaching, however, is also helpful for Christians. Whose heart has yet fully appreciated the goodness of God to us in providing for our salvation in Christ? Who of those hearing the next sermon you preach has fully comprehended God's love for us in Christ? Whose gratitude is as full as it can be? Whose hope as sharp? Whose faith as strong? All of this can happen by searching presentations of the gospel through preaching that exposes God's word. Passages that explore God's holiness, contemplate his rights, consider our purpose, trace out our sin, meditate on Christ, delineate various aspects of his work, tease out the nature of faith, or expose false repentance — all of these can be the subject of sermons that, by exposing God's people to God's word, not only hold out the gospel to those who never heard it, but build up those who have. Expositional preaching should be, by its very nature, evangelistic and edifying. John Piper defines preaching itself simply as "the heralding of the good news by a messenger sent by God."[3] Good evangelistic preaching should always edify God's people merely by carefully holding out God's gospel.

Such evangelistic preaching is important for Christians to hear because it helps us to better understand the gospel we claim to believe. And along with our head's understanding, our heart's appreciation grows and deepens. What believer would not profit from having a clearer grasp of God's holiness, his coming judgment, human purpose, our sin, Christ's person and work, or the required response of repentance and faith?

What results from such a growing gospel understanding among Christians? There are several results, but let me name just three. First, a growing gospel understanding among Christians leads us to praise. God desires that we praise him. His word is full of encouragements for us and even exhortations to us to praise him (Deut. 8:10; Ps. 33; Isa. 12:4; Acts 15:14; Rom. 9:17; 1 Peter 2:9). Eternity will not be long enough for us to adequately thank God or to explore the fullness of the reasons we should praise him. Proclaiming his gospel displays his character to us at its most gracious and loving point. As Samuel Crossman's beautiful hymn declares:

> My song is love unknown,
> My Saviour's love to me;

Love to the loveless shown,
That they might lovely be.

Crossman goes on to detail ways in which God loved us, none more poignant than this observation:

In life, no house, no home
My Lord on earth might have;
In death, no friendly tomb,
But what a stranger gave.
What may I say?
Heaven was His home;
But mine the tomb
Wherein He lay.

A growing understanding of our Savior's love for us causes us to praise God.

Another result of such gospel-oriented evangelistic preaching in the lives of Christian hearers should be an increasing integration of biblical knowledge with their everyday lives. As the gospel is explored and explained, as implications are drawn out and false conclusions confuted, the gospel becomes more woven into the warp and woof of our lives. It forms the filter through which we understand the world. It acts as a protection from sin and a guide to holiness. A healthy appreciation for God's holiness causes us to grow in our respect for God and in our esteem for his abilities. We may defend the inerrancy of his word not based upon a high conception of the human authors, but rather based upon a high conception of God and of his ability to create creatures who can understand what he reveals. A growing understanding of our having been made in God's image may help us to understand how good can be produced by non-Christian artists or novelists or business owners or scientists, or how non-Christians can have good marriages and good homes. We are not baffled by that. We understand that we are made in the image of God. Increased appreciation for the gospel may result in a deepened grasp of the offensiveness of sin to God and therefore in our living more holy lives. We could proceed through every head of theology as it flows from the gospel and consider how a greater understanding of each one of these causes the gospel to stand in more immediate connection with every thought we have during the day and with every aspect of our lives.

If this is the case, then a third result of such expositional preaching that faithfully points to the gospel is that our own personal evangelism should become more pervasive and more natural in our lives. If we clearly see the connection between the gospel and the worldview espoused in this movie or that editorial, this decision your child makes or that ethical dilemma your friend at work faces, then the gospel comes much more naturally into our conversations. Instead of abruptly changing topics with a non-Christian friend, such equipped Christians can see how the gospel is the topic at the root of the matter being discussed. Certainly one could caricature such readiness with the gospel in conversation, but a congregation well instructed in the gospel and its implications in our daily lives should be a congregation that evangelizes much more naturally and therefore regularly.

For all these reasons, and more, it is both biblically right and practically helpful for pastors regularly to preach expositional sermons evangelistically to their own congregations. Both Christians and non-Christians need to hear the gospel preached.

How to Preach Expositional Sermons Evangelistically

The question people may ask is, How can a sermon be both faithfully evangelistic and faithfully expositional? Perhaps the questioner would understand how that can be the case with certain passages as the text, but can every text of Scripture be expounded with the expectation that the gospel will be central to that exposition? It is the conviction of this author that the answer to that question is a definite yes!

Little has been written on preaching that is both evangelistic and expositional, but surely it is in the nature of good biblical preaching to be both. Expositional preaching can be the best evangelistic preaching. Who can have heard or read the preaching of James Montgomery Boice through the early chapters of Genesis or Romans or of D. Martyn Lloyd-Jones in Ephesians 2 and not agree with that sentiment?

Though the argument is not made in this chapter that exposition and evangelism are synonymous—nor even quite inseparable—it should be clear that they are normally deeply related and that great benefit should flow to the hearers when the message has both exposition and the gospel carefully integrated.

How precisely can we preach such biblical, evangelistic sermons? That is the topic of the remainder of this chapter. But before we turn to such practical matters that may help us to do this, we must first check our own understanding of what the message of the Bible is.

As those who handle the word of God publicly, preachers and teachers must understand that the whole Bible is gospel-shaped. The stories in Genesis and Exodus, the wisdom of the Psalms, the warnings and prophecies of Isaiah and Ezekiel, the parables of Jesus, and the letters of Paul—all are gospel-shaped. They contain and convey the great themes of who God is, why he made us, how we failed, what God did in Christ, and the repentance and faith we are now called to in light of all this. In our preaching, we should not merely insert a gospel outline in an otherwise moralistic message from the Old Testament; rather, we need to understand how God's law drives us to God's gospel. And we need to do that in the teaching of every passage of Scripture. With that understanding of the Bible in place, expositional sermons much more naturally become conduits for the gospel. Making sure we have that understanding is the first practical step we can make to bring our expositions and our evangelism together.

Assuming this gospel-shaped understanding of the Bible, there are a number of particular ways our own expositional preaching ministry can be more faithfully evangelistic.

Accommodation

The main weekly Lord's Day gathering of a church is primarily for Christians, not non-Christians. Therefore we should deliberately set about to plan the service—including our preaching—with our primary end as the glorification of God through the edification of his church. Certainly evangelism can be a part of that—as I argue above—but it is never the main point. Our expositional sermons are preached to feed the flock entrusted to our care.

Of course, when you preach well expositionally, you necessarily preach evangelistically. This is why we so often find the ministries of great expositional preachers so blessed evangelistically. God honors the preaching of his word. We realize that our Sunday morning congregations are not stationary Billy Graham rallies. They are not audiences to be lured and kept, but congregations to be shepherded and fed. And yet, as we preach God's word faithfully, hypocrites will find the new birth. And non-Christians will see the change in their family and friends, and they, too, will, by God's grace, inevitably come.

Therefore it is appropriate for us to take into account the presence of non-Christians in our services. Our services can be properly sensitive and friendly to non-Christians without calibrating everything to the level of a first-time visitor. When we gather as a church, we gather as a family in need of sustenance. Part of what we do during that time will be quite naturally to pray for and preach to those who are not yet Christians. And in doing that we should use language they can understand. We should remind people occasionally why we do what we do in the service. We should preach from a translation that people can understand. We may even explain from time to time what chapter and verse numbers are and other things that those of us who have been Christians for years take for granted. But no believer is ever hurt by having the truth explained to them briefly and simply, even as no unbeliever is hurt by having Scripture preached powerfully on points they do not fully understand. When the church all around is helped, they too will be helped.

Title

Even sermon titles can be provocative for drawing people to consider their lives and to consider coming to hear the sermon. Coaxing interest need not compromise content. You could entitle a series in Exodus "A New Start." You could give the following names to a series through 1 John called "Basic Questions":

- ✧ "What Do I Do with Sin?" (1 John 1:1–2:2)
- ✧ "How Can I Know That I Have Eternal Life?" (1 John 2:3–27)
- ✧ "What Is True Love?" (1 John 2:28–3:24)
- ✧ "How Can I Face Judgment?" (1 John 4)
- ✧ "What Is Faith?" (1 John 5)

Such titles are both faithful to the content of the texts to be expounded and, at the same time, help to call attention to the relevance of the content for those who are not yet Christians. They should naturally be of interest to non-Christians and Christians alike. Just because your non-Christian friend is not interested in a series of sermons advertised as being "on 1 John" does

132

not mean he or she would not be interested in hearing sermons addressing the matters John addressed in those letters. That is what the titles listed above are intended to do—to expose the content of the text and to suggest something of the way it might intersect with their lives.

Even the events of our lives conspire to create interest in God's word. Titles can reflect such interest. Times of cultural interest in Christianity provided by crises (like the events of September 11, 2001), unusual events (like the new millennium), or regular seasons (Thanksgiving, Christmas, New Year's, Easter) can be well used for gospel ends. With a little thought, relevant and even provocative titles can be provided for advertisements.

Introductions

Our sermon introductions, too, can evidence the evangelistic intent that we have in expounding God's word. We can begin our sermons expectantly, but not wrongly presuming the interest of those gathered. Certainly the faithful members of the congregation *should* be interested, but they are not always. Some will be distracted, others hardened, others uninformed, and still others weary. All of these will be helped if they are first told why they should listen to the sermon before they are actually made to do it. Reminding ourselves of why and how the doctrinal center of our text is important is a useful exercise in an introduction.

And if introductions are so useful for our Christian hearers, they are certainly no less so for our non-Christian hearers. Introductions that highlight and seek to demonstrate the relevance, to carefully delineate the difficult points, to admit uncertainties on a popular topic, all serve to encourage hearers to give their careful attention to the sermon.

Doctrinal Exposition

Good evangelistic expositions should clearly explain the gospel itself to people. While the whole Bible—and every text in it—is gospel-shaped, it is still useful to have some time in a sermon where the good news itself is clearly and simply stated. Paul did this at the beginning of 1 Corinthians 15. We, too, can follow this practice. Consider having some simple explanation, like this one:

This holy Creator made us for himself. We have sinned and separated ourselves from him. But we will give an account to him. We may ignore him for a time; we will never avoid him forever. At that accounting, he will rightly judge us for our sins. His mercy that we've enjoyed to that time will end; his justice will begin. Our only hope is in what he has done in Christ. God became a man, lived a perfect life, and took on himself all the sins of all those who would ever turn from their sins and trust in him. In his death on the cross he bore the sins of all his people. Christ the plaintiff became the punished for us, the guilty people. He became our substitute. And he calls us now to recognize in his resurrection God's acceptance of this sacrifice, that his justice toward those in Christ is exhausted, and to repent of our sins and trust in Christ and so find forgiveness and new life.

Evangelistic expository sermons should include some simple statement like this, perhaps explaining one or more of these ideas at length, depending on the topic of the text being expounded. A clear summary can add luster to all the other aspects of the gospel brought out in the text. Like the rays of a beautiful sunset, they can go back over the territory covered in the sermon, causing us to review it all in the fresh, warm brilliance of God's self-giving and saving love for us in Christ. When we do this, we hold forth the good news.

When we hold forth the good news in our preaching, we should particularly beware of presenting this gospel as an option to be exercised for the betterment of sinners' lives. After all, what would a carnal person consider better? Leading questions like "Are you scared of death?" or "Do you want happiness?" or "Would you like to know the meaning of your life?" are all well intentioned, and any of them may be used by God's Spirit to convict someone and to lead to their conversion. But such questions may also be answered by a simple no. To use such questions as if they are the starting point for those considering the gospel is to make it sound all too optional.

To speak personally for a moment, when I am in a situation in which I am called upon to preach, as Baxter said, "as a dying man to dying men," I do not care if my hearers are scared of death, wanting happiness, or searching for meaning in life; I know that they will die and stand before God to give an account of their lives. Furthermore, I know that they will fail in their attempt to justify themselves, and I know that God will therefore rightly condemn them to an eternal hell.

As one who shares their common weakness and depravity, my sympathy with them compels me to tell them the truth, and that is not dependent upon their passing interest or my ability to find the right marketing introduction to snag them. They are in fact accountable to God. He is their Creator, and he will just as certainly be their judge. So I find verses like Mark 8:38 useful, where Jesus taught, "If anyone is ashamed of me and my words in this adulterous and sinful generation, the Son of Man will be ashamed of him when he comes in his Father's glory with the holy angels." Or Paul's statement in Acts 17:31: God "has set a day when he will judge the world with justice by the man he has appointed. He has given proof of this to all men by raising him from the dead." Or again, Romans 3:19–20: "Now we know that whatever the law says, it says to those who are under the law, so that every mouth may be silenced and the whole world held accountable to God. Therefore no one will be declared righteous in his sight by observing the law; rather, through the law we become conscious of sin." Or Hebrews 9:27: "Man is destined to die once, and after that to face judgment." These verses underscore the inevitability of God's judging us, regardless of our interest in God at any given point in our lives. This demand — rather than a marketer's appeal — is to be the basis of the evangelistic call in our sermons. Our gospel sermons are not to sound like the solicitations of a sales representative, but the summons of a judge.

Illustration

Good evangelistic illustrations can fall short of containing the whole gospel in them. Existentialist literature well captures some of the emptiness and pointlessness of life without God. Popular novels, films, editorials, and political situations can expose hypocrisy, greed, shattered illusions, responsibility, and so many other themes nearly related to the gospel. Use of such material can help our non-Christian listener to consider what we are saying, just as the Greeks listened to Paul in Acts 17 as he quoted their own inscriptions and poets. We all tend to listen better to someone when we think they understand where we are coming from. Our non-Christian friends are no different in this.

One particularly appropriate kind of illustration of biblical truth is the personal testimony. Certainly a testimony of "what Jesus has done for me" may not include a clear presentation of the gospel; but just as certainly it may, and it will if we have that in view. Include in your sermons examples of gospel truths being brought home in people's lives — whether at conversion or some later point. The vividness of such illustration can help a salient

135

point to live on in someone's mind. It can explain things by analogy in ways that no amount of close reasoning will do. God is glorified by testimonies of his grace. Illustrate it in your preaching.

Application

And, of course, our applications can be evangelistic in a number of ways. Even the very implications we draw out from the text can help to expose the shallow righteousness of this world and of human-made religious solutions. Expositions that expose the insufficiency of answers apart from Christ can be as useful in setting forth the gospel as a doctor's diagnosis can for compelling someone to take a prescribed medicine. As they say, "a good diagnosis is half the cure."

Christian preachers should be especially careful to speak the truth about sin. Our sermons are never to be negotiated finally by what we think our hearers can emotionally bear, let alone by what we think non-Christian hearers in our community would agree with. The goal of our sermons is not to enhance our hearer's self-esteem, but to see them inherit eternal salvation. Lovingly exposing sin is a necessary part of our call to truth telling. Such exposing will often be initially unpopular. A sinner in the flesh will never agree that he or she should be convicted, until the Holy Spirit does his convincing and convicting work. We should proclaim the truth about human sin, with the humility that is appropriate when one sinner speaks to others about such matters. We should proclaim the truth about human sin as surely as we hope our own doctors tell us the truth about our own health, particularly when the news is bad and most particularly when it is dire. As the ancient Greek proverb put it, the opposite of a friend is not an enemy, it is a flatterer. When we flatter our hearers we help no one, least of all those who most need it.

Exploring the truth about sin, tracing its ways in our hearts, and exposing the truth about God's verdict on it and its ruinous end is one of the most important functions Christian preaching has. We must commit ourselves to faithfully expounding the word, especially in those places where it would correct or convict us. When we go wrong is when we most need to be put right. Politeness is a poor substitute for honesty. If that is true in passing human relationships, how much truer is it in our eternal relationship with God? Furthermore, something in even the most depraved human heart witnesses to the truth of God's revelation of our sins. God's image in us, our conscience, cries out in every heart, even if its cry is often muted or inconsistent. We must go into our pulpits not trying to win our non-Christian friends' approval, but their souls. God's Spirit will use the faithful proclamation of the truth to do that.

One method that I find helpful in preparing to apply Scriptures both carefully and evangelistically is to make a grid, with rows going across for each point of the sermon and with columns going down. The columns help me to consider, in turn, what is unique in salvation history in this text, what the application of the text is to the non-Christian and for our public lives in society, how it is fulfilled in Christ, what the application is to the individual Christian and for us as a local church.

While there is rarely time to work out all these applications for each point in any one sermon, the exercise of carefully considering implications and applications across the board like this has the effect of helping me to hear the Scripture as a non-Christian friend might hear it and so to pray about which parts to lean on and to press home in the sermon. It is always good before preaching to review the sermon notes prayerfully in order to consider where the gospel points of human need and divine provision might best be pressed home.

Yet in evangelistic expositional preaching, the gospel should be presented not merely by means of some slender connection I happen to notice (e.g., an imagined connection between the scarlet cord in Josh. 2 and 6 and the color of Christ's blood) but by the structure of the story itself (e.g., Rahab believes the truth of God's word told to her by the spies and so effectively repents and believes and is thus incorporated savingly into the people of God). In this way, the non-Christian is helped to see the unified testimony of God's word and saving actions across the centuries, all pointing to the non-Christian's need and to God's provision in Christ. The thoroughness of pressing home a passage, along with its implications for several different areas of life, exposes the shallowness of life without Christ and the richness of the life that God calls us to. We must apply the text evangelistically.

Invitation

No exposition of God's word should ever be given without an invitation to respond. More than an invitation, really a demand should come in the sermon that all those listening submit themselves to God, confess their sins and his lordship, repent from their sins, and trust in Christ for salvation. In this

137

age, words from our holy Creator to sinful creatures like us must always include the imperatives *repent* and *believe*. How else can we faithfully represent any portion of Scripture if we do not reflect the saving purposes of God?

Part of our inviting people to respond can be an offer to speak with them after the service at some designated place or time. It could be encouraging them to speak to those around them or to some Christian friends. We can offer them literature or a series of Bible studies. It is best to avoid any kind of invitation that would lead them to think that in responding to our invitation they have responded savingly to Christ. The confusion and carnality that reigns in so many evangelical churches today shows the disaster that such well-intentioned mistakes work in people's lives. Nevertheless, with cautions duly noted, we must call people earnestly and urgently to respond to the gospel. To do anything less is to default on the very call that God has given his ministers to proclaim his word.

Here it must be said that if we do not in our normal, everyday lives have a heart for the lost, there is little chance that our sermons will burn with the evangelistic passion that so becomes the gospel. We must be impassioned by the gospel that has called us and that we are now called to proclaim.

Conclusion

These then are some of the elements that will help us to preach our expositional sermons with evangelism in view. We should understand the gospel centeredness of the whole Bible. We should take account of the presence of non-Christians—known or unknown to us—among us. We can announce that we will preach on topics that might interest them (even when the sermons themselves are straightforward expositions of Hebrews or Malachi). We can introduce the sermons themselves in ways that help to show the relevance of the Scriptures to common concerns. We can clearly state the gospel, illustrate it movingly and personally, pray to apply it searchingly, and clearly and earnestly call for a response. In all of these ways our expositional sermons can hold forth the gospel.

One reason I can be so confident of the power of evangelistic expositional sermons is a series of messages I heard one summer when I was in college. I was at the camp of a college fellowship, and James Montgomery Boice preached expositionally through the first few chapters of Genesis and then through the first few chapters of Romans. The messages were some of the most powerful expositions I had yet heard. The word was unfolded, and the very clarity of its presentation made the already-glorious truths more glorious still. The darkness of our sins and the depth of God's mercy had never been more obvious to me. At the same time, these messages were some of the clearest explanations of the gospel I had ever been given. The cross of Christ and the necessity of repentance and faith could not have been clearer. There, in the middle of those thick Bible expositions were some of the most powerful evangelistic sermons that my Southern Baptist, revival-going ears had ever heard. God's grace was clearly magnificent. The intervening decades have not dimmed my memory of the happy marriage of evangelism and exposition in those sermons.

And, in God's good providence, I have many other times been blessed by hearing sermons that are both evangelistic and expositional. I would like to think that with his help that is how I, too, have preached. And, if you are still reading this chapter, my guess is that you, too, may have done the same. If we do not preach as well as the giants, we can at least preach the same message and to the same end—that God may be glorified in the salvation of sinners and in the edifying of his church.

If you are a preacher that still has questions about this, the next time you try to preach evangelistically without preaching expositionally, consider how your message might be strengthened, your points illustrated, your passions stoked, your framework deepened by preaching to the same group from one passage of Scripture. Would a particular text be useful for your hearers, to try to come to grips with, to understand, and to remember? Would such expositional preaching be an enhancement of your evangelism?

And even more, the next time you preach expositionally, consider what it might be like to do it without preaching evangelistically. Can you really explore the themes of the law in the Old Testament without going to the gospel? Can you understand David's delight in God and his word apart from Christ? Can you present Isaiah's hope or Ezekiel's vision without an understanding of what God would do in Christ? Can you expound the teaching of Jesus or the letters of John without clearly talking of God's holiness, our sin, Christ's sacrifice, and our needed response of repentance and faith? Often, to evangelize well will entail carefully expounding God's word. Carefully expounding God's word will *always* entail evangelizing. Neither can be neglected; both must be done in our preaching if we are to preach God's word to God's people.[4]

139

7

READING AND PRAYING THE BIBLE IN CORPORATE WORSHIP

TERRY L. JOHNSON AND J. LIGON DUNCAN III

One of the striking things about evangelical corporate worship in our times is the evident paucity of Scripture. There is relatively little Scripture read, prayed, or sung in our assemblies. While high liturgical traditions continue to infuse services with scriptural language via lectionaries and other devices, even when there is little actual clerical or congregational esteem for the final authority of God's word written, it is a supreme irony that in evangelical worship (the gathered praise of those who among all Christians profess to take the Bible most seriously) the Bible often almost disappears.

This chapter is a call to the reclamation of the public reading and praying of Scripture in the corporate worship of God. What we are looking for is very simple: for the regular reading of a substantial amount of Scripture to reappear in congregational worship; for that reading to be distinct from the sermon text; for that reading to be accompanied by a compendious introduction that will help God's people understand the portion they are about to hear (and thus help them learn how to read God's word for themselves); and for the local church ministry to cultivate an expectation of, a longing for, and an appreciation of the significance of the public reading of the word of God among the members of the congregation, so that they will sense a personal loss if the service of worship fails to contain a substantial presentation of God's word.

Additionally, we aim here to motivate ministers to a higher estimation of the importance of their pulpit prayer. Spurgeon once quipped, "Well, if I had to choose between the sermon and the prayer, I guess the sermon would have to go." That sentiment came from a man who by no means denigrated, in principle or practice, the centrality of the preached word in the public worship of almighty God. John Currid, an Old Testament scholar and commentator, while expounding and applying Exodus 32 and Moses' intercessory prayer, comments:

> The Westminster Confession of Faith (1645) lists eight primary duties of the office of pastor. It is quite significant that the first one deals with the issue of intercessory prayer. "First, it belongs to his office, to pray for and with his flock, as the mouth of the people unto God, Acts 6:2, 3, 4 and 20:36, where preaching and prayer are joined as several parts of the same office. The office of elder (that is, the pastor) is to pray for the sick, even in private, to which a blessing is especially promised; *much more therefore ought he to perform this in the public execution of his office as a part thereof.*"[1]
>
> There is no greater task for the pastor (and ruling elders) than to pray for his flock. Unfortunately there is an almost total lack of attention given to this subject by denominations, seminaries and individual churches. And many pastors seem to have made intercessory prayer supplemental rather than fundamental. It is no wonder that the rot of materialism and secularism is corrupting the church today.[2]

Recovering the reading of God's word and regaining the robust practice of public pastoral intercession with prayers suffused with the language and thought of Scripture would surely be a boon for the church today.

Reading the Word in Worship

Hughes Old establishes beyond doubt the central importance of the reading of the word of God as an essential component of Christian worship in the total history of the church.[3] But one does not have to look any further than Paul and the Pastoral Epistles in the New Testament to find an explicit directive being given to a church planter regarding the regular public reading of God's word. Paul told Timothy: "Until I come, give attention to the *public* reading *of Scripture*, to exhortation and teaching" (1 Tim. 4:13). And

141

this was not a new thing. The public reading of the Bible has been at the heart of the worship of God since Old Testament times. What we need today is ministers who take this directive seriously, for rare is the evangelical church whose service can be characterized as full of Scripture.

In the reading of God's word, God speaks most directly to his people. And so, this act of worship, in which the verbal self-revelation of God is addressed unedited to the hearts of his gathered people, ought not to be ignored, skipped, or squeezed out. It is irritating enough to have to endure preachers who say "I do not have time to read my text today" (as if to say, "we need to hurry on past God's word to get to mine!"), but to have whole worship services in which the formal reading of God's word is absent is a self-imposed famine of the word.

Furthermore, as John Reed Miller is known to say, "The reading of the word of God ought to be an event." It ought to be arresting to the congregation. It ought to grab their attention. It ought sometimes to make them tremble and other times rejoice. It ought to be elevated to the same status and gravity as the other biblical elements of worship and seen in combination with pastoral preaching and prayer as part of the essential *triplex munus* of the gospel minister in public worship. Thus it needs to be prepared for just like public prayer, just like the sermon, just like the totality of the worship service. The minister of the word can convey the supreme importance of the reading of the word just in the way he does it.

So how does one do it? How ought we to approach this in our corporate worship? The prescription of the Westminster Directory for Public Worship is just what the doctor ordered:

> Reading of the word in the congregation, being part of the public worship of God (wherein we acknowledge our dependence upon him and subjection to him), and one mean sanctified by him for the edifying of his people, is to be performed by the pastors and teachers.
>
> Howbeit, such as intend the ministry, may occasionally both read the word, and exercise their gift in preaching in the congregation, if allowed by the presbytery thereunto.
>
> All the canonical books of the Old and New Testament (but none of those which are commonly called Apocrypha) shall be publicly read in the vulgar tongue, out of the best allowed translation, distinctly, that all may hear and understand.

How large a portion shall be read at once, is left to the wisdom of the minister; but it is convenient, that ordinarily one chapter of each Testament be read at every meeting; and sometimes more, where the chapters be short, or the coherence of matter requires it.

It is requisite that all the canonical books be read over in order, that the people may be better acquainted with the whole body of the Scriptures; and ordinarily, where the reading in either Testament ends on one Lord's Day, it is to begin the next.

We commend also the more frequent reading of such Scriptures as he that reads shall think best for edification of his hearers, as the Book of Psalms, and such like.

When the minister who reads shall judge it necessary to expound any part of what is read, let it not be done until the whole chapter or psalm be ended; and regard is always to be had unto the time, that neither preaching, nor other ordinances be straitened, or rendered tedious. Which rule is to be observed in all other public performances.

Beside public reading of the Holy Scriptures, every person that can read, is to be exhorted to read the Scriptures privately (and all others that cannot read, if not disabled by age, or otherwise, are likewise to be exhorted to learn to read), and to have a Bible.[4]

There are eleven pieces of exceedingly wise biblical and pastoral counsel here:

1. The public reading of Scripture is a part, an element to be exact, of corporate worship. It is not an option. When it is neglected, an essential aspect of Christian worship is lost irreparably. As the Westminster Confession of Faith notes: "The reading of the Scriptures with godly fear; the sound preaching; and conscionable hearing of the word, in obedience unto God with understanding, faith, and reverence; singing of psalms with grace in the heart; as also, the due administration and worthy receiving of the sacraments instituted by Christ; are all parts of the ordinary religious worship of God" (21.5). Not reading the Scriptures is on the same order as not having a sermon or omitting congregational singing.

2. The public reading of Scripture is a means of grace. It not only serves as an opportunity whereby we openly and corporately sit

under his word—acknowledging his authority, acknowledging our dependence upon the initiative of his self-revelation, acknowledging our glad surrender to the lordship of his word—but it is also a God-appointed means whereby we are strengthened by and receive his favor. The Lord has deigned to bless and edify his people by it.

3. The public reading of Scripture ought to be done by those responsible for the preaching of the word. It is not uncommon to see congregation members invited to lead the church in the reading of Scripture in various ecclesiastical traditions. Sometimes this is done with the desire to make the church service more participatory. Sometimes it is done to stress a positive form of anticlericalism or the priesthood of all believers. Sometimes it is done (one suspects) to prove to a suspicious culture that conservative evangelical churches are not knee-jerk reactionaries in their stance against women preachers, and so sometimes women are invited to lead the church in this area, if not in proclamation. Now, we do not doubt for a moment that many who follow the practice of having non-pastors read Scripture publicly in the services of the church do so with a clear conscience that they are acting biblically. However, the Westminster Assembly argues against this practice and does so on biblical grounds: not only because of its high view of church office but also because of its high view of the reading of the word. In the Larger Catechism Q. 156, the divines said that "all are not to be permitted to read the word publicly to the congregation" (based upon the example of the Old Testament priesthood). The Form of Church Government elaborates upon this argument, but the fundamental reason was that in the reading of God's word, God speaks most directly to his people. Since the preaching of God's word is to be the unique responsibility of the ministry, so also is the reading of that same word. It is all about the coordination of the read and proclaimed word. The read word is not on some lower order of significance than the proclaimed word, but that is the inevitable message sent if preaching in a church is restricted to ministers and elders and the reading of the word is not. The Presbyterian Church of America's Book of Church Order: Directory of Worship picks up on this same theme and says: "The public reading of the Holy Scriptures is performed by the minister as God's servant. Through it God

speaks most directly to the congregation, even more directly than through the sermon. The reading of the Scriptures by the minister is to be distinguished from the responsive reading of certain portions of Scripture by the minister and the congregation. In the former God addresses His people; in the latter God's people give expression in the words of Scripture to their contrition, adoration, gratitude and other holy sentiments."[5]

4. The minister ought to endeavor to read all of Scripture to his people. The whole canon is "profitable for teaching, for reproof, for correction, for training in righteousness" (2 Tim. 3:16), and so the people of God need to hear from that whole body of God's word: not only the well-known parts and the encouraging passages or the New Testament and the Psalms, but also the Pentateuch, Prophets, Wisdom literature, Historical Books, Gospels, Epistles, Acts, and Revelation. The Reformers not only believed in *sola scriptura*, they believed in *tota scriptura*. The Puritans often criticized the court divines of their day for failing to read consecutively through the balance of Scripture. This does not mean that we have to start at Genesis and end at Revelation, but it does mean we ought to be following a method of reading and that we ought to be reading through whole books, chapter by chapter or significant portion by significant portion.

5. The minister ought to read from the best available translation. Now, of course, we could strike up a quick debate about which translation is the best available. But do not miss a good point here. The minister ought to read from a sound version to which the people have access—a translation. Every once in a while, I run into starry-eyed seminary students who swoon when their Old Testament professor reads from the Hebrew text before the morning sermon. They dream of sweeping their congregations off their feet with their eloquent on-the-spot renderings of complex Hebrew narrative. Well, I could stand up and give my own translation too, but nobody in the room but me would have any permanent written access to it or be able to study it for themselves after the service was over. No, even good Greek-, Hebrew-, and Aramaic-reading preachers ought to read from the best available literal translation as a deliberate act of pastoral care. This will promote what the Westminster Assembly

desired when it said, "Every person that can read, is to be exhorted to read the Scriptures privately, . . . and to have a Bible." A capable exegete can always bring his insights to the exposition of a passage he has read aloud from a good vernacular translation, but few if any of his audience will ever be able to read and study his private rendering, so he ought to use a translation they can access and memorize and study.

6. The minister ought to exercise common sense in deciding how much Scripture to read at once. If a congregation has never had a large portion of Scripture reading in its service, I cannot think of a better way to kill the reading of the word than to start plowing through Numbers, Leviticus, Chronicles, or Job a chapter at a time. Use discretion! Start with something easy and well known. Be committed to getting to the point of reading a substantial portion, but take smaller bits at first. Break up overlong chapters. Mark out natural pericopes. Ease the people of God into the habit. Let them drink from the water fountain first, not from the fire hydrant. Try a gospel first—say Mark. Divide up the chapters. Give them a feel for the total story of Jesus' ministry and work. You can read through it in less than half a year, even at a less aggressive pace, and then move on to more challenging matter.

7. The minister ought to keep a balance of reading between the two Testaments. If you are preaching through a New Testament book in your service, then read from the Old Testament. If you are preaching through an Old Testament book, read from the New Testament. The Westminster Directory contemplated a chapter from the Old Testament and a chapter from the New Testament at every service, in addition to the sermon text and message! That is probably a little aggressive for today and for our typical service lengths, but the principle of paying attention to the balance of Old and New in your reading is as wise as when they first said it. Depending upon the duration of your service, it may eventually become possible to have more than one reading.

8. The minister ought to develop an orderly plan for reading through the Scripture. The directory says that "it is requisite that all the canonical books be read over in order, that the people may be better acquainted with the whole body of the Scriptures." As we men-

tioned under point 4, the minister needs to develop and follow a practical and rational plan for working through the Scriptures. He may move chronologically or between alternate types of biblical literature or in canonical order. But whatever the case may be, there needs to be some method to his practice.

9. The minister ought to pick up where he left off. Following on the last point, the directory advises that "ordinarily, where the reading in either Testament endeth on one Lord's Day, it is to begin the next." The Puritans often poked fun at the court divines for the endless skipping around in their brief readings. Their path resembled rabbit trails, the Puritans said. Remind the people what they read last, show them the connections with today's reading, give them a feel for the big picture, and remember—sad to say—that many in your hearing will not have picked up a Bible at any point during the week. This may be the only time they hear the word read or read it for themselves all week. This reading, then, is important.

10. The minister ought to make regular use of exceptionally edifying portions of Scripture like the Psalms. There are some parts of Scripture that lend themselves to greater profit in being read aloud. It is not that they are more inspired, but who can doubt that Psalm 51 is capable of yielding an immediate and obvious benefit that would escape most hearers of the genealogy in 1 Chronicles 6? The reading and hearing of the Psalms, for instance, provides resources for a profound spirituality, a piety that equals the exigencies of our experience. The Book of Psalms deals with the realities of life and reveals a soul poured out to the living God—the complaints, the heartaches, the emptiness—and yet alongside these, it acknowledges a God who is incomparably great, whose plans and purposes are far above our agendas and understandings, but who also loves us with an everlasting covenant love. Thus, we see in the Psalms a perfect biblical balance of objective and subjective in spiritual experience. In the Psalms, God and his word are clearly dominant in the believer's experience without any diminution whatsoever of the wounds and quandaries and questions of life in a fallen world. No wonder the Reformers thought we ought to sing psalms and read psalms in worship—they saw them as the very core of a well-rounded Christian experience. So, it is natural that the Book of Psalms might

be featured with a prominence in our cycle of public readings that, say, 2 Samuel would not share.

11. The minister ought to offer brief explanatory remarks about the reading but those remarks ought not to be overlong or overshadow the event of the reading of the word. In a famous story from the tragic life of Edward Irving, on one occasion when the great Thomas Chalmers was invited to preach at Irving's church, the troubled and eccentric Irving gave the Scripture reading and expounded the Scripture reading for some forty minutes, so that when time came for the sermon, Chalmers felt he ought not get up and preach after so long an explanatory word. This was precisely the kind of practice the assembly did not want to see in connection with the regular reading! The divines expressly said: "Regard is always to be had unto the time, that neither preaching, nor other ordinances be straitened, or rendered tedious." The Scripture reading and its accompanying words of explanation ought not to crowd out the preaching of the word, the singing of praise, the administration of the sacraments, or the pastoral prayer.

Praying the Word in Worship

Offering prayer in public is an aspect of leading in worship that also deserves focused attention.[6] Because the Lord's Day worship service is a *public* service, the prayers in those services are of necessity public and partake of the qualities of public ordinances. This means that public prayer will differ from private prayer in both its subject matter and its aim. Namely, public prayer must edify the public. Prayers offered in public are audible, not silent, and must be intelligible because they aim at not personal but public edification. Their purpose is to bless both God and the congregation. There are two audiences, one on earth and one in heaven. This is precisely the Apostle Paul's point in 1 Corinthians 14:14–19. If one prays "in the spirit" (whatever exactly that means) so that one cannot be understood, the prayer may be a sincere expression of thanksgiving, but (and here is the crucial point) "the other person is not edified" (14:17). Better are five intelligible words that may "instruct others" than "ten thousand words in a tongue" (14:19). Public prayer, while addressed to God, is for public edification and instruction. It is another kind of pulpit speech, closely related to preaching.

148

This understanding of public prayer was typical of early Protestantism and the whole subsequent free-church tradition (Presbyterian, Congregational, Baptist, Methodist). Skill in praying publicly was considered a gift given by God to those whom he calls into the public ministry and was to be cultivated through prayer disciplines and the careful study of the devotional language of the Bible. Because faith comes by hearing the word of God (Rom. 10:17), the use of scriptural language and allusions in prayer was understood to be of critical importance. The congregation will be edified as Scripture-enriched, impassioned prayers are offered in public worship.

Convictions like these lie behind the liturgical reforms of Bucer, Farel, Calvin, and Knox, as they wrote Scripture-based prayers in their orders of worship and encouraged free prayers.[7] They are clearly evident in the attempted reforms of the English Puritans, as seen in the Middleburg Liturgy, the Westminster Directory for the Public Worship of God, and Richard Baxter's Savoy or Reformed Liturgy, presented to Charles II in Puritanism's final attempt to reform the prayer book. Throughout the Reformation and Second Reformation period of over one hundred years, the theme is the same: written prayers must be more scriptural, and free prayers must be permitted so that the people may be edified as the church prays.[8] Pastoral concern drove these liturgical reforms.

Following the Acts of Uniformity and the Great Ejection of the Puritans from the Church of England in 1662, Anglicanism returned to a strictly liturgical worship, consisting of fixed forms and allowing no divergence from these forms. But the dissenting churches continued to emphasize Scripture-enriched free prayers. For generations, ministers of the Scottish Presbyterian, British Nonconformists, and their American sibling churches learned to pray by consulting Matthew Henry's *Method for Prayer* or Isaac Watt's *Guide to Prayer*. The former of these appeared in over thirty editions between 1712 and 1865.[9] Henry understood that the one who prays publicly must not only look within his own heart as he prays, but must seek "the edification also of those that join with him; and both in matter and words should have an eye to that."[10] He designed his book as a help for those who lead in prayer, organizing his work according to the standard categories of adoration, confession, thanksgiving, and intercession, as well as providing a few examples or forms of prayer for various occasions. He restricted himself almost entirely to the language of Scripture, the only exceptions being some section headings. He goes on in this fashion, Scripture phrase after

Scripture phrase for nearly two hundred fifty pages! Remarkably, he says in his introduction (as he explains that much more could have been written), "I have only set down such *as first occurred to my thoughts.*"[11]

Henry wrote in 1710 and according to Old "for generations shaped the prayer life of Protestantism."[12] Writing a generation later, Watts stressed the same themes; and in 1849 Samuel Miller published *Thoughts on Public Prayer*,[13] carrying this same theme forward to the turn of the twentieth century. Public prayer, they all agreed, like public preaching, must edify the whole congregation, and to do so it must be rich with scriptural language and allusions.

Given this perspective, it is not surprising to learn that most of the older manuals on preaching (e.g., Perkins, Doddridge, Dabney, Dale, Beecher, Broadus, Jowett)[14] included instruction on and urged the use of Scripture in public prayer. They perpetuated the prevailing Protestant understanding that preaching and prayer are parallel forms of edifying public speech, even as William Perkins labeled it "the second aspect of prophesying" years before.[15] For example, Henry Ward Beecher, delivering the first of the famous Yale Lectures on Preaching in 1872, entitled a section of his work, "Prayer as an Element of Preaching." Later Yale lecturers Brooks, Dale, and Jowett continued to reflect the same concerns. Similarly most of the older manuals on pastoral theology (e.g., Fairbairn, Murphy, Porter, Shedd, Spurgeon)[16] included sections on public prayer, typically under the heading of "preaching" or "homiletics," urging all the same themes. A solid consensus on the nature and language and value of public prayer can be traced from the Reformers to the beginning of the twentieth century.

Recent Times

Strange amnesia, however, seems to have set in around the middle of the twentieth century. Few books have been written recently on the subject of public prayer, and few of the older manuals were republished for wide circulation until Miller's (mid-1980s) and Henry's (1994) books were reprinted, no doubt as part of the neo-Puritan publishing revival.[17] Those few authors who did write on public prayer did so in a historical vacuum with respect to this free-prayer tradition. For example, Andrew Blackwood, professor of practical theology at Princeton Theological Seminary from 1930 to 1950, wrote numerous books on pastoral practice including, *The Fine Art of Wor-*

ship and *Leading in Prayer,*[18] and must be considered a leading influence on twentieth-century pastoral practice. He writes of public prayer with reverence and evangelical warmth and provides sound advice, but seemingly without any awareness of Henry, Watts, or Miller and without any stress upon the use of scriptural language and its potential for edification.

Among more recent works, Thomas Oden's encyclopedic *Pastoral Theology* includes a seven-page section on public prayer. He passes along helpful suggestions offered by Phillip Doddridge, including "let prayer be informed by Scripture and Christian memory," but says no more.[19] The *Leadership Handbook of Practical Theology,* volume 1: *Word and Worship,*[20] is five hundred pages long. It allocates space in the following proportions:

- ✧ preaching—136 pages
- ✧ worship—124 pages
- ✧ music—95 pages
- ✧ sacraments—73 pages
- ✧ weddings and funerals—88 pages

Included in these pages is a 22-page section entitled "Balancing Tradition and Innovation," which provides guidelines for use of art, drama, dance, and multimedia in worship. Public prayer, by way of comparison is handled in 20 pages. In those 20 pages, not one word is said about the pastoral value of public prayer, of its power to edify, or of the use of scriptural language in prayer. Given the central role that *Leadership Magazine/ Christianity Today* plays in contemporary evangelicalism, this perhaps symbolizes as well as anything the marginalization of prayer in public worship generally and of Scripture-based public prayer specifically among conservative Christians.

Contemporary books on preaching,[21] unlike those of previous generations make no reference to public prayer. William H. Willimon is an exception to this rule in his *Preaching and Leading Worship.*[22] He notes that "our liturgical speech should attempt to be biblically based. . . . The Bible is a helpful guide for liturgical language."[23] A number of works on public worship discuss the practice of public prayer. But among those few written from a Reformed perspective since World War II (e.g., von Allmen, Maxwell, Rayburn, Macleod, Nichols),[24] most of the discussion has to do with the history, use, and placing of the five major types of prayer (invocation, confession, intercession, illumination, benediction). Little or nothing is said about learning the biblical language of prayer or the pastoral value of such prayers.

We may look closer to home as well. Jay Adams's *Shepherding God's Flock*[25] treats numerous pastoral issues, including personal habits, pastoral visits, hospital visits, counseling, leadership, finances, and evangelism, but says nothing about worship or public prayer. An important volume honoring Edmund P. Clowney, ambitiously entitled *Practical Theology and the Ministry of the Church, 1952–1984,*[26] contains essays on pastoral ministry, practical theology, ecclesiology, preaching, evangelism, and worship. Robert G. Rayburn's chapter, entitled "Evangelical Worship in Our Day," complains that evangelical seminaries "have placed such little emphasis upon corporate worship, and that they have given practically no instruction as to the minister's responsibilities in teaching the congregation how to worship and in the conducting of common worship."[27] But the volume as a whole has almost nothing to say about the pastor's public prayer. A work recently produced by The Master's Seminary entitled *Rediscovering Pastoral Practice* represents the thinking of serious, conservative, noncharismatic, Reformed-friendly evangelicals, but like the rest of the books surveyed, says nothing about Scripture-based public prayer.[28]

A survey of evangelical periodicals likewise offers little encouragement. *Leadership* began publishing in 1980 with the express purpose of addressing "the greatest practical needs of the pastor" and other church leaders and of focusing on "the practical problems of ministry."[29] Yet in seventeen years and sixty-eight issues (through 1996) only one article was published on public prayer.[30] The *Banner of Truth* magazine, from which more attention might have been expected, published exactly one article on the subject during its first thirty years (1955–85), other than the occasional short reprint.[31] Since then "Spurgeon's Pulpit Prayers," has been published,[32] and in 1994 public prayer was treated three times in the first seven months, perhaps signaling a revival of concern.[33] *Reformation and Revival: A Quarterly Journal for Church Leadership*, while purporting to seek the reformation of the whole life of the church, has not dealt with public prayer in its five years and twenty issues. *Reformed Worship: Resources for Liturgy and Music* defines its purpose as that of providing "practical assistance to worship leaders of the Christian Reformed Church and other Reformed/Presbyterian churched in planning, structuring, and conducting worship," all in accord with the Reformed tradition. The inaugural issue had a fine article by William S. Barker on written versus spontaneous public prayers. Eight years later a second article appeared urging written prayers.[34] Over the years there occasionally have been articles on public prayer, typically highlighting the liabilities of the "monologue" pastoral prayer and suggesting alternatives.[35] Otherwise little has been said. The editors seem to have little affinity for the practice of free prayer and know nothing of the Reformed tradition of Scripture-enriched public prayer, remarkable for a journal entitled *Reformed Worship*.

If I may include in this survey my own experience and admittedly unscientific observations, not once in over forty years has anyone suggested to me that I ought to make use of Scripture in my public prayers. Not once has anyone suggested that there is a unique sanctifying power in public prayers enriched by scriptural language and allusions. Not once has anyone urged consideration of public prayer as an important means of grace paralleling preaching itself. The subject was never mentioned through years of Sunday school and church attendance in my childhood and youth. It was not mentioned during four years of college parachurch Bible studies, camps, and conferences. It was not mentioned during four years of seminary. It was not mentioned during the first fifteen years of postseminary ministry.

This brief survey, by no means exhaustive, surely is illustrative. When reviewing the work of evangelical leaders who have done much to revive other areas of neglect, one wishes not to appear as if, say, one were criticizing Columbus for not discovering Australia. For example, Adams in counseling and preaching, MacArthur in preaching, and Rayburn in worship have made unique and important contributions that have enriched evangelical and Reformed pastoral practice. Nevertheless, the pastor's prayers have received scant attention in recent decades as to either their practice or pastoral value. When they have been discussed, little has been said about enriching them with scriptural language and allusions. Beyond this and fundamental to the whole discussion, there is no vision for the pastoral value of public prayers. Prayer—like preaching—is a means of grace, as any child brought up on the Shorter Catechism knows (Q. 88). This is true not just of private prayers, but public as well. Troubled souls at times need not counsel, even nouthetic counseling, but passionate and biblical prayer. A pastor's scripturally enriched public prayers may soothe the troubled, calm the

153

anxious, answer the doubting, stiffen the wavering, break the unrepentant, and in so doing remove the need of further counseling or preaching. The role of public prayer as a means of grace is little understood today. Too often public prayer is seen as a burden to bear, not a blessing to receive.

The lone exception in this disappointing survey is Hughes Oliphant Old, who for over two decades has been something of a voice crying in the wilderness. Following his seminal study *The Patristic Roots of Reformed Worship*,[36] he has three times published works calling for a renewed study of Matthew Henry and a return to Scripture-based prayer.[37] His latest, *Leading in Prayer* purports to be a Henry or Watts for the 1990s. "I publish this book," he says, "much in the same spirit as Matthew Henry published his *Method of Prayer* or Isaac Watts published a similar sort of volume a generation later."[38] Prayer, he says, has "its own language, its own vocabulary, and its own imagery. This language is not simply a matter of style. Prayer, particularly Christian prayer, *uses biblical language*."[39]

While Old stands alone today, the Protestant past, as we have seen, stands with him. A revival of the historic Protestant practice of Scripture-enriched prayer stands at or near the top of the reforms that are crucial to the health of the church today.

Personal Experience

Given the lack of instruction mentioned above, my own pilgrimage to these convictions has been slow, accidental (in a Presbyterian sense), and at times painful. Yet I am sure that my experience parallels that of many others as well, who, upon reflection, may recall similar incidences.

My first serious thoughts about public prayers began dramatically in the spring of 1978, as an intern at St. David's Broomhouse Church of Scotland in Edinburgh. C. Peter White, the minister, was ill one Sunday, leaving me to lead the services and preach. It was the practice of the leadership of the congregation to gather thirty minutes or so before the beginning of worship and pray for the services of the day. A group of about fifteen took their seats in a large circle in a private room. When it looked like all who were coming were present, they rose up, turned and faced their chairs, knelt down on their knees, and began to pray. Though this was a working-class congregation and though none of those present were college educated, and even a few were functionally illiterate, I soon realized that I was

154

in way over my head. I came to Scotland from Southern California via Trinity College in Bristol, England, arriving full of hope that I might be the means of ushering in revival in Scotland. After all, I knew the essential principles of small-group discipleship and was armed with all the latest choruses and "Scripture songs." As the Scots began to pray, I realized that something was seriously amiss. I had never heard such prayers. They were full of God, full of Scripture, full of passion, full of reverence, and full of humility. My prayers, by comparison, had always been of the "just really" variety—trite, self-centered, too casual, and too familiar. The spiritual maturity of their prayers exposed my spiritual poverty. The God that they knew was almost a different God. That short experience had a devastating impact on me. I could just barely persuade myself to go on and lead the service. I had no business leading these people in worship, I thought. They should be leading me. I returned to Trinity College humbled, seriously questioning my call, unsettled for another six months. That summer I returned to what was then my home church, the Lake Avenue Congregational Church in Pasadena, a church in which I had served as a summer intern, and refused to be involved in any leadership in ministry. I needed to sit quietly and learn, I told them.

The next year back in Bristol I began to attend the Buckingham Baptist Church pastored by Ron Clark. He was preaching on Psalm 23. Week by week, his sermons were profoundly moving, using Scripture in a way that gave them a unique unction. Equally moving were his prayers. I was not consciously aware of why they were so moving, but looking back I now remember—they were full of Scripture language and allusions.

Several years later a friend loaned me a tape of a Lloyd-Jones sermon on evangelism. In the first half of the sermon he attacked the Arminians for unbiblical preaching. As all the Calvinists were saying "amen," he turned his considerable artillery on them with devastating effect. I was at the time putting a fence in a friend's backyard. I had to stop to dry my eyes. Never had I heard such preaching. Then Lloyd-Jones began to pray. I can still recall a few of the phrases: "In wrath remember mercy"; "turn us and we shall be turned"; "revive thy work in the midst of the years." Full of lament and passion, he prayed on. It was overwhelming. I was utterly undone by the extraordinary power of that concluding prayer.

Years later at Independent Presbyterian Church, I began to notice that several of the laypeople who gathered weekly at 6:30 on Tuesday morning

155

for our prayer meeting prayed with unction and made, not coincidentally, pointed use of Scripture as they prayed. One man in particular arrested my attention as he prayed: "O Lord, our Lord, how majestic is Your name in all the earth!" (Ps. 8:1). The conviction that one ought to use Scripture in prayer was growing through the years. The clincher came just a few years ago when I began to read Henry's *Method for Prayer*.

Over a fifteen-year period I slowly came to realize the importance of using Scripture language in prayer. Those coming out of a low or nonliturgical church tradition are often amazed at the amount of Scripture found in the traditional liturgies, far more than in the average evangelical church. One reason for this is that the church of late antiquity responded to various heretics by banishing from its liturgy all nonscriptural language, especially hymns, which the heretics (such as Arius) were especially skilled at composing. The liturgies of the Lutheran, Anglican, Orthodox, and Roman churches still reflect this scriptural emphasis. Previous generations of Presbyterians and Baptists did not find this emphasis so remarkable because their "free" worship, with metrical psalms, Scripture-based prayers, Bible reading, and biblical preaching, was equally rife with the language of Scripture. But today, even those churches that are not on the "Durham Trail," as D. G. Hart calls it, that is, churches that are not deconstructing traditional worship in order to appeal to tastes shaped by America's popular culture, retain very little of Scripture in their services.[40] Not much is read. Sermons are more topical than expository. Fragments, at best, are sung. As for the prayers, "one has to admit," says Old, "that the spontaneous prayer one often hears in public worship is an embarrassment to the tradition."[41]

Recommendations for Public Prayer

Let me make several recommendations for the improvement of public prayer in light of what we have discussed so far.

Pray the Language of Scripture

First and most obvious is that we pray in the language of Scripture. Listen to the voices from the past as they universally urge this practice:

Matthew Henry: "I would advise that the *sacred* dialect be most used, and made familiar to us and others in our dealing about *sacred* things; that language Christian people are most accustomed to, most affected with, and will most readily agree to."[42]

Patrick Fairbairn: "[Prayer] should be cast much in the mould of Scripture, and should be marked by a free use of its language."[43]

R. L. Dabney: "Above all should the minister enrich his prayers with the language of Scripture. . . . Besides its inimitable beauty and simplicity, it is hallowed and sweet to every pious heart by a thousand associations. It satisfies the taste of all; its use effectually protects us against improprieties; it was doubtless given by the Holy Spirit to be a model for our devotions. Let it then abound in our prayers."[44]

Samuel Miller: "One of the most essential excellencies in public prayer, and that which I feel constrained first of all, and above all to recommend, is, that it abound in the language of the word of God."[45]

Thomas Murphy: "The prayer of the sanctuary should be thoroughly saturated with scriptural thought and expression. The language of the Bible is that which the Spirit prompted, and which must therefore be most in accordance with the mind of God. For the same reason it must be Bible language which is best calculated to express those devotional feelings which are the work of the Spirit in the heart."[46]

John Broadus: "The minister should be consistently storing in his memory the more directly devotional expressions found everywhere in the Bible, and especially in the Psalms and Prophets, the Gospels, Epistles, and Revelation . . . most of us greatly need in our prayers a larger and more varied infusion of Scripture language."[47]

But perhaps some are still unpersuaded or are concerned that what worked in the past may not work today. Consider the following.

This is the pattern found in Scripture itself. This is not merely the opinion of the Reformers or of eighteenth- and nineteenth-century evangelical theologians. It is also the pattern that we see in Scripture. The biblical saints learned God-pleasing devotional language from the Bible. They often used the language and themes of Scripture to interpret and express their experience. Consider for instance Moses' seminal revelatory experience in Exodus 34:6–7:

> Then the Lord passed by in front of him and proclaimed, "The Lord, the Lord God, compassionate and gracious, slow to anger, and abounding in lovingkindness and truth; who keeps lovingkindness for thousands, who forgives iniquity, transgression and sin; yet He will by no means leave *the guilty* unpunished, visiting the iniquity of fathers on the children and on the grandchildren to the third and fourth generations."

The echo of this revelation is heard on at least eleven additional occasions in the Old Testament as later prophets learned from Moses how to praise God (Num. 14:18; 2 Chron. 30:9; Neh. 9:17, 31; Pss. 103:8; 111:4; 112:4; 116:5; 145:8; Joel 2:13; Jonah 4:2). At the annunciation, Mary drew upon the Song of Hannah (Luke 1:46–55; cf. 1 Sam. 2:1–10); at the dedication of the temple, Solomon incorporated Psalm 132:8–9 (2 Chron. 6:40–42); on the cross Jesus used the words of Psalms 22:1 and 31:5 (Matt. 27:46; Luke 23:46); and in the face of persecution, the early church cited Psalm 146 and Psalm 2 (Acts 4:24–30). In each case the language of Scripture provided the language for prayer.

Where then are we to learn the language of Christian devotion if not from Scripture? That this is less than self-evident to a tradition whose defining principle has been that worship must be regulated by God's word is surprising indeed. Since our minds are "factories for idols," borrowing Calvin's phrase, we must be taught the language of prayer. Is that not the point of the disciples' request of Jesus, "Lord, teach us to pray" (Luke 11:1)? Is that not indeed the point of the Book of Psalms? Were the Psalms not provided to teach the people of God the language of devotion with which God is pleased? If Jesus in the supreme crisis of his life drew upon the Psalter in order to understand and express his devotion and experience, then we can do no less.

It then follows that there is special efficacy in Scripture-based prayer. No prayers more accurately reflect the will of God than those which use the language that God himself puts into our mouths. No request is surer to be granted than that which expresses what God himself has promised to fulfill. No petition is surer to be answered than that which pleads for that which God already commands. Pray the promises and commands of Scripture. This principle is evident in James 1. Does God command that we be wise? Of course he does. It follows then that we should ask for it: "But if any of you lacks wisdom, let him ask of God, who gives to all generously and without reproach, and it will be given to him" (James 1:5). Similarly, pray the promise of 1 John 1:9, that "if we confess our sins, He is faithful and righteous to forgive us our sins and to cleanse us from all unrighteousness." Claim the promise of John 3:16 in prayer, that "whoever believes in Him shall not perish." Plead that the people of God will be holy even as God is holy (1 Peter 1:16). Plead that they will love one another and bear one another's burdens (Gal. 6:2). Faith comes by hearing the word of God (Rom. 10:17). The word prayed in the hearing of the congregation will be efficacious to the salvation of their souls.

There is a special comfort in scriptural prayer. It is one thing to pray, "Lord, please be with us through this day." It is quite another to pray, "Lord remember your promise, 'I will never leave nor forsake you' " (Heb. 13:5). Can you sense the difference? It is one thing to pray, "As we begin our prayer, we thank you for the privilege of bringing our petitions to you." It is quite another to pray, "We come at your invitation, O Christ, for you have promised, 'Ask, and you shall receive; seek, and you shall find; knock, and it shall be opened to you.' And so we come asking, seeking, and knocking" (Matt. 7:7–8). It is one thing to pray in the middle of tragedy, "Lord we know that you have a plan." That is a true, valid, and comforting thing to pray. Even so, it is quite another to pray, "O Lord, you have numbered the hairs upon our heads. You are working all things after the counsel of your will. Not even a sparrow may fall from a tree apart from you. You cause all things to work together for good for those who love you, and are called according to your purpose" (Matt. 10:29–30; Eph. 1:11; Rom. 8:28). More effectively comfort the hearts of your people by echoing the promises of Scripture in your prayers.

Scriptural prayer reinforces the ministry of the word. As noted above, one reason why previous generations of evangelicals were more biblically literate than ours is that there was more Bible content in their services than in ours. The word preached and the word prayed and the word sung were constantly reinforcing each other. The romanticism of the late-nineteenth and early-twentieth centuries emptied our hymns of most of their biblical and theological content. As noted above, only fragments of scriptural expression remain in our songs. We have already commented on the state of preaching and praying. The irony that churches that profess to believe in the inerrancy of Scripture make such little use of Scripture and are becoming increasingly ignorant of Scripture is bitter indeed. What a difference it will make if you will call the people to worship with Scripture, invoke the presence of God with scriptural praise, sing a metrical psalm, confess sins using Scripture language, read the Scripture, preach an expository sermon, sing a scriptural hymn, build your intercessions around the five categories found in Scripture, used by the early church, and revived by the Reformers, and conclude with a scriptural benediction.[48] This done, Sunday morning and evening, fifty-two weeks a year, year after year, will build a strong church, one characterized by scriptural literacy and spiritual maturity. If you worship in this way, your growth may be slower than is acceptable to many. It may require that one take a longer view than is customary today. One may not gather large crowds overnight. But in the long run a church that builds a foundation like this on the words of Christ will endure like a rock and not be shaken.

Now we will look at how to become proficient in praying in the language of Scripture.

Study and use the prayers in Scripture. Are there any better prayers of praise than those of David in 1 Chronicles 29 or the composite prayer of Paul in 1 Timothy? Listen to them:

> Yours, O Lord, is the greatness and the power and the glory and the victory and the majesty, indeed everything that is in the heavens and the earth; Yours is the dominion, O Lord, and You exalt Yourself as head over all. Both riches and honor *come* from You, and You rule over all, and in Your hand is power and might; and it lies in Your hand to make great and to strengthen everyone. Now, therefore, our God, we thank You, and praise Your glorious name. (1 Chron. 29:11–13)

> Now to the King eternal, immortal, invisible, the only God, *be* honor and glory forever and ever. Amen. . . . He who is the blessed and only Sovereign,

the King of kings and Lord of lords, who alone possesses immortality and dwells in unapproachable light, whom no man has seen or can see. To Him *be* honor and eternal dominion! Amen. (1 Tim. 1:17; 6:15–16)

Are there any better prayers of confession than David's in Psalm 51 or Daniel's in Daniel 9? Are there any better prayers of illumination than those of Psalm 43 and Ephesians 3?

> O send out Your light and Your truth, let them lead me;
> Let them bring me to Your holy hill
> And to Your dwelling places. (Ps. 43:3)

May [we] be able to comprehend with all the saints what is the breadth and length and height and depth, and to know the love of Christ which surpasses knowledge, that [we] may be filled up to all the fullness of God. (Eph. 3:18–19)

Are there any better prayers of intercession for the saints than Paul's for the Ephesians (1:15–23), Philippians (1:9–11), and Colossians (1:9–12)? The following is a partial list of the major prayers found in Scripture, whose study will pay spiritual dividends:

- ✧ Abraham—Genesis 18:23–33 (intercession)
- ✧ Moses—Exodus 15:1–18 (praise); 32:11–14 and 33:12–16 (intercession); Numbers 11:10–15 (complaint); 14:11–19 (pleading)
- ✧ Hannah—1 Samuel 2:1–10 (praise)
- ✧ David—2 Samuel 7:18–29 (thanksgiving); 1 Chronicles 29:11–19 (praise)
- ✧ Solomon—1 Kings 3:6–9 (for wisdom); 8:22–53 and 8:54–61 (praise); 2 Chronicles 6:14–42 (praise and petition)
- ✧ Hezekiah—2 Kings 19:14–19 (intercession)
- ✧ Ezra—Ezra 9:5–15 (confession)
- ✧ Nehemiah—Nehemiah 9:5–37 (praise and petition)
- ✧ Jeremiah—Jeremiah 32:16–25 (praise and questioning)
- ✧ Daniel—Daniel 9:1–19 (confession and petition)
- ✧ Habakkuk—Habakkuk 1:12–17 (questioning)
- ✧ Mary—Luke 1:46–55 (praise)

✧ Zachariah—Luke 1:68–79 (praise)
✧ Simeon—Luke 2:29–32 (praise)
✧ early church—Acts 4:24–30 (praise and petition)
✧ Paul—Ephesians 1:15–23; Philippians 1:9–11; Colossians 1:9–12 (praise and petition)
✧ church triumphant—Revelation 4:8–5:14 (praise)

Incorporate the language of Scripture in your prayers. Not only pray the prayers of Scripture, but let both your terminology and content reflect Scripture's terminology and content. Do not just open the worship by praying whatever pops into your head. Pray, "O Lord we have come to worship and bow down, to kneel before you, the Lord our maker; for you are our God, and we are the people of your pasture, the sheep of your hand" (Ps. 95). Do not just pray, "Lord save our covenant children." Pray instead, "Lord remember your promise to be a God to us and to our children, and so save our covenant children." Pray back to God his promises. Pray back to God his revelation of his own nature. Pray back to God those things that he requires of us in his word. For example, why not turn Ephesians 5:1–17 into a prayer?

> We pray that we might be imitators of God, as beloved children, and walk in love, just as Christ also loved us. We pray that immorality, and impurity, and greed might not be named among us; nor filthiness and silly talk, nor coarse jesting, nor anything else that is improper or not fitting. Help us to walk as children of light, in goodness, righteousness, and truth. Teach us what is pleasing to you. Use us to expose the unfruitful deeds of darkness. Guide us, that we might walk, not unwisely, but wisely, making the most of our time, because the days are evil. Keep us from foolishness, and give us an understanding of your will.

Find key phrases and precious promises and turn them into prayer. There is almost no limit to what can be done. Even historical allusions can be profitably employed in prayer. Miller provides several examples. In a time of struggle for the church:

> O Thou who didst of old, deliver thy covenant people from the bondage of Egypt, and didst open a way through the sea for them to pass in safety; so may

it please thee now to deliver thy afflicted and struggling Church, to disappoint those who seek her hurt, to sanctify to her all her troubles, and bring her out of them all with increasing purity, and peace, and joy.[49]

To cry for freedom from the corruption of sin:

We are by nature carnal, sold under sin; but we rejoice to know that, as thou didst once bring thy people out of bondage, and make them the Lord's freemen in their own land; so thou hast promised, by the Lord Jesus Christ, to proclaim liberty to the captives, and the opening of the prison to them that are the bond slaves of Satan. We rejoice to read in thy word, that, as Moses lifted up the serpent in the wilderness, even so the Son of man has been lifted up, that whosoever believeth on him should not perish, but obtain eternal life.[50]

In addition to the older volumes already cited, especially helpful in the study of prayer are Richard L. Pratt's *Pray with Your Eyes Open,* W. Graham Scroggie's *Paul's Prison Prayers,* Donald Cogan's *Prayers of the New Testament,* and Herbert Lockyer's *All the Prayers of the Bible.*[51] Better yet, get a copy of Henry's *Method for Prayer* and read it over and over again.

Plan Public Prayers

Second, we recommend for the improvement of public prayers that they should be planned. This is obviously necessary if the preceding point is to be realized, if you are to pray the actual terminology of the Bible. But it is necessary for other reasons as well. It is sad to hear the careless language, the imprecision, and the incoherence of many pulpit prayers today. I suspect, though I cannot prove, that many ministers give no thought whatsoever to what they intend to pray beforehand. Willimon complains that "many of our pastoral prayers are a maze of poorly thought out, confusing cliches, hackneyed expressions, shallow constructions, and formalized, impersonal ramblings."[52] All of the old commentators are of one mind on the need of planning public prayers. One ought no more pray without preparation than preach. Fairbairn says, "I would earnestly advise a certain measure of special preparation for the devotional work of the sanctuary."[53] He encourages the use of an outline and even the practice of writing out one's prayers, not in order to read them, but in order to organize one's thoughts.

Shedd says the minister "ought to study *method* in prayer, and observe it. A prayer should have a plan as much as a sermon."[54] He continues:

> In the recoil from the formalism of written and read prayers, Protestants have not paid sufficient attention to an orderly and symmetrical structure in public supplications. Extemporaneous prayer, like extemporaneous preaching, is too often the product of the single instant, instead of devout reflection and premeditation. It might, at first glance, seem that premeditation and supplication are incongruous conceptions; that prayer must be a gush of feeling, without distinct reflection. This is an error. No man, no creature, can pray well without knowing what he is praying for, and whom he is praying to. Everything in prayer, and especially in public prayer, ought to be well considered and well weighed.[55]

Dabney writes, "I deem that the minister is as much bound to prepare himself for praying in public as for preaching. The negligence with which many preachers leave their prayers to accident, while they lay out all their strength on their sermons, is most painfully suggestive of unbelief toward God and indifference to the edification of their brethren." He labels the idea that one should trust in the leading of the Holy Spirit in prayer rather than prepare ahead of time "a remnant of fanatical enthusiasm." "To speak for God to men is a sacred and responsible task. To speak for men to God is not less responsible, and is more solemn. . . . The young minister should no more venture into the pulpit with an *impromptu* prayer, than with an *impromptu* sermon."[56] Both Dabney and Miller (like Murphy) encourage the discipline of what they call "devotional composition," "not so much to recite these written prayers in the pulpit," explains Dabney, "as to train his own taste, and to gather a store of devotional language."[57] Among modern writers Rayburn agrees: "If a minister wishes to be effective in leading the prayers of his congregation he must prepare for his public prayers."[58] When we argue that one should prepare for prayer and study to lead in public prayer, we are not, of course, saying that the prayer should be read aloud from a manuscript. Free prayer, rich scriptural free prayer, is too valuable a commodity to be lost to the church. It is studied prayer, not read prayer that we are advocating here.

Let us, then, make a few recommendations about the prayers that you plan:

164

1. Plan so as to offer brief prayers. Do not try the patience of your people by rambling on and on. Even the nineteenth-century writers recommend brevity. Murphy recommends that the main prayer should be five minutes, no more than eight. Miller complains of the "excessive length" of some prayers.[59] Careful planning will help avoid the "verbiage and repetition" about which Shedd complains.[60] It will also guard against the frequent and mechanical repetition of favorite phrases, titles of God, and any other formula or words, of which Dabney complains: "This mechanical phrase is obnoxious to every charge of formalism, monotony and lack of appropriate variety, which we lodge against an unchangeable liturgy, while it has none of its literary merit and dignified and tender associations."[61] Wandering prayers, meandering at length here, there, and everywhere, will also be corrected by planning.

2. Plan so as not to preach. Dabney warns of the "painful absurdity in our going about formally to instruct God of his doctrinal truth" or our seeming "to preach to God instead of praying to him."[62] Shedd warns of "didactically discoursing in prayer."[63] Murphy calls it "a great abuse of public prayer to use it for preaching to the audience or for rebuking them, or even, as is often done, for giving information to the Lord."[64] You have heard ministers pray, "Lord, we thank you for the prayer meeting that is held in the chapel on Wednesday evening at seven o'clock, just after the fellowship supper and just before choir rehearsal. And we know that you want all your people to come unless providentially hindered. Help us to make it a priority." This is "a great abuse of public prayer" (not to mention silly) and must be avoided.

3. Plan so as to use appropriate terminology. Choose suitable language in addressing the almighty. The old authors denounce, with surprising vehemence, the use of overfamiliar language in prayer. "Familiarity is the worst of faults in prayer," says Shedd.[65] Dabney heaps scorn on "half-educated or spiritually proud men" who "frequently indulge in an indecent familiarity with the Most High, under the pretense of filial nearness and importunity."[66] Spurgeon counsels that one avoid "an unhallowed and sickening superabundance of endearing words." He says, "When 'Dear Lord,' and 'Blessed Lord,' and 'Sweet Lord,' come over and over again as vain repetitions, they are among the worst

of blots." He wishes that "in some way or other" those who indulge such "fond and familiar expressions" could come "to a better understanding of the true relation existing between man and God."[67] He counsels that one be "scrupulously reverent" in one's language.[68]

Application

It remains for us now to illustrate the way in which such prayers are actually prayed and apply the above principles to the five major prayers of the worship service. As you invoke the presence of God, fill your praise with the language of Scripture. Your congregation needs to hear you humbly exalting the greatness and majesty of God. Remember that they are likely to learn how to pray in large part from listening to their minister. Study the great prayers of praise and glean from the Psalms their rich devotional expressions. Week by week provide for the congregation a vision of the power and glory and goodness of the God whom they worship, a God for whom nothing is impossible, a God who can do all things, and a God to whom homage and adoration is due.

As you move on to the prayer of confession, use the deep, prolonged, detailed language of Scripture. Your people come to church each week bruised and battered by sin. They come burdened with guilt, knowing something of what they ought to be and their failure. Let them hear you humbly grieving for sin on their behalf as you confess idolatry, greed, covetousness, pride, lust, selfishness, jealousy, envy, and gossip. Confess that you have not loved God with all your heart, mind, soul, and strength and not loved your neighbor as yourself. Use, for example, the language of David and confess:

> I know my transgressions,
> And my sin is ever before me.
> Against You, You only, I have sinned
> And done what is evil in Your sight. . . .
> I was brought forth in iniquity,
> And in sin my mother conceived me. (Ps. 51:3–5)

And then begin to plead, with David:

> Be gracious to us, O God, according to your lovingkindness; according to the
> greatness of your compassion blot out our transgressions. Wash us thoroughly

from our iniquity, and cleanse us from our sin. Purify us with hyssop, and we shall be clean; wash us and we shall be whiter than snow. Hide your face from our sins, and blot out all our iniquities. Deliver us from blood guiltiness, O God, the God of our salvation. Create in us clean hearts, O God, and renew a steadfast spirit within us. Restore to us the joy of your salvation, and sustain us with a willing spirit. O Lord, open our lips, that our mouth may declare your praise.

Your people are struggling to believe the gospel and struggling to experience forgiveness. They may have confessed their sin privately, and yet they have not found relief. Often the problem is that they have not gone deeply enough. Their brokenness has been healed superficially with flippant promises that " 'all is well, all is well'; but there is no peace" (Jer. 8:11). They need to hear you earnestly acknowledging and grieving sin and claiming the promises of God on their behalf. I mentioned above how I hated the prayer book my first six months in Britain. Eventually I learned to love it and even to look forward to going to chapel each day, in no small part so that I could pray Cranmer's beautiful general confession. I found it therapeutic, though I hesitate to use that word, to deal with God with my sins in corporate worship each day. This is what people need to do in our worship. They need to deal with God. You need to lead them there with praise and then confession. Let them hear you conclude your confession with a rehearsal of the promises of God. Give thanks for the promise of 1 John 1:9, that "if we confess our sins, He is faithful and righteous to forgive us our sins and to cleanse us from all unrighteousness." Give thanks that Jesus "bore our sins in His body on the cross" (1 Peter 2:24), that he gave "His life a ransom for many" (Matt. 20:28), that though he "knew no sin" he became sin "that we might become the righteousness of God in Him" (2 Cor. 5:21). Give thanks that we now have "no condemnation" and "peace with God" in Christ (Rom. 8:1; 5:1). Even pray for them the extended promises of Psalm 103:

> The Lord is compassionate and gracious,
> Slow to anger and abounding in lovingkindness. . . .
> He has not dealt with us according to our sins,
> Nor rewarded us according to our iniquities.
> For as high as the heavens are above the earth,

167

So great is His lovingkindness toward those who fear Him.
As far as the east is from the west,
So far has He removed our transgressions from us.
    (Ps. 103:8, 10–12)

As you move into intercessions, plead for the sanctification of your people, let them hear compassion and urgency in your voice as you pray that the ideals of the Christian life might be realized in their lives. They need to hear you praying week after week that they might be holy even as God is holy (1 Peter 1:15–16), that they might be imitators of God as beloved children and walk in love (Eph. 5), that they might be conformed to the image of Christ, bearing the fruit of the Spirit (Gal. 5:22–23). Let them hear you pleading that they will not love the world or the things of the world and that they will not be seduced by the lust of the eyes, the lust of the flesh, and the boastful pride of life (1 John 2:15–16).

Move on then into four other areas of intercession found in Scripture, used by the early church, and revived by the Reformers. Pray for the (1) civil authorities (Rom. 13:1–7; 1 Tim. 2:2), (2) the Christian ministry (Matt. 9:36–38; 1 Tim. 2:1–2), (3) the salvation of all people (1 Tim. 2:1, 3–4), and (4) the afflicted (2 Cor. 1:3–4, 11; James 5:13–18).[69] They need to hear the breadth of your prayers. They need to hear your prayers circle the globe as you pray for the progress of Christian missions, for ministers and missionaries, for the nation, and for the needy.

What about the prayer of illumination? Does not the congregation need to be reminded that "the natural man does not accept the things of the Spirit of God" (1 Cor. 2:14)? Will not your people benefit from a weekly reminder that we are dependent upon the Holy Spirit if we are ever to understand the word of God? Pray for illumination before you read Scripture or before you preach. Pray that eyes will be opened (Ps. 119:18), that ears will be unstopped, that stony hearts will be softened, that stiff necks will be loosened. Pray that the eyes of the heart might be enlightened (Eph. 3:18), that the Lord might teach us his truth (Ps. 86:11–12) and give us understanding (119:33).

Finally, they need to hear you pray the blessing of God upon them. Bless them with the apostolic (2 Cor. 13:14) or the Aaronic (Num. 6:24–26) or some other benediction (e.g., Heb. 13:20–21). Let them leave with one of these scriptural blessings ringing in their ears. Will that not encourage them as they leave? Does this not conclude the service on the gospel's optimistic note?

Can you see now why we have said that the minister needs to lead in prayer? Who in the congregation is trained to pray in this manner? Who is most aware of the pastoral needs of the congregation? Who has been set apart for three years of biblical and theological education? Who spends extended time each day in the study of Scripture? Who labors daily on his knees in private prayer for the souls of the saints? Who consequently is capable of praying in the rich devotional language of Scripture as well as in a manner that is theologically sound? Public prayer is not merely a matter of you or anyone else standing up and praying off the top of your head. The first thing into most of our minds, as Spurgeon once said, is "mere froth." Even as it makes sense to have the minister preach and administer the sacraments, it makes sense to have him pray. The prayers that we envision are those offered by a man called by God, who saturates his mind with the word of God and spends hours each week on his knees before God. Even as the church has deemed it wise to apply the New Testament admonitions to "guard the gospel" by entrusting its proclamation through word and sacrament only to those ordained to do so, so also it is both pastorally and theologically wise to leave leadership in prayer in the hands of the minister.

Have you been giving to public prayer the attention it deserves? Do you see how public prayer is a means of grace that builds the church? Begin now to practice "studied prayer" (as the Puritans called it) or "conceived prayer" (Watts's term). Plan your prayers, fill them with scriptural language and allusions, and watch the sanctifying impact that they make upon the congregation multiply to the glory of God.

8

BAPTISM: JOYFUL SIGN OF THE GOSPEL

D. MARION CLARK

Baptism is God's gift to his church to fill his people with joy, to powerfully communicate the gospel, and to build the faith and unity of the Christian community. The purpose of this chapter is to explore the significance of baptism in Reformed worship, and there is much to explore! Many excellent expositions of baptism already exist, but most are written from the perspective of promoting either paedobaptism or credobaptism. Unfortunately, the result is that the issue of paedobaptism versus credobaptism has become the focus whenever baptism is raised as a subject. The assumption is that after one has decided which position to take there is nothing more to consider. Even an author who presents a thorough study of baptism's significance inevitably goes on to demonstrate how one ought to conclude that such and such a position on paedobaptism is necessary, thus making the earlier presentation immediately suspect to the reader who disagrees with this conclusion.

This chapter is not a contribution to the paedobaptism/credobaptism debates, but rather an exposition of what makes baptism the joyful celebration that it ought to be in Reformed worship. Or, if I may be allowed to express it this way—what makes baptism so much fun for a pastor to administer. We will consider what baptism signifies, the mindset in which it ought to be received, its function as a seal, and the role of the minister in administering it.

The Joyful Sign

Baptism signifies the gospel. It communicates the atonement of Christ, our union with him, the sanctification of the Holy Spirit, and entry into God's covenant. The Westminster Confession states that it is "a sign and seal of the covenant of grace, of his [the believer's] ingrafting into Christ, of regeneration, of remission of sins, and of his giving up unto God, through Jesus Christ, to walk in newness of life" (28.1).

The Second Helvetic Confession (20.2) powerfully presents the same message:

> Baptism, therefore, does call to mind and keep in remembrance the great benefit of God performed to humankind. For we are all born in the pollution of sin and are the children of wrath. But God, who is rich in mercy, does freely purge us from our sins by the blood of his Son, and in him does adopt us to be his sons, and by a holy covenant does join us to himself, and does enrich us with diverse gifts, that we might live a new life.

What a joyful sign! Baptism is a neon light flashing "Gospel, Gospel, Gospel." Consider all that is expressed through this sign.

The Atonement of Christ

First is Christ's redemption and the remission of our sins. In Colossians, Paul, linking together circumcision and baptism with the crucifixion and resurrection, proclaims that in baptism we are buried and raised with Christ, who is our circumcision. What does this mean? He explains:

> When you were dead in your sins and in the uncircumcision of your sinful nature, God made you alive with Christ. He forgave us all our sins, having canceled the written code, with its regulations, that was against us and that stood opposed to us; he took it away, nailing it to the cross. And having disarmed the powers and authorities, he made a public spectacle of them, triumphing over them by the cross. (Col. 2:13–15)

171

God forgave us! That is what baptism proclaims. He forgave us because of the baptism his own son undertook for us (cf. Mark 10:38; Luke 12:50). Each baptism of a child of God replays the baptism of the cross. As the minister enacts the ritual, he is showing the redemption of Christ.

God forgave us because our sins were washed away. This perhaps is the clearest message conveyed in this sacrament. However the water may be applied, we all can attest to the answer given to Q. 69 in the Heidelberg Catechism: "How are you admonished and assured by holy baptism that the one sacrifice of Christ upon the cross is of real advantage to you?" The answer: "That Christ appointed this external washing with water, adding thereto this promise, that I am as certainly washed by his blood and Spirit from all the pollution of my soul, that is, from all my sins, as I am washed externally with water, by which the filthiness of the body is commonly washed away."

This is the meaning that Peter expresses in his epistle: "And this water symbolizes baptism that now saves you also—not the removal of dirt from the body but the pledge of a good conscience toward God. It saves you by the resurrection of Jesus Christ" (1 Peter 3:21).

Baptism, therefore, depicts Christ's redemptive baptism of death and resurrection.

Our Union with Christ

Second, baptism signifies our "ingrafting into Christ." The outer sign represents the inner grace of union with God the Son. A number of scriptural texts emphasize this union:

> Or don't you know that all of us who were baptized into Christ Jesus were baptized into his death? . . . If we have been united with him like this in his death, we will certainly also be united with him in his resurrection. (Rom. 6:3, 5)

> For we were all baptized by one Spirit into one body. (1 Cor. 12:13)

> You are all sons of God through faith in Christ Jesus, for all of you who were baptized into Christ have clothed yourselves with Christ. . . . For you are all one in Christ Jesus. (Gal. 3:26–28)

> In him you were also circumcised, . . . having been buried with him in baptism and raised with him. (Col. 2:11–12)

Note the phrases "baptized *into* Christ Jesus," "baptized by one Spirit *into* one body," "baptized *into* Christ," "*in* him you were also circumcised." Baptism signifies the inner baptism of the Holy Spirit that unites us with Christ or ingrafts us into him.

How does baptism signify this reality? Through the word spoken: "Jean Clark, I baptize you in the name of the Father and of the Son and of the Holy Spirit." We get that formula, of course, from Jesus' command: "Therefore go and make disciples of all nations, baptizing them in the name of the Father and of the Son and of the Holy Spirit" (Matt. 28:19). The preposition *in* is the same Greek preposition—*eis*—translated "into" in the first three passages quoted above. In other words, I do not as a minister baptize an individual simply on behalf of the Trinity, but *into* the Trinity, that is, into communion with the triune God.

Expressing the same idea, Edmund Clowney refers to baptism as a naming ceremony:

> The baptized person is given a name, not the name on a baptismal certificate, but the name of the triune God. A flustered pastor performing an infant baptism may address little Martha as Margaret, but he is not giving her that name. The name that he gives her is the name of the triune God. Baptism gives Christians their family name, the name they bear as those called the children of God (Isaiah 43:6b–7).[1]

Baptism is a statement that the recipient is in the family. The disciple of Christ has been brought into Christ, and because the disciple has been brought into Christ, the disciple abides in the Father and Spirit as well. Regarding the Father, Jesus says, "If anyone loves me, . . . my Father will love him, and we will come to him and make our home with him" (John 14:23). Regarding the Holy Spirit he promises to send the Counselor who "lives with you and will be in you" (14:17).

Sanctification of the Holy Spirit

This ingrafting in Christ occurs through the work of the Holy Spirit applying the Son's redemptive work by the Father's saving grace. The water signifies, then, not only the cleansing blood of Christ, but the anointing of the Holy Spirit. It is the Holy Spirit who sprinkles the blood of Christ on the soul of the baptized (cf. 1 Peter 1:2). The Spirit enters and regenerates the heart:

I tell you the truth, no one can enter the kingdom of God unless he is born of water and the Spirit. Flesh gives birth to flesh, but the Spirit gives birth to spirit. (John 3:5–6)

I will sprinkle clean water on you, and you will be clean; I will cleanse you from all your impurities and from all your idols. I will give you a new heart and put a new spirit in you; I will remove from you your heart of stone and give you a heart of flesh. And I will put my Spirit in you and move you to follow my decrees and be careful to keep my laws. (Ezek. 36:25–27)

Baptism also depicts the change in the baptized: "His giving up unto God, through Jesus Christ, to walk in newness of life" (Westminster Confession 28.1). We who have died in Christ have risen with Christ so that we might live for Christ. As Paul explains in Romans 6:4–14, we have been buried and raised with Christ through inner baptism (which our outer baptism represents). Thus, we are going to live new lives. We are freed, no longer under bondage to sin. Our baptism signifies this change. We were therefore buried with Christ through baptism into death in order that, just as Christ was raised from the dead, we too may live a new life, that we should no longer be slaves to sin. In the same way, we count ourselves dead to sin but alive to God in Christ Jesus.

Count yourselves changed: stone hearts turned to flesh, enslaved bodies now freed. In *Foundations of the Christian Faith*, James Boice contends that this element of change is inherent in the meaning of *baptizō*. First, he establishes its use in the processing of pickling, which clearly indicates making a change in the object being baptized. He then explores several texts, demonstrating the change that occurs under each instance of baptism: peace to fear (Isa. 21:4), identification with Christ (Gal. 3:27; Mark 16:16), and rebellion to obedience (1 Cor. 10:1–2).[2]

Entry into God's Covenant

Baptism, furthermore, signifies entrance into the new covenant to which we belong, namely, the covenant of grace in Christ. Abraham Keach's catechism, prepared for instruction in the Baptist Confession of 1689, reiterates the same language as the Westminster Shorter Catechism in this regard: "Baptism is an holy ordinance, wherein the washing with water in the name of the Father, the Son and the Holy Spirit, signifies our engrafting into

Christ *and partaking of the benefits of the covenant of grace,* and our engagement to be the Lord's" (Q. 100 [emphasis added]).

At this moment our credobaptist kin may be getting nervous, wondering where this is leading, while our paedobaptist kin are rubbing their hands in anticipation of where this is going! Let both draw their own conclusions; we are going only so far as what baptism signifies, and all can certainly agree on entrance into the new covenant.

Baptist pastor Erroll Hulse notes, "It is wrong to assume that interest in the subject of covenant theology and the covenant of grace has been wholly confined to Calvinistic non-Baptist theologians. English Baptists found no reason to quarrel with the subject when they used the Westminster Confession as a basis for their own Confession published in 1689."[3] He then proceeds to give a succinct recount of covenant theology, borrowing from John Murray and Meredith Kline and concluding that an understanding of the role of covenant obviously leads to a credobaptist position!

God has made a covenant with us to be his people. As the writer of Hebrews explains, "For this reason Christ is the mediator of a new covenant, that those who are called may receive the promised eternal inheritance — now that he has died as a ransom to set them free from the sins committed under the first covenant" (Heb. 9:15). As circumcision signified the covenant made with Abraham for his descendents, so baptism signifies the covenant made with Christ for his. But here is the key difference: Christ through his body bore the guilt incurred in the first covenant and ratified the second. Thus, when we enter the covenant, our baptism signifies the work that Christ has already done to fulfill its conditions. It is a sign that points us to the finished work of our Redeemer.

But God has not made many covenants with many persons. He has made one covenant with his people in Christ. We are baptized into God's covenant family. That is why baptism ought to be enacted in God's gathered assembly. I was told of a man who baptized his own sons in his home. Setting aside for the moment who ought to administer baptism, this man peeled away an essential aspect of what baptism means. He taught his children through this action that belonging to the church of Christ is an extra in God's plans for them.

Baptism is not "just between God and me." If anything, this sacrament ought to break the mindset of individualistic religion. As Christians we are a people, not a group of persons who find it convenient to congregate for spiritual services. If we are united in Christ, then we are united to one another.

This is where the church comes in as the local gathering of Christ's body. In encouraging the church body to gather for the ordinance of baptism, Don Whitney writes, "When God brings a person into spiritual life, that person enters into the spiritual and invisible body of Christ—the universal church. When that spiritual experience is pictured in water baptism, that is the individual's symbolic entry into the tangible and visible body of Christ—the local church."[4]

Redemptive Judgment

Under the idea of baptism being a covenant sign, Meredith Kline advocates an understanding of baptism as judgment. In *By Oath Consigned*, he demonstrates how circumcision served as the ratifying sign of God's covenant with Abraham. The ratification invokes sanctions and punishment for breaking those sanctions. Thus, circumcision was a sign of judgment should the covenant be broken. Water baptism serves the same purpose. Kline explains how water served as a judgment sign in the Old Testament, using the Noahic flood and the Red Sea crossing as examples. They are instances of "redemptive judgment."[5] The waters exercise judgment on the condemned and save the redeemed. Kline appeals to 1 Peter 3:21, which links baptism with the Noahic flood, and 1 Corinthians 10:2, which does the same with the Red Sea crossing, to contend that Peter and Paul viewed baptism in the same manner.[6]

This idea brings to baptism a solemnity both for what it recalls has been done for the baptized and for what it calls upon the baptized to be and do. We are not cleansed merely because God the Spirit has given us a spiritual bath; we are cleansed by the blood shed by our Lord Jesus Christ. He has undergone his baptism (Luke 12:50) of judgment on our behalf to mediate for us the new covenant (Heb. 9:15).

Our Consecration

Let's review. Baptism signifies Christ's atonement for our sins. It signifies our union with him and the Holy Spirit's work of sanctification. Baptism is the sign of God's covenant with us, a sign of redemptive judgment. These are the privileges signified to us. But along with privilege comes obligation as well.

176

Baptism consecrates us for service to the Lord. To receive God's family name and be brought into his covenant sets us apart from the world. Baptism publicly marks us as belonging to God's kingdom, that our allegiance belongs to him. As Paul explains, if baptism signifies a change in us, then we must act accordingly:

> Therefore do not let sin reign in your mortal body so that you obey its evil desires. Do not offer the parts of your body to sin, as instruments of wickedness, but rather offer yourselves to God, as those who have been brought from death to life; and offer the parts of your body to him as instruments of righteousness. For sin shall not be your master, because you are not under law, but under grace. (Rom. 6:12–14)

Our baptism obligates us to live in righteousness so that we honor, not shame, our Lord with whom we have been buried and raised to life in baptism. We cannot go back. We have entered into the new covenant; we have sworn allegiance to our king. Now we must live as citizens and servants of his kingdom.

But the baptism that obligates us to live in righteousness also holds us steady when we are pummeled by the assaults of Satan, the flesh, and the world, and it reassures us the many times we do fail. Christ Jesus has been baptized on our behalf. He has gone through the waters of judgment and has arrived safely to the side of resurrection. His body is now our ark that bears us safely. The waters of judgment are also the waters of salvation. We too when doubts assail us cry out with Martin Luther, "I have been baptized!"

"Go forth," our Lord commands us in baptism. "Go forth on behalf of me and the gospel to live as a true disciple, obeying everything I have commanded you. But know that you go forth in my name under my protection. You bear my mark. Know that I am with you always, to the very end of the age."

What a glorious sign! Truly it is a solemn joy to display the sign that speaks of our Lord's sacrifice for his people, that communicates the blessings of redemption and remission of sin, that calls us to live lives of purpose and true worth, and then assures us that he will cause us to persevere.

From God to Us

Knowing what baptism signifies should lead us to understand that the sacraments are God's signs to us—and not ours to him. Essential to

Reformed theology is the idea that God is the initiator in his relations with his people. No one comes to Christ unless the Father draws him (John 6:44). This concept of God as initiator applies to the sacraments as well.

Baptism is not the act by which a convert comes before God and says, "I want to give you a sign that I have now decided to be identified with you." Nor is it an opportunity for parents to let God know that they will raise their child for him as best they can. No, God calls forth the person whom he has regenerated, saying, "Here is my sign to you that I have decided to identify you with me. Here is my sign to you that I have already baptized you through the Holy Spirit." To parents he is saying, "Bring your child to me. Here is my sign that your child belongs to me and that you are to raise her as such. She is not to be treated as one outside my covenant family."

More attention needs to be given to this point, which distinguishes the Reformed approach to baptism from the Arminian. Often the pastor will introduce a baptism ceremony by noting that John Smith desires to be baptized. John may so desire, but to say nothing more lends to the notion that baptism is a sign that John chooses to display. The truth, however, is that as much as John may desire to be baptized, he is responding to a command from God to receive the sign that God has chosen to impart his message to John and witnesses.

Now, it is true that baptism involves the action of the believer (or believing parents) to signify his faith. Calvin expresses this well:

> Baptism serves as our confession before men. Indeed, it is the mark by which we publicly profess that we wish to be reckoned God's people; by which we testify that we agree in worshiping the same God, in one religion with all Christians; by which finally we openly affirm our faith. Thus not only do our hearts breathe the praise of God, but our tongues also and all members of our body resound his praise in every way they can.[7]

Baptism is the means by which we declare to whom we owe allegiance. This is the very reason it is such a significant decision for converts to make in societies hostile to the Christian religion. Such an act will bring ostracism, even death for some. It requires a courageous faith. Even in America, baptism has become a countercultural act because of the growing contrast between the church and secular society.

Even so, or especially so, ministers as stewards of the sacraments must make clear that God gives this sign for his people for our benefit. God is our bridegroom, who has chosen us, paid the dowry, and given us his ring so that all may know that we belong to him. Even more, he has done so to make clear to us that we are his. The ceremony of baptism asserts that his love for us is not a dream, but a reality.

This aspect of baptism is more important than ministers often realize. Many in our flocks are beset with worry that they do not really belong in God's family, or that if they do, they are let in begrudgingly. Many live as though God might at any time kick them out of the house. They have got to keep up their good works or their feelings of faith. For many, baptism haunts them rather than comforts them. They feel that they have let God down. They publicly signified that they were committed to Christ or would raise their children to be committed, but they have failed time and again. God must really be angry now.

If the emphasis of baptism is on our professed commitment to God, then we do have much to worry about. But baptism is not so much about our profession for God as it is God's acknowledgment of us. God is not thanking us at baptism for accepting him. He is not grateful for our profession of faith, as though he is thankful to have such committed followers as we. He is no more impressed with our vows of unwavering faith than Jesus was with Peter's avowal to die with him.

When we declare our allegiance to God and determination to follow him, picture him smiling indulgently on us, patting us on our heads, and saying, "That is a nice sentiment, but you are going to blow it, just like Peter did. What I want you to know by this sign is that I have made a commitment to you, and I *will not* blow it. Every time you fall, I will pick you up. Every time you sin, I will remain as ever faithful to my covenant as before. I will not give up on you or let you be snatched away."

Again, Calvin articulates so well what is involved:

For inasmuch as it is given for the arousing, nourishing, and confirming of our faith, it is to be received as from the hand of the Author himself. We ought to deem it certain and proved that it is he who speaks to us through the sign; that it is he who purifies and washes away sins, and wipes out the remembrance of them; that it is he who makes us sharers in his death, who deprives Satan of his rule, who weakens the power of our lust; indeed, that it is he who

179

comes into a unity with us so that, having put on Christ, we may be acknowledged God's children. These things, I say, he performs for our soul within as truly and surely as we see our body outwardly cleansed, submerged, and surrounded with water.[8]

What the baptized is primarily confessing is not undying devotion to God, but God's unfailing devotion to redeeming, cleansing, sanctifying, and ultimately glorifying this weak sinful believer. The sacrament of baptism is intended by God to feed our faith, to comfort and assure us. Thus, the focus of this ordinance must be on what God has done and is doing for us, and not on what we have, are, or will be doing for God. Otherwise, the sacrament will serve only to burden and ultimately condemn us.

There certainly is a place for the participants to confess allegiance to Christ. As stated earlier, baptism places obligations upon the recipients. Baptism is a time for the baptized to make profession of faith and commitment to Christ. Furthermore, the sacrament bears witness against the unrepentant and mocker of God's redemption. Many will say to God, "Have I not been baptized?" and God will reply, "Your very baptism condemns you, for you professed what you did not believe." Thus we ought to warn those who receive baptism not to do so lightly.

In my own experience as a pastor I have dealt with the unfounded fears of sincere believers who are weak in their assurance. It is to build up, not undermine, the faith of his people, that Christ instituted this sacrament. He did not command that baptism be yet another work for his followers to prove their faith and commitment; he commanded this sign to be kept so that his followers would put their trust and hope in him alone. He commanded the sacrament to be kept so that in our times of doubts and failure we would not be fearful of his disgust with us. Instead, in such times we should be ever more awed by his faithfulness to us.

By the way, those who advocate immersion have a strong point that such a mode best illustrates the concept of dying and rising with Christ, but infant baptism also illustrates the activity of God in regeneration. Spiritual regenerative baptism takes place while we are oblivious to what is going on. The Holy Spirit administers baptism to us while we are drooling and babbling in our unregenerate state, just like the infant we hold in our arms. One might say that the water-baptism ceremony reenacts the spiritual-baptism ceremony administered by the triune God.

Grace Bestowed

We have considered what baptism signifies and who is giving the sign to whom. As a sign, baptism is very meaningful, but we must go further in our understanding of it as a seal. Of course, this is where we move into more difficult territory because it is harder to grasp the activity of baptism. What does baptism actually do?

In the Reformed community we are clear about what the sacraments do not do. They do not confer salvation. They signify the saving work that the Holy Spirit already has done. Baptism signifies regeneration, but it is not itself the means of regeneration.

"Signifying" is a good, safe word. It is the "sealing" part that causes some confusion and makes many of our Baptist kin uneasy. Neither the London Confession of Faith nor Spurgeon's catechism nor Keach's catechism uses the word *seal*, even though they are indebted to the Westminster Confession for much of their substance. But dropping the word *seal* from the definition of sacrament (or ordinance) of baptism diminishes an important aspect of understanding its significance.

What, then, does the term *seal* add to the function of baptism? Paul helps us with this in his discussion of the function of circumcision for Abraham:

We have been saying that Abraham's faith was credited to him as righteousness. Under what circumstances was it credited? Was it after he was circumcised, or before? It was not after, but before! And he received the sign of circumcision, a seal of the righteousness that he had by faith while he was still uncircumcised. So then, he is the father of all who believe but have not been circumcised, in order that righteousness might be credited to them. (Rom. 4:9b–11)

In his commentary on Romans, James Boice applied this passage to the sacraments:

What is a seal? We do not use seals very often today, but we have enough examples to illustrate their meaning and importance. Suppose you want to go abroad. You have to secure a passport issued by the government of the United States. You apply for it, submitting two recent pictures of yourself. When it comes you find that one of the shots has been affixed to the passport with a seal: the great seal of the United States. It is stamped into the passport in such a way that it is impossible to remove or alter the photo without damaging and thus invalidating the document. This seal indicates that the authority of the United States government stands behind the passport in affirming that the person whose picture appears there is a true citizen of the United States. . . .

Sacraments operate in this way. In the case of Abraham, Paul says that circumcision was "a seal of the righteousness that he had by faith while he was still uncircumcised." That is, after Abraham had believed God and God had imparted righteousness to him, God gave the seal of circumcision to validate what had happened. In the same way, baptism is a seal that the person being baptized has been identified with Jesus Christ as his disciple.[9]

Thus, baptism does more than signify the work of Christ and the Holy Spirit. It validates the benefits of Christ's work that have been applied by the Holy Spirit in the recipient. The recipient himself or herself is validated as now being in Christ. It is one thing for a new creature in Christ to be shown a sign of salvation; it is another to have the seal of salvation stamped on the believer to authenticate one's salvation experience. Hanging on the wall a picture representing one's alma mater might produce warm feelings, but of far greater meaning is to have a diploma on the wall that not only generates old memories, but authenticates the person named as a bona fide graduate of that school. That is what baptism also serves to do as a seal.

Another way of viewing sealing is as God's mark of approval. Consider Jesus' use of the term in John 6:27: "Do not work for food that spoils, but for food that endures to eternal life, which the Son of Man will give you. On him God the Father has placed his seal of approval." Jesus then explains that the approval is based on faith in him. What a blessing both of these aspects are to the one receiving baptism! God is saying to the one baptized, "You are mine; I delight in you. Here is my seal of identification and approval."

The function of baptism can be understood further in its role as a "means of grace." Note for example how Keach's catechism (which corresponds with the London Baptist Confession in the same way that the Larger and Shorter catechisms correspond with the Westminster Confession) presents the ordinances as "means of salvation" (emphasis added):

Q. 95. What are the outward and ordinary means whereby Christ communicates to us the benefits of redemption?

A. The outward and ordinary means whereby Christ communicates to us the benefits of redemption are his ordinances, especially the word, baptism, the Lord's Supper and prayer; *all which are made effectual to the elect for salvation.*

Q. 98. How do baptism and the Lord's Supper become *effectual means of salvation?*

A. Baptism and the Lord's Supper become *effectual means of salvation,* not from any virtue in them or in him that administers them, but only by the blessing of Christ and the working of his Spirit in them that by faith receive them.

Q. 99. Wherein do baptism and the Lord's Supper differ from the other ordinances of God?

A. Baptism and the Lord's Supper differ from the other ordinances of God in that they were specially instituted by Christ to represent and *apply to believers the benefits of the new covenant* by visible and outward signs.

Clearly the composers of the Baptist Confession and Catechism believed that God confers some form of blessing to the recipients through the ordinances. To be sure, as the Westminster divines also were careful to explain, these blessings had to be received by faith and because of faith. One must already have been exercising saving faith, as well as understand and believe what he or she is receiving. Grace is not being infused into the recipient as though the sacraments themselves dispense salvation or a measure of salvation. Nevertheless God has chosen to communicate the blessings of his covenant with us through these sacred signs, which Christ instituted for his people.

Indeed, to appreciate more fully the sacraments, Protestant Christians need to recover the reality of biblical blessing. We have reduced blessing to the subjective experience of feeling blessed: "I was so blessed by that song." "You are such a blessing to me." The parents who brought their children to be blessed by Jesus came to him not because he was such a nice man that he was a blessing to be around, but because they recognized him as being a man of God who could confer special blessing. The stories of Isaac's blessing Jacob and Esau and of Jacob's blessing his sons are filled with solemnity and drama because of the very real act of passing on blessing. Paul's blessings in his epistles are not mere wishes of well-being; he understands his role as an apostle of Jesus Christ to impart the blessings of

Christ. And we ministers of the gospel are called to impart the blessings of that gospel to our people as we administer the sacraments to them.

Do we understand precisely what we are doing when we administer the sacraments? Of course not, but we do recognize that more is happening than simply some people reenacting a ceremony that makes them feel good. There is mystery involved. In our fear of becoming "like the Catholics" and investing too much power in the sacraments, we must be careful of the greater danger of turning God's sacred institutions into rituals that have only the meaning that we invest in them. Then we fall into postmodern reasoning, which asserts that anything outside of us carries only the meaning and value we give it.

When we administer the sacraments, let us say to our people that more is happening than we know. Let us say that Christ is present and bestowing his blessing on his people. The Good Shepherd is present feeding and nourishing his flock. Yes, we mean that he is present spiritually and that this is to be received by faith, but he is present, nevertheless, through means that he has specially ordained. Something sacred, something mysterious is taking place.

This mystery justifies keeping the term *sacrament* for baptism and the Lord's Supper. Calvin points out that "the ancients" used the Latin term *sacramentum* to translate the Greek word *mystērion* in passages such as Ephesians 1:9: "And he made known to us the mystery of his will according to his good pleasure, which he purposed in Christ."[10] It is worth having to explain what we mean by the term *sacrament,* so that we might retain such a rich expression of the gospel that it signifies. The term *ordinance* may keep us from confusing how Protestants and Catholics view baptism and the Lord's Supper, but it tends to dilute the very real presence and activity of the Holy Spirit that makes us partakers of the benefits of the covenant of grace.

The Role of the Pastor

Make It Clear

Let's consider the role the pastor plays in administering baptism, as the "steward of the mysteries of God."[11] Many ministers do not know the power of the means of grace by which to minister to their people. The juxtaposition of two articles in *Leadership Journal* helps bring out this problem. The first article was an interview with economist Jim Gilmore who presented the latest approach in retailing and marketing—providing "an experience." He pointed out that what shoppers are seeking (and smart retailers are providing) when they venture out to the stores is not a particular item, but a pleasurable or meaningful experience. The obvious question was then asked, "So how does all this 'experience providing' apply to the church?" Note his perceptive response:

> It doesn't. When the church gets into the business of staging experiences, that quickly becomes idolatry. . . . Increasingly you find people talking about the worship *experience* rather than the worship *service*. That reflects what's happening in the outside world. I'm dismayed to see churches abandon the means of grace that God ordains simply to conform to the patterns of the world.[12]

Compare that insight to the comments in the next article written by a minister:

> People are on a search for the spiritual, and what they are looking for is far more experiential than cerebral. Instead of thinking their way into feeling, they often feel their way into thinking. As a result, believers need to express themselves like never before, and seekers need to see a life engaged in the spiritual like never before. Thus our services involve many more moments designed to directly engage the soul and expose it to the holy—allow it to respond in kind.[13]

The marketer warns the church not to market worship; the minister "designs" worship to meet marketing demands! I bring this up not to disparage the value of experience in worship, but to demonstrate the error many of us ministers make in our eagerness to experience meaningful worship. Early in my ministry I grew weary of dry worship. Typical of a small church, singing was poor, and the hymnbook had a thin selection of standard hymns. Certainly no one would have attended that church service for the worship experience. As good Presbyterians, we remained quiet throughout the service; no display of emotion. I wanted something more, and I turned to the charismatic movement for what I perceived to offer a real experience with God.

185

It was at Tenth Presbyterian Church, though, where I recovered the "experience" that God provided through his means of grace. It did not take long under Jim Boice's influence to find my greatest joy in exploring the truths of God's word. What is more glorious than the revelation of God and his redemption? The next personal revelation came when he assigned me the duty of the pastoral prayer. After a period of time, worshipers would greet me at the door and thank me for how the prayer ministered to them. I learned then the power of ordinary prayer. Eventually, Tenth Presbyterian Church instituted a weekly Communion service, which I led. Through that I learned the power of the sacraments to communicate the gospel, especially Christ's promise of forgiveness. In brief, my pilgrimage to find meaningful worship led me to the ancient forms of worship instituted by Christ and practiced through the centuries—preaching, prayer, and the sacraments. My problem in worship had not been poor singing or the lack of charismatic activity; my problem was in not realizing the treasures for worship that exist in the means of grace.

The glorious joys of these means hit home one Sunday when I participated in the services of two churches. I led the early service at Tenth Presbyterian Church, which included preaching, praying, and administering Communion. I then rode to a nearby church where I ordained two elders and administered baptism. I grew more enthused as I carried out each element of worship, because each became yet another means of proclaiming the same gospel message. That is what the means of grace are about—proclaiming the glorious gospel of Jesus Christ!

Pastors, get that across to your congregations. Recover for yourselves and then recover for them the joy of God's word proclaimed in preaching and of the message of redemption and reconciliation displayed in the sacraments. You do not need to design a meaningful worship experience. You need to present clearly the glory of the gospel through the means that Christ has already given you.

Thus, your role as minister in administering baptism is to take time to explain clearly what baptism signifies. Reformed teaching makes clear that the word must accompany the sign to prevent confusion about the sign's meaning. It certainly is fitting to preach a sermon on baptism. But whether you preach a sermon, you must always present clearly what baptism signifies and what is, and is not, taking place. Because baptism is so rich in meaning, it is not necessary to present every point each time. Indeed, you can dilute its significance by turning the explanation into a tedious checklist of everything to remember. Make sure that the gospel message is presented and, then, as each occasion presents itself, emphasize one particular aspect.

For example, in baptizing young people who have grown up in the church, it would be fitting to emphasize that they are being consecrated for service to the Lord. This is the moment for them to make a public stand for Christ and to commit themselves to living as his people. For one who has been delivered from addiction or a wicked lifestyle, the pastor may emphasize the assurance this sign gives that Christ has the believer now and will not let go. To young parents of an infant, let them know how much God cares for their child and will be there for them in raising the child.

See how powerful baptism can be, especially when accompanied with the spoken word? Clear explanation of the sacrament brings forth a truly powerful experience, contrary to what advocates of mystical experiences contend. Consider Joseph Campbell's attempt to help us in the matter of presenting our symbols of faith. His solution to stale worship services is to make the sacraments appear magical:

> Where the synagogues and churches go wrong is by telling what their symbols "mean." The value of an effective rite is that it leaves everyone to his own thoughts, which dogma and definitions only confuse. Dogma and definitions rationally insisted upon are inevitably hindrances, not aids, to religious meditation, since no one's sense of the presence of God can be anything more than a function of his own spiritual capacity. Having your image of God—the most intimate, hidden mystery of your life—defined for you in terms contrived by some council of bishops back, say, in the fifth century or so: what good is that? But a contemplation of the crucifix works; the odor of incense works; so do, also, hieratic attires, the tones of well-sung Gregorian chants, intoned and mumbled Introits, Kyries, heard and unheard consecrations. . . . If we are curious for meanings, they are there, translated in the other column of the prayerbook. But if the magic of the rite is gone. . . .[14]

Mumbling and making the sacrament feel mysterious may work to manipulate the experience of worshipers, but to give worshipers a true experience of the majesty and graciousness of God, the minister must explain as clearly as possible what is taking place. Baptism does not need to be made to feel mysterious; the gospel that it signifies is by far the most wondrous of all mysteries. Make the gospel known through the sacrament, and the people will experience mystery—the mystery of the holy God who graciously saves sinners through the Son's sacrifice. Keeping the sacrament vague allows us to keep it under control; opening its message and its significance for the believer frees it to overwhelm us with wonder and joy.

Value the Sacrament

But you, the minister, must first be caught up in the glory of the sacrament, just as you must first be struck by the gospel you are preaching, if you want your congregation to be struck with the message. Both paedobaptists and credobaptists are too often concerned with defending their positions about baptism to give adequate attention to the blessing of the baptism for the recipient. Use this time of the ritual to build and encourage the faith of your fellow worshipers.

What of the use of visuals and sound to enhance worship? Many ministers are turning to media technology and to the drama and music stage to spice up their preaching and worship. The reasoning is that people today are visual and feeling oriented. To reach them we must appeal to the senses and to the emotions. However that is debated, at least understand that the best visual and sound presentation, the best drama, is found in the sacraments. See and feel the water of baptism that signifies the washing away of sin. Hear the words "I baptize you in the name of the Father, the Son, and the Holy Spirit" pronounced by the pastor as he lays his hands on the head or immerses the body of the baptized. In the Lord's Supper, see, hear, feel, and taste the ritual of the sacrament. I assure you that a minister who faithfully administers these holy rites, which are not borrowed from the stage or corporate seminars but instituted by our Lord, will bless his people with an experience that truly gives them an encounter with God and builds their faith.

Keep It Simple and Focused

How then do we faithfully administer baptism? The key word is simplicity. Just as your goal in preaching is to convey the message of God's word as clearly as possible, so should be your goal with baptism. There is but one symbol—water. Do not add more such as prescribing special clothing or applying the water by special means. I am told of one minister who sprinkled water with a white rose. Besides being a poor symbol, the rose serves only to distract from the symbol of the water.

The minister must also be careful in the matter of consecrating the water. Indeed, one wonders if this expression should be used. It can confuse what is happening in baptism and lead the recipients and worshipers to have a superstitious regard for the water. The Reformers were careful to avoid such an attitude. The elements of the sacraments are signs. As significant as these signs might be, they are not to be confused with the spiritual reality signified. Water does not cleanse the soul, but we confuse this message in the minds of our people when we set apart the water for sacred use. They believe that some power has now been invested in the water. Their faith becomes directed toward the water rather than the blood of Christ.

Where does the efficacy of baptism lie? It is in the faith of the recipient (or parents) in the work of Christ that baptism signifies — not faith in the water. Keep the eyes of your people on Jesus Christ. When they are receiving or observing the sign of baptism, they should be focused upon the mercy of God shown in the redemptive work of his Son. Do not let them walk away thinking that the water has done the work, which is reserved for Christ's atonement and the Holy Spirit's sanctification. Do not let parents think that the souls of their children are now safe because water has touched their bodies. Do not let professing recipients think that they are safe now that they have done the "baptism thing." What matters is faith in Jesus Christ.

Presbyterian and Baptist ministers face the same problem in their people bringing a false assumption to the sacrament. Both have people in their church vainly assured of their salvation because of a heretical understanding of baptism. At heart, many Protestants are Roman Catholics: "Yes, I'm saved. I got baptized." What they mean is . . . well, that is all they mean: They got baptized. Question them about their faith, and they reveal no understanding of the gospel. But, again, they were baptized, so why worry?

Prayer can cultivate the proper attitude toward baptism. Make your baptism prayer the same as your prayer before you preach. Pray for the blessing of the Holy Spirit to make the sacrament effective in the heart of the recipient. Pray for the Spirit to give understanding and faith. Pray that the sign will point the recipient to Christ's redemption and the Holy Spirit's sanctification. Keep the focus on Jesus.

The Role of the Participants

To keep proper focus, it is necessary that the participants express their faith. This may be done through testimony and having them affirm questions that articulate their faith in Christ and their understanding of baptism. It would seem wise for the minister to address the participants directly with a question that puts baptism in proper perspective. For example, individuals receiving baptism upon profession of faith might be asked:

> Do you receive by faith this sacrament (ordinance), to be a sign given to you by Jesus Christ of being united with him, of the forgiveness and cleansing of sin by his blood and by regeneration of the Holy Spirit, and of being received into his covenant church? Do you receive it as God's seal that you belong to him?

After which, they would then be charged to maintain their profession of faith and commitment to follow Jesus Christ and to serve in his church. A similar question and charge may be given to the parents of children being baptized. The questions laid forth in the Presbyterian Church of America's Book of Church Order 56-5 fill this function well.

The minister should also consider addressing questions and a charge to the congregation as well. If baptism signifies entry into the church, then the church ought to acknowledge its obligations to the baptized. As Reformed churches, we rightly insist that baptism be administered publicly in the church. If so, then we ought to engage the congregation as more than spectators. Often in infant baptism, the congregation is asked a question such as, "Do you as a congregation undertake the responsibility of assisting the parents in the Christian nurture of this child?" (Presbyterian Church of America, Book of Church Order, 56-5). For some reason, that is listed as an optional question. There is no suggestion of asking the congregation anything at a professor's baptism. If we want our people to understand the concept of a covenant people, let us start with the sign of entry into the covenant. Call upon your people to commit to one another at each baptism. Charge the baptized to honor the sign given by living in unity with the church; charge the congregation to be truly a family for the new believer. Charge the parents to raise their children to love the church; charge the congregation to care for the child as their own.

I would discourage pastors from baptizing for sentimental reasons the children of parents who have left your church and yet desire to return. In such a case, the congregation watching is rendered superfluous, as well as the absent congregation in which the child will actually be raised. The same is true for a professor of the faith. To be baptized outside the church, even in a church activity such as a youth retreat, enforces the concept that "my salvation is between only God and me."

Understand that the circumstances of baptism either support the sign's significance or detract from it. If sacramental churches are guilty of over-ritualizing baptism, many of our churches are guilty of undermining its import. This, by the way, is the tremendous aid of tradition, which gives added influence in making the baptism ritual meaningful and protects us from hasty "redesigning" because someone thought a change would be nice.

Judging Valid Baptisms

A practical concern for ministers is judging the validity of a previous baptism. Is a Catholic baptism valid? What about a baptism performed by a liberal minister? What if a person who was baptized upon profession of faith says that he or she really was not a Christian at the time and only later was converted? What if the individual was not sure if the person doing the baptism was a minister?

A helpful discussion of these issues can be found in the majority and minority reports of a Presbyterian Church of America study committee on the validity of certain baptisms.[15] I cannot add to the discussion in determining validity, but I would note pastoral concerns. The pastor must be careful in deliberating the issues and especially in counseling the person concerned not to foil the intent of our Lord when instituting the sacraments. The purpose, remember, is to build up the faith of Christ's sheep, not to create fear and doubt. Handled unwisely, the sacrament intended to strengthen faith and unity in the body can instead undermine faith and create disunity. Do not let your uncertainty of a person's baptism lead to a questioning of one's salvation or place in Christ's church (unless, of course, you have serious doubts about this person's salvation). Be especially cautious of barring someone from membership in the church or from partaking of the Lord's Supper because you are not sure his or her baptism was valid. It is just as serious to withhold such privileges from those who are deserving as it is to grant them to the undeserving.

The pastor must also be careful to make decisions objectively and to lead the individual in question in such a process. First, it ought to be a decision made in counsel with other ministers and/or elders. No individual, neither the person in question nor the minister, should make a decision based on subjective feelings. Again, tradition and the consensus of ordained elders play a strong role. The decision is not determined by what feels right or what would be nice to do. No one should be rebaptized simply because it would be a nice experience. The validity of the previous baptism must be at question, and that validity must be objectively based. Otherwise, baptism is subjected to the same relativism that is attacking the rest of worship—whatever feels right.

Conclusion

What the minister needs to do for his people is keep before them the meaning and purpose of baptism. He needs to keep before them the gospel that is expressed (the meaning) and the blessing for God's people (the purpose). There is, of course, a proper place for the defense of paedobaptism or credobaptism, but where you, the minister, do not need to do that is in the act of administering the sacrament. You are in your church administering the sacred sign to your people. Keep their attention on the glorious promises of the gospel communicated in this blessed sign. Lift up their eyes to their Lord, who has cleansed them from sin and welcomes them into his family. Leave them with the hope and the joy that baptism was intended by our Lord to give.

9

THE LORD'S SUPPER: AN OVERVIEW

RICHARD D. PHILLIPS

It has been aptly remarked that the history of theology consists of the flight from one error into the arms of another. One of the theologian's greatest challenges is to avoid just this, for in fleeing the extremes of another, we all too easily cultivate extremes of our own. There is perhaps no arena of theology and pastoral practice in which this tendency has been more evident than that of the sacraments in general and the Lord's Supper in particular. Therefore, if we seek to honor the Lord through obedience to his word and to benefit rightly from the means of grace he has provided, we will want to exercise particular care in our study of this matter.

The goal of this chapter is to provide an overview and introduction of the Lord's Supper, with an emphasis on the pastoral implications for this element in the worship of God. First, we will turn to the biblical institution to discern the nature and function of the Lord's Supper. Next, we will undertake a compact treatment of key theological issues. Finally, we will draw forth pastoral considerations for the faithful and beneficial administration of this blessed sacrament for the betterment of God's people.

The Biblical Institution

The Lord's Supper receives its name from Paul's usage in 1 Corinthians 11:20. Other common names deriving from Scripture are the Eucharist (from

11:24) and Holy Communion (from 10:16). The Roman Catholic term *Mass* derives from the Latin word *missa*, which was used in early times to dismiss noncommunicants prior to the sacrament but later for dismissing all the people at the end of the liturgy. There is no biblical support for this term.

The Reformers emphasized that a sacrament—that is, a sacred and divine mystery—must have been instituted immediately by our Lord. The Lord's Supper meets this qualification, as recorded in four Bible passages. Three of them come from parallel accounts of the Last Supper in the Synoptic Gospels (Matt. 26:26–30; Mark 14:22–26; Luke 22:19–20), to which Paul adds a fourth account in 1 Corinthians 11:23–26. Matthew 26:26–28 presents the basic biblical institution:

> While they were eating, Jesus took bread, gave thanks and broke it, and gave it to his disciples, saying, "Take and eat; this is my body." Then he took the cup, gave thanks and offered it to them, saying, "Drink from it, all of you. This is my blood of the covenant, which is poured out for many for the forgiveness of sins."

Christ's words establish the basic pattern for the supper, namely the use of bread to signify his body and wine to signify his blood. As these are respectively broken and poured forth, testimony is given to Christ's sacrificial death on the cross. Participation takes the form of eating and drinking. Paul's statement in 1 Corinthians 11:26 further establishes the ongoing and perpetual establishment of the sacrament until the return of Christ: "For whenever you eat this bread and drink this cup, you proclaim the Lord's death until he comes." Finally, the biblical data presents the Lord's Supper in continuity with the Old Testament Passover meal and sets it forth as a sign and seal of the covenant of grace in Christ.

The Lord's Supper and Passover

Benjamin Warfield writes: "Nothing can be more certain than that [Jesus] deliberately chose the Passover Meal for the institution of the sacrament of his body and blood."[1] Mark 14:12 and Luke 22:7–8 make clear that Jesus and his disciples were gathered in the upper room for the Passover meal. By instituting the Lord's Supper on that occasion Jesus intended for this new ordinance to supersede the Passover in the religious life of his disciples.

Not surprisingly, the institution presents a clear continuity with the

Passover. Both are religious feasts in which participation takes the form of eating and drinking. The New Testament elsewhere makes plain that the paschal lamb typified Jesus Christ in his atoning work (John 1:36; 1 Cor. 5:7; 1 Peter 1:19). This same significance is precisely assigned by our Lord to the bread and wine that he held forth in his hands. Any doubt that these signify his death is removed by Paul in 1 Corinthians 11:26: "Proclaim the Lord's death until he comes." Warfield therefore asserts, "The Lord's Supper is the Christian Passover Meal. It takes, and was intended to take, in the Christian Church, the place which the Passover occupied in the Jewish Church. It is the Christian substitute for the Passover."[2]

This being observed, it is worth giving consideration to the Passover meal celebrated in the Old Testament and in the time of Christ. The Passover was a memorial to Israel's exodus deliverance and in particular to the angel of death's passing over the Israelite houses. The first Passover meal was eaten in Egypt on the night of the plague on the firstborn. Exodus 12:3 tells us that the lambs were brought into the Israelite houses to be cared for, indicating an intimacy between the people and the sacrifice. They were to be spotless lambs, which represented fitness to be offered up to the holy God (1 Peter 1:19). The lambs were slaughtered and their blood spread on the sides and tops of the doorframes as a sign, not only for the people but for God. "When I see the blood," said the Lord, "I will pass over you" (Ex. 12:13 [emphasis added]). That night, while the plague brought terror to the homes of Egypt, the Israelites ate the roasted lamb along with bitter herbs and unleavened bread. "This is how you are to eat it," they were told: "with your cloak tucked into your belt, your sandals on your feet and your staff in your hand. Eat it in haste; it is the Lord's Passover" (12:11).

From the first, the Passover was intended as a perpetual memorial. Prominent in its observation was the removal of yeast not merely from the bread but from the entire household. Deuteronomy 16:3 describes unleavened bread as a symbol of haste and affliction — it could be carried conveniently on a long journey and was the kind of bread one prepared on short notice. The New Testament also understands this as a call to holiness through the removal of sin (1 Cor. 5:6–8).

The Passover feast was to be observed by all the covenant community, but by them only. Slaves or resident aliens could partake only after they had received the covenant mark of circumcision (Ex. 12:43–48). An interesting detail is that none of the lamb's bones were to be broken.

Furthermore, according to Deuteronomy 16:16, Passover was one of the three feasts for which the people must appear before the Lord in Jerusalem after Israel had entered into the land. By this means, the descendants of Israel would remember the Lord's deliverance in the exodus and the blood that caused the angel of death to pass over. Three times in the Book of Exodus, fathers are explicitly commanded to tell their children the story of their deliverance by means of the Passover celebration (Ex. 12:26; 13:8, 14). While the exodus was a once-for-all, unrepeated act of deliverance, the Passover was a repetitive rite by which successive generations were bound to that salvation. Hughes Oliphant Old comments: "By participating in the meal, each new generation was added to that people who had been saved from the armies of Pharaoh and the slave-masters of Egypt."[3]

The Lord's Supper as a Sign

Like the Passover, the Lord's Supper was instituted as a sign to the disciples and their future generations. Both Luke and Paul record Jesus saying, "Do this in remembrance of me" (Luke 22:19; 1 Cor. 11:25). The central fact and event signified is the death of Jesus Christ, which our Lord anticipated as imminent. Jesus handed them the bread and said, "This is my body given for you" (Luke 22:19). Then he passed the cup, saying, "This cup is the new covenant in my blood, which is poured out for you" (22:20). Thus the bread and the wine together, as presented with Christ's words, signify Christ's death for his disciples as an atonement for sin. Charles Hodge observes: "Redemption therefore, is not by power, or by teaching, or by moral influence, but by expiation. It is this truth which the Lord's Supper exhibits and authenticates."[4]

In instituting this sacrament, our Lord bore testimony to the primacy of his atoning death at the very heart of the Christian religion. Louis Berkhof adds: "The central fact of redemption, prefigured in the sacrifices of the Old Testament, is clearly set forth by means of the significant symbols of the New Testament sacrament. The words of the institution, 'broken for you' and 'shed for many,' point to the fact that the death of Christ is a sacrificial one, for the benefit, and even in the place, of His people."[5]

Warfield reflects on the substitution of elements, from the paschal lamb to the bread and cup, in signifying a sacrificial death. For all the supper's continuity with the Passover meal, a new form is unmistakably given. The main reason for this change, he says, has to do with the central act of re-

196

demptive history that was unfolding even as the Lord gathered that last time with his disciples before his arrest. Warfield writes, "He to whom all the Paschal lambs from the beginning had been pointing was about to be offered up. The old things were passing away; behold, all things were to become new."[6]

This transition was made vivid in the actual events of Jesus' last week, since his triumphal entry into Jerusalem coincided with the masses of lambs being shepherded into the city and his crucifixion coincided with the lambs' slaughter in the Passover celebration. The antitype having come, therefore, it could no longer be fitting to set forth the type that so long had represented it. A number of changes, Warfield notes, were linked to this great fulfillment and transition. The Jewish state was to be dissolved, along with the ritual law and its sacrifices. In keeping with the finished work of Christ's atoning death, this sacrament required no altar. Furthermore, in line with the universal character of the redemption offered up by Christ, no central location was prescribed. While the symbolism remained essentially the same—wrath passing over because of a sacrifice's shed blood—the symbols were changed to represent the newness of a saving event that would explode the bounds of Israel's prior redemptive experience.

The elements of the Lord's Supper present Christ's death to the senses of his people. But more is signified in its administration. The eating of the elements by believers signifies their participation in the crucified Christ. Berkhof teaches: "They symbolically appropriate the benefits secured by the sacrificial death of Christ."[7] Additionally, the partaking of the sacrament signifies the effect of Christ's death in giving life and strength to the soul, as food and drink sustain the body. Furthermore, just as the sacrament symbolizes the believers' union with Christ, it also places a visible difference between members of Christ's church and the world, while signifying believers' communion one to another in him.

The Lord's Supper as a Covenant Seal

The Westminster Confession of Faith refers to this sacrament and baptism as "holy signs and seals of the covenant of grace" (27.1). Perhaps the best way to understand the idea of a covenant seal is to realize that the Passover was not merely a religious feast but was also a covenant meal at which God identifies his people, accepts them as his own, and spreads before them his provision.

197

The Book of Genesis records the importance of meals in establishing a covenant relationship. We think of Abraham receiving bread and wine from the hands of Melchizedek after he had tithed the spoils of his victory over the eastern kings (Gen. 14), as well as the meal he prepared the angelic visitors (Gen. 18). Significantly, Isaac sent his son Esau to prepare a meal for the occasion of his dispensing the covenant blessing (27:4). When the Lord confirmed his covenant with Moses and the people at Mount Sinai, he called Moses and Aaron and the seventy elders onto the mountain. Moses sprinkled the blood of the covenant on the altar and on the book of the covenant; then he and the elders went up to the Lord, looking upon him in the sapphire sea: "They saw God, and they ate and drank" (Ex. 24:11). Finally, the ongoing history of Israel shows the importance of the covenant meal at times of confirmation and recommitment. When Joshua led the second generation across the Jordan and into the promised land, he first brought them before the Lord to reconfirm the covenant, to receive the covenant sign of circumcision, and then to eat the Passover meal before the Lord (Josh. 5:10). Centuries later, when Josiah rediscovered the book of the law in the temple he tore down the idols and renewed the covenant. Prominent in the biblical account of this return to covenant faithfulness was the reestablishment of the Passover celebration, which had been neglected during the years of infidelity (2 Kings 23:21–23).

Therefore, when the minister today holds forth the bread and the cup of the Lord's Supper, he does so on Christ's behalf as Christ sets forth a meal before his covenant people. This is foreshadowed in the Passover, which was more than a memorial meal. Those who gathered at the table entered into covenant with the Lord and thus received the benefits of his saving provision. Just as the blood marked the houses of those who would be passed over by the angel of death, Jesus marked the disciples as his own, holding forth the cup and saying, "This cup is the new covenant in my blood" (1 Cor. 11:25). In this way, Jesus sealed them to the benefits of his atoning death, bringing them into the bonds of his new covenant of salvation. Old comments: "Jesus bound his disciples to himself in this covenant meal before he went to the cross and passed from death to life."[8] Likewise today, partaking of the Lord's Supper by eating and drinking is a way of entering into covenant with Christ, for the benefits and obligations thus involved.

The Lord's Supper seals God's people by giving them a reliable attestation of their participation in Christ. It is Christ who thus identifies his own, stretching forth his hand to give them the bread and the cup of his covenant meal. John Murray says: "When we partake of the cup in faith, it is the Lord's own certification to us that all that the new covenant in his blood involves is ours. It is the seal of his grace and faithfulness."[9] Berkhof points out that this sealing assures us that we are the recipients of Christ's atoning work: The Lord's Supper "seals to the participant the great love of Christ . . . it assures the believing participant . . . that he was personally the object of that incomparable love." Furthermore, it confirms to the believer that all the promises of the covenant and all the blessings of salvation "are his in actual possession." Finally, it is a reciprocal seal whereby believers through participation "profess their faith in Christ as Savior and their allegiance to Him as their King, and they solemnly pledge a life of obedience to His divine commandments."[10]

Theological Issues

To surely a majority of professing believers today, the various theological issues surrounding the Lord's Supper are at best a subject of academic interest and at worst a needless source of division. This, perhaps more than any other distinction, marks the divergence between our contemporary mindset and that of our Protestant forebearers.

The issue of the presence of Christ has played an especially prominent role in theological dispute since the Reformation. It was this issue that thwarted union between the German Lutherans and the Swiss Reformed in the crucial early years of the Reformation, with the result that Zurich was bereft of aid and fell to the Roman Catholic sword. In the English Reformation, it was this that supplied the formal cause for the death of the Marian martyrs at Smithfield. If one were to ask such martyrs as Ridley and Latimer why they were willing to die for a matter of merely academic interest, they would have rightly replied that what they were dying for was the gospel.

Other theological issues necessary to an overview of the Lord's Supper deal with the nature of its efficacy and the question of its necessity. These may appear to be matters of slight import, in which we may safely let each professing believer act as seems best. But, in fact, these matters exert a controlling influence on our whole practical system of religion. The questions they treat include how sinners may apprehend the benefits of Christ's atoning work, and as such they shape our whole approach to the matter of salvation. Therefore, upon inspection, resentment toward a consideration of these theological issues reveals not a laudable practicality but an ominous disinterest in salvation truth.

The Presence of Christ

The question arises as to whether and in what sense Christ may be seen to be present in the sacrament. There are three basic views, namely that Christ is *not* present in the supper, that Christ is *physically* present, and that Christ is *spiritually* present.

Christ not present in the sacrament. The view that Christ is not present is generally attributed to the Swiss Reformer Zwingli and is often represented today as "the Zwinglian view," although it fails to do justice to all of Zwingli's writings, especially his later views. According to this position the Lord's Supper is a simple sign, a commemoration of Christ's atoning death, and an emblem of the believer's trust in him. This position is especially directed against an unintelligible mysticism or a magical understanding of the supper, and it places particular emphasis on the role of faith in the Lord's Supper. Zwingli especially directed his own view against the corporeal presence of Christ in the sacrament as understood by the Roman Catholic Church.

Hodge cites the "Sincere Confession of the Ministers of the Church of Zurich," dated 1545, as the best presentation of this view. Here we read not merely that the benefits of the Lord's Supper require faith in the recipient, but that the sacrament contains no spiritual blessing that cannot equally be had elsewhere by faith. It emphasizes that Christ is neither more nor less present in the sacrament than anywhere else: "He has truly eaten the bread of Christ who believes on Christ. . . . Believers have in the Lord's Supper no other life-giving food than that which they receive elsewhere than in that ordinance. The believer, therefore, receives both in and out of the Lord's Supper, in one and the same way, and by the same means of faith, one and the same food, Christ." The Lord's Supper, then, is no more than a memorial that sets forth the symbols so as to prompt the exercise of faith, although it is an occasion "accompanied with a testifying, thanksgiving, and binding service."[11]

Among those who strongly object to this teaching is John Calvin, who saw in this an overemphasis on human activity against that of God, as well as on the past work of Christ against his present spiritual work through the Holy Spirit.[12] In terms of biblical support, the Zwinglian view fails to incorporate all the data offered by the our Lord and the apostles, much of which goes beyond mere memorial language. Christ, for instance, did not merely display the elements for the disciples to look at and remember, but he offered them for the disciples to eat. Surely these actions indicate the way in which the sacrament confers spiritual blessing and thus demand that we go far beyond the memorialist view. Furthermore, the Apostle Paul makes plain that partaking of this meal involves genuine spiritual reality, so that recipients participate in the blood and body of Christ (1 Cor. 10:16), and an unworthy partaker not only offends the Lord but "eats and drinks judgment on himself" (11:29).

The Zwinglian or memorialist position protects its adherents from Roman Catholic sacerdotalism and superstition, but it runs into an error of rationalism on the other extreme. It is no surprise, therefore, that this view of the sacrament as a bare memorial is typically accompanied by a de-emphasis in its significance and an infrequency of its celebration. Surely this low view of the spirituality of the Lord's Supper has contributed to a readiness to substitute human inventions such as the revivalist's altar call, which under this view may seem to offer no worse and perhaps a more persuasive impetus for drawing forth faith.

Christ physically present in the sacrament. The view that Christ is physically present is held by both Roman Catholics and Lutherans, although considerable differences exist between the two. In the Roman view, there is no sacramental union at all, that is, a union in which the thing signified is present by means of the sign. Instead, they maintain that there is a transformation of the former elements into the corporeal body of Jesus Christ. Berkhof summarizes: "When the priest utters the formula, '*hoc est corpus meum*,' bread and wine change into the body and blood of Christ."[13] The elements continue to look like bread and wine, but in that form the physical body and blood of Christ are physically present. For this reason, the elevation and adoration of the physical elements of the supper is justified and encouraged, as indeed it must be. One Roman Catholic explains: "We treat them as we would treat God, because that is what they are."[14] The Roman Catholic catechism affirms this view: "Under the consecrated species of bread and wine Christ himself, living and glorious, is present in a true, real, and substantial manner: his Body and his Blood, with his soul and his divinity."[15] This consideration greatly shapes the Roman view of the efficacy of the sacrament, as we will see below.

Luther rejected this doctrine of transubstantiation, holding instead to a view known as consubstantiation. According to him, the elements are not transformed into body and blood, but rather in a mysterious and miraculous way Christ's whole person — body and blood — is present in, under, and along with the elements of the sacrament. In this way, the physical body of Christ is locally present in the Lord's Supper, although the elements themselves undergo no transformation. Therefore, while emphasizing the role of faith along with the Zwinglians, Lutherans also agree with Rome that in the sacrament Christ's body and blood are physically eaten "with the bodily mouth."

Both the Roman and the Lutheran view of the physical presence of Christ's body and blood rely on an absolutely literal interpretation of Christ's words as he handed the bread and the cup to the disciples: "This is my body . . . this is my blood." (The Roman position, however, is more literal here than the Lutheran.) But contrary to this, it is obvious that the relationship between these elements and Christ's body and blood was representative and sacramental. Jesus was bodily present at the time: it was his hands that held forth the bread; it was before his blood was yet spilled on Calvary that he lifted the cup. Berkhof notes: "It is quite impossible to conceive of the bread which Jesus broke as being the body which was handling it; and it should be noted that Scripture calls it bread even after it is supposed to have been transubstantiated, 1 Cor. 10:17; 11:26–28."[16] As R. L. Dabney points out, Christ elsewhere refers to himself as the way, the vine, and the door, yet no one doubts the figurative sense in which these are spoken; to likewise deny the figurative meaning of the bread and wine as Christ's body and blood is to enter into the absurd.[17]

Additional support for the physical view of Christ's presence is drawn from Jesus' remarks in John 6:50–59, on the occasion of his feeding the five thousand: "This bread is my flesh, which I will give for the life of the world. . . . Whoever eats my flesh and drinks my blood has eternal life, and I will raise him up at the last day" (John 6:51, 54). The argument is made that this proves that the sacrament involves eating the flesh of Christ.

Two points refute this argument, however. First is careful consideration of the text. In verse 63 Jesus argues that his meaning is spiritual in nature; already in verses 35, 40, and 47 he links the idea of eating his flesh to "coming to him" and "believing in him." Therefore the bread of John 6 directs us to Christ's atoning death received by faith, not to the sacrament of the Lord's Supper. The bread with which Jesus fed the multitude was a sign, but it did not signify another sign. Rather, it set forth the same reality depicted both in the miracle of the loaves and in the sacrament. The episode and discourse of John 6 is indeed analogous to the institution of the Lord's Supper, but it does not directly refer to it. Like the sacrament, it refers us to the death of our Lord; and like the sacrament, it informs us that we must partake of Christ's death by faith.

For these reasons, John 6 is better seen as militating *against* the idea of our partaking Christ's physical presence in the sacrament literally by eating and drinking, instead arguing for our spiritual partaking of him by faith. This first argument, from the text itself, is sufficiently persuasive. But second, this sacramental understanding of John 6 requires Jesus to have taught the necessity of the sacrament before it was even instituted and implies the automatic salvation of everyone who simply participates in the rite. As Dabney argues, "The Lord's Supper was not even instituted; it is absurd to suppose that our Saviour would use language necessarily unintelligible to all His followers, the subject never having been divulged to them."[18]

The Westminster Confession of Faith directs its rejection of Christ's physical presence specifically against the Roman doctrine of transubstantiation, without direct consideration of the Lutheran view: "That doctrine which maintains a change of the substance of bread and wine, into the substance of Christ's body and blood (commonly called transubstantiation) by consecration of a priest, or by any other way, is repugnant, not to Scripture alone, but even to common-sense and reason; overthrows the nature of the sacrament; and has been, and is the cause of manifold superstitions, yea, of gross idolatries" (29.6). Both the Roman and the Lutheran views of Christ's physical presence involve implications fatal to the theology of salvation, implications they themselves would deny but that logically follow from the physical presence of Christ in the sacrament. This teaching requires Christ's human body to be universally present, and such ubiquity necessitates its partaking in the attributes of divinity. In that case, Christ's true humanity is compromised, even violated, so that he is disqualified from his mediatorial work on which our salvation entirely depends. Calvin argues the vital significance of this point and pleads that it constrain any views of the physical presence of Christ in the sacrament: "Let nothing inappropriate to human nature be ascribed to his body, as happens when it is said either to be infinite or to be put in a number of places at once."[19]

Christ spiritually present in the sacrament. Our critique of the memorialist view noticed that the biblical institution mandates the true presence of Christ in some sense (see again 1 Cor. 10:16; 11:29). We do not merely reflect upon Christ's death, but we in some way eat what is offered. The view that Christ is spiritually present, which is the main Reformed doctrine on this matter, incorporates this realization with a rejection of a physical presence. Christ himself is present in the sacrament by means of the Holy Spirit. The Westminster Larger Catechism explains: "The body and blood of Christ . . . are spiritually present to the faith of the receiver, no less truly and really than the elements themselves are to their outward senses." Therefore, the communicant "feed[s] upon the body and blood of Christ, not after a corporal and carnal, but in a spiritual manner; yet truly and really, while by faith they receive and apply to themselves Christ crucified, and all the benefits of his death" (Q. 170).

Important to this approach is an understanding that "the sacrament is connected not merely with the past work of Christ, with the Christ who died . . . but also with the present spiritual work of Christ, with the Christ that is alive in glory."[20] Christ is present not in the elements, which serve the purpose of signifying his atoning death, but rather as the one who offers the benefits of that death through the ministry of the Holy Spirit by which he is truly present to the believer in the sacrament. Hodge elaborates: "Anything is said to be present when it operates duly on our perceiving faculties. . . . Christ is present when He thus fills the mind, sheds abroad his love in our hearts by the Holy Ghost given unto us; and not only communicates to us the benefits of his sufferings and death, that is, the remission of our sins and reconciliation with God, but also infuses his life into us." He concludes: "Nothing is plainer from Scripture than that there is this communication of life from Christ to his people. . . . This is a presence to us and in us which is not imaginary, but in the highest sense real and effective."[21]

The Efficacy of the Sacrament

Inseparable but distinct from the question of Christ's presence in the Lord's Supper is the nature of its efficacy. Here we will first consider what is the grace conferred in the supper, followed by a consideration of the manner in which such grace is communicated.

The grace conferred. The question arises as to what benefit, spiritual or otherwise, the communicant receives through the right partaking of the Lord's Supper. Again we should take our first cues from the institution, which indicates that the spiritual benefits we receive in the sacrament are analogous to those benefits received by the body through eating and drinking. In the Lord's Supper, then, the believer is strengthened and fed, receiving sustenance and life. In keeping with the sacrament as a sign, we gain from it a quickened faith; as a seal of Christ's covenant we gain increasing assurance of salvation and communion with God. Old sums up our benefit in the sacrament in terms of the union between the sign and the reality signified: "The outward sign of the meal speaks of nourishment for eternal life. The worshiper taking part in the service can be sure that what the outward and visible sign promises will take place inwardly and invisibly. This . . . is the work of the Holy Spirit."[22]

According to Roman Catholics, the Lord's Supper is not only a sacrament, but it is also a *sacrifice*, a renewal of Christ's death upon the cross. Berkhof explains: "The sacrifice of Christ in the Lord's Supper is considered to be a real sacrifice, and is supposed to have propitiatory value."[23] In carefully worded language the Roman Catholic catechism denies that a different sacrifice is offered than that of the cross, but rather "it re-presents (makes present) the sacrifice of the cross, because it is its memorial and because it applies its fruit. . . . In this divine sacrifice which is celebrated in the Mass, the same Christ who offered himself once in a bloody manner on the altar of the cross is contained and is offered in an un-bloody manner."[24] As such, the sacrament not only gives assurance of redemption, but itself actually remits sins for which it is offered. Just as communicants commit fresh sins, so the sacrifice of Christ is freshly offered for them in the Mass.

This understanding of the Lord's Supper as a sacrifice must be rejected as denying the vital matter of the sufficiency of Christ's once-for-all atoning death (Rom. 6:10; Heb. 7:27; 9:12, 26; 10:10). Instead of as a sacrifice that creates grace, as Rome understands it, the sacrament must be seen as strengthening grace that is already present by virtue of Christ's once-for-all offering of his blood and that is received through faith in the gospel.

The manner in which grace is conferred. Crucial to our understanding of the Lord's Supper is the issue of how it works. The answer to this question is inevitably linked to the view of the Lord's presence in the supper. In general, we may understand that the Zwinglian view sees no grace being conferred, properly speaking, while the view of a real physical presence considers that the physical eating of the elements confers the grace. The

Reformed doctrine of a real spiritual presence sees the grace conferred by the ministry of the Holy Spirit as Christ is received by faith. In this latter view, grace is received via the sacrament in the same manner as through the word, namely, through faith.

According to Roman Catholics, the benefits of the Lord's Supper are received *ex opere operato,* that is, by the doing it is done. This is because the grace is contained in the elements themselves, the priest having caused the change of its substance into divine matter. Everyone who partakes, therefore, regardless of their faith or unbelief, piety or irreligion, automatically receives the benefits of the sacrament, including remission of their sins. Rome does allow that this conveyance may be frustrated by an indisposition of the receiving soul to the blessings so offered, except in the case of so-called mortal sins.[25]

Lutherans do not hold this same position, since for them faith is necessary to any real blessing. In a view that is not easily summarized, they hold that the virtue of the sacrament is inherent in the elements themselves, having Christ's physical presence, independent of both the Holy Spirit and the faith of the recipient. But even though the virtue or power of Christ's blessing is in the elements, faith is necessary to our receiving the blessing, because it is faith that leads the communicant to the Lord's Supper. Luther illustrated this with the woman whose issue of blood was healed in the gospels. The power was in Christ himself, but it was touching the hem of Christ's robe that healed her. It was only by faith that she touched the garment and received benefit from the virtue inherent in Christ.

The view that best accords with the biblical evidence we have already examined is the Reformed view, which denies that any efficacy is found in the elements themselves. Hodge explains: "The efficacy does not reside in the elements . . . in the bread and wine used in the Lord's Supper. It is not in the sacramental actions . . . [or] from the person by whom they are administered. . . . The efficacy of the sacrament is due solely to the blessing of Christ and the working of his Spirit. . . . [God] has promised, through the attending operation of his Spirit, to render the sacraments effectual."[26] Christ is present at the table by means of the Holy Spirit, and it is the Spirit who applies Christ's redemptive benefits to the communicant who believes.

There are two ways of considering this spiritual blessing, however. In the first, the Spirit is considered to bring mystical union with Christ in heaven, in terms of both his human and his divine nature. This was emphasized by

Calvin, who saw the believer spiritually and mystically communing with Christ in his entire person, body and blood. Thus he understood that believers are blessed in the Lord's Supper by being lifted up into heaven where Christ now is, to mystically feed upon him wholly. This view is not universally accepted in Reformed circles, although in a carefully crafted paragraph the Westminster Confession does not go out of its way either to explicitly endorse or refute it. The confession says that the worthy receiver does "spiritually, receive, and feed upon, Christ crucified, and all benefits of His death" (29.7).

A. A. Hodge, in his commentary on the Westminster Confession, steers the reader away from inferring Calvin's view from that language.[27] Dabney writes convincingly when he says the confession means to limit our understanding so that "the thing which the soul actually embraces is not the corporeal substance of His slain body and shed blood, but their Redeeming virtue,"[28] that is, the spiritual blessings of his atoning death. Dabney suspects that Calvin was motivated in this matter by "personal attachment to Melanchthon [a Lutheran leader], and by a desire to heal the lamentable dissensions of Reformed and Lutherans." He, like many others in the Westminster tradition, looks upon Calvin's teaching on this point as a curious inconsistency in his normally coherent thought. In support of Dabney's view, we observe that the Westminster Larger Catechism's strong statement that "the body and blood of Christ . . . are spiritually present to the faith of the receiver," is then qualified by the conclusion that what we receive thereby is "Christ crucified, and all the benefits of his death" (Q. 170). Therefore, while extolling the blessing of mystical communion with the body and blood of Christ, the Westminster Standards take care to focus this spiritual blessing as arising out of Christ's body as crucified for us, rather than out of Christ's corporeal humanity as such.

Francis Turretin, however, writes in support of Calvin's view, helpfully putting it in these terms: "Christ is inseparable from his benefits. The believers under the Old Testament are rightly said to have been made partakers of Christ himself and so of his body and blood, which were present to their faith. Hence they are said to have drunk of the rock, which was Christ (1 Cor. 10:4)."[29]

The way of understanding this matter of spiritual blessing most broadly held among the Reformed is that through the Supper the Holy Spirit confers the benefits of Christ's atonement to the believing recipient. Here, the emphasis is not on the bread and blood as representing the corporeal body of Christ, but as they are broken and shed for us in his atoning death. This is most consistent with Christ's own institution, in which his body was set forth not as such but as given for us on the cross, not merely his blood as such but as it was poured out through pierced feet and hands. What the believer feeds upon, therefore, is not Christ's body as such but the redemptive benefits that he offers through his saving death. This is what the Lord's Supper especially sets before us: Christ crucified, who in the sacrament conveys to our faith all the blessings contained in the giving of his life for those who believe.

This is consistent with the functioning of all ancient sacrificial meals, that by partaking of the sacrifice one claimed a part in the benefits so procured. Likewise, we by eating and drinking in faith partake of the blessings that Christ provides through his sacrifice. Surely these blessings in Christ are not different from the ones extolled in Paul's hymn of praise in Ephesians 1: a seal of election, adoption into God's family, redemption with forgiveness for our sins, the deposit of the Spirit in anticipation of our full inheritance. All these blessings are applied to our faith by the ministry of the Holy Spirit, whom the living Christ sends from heaven. The sacrament is not a converting ordinance; that is, it does not convey these blessings to those who have never known them before. Rather, for those who have already received them through faith in the gospel and by the ministry of God's word, the apprehension of these great and saving blessings is "increased and strengthened" (Westminster Confession of Faith 14.1).

In this understanding, it is not we who ascend to heaven, as Calvin puts it, but Christ who comes to us by the Spirit among the trials of this world. The blessings come across to us from beyond the Jordan, while still we journey through this desert life toward the promised land ahead. As Joshua and the spies brought back to Moses the abundant and extraordinarily large fruit of Canaan—fruit that heartened the soul with anticipation just as its juice gave joy to the mouth—so also the Holy Spirit brings into our life of difficulty the very sweets of heaven, leading us onward toward our destination with renewed vigor and gladness of soul.

In all the above, we are stressing the objective nature of the sacrament in its gracious efficacy. The Westminster Confession adds to this the importance of our being "worthy receivers," saying that "all ignorant and ungodly persons, as they are unfit to enjoy communion with him, so are they unworthy of the Lord's Table" (29.7–8). In 1 Corinthians 11:28, Paul writes that "a man ought to examine himself before he eats of the bread and drinks of the cup." This is a matter we will take up later in this chapter. For now it will suffice to observe that, as in all the Christian life, the grace offered in the sacrament is an objective grace that presents itself to the subjective repentance and faith of the receiver. Christians do not have to work up in themselves the grace they are seeking from Christ; they merely have to present themselves sincerely, trusting and seeking with a readiness to do the will of the Lord who blesses them with his body and blood.

The Necessity of the Sacrament

The final theological issue for us to consider is the necessity of the Lord's Supper. Roman Catholics and Lutherans hold that the sacrament is necessary to salvation in that the grace thus conveyed is not otherwise available. The Reformed view denies this necessity, asserting that the grace received in the sacrament is otherwise available through faith in the word of the gospel. Berkhof argues this on four considerations: (1) Given "the free spiritual character of the gospel dispensation . . . God does not bind His grace to the use of certain external forms." (2) Scripture regards only faith as "an instrumental condition of salvation." (3) The sacraments are not necessary because they "do not originate faith but presuppose it, and are administered where faith is assumed." (4) The Bible shows many people being saved without the use of the sacraments.[30]

The Lord's Supper is not necessary in and of itself as a means of salvation, yet we must acknowledge a necessity resulting from Christ's command. Hodge explains: "No one would be willing to say . . . that it is unnecessary to obey an explicit command of Christ. And as He has commanded his disciples . . . to commemorate his death by the celebration of the Lord's Supper, the strongest moral obligation rests upon his people to obey these commands."[31] The sacrament itself is not necessary to salvation, but obedience to Christ's command with regard to the Lord's Supper is, and in this limited sense we rightly think of the sacrament as necessary and are thus obliged to celebrate it regularly and faithfully.

While few in Reformed circles would openly assert the necessity of the sacraments in the former sense, in that its grace is not otherwise available, a neo-sacerdotalism rising today so emphasizes the Lord's Supper as to convey this impression. This Reformed sacerdotalism is seen when zealous proponents read the sacraments into key passages about Christ's saving work, such as John 3:5; 6:47–58; and Romans 10:4. These passages make contributions to our understanding of the sacraments, but they refer to the reality of partaking in Christ through faith, not to the sacraments themselves. It is noteworthy that two of these passages were taught by our Lord before the sacraments were even instituted. Nonetheless, many interpreters download a sacramental meaning as if a reference to the reality necessitates the sign. Such an overemphasis gives the impression that Christ died so as to offer us the sacraments, through which we receive the benefits of his saving work.

The best way to avoid an unbalanced sacerdotalism is to properly distinguish between the word, which is necessary to salvation, and the sacraments, which do not share this quality. The Lord's Supper is not a converting ordinance, since it presupposes faith, and it is not able to replace the word as a most singular means of grace. Still, the sacrament is greatly blessed by our Lord as it is joined to the word as a powerful but supplemental means of grace for those who belong to Christ.

Pastoral Considerations

Given the weightiness of the matters we have considered and their implications for the right approach to the Lord's Supper, we see how important is the pastoral practice with which it is set before the congregation. Along this line we will consider the sacrament's presentation to the congregation, the right practice of restricted Communion, the matter of worthy partaking, and the frequency with which the Lord's Supper should be celebrated.

Presentation of the Lord's Supper

My first pulpit ministry took place in a service that included the weekly celebration of the Lord's Supper. Thus, I concluded each sermon at the table, reading the words of the institution and making connections between what I had said and what I now set forth. Robert Godfrey writes about what a difference it would likely make in much of our preaching "if every sermon had to end in the Lord's Supper. Would it give a healthy new dimension to the way our sermons develop and conclude? Would it force us back to the central things of the gospel?"[32] My own experience is that it does.

210

Surely it is a healthy gauge of our preaching to ask whether what we have said in the sermon would be of any help in explaining the bread and the cup set forth on the table of the Lord.

It is essential that the physical elements of the Lord's Supper be accompanied by the words of our Lord's institution, normally those given by Paul in 1 Corinthians 11:23–26. This establishes both the authority with which we offer his grace and a biblical explanation of its meaning. This should be done simply and without elaboration. Then, the minister should make brief and forceful comments pressing upon the people the solemnity of the occasion, relating the sacrament to the sermon's redemptive message and briefly instructing the people as to their participation.

Ministers should realize the great pastoral value of the Lord's Supper as it personally confronts each person present with the reality of their own relationship to God. People may endure the sermon with studied indifference, but when the bread and wine are set before them they must make a decision about what they are going to do and what it means to them. The minister's remarks should bear this in mind and should directly challenge them to assess the state of their spirit and the actual religion they profess. The minister is wise to confront false ways of approaching the supper, especially those of unbelief and of works righteousness, but also to encourage the true believer who is faint of heart. Here is the true altar call that ministers are to give the people of God, where weary Christians are called to revival and the unbelieving world is called to repent and believe.

Given that this volume is presented in honor of James Montgomery Boice, two choice examples come to my mind from his ministry. On one occasion Dr. Boice preached a passage from the Gospel of Matthew that clearly explained the death of Christ for sinners. It happened to be a Sunday on which we were celebrating the Lord's Supper. Dr. Boice approached the table gravely, read Paul's words of institution from 1 Corinthians 11, then looked out upon the congregation and stopped. Gazing into the eyes seemingly of every man, woman, and child present, he solemnly exclaimed: "Let no one here today, in life or in death, ever declare that they have not heard the Gospel of Jesus Christ." Then he briefly pressed upon us the eternal significance of what we had heard and the need to submit our hearts to God if we hoped to be saved. The simplicity and directness of his presentation worked a memorable solemnity upon the proceedings, so that the word and sacrament combined to powerfully set forth the gospel's demands.

211

The second instance was at the conclusion of a New Year's Eve watch-night service held annually at Tenth Presbyterian Church. This is a service of open sharing of testimonies, followed by a brief reception, with the congregation regathering in the sanctuary to celebrate the Lord's Supper as the new year rings in at midnight. Given the church's location in downtown Philadelphia, with the city's worldly revelry forcing itself into the quiet of the sanctuary, this is a solemn occasion in which the church is vividly set apart from the world.

This was especially the case on December 31, 1999, the last of these services officiated by Dr. Boice. Millennium excitement filled the media, and excessive anxiety attended the Y2K computer scare. None present will ever forget, therefore, Dr. Boice standing before the Lord's Table and telling us how he had been watching the television reports of the new millennium rolling into one time zone after another, as it now entered into our own. He commented on the great focus given to the threat to our computers and then said words to this effect: "Understand, however, that your problem is not that your computer might stop working, but that you are going to die. Having died, you are going to stand in judgment before God and if you have not come to him through Jesus Christ, as represented here in his death on the cross, then you will condemned forever." Not a sound was heard, and with the greatest sobriety the congregation received in faith the supper of our Lord. Little did we know that it was James Boice who soon would die, and many remembered that New Year's Eve celebration and commented that he was prepared for death because of his confidence in the great atoning work he set before us with the bread and wine.

In presenting the Lord's Supper, ministers will find no end of opportunities to connect it with the redemptive themes of their sermons. This is no surprise, since all of our life in Christ, the whole spectrum of Christian salvation, passes through the cross of our Lord, which is the explicit subject of the Lord's Supper. I would like, however, to suggest a few redemptive themes that are especially connected to the Eucharist and that may serve as examples for the much larger whole of related themes.

I have already mentioned the Passover, and our congregations should be thoroughly familiar with this theme in connection with the Lord's Supper. They should hear of Israel's deliverance from bondage to Pharaoh and of our redemption from the Egypt of our sin. They should know of the angel of death that passed by because of the blood and how God's wrath is propitiated by the blood represented on the table. They should remember our pilgrim status and the bitterness of life and the afflictions recalled to us by the unleavened bread. The Passover is a theme that ministers should regularly recall in their presentation of the sacrament. On the occasion of Holy Communion we should sing hymns like this from John of Damascus:

> Come, ye faithful, raise the strain
> of triumphant gladness;
> God has brought his Israel
> into joy from sadness;
> Loosed from Pharaoh's bitter yoke
> Jacob's sons and daughters;
> Led them with unmoistened foot
> through the Red Sea waters.

It is helpful for ministers to rehearse the events of that night on which our Lord instituted the supper and was later arrested. We should speak of the dismay with which the disciples heard of the cross, but the words of comfort Jesus gave. Christians should know of the two cups spoken of on that night. Handing over the wine, the cup of fellowship and gladness, it is noteworthy that Jesus himself did not drink it (Matt. 26:29). Instead he withdrew to the garden of Gethsemane, where with blood-tinged sweat he prayed to the Father about the other cup he would drink to the bottom (26:39, 42). Jesus drank the cup of wrath on the cross, down to its bitterest dregs, so that he might extend to us the cup of blessing in salvation.

This points us forward as well to the wedding feast of the Lamb to which we are invited through Jesus' death (Rev. 19:9), the very wine of heaven which we now drink indeed by faith. Horatius Bonar thus writes of the Lord's Supper:

> This is the hour of banquet and of song;
> this is the heavenly table spread for me:
> Here let me feast, and feasting still prolong
> the brief bright hour of fellowship with thee.

The Lord's Supper contains within itself a lesson on the history of redemption. It directs our attention to the past, even as our Lord commanded us to "do this in remembrance of me." Christians are people who look back on the death of Christ as the pivotal moment in all history. But Christians also look forward, even as Paul tells us, "Whenever you eat this bread and drink this cup, you proclaim the Lord's death until he comes" (1 Cor. 11:26). We are those whose eyes are fixed on the future horizon when our Lord returns in glory and in power.

But the sacrament also speaks to the present. Christians gather before the Lord's Table like Israel in the desert seeking provision. We are pilgrims on our sojourn to Canaan, and here is the spiritual manna through which we gain strength for the long journey yet ahead. Here is the drink for the parched lips of our souls, brought forth not by the striking of the rock but by the striking of Christ upon the cross. Like Abraham coming to Melchizedek from the weariness of his battles, we come to God through Christ to be fed, provisioned, refreshed, and renewed. The sacrament is a mighty lesson in the history of redemption and therefore on God's provision for us in the trials of this life. Bonar, again, puts it so well:

> Here would I feed upon the bread of God,
> here drink with thee the royal wine of heaven;
> Here would I lay aside each earthly load,
> here taste afresh the calm of sin forgiv'n.

Restricted Communion

Given God's promise of blessing through the sacrament, many find it difficult to understand why we must keep people from communing. But study of Scripture reveals a clear mandate to restricted Communion, to which ministers are bound to adhere and communicants to observe.

Murray explains the principle of restricted Communion: "Not all without distinction are eligible to come to the Lord's Table. . . . When Jesus preached the gospel he made no difference between men. . . . But when he instituted the Lord's Supper he sat down with his disciples. This betokens its distinguishing character; it is for disciples."[33] Murray explains the principles by which the table is to be fenced:

> The Lord's Supper is not for all indiscriminately as the gospel is. The Lord's Supper is chiefly commemoration and communion. It is for those who discern the Lord's body, who can commemorate his death in faith and love. And

since the supper is also Communion it is obviously for those who commune with Christ and with one another in the unity of the body which is the church. . . . It is part of the whole counsel of God that those conditions be clearly and insistently set forth, to the end that those who are eligible partake and those who are not refrain.[34]

The New Testament clearly articulates certain categories according to which people should refrain from the Lord's Supper. The first of these is that nonbelievers must not participate in the sacrament. Paul writes: "Anyone who eats and drinks without recognizing the body of the Lord eats and drinks judgment on himself" (1 Cor. 11:29). This applies to Christians who irreverently partake, a particular concern of Paul's in 1 Corinthians, but in general to all who look upon the bread and wine without perceiving their spiritual meaning.

Furthermore, Paul plainly warns against believers who participate in "an unworthy manner" and are thus "guilty of sinning against the body and blood of the Lord." To guard against this, he says, "A man ought to examine himself before he eats of the bread and drinks of the cup" (11:27–28). A separate treatment of worthy partaking follows below, but we should note here that willfully unrepentant sin compromises our communion with Christ. Christians should be warned to repent of sins that are brought to mind in their self-examination. If they are unwilling to repent—and this should be sharply differentiated from weakness in carrying through with repentance—they must refrain from the supper, which is, Paul says, participation in Christ's body and blood (10:16).

Third, the Lord's Supper should be restricted to those in unbroken communion with their fellow Christians. The reason for this is that the sacrament entails a real participation in the church's spiritual unity in Christ, as Paul asserts in 1 Corinthians 10:17. Ordinarily, this will mean membership in a gospel-believing church, since membership (upon a credible profession of faith and receipt of the initiatory sacrament of baptism) is the normal expression of being a part of the church's communion. This also means that Christians who are under the discipline of the church or who have unreconciled hostility with another member of the congregation are to refrain from the supper.

In this latter respect, frequent partaking is a great aid in resolving church divisions and promoting fervent spiritual brotherhood. Calvin observes: "As often as we partake of the symbol of the Lord's body, as a token given and received, we reciprocally bind ourselves to all the duties of love in order that none of us may permit anything to harm our brother, or overlook anything that can help him."[35] Christians ought therefore to prepare for the supper by seeking reconciliation with others as needed. In the absence of heartfelt fellowship with all others in the congregation, they must then refrain from the table. We should additionally consider our Lord's words in Matthew 5:23–24 as having bearing on this same matter: "If you are offering your gift at the altar and there remember that your brother has something against you, leave your gift there in front of the altar. First go and be reconciled to your brother; then come and offer your gift."

It should be obvious from all this that children who have not given a recognized confession of faith are not eligible to commune. This is for the children's benefit, both in protecting them from the penalties of unworthy Communion and in calling them to a clear response to the gospel. It is this need for care that produces the distinction between communing and non-communing members of the church, the latter group consisting of baptized children who are not admitted to the Lord's Table.

While recognizing that the Bible does not specify a definite age of consent and maturity, churches are wise to recognize matters of development and maturity in assessing a child's profession of faith. With regard to the sacrament, this counsels a conservative stance. Since communicants are asked to examine themselves soberly, it is reasonable to restrict this, as the Westminster Larger Catechism puts it, "only to such as are of years and ability" to do so (Q. 177). Churches are therefore prudent to ask children to wait before entering into full and communing membership in the church. This consideration also argues in favor of a structured process of confirmation. Here, baptized children of sufficient maturity may be thoroughly taught, have an opportunity to give clear and public confession of faith, and then may formally enter into full Communion as members of the church.

Restricted Communion must be taught and adhered to by the church but should not be enforced upon the congregation, since the duty of worthy partaking in 1 Corinthians 11:27–28 is given to the individual Christian and not to the church leadership. This means that, except in the cases of those suspended by formal church discipline, Communion should be left to the conscience of individuals after they have been appropriately instructed. We must recognize, however, that the church's duty to restrict Communion mandates effective church governance, including the practice of thorough church discipline. In situations where the norms of church structure and membership are not in view, such as in a military chapel or an evangelist's work of church formation, the absence of formal structures of membership and discipline ought not to cause the sacrament to be withheld from true and worthy believers. The overarching principle of restricted Communion is that those present should know the terms of partaking, with those suspended by church discipline denied the elements and all others invited to the table according to the exercise of their own conscience and voluntary choice.

Worthy Partaking of the Lord's Supper

We noted above that in 1 Corinthians 11:27–28 Paul warns against partaking of the sacrament in an unworthy manner. Most pointedly, as the next verse shows, the apostle targets his remarks against eating and drinking the elements without faith in what they signify, namely the atoning death of Christ. Paul's comment that "a man ought to examine himself before he eats of the bread and drinks of the cup" (11:28) alerts us to the need of a broader preparation than that of doctrinal affirmation only. Berkhof widens the bounds of this self-examination to a healthy extent, writing that the sacrament is for believers who "earnestly repent of their sins, trust that these have been covered by the atoning blood of Jesus Christ, and are desirous to increase their faith, and to grow in true holiness of life."[36]

At this point a word of caution is in order. Although communicants are warned to approach in a worthy manner, the sacrament does not rely on their spiritual attainment in order to "work." The blessing of the Eucharist comes as God's gift of grace by means of promise; it is worthily received by faith and not by works. Yet ministers are wise to realize how easily the call to worthy partaking may lead us in this subjective direction. Michael S. Horton, recalling his own youthful confusion on this matter, writes: "My focus was on trying to make it really 'work.' . . . Was I sad that Jesus died? And what if I had some unconfessed sin that I could not recall: that could make whatever was supposed to happen not happen, couldn't it? It seemed that so much depended on the combined imaginations of the preacher and my own, along with the special music that accompanied the distribution." Horton summarizes the error into which he had been encouraged: "I had, without malice but with plenty of ignorance, turned the Sacrament of Christ's doing into my sacrament of feeling and remembering."[37]

217

Horton is not the only one who worries about an excessive emphasis on worthily partaking. Calvin is another, and he complained in the *Institutes* about the practice of some that he observed:

> Commonly, when they would prepare men to eat worthily, they have tortured and harassed pitiable consciences in dire ways. . . . They said that those who were in state of grace ate worthily. They interpreted "in state of grace" to mean to be pure and purged of all sin. Such a dogma would debar all the men who ever were or are on earth from the use of this Sacrament. . . .
>
> By its immoderate harshness it deprives and despoils sinners, miserable and afflicted with trembling and grief, of the consolation of this Sacrament; yet in it, all the delights of the gospel were set before them. . . . Therefore, this is the worthiness—the best and only kind we can bring to God—to offer our vileness and (so to speak) our unworthiness to him so that his mercy may make us worthy of him; to despair in ourselves so that we may be comforted in him; to abase ourselves so that we may be lifted up by him; to accuse ourselves so that we may be justified by him.[38]

Worthy partaking, then, does not mean making the sacrament work in our own spiritual strength or presenting a supposed righteousness of our own, but instead ensuring that ours is a faith that is credible and real. The Westminster Standards, along these lines, employ self-examination not as a means of gaining approval for Christ's table, but rather of embracing the sobriety of communion with our Lord and seeking the maximum benefit from this means of grace. The Larger Catechism urges Christians to prepare "by examining themselves of their being in Christ, of their sins and wants; of the truth and measure of their knowledge, faith, repentance; love to God and the brethren, charity to all men, forgiving those that have done them wrong of their desires after Christ, and of their new obedience; and by renewing the exercise of these graces, by serious meditation, and fervent prayer" (Q. 171). By such preparation, Christians honor Christ in the manner of their communion with him and seek to make best use of the sacrament for godly advancement.

The Larger Catechism gives helpful counsel as to the Christian's spiritual exercise during the administration of the Lord's Supper. In receiving the elements "with all holy reverence and attention," Christians "wait upon God in that ordinance, diligently observe the sacramental elements and actions, heedfully discern the Lord's body, and affectionately meditate on his death and sufferings, and thereby stir up themselves to a vigorous exercise of their graces; in judging themselves and sorrowing for sin; in earnest hungering and thirsting after Christ, feeding on him by faith, receiving of his fullness, trusting in his merits, rejoicing in his love, giving thanks for his grace; in renewing of their covenant with God, and love to all the saints" (Q. 174). Afterward Christians are likewise to seek to best employ God's grace to the fullest extent by progressing in the faith (Q. 175).

There is a great and fundamental difference between trying to make the sacrament work and seeking to improve upon the grace therein received. Nonetheless, this difference is not immune to confusion. Therefore, wise ministers will not only press forth the command to partake worthily, but will urgently remind the congregation that God's grace is for sinners and not the righteous, for the weak and not the strong, for bad people and not good people. Recognizing these things is the best worthiness we can have to partake of Christ's Supper, when combined with a desire for his saving grace. With regard to our improvement of God's grace through growth in sanctification, our emphasis is on receiving God's help to do those things that are far beyond the reach of our flesh but that we may indeed attain by his grace in the power of the Spirit. Calvin places these both together in a fitting summary: "It is a sacrament ordained not for the perfect, but for the weak and feeble, to awaken, arouse, stimulate, and exercise the feeling of faith and love, indeed, to correct the defect of both."[39]

Frequency of Administration of the Lord's Supper

The final matter to discuss is one that is receiving an increased amount of attention today. How often should our church celebrate the Lord's Supper? The biblical data is helpful but indecisive. Jesus spoke of frequency only in terms of "whenever you eat this bread and drink this cup" (1 Cor. 11:26). A well-known passage in Acts (2:42–47) speaks of the earliest church breaking bread as part of their regular daily meeting: "They broke bread in their homes and ate together with glad and sincere hearts" (v. 46). It is not certain, however, that this communal eating consisted of the sacramental supper instituted by Christ, although that impression is natural enough. Likewise, Paul's admonition to the Corinthians implies that the sacrament was a regular feature of their frequent meetings (1 Cor. 11:20–22). What is not certain, however, is that Paul commends this practice; indeed, it seems that he would be happier with less frequent and more careful partaking of the supper of the Lord.

Historically there are two poles on this matter, those who commune with great infrequence, perhaps only once a year, and those who receive the sacrament on each occasion of their gathering together. The former was practiced by a number of churches in the Puritan and Scottish Presbyterian traditions and was motivated by a desire not merely to fence the table but to effectively enforce restricted Communion. A pastoral examination assessed one's worthiness to commune based on knowledge of the confession and a consideration of his godliness. Only then would permission be granted and a token be issued to attend the annual celebration of the sacrament. While such zeal for proper discipline may be commendable, it is hard to imagine that this level of infrequency accords with the sacrament's place as instituted in Scripture.

The biblical support for the other extreme is much stronger, as stated above, but not without qualification. Calvin weighs in strongly on the side of frequent Communion. He writes that the sacrament "was ordained to be frequently used among all Christians in order that they might frequently return in memory to Christ's Passion, by such remembrance to sustain and strengthen their faith."[40] On that basis Calvin advocates the administration of the Lord's Supper "at least once a week,"[41] although we should note that the Geneva city council refused this advice and directed that Communion be held no more than four times a year.

Prudence may dictate that weekly Communion militates against meaningful preparation and improvement. My own experience with weekly Communion is that when practical it is of the greatest benefit to the church; the dangers of excessive familiarity are in my view overstated and are easily overcome with proper pastoral oversight and presentation. Given the balance of the biblical and pastoral considerations, the Lord's Supper ought to be celebrated no less frequently than monthly and may be administered weekly with real blessing to Christians and to the whole church.

Conclusion

A thorough consideration of the Lord's Supper reveals the richness of its blessing to the people of God, for which we ought to be moved to the most profound thanksgiving. It also shows how much care must be given to its administration and receipt. Surely these are not unwarranted conclusions for something so holy as that set before us as signs and seals of Christ's sacrificial death and the covenant of grace. The minister of the gospel is especially rewarded in his meditation on the depths of what is here symbolized and sealed. The church will be blessed by careful, thoughtful, and expectant preparation, both on the part of the minister in setting the sacrament forth and on the part of those who come in weakness but depart in the strength of the joy of the Lord.

10

Hymnody in a Post-Hymnody World

PAUL S. JONES

Praise the Lord.
Sing to the Lord a new song,
    his praise in the assembly of the saints. (Ps. 149:1)

Fifty years ago the idea that one would need to argue in support of the existence and use of hymns in the worship of the church would have been laughable. With the exception of those who held to exclusive psalmody, hymns were an element of Christian worship as customary as bread at mealtime. In the postmodern, post-Christian age in which we live, however, we should not be surprised that worship and worship music in evangelical churches have followed the path of our culture. Under closer examination one finds that our value system, musical and otherwise, reflects society's primary philosophy (pragmatism), object of attention (ourselves), and occupation (our own amusement). In this system, psalms and doctrinal poems set to music in the traditional form of Reformation congregational song do not appear relevant.

We hear questions, statements, and arguments about their use: "Hymns? Why should we sing hymns? Are they not old fashioned? Young people will not like them. Is it not time to put the hymnal down and focus on things more current? Are we not to sing a *new* song? That is just not *my* kind of music. It does not *minister* to me. You will not win anyone with *that* music. Hymns are too hard to understand." And so on. Most of these perceptions emanate from a lack of information and education rather than from an antihymn agenda.

Those questions and statements may sound familiar to the majority of readers. For some others, like strict followers of John Calvin, there is no place for hymnody in the church for another reason—the belief that only canonical psalms should be sung in worship. The two references to singing "psalms, hymns, and spiritual songs" in the New Testament are interpreted by theologians on both sides of the exclusive-psalmody debate in support of their respective positions. At times the goal of singing to the glory of God and for the instruction and edification of his saints becomes obscured by polemics. Then, for many modern believers Calvin, psalms, and hymns are all somewhat of a mystery. Their reading material is predominantly futuristic Christian fiction, and the church music with which they are familiar consists of contemporary praise choruses.

The postmodern church, like the rest of Western culture, is self-obsessed and seems uninterested in the rich heritage of church music imparted to us from saints of previous generations. Although worship has become a buzzword in all ecclesiastical circles, minimal attention is given to biblical teaching regarding worship. As a result, we find evangelicals slipping away from biblical worship and justifying their practices on the basis of the *Zeitgeist*. A hedonistic, narcissistic, relativistic, "me-focused" age, though, is hardly one that should inform and define our approach to God. And yet, it does. We measure our success by numbers, our relevance by how technologically integrated and up-to-date we are, and our worship by how good it makes us feel. In the minds of contemporary saints, hymns clash with the spontaneity, simplicity, and style that have come to rule in the modern evangelical church.

Our goal in this chapter is to revisit biblical support by example and inference, not only for the validity of hymnody, but also for the importance of hymnody in the worship of the church of the twenty-first century. We shall proceed from an overview of song in the Bible to a brief discussion of Reformation hymnody in the sixteenth and twentieth centuries, followed by commentary on the important roles of hymn-singing in Christian worship. From there, practical suggestions for the local assembly will be offered, including ideas about how to introduce new hymns to the repertoire by means of education and composition.

Great hymns serve as praise, prayer, and proclamation in the context of worship. They say something we still need to hear, something we must believe, sing, and share. They often paraphrase a psalm, distill the teaching of a specific scriptural passage, or relate a doctrine or other spiritual truth by drawing on several biblical texts. Hymns are not emotionless. They make demands on the whole person—on the heart, soul, and mind—and they have special power to communicate spiritual truth and encouragement particularly through association with a fitting tune. While some hymn texts and tunes are ancient, hymns are not antiques. They are a living genre, important, even vital to the church; in fact, hymns are still being written today. While the church has shunned psalm and hymn singing, particularly in the last two decades of the twentieth century, both activities are biblical and necessary. As Donald Hustad points out, "Though mainline evangelicals claim to be leaders in Scripture study, biblical research to determine worship practice seems to be at the bottom of their priority list."[1] Let us, then, begin by turning to Scripture for guidance.

Song in the Bible

Psalms

The Book of Psalms has been called "the hymnbook of Israel" and is divided into five books (1–41, 42–72, 73–89, 90–106, 107–50). The Book of Psalms was the primary source of praise, prayer, and lament for God's people in living worship. The psalms' function in worship changed throughout Israel's temple history, and their employment in the synagogue and New Testament church was transformed as well. Psalms were understood as praise when first used in Israel's worship. The two primary times that psalms were sung in Solomon's temple were upon entering the temple and at the immolation of the sacrifice.[2] Later, in the synagogue, the psalms became spiritual sacrifices that replaced the need for animal sacrifice. The early church kept many of the synagogue's worship traditions, including the singing of psalms, predominantly in the context of prayer. Psalm 118:27 provides a good example of the changing use of psalms: "With boughs in hand, join in the festal procession up / to the horns of the altar." In temple worship

224

the action sung about here was literal; the animal would have been bound. In synagogue worship this was symbolic since worshipers were not actually tying a sacrifice to the altar. And in the early church, this verse would have been understood as a celebration of Christ's death and resurrection. Christ had fulfilled the demand for sacrifice and thereby abolished the need for such a practice in worship.

Psalm singing is commanded as part of New Testament worship in Ephesians 5:19 and Colossians 3:16.[3] These passages direct us to sing psalms, hymns, and spiritual songs (or odes). Some argue that the three designations are simply three interchangeable words for canonical psalms, pointing out that the Septuagint uses all three words in psalm subtitles, making them terms with which Paul and believers of his day would have been familiar.[4] On the other hand, Wesley Eisenberg writes: "The very use of diverse terminology such as this suggests that the early church encouraged a creative variety of musical and poetic expression in its corporate worship. Had the church sought to discourage such expression, the variety of terms would eventually have given way to a single term, by which we would now be able to define and delimit the 'hymn form.' "[5]

Regardless of one's conclusion about the terminology, singing psalms is not an optional activity, and yet we find it missing from many worship services in our time. It is insufficient to sing choruses based on a few verses of a psalm; in fact, this practice more often ignores the reasons the psalms give for worshiping God. Such reasons should be recalled if our thanks, praise, and prayers to God are to be properly contextualized.

However, psalms are not the only appropriate worship songs of the people of God. From New Testament examples, worship should also include our Christian response to the finished work of Calvary, what could be called a "Christian interpretation of the Psalms" through hymns, canticles, biblical songs, and present-day hymns. According to Hughes Oliphant Old, "the doxology of the earliest Christians kept psalmody and hymnody in a dynamic balance."[6] Without Christian hymns, our praise of God through psalms would be rich, but it would be missing our acknowledgment of and gratitude for the manner in which Christ has redeemed us and fulfilled that which the Old Testament promised.

Psalms teach us how to worship, and they provide fitting, biblical language with which to thank, praise, implore, and glorify God. They also demonstrate confession and lament. Many are messianic; some recount Israel's redemption history. A historical study of psalms sung in church worship reveals a number of traditions—from Gregorian psalmody to the metrical psalms of the *Strasbourg Psalter* (1539) and *Genevan Psalter* (1562) to the *Bay Psalm Book* (1640), Anglican chant, and the psalm-hymns of Martin Luther, Isaac Watts, and James Montgomery. In other words, psalms should be sung, but the manner (language, mode, music) in which they should be sung is a matter of choice.

Canticles

As one studies the Bible, it becomes apparent that singing hymns of praise was the response of many saints to God's deliverance and other blessings. Like the psalms, these biblical songs, recorded in written form, were passed on by oral tradition. Although the Old Testament also includes laments, canticles typically rehearse the attributes of God and his mighty acts on behalf of his people. They give glory to God and manifest a spirit of joy and thankfulness for his work and deliverance:

- ✧ Moses and Miriam and all Israel sang after the nation was delivered from the hand of Pharaoh at the Red Sea (Ex. 15).
- ✧ Deborah and Barak sang when God gave victory to the Israelites over the Canaanites (Judg. 5).
- ✧ David sang as the Lord delivered him from the hand of all his enemies and from Saul (2 Sam. 22).
- ✧ Mary sang upon seeing Elizabeth, who understood that God's promise of a Redeemer was going to be realized through Mary (Luke 1—*Magnificat*).
- ✧ Zechariah sang following the return of his speech as he was filled with the Holy Spirit and verified his son's name—John, the one who would prepare the way for the Savior (Luke 1—*Benedictus dominus*).
- ✧ Simeon had a similar response when he held Jesus the Messiah in his arms, having entered the temple "in the Spirit" (Luke 2—*Nunc dimittis*).

There are other songs in the Old Testament: Jacob's (Gen. 49), Moses' (Deut. 32), and Hannah's (1 Sam. 2:1–10), as well as numerous *cantica minora* in Exodus, Deuteronomy, 1 Samuel, 1 Chronicles, Isaiah, and

Habakkuk. The three New Testament canticles listed above are also known as the Lukan psalms, and they evidence the continued writing and singing of inspired Christian psalms, apart from apocryphal songs, after the writing of the canonical psalms concluded. Old notes that "these are clearly Christian psalms written in the literary genre of the Hebrew votive thanksgiving psalms. . . . The Old Testament Psalms had for generations cried out for the Lord's anointed; now the New Testament psalms confessed that the cry had been heard and the promise fulfilled."[7]

The majority of these biblical songs were the response of Spirit-filled people to God's salvation. The biblical model is to sing of God's deliverance, to sing what we preach. We preach Christ's work of redemption—his birth, life, death, and resurrection—the message of the book. The Bible sings this gospel time and time again, and so should we.

Canticles such as the *Magnificat* and the *Nunc dimittis* are sung regularly in vespers and evensong, and there are numerous places where these and other canticles reside in the Lutheran, Anglican, and Roman Catholic traditions. Perhaps their prominence in liturgical and non-Protestant traditions is among the excuses for not employing them in modern evangelical worship. But because they are Holy Spirit–inspired biblical songs, we would be well advised to sing them. Not to do so is to deprive ourselves of their value and to ignore some of the rich hymnody of the Scriptures.

Hymns of Christ

In addition to extensive quotations from the psalms and canticles of the Old Testament, particularly in Romans and Hebrews, in several New Testament passages one finds heightened poetic language and hymn fragments (John 1:1–5, 9–11; Rom. 10:9–13; 1 Cor. 12:3; Eph. 5:14; Phil. 2:6–11; Col. 1:15–20; 1 Tim. 2:5–6; 3:16; 2 Tim. 2:11–13; Heb. 1:3; 1 Peter 3:18c–19, 22). There is no conclusive way to distinguish between poetry and hymnody in the New Testament, as both contain the fundamental features of Hebrew poetry. Usually, such passages are christocentric and may be indicated in modern translations by indented margins, italic type, or quotation marks. While one can read of Christ in the various psalms, they largely focus on the praise, worship, attributes, and acts of God the Father rather than on the Son, as one would expect before his first advent. These portions of the gospels and epistles, on the other

227

hand, poetically celebrate the lordship of Christ and provide hymns specifically to and about Christ—a new genre of biblical song. As Ralph Martin puts it:

> It was in worship that the decisive step was made of setting the exalted Christ on a level with God as the recipient of the church's praise. Hymnology and Christology thus merged in the worship of one Lord, soon to be hailed after the close of the New Testament canon as worthy of hymns "as to God" (Pliny's report of Bithynian Christians at Sunday worship, a.d. 112).
>
> It was this close drawing together of the persons of the Godhead which laid the foundation for the Trinitarian creeds, and raised a bulwark against classical gnosticism in the late second century. . . . While "messianic psalms" played their role in defining and defending the church's belief in the fulfillment of Old Testament types and prefigurements, it required a new species— the "hymn to Christ"—to open fruitful avenues of Christological and soteriological inquiry that set the church from its early days on a course that led eventually to Chalcedon and the *Te Deum:*
>
> You are the King of Glory, O Christ,
> You are the everlasting Son of the Father.[8]

The *Te deum laudamus* is one of the greatest hymns of the early church. Many hymns to Christ were written by church fathers in their letters, apologies, and homilies. Such christological Greek and Latin hymns are not to be confused with gnostic hymns that were written with the intention of replacing the psalms; on the contrary, many of the early church's hymns were written by orthodox theologians to counteract the work of gnostic hymn writers.

Isaac Watts authored psalm paraphrases and hymns with a related purpose—the quest to "Christianize" the psalms. Like Luther, he wanted believers to benefit from psalm singing, so that this was not an intellectually or culturally remote activity, but one from which they would learn and with which they could associate. We see in Watts's work what Horton Davies calls a desire to create a "Christian re-orientation of the Psalms."[9] To do so, Watts would abbreviate lengthy psalms and avoid potentially confusing metaphoric language. Further, he makes direct reference to Christ or the gospel in many of his psalm paraphrases in at least one stanza. For example, the final stanza of "O Bless the Lord, My Soul" (Ps. 103) reads:

His wondrous works and ways
He made by Moses known,
But sent the world his truth and grace
By His beloved Son.

Another example is "The Heavens Declare Your Glory, Lord" (Watts's paraphrase of Ps. 19), where we find this stanza:

Nor shall your spreading gospel rest
Till through the world your truth has run;
Till Christ has all the nations blessed
That see the light, or feel the sun.

While we understand many psalms to have their prophecies fulfilled in Christ, the psalm texts do not refer to Jesus or to the gospel by name. Watts wanted to make Christ's fulfillment of them evident: "In all places I have kept my grand design in view; and that is to teach my author to speak like a Christian."[10] He instructed congregants to carry psalm books with them and asked the clerk to read aloud the psalm before it was sung so that people might better understand what they were to sing. In so doing, he restored Christian praise to its rightful place in the worship of the dissenting church of the early eighteenth century. Understanding biblical principles of worship would have a similar restorative effect on the church in our day—it would enrich our worship and help to guard against the dangers of Gnosticism, narcissism, and anthropocentrism.

Doxologies

The New Testament includes numerous excerpts from benedictions, prayers, creeds, eulogies, responses, and doxologies. Doxology encompasses the full gamut of praise to God and can be referred to as "the theology of worship."[11] Extended doxological passages occur in Romans 11:33–36; Revelation 1:5–7; 4–5; 7:10–12; 11:15–18; 15:3–4; and 19:1–8.

Romans 11:36 closes the great doctrinal chapters of the Book of Romans and acts as the climax of the Apostle Paul's testimony to all he has written. James Boice puts it this way: "As Paul contemplated the mercies of God, he was so lost in wonder that he composed the doxology . . . as an outpouring of praise . . . the song of the redeemed."[12] This doxology, which quotes both

Isaiah and Job, concludes that all things come both from and through God himself and lead rightly to the worship of God by his redeemed creation. This is the only acceptable Christian worldview. All things are to bring glory to God and to him alone.

Five doxological hymns in Revelation 4–5 are sung by the seraphim, cherubim, four living creatures, twenty-four elders, and all creation. These songs are continuous. The first two praise God the Father; the next two praise Christ, the Lamb; and the fifth praises both the Father and the Son. God is worshiped for his holiness, for his everlasting existence, and for his creation. Christ is praised for his worthiness to open the seals and for his saving act of redemption. A *"crescendo* of praise" is evident in these hymns as well. The first is sung by the four living creatures; the second and third by the four living creatures and the twenty-four elders; the fourth by the four living creatures, the twenty-four elders, and myriads of angels; and the fifth by every creature in heaven and on earth and under the earth and on the sea.

Our understanding of heaven's eternal worship as expressed in Revelation also informs our understanding of worship following the death and resurrection of Christ, for "eternal" worship must include the past, present, and future. As Old points out, "one is struck by the fact that in Revelation's report of the heavenly worship there are constant echoes of the psalms and canticles of the Old Testament and yet no example of a direct and simple use of one of the canonical psalms. In every case what we have is a Christian paraphrase."[13] Since this information is the revealed word of God demonstrating at least a veiled picture of perfect, heavenly worship, it would seem appropriate to imitate this revelation in our present-day worship in the church.

Reformation Hymnody

We shall not recount the history of hymnody, as this has been accomplished in fine books by Erik Routley, Paul Westermeyer, Donald Hustad, and others. It shall suffice to consider the roots of Reformation hymnody, which can be understood as a rebirth and outgrowth of the worship of the early church, and to compare this to music employed in the worship of our time.

230

Sixteenth Century: The Contribution of Martin Luther

Hymns played an important role in the Reformation and contributed to its widespread success across the Continent. This influence was more prominent in Lutheran lands than in those that chiefly adhered to a Reformed perspective. It has been said that Luther recovered the congregation's singing, Zwingli denied it, and Calvin restricted it.[14] Zwingli did not dislike music; quite the contrary, he was trained in virtually all instruments and was a good composer. He understood the power of music but felt it had no place in worship. He believed silence was the answer for hearing the word and for contemplation. Calvin, on the other hand, was not a musician. Like Zwingli and Luther, he knew that the power of music could be misused, so the solution was to carefully restrict its use. Although he encouraged singing, Calvin limited sung text to the Book of Psalms and believed that the music must have "weight" and "majesty." He advocated, for the Reformed church, the strictures of metrical psalms, and a single monophonic line, and he forbade instruments or choirs (except a group of children who led the congregation's unison/octave singing). Interestingly, these restrictions were for corporate worship only; at home, the same texts could be sung polyphonically for family worship and could include instruments.[15]

Any Protestant church that encourages the use of instruments, hymn-singing, reharmonization, part-singing, improvisation, contrapuntal texture, or psalms other than metrical ones is an heir of Martin Luther. Luther was a talented lutenist and composer who had more than a casual appreciation for music; in fact, he wrote: "Next to the Word of God, music deserves the highest praise. She is a mistress and governess of those human emotions which control men or more often overwhelm them."[16] And: "Nor am I of the opinion that through the Gospel all arts should be cast to the ground and should perish, as some misled religious people claim. But I want to see all the arts, especially music, used in the service of Him who has given and created them."[17]

With his friend and musical collaborator Johann Walter (1496–1570), Luther worked to propagate the gospel and Lutheran doctrine through music by writing chorales (German hymns). Luther is rightly called the "father of congregational song" for his contribution to the development of hymnody. He knew that doctrine and theology could be taught by singing hymns and that young people especially would benefit from exposure to

231

wholesome music. To this end, he wrote quite a number of hymns with Walter; at least thirty-six chorales are ascribed with some certainty to him. Leonard Payton reminds us that Roman Catholic leaders in the middle of the sixteenth century believed they would have been able to suppress "that 'Lutheran Heresy' as they called it, except for its hymnody."[18]

The claim is right that Lutheran hymnody was the point at which the doctrine of the priesthood of all believers received its most concrete realization.[19] The Latin chants, psalms, and canticles previously reserved for trained priests and monks to deliver were now transformed into doctrine-infused hymns and prayers for the congregation to sing in its native tongue. There was no need for an earthly intermediary as Christians could, in Protestant worship, communicate directly to God through song.

Luther held that our understanding of the arts must be informed by our theology and that our theology will benefit from artistic insight and expression. Since music is a gift from our Creator, it has a role to play in teaching more about him. Music and the other arts should be offered as sacrifices of praise to God and should function as vehicles to serve our worship of him—to pray and even to proclaim his word. This does not align with the utilitarian, pragmatic, and social roles to which music and art are often relegated in modern evangelicalism, where a general shunning of the arts and trivial approaches to worship reveal bad theology.

Twentieth Century: The Contribution of James Montgomery Boice

A twentieth-century hymn-writing counterpart to the sixteenth-century Luther was James Montgomery Boice, who authored twelve Reformation-like hymns during his final year that are rich in doctrine and theological content. These hymns are sermons in verse form whereby their author continues to preach wherever and whenever they are sung. Other hymn writers of note, particularly in England and America, most certainly could be included in a discussion of twentieth-century contributors to the repertory. Hymn writers in the modern Reformed tradition include Eric J. Alexander, Edmund Clowney, and R. C. Sproul, to name just a few. As this is a Festschrift for James Boice, we shall focus on his contribution of a new genre of Reformation hymns.

As one discovers Luther's purposes for hymn development in his prefaces to hymnals and other writings, so too with Boice. The pastor-scholar's own words help to clarify his goals for hymnody and his understanding of its significance. In his sermon on Revelation 4:9–11, Boice spoke about the importance of music and singing in worship:

> Isn't it interesting that heaven's worship is expressed in words set to music, in words that are sung? This is more than interesting, of course. It is important, for music is a gift from God that allows us to express our deepest heart responses to God and his truth in meaningful and memorable ways. It is a case of our hearts joining with our minds to say, "Yes! Yes! Yes!" to the truths we are embracing. . . . It is what the four living creatures, elders, angels and the entire creation are doing today in heaven. We join that great heavenly choir rightly, wisely and joyously when we sing.[20]

With *Hymns for a Modern Reformation* Boice and I attempted to revisit Luther's goals for his own hymns—to teach the Bible in a meaningful, memorable, life-changing manner. Boice emailed me in August 1999 with a statement that delineated the *raison d'être* for our collaborative effort: "I am thinking that if we are going to have a modern reformation, we are going to need new reformation music. Bible doctrines have always gotten a hold on people this way." His hymns sprang directly from contemplating and teaching a biblical passage. For example, in reviewing his *sola gratia* hymn on Ephesians 2:1–10, we find that the poem is written in the first-person singular and can be understood as the author's personal testimony. The titles for the chapters he wrote explicating the Ephesians passage also outline his thoughts for this hymn. The following section titles and two paragraphs are excerpted from *Hymns for a Modern Reformation* and Boice's commentary on Ephesians:

1. The Way We Were (2:1–3)
2. But God (2:4–5)
3. Risen with Christ (2:6–7)
4. Saved by Grace Alone (2:8–9)
5. God's Workmanship (2:10)

The five hymn stanzas mirror these five divisions of the passage precisely as they trace the Christian's past, present and future in a cogent manner. We were dead to God in our transgressions and enslaved by our sins. As such, by nature we were objects of God's wrath and under his just sentence for our sin. "But God" has made us alive in Christ. Boice wrote, "May I put it quite

233

simply? If you understand those two words—'but God'—they will save your soul. If you recall them daily and live by them, they will transform your life completely." Why did God do this? Because of his love (v. 4), his mercy (v. 4), his grace (v. 5), and his kindness (v. 7). God made us alive together with Christ, raised us up together with him, and made us sit down together with him in the heavenly realms. "Before, we were dead; now we are alive. Before, we were enslaved by our sins and carnal nature; now we are emancipated. Before, we were objects of wrath; now we experience God's love."

We are saved "by grace" alone, "through faith." But this is not by our own doing; it is God's work and God's gift. "Faith is not from ourselves. . . . If it were a virtue, then we would be able to boast in heaven. . . . No, not even faith is a work. Nothing that you or I can do, however great or small, can get us into salvation. . . . Salvation is by grace alone." Paul quickly moves from rejecting any notion of good works being part of our salvation to insisting that good works are precisely what God has created us to do. In fact, God created us in Christ Jesus to do good works that were specifically "prepared in advance for us to do." This "is the re-creation of a man or woman who before was spiritually dead, utterly incapable of doing any good thing that could satisfy God, but who now, as the result of God's working, is able to do truly good 'good works.' "[21]

Compare the biblical passage, Boice's outline and teaching of the passage, and his five stanzas of "Alive in Christ" (fig. 10.1). This is not poetry for poetry's sake, but verse written for the purpose of instruction. It is lyrical and creative, but has as its motivating force and ultimate intent the desire to communicate the truth of God's word. It is proclamatory. It is illuminating. It shares the message of the gospel of grace. Luther and Boice understood that proclamation—together with praise and prayer—was one of the primary roles of hymnody, roles that we will now consider in more detail.

The Roles of Hymnody

Hymns as Praise

That psalms and hymns have as their most common theme the praise of God will not be contested. While other themes exist, that of praising God

Alive in Christ

But. . . God, who is rich in mercy, made us alive with Christ. Eph. 2:4-5

1. I once was re - bel - lious, cor - rup - ted by
2. But God who is rich in com - pas - sion and
3. God lif - ted me up to the heav - en - ly
4. Since grace is the source of the life that is
5. Yet now I am liv - ing with work to be

sin, pur - su - ing the dev - il's dark path,
love, not leav - ing my soul to the grave,
realms where seat - ed with Christ I am free;
mine — and faith is a gift from on high —
done for I am God's work - man - ship too,

— O - bli - vi - ous, dead to the state I was
— Has giv - en me life; born a - gain from a -
— In a - ges to come he will show me more
— I'll boast in my Sav - ior, all mer - it de -
— Cre - a - ted in Christ with a race to be

in, an ob - ject of God's dread - ful wrath.
bove, by God's sov - 'reign grace I've been saved.
grace — so great is his kind - ness to me.
cline, and glo - ri - fy God 'til I die.
run, which God has or - dained me to do.

Based on Ephesians 2:1-10
James Montgomery Boice, 2000

SOLA GRATIA 11.8.11.8.
Paul S. Jones, 2000

Figure 10.1

235

for his word, acts, and attributes recurs frequently. Hymns to Christ and canticles are most often hymns of praise as well (e.g., Zechariah's song: "Praise be to the Lord, the God of Israel, / because he has come and has redeemed his people"; Luke 1:68). Doxologies and benedictions likewise commence or conclude passages, chapters, or books with an ascription of praise (e.g., Rev. 1:6: "To him be glory and power for ever and ever! Amen"). Psalms of praise are typically marked by a call to give God praise for deliverance and often are accompanied by sacrifices of thanksgiving (e.g., Ps. 30 or 124). Particularly praise oriented, the last five chapters of the Book of Psalms invoke all of creation to praise the Lord and to do so with singing, dancing, music, and instruments. Three examples of praise-oriented hymns are "Praise, My Soul, the King of Heaven" (Henry F. Lyte, based on Ps. 103); "All Praise to God, Who Reigns Above" (Johann J. Schütz); and "Now Thank We All Our God" (Martin Rinkart).

The first Boice hymn written was entitled "Give Praise to God" and is based on the Pauline doxology in Romans 11:33–36. This doxology acts as the climax and testimony to the great doctrinal chapters leading up to it:

> Oh, the depth of the riches of the wisdom and
> knowledge of God!
> How unsearchable his judgments,
> and his paths beyond tracing out!
> "Who has known the mind of the Lord?
> Or who been his counselor?"
> "Who has ever given to God,
> that God should repay him?"
> For from him and through him and to him
> are all things.
> To him be the glory forever! Amen.

Boice's hymn may rightly be called "Hymn of the Father." His sermons on this passage appear under the same heading as this hymn—*soli deo gloria* (glory to God alone). In particular, his message on verse 36 (which he used as the key verse in defining a proper Christian worldview) was titled after the Reformation motto. Boice's hymn proclaims the theology of this passage, but arranges the thoughts in a context of poetic praise, with the refrain serving as our only appropriate response to it:

Give praise to God who reigns above
For perfect knowledge, wisdom, love;
His judgments are divine, devout,
His paths beyond all tracing out.

No one can counsel God all-wise
Or truths unveil to his sharp eyes;
He marks our paths behind, before;
He is our steadfast Counselor.

Nothing exists that God might need
For all things good from him proceed.
We praise him as our Lord, and yet
We never place God in our debt.

Creation, life, salvation too,
And all things else both good and true,
Come from and through our God always,
And fill our hearts with grateful praise.

Refrain:
Come, lift your voice to heaven's high throne,
And glory give to God alone!

Another Boice hymn could be called "Hymn of the Son"; based on the doxology in Revelation 1:5–7, it is entitled "All Praise to Christ." Preaching on this passage Boice said,

Earlier in this study I referred to the last words of verse 6 as a doxology, which they are. But in a broader sense everything in verses 5–7 is a doxology or, to put it differently, a hymn to be sung with joy by God's people. . . . It is a communal hymn, for the repetition of "us" and "our" draws John and his readers together as a confessing community of faith. This is what hymns are meant to do. They are a means given by God by which we join in confessing our beliefs, lift up our flagging spirits, encourage our hearts, and worship God together. Can anything be more joyful and uplifting than that? Nothing at all, until we do it perfectly in the presence of our Savior and God.[22]

237

The fourth and final stanza of Boice's hymn gives us a glimpse of heavenly worship, where the new creation is singing together with heavenly beings and saints of past ages. This eternal song is quoted, and then our present response of praise is given in the refrain:

> With angels, saints, and seraphim
>   the new creation sings,
> "All glory, pow'r and praise to him
>   who made us priests and kings."

> *Refrain:*
> All praise to Christ from grateful men
>   forevermore. Amen.

Hymns as Proclamation

Luther realized the significant role that music could play in the spiritual growth of the Christian. He declared: "Music and notes, which are wonderful gifts and creations of God, *do help gain a better understanding of the text*, especially when sung by a congregation and when sung earnestly." And: "We have put this music to the living and holy Word of God *in order to sing, praise and honor it*. We want the beautiful art of music to be properly used to serve her dear Creator and his Christians. He is thereby praised and honored and *we are made better and stronger in faith* when his holy Word is impressed on our hearts by sweet music."[23] Westermeyer expands on these statements:

> Luther was not simply fond of music. Luther thought music has a theological reason for being: it is a gift of God, which comes from the "sphere of miraculous audible things," just like the Word of God. Music is unique in that it can carry words. Since words carry the Word of God, music and the Word of God are closely related. . . . It almost seems as if Luther sees music in its own right as a parallel to preaching. . . . But the weight falls on its association with the Word and words that carry the Word.[24]

With Walter, Luther compiled and edited several hymn collections, and for some of these he wrote prefaces. As previously mentioned, one of Luther's goals was to properly educate the youth of his day:

238

Therefore, I too, with the help of others, have brought together some sacred songs, in order to make a good beginning and to give an incentive to those who can better carry on the Gospel and bring it to the people. . . . And these songs were arranged in four parts for no other reason than that I wanted to attract the youth (who should and must be trained in music and other fine arts) away from love songs and carnal pieces and to give them something wholesome to learn instead. . . . It is unfortunate that everyone else forgets to teach and train the poor young people; we must not be responsible for this too.[25]

Obviously Luther did not invent the notion that music and the proclamation of the gospel are related. He found its basis in Scripture. There are more than six hundred references to music in the Bible, and we know that singing is an eternal activity. Singing and music are actually to be a daily occupation of the believer. Luther believed music should be composed to teach doctrine and to instruct young people, that by singing the word of God our faith would be strengthened. So did Boice. In his commentary on Psalm 9:9–10, Boice wrote:

It is striking that in each part the psalmist combines singing with preaching. And, it is interesting to remember that great periods of church history have always been marked by both. At the time of the Reformation, Martin Luther's hymns were on the lips of the German people as much as his words were in their hearts. At the time of the Wesleyan Revival in Great Britain, the recovery of the gospel was accompanied by an equally stirring recovery of gospel singing, as the hymns of John and Charles Wesley, August Toplady, William Cowper, John Newton and others show.[26]

Perhaps history will show that a reformation in the twenty-first-century church found the hymns of Boice on its members' lips as well.

Within the context of proclamation, we expect to find elements of exhortation and admonition, of teaching and pedagogy. Watts's position on this is clear: "His belief in the didactic value of praise, as in his insistence upon intelligibility, his aim, like that of the Puritans, was edification."[27] What does the Bible witness about the instructive use of music? We know that a number of the psalms record the works of the Lord so that these might be passed on by oral tradition from priests to people and from parents to children.[28] A New Testament statement is found in Colossians 3:16–17: "Let the word of Christ dwell in you richly as you teach and admonish one another with wisdom, and as you sing psalms, hymns and spiritual songs with gratitude in your hearts to God." Music, and singing in particular, is advocated for teaching and admonishing one another. Therefore, the Bible is clear in stating that sacred music has an instructive purpose.

There is also biblical support for the idea that singing the word of God will strengthen our understanding of it. Singing should, in fact, be a result of hearing and meditating on God's word as well, as the psalmist said in the last section of Psalm 119:

> May my lips overflow with praise,
>> for you teach me your decrees.
> May my tongue sing of your word,
>> for all your commands are righteous.
> . . . .
> I long for your salvation, O Lord,
>> and your law is my delight.
> Let me live that I may praise you,
>> and may your laws sustain me. (Ps. 119:171–72, 174–75)

Also in Psalm 119, that great psalm of the word, which itself is both an extensive acrostic poem and a song, we read, "Your decrees are the theme of my song / wherever I lodge" (v. 54).

In 1 Corinthians 15, Paul articulates for his Corinthian believers the gospel that he had preached and proclaimed to them. The *euangelion* (good news) was the death, burial, and resurrection of Jesus Christ. Christ's resurrection power over death is celebrated, particularly at the end of the chapter: "Death is swallowed up in victory. O Death, where is your sting? O Grave, where is your victory?" (Authorized Version, modified). Here Paul quotes Isaiah 25:8, which is a song of praise, and Hosea 13:14, which delivers God's word through the prophet. Intentionally or unintentionally, Paul relates song and the proclamation of the gospel, something he does again in Ephesians 5:19 and Colossians 3:16. Luther's commentary on 1 Corinthians 15 finishes this way: "And now St. Paul appropriately concludes with a song which he sings: 'Thanks and praise be to God, who gave us such a victory!' We can join in that song and in that way always celebrate

Easter, praising and extolling God for a victory that was not won or achieved in battle by us . . . but we must . . . sing of this victory in Christ."[29] And, in his foreword to one of Walter's hymnals Luther wrote: "We may boast, as Moses does in his song in Exodus 15, that Christ is our praise and our song and that we should know nothing to sing or say but Jesus Christ our Savior, as Paul says in 1 Corinthians."[30]

Luther frequently employed the terms *sing* and *say* to describe the proper work of a believer. The content of the proclamation is always the gospel—the work of Christ. He wrote in his commentary on Psalm 118: "They [the righteous] praise only God's grace, works, words, and power as they are revealed to them in Christ. This is their *sermon and song*, their hymn of praise."[31] One of his best loved and known Christmas hymns, "Vom Himmel hoch," states it this way:

> From heav'n above to earth I come
> To bear good news to every home;
> Glad tidings of great joy I bring,
> Whereof I now will say and sing [davon ich sing'n
>   und sagen will].

Many proclamatory hymns focus on the basic tenets of the gospel—the birth, life, death, and resurrection of Christ—and the life available to us because of Christ's sacrifice. Some examples of such hymns are "Arise, My Soul, Arise" (Charles Wesley); "My Hope Is Built on Nothing Less" (Edward Mote); and "Alas! And Did My Savior Bleed?" (Isaac Watts). Personally, I define musical proclamation broadly so as to include any text that teaches or sets a passage of Scripture, recounts God's work, issues a call to repentance, or reminds us of God's promises.

The Boice hymn "How Marvelous, How Wise, How Great" (fig. 10.2), based on Romans 8:28–31, proclaims the cardinal doctrines of Calvinism as it reflects and expounds on this "golden chain" passage. Its language is both proclamatory and instructive. This is not a hymn of praise, although an appropriate response to its teaching is the praise of God. Neither is it a hymn of prayer, nor a lament, nor simply a spiritual poem. It is a short sermon that outlines and explains a difficult passage of Scripture, yet it does so in poetic language and form. This accounts for the interlocking rhyme scheme that pervades and links the four stanzas.[32] The stanzas follow the

241

biblical text. The first marvels at God's purpose to regenerate faithless, fallen man. The second reflects on the election of the individual and notes that God's predestining purpose is to conform him to the likeness of Christ. After rejoicing in our justification and glorification in stanza three (as does Rom. 8:30), the hymn concludes in stanza four by saying that nothing remains for us now but to embrace God and his grace, run our race well, and praise God forever—the application of the sermon to daily life.

Hymns as Prayer

The role of hymnody in worship is not limited to praise and proclamation, however. Hymns can also serve as prayers, as is the case with many of the psalms. Many passages from the psalms, canticles, hymns of Christ, and various *cantica minora* address God directly. Direct address is one of the most recognizable characteristics of a prayer hymn. Likewise, many hymns and choruses directly address God: "Be Thou My Vision"; "Holy, Holy, Holy"; "My Jesus, I Love Thee"; "Come, Thou Fount of Every Blessing"; "Day by Day"; "I Love You, Lord"; "Create in Me a Clean Heart, O God"; and so on. Thinking of them as anything other than prayers is simply unsupportable. One can find prayer hymns addressed to each person of the Trinity:

- *Father:* "Dear Lord and Father of Mankind" (John Greenleaf Whittier)
- *Son:* "O Jesus, I Have Promised" (John Bode)
- *Spirit:* "Breathe on Me, Breath of God" (Edwin Hatch)

It seems both logical and biblical to conclude that *any* communication to God—verbal or nonverbal, spoken, sung, written, or thought—is prayer. Communication does not stop when one sings, and yet subconsciously we often separate the act of singing from the acts of thinking, speaking, or "meaning." Perhaps this is somehow tied to the flawed idea that prayer must be spontaneous—that unless it is improvisatory in nature, it is not Spirit directed. Such thinking does not align with canonical psalms and other biblical songs being prayers. These prayers are recorded and have been used in worship in both ancient and modern times.

Calvin understood the singing of psalms to be prayer, which matches the teaching of the last verse of the second book of the Psalms: "This con-

How Marvelous, How Wise, How Great

For those God foreknew he also predestined... called... justified... glorified.
Rom. 8:29-30

1. How mar - ve - lous, how wise, how great, how in - fi - nite to con - tem - plate: Je - ho - vah's sav - ing plan. He saw me in my lost es - tate yet pur - posed to re - gen - er - ate this faith - less, fal - len man.

2. Fore - known be - fore the world be - gan, ac - cord - ing to his gra - cious plan, God des - tined I must be con - formed to Je - sus Christ, the man, who lived and loved as no man can: a glo - ri - ous de - cree.

3. He bore my sin on Cal - vary's tree and right - eous - ness be - stowed on me that I might see his face. God jus - ti - fied me, set me free, and glo - ri - fied I soon will be: how mar - ve - lous this grace.

4. What have I now but to em - brace the God who saved me from dis - grace and love him ev - er - more; and with con - tent - ment run my race my eyes fixed ev - er on his face to praise him and a - dore.

Based on Romans 8:28-31
James Montgomery Boice, 1999

SPRUCE STREET 8.8.6.8.8.6.
Paul S. Jones, 1999

Figure 10.2

cludes the prayers of David son of Jesse" (Ps. 72:20). "Spontaneous prayer only" would rule out use of the inspired Psalter. On the other hand, praying only the psalms excludes obvious New Testament passages and examples from the early church, such as the Lord's Prayer or the "Sovereign Lord" prayer of Acts 4:23–26. Both fixed and spontaneous prayers are valid and supported by the example of Scripture. Other New Testament passages also relate singing and praying:

- ✧ "Is any one of you in trouble? He should pray. Is anyone happy? Let him sing songs of praise." (James 5:13—this is in the context of James's discussion of prayer and faith)
- ✧ "I will pray with the spirit and I will pray with the mind also; I will sing with the spirit and I will sing with the mind also." (1 Cor. 14:15 New American Standard Bible)[33]

Prayer and singing are closely associated in these texts, and we see that both should be done with the spirit (with energy, with emotion) and also with the mind (with thought). Neither element should be missing. In other words, we should *mean* what we pray with all our hearts, and we should *know* what we mean. We should also mean what we sing and know what we are singing. A lapse in either element (intention or understanding) often renders the singing of hymns and the worship of God irrelevant, even *irreverent*. Watts had this in mind when creating Christian paraphrases of the psalms: "I would neither indulge any bold metaphors, nor admit of hard words, nor tempt the ignorant worshiper to sing without his understanding."[34]

One welcome addition the charismatic church has reintroduced to modern Christianity is the importance of emotion in worship and what it means to worship God with all of our hearts. These elements have been missing from hymn and psalm singing in many Reformed and evangelical churches. Unfortunately, the "packaging" and "success" of these elements in the Contemporary Christian Music movement has led to a consumer-oriented church music industry, which holds up the seeker-sensitive megachurch as the ideal for young and middle-aged pastors. Since most pastors have not had musical training and received little (or no) church music or worship instruction in seminary, they frequently succumb to the pragmatic path of least resistance fostered by church-growth experts. In hope of bringing vitality to church (and giving the people what they want), contemporary services with all the trimmings are added, often to the demotion or exclusion of psalms and hymns from worship. The primary flaw in this thinking is the belief that musical style will cause growth in church attendance and that such numerical growth can be equated with spiritual growth. We must remember that it is God who builds his church.

Old states in his book on worship for pastors, entitled *Leading in Prayer*:

> Choosing appropriate hymns is an important part of leading the congregation in prayer. We may not always regard hymnody as prayer, but theologically that is how it makes the best sense. In hymns the people of God pray together with one voice. As Luke puts it in his report of an early Christian prayer meeting, "they lifted their voices together to God" (Acts 4:24). Luke actually says this about psalm singing, but the same is true of hymnody as well. Uniting our voices together is just what we do when we sing.[35]

German Protestants actually refer to their hymnals as "prayer books." Lutheran church composer Johann Sebastian Bach (1685–1750) understood the singing of chorales to be prayer—that hymn-singing was a manner of communicating with God. If we realized that many of our hymns are prayers, we might approach them and sing them differently. When we sing psalms and great hymns of the faith together, we are corporately praying not only in the present but also in solidarity with saints of the past who have walked with God and who have uttered the same words.

Eric J. Alexander of Scotland has written several prayer hymns, among them "O Lord God, How Great Your Mercy" (in response to Rom. 12:1–2); "Sovereign Lord of All Creation" (in response to Acts 4:23–30); "My Gracious Lord, Your Love Is Vast" (a hymn based on biblical teaching regarding God's love); and "Lord Jesus Christ, How Far You Came" (in response to Phil. 2:5–11; see fig. 10.3). The latter responds to the great passage from Paul's letter to the Philippians that describes for us the humility of Jesus and the doctrine of the *kenosis*. Earlier we identified this passage as one of those Pauline poems that functions solidly as a hymn of Christ. It describes our Lord's nature and ascribes praise to him to the glory of God the Father. It makes perfect sense to teach, rehearse, and pray this passage through song—to respond to its truth and power by creating a hymn and by singing it.

Lord Jesus Christ, How Far You Came

...He humbled himself and became obedient to death... Php. 2:8

1. Lord Je - sus Christ, how far you came from
2. Lord Je - sus Christ, how deep your love for
3. Lord Je - sus Christ, how great your grace to
4. Lord Je - sus Christ, ex - al - ted high by

heav - en's high - est throne, to take on you our
sin - ners, poor and lost, that you should come from
die the death you died: ac - cur - sed for a
God the Fa - ther's Word; O speed the day when

hu - man frame and wear our na - ture, bear our shame, for
heav'n a - bove, a ser - vant be, our sins re - move, and
sin - ful race, we scarce can look up - on your face: our
all will cry, in heav'n and earth and sea and sky, that

our sin to a - tone,___ for our sin to a - tone.
save at such a cost,___ and save at such a cost.
Lord is cru - ci - fied,___ our Lord is cru - ci - fied.
Je - sus Christ is Lord,___ that Je - sus Christ is Lord!

In response to Philippians 2:5-11
Eric J. Alexander, 2001   ©2001 Eric J. Alexander & Paul S. Jones. All rights reserved.

KENOSIS 8.6.8.8.6.6.
Paul S. Jones, 2001

Figure 10.3

Hymns in Your Church and Worship

Sing to the Lord, you saints of his;
praise his holy name. (Ps. 30:4)

When the value of hymnody is grasped, one may have a desire to increase the use of hymns in worship as a church or as an individual. There can be obstacles to overcome in the effort to recover old or to introduce new hymns to a personal or collective repertoire. Education is the best means of introducing hymns or a more challenging musical language to one's congregation. Explaining the meaning of particular texts, their scriptural origin, or something of their composition, form, author, or composer will assist in heightening the appreciation and understanding of a hymn's value. The following are some suggestions to assist in bringing about a modern reformation of hymnody in personal and corporate worship.

Personal Worship

Since we can rightly consider the hymnal to be a prayer book, it would be fitting to own and use one or several. Use them personally or with family members. Include the hymnal as an aid in your devotional life. One might employ a scriptural index or index of scriptural allusions to search for a hymn that corresponds to a passage of Scripture being studied. A hymn can be chosen to help one pray, and it can then be memorized and sung as a prayer each day for a week or throughout a month. Many people discover that the tune will spontaneously appear in their ear or thoughts throughout the day, bringing the text to mind. This can truly help one to remember the teaching of the text and to maintain a spirit of prayer before the Lord. Take time to think through the text and explain it to children. A text understood is one that can be meaningfully sung—worship must be intentional.

Corporate Worship

Congregational singing may seem like the most obvious of places for hymns to be employed, but hymn selection and singing should be anything but routine. Irrespective of whether it is the minister or the music director who chooses congregational song, the same criterion should apply. The text should be biblically sound and meaningful, and the music that accompa-

247

nies the text should be excellent and should facilitate our understanding of the text. For ministers without musical training or musicians without doctrinal clarity, this is a precarious task that would be best done in partnership with an informed colleague. In the flow of the worship service, care must be taken to include elements of praise, confession, and thanksgiving. Hymns may be linked to a common theme for the service or may be tied in some fashion to Scripture readings.

Most modern hymnals provide helpful indexes that should assist in hymn selection. For example, the index of scriptural quotations or allusions can quickly direct one to texts that may be appropriate to the sermon text. Subject headings may help one locate hymns that deal with the sovereignty of God or stewardship or another relevant topic. The metrical index will indicate other tunes with an identical meter, so that if a strong text in a particular hymnal is accompanied by an unknown or lousy tune (yes, there are some), it can be matched with a better or more familiar one. At times this alternate pairing will heighten the congregation's interaction with the text.

Hymn Services

One method of introducing hymns to a congregation or Bible study group is through a short hymn service. This might last ten to twenty minutes and include three or more hymns. It is helpful for the person leading such a service to have consulted resources for the purpose of learning about the hymn's author or composer.[36] This information can then be shared with the congregation. A theme will help unify such a service; for example, "Hymns of Luther," "Hymns of Philip Doddridge," "Hymns of Joy," "Passion Hymns," "Hymns from 1 Corinthians 15," "Evening Hymns," or "Hymns Written by Missionaries."

More significantly, the leader should have considered the role(s) of the hymn—praise, proclamation, prayer, and so on—and should share such insights with those who will be singing. The central focus must be on God and his word. A verse or passage of Scripture upon which the hymn is based can be read and its place in the hymn noted so as to draw attention to the teaching of the word of God. Such preplanned hymn services with teaching enrich and enliven the hymn-singing experience and are more significant than choosing favorites or singing random songs. The choir can also assist in introducing new tunes or by singing a median stanza as a means of setting it apart.

248

Hymn-of-the-Month

Another helpful way to introduce hymns to one's congregation or household is to select one hymn each month and sing it each day or each Sunday at one service consistently throughout that month. Permission to print the hymn as a bulletin insert can be obtained from the publisher if required, and the hymn could travel home with families so that it may be learned together. The same hymn could appear in the Sunday school curriculum or at the youth group meeting, making it a church-wide effort. This would demonstrate its value to the entire congregation and make hymn learning a shared experience. Singing hymns is a unifying activity, and it is our common heritage.

An explanation of the hymn or information concerning its provenance can appear in the bulletin or be recounted by a song leader. If the church has a choir, the choir can prepare the hymn and introduce it immediately before the congregation sings it for the first time or simply serve as a force to help lead the singing. Choirs can function as corporate teaching ensembles and should be employed in helpful, creative ways in worship. They need not be limited to performing an anthem or static service music week after week.

Hymn Festivals

Any time of year is a good time for a hymn festival, but certain seasons or events are especially well suited: Advent, Christmas, Lent, Easter, Pentecost, Reformation Day, the opening of a new church, the dedication of a new pipe organ, the installation of a new pastor. At a hymn festival, one can take the concepts of a hymn service into a grander context in a fully integrated service of sixty to ninety minutes. This is a wonderful chance for pastors and music directors to work together to prepare a meaningful service of worship, particularly if such collaboration is not their regular practice. Planning is an essential aspect. Theme, timing, and texts all need careful consideration. The structure of the service should be solid. The flow of events, ideas, keys, and mood should be thought through, and a printed order of service is of excellent help and guidance to those attending. A hymn festival can center around one doctrine, era, country, theme, or composer—or it can have considerable diversity. Employing rehearsed choirs and instrumental ensembles contributes to the effective leading and accompanying of hymns. Here are the elements in a hymn festival held on Reformation Sunday 2000 at Tenth Presbyterian Church:

Prelude
Welcome
Call to Worship/Prayer
Hymn: "A Mighty Fortress Is Our God" {Ein' feste Burg}
Historical Commentary: "The Context of the Reformation"

I. *Sola scriptura (Scripture alone)*
   Scripture: 2 Timothy 3:10–17
   Hymn: "God's Amazing Word" {Sola Scriptura}

II. *Sola fide (faith alone)*
    Scripture: Romans 3:21–28
    Hymn: "Heaven's Gift" {Sola Fide}

III. *Sola gratia (grace alone)*
     Scripture: Ephesians 2:1–10
     Hymn: "Alive in Christ" {Sola Gratia}

IV. *Solus christus (Christ alone)*
    Hymn: "O Sacred Head, Now Wounded" {Passion Chorale}
    Prayer
    Offering/Offertory
    Scripture: 1 Corinthians 1:18–31
    Hymn: "Christ Alone" {Solus Christus}
    Sermon: "Christ Alone" (1 Corinthians 2:2)

V. *Soli deo gloria (glory to God alone)*
   Hymn: "Now Thank We All Our God" {Nun danket alle Gott}
   Scripture: Revelation 4:1–2, 6–11; 5:6–14
   Hymn: " 'Round the Throne in Radiant Glory" {Qadosh}
   Hymn: "Give Praise to God" {Soli Deo}
   Benediction: Romans 11:33–36
   Postlude

Accompanying Hymns

The church may have a pianist, keyboard player, or organist who follows a song leader; there may be a worship team; or everything may be led from

250

the organ console. In any case, the way one plays affects the way the people sing. Most accompanists, music directors, and pastors probably acknowledge this at some level, but the full extent and responsibility of this role are seldom conceived or realized.

The accompanist's ability and choices directly influence the way people sing. This is true not only of congregations, but of choirs as well. An accompanist can influence the choir as much or more than the choir director. Why? Because in music we respond to what we hear more than to what we see, read, or are told. In a band or orchestra, the percussion section must be attentive to the conductor and be especially accurate. If the snare-drum player moves a little faster or slower than the conductor, the whole group will go with the drum. The percussive nature of the piano has a similar effect. A choir or congregation will typically move with what they hear. The organ, if it is a good one, has the power and volume to lead with force, but the organist's articulation (length of notes and silences) and other factors make considerable difference in what results.

In addition to tempo and rhythm, which have already been mentioned, the accompanist influences the congregation in terms of volume and dynamic as well as by pacing and style (time between verses, how long chords are held, how articulately one plays). Breathing and ensemble are affected. Most significantly, through these various parameters one can stimulate the individual worshiper's thinking as well as his or her connection to the truths being sung.

This last matter is the most important, and all the others are tied up in it. There is a great lack of thinking in worship today. Some are much more concerned about feeling, about their own emotional connection and what they are getting out of the worship experience. Others act as spectators from the pew, never becoming involved in singing or praying. And, we must realize that our singing is not directed to each other but to God. If we truly grasped that when we sing we are praising him or praying to him, that we are in the presence of the King of Glory, and that we should have come to thank him, praise him, and ascribe worth to him (not to make ourselves feel better), we would begin to understand how important it is to know *what* we are singing. This is one reason, among others, that hymns have fallen out of popularity and use in many circles. It is because they require thought, and we do not want to think. "I come to church to be refreshed—not to work" is a common attitude. But proper worship does take work, thought, preparation, and action.

Hymns deliver Christian doctrine directly from Scripture or relay a message of challenge or encouragement to fellow believers. Likewise, choruses that set Scripture to music can deliver God's word to us. How we think about these pieces and how we sing them matters. The accompanist has a lot to do with that. In fact, I would go so far as to say that supporting and influencing congregational song is the single most important thing one does as a church accompanist. Effective hymn-playing requires practice and thought about the *introduction* (which will set key, tempo, mood, character, and volume and will acquaint the ear with the tune), *breathing* (which should occur with grammatical punctuation where it makes sense—by lifting the hands off the keys and rearticulating with the new word), *articulation* (the attack, the amount of space between notes, the use of damper pedal, the length of notes, emphasis—all of these things affect the sound and character of the music), *registration* (contemplate the text when choosing the color, volume, and character of the accompaniment), and *improvisation* through alternative keys or harmonies (what is altered should enhance the text or music without drawing unnecessary attention to the player). One should review the hymn before it is sung in worship and consider the above parameters in preparation. Being prepared does not mean the accompanist is trapped within a box or some sort of invariable environment. There is room for spontaneity and for inspiration, but being prepared strongly corresponds to being effective.

Writing Hymns

Many people have asked me about the process of writing hymns. How is it done? Who writes hymns? Since I am convinced of the need for *canticum novae* and am engaged in the ongoing activity of composing biblical hymns to aid our worship of God, I wish to offer a brief reflection on the process of hymn-writing in the hopes of stimulating other readers who may have such gifts to exercise their hands and minds.

Author

Often the best hymn writers are ministers who penned hymn texts to summarize and imprint the salient points of their sermons in the minds of congregants. Seasoned pastors are especially well suited to hymn-writing, as a survey of Protestant hymnody readily verifies. Biblical learning, life experience, and knowledge of great literature and other hymns provide requisite subject matter, poetic models, and ample fare for allusion.

Whether preacher or poet, hymn writers find inspiration in the same places that all Christian poets do—in Scripture, in nature, in a life experience that prompts reflection upon spiritual neediness, or in an overpowering awareness of God's glory. Hymn-writing can be an act of Christian devotion. It both germinates and develops through study of the Bible, and it may, in fact, lead one to deeper levels of spiritual discovery.

Not every good poem makes a good hymn, and not every good hymn necessarily meets the criterion of great poetry. Hymn poetry, in general, should be limited to six or fewer strophes of consistent length. Four to six lines per stanza will be best managed, and each should maintain parallel meter, rhythm, and stress with its corresponding line in other stanzas to avoid an awkward rendering when sung. Strong and weak syllables should appropriately correspond to the musical beats, something that cannot occur if the hymn writer is inconsistent. Most hymn texts rhyme, and there are numerous rhyme scheme options (although good hymns and psalm paraphrases exist that do not rhyme).

Since the melody and rhythm cannot be altered strophe by strophe, a consistent mood in the poetry works best, as the hymn will be stronger if its verbal and musical sentiments agree. A refrain provides opportunity for a change of spirit or direction, or it can serve to summarize or reinforce the theme. Further, while a hymn text may contain figures of speech, the primary goal of a hymn—as with a well-crafted sermon—should be the delivery of an identifiable message. Hymn-singing is a forum in which a broad public encounters Christian doctrine, so the poetry should permit the least educated to comprehend (although not necessarily at first reading), yet give the discerning mind something to ponder.

Composer

A good composer chooses a worthy poem, considers its meaning, and identifies its rhyme scheme, metrical pattern, and syntax. The composer will want to allow time for the text to work itself into his or her consciousness. A standard or modified hymn form will probably suggest itself on the basis of the text's pattern, and the composer will be mindful of this in out-

253

lining the tune. One seeks to discover the architecture and overall sense of the poem—metrical rhythm, mood, energy, and pacing. On these bases a key and range befitting the spirit of the poem are chosen. Keys and modes, by virtue of their physical properties within the equal system of tuning and corresponding overtone series, have colors and qualities. Some are more powerful than others; some are brighter or more melancholy. It is also important to pick a range that can be ably managed by untrained voices.

The melody is what the singer will remember most vividly, and thus it should be singable, lyrical, and logical, yet fresh and not overly predictable. It should creatively strengthen the singer's attention to and understanding of the text. Several rhythmic choices may present themselves after studying the text, but the composer must determine if one draws attention toward or away from the meaning more than another and whether the rhythm helps the meter and rhyme of the verse to avoid seeming trite or commonplace. Often one "hears" the harmony while conceiving the melody, but this basic chord structure can be refined once melodic and rhythmic elements are determined. The value of "line" within voice parts should not be underestimated. Too many hymns leave the altos with two notes side by side over multiple measures.

Once written, the whole work should be examined and proofread multiple times, leading to more subtle changes of tone or nuance, in the same manner that one might polish a poem or essay by selecting a more colorful word or fashioning a more economical phrase. Hopefully, the result will be a welcome addition to the rich repertory of hymns from which we benefit and will find resonance in the congregations of churches who value this heritage.

Conclusion

In answer to the question of whether hymns should be utilized in worship, we must conclude that there are too many examples of hymns throughout Scripture to ignore or to forbid their use in present-day worship. In answer to the concern that only canonical psalms should be sung, we must acknowledge that there are commands in Psalms, Isaiah, Revelation, and elsewhere to "sing a new song" and numerous accounts where the saints in both Old and New Testaments sang new songs of praise and deliverance. Therefore, to cease creating and singing new hymns of praise to our great God would be contrary to the teaching of Scripture. Further, the pictures of perfect, heavenly worship in Revelation reveal echoes of psalms and hymns in paraphrase, combining the praises of all ages in an eternal song that is both old and new. Surely this must inform our current worship practices.

We must also acknowledge the instruction of the Apostle Paul in the epistles to the Ephesians and Colossians to "sing psalms." Singing psalms in worship is a biblical mandate—not an optional activity. Whether psalms are sung as unison chant or four-part harmony, with instruments or *a cappella*, in a metrical form or as a paraphrase, in English, French, or Hebrew, appear to be extrabiblical decisions. We no more sing in the same style as the early church did than we gather together in the same types of physical structures or arrive for corporate worship by the same method of transportation or understand things with the same sociocultural perspective. It is not the make of the vehicle delivering the psalm that is so significant, but that the inspired word of God is sung back to him for his glory and for our edification and instruction. The vehicle, however, should suit the text and must not contradict it. Further, the quality of the mode through which we meet our king should be our finest offering possible.

In church music, the quality of the music itself—melody, harmony, rhythm, and form—plays a significant role in terms of both the interpretation of the text and the delivery of its truth. If the musical setting communicates a message contrary to the text, its meaning can be thwarted or even miscommunicated. This is the unfortunate case with much of the new music of the last few decades. While there may have been a positive return to singing Scripture in some segments of the Contemporary Christian Music movement, there are not many examples where the form or other musical elements suitably support the weight and meaning of a text, when it is one worthy of being sung.

We should answer the call to sing *canticum novae* by following the examples of Luther, Watts, and Boice. Their hymns are biblically derived, artistically conceived, theologically sound, and exegetically purposeful. They fulfill and reinforce biblical patterns of praise, proclamation, and prayer as the rightful roles of church music. We must be willing to educate our congregations so that they sing with understanding—with the heart and the head. We must support properly—both philosophically and financially—the ministry of music in our local congregations, engaging and compensating church musicians who are professionally skilled and biblically mindful. Such musicians will understand both the seriousness and joy of their office, will measure their creations by Scripture, and will be unwilling to offer less than the best they can to the King of kings.

If there has ever been an age so myopically transfixed by its own importance and significance and a people so quick to dismiss its spiritual heritage, the age is ours and the people are evangelical Protestants. One of James Boice's chief goals in preaching to the evangelical church at large was to reawaken it from its worldliness—from self-obsessed, relativistic, pluralistic values and theology—by reclaiming the doctrines of grace expressed in the *solae* of the Reformation. He believed the cure for evangelical worldliness was to view all of life through the lens of Romans 11:36, where God reigns supreme, since all comes "from him and through him and to him." In his last few years, and in the final twelve months in particular, he preached more strongly than ever the message that spirited singing of biblical hymns was an excellent and necessary way by which to exercise the mind and soul, that this was a worthy and essential spiritual occupation of every Christian. After all, it will be our occupation and delight for all eternity as we sing the old songs and the new, psalms and hymns, law and grace—the songs of Moses and of the Lamb.

> They held harps given them by God and sang the song of Moses the servant of God and the song of the Lamb. (Rev. 15:2–3)

11

RESTORING PSALM SINGING TO OUR WORSHIP

TERRY L. JOHNSON

When I was a freshman in college, the minister leading our Bible study asked us to turn to Psalm 92, which he then began to lead us in singing to the tune of "If I Were a Rich Man":

> It is good to give thanks,
> And sing praises to the name of the Lord, O Most High;
> To declare Your lovingkindness,
> In the morning and by night.
>
> It is good to give thanks,
> And sing praises to the name of the Lord, O Most High;
> To declare Your lovingkindness,
> In the morning and by night.
>
> And with the ten-stringed lute and with the harp,
> With resounding music on the lyre.
> For You, O Lord, have made me glad by what You have done,
> I will sing for joy at the works of Your hands.
> How great are Your works, O Lord!
> Your thoughts are very deep.

It is good to give thanks,
And sing praises to the name of the Lord, O Most High;
To declare Your lovingkindness,
In the morning and by night.[1]

In my California Christian way, I thought that it was "neat." The psalms were meant to be sung, and we were singing them—or, at least one of them. What could make more sense? What a great way to memorize Scripture, I thought.

That for me was the beginning of a fascination with the psalms that has continued to the present. Nearly five years passed before I received any more encouragement. In March 1978, I rode British Rail up to Edinburgh to begin a one-month internship at St. David's Broomhouse Church as part of my degree requirements at Trinity College in Bristol. The first Sunday there I learned that more psalms than just the ninety-second had been put to music. The hymnal of the Church of Scotland had nothing but psalms in the first 190 pages—all 150 were rhymed and metered for singing. I was amazed. Where had these been hiding all my life? Why did not American churches use them? It seemed odd to me. Why would Bible-believing Christians in America not care about singing the psalms? For me this was what we would later call a "no brainer." God wrote the psalms. He wrote them to be sung. Therefore, we ought to sing them.

The psalms are the 800-pound gorilla of evangelical worship. There they sit in the middle of our Bibles, the book that provides the content of our worship. They make up the longest book in the Bible. They are the only canonical hymnbook. Yet they are mostly ignored even by those with high views of Scripture. Nearly a decade has passed since the *Trinity Psalter* set all of the psalms to familiar and singable tunes.[2] The whole Psalter is easily and inexpensively accessible to hymnal-using congregations. Though nearly twenty-five thousand copies have been sold, this number represents less than 10 percent of the membership of the Presbyterian Church of America, James Boice's denomination. The anecdotal evidence is that few congregations in the Presbyterian Church of America sing psalms on a regular basis from any source. Extend the survey to include the broader evangelical world and one would probably find that the typical worshiper is more likely to be struck by lightning on Sunday morning than to sing a psalm in church. What has been obvious to me for the last quarter of a century—

that psalms should be sung — is obvious to only the tiniest of remnants. The 800-pound gorilla sits, largely ignored.

Toward the end of his life Dr. Boice complained with increased volume about the replacing of the great hymns of the church "with trite jingles that have more in common with contemporary advertising ditties than with the psalms."[3] In his last written work (published posthumously) the direction of this thought is clear. There he notes that the "praise songs of the Psalter" do not fall into the trap of narcissism that characterizes so many "contemporary praise songs." Instead of self-absorption, they are focused on God, and for that reason, he argues, "they are such good models for our worship and . . . *should be used in worship more often than they are.*"[4]

It is upon this growing conviction of Dr. Boice that I would like to build. The psalms should be used — that is, sung — in worship more often than they are. The case is essentially a simple one, requiring merely that evangelical pastors admit the existence of the 800-pound gorilla and begin to use it as God intended that it be used. It is helpful at times to step back from familiar things and practices and ask "Why is this here?" or "Why do we do (or not do) this or that?" Let's ask these questions about the Psalter.

What are the implications of a psalter in the canon of Scripture? Is it not that the psalms should be sung as a regular part of our worship? Let's begin our review with a survey of the nature and virtues of the psalms and then examine the value of singing (as opposed to merely reading) them.

The Psalter

The canonical Book of Psalms may correctly be viewed as the Bible's own devotional book. Bonhoeffer made this point in his brief work *The Psalms: Prayer Book of the Bible.*[5] Indeed the Book of Psalms is the primary source from which all other devotional books have drawn. Thomas à Kempis (1380–1471), for example, quotes the Psalms more than the gospels in *The Imitation of Christ*, which is "the most popular of all Christian devotional books."[6] The Psalter provides the people of God with the verbal images, names, and terminology with which to understand God and how we are to relate to him. They teach us how to speak to God, providing us with the language to use in each of the following categories (included are a few examples of each):

1. Praise:

> O Lord, our Lord,
> How majestic is Your name in all the earth. (Ps. 8:1a)

> The heavens are telling of the glory of God;
> And their expanse is declaring the work of His hands. (Ps. 19:1)

> The earth is the Lord's, and all it contains,
> The world, and those who dwell in it.
> For He has founded it upon the seas
> And established it upon the rivers. (Ps. 24:1–2)

2. Confession:

> I acknowledged my sin to You,
> And my iniquity I did not hide;
> I said, "I will confess my transgressions to the Lord";
> And You forgave the guilt of my sin. (Ps. 32:5)

> Be gracious to me, O God, according to Your lovingkindness;
> According to the greatness of Your compassion blot out my
>   transgressions.
> Wash me thoroughly from my iniquity
> And cleanse me from my sin. (Ps. 51:1–2)

3. Sorrow and complaint:

> My God, my God, why have You forsaken me?
> Far from my deliverance are the words of my groaning. (Ps.
>   22:1)

> Out of the depths I have cried to You, O Lord.
> Lord, hear my voice!
> Let Your ears be attentive
> To the voice of my supplications. (Ps. 130:1–2)

4. Thanksgiving:

Bless the Lord, O my soul,
And all that is within me, *bless* His holy name.
Bless the Lord, O my soul,
And forget none of His benefits. (Ps. 103:1–2)

Give thanks to the Lord, for He is good,
For His lovingkindness is everlasting.
Give thanks to the God of gods,
For His lovingkindness is everlasting. (Ps. 136:1–2)

5. Trust:

The Lord is my shepherd,
I shall not want. (Ps. 23:1)

Do not fret because of evildoers,
Be not envious toward wrongdoers. (Ps. 37:1)

God is our refuge and strength,
A very present help in trouble. (Ps. 46:1)

He who dwells in the shelter of the Most High
Will abide in the shadow of the Almighty. (Ps. 91:1)

I will lift up mine eyes unto the hills,
from whence cometh my help. (Ps. 121:1 Authorized Version)

These fourteen psalms are but the tip of the iceberg, 10 percent of the Psalter, whose richness has stretched the capacity of commentators to express. "There is no one book of Scripture that is more helpful to the devotions of the saints than this," says Matthew Henry, "and it has been so in all ages of the church, ever since it was written."[7] Authors from ancient to modern times note the following virtues.

The Doctrinal Completeness of the Psalms

In his 1528 "Preface to the Psalter," Luther refers to the Psalter as a "little Bible." He says, "In it is comprehended most beautifully and briefly everything that is in the entire Bible." He calls it a "short Bible," in which is provided an "entire summary" of the whole "comprised in one little book." Before him Athanasius (ca. 296–373) referred to the Psalter as an "epitome of the whole Scriptures." And Basil (ca. 330–70) called it a "compend of all divinity."[8] All that the Bible teaches is found in summary form in the Book of Psalms.

The Christological Completeness of the Psalms

The Psalms prophesy Christ's life and ministry and especially his suffering. Note the following references to Jesus' life and ministry:

- ✧ deity: Psalms 8:4–6; 27; 45:6–7; 102:25–26; 104:4 (Heb. 1:5–2:9)
- ✧ incarnation: Psalms 22:9–10; 40:6–8; 98 (Heb. 10:5–7)
- ✧ adoration of the magi: Psalm 72:9–15 (Matt. 2:1–11)
- ✧ baptism: Psalm 2:7–8 (Mark 1:9–11)
- ✧ temptation: Psalm 91:11–12 (Matt. 4:1–11)
- ✧ ministry: Psalm 146:7–9 (Luke 4:16–26)
- ✧ obedience: Psalm 40:6–10 (Heb. 2:10; 10:5–7)
- ✧ teaching: Psalm 78:1–6 (Matt. 13:34–35)

In addition one finds references in the Psalms to the last week of Christ's earthly life:

- ✧ triumphal entry: Psalm 118:20–29 (Matt. 21:1–11)
- ✧ cleansing of the temple: Psalm 69:9 (John 2:13–17; Matt. 21:12–17)
- ✧ betrayal: Psalm 41:7–9 (John 13:12–30; cf. Ps. 55:12–14)
- ✧ rejection: Psalm 35:19–21 (John 15:18–27)
- ✧ trial and mocking: Psalm 69:17–21 (Matt. 27:24–34)
- ✧ crucifixion: Psalm 22:13–18 (John 19:17–24)
- ✧ insults: Psalm 22:6–8 (Matt. 27:35–44)
- ✧ forsaken: Psalm 22:1–3 (Matt. 27:45–49)
- ✧ committal: Psalm 31:1–5 (Luke 23:46–49)
- ✧ death: Psalm 34:15–20 (John 19:28–37)

❖ resurrection: Psalm 16:8–11 (Acts 2:22–32)
❖ ascension: Psalm 110 (Acts 2:33–36)

Nowhere in the New Testament is the internal suffering of Christ described as in the psalms (especially Ps. 22). There is a sense in which all psalms are messianic (Luke 24:27). Augustine says: "The voice of Christ and His church is well-nigh the only voice to be heard in the Psalms."[9] The lack of gospel content is not a defect that may rightly be attributed to the psalms. Luther labeled his favorite psalms the *psalmi paulini* (Pauline psalms). He had in mind several of the penitential psalms (Pss. 32, 51, 130, 143), where clearly and forcefully human depravity and guilt, spiritual repentance, and free grace are taught. Luther says in his "Preface to the Psalter" (1528) that the Book of Psalms "should be precious and dear to us if only because it most clearly promises the death and resurrection of Christ, and describes His kingdom, and the nature and standing of all Christian people." Bishop William Horsley (1774–1858) put it this way: "There is not a page of this Book of Psalms in which the pious reader will not find his Savior, if he reads with a view of finding Him."[10] Henry observes: "So much is there in it of Christ and His gospel, as well as of God and His law, that it has been called the abstract, or summary, of both testaments."[11]

The Experiential Completeness of the Psalms

The whole range of Christian experience finds expression in the psalms. Athanasius says that they "embrace the whole life of men, the affections of his mind, and the motions of his soul." One may find, he says, "a Psalm suited to every occasion, and thus will find that they were written for him."[12] Whether one has plunged to the "depths" (Ps. 130:1) or to the "lowest pit" and the "dark places" (88:6) or is stuck in the "deep mire" (69:1–2, 14–15), there is a psalm suited to the occasion. Pursued by enemies (7)? God seem distant (10)? Lonely or afflicted (25:16–22)? Needy (86:1)? Despairing (42–43)? Encompassed by the cords of death (116:3–4)? Walking through the valley of the shadow of death (23)? On the other hand, are you delighting in God and his law (1:2; 19; 37:4; 40:8; 73:25; 94:19; 112:1; 119:16, 24, 35, 77, 97, 103, 162, 174)? Are you glad and exulting in God (4:7; 9:2; 122:1)? Rejoicing in the Lord and enjoying his pleasures (16:11; 32:11; 33:1, 21; 87:7; 89:16; 100:2; 104:34; 105:2–3; 145:7)? Experiencing satisfaction or fulfillment in him (17:15; 63:3–8; 65:4; 90:14)? Have you tasted and seen

263

that the Lord is good (34:8)? Are you thirsting, yearning, for his presence (42:1–2; 63:1; 84:1–2; 143:6)?

The positive side of Christian experience is given full play as well. Luther says: "In whatever situation he may be," the Christian will find "in that situation Psalms and words to fit his case." Indeed he will find words better than his own, "so that he could not put it better himself, or find or wish for anything better."[13] Calvin concurs in this judgment, referring to the psalms as "an anatomy of all the parts of the soul" in which "there is not an emotion of which anyone can be conscious that is not here represented as in a mirror." The Holy Spirit, he says, "has here drawn to the life all the griefs, sorrows, fears, doubts, hopes, cares, perplexities, in short, all the distracting emotions, with which the minds of men are want to be agitated."[14]

There is a wholeness to the psalms as designed by their divine author that addresses the whole of human life. There is a realism as well, teaching the positive and negative sides of spiritual experience: the light and the dark, the delightful and the degrading, the victorious and the defeating, the hopeful and the discouraging. Upon these three virtues of doctrinal, christological, and experiential completeness authors both ancient and modern agree. Basil summarizes this view: "The Book of Psalms is a compendium of all divinity; a common store of medicine for the soul; a universal magazine of good doctrines, profitable to everyone in all conditions."[15]

On September 11, 2001, the United States suffered the worst terrorist attack in the history of the world. Thousands died, billions of dollars of property damage was suffered, landmarks were destroyed. The American people were profoundly shaken. The next morning I happened to turn to a contemporary Christian radio station. A very serious, pastorally sensitive discussion was taking place. Naturally enough, this discussion was broken up by the broadcasting of songs from the world of contemporary Christian music. Invariably the songs were utterly ill suited to the mood of the occasion or even of the rest of the program. There seemed to be nothing in their collection of contemporary genre that could express in word or music the sorrow, grief, tears, complaints, pleas for justice, or cries for God to avenge the blood of the innocent. So back and forth the morning program went, from serious, somber discussion to upbeat, exuberant, happy, and frankly frivolous songs, and back again.

The following Wednesday (September 12) our congregation concluded a special service of prayer by singing Psalm 94 to the tune Austrian Hymn ("Glorious Things of Thee Are Spoken"). The contrast was notable:

God of vengeance, O Jehovah,
God of vengeance, O shine forth!
Rise up, O You Judge of Nations!
Render to the proud their worth.
Lord, how long shall the wicked,
How long shall the wicked boast?
Arrogant the words they pour out,
Ill men all, a taunting host. . . .

Can destructive rulers join You
And by law disorder build?
They conspire against the righteous,
Sentence just ones to be killed.
But the Lord is still my stronghold;
God, my Refuge, will repay.
He'll for sin wipe out the wicked;
Them the Lord our God will slay.

I doubt if any song written in the last hundred years compares with these pleas to avenge, from "God of vengeance, O Jehovah, / God of vengeance, O shine forth!" to its powerful conclusion: "He'll for sin wipe out the wicked; / them the Lord our God will slay." When one is a victim of wicked violence and remains vulnerable to further attacks, these are profoundly comforting and satisfying words. That such expressions may sound strange to modern evangelicals is a fact to be seriously pondered, especially as we examine what evangelical piety has become today. Doubters may wish to consult Romans 13:4 and Revelation 6:10.

That Friday (September 14) the president asked for "Services of Prayer and Remembrance" at noon throughout the nation. We organized a service in which, among other things, we sang psalms. First we sang psalms of grief:

- ✧ Psalm 130:1–2, 5–6, to the tune Martyrdom ("Alas! And Did My Savior Bleed?")
- ✧ Psalm 13:1–6, to the tune Passion Chorale ("O Sacred Head, Now Wounded")
- ✧ Psalm 25:16–20, to the tune Trentham ("Breathe on Me, Breath of God")
- ✧ Psalm 142:1–6, to the tune Rockingham Old

265

We sang "Lord, from the depths to Thee I cried. . . . O hear my voice and hearken to my supplicating plea" (Ps. 130:1), "O Lord, my God, consider and hear my earnest cries" (13:3), and "My griefs of heart abound; my sore distress relieve. . . . Consider Thou my foes because they many are; and it a cruel hatred is which they against me bear" (25:17, 19). We concluded this section of the service with this psalm:

> All unprotected, lo, I stand,
> No friendly guardian at my hand,
> No place of flight or refuge near,
> And none to whom my soul is dear.
> O Lord, my Savior, now to Thee,
> Without a hope beside, I flee,
> To Thee, my shelter from the strife,
> My portion in the land of life. (Ps. 142:4–5)

When one has plunged into the depths, is feeling unprotected, or needs refuge and shelter, it is deeply comforting to express in song these emotions with the words that God himself has given to us.

Second, we sang psalms that cry for protection and justice (see also Pss. 28; 58:6–11; 60:2–5, 11):

✧ Psalm 54:1–7, to the tune Ebenezer ("O the Deep, Deep Love of Jesus)
✧ Psalm 57:1–5, to the tune Germany ("Jesus, Thy Blood and Righteousness")
✧ Psalm 71:1–6, to the tune St. Christopher ("Beneath the Cross of Jesus")

Again, it was deeply comforting and satisfying to identify our wicked oppressors, those "strangers" who "have come up against [us], even men of violence," who "seek my life's destruction" (54:3); to plead in song for God to defend us from those "who would [my] life devour," from "cruel men" who are "like hungry lions wild and fierce," "whose teeth are spears," whose words are "envenomed darts and two-edg'd swords" (57:3–4); to cry for deliverance from "wicked hands . . . hands cruel and unjust" (71:4). "Now save me," we sang. "Grant me justice by your strength." Yes, even "in your truth destroy them all!" (54:1, 5):

> Thy mercy, God, to me extend;
> On Thy protection I depend,
> And to Thy wings for shelter haste
> Until this storm be overpast. (57:1)

They tried to snare us in their net; yet "they are fallen, by Thy decree, into the pit they dug for me" (57:6):

> Be Thou my rock, my dwelling place,
> My constant safe resort.
> Thou my salvation hast ordained;
> Thou art my rock and fort. (71:3)

Third, we sang psalms of trust:

- ✧ Psalm 23, to the tune Crimond
- ✧ Psalm 37:1–2, 10–19, to the tune Forest Green
- ✧ Psalm 46:1–3, 10–11, to the tune Bethlehem
- ✧ Psalm 91:1–12, to the tune Hyfrydol ("Jesus! What a Friend for Sinners")

For us to sing "The Lord's my shepherd, I'll not want," "Have no disturbing thoughts about those doing wickedly," "God is our refuge and our strength, in straits a present aid," and "Who with God Most High finds shelter, in the Almighty's shadow hides," was remarkably comforting, bringing unparalleled words of unequaled spiritual power to bear upon our hearts.

Scripture and History

Our rich experience of the psalms during the week of September 11, 2001, only underscores the testimony of the saints throughout the ages. Because the Psalter is God's hymnbook, given by the inspiration of the Holy Spirit ("by the Holy Spirit, *through* the mouth of our father David"—Acts 4:25), we find that they are what we would expect: theologically, christologically, and experientially complete. God has provided a psalm for every occasion, a psalm for every need. Because they are not merely human words but God's, their spiritual efficacy is experienced through their use without respect to the generation, age, race, or culture of the user. The psalms are a powerful means of shaping a distinctive biblical piety. They express the inner experience of believing hearts even as they transform them.

Thus from the Scottish Covenanters to the Benedictine monks (what Hughes Oliphant Old suggests might be seen as the "infrared and ultraviolet of the liturgical spectrum"), one finds "a determined commitment to the use of psalms as Christian prayer."[16] This determined commitment goes back to Israel itself, which from the time of David wrote and compiled these psalms for use in temple and synagogue worship.[17] The glimpses of the worship of the apostolic church in the New Testament demonstrate what Old claims: "The Psalms formed the core of the praises of the New Testament church."[18] When the church gathered for prayer as recorded in Acts 4, they sang ("lifted their voices . . . with one accord") first from Psalm 146 and then from Psalm 2 (Acts 4:24–26). Apparently they had no trouble in making the transition from the old covenant to the new. The psalms were immediately, even instinctively seized upon as suitable Christian devotional literature. Paul commanded both the Ephesian (5:19) and Colossian (3:16) churches to sing psalms, and he observed that the church at Corinth did so (1 Cor. 14:15, 26). James instructs his readers ("the twelve tribes who are dispersed abroad," apparently a way of referring to the whole church) to sing psalms (*psallō*; James 5:13). Moreover there are 55 citations of the psalms in the New Testament[19] and by one count nearly 150 additional clear allusions to the Psalter and still another 200 fainter ones.[20]

This instinct to own and christologically interpret the psalms has continued throughout the centuries, as is clear from the earliest Christian writings and liturgies.[21] The writers of *The Psalms in Worship* and others collected a number of testimonies from the church fathers that survive to this day. For example, Tertullian, in the second century, testified that psalm singing was not only an essential feature of the worship of his day, but also had become an important part of the daily life of the people. Athanasius says it was the custom of his day to sing psalms, which he calls "a mirror of the soul."[22] Bishop Eusebius of Caesarea (ca. 260–ca. 340) left this vivid picture of the psalm singing of his day: "The command to sing Psalms in the name of the Lord was obeyed by everyone in every place: for the command to sing is in force in all churches which exist among nations, not only the Greeks but also throughout the whole world, and in towns, villages and in the fields."[23] Augustine (343–430) in his *Confessions* 9.4 says of them:

"They are sung through the whole world, and there is nothing hid from the heart thereof."[24] Jerome (died 420) said that he learned the psalms when he was a child and sang them daily in his old age. He also writes:

> The Psalms were continually to be heard in the fields and vineyards of Palestine. The plowman, as he held his plow, chanted the Hallelujah; and the reaper, the vinedresser, and the shepherd sang something from the Psalms of David. Where the meadows were colored with flowers, and the singing birds made their plaints, the Psalms sounded even more sweetly. These Psalms are our love-songs, these the instruments of our agriculture.[25]

Apollinaris Sidonius (ca. 431–ca. 482) represents boatmen working their heavy barges up the waters of ancient France and "singing Psalms till the banks echo with 'Hallelujah.'" Chrysostom (died 407), renowned Greek father and patriarch of Constantinople, says:

> All Christians employ themselves in David's Psalms more frequently than in any other part of the Old or New Testament. The grace of the Holy Spirit hath so ordered it that they should be recited and sung night and day. In the Church's vigils the first, the middle, and the last are David's Psalms. In the morning David's Psalms are sought for; and David is the first, the midst, and the last of the day. At funeral solemnities, the first, the midst, and the last is David. Many who know not a letter can say David's Psalms by heart. In all the private houses, where women toil—in the monasteries—in the deserts, where men converse with God, the first, the midst, and the last is David.[26]

He says again:

> David is always in their mouths, not only in the cities and churches, but in courts, in monasteries, in deserts, and the wilderness. He turned earth into heaven and men into angels, being adapted to all orders and to all capacities.[27] (Sixth Homily on Repentance)

During the early centuries of the church these many observations of ordinary believers carrying out common tasks with the psalms constantly on their lips tell us much about the worship of the early church, as well as about the piety of the early Christians.

Indeed over against this devotion to singing psalms was a growing skepticism about hymns "of human composition" throughout this period because of the use to which they were put by heretics. For this reason the Council of Braga (350) made the following enactment: "Except the psalms and hymns of the Old and New Testaments, nothing of a poetical nature is to be song in the church."[28]

The important Council of Laodicea, which met about 360, forbade "the singing of uninspired [i.e., noncanonical] hymns in the church, and the reading of uncanonical books of Scripture" (canon 59). While these were not ecumenical councils, nearly one hundred years later, the Council of Chalcedon (451), the most important and largest of all the general councils, confirmed the Laodicean canons. We cite these decisions, not in order to promote exclusive psalmody, but to make the point that the Psalter clearly was the primary songbook of the early church: "From the earliest times the Christian community sang the Psalms following the practice of the synagogue," says Mary Berry.[29]

The use of psalms by medieval monastic orders (which typically sang their way through them each week), by the Reformers, and by all branches of Christendom testifies to the central role that the psalms should play in the life of a healthy Christian community. "The use of the Psalms in centuries of Christian worship is sufficient to show that . . . there is no part of the Old Testament in which the Christian finds himself more easily and more completely at home," says J. A. Motyer.[30] *The New Bible Dictionary* chimes in: "Moreover from earliest times the Psalter has been both the hymn-book and the prayer book of the Christian Church."[31]

The Psalms Sung

Perhaps it would be wise to pause at this point and collect our thoughts. We have, after all, told only half of the story. But given the woeful ignorance of the Psalter in our day, it is a story that had to be told. It may be that some are now persuaded to give more emphasis to the psalms in public worship. It may even be that most of our readers have been persuaded of this all along. What remains unproven, they might say, is the argument that they must be *sung*. Why not just read them, even read them responsively?

Our answer would be that reading the psalms should be encouraged, not disparaged. But better yet is to use a thing in the manner for which it has been designed. My son may say, "But, Daddy, I like to ride my two-wheel bike by dangling my feet to the ground and pushing myself along." I would answer him, "You can do that and enjoy yourself, but it works so much better if you use the pedals for their real purpose." Given the texts that specify that psalms were sung or are to be sung (Acts 4:24–26; 1 Cor. 14:15, 26; Eph. 5:19; Col. 3:16; James 5:13) and given the testimonies from the early church that they were sung (Tertullian, Eusebius, Athanasius, Augustine, Jerome, and Chrysostom), we would answer the psalms were made to be sung. They are not merely a collection of the poems to be recited. They are songs to be sung. "The Psalms may be spoken," says Westermeyer, "but they cry out to be sung."[32] That in itself is worth pondering. "The Psalms are poems," adds C. S. Lewis, "and poems intended to be sung."[33]

The command to sing is the most frequently repeated command found in Scripture. Thirty-nine times we are commanded to sing. Thirty-two additional times we declare that we will sing (e.g., Pss. 30:4; 47:6–7; 66:1–2; 81:1; 100:1–2; 149:1; Col. 3:16; Eph. 5:18–19). "No command is more frequently and emphatically imposed upon God's people in the Old Testament than is the duty of singing praise to God. In the New Testament these commands are renewed and made emphatic."[34] It would seem that God is keenly interested in both *that* we sing and *what* we sing: "Language in the form of a command could not insist more clearly and distinctly upon the duty of singing praise to God."[35]

Singing must have its own inherent properties that God values. So we ask, What is it about singing that God values? What are its positive properties? This is a subject concerning which evangelical Christians have paid little attention. The two components of song, words and tunes, are both almost universally assumed to be secondary issues, matters of taste or personal preference. Many ministers, who typically have the highest level of theological and pastoral training in a given congregation, turn music matters over to music directors and worship teams. He may have no opinions on these things at all. This indifference flies in the face of the common consent of humanity going back to the Greeks, Hebrews, Reformers, and Enlightenment and post-Enlightenment philosophers and scholars. Carson Holloway demonstrates the utmost seriousness with which the philosophers from Plato to Aristotle to Rousseau to Nietzsche have taken music. He notes the "lack of seriousness" today "about music and a failure to come to grips with its power."[36] By way of contrast, in his *Republic* Plato gives the first place in education to music because of the capacity of "rhythm and harmony" to "insinuate themselves into the inmost part of the soul" and "most vigorously lay hold of it."[37] Aristotle argues much the same, observing that "we are altered in soul when we listen to such things."[38] Essentially their argument was that good music has the capacity to order and discipline the soul, teaching young people in particular to practice restraint and self-control. Control of one's passions and impulses makes a life lived for noble ends possible since it frees one from the disordered and random pursuit of immediate gratification. Bad music, however, has the opposite effect. It breaks down discipline and encourages the casting off of restraint, resulting in a disordered and consequently unworthy manner of living.

The Reformers (Calvin[39] in particular) were very attuned to this power in music. Building upon the thought of Augustine, Calvin recognizes that music is a "gift of God" whose aim is "recreating man and giving him pleasure." However, he urges its moderate use lest it become the "occasion for our giving free reign to dissolution, or making ourselves effeminate in disordered heights" or "become the instrument of lasciviousness" and "shamelessness." Taking a cue from Plato (whom he names) Calvin observes: "There is scarcely in the world anything which is more able to turn or bend this way and that the morals of men, as Plato prudently considered it. And, in fact, we find by experience that it has a sacred and almost incredible power to move hearts in one way or another."

Because of this "incredible power," the use of music ought to be carefully regulated. Calvin cites the precedent of the "ancient doctors of the church" who denounced the "dishonest and shameless songs" to which their contemporaries were "addicted" as "mortal and Satanic poison for corrupting the world." He distinguishes words from tunes, arguing that when bad words are joined to appealing melodies, the song "pierces the heart much more strongly, and enters into it, in a like manner as through a funnel, the wine is poured into the vessel; so also the venom and the corruption is distilled to the depths of the heart by the melody."

Calvin's solution to this potential corruption is words that God himself selected and tunes that are appropriate. Respecting the words he said:

> Moreover, that which St. Augustine has said is true, that no one is able to sing things worthy of God except that which he has received from him. Therefore, when we have looked thoroughly, and searched here and there, we shall

not find better songs nor more fitting for the purpose, than the Psalms of David, which the Holy Spirit spoke and made through him. And moreover, when we sing them, we are certain that God puts in our mouths these, as if he himself were singing in us to exalt his glory.

Regarding tunes:

Care must always be taken that the song be neither light nor frivolous; but that it have weight and majesty (as St. Augustine says), and also, there is a great difference between music which one makes to entertain men at table and in their houses, and the Psalms which are sung in the Church in the presence of God and his angels.

In contrast to the world, whose songs are "in part vain and frivolous, in part stupid and dull, in part foul and vile, and in consequence evil and harmful," Calvin insists that psalm-singing Reformed Christians should use melodies that are "appropriate to the subject" and "proper for singing in the Church." The church, in other words, is to have its own distinctive music that is, unlike that of the world, characterized by "weight and majesty."

A narrow biblicist might object that "the Bible says nothing about this alleged power of music" or about the suitability of one kind of music over another. Calvin and his tribe might respond that this is a matter of wisdom. The Bible says nothing about the relative properties of rocks, sand, and buildings, yet Jesus expects us to be wise about the nature of things and build accordingly (Matt. 7:24–27). The Bible says nothing about the relative properties of wine and wineskins, yet Jesus expects that we should be shrewd enough observers of the nature of things to know not to put new wine into old wineskins (9:16–17). The essence of biblical wisdom is this understanding of the nature of things: whether one is a farmer (Prov. 10:5–6; 12:11), sheepherder (27:23), orchardist (27:18), a person walking down the street (7:6–23), or an attendant of the king (23:1–2; 25:6–7), one is to carefully discern the nature of people, things, and circumstances and bring one's life into conformity with the realities uncovered. Consequently the wise person will pay attention to the relative properties of music and human nature and draw correct conclusions about its power to influence and corrupt. It has not been wise of evangelicals to ignore the issues raised by tunes, words, and tunes and words in combination.[40] Regrettably, those who raise concerns are often branded as elitists, legalists, and narrow-minded funda-mentalists and ignored.[41]

One might summarize the commonly noted properties of music as follows:

1. Music has the power to move and express the emotions. Even as David was able to soothe Saul's troubled spirit with his harp (1 Sam. 16:23), so there is music that saddens, gladdens, arouses a martial spirit, entices lust, readies for sleep, and so on. Music may both arouse the whole range of human emotions and provide a vehicle for expressing them when they are already present.
2. Music has the power to stimulate the memory. As anyone who learned the A-B-C song knows, music is a great aid to the memory.
3. Music has the power to discipline or corrupt the soul. This at least is the argument of the philosophers and theologians. Good music — that which consists of ennobling lyrics and moderate tunes — edi-fies and disciplines the soul. Bad music — that which consists of unworthy lyrics and tunes — inflames the passions, breaks down re-straint, and corrupts the soul.

Thus the right words (God's own) with appropriate tunes are a powerful tool of sanctification. This is the primary virtue of the psalms. They carry all the sanctifying power of God's word, but driven more deeply still into the soul by the music. So God commands, "Sing!" But it is critical that these things be kept in proper proportion.

Recommendations

Sing the Biblical Psalms

Why sing biblical psalms? Because psalms are God's word and as such possess all the power of inspired Scripture. Those who are not currently singing psalms as a regular part of public worship might perhaps ask the ques-tion: What is worship? Or more to the point: What are we to do in worship? The correct answer is twofold: we listen as God speaks to us in his word; and we speak back to him in the way that he himself commanded. This includes using the language that he provided ("Lord, teach us to pray"). New Testa-ment worship is both spiritual and simple (John 4:20–26). We simply:

274

1. Listen as God speaks to us:
   - ✧ read the Bible
   - ✧ preach the Bible
   - ✧ administer the "visible word" (as Augustine called the sacra-
     ments)
2. Speak back to God in the language he has provided:
   - ✧ pray the Bible
   - ✧ sing the Bible[42]

The reason for this Bible centeredness is obvious: faith comes by hearing the word of God (Rom. 10:17). It is by the word that we are born again (1 Peter 1:23–25). We grow by the "pure milk of the word" (2:2). We are sanctified by the truth of God's word (John 17:17). God's word is profitable and equips us for every good work (2 Tim. 3:16–17). God's word is "living and active and sharper than any two-edged sword . . . and able to judge the thoughts and intentions of the heart" (Heb. 4:12). It is the sword of the Spirit (Eph. 6:17). It is the power of God unto salvation (Rom. 1:16; cf. 1 Cor. 2:4; 1 Thess. 1:5.) It performs its work in us (2:13). It is "like fire . . . and like a hammer which shatters a rock" (Jer. 23:29). It does not return void, God says, "without accomplishing what I desire, / and without succeeding *in the matter* for which I sent it" (Isa. 55:11). If these things are so and if today's Christians believe them, then why have the innovations in worship of the past fifty years gradually reduced the biblical content of evangelical Protestant worship services? Less Bible is read, preached, prayed, sung, and administered. One might quibble about particular churches and particular practices, but the trajectory is emphatically undeniable. Our particular concern is the word sung. The transition in the church from the metrical psalms of the sixteenth–eighteenth centuries to the classic hymns of the eighteenth century (e.g., Watts, Newton, Cowper, Wesley) to the gospel songs of the late nineteenth to mid-twentieth centuries to the Scripture songs of today demonstrates a dramatic reduction of the theological and biblical content of the church's songs. If God's word has the converting, sanctifying, and edifying properties noted above, this reduction is a spiritually disastrous development that begs to be reversed. As the psalms are sung, their converting and sanctifying power will be released.

Sing Whole Psalms and the Whole Psalter

It will not do merely to sing psalm fragments. John D. Witvliet points out that one of the distinguishing dynamics of Reformation-era psalm singing was "the singing of whole or large portions of individual Psalms rather than the versicles used in the medieval Mass."[43] Regrettably "versicles," or fragments of psalms, are virtually all that have been available in recent years. This is true of the partial collections of psalms (containing sixty-five to eighty psalm settings) found in the Presbyterian hymnals of the last century (e.g., *The Presbyterian Hymnal* [1933], *The Hymnbook* [1955], *Trinity Hymnal* [1961, 1980]), as well as what Old calls their compilers' "too prissy" editing of those that were included. With regard to the imprecatory psalms, Old says that *The Presbyterian Hymnal* "went much too far in trying to clean up the treasury of David."[44] This criticism would also include the practice of isolating particular verses of psalms to be sung, as in many of today's Scripture songs. To sing psalms is to sing the Psalter. The Book of Psalms as a whole is characterized by the theological, christological, and experiential wholeness noted above. It was given by the Holy Spirit as a complete collection whose strengths are collective—laments not isolated from praise, imprecations not isolated from confessions of sin—but all together. The whole gospel of the whole Christ is found in the whole Psalter. Our recommendation is that churches commit to singing at least one psalm in every service of worship.[45]

Sing Psalms with Appropriate Tunes

The key word with regard to tunes is "appropriate." Can this ever be anything other than a subjective judgment, a personal opinion, or preference? Indeed it can be and must be. The Scriptures regularly ask us to make judgments on the basis of what is proper or fitting. This includes such things as hair length (1 Cor. 11:14), speech (Titus 2:1), and clothing (1 Tim. 2:9–10). Most of our decisions in life, including worship, are wisdom issues:

- ✧ what to say or not say
- ✧ what to wear or not wear
- ✧ what it means to love my neighbor in a given situation
- ✧ what it means to live with my spouse in an understanding way
- ✧ what it means to practice wise stewardship
- ✧ what it means to let my mind dwell on things that are excellent and lovely (Phil. 4:8)

In each of these cases wise judgments must be made. Miss the mark, and one falls into sin. Say something unseemly or unkind, wear something immodest, fail to love or be understanding or make the most of my time or resources (Eph. 5:15–16), or become absorbed with the unlovely, the unworthy, and the mediocre, and I fall short of the will of God.

It is no different with worship and music. The music we use must be lovely, excellent, and appropriate. This outlook is clearly behind Calvin's distinction (noted above) between tunes that are light and frivolous and those that have weight and majesty. The latter have a place in worship conducted in church "in the presence of God and his angels," the former do not. The tunes used in singing psalms should underscore the message. Music, as Luther said, is the handmaiden of theology. This leads to the following principles:

1. The tunes should be well crafted (Ps. 33:3), blending melody, harmony, and rhythm in balanced proportions.
2. The tunes should be lovely (Phil. 4:8), exhibiting true beauty by reflecting the beauty of God (Pss. 27:4; 50:2; 96:6).
3. The tunes should be universal in their appeal. By this I mean that they should avoid narrow generational or cultural classification in the same way that the psalms transcend sect, race, generation, and party. The psalms are truly catholic, the songs of the whole church, not merely of Watts and the evangelicals, of Keble and the high church, of Sankey and the revivalists, or of Maranatha Music and the charismatics. The best tunes in our hymnals, psalters, and songbooks do just this. Because they tap into universal aesthetic principles, they transcend the "cultural moment"—the time, place, and group out of which they have arisen—and appeal broadly.[46] Whether our tunes have medieval Jewish, Greek, or Latin roots or arise out of the timeless European folk traditions or are of African, Asian, Latin American, or contemporary origins, they should appeal beyond the circumstances of their composition.
4. The tunes should be emotionally suited to the words. Centuries ago Augustine wrestled with the relationship between the words and the tune. He was eager in the first instance that the tune should never overpower the words. Indeed in his *Confessions* he labels it "a grievous sin" when he finds "the singing itself more moving than the

truth which it conveys."[47] He also argued that the tune should fit the words, the sound corresponding to the mood communicated by the words. Augustine's view is that "there are particular modes in song and in the voice, corresponding to my various emotions and able to stimulate them because of the mysterious relationship between the two."[48] The tunes should fit the words, matching their mood or tone.

5. The tunes should be singable. That is, they should not be beyond the reach of the congregations. They should not be overly difficult because of complexity or what Witvliet calls "idiosyncratic rhythms."[49] Neither should they be comparatively trite, insulting the taste and ability of the congregation (what we might call the "Deep and Wide" phenomena). Again, wisdom is needed.

Inclusive Hymnody

Most churches today practice exclusive hymnody or exclusive "chorusody." They sing only hymns or choruses and rarely or never sing whole psalms. The subject of this essay is inclusive psalmody. The word *inclusive* is a play on the word *exclusive*, which refers to the position of those who say that only psalms may be sung in worship. Inclusive, then, means that psalm singers need to be persuaded to include some hymns in their worship. Clearly this is not the focus of our concern. What we really are arguing is for exclusive hymnody to become inclusive hymnody—hymnody that makes room for the practice of the psalm singing. Today few evangelical congregations ever sing metrical psalms outside of the obligatory Psalm 100 ("All People That on Earth Do Dwell") and Psalm 23 in the Scottish metrical version ("The Lord's My Shepherd"). The standard evangelical hymnals have few psalm versions if any beyond these two.[50] If persuading psalm singers to begin singing hymns is a crying need, we will leave it to others to make the case. Our goal is to persuade the thousands and thousands of exclusively hymn-singing congregations to begin singing psalms. There remains for us yet two tasks before we complete this work: first, to summarize our argument; second, to answer pragmatic concerns.

Let me summarize our arguments for psalm singing:

1. Psalm singing is biblical. The songs we wish to sing are the canonical psalms, given by the Holy Spirit to be sung. Moreover, we are

commanded to sing psalms and are given examples of the New Testament churches singing them.

2. Psalm singing is historical. It was the practice of the early church (as attested by the church fathers), of the medieval monastic orders, of the Reformers, and of virtually all Protestants until the middle of the nineteenth century.

3. Psalm singing is beneficial. Because the psalms are Scripture, they partake of all of the inherent spiritual virtues of Scripture to convert sinners and sanctify saints.

4. Psalm singing is satisfying. Its theological, christological, and experiential richness provides God's people with the language with which to understand and express the vicissitudes of life. Nothing touches the hearts of God's people like the psalms, particularly sung.

5. Psalm singing is unique. The act of singing (not merely reciting as poetry) the whole Psalter (not merely hymns or even psalm fragments), given the divinely balanced content of the Psalter as a whole, has a unique capacity to shape and mold a biblical piety. A distinctive contribution to the health and vitality of the body of Christ is made by the singing of psalms.

I will now attempt to answer the pragmatic concerns that might lie behind the neglect of the psalms today. Perhaps the primary reason why most evangelicals are not committed to psalm singing is ignorance. Few know that the psalms have been sung historically, and few have ever been exposed to its actual practice. We have long been convinced that those who try psalm singing grow to love it. But the chief secondary reasons for not singing the Psalms are probably pragmatic. Ministers and music leaders who know that they ought to sing them do not because they think that it will not work for one reason or another. They may be intimidated by their own lack of musical background. They may think that it would not be user friendly enough for a church interested in attracting visitors and growing. They may have a variety of objections such as preference for other forms of psalm usage or more contemporary musical forms. Let me try to answer some of these concerns.

Currently Available Versions of the Metrical Psalms Are Inadequate

The current metrical psalm versions that are available (e.g., *Trinity Psalter, Scottish Psalter, The Book of Psalms for Singing, Book of Praise:*

Anglo-Genevan Psalter) are better than those that are nonexistent. This point here is similar to that made by D. James Kennedy in answering critics of *Evangelism Explosion:* "I like the method of evangelism that I use better than the one which you do not use." Traditional metrical psalm singing is not without its limitations, but complete psalters are available: for example, the *Trinity Psalter* (with whose publication I was involved) is ready to use today and contains every verse of all 150 psalms. Critics periodically note what they regard as the poetic weakness of English-language psalmody. One critic refers to "artlessly rhymed psalms"[51] as characteristic of the whole tradition. Among the Scots, whose 1650 psalter is the primary English-language version and the basis for nearly all subsequent English-language psalters, the importance of poetic quality has long been debated. It needs to be noted, though, that compromises must always be made when moving from one language to another. English-language versions have always favored textual accuracy over poetic grace. For some observers this is a weakness; for others it is a virtue. When revisions were being considered in the early 1800s in Scotland, no less a literary authority than Sir Walter Scott shared little enthusiasm for the project. He argued that "the ornaments of poetry are not perhaps required in devotional exercises." He claimed that though the old versions were "homely," they were "plain, forceful, and intelligible," possessing, he said, "a rude sort of majesty which perhaps would be ill exchanged for more elegance." He urged that they be touched only with a "lenient hand."[52] "Literal simplicity" has been the goal of English-language psalmody rather than poetic grace. The very title page of the 1650 *Scottish Psalter* boasts, "The Psalms of David in metre, more plain, smooth, and agreeable to the Text than any heretofore." As Millar Patrick points out, the aim has not been "to satisfy literary critics."[53] Moreover, he claims, "Critics of weight have been found to praise these psalms because of the suitability of their style to the purpose they were meant to serve, and to regard their very lack of the smoother graces as a count in their favour."[54] We would maintain the same point today. Current versions are suitable to the purpose that they were meant to serve, though certainly there is room for improvement. Better renderings may need to be written for some psalm versions. Better music may need to be composed for others (see below). But there is no sense in damning the imperfections of what we have now until there is something better with which to replace it. Any such replacement is at least a decade away even if a monumental effort were begun today.

Musical Forms Associated with Metrical Psalm Singing Are Outdated

The form of the psalm itself will determine to a significant degree the form of the music. The hymn/psalm tune style has developed over many centuries to its present form. It is the best style or form of music for congregational singing that the church has been able to produce given the requirements of the psalm form. Specifically, a psalm is a song that develops a theme over multiple lines and stanzas, using minimal repetition (e.g., Pss. 57, 99, 136). Consequently, if the psalms are to be sung, then musical forms must be developed that are multistanza, multiline, with multiple beats, syllables, or words to each line. Tunes must be capable of handling sentences long enough to express a thought, enough lines to develop the thought, and enough stanzas to complete the thought, while remaining singable by congregations. They must look, in other words, like the hymn-tune form that Christendom has developed over the past two thousand years. This has nothing to do with when the tunes were written. Indeed the hope is that the current generation will add quality tunes to the current musical treasury of the church. There may be other forms that may serve the church equally well, but they have yet to be developed. If they exist, we have yet to discover them.

Chanting Is a Better Form of Psalm Usage Than Singing

Some readers will find psalm chanting to be a remote issue, given the relative difficulty of chanting and the minuscule interest in it. But since some raise the issue we will try to answer it. Chanting has the advantage of leaving the prose text unchanged and making the "music" fit the text rather than the text fit the music. This advantage seems significant at first, but upon reflection is less so than initially thought. The reasons are as follows:

1. Compromises inherent in the process of translating songs and poetry from one language to another go beyond the problems associated with translating prose. Rhyme, rhythm, cadence, wordplays, and letterplays are often lost. A strict English translation may literally convey the meaning of the text, but may not be its "dynamic equivalent," to use a term employed by translators. What is the dynamic equivalent in modern English of the songs of the ancient Hebrews? It may be that rhymed and metered renderings do a bet-

ter job of conveying Hebrew poetry and song than do more prosaic chant versions. What our culture sings is typically rhymed. What our culture sings collectively usually follows a regular meter for the sake of simplicity and group participation. Moreover the metrical psalms in the English/Scottish tradition purport to be rhymed and metered translations. They were not viewed as paraphrases but as translations, though translated in a scheme of meter and rhyme. French metrical psalms were more like paraphrases. English language psalmody sticks close to the original text.

2. Chants are difficult. Witvliet points out that Calvin deliberately promoted metrical psalmody over the current Roman Catholic psalmody in which the actual words of the biblical text were used. He favored a poetic reworking of the text because, says Witvliet, "the Psalms needed to be rendered in a singable musical form and metrical psalmody was judged to be the most singable."[55] A fundamental principle of Protestant worship is simplicity. Whatever songs are sung in church must be simple enough to be sung by ordinary laypeople. Congregations rarely, if ever, are able to master chants. The history of their use follows a straight line from their introduction to the formation of specialized choirs that alone were able to sing them properly. Rare is the layperson or congregation that can sing them well.[56] If our goal is congregational singing, chanting is probably not a viable option.

3. Chanting lacks the dynamic of singing. It lacks the emotional punch, the power to move the passions that is characteristic of singing. We might even ask, in what sense is chanting singing? Of course it falls broadly under the category of song, but it is called chanting because it is significantly unlike singing. Its lack of regular rhythm distinguishes it from ordinary song and the powerful emotive impact that results when we make a "melody" in our heart (Eph. 5:19).[57]

Psalm Singing Inhibits Church Growth

In response to the issue that psalm singing inhibits church growth, let me ask, Will Bible reading inhibit church growth? Will Bible exposition? Will biblical praying? Regrettably there are those whose answer to all of the above is yes. Consequently they have eliminated all but token elements of each in their services of public worship. To such we really have nothing to say. The Bible either has converting and sanctifying power or it does not. If faith comes by hearing the word of God (Rom. 10:17), then the key to creating and building faith in sinners and saints is God's word. Psalm singing will build the kingdom of God. That does not mean that there is not a learning curve. That does not mean that one does not need to proceed slowly and wisely in introducing new words and music. But unless one has lost all confidence in the power of God's word, the question of church growth should not be an issue.

We could also point to historical precedent. Church growth? Yes, indeed. Partial versions of the *Genevan Psalter* were published in 1542 and 1547. They were instantly embraced by the French refugees streaming into Geneva in large numbers. Louis F. Benson, the leading hymnologist of a previous generation, wrote a series of scholarly articles in 1909 for the *Journal of the Presbyterian Historical Society* entitled "John Calvin and the Psalmody of the Reformed Churches."[58] In these articles he discusses the impact that the *Genevan Psalter* had upon the French exiles in Geneva as they first encountered psalm singing:

> The sight of the great congregation gathered in St. Peters, with their little Psalm books in their own hands, the great volume of voices praising God in the familiar French, the grave melodies carrying holy words, the fervor of the singing and the spiritual uplift of the singers, — all of these moved deeply the emotions of the French exiles now first in contact with them.[59]

As these refugees flowed in and out of France, they took with them a love for the psalms that they had learned in Geneva. By 1553 the Genevan psalms were sung in all of the Protestant churches of France.[60] In 1559 the *Genevan Psalter* became the official hymnal of the Reformed churches of France. Rather than inhibiting the growth of the French churches, the psalms played a great part in "spreading the Genevan doctrines in France," says Benson.[61] When the first complete edition was published in 1562, it was immediately consumed, going through twenty-five editions in its first year of publication.[62] Yet during this time of fervent devotion to the psalms, the French church grew with extraordinary speed. In 1555 there were 5 underground churches in France. By 1559 the number had jumped to more than 100. By 1562 there were estimated to be more than 2,150 churches established in France with approximately three million attending.[63] Growth from 5 to 2,150 in only seven years is phenomenal growth by anyone's standard, not in spite of, but in part because of psalm singing. Witvliet maintains that "metrical Psalm-singing was a maker of the Reformation."[64] It popularized Reformed piety, "opening up the Scriptures to the laity,"[65] says Miriam Chrisman. Joining the sermon and catechism, says Witvliet, it was one of "the chief means of spiritual formation."[66] There is no reason, besides blinding personal preference, for thinking that psalm singing is not compatible with church growth today.

In addition to all the reasons for returning to psalm singing argued in the preceding pages, we would also note that we are, in one sense, only urging that evangelical Christians return to their roots. Most Christians of the conservative or Bible-believing sort are keenly aware that the cultural trends of the last hundred or more years, and especially of the last fifty years, have not been conducive to serious Christian discipleship. Evangelical Christianity has struggled to stay afloat among the flood of secular, materialistic, and hedonistic influences. A bolder, more militant spirituality is needed if we are to meet the challenges of today with the same courage and resolve as did our ancestors. The psalms will nurture such a piety, stiffening the resolve of Christians today as they did in the past. All evangelical Protestant denominations have psalm-singing roots. Let's briefly review the story.

The early French and Swiss Protestants, under the leadership of Zwingli and Farel, made no provision for congregational singing in their liturgies. Calvin first urged the singing of psalms in his Articles of Church Order presented to the Genevan civil authorities in January 1537. At the time, no singable version of the psalms existed. Over the next twenty-five years, through his urging the metrical versions of Clément Marot (the leading poet of his day) and of Theodore Beza (Calvin's assistant in Geneva) were collected. They were joined to tunes written by Louis Bourgeois and others. In 1562 the complete *Genevan Psalter* was ready. As noted above, it proved to be a providential benefit for the French Protestants, as attempts at reconciliation with Rome and the French crown failed and civil war broke out that very year. "They found in it," Benson says, "a well opened in the desert, from which they drew consolation under persecution, strength to resist valiantly the enemies of their faith; with the assured conviction that God was fighting for them, and also (it must be added) would be revenged against their foes."[67] "To know the Psalms," says Benson, "became a primary duty" for the Huguenots, as French Protestants became known. The powerful appeal of the psalms sung "made Psalmody as much a part of the daily life as of public worship." Families at home and men and women in the workplace or engaged in daily tasks were recognized as French Protestants because they were overhead singing psalms. "The Psalter became to them the manual of the spiritual life." Moreover, the psalter "ingrained its own characteristics deep in the Huguenot character and had a great part in making it what it was," says Benson. For the Huguenot, "called to fight and suffer for his principles, the habit of Psalm-singing was a providential preparation":

> The Psalms were his confidence and strength in quiet and solitude, his refuge from oppression; in the wars of religion they became the songs of the camp and the march, the inspiration of the battle and the consolation in death, whether on the field or at the martyrs' stake. It is not possible to conceive of the history of the Reformation in France in such a way that Psalm singing should not have a great place in it.

A similar story can be told of the Scottish Presbyterians. As John Knox and other Protestant refugees returned to Scotland from exile in Geneva in the late 1550s, they came with a zeal for an English-language psalter corresponding to the *Genevan Psalter*. The result eventually was the *Scottish Psalter* of 1564, then of 1635, and finally of 1650. The last of these became the standard psalter for the Scots and "passed straight into the affections of the common people."[68] "It was a godsend," Patrick says, published a few years before the enormous suffering of the "Killing Times" (1668–88), by which time "it had won its place in the people's hearts, and its lines were so deeply imprinted upon their memories that it is always the language thus given them for the expression of their emotions, which in the great hours we find upon their lips." Note what he says: the language that they used to interpret and express their experience was the language of the psalms that they sang. Patrick continues: "You can imagine what it would be to them. Books in those days were few. The Bible came first. The Psalm-book stood next in honor. It was their constant companion, their book of private devotion, as well as their manual of Church worship. In godly households it was the custom to sing through it in family worship."

They turned to their psalms, Patrick says, "to sustain their souls in hours of anxiety and peril," and from them they "drew the language of strength and consolation." He continues: "It was there that they found a voice for faith, the patience, the courage, and the hope that bore them through those dark and cruel years." The Scottish metrical psalms, Patrick says, "are stained with the blood of the martyrs, who counted not their lives dear to them that by suffering and sacrifice they might keep faith with conscience and save their country's liberties from defeat."

The singing of psalms has been an important part of the "strength and consolation" of all the churches. The Reformed and Presbyterian churches were exclusively psalm singing for over 250 years, as were the Congregationalists and Baptists. The first book published in North America was a psalter. The enormously popular *Bay Psalm Book* (1640) was the hymnal of American Puritanism, undergoing seventy printings through 1773. When the *Bay Psalm Book* and the favorite among Scots-Irish immigrants, the 1650 *Scottish Psalter*, were eventually superseded, it was by a book that purported to be yet another psalter: Isaac Watts's *Psalms of David Imitated* (1719). Ironically Watts's hymns and psalm paraphrases were the primary vehicle through which hymns finally were accepted into the public worship of Protestants. Yet even then it was not until the middle of the nineteenth century that hymns began to overtake the psalms in popular use. In addition to the Presbyterians, Congregationalists, and Baptists, the Anglican and Episcopal churches boast a 300-year history of exclusive psalmody, singing first from Sternhold and Hopkin's *Old Version* (1547, 1557), then from Tate and Brady's *New Version* (1696, 1698). Not until the publication of *Hymns Ancient and Modern* in 1861 did hymns gain entrance to the Anglican liturgy.

Our ancestors were psalm singers! The Psalter gave to their faith the bold, robust quality that we still admire today. A revival of their use has begun in our time. May it continue with vigor and may the modest hopes of Dr. Boice be fulfilled. Perhaps we will yet see the "praise songs of the Psalter . . . used in worship more often than they are."[69] Indeed, may they become a fixed element in the worship of evangelical Christians once more.

Part 3

PREPARING FOR BIBLICAL WORSHIP

orship encompasses all of life. There is not an aspect of our humanness from which worship is not the requisite response. Cranmer's prayer-book liturgy spoke of worship "not only with our lips, but in our lives." Our bodies are to be offered as living sacrifices—an act of "spiritual . . . worship" (Rom. 12:1 English Standard Version). It is interesting to note that the Directory for the Public Worship of God (1645) made specific mention of the need for preparation for (*public*) worship in terms "of the Sanctification of the Lord's Day" (see that heading):

> That there be private preparations of every person and family, by prayer for themselves, and for God's assistance of the minister, and for a blessing upon his ministry; and by such other holy exercises, as may further dispose them to a more comfortable communion with God in his public ordinances.
>
> That all the people meet so timely for public worship, that the whole congregation may be present at the beginning, and with one heart solemnly join together in all parts of the public worship, and not depart till after the blessing.

Donald Whitney writes about private worship somewhat reluctantly! He readily confesses that "the weight of Scripture tilts the scale decidedly in favor of the priority of public worship."

Still, few have done more to help us in terms of a Reformed view of spirituality than Whitney. Arguing cogently and decisively that the regulative principle applies to private as well as public worship (only differently!), Whitney makes the case for a Bible-centered, Bible-structured daily activity with God. To the guilt ridden (and who is not in this area?), he concludes that it is "amazing how much progress one can make by moving forward just a little at a time."

Family worship was a feature of the homes of the godly in a bygone era and an area that needs to be recovered today. Ligon Duncan and Terry Johnson, whose book *Family Worship* has helped so many, explain and advocate a resurrection of family worship.

William Edgar writes on worship in all of life, focusing particularly on Romans 12:1–2. With one eye on postmodernity and another on the state of the church, Edgar argues that we are to be salt and light in a broken, sin-cursed world. And we can be such only if our lives are given over entirely to the praise of God.

Few things are more difficult to define accurately than the role of emotions (or, as our ancestors might have said, the affections) in worship. Sections of the church at large have often criticized Reformed worship as too cerebral, deficient in suitable "emotional" commitment and response. The charge is, of course, as are all general criticisms, wildly inaccurate. Robert Godfrey addresses this issue head-on, arguing carefully for the theology of affections in human experience. Critical, in part, of Jonathan Edwards's formulation, Godfrey sees Calvin's contribution at this point as definitive and crucial. A Reformed approach to worship, he concludes, "is as much concerned with the heart in worship as with the form of worship."

12

PRIVATE WORSHIP

DONALD S. WHITNEY

If you had asked me during my first decade of pastoral ministry which was most important, private worship or corporate worship, that is, worship alone or worship with the church, in a heartbeat I would have said private. But after reading one sermon—"Public Worship to Be Preferred before Private"[1]—I completely changed my view. David Clarkson, assistant to and successor of the prodigious Puritan theologian John Owen, preached this sermon in the 1600s. Clarkson's work still speaks centuries later, and it greatly influenced my publications on worship.[2]

I also find it significant when considering the relationship between private worship and public worship that nearly every glimpse given to us in Scripture of worship in heaven reveals only congregational worship. And the two exceptions (Rev. 19:10; 22:8–9) are instances of false worship where the Apostle John is so overwhelmed by what has been revealed to him that he falls to worship at the feet of the angel who shows them to him—and is rebuked for this act. Will there be private worship in heaven? If we ever walk in solitude in heaven, then I'm confident there will be solitary worship. But we must admit that all that has been revealed to us of the worship in heaven is congregational in form.

Congregational worship is thus more like heaven than private worship.

Moreover, God is glorified more in public worship than in private worship, for his glory is more widely declared there than in secret worship. In addition, corporate worship is generally more edifying than private worship because of the presence and gifts of others that are unavailable when you are worshiping alone. So even on those occasions of public worship that seem less edifying than a given experience in private worship, the potential is always present for more edification via the preaching, prayers, voices, and gifts of others than you could receive when worshiping God individually. Besides, your participation in congregational worship is more edifying to others than when you worship God by yourself. And while the Bible does refer to the individual Christian as "a temple of the Holy Spirit" (1 Cor. 6:19), where God can be experienced in worship, it far more often speaks of Christians collectively as the temple of God (1 Cor. 3:9, 16–17; 2 Cor. 6:16; Eph. 2:19–22; 1 Peter 2:5). Consequently we can expect the Lord to manifest his presence to us in congregational worship in ways unique to that much larger and more gloriously multifaceted temple.

And so I acknowledge at the outset that when trying to find the balance between worshiping alone and worshiping with the people of God, the weight of Scripture tilts the scale decidedly in favor of the priority of public worship. But recognizing the priority of public worship is not to say that God considers our private communion with him to be light or insignificant. Knowing that three bars of gold outweigh two is not the same as thinking that the two bars are weightless. Lighter, yes, but their value is great.

The Value of Private Worship

Countless people think they have no need for the church or public worship. Among them are many who consider their individualized "spiritual experiences" sufficient for the needs of their souls. They confidently pronounce events like a round of golf, a walk in the woods, or a few hours in a fishing boat or the garden equivalent in the eyes of God to Lord's Day worship where the Bible is preached and praises are sung to God by his people. So I rejoice when anyone rejects this heretical privatization of religion and magnifies the importance of biblical worship in the church.

But some who make this appropriate theological correction swing too far and overcorrect. In their insistence on the necessity of public worship, they allow private worship to fall into the shadows. And in some cases the problem is not simply a kind of benign neglect; rather, congregational worship holds such a multidimensional splendor for them that personal worship seems relatively trivial by comparison. When they are alone before the Lord there is no powerful preaching, no glorious congregational singing such as they hear on Sunday, and as a result private worship is minimized or abandoned. In addition to those folks, there are habitual churchgoers who never worship the Lord privately because they simply never think about it. Sunday morning attendance adequately placates their conscience in regard to the worship of God; nothing more seems necessary.

However, can once-a-week worship, regardless of quality, satisfy the heart of a man or woman who longs to fulfill the greatest commandment and "love the Lord your God with all your heart, and with all your soul, and with all your strength" (Mark 12:30)?

Not according to Welsh pastor Geoff Thomas: "There is no way that those who neglect secret worship can know communion with God in the public services of the Lord's Day."[3] Another twentieth-century pastor, the prophetic A. W. Tozer, felt the same way about how the absence of weekday worship affects the quality of Lord's Day worship: "If you will not worship God seven days a week, you do not worship Him on one day a week."[4] And the beloved old Bible commentary by Matthew Henry asserts: "Those cannot worship God aright who do not worship Him alone."[5]

The Value of Private Worship to Jesus Christ

Our master, the Lord Jesus himself, saw the value and felt the necessity of private worship. Though he was fully God and though the urgency and magnitude of his work would seemingly have excused him from it and though Luke reminds us that Jesus' custom was to gather each week in the synagogue for public worship (Luke 4:16), our king and perfect example made a priority of private worship. Not only did he teach its importance when he said, "But you, when you pray, go into your inner room, close your door and pray to your Father who is in secret" (Matt. 6:6), but he also modeled it. Mark 1:35 tells us that "in the early morning, while it was still dark, Jesus got up, left *the house*, and went away to a secluded place, and was praying there." And this private worship was not just an occasional practice, for as Luke explains, "Jesus Himself would *often* slip away to the wilderness and pray" (Luke 5:16). So the man who was God in the flesh, filled with the Holy Spirit every moment of his life, a man with more and heavier re-

291

sponsibilities than any of us can imagine, required and delighted in much time alone with "our Father who is in heaven."

Many other people in the Bible flourished spiritually in relation to their practice of private worship. Among them is David, the man after God's own heart (Acts 13:22), who declared: "In the morning, O Lord, You will hear my voice; / in the morning I will order *my prayer* to You and *eagerly* watch" (Ps. 5:3). The sons of Korah likewise said: "In the morning my prayer comes before You" (88:13). Then there is that famous episode in the life of Daniel that resulted in his being dropped into a den of lions. Do you remember what triggered the event? Daniel's political enemies knew that he consistently worshiped God in private. So they manipulated King Darius into signing an irrevocable law decreeing that for thirty days anyone who prayed to any god or man other than the king would be executed. "Now when Daniel knew that the document was signed," we are told in Daniel 6:10, "he entered his house (now in his roof chamber he had windows open toward Jerusalem); and he continued kneeling on his knees three times a day, praying and giving thanks before his God, as he had been doing previously." As a result Daniel was cast into the lions' den where, no doubt, he also worshiped privately (if you can call praying in a pride of lions private) while God shut the lions' mouths until Daniel's safe removal in the morning. One instance of private worship in the New Testament is where the Apostle "Peter went up on the housetop about the sixth hour to pray" (Acts 10:9).

The Value of Private Worship to the Heroes of the Church

Our heroes from Christian history also considered private worship absolutely essential to communion with God and to Christlike living. The daily prayer life of church reformer Martin Luther, for example, is the stuff of legend. Yet despite all his insight, Christian maturity, and world-transforming spiritual victories, near the end of his life he remarked, "I still find it necessary every day to look for time during which I may pray."[6]

In the century after the Reformation, an Englishman named Lewis Bayly wrote a Puritan devotional manual called *The Practice of Piety*, which went through some seventy editions in 170 years, making it one of the most popular books in England. A large part of the book's appeal was Bayly's clarity and simplicity, as illustrated in one of his first words of advice: "As soon as ever thou wakest in the morning, keep the door of thy heart fast shut, that no earthly thought may enter, before that God come in first; and let him, before all others, have the first place there. . . . Begin, therefore, every day's work with God's word and prayer."[7]

One of the brightest of God's lights in the eighteenth (or any other) century was pastor/theologian Jonathan Edwards of Massachusetts. "Edwards' whole ministry," writes biographer Iain Murray, "as that of the Puritans, was based upon the conviction that the usefulness of a preacher's work is invariably related to the nature of his inner life. Personal communion with God must come first."[8] But Edwards believed that the inclination to personal communion with God was common to every Christian: "True religion disposes persons to be much alone, in solitary places, for holy meditation and prayer. . . . True grace . . . delights in retirement, and secret converse with God."[9]

A century later, George Müller, one of the most famous men of faith who ever lived, said that "the first thing the child of God has to do morning by morning is to *obtain food for his inner man.* . . . I dwell so particularly on this point because of the immense spiritual profit and refreshment I am conscious of having derived from it myself, and I affectionately and solemnly beseech all my fellow believers to ponder this matter. By the blessing of God, I ascribe to Him this mode the help and strength which I have had from God."[10]

Müller's contemporary, London preacher Charles Spurgeon, believed that "the habit of regular morning and evening prayer is one which is indispensable to a believer's life."[11] Of his own such times he testified, "My happiest moments are when I am worshiping God, really adoring the Lord Jesus Christ, and having fellowship with the ever-blessed Spirit. In that worship I forget the cares of the church and everything else. To me it is the nearest approach to what it will be in heaven."[12]

The value of personal worship was seen in the first half of the twentieth century by Olympic champion and missionary martyr Eric Liddell:

> He seemed to get his strength and self-discipline and his air of quiet serenity from his early-morning sessions of prayer, meditation and Bible study. He would come out from that and stride through the rest of the day as though the Sermon on the Mount was still ringing in his ears. Whatever it was that he received in those morning sessions he spent the rest of the day giving out to others. . . . Somewhere in this daily discipline of faith lay the secret of the man. . . . He never deviated from the practice that had

become his routine, of rising early and hallowing the "Silent Hour" which shaped the rest of his day.[13]

A little later Martyn Lloyd-Jones, one of the most influential men of God for decades during the 1900s, was described this way by his associate: "To take time alone every day for the reading of Scripture and for prayer was foundational to his view of living as a Christian."[14]

The Value of Private Worship in Daily Experience

No wonder our heroes thought private worship so important. How can anyone consider it inconsequential when they realize what it is? This is meeting with God. This is the greatest encounter possible. This is the soul's coming home to God and feasting on the banquet of God himself. In private worship God reveals himself through his word, shining divine light upon the divine book so that we might find our minds instructed by God, our decisions guided by God, our hearts encouraged by God, our sins confronted by God, our hopes refreshed by God, and our spiritual hungers satisfied by God. Here we can delight in God, sing to God, weep to God, pour out our thoughts to God, confess our sins to God, and feel the worth of God. When alone with God we can rejoice in his forgiveness, revel in his goodness, thank him for his blessings, and bask in his love.

In addition to these reasons, meeting God in personal worship has the effect of keeping us in close orbit to the heart and mind of God throughout the day. The imprint of his words on our thoughts and the heartprint of his presence upon our souls stoke the fires of our affection for God and the things of God so that they burn long after the meeting of the morning. Without the habit of coming to the Lord in the intimacy of private worship, however, a spiritual frost forms on our hearts, and our minds are more easily distracted from the things of God. And when this spiritual distraction sets in, the world, the flesh, and the devil usually empower it and develop it into temptation of various kinds. Then it is so much easier for one or more of these temptations to become a preoccupation as we glance less and less at God himself. Our bodies may remain in the public worship of God, our combined voices may mouth words to or about God, but our spiritual passion and vision may decrease even though surrounded by the light of God. Then like Samson who did not know until it was too late that the Lord's strength had left him, we do not realize that a kind of protection has been withdrawn. And the results of this loss are sometimes disastrous.

One of the leading Baptists in South Africa, Martin Holdt, told me a story I asked him to repeat in an email. He wrote:

> The story I told you was about a friend of mine who was a principal of a Bible college who after his fall came to see me and told me that on the basis of two things he fell: he had become so busy in the Lord's work that he simply neglected to read the Scriptures and pray. The long-term effects of this neglect, he believes, led to his adultery. When I shared this with a minister from England earlier this year when he was in South Africa, his words to me were, "I almost interrupted you before you told me the two things because I wanted to say that I knew exactly what they were in light of discovering this to be true of every known case of ministerial adultery in the U.K.!" He went on to tell me that a leading theologian in England whose once widely accepted ministry had fallen into disfavor admitted to him that he felt that he had outgrown the reading of the Scriptures!

Such will not happen to everyone who neglects private worship, but it has happened to many who thought it could never happen to them. The risks of rushing through life without resting beside the quiet waters of daily worship, virtually unmindful of God, are many and great. But so are the benefits and blessings.

John White puts it succinctly:

> Private devotions work. They produce changes—changes in us if we engage in them and changes in people around us.
>
> We will see people differently. . . . We will approach problems differently and feel different about our day's work, our studies, our job, our future. Our goals will changes and life will take on new meaning. . . . Since we are influenced by the people with whom we associate, it follows that if we spend time daily in the company of our Creator God, a profound impact will be made on our existence.
>
> To have personal devotions regularly will produce beneficial changes in our character. But I don't want merely to peddle a secret in character development. . . . Don't decide to meet regularly with God merely as an exercise in self-cultivation.

295

I recommend private devotions on many grounds. . . . To commune with God is to touch both infinity and eternity, not metaphorically but in very deed. . . . In prayer we are invited to private tutorials with the Fountain of infinite wisdom, to a daily audience with the Author of history, to fellowship and communion with the Source of all holiness and love. There is no charge for such privileges. . . . The glories of heaven are ours for the taking. The wisdom of the ages is proffered free. We are bidden to bring our empty hearts to have them filled from cataracts of healing and love.

What then is the value of meeting regularly with God? We will escape the pettiness of the earth-bound; we will commune with ultimate wisdom, infinity and love.

Yet not for these reasons, but for love's sake, we must seek God. For who he is, not for any advantage we may gain.

Come, then, for love's sake. Come boldly defying fear. Enter into a love-pact to meet Christ daily. We can bring our trembling with us and tell him our inadequacies. He is gentle and will understand. He will not force us or hurry the pace beyond what we are able to tolerate.

Come trusting to his footstool. And come for love of him.[15]

What should we *do* in private worship so that we might expect to experience God in these ways?

The Activities of Private Worship

Two of the most influential confessions of faith in history are the Presbyterian document of 1647 known as the Westminster Confession of Faith and the Baptist Confession of Faith of 1689 (also called the Second London Confession). They are the ancestors of several other confessional statements, and both continue to be used by churches worldwide today. Much of the Baptist document was lifted verbatim from the Presbyterian one, with the result that entire paragraphs are identical in both documents, including these on worship:

But the acceptable way of worshiping the true God is instituted by himself, and so limited by his own revealed will, that he may not be worshiped according to the imagination and devices of men, or the suggestions of Satan, under any visible representations or any other way not prescribed in the Holy

296

Scriptures. (Westminster Confession of Faith 21.1; Baptist Confession of Faith 22.1)

Neither prayer, nor any other part of religious worship, is now, under the gospel, either tied unto, or made more acceptable by any place in which it is performed, or towards which it is directed: but God is to be worshiped every where in spirit and truth; as in private families daily, and in secret each one by himself, so more solemnly in the public assemblies, which are not carelessly or willfully to be neglected or forsaken, when God, by his word or providence, calls thereunto. (Westminster Confession of Faith 21.6; Baptist Confession of Faith 22.6)

These carefully crafted words express what has become known as the regulative principle of worship. The essence of the regulative principle of worship is that Scripture, not tradition or the preferences of worshipers, should regulate the worship of God. Those who hold this view argue that God has revealed in the Bible how he wants to be worshiped, and for us to worship otherwise—regardless of the purity of our motives—is unacceptable to God because it is not the way of worship he himself prescribed. It is important to know that the regulative principle of worship distinguishes between the *elements* of worship and the *circumstances* of worship. Elements include activities such as preaching, prayer, and praise (among others), while circumstances involve matters like the time, place, and length of the service, the use of hymnals, air conditioning, and so on. According to the regulative principle, God has shown in Scripture all the elements of worship that please him, but not the circumstances. The circumstances themselves are neutral and are quite flexible from culture to culture and from church to church, but they should always "be ordered by the light of nature and Christian prudence, according to the general rules of the word, which are always to be observed" (Westminster Confession of Faith 1.6; Baptist Confession of Faith 1.6).

Ever since the regulative principle of worship was first articulated in the mid-1500s it has competed with what became known as the normative principle of worship. The regulative principle of worship was championed by Presbyterians, Baptists, Congregationalists, and in general by those who called themselves Reformed; the advocates of the normative principle of worship were Lutherans, Anglicans, and Methodists. Advocates of the nor-

297

mative principle agree with adherents of the regulative principle in that we ought to do those things that God tells us in Scripture to do in worship, but they differ from it by saying that we are not limited to those things. And while most church leaders nowadays have heard of neither the regulative principle nor the normative principle of worship, by default the great majority of churches today worship according to the normative principle. Unless the Bible forbids an activity, most feel free to do just about anything in worship if it works—that is, if it increases attendance, is enjoyed by the people, enhances the sense of relevance, and so on.

For reasons I do not have space to articulate here, I believe the Bible teaches that the worship of God is prescribed by God and limited by him to the elements he has revealed in Scripture. Which is to say, I hold to the regulative principle. I could explain the regulative principle of worship in greater detail, but the relevance of it at this point is this: does the regulative principle of worship apply to private worship? To put it another way, may those who adhere to the *regulative* principle in *public* worship follow the *normative* principle in *private* worship? Here's what I believe: if God has revealed to us the kind of worship that pleases him, then these standards apply whether that worship is public or private.

That does not mean, however, that there are not both practical and biblical differences between the application of the regulative principle to public worship and to private. Some aspects of worship prescribed by the regulative principle of worship are congregational by nature. The preaching of God's word, for example, is not a private activity, but one that requires both a preacher and hearers. (Yes, we now have various media by which we can listen to preaching while alone, but for most of history this was not so and still is not so for many Christians around the world.) The ordinances are another part of biblical worship never intended for private practice. Moreover, when the confessions of faith in the tradition of the regulative principle of worship quote Scripture to say that "teaching and admonishing one another in psalms, hymns, and spiritual songs" (Baptist Confession of Faith 22.5, referring to Col. 3:16 and Eph. 5:19) is part of God-ordained worship, it is obvious that while such singing can and should characterize our private worship, the "one another" aspect is impossible when worshiping alone.

Therefore all the biblical elements of public worship that can be legitimately practiced in isolation from other believers constitute the elements

298

of private worship. And while these elements may take somewhat different forms (for instance, one person might pray aloud in private worship, another silently), these elements are few and simple. This simplicity is not surprising since God has believing children of a wide variety of ages, intellectual capacities, and educational levels. So in the private worship of God, the basic elements are intake of the word of God, prayer, and worshipful song.

The most important of these elements is exposure to the revelation of God. As important and necessary as prayer and song are in worship, it is more important for us to hear from God than for God to hear from us.

Intake of God's Word

Since worship is focusing on and responding to God, and since the invisible God must be revealed to us before we can focus on him and respond in worship, the written self-revelation of God is the foundation of all true worship. Everything we know infallibly about our unseen God, including how to relate to him, comes from his self-revelation known as the Bible. Through it God can be encountered as we read, study, memorize, pray, sing, and meditate on his word. Here are a few thoughts and suggestions about each activity.

Reading God's word. Reading Scripture is basic to the Christian life. Just as in congregational worship we should "give attention to the *public* reading *of Scripture*" (1 Tim. 4:13), so we should give attention to reading it in our private worship. The Bible is food for the soul, and just as our bodies need daily food, so do our souls. So try to feed your soul with God's word every day. Moreover, since "man shall not live on bread alone, but on every word that proceeds out of the mouth of God" (Jesus in Matt. 4:4), regularly read through every word of the book that has come out of the mouth of God. Some read the entire Bible every few months: George Müller read through it four times annually. Some go for a two-year plan, and some just read at their own pace until they finish, then start again. But surely the most common timetable among those who read through the Bible habitually is the once-a-year plan. By reading just four chapters a day you will read all 1,189 chapters of the Bible in less than ten months, and still have sixty-eight days in the year—more than one day each week—to make up for those times when you were unable to read.

Starting in Genesis and working your way straight through the entire

Bible is one method, but it is not the only one. Sometimes people enjoy reading the books of the Bible in a random sequence. With my favorite plan I start in more than one place and read equal amounts in each section. For instance, I will begin in Genesis, then turn to Joshua and read the same amount there, then do likewise in Job, Isaiah, and Matthew. When I have read through each of the five sections of Scripture that start with these books, I have read the entire Bible. Some prefer to do this in three places instead of five, and start in Genesis, Job, and Matthew. People have told me that not only do they enjoy the variety of reading in more than one book at each sitting, but that this kind of scheme also helps them maintain the momentum they sometimes lose when reading some of the more difficult parts of Scripture. And, of course, there is no lack of Bible reading plans in some study Bibles, devotional books, magazines, pamphlets, and other publications, where preassigned readings for each day are listed.

There may be times—even a whole year—when you will sense that you should break the rhythm of reading according to schedule. Instead of plowing through the Prophets according to your plan, for example, you may feel the need of your heart is to walk with Jesus in one of the gospels or to saturate your soul for a month in an epistle like Ephesians so that you will really absorb it. Break away from your regular routine if necessary, or simply go to these other places in addition to your scheduled reading. But think of reading through the entirety of Scripture like a balanced diet. Over time, feast your soul on the buffet of "every word that proceeds out of the mouth of God."

Studying God's word. To study the Bible may entail nothing more than taking notes while reading and comparing cross-references, or it can be as involved as using stacks of reference books and CDs. The study of Scripture, like the study of anything, deepens our understanding of it (and in this case, our understanding of God, ourselves, etc., as well) in ways that reading cannot. Through study we gain insight, identify patterns and relationships, and discern causes and effects that otherwise go undetected.

I'm always impressed by the value put on Bible study by the Apostle Paul in 2 Timothy 4:13. Though he is in Roman custody and knows that he is near the end of his earthly life, in the last inspired chapter of Scripture he ever wrote, Paul asks Timothy to bring a warm cloak he'd left at Troas "and the books, especially the parchments." He knows he will soon enter heaven, but Paul wants to study the word of God. And clearly the purpose of his study was not merely the acquisition of information; Paul wanted to meet with and worship the God of the word.

So make sure that your study of God's word, especially when you study it as part of your private worship, is a worshipful study. While all contact with Scripture should result in some degree of worship, there is a difference between Bible study done primarily to prepare for a class and poring over the Scriptures in the worship of God. To study the names of God in order to make an exhaustive list of those found in the Old Testament is a worthwhile endeavor, but it is not the same as praying over them, praising the attributes of God represented by each, and seeking to experience the benefits signified by the names. Jonathan Edwards had it right: "Whether wrestling with Scripture, preparing sermons or writing in his notebooks, he worked as a worshiper. Thought, prayer and writing were all woven together."[16]

Memorizing God's word. Likewise, memorizing Scripture can be done when the worship of God is the primary pursuit or the secondary one. If the Bible is properly internalized through memorization, worship will inevitably follow. But often the process of Scripture memory is perceived (at least at the moment) as almost exclusively a learning time. If the time at hand is learning time, then viewing Scripture memory entirely as Christian education is appropriate. At this point be aware that because it is the intake of God's word, Scripture memory can also be an act of worship. So if you desire "the word of Christ [to] richly dwell within you" (Col. 3:16) by this means during private worship, take care to maintain your Godward focus in the process.

Praying God's word. I know of no faster or better way to enrich your prayer life than to pray God's word in worship. I find this especially true when praying through one of the psalms. Praying as most of us tend to pray, that is, by routinely saying the same old things about the same old things, will freeze the heart of prayer. But to pray through a passage of Scripture means to take living words that have been inspired in the very heart and mind of God and flow them through your heart and mind back to God. And to do this from the Book of Psalms is to use the one book of the Bible inspired by God for the express purpose of being returned to God verbally (the Book of Psalms was Israel's God-given songbook).

301

Jesus prayed the psalms (Matt. 27:46), and so did the Christians in the Book of Acts (4:24–26). Why not you? You will not only see reminders to pray for the concerns you want to pray about daily (such as your family, your future, your work, etc.) springing out of every psalm, you will also find yourself prompted by the text to pray about matters you'd never think about otherwise. Best of all, by using the words of Scripture as your own you will pray in fresh new ways every time, even when praying about the "same old things."

Although the benefits of praying through a passage of Scripture are many, one of the most valuable is the sense of worship and intimacy with God that accompanies it. After praying through Scripture for the first time, many have said to me, "It's like a real conversation with a real person." And that is what prayer should be.

Singing God's word. To sing Scripture is another way to respond in worship to the revelation of God. Not only were the psalms inspired for God's people in the old covenant to sing, but also twice in the new covenant God commands his people to sing "psalms and hymns and spiritual songs" (Eph. 5:19; Col. 3:16). And since the presence of others is not necessary for singing praise to God, singing psalms and other parts of Scripture when we privately worship God no doubt sounds very sweet to the ears of God.

Do you need practical suggestions for singing God's word? Get a hymnal and check the Scripture index at the back. From there you can see which of the songs you already know are based upon a psalm or another part of the Bible. Also, do not overlook simply composing a tune spontaneously and singing to the Lord some of the words of Scripture you just read.

Meditating on God's word. The need to meditate on God's word is the most overlooked and yet possibly the most important part of private worship. Even among the most faithful Bible readers many close the book each day and would have to confess, "I do not remember a thing I read." Their much reading makes little impact. Reading is the *exposure* to Scripture; meditation is the *absorption* of Scripture. We feel the life-giving power of the living water of Scripture most refreshingly when it percolates by meditation down into the soul. We live more intentionally in the spiritual realm, as well as in the physical one. Heaven seems nearer.

In James 1:25 God promises one of his broadest and most far reaching blessings, not on the one who merely looks regularly into his word, and certainly not to the one who forgets what it says, but to the one who looks intently, that is, who meditates on it and then obeys it. Here's the promise and its conditions: "But one who looks intently at the perfect law, the *law* of liberty, and abides by it, not having become a forgetful hearer but an effectual doer, this man will be blessed in what he does." The first of those blessings begins immediately as the meditation enriches the sense of the presence of God in your private worship.

Meditation on Scripture is not just leaning back and staring at the ceiling after reading a bit of the Bible. Meditation as worship means focused thinking on the text of Scripture and thus on God and the things of God revealed in the words of Scripture. In terms of actual methods of doing this, there is no one right way, but I will mention several I use. After selecting a verse or phrase from your reading, you could slowly repeat it with emphasis on a different word each time or rewrite the verse or phrase in your own words. You could ponder the text for the purpose of discovering at least one application of it, that is, some way the Lord would have you respond to it. Praying your way through the text is not only a good way to pray, but a good method of meditation as well. For centuries Christians have kept a short list of questions ready that they ask of a text in order to meditate on it. If you want to meditate on more than just a line or two, you could look for a theme or common thread between all the chapters or paragraphs you read. Some even like to make diagrams, sketches, or drawings as a way of clarifying or imprinting the words of God into their minds and hearts.[17]

Remembering the distinction that the regulative principle of worship makes between the elements of worship and the circumstances of it, consider using a journal or notebook as a circumstance to help your private worship. For some, a journal is a means of worship because through it they express their Godward thoughts and prayers. But a larger percentage of private worshipers take advantage of a journal simply as a place to write their meditations on Scripture and their reflections on life from a scriptural perspective.[18]

As mentioned earlier, the essence of worship is focusing on and responding to the revelation of God. Thus far I have referred only to the clearest and most important revelation of God, the Bible. But there is also a revelation of God in creation (which the Bible recognizes in places like

Rom. 1:20), and despite its limitations it is a revelation of God nonetheless and thus should prompt our worship. When King David considered the heavens as the work of God's fingers he exclaimed in worship, "O Lord, our Lord, / how majestic is Your name in all the earth!" (Ps. 8:3, 9). Such personal worship experiences do not have to be merely incidental and unplanned events in our walk with God, but can be regular aspects of our devotional life, if we so choose, for one of the liberties available in private worship is the ability to make greater use of general revelation than congregational worship usually affords. I'm not saying that a walk in the woods can substitute for reading the word. Creation does not tell us of Christ or of countless other things in Scripture. But supplemental to and informed by the Bible, the revelation of God in creation can provide both a glorious venue for and stimulus to our private worship. The godly Edwards found it so. He once wrote in his journal: "I rode out into the woods . . . having alighted from my horse in a retired place, as my manner commonly has been, to walk for divine contemplation and prayer."[19] In fact, many love to combine the two means of revelation, worshiping God through his word while walking in his world. Müller said, "I find it very beneficial to my health to walk thus for meditation before breakfast, and am now so in the habit of using the time for that purpose, that when I get into the open air, I generally take out a New Testament of good sized type, which I carry with me for that purpose, besides the Bible: and I find that I can profitably spend my time in the open air."[20] Whenever possible, I myself take to the woods and fields near my home to walk and pray through one of the psalms.

The intake of God's word, or rather encountering God through his word, is thus the foundation upon which the rest of worship is a response.

Prayer

One of the God-ordained responses in worship—whether the worship is public or private—is prayer. God, through the Bible, commands us to pray ("devote yourselves to prayer"; Col. 4:2). In fact, in some sense he expects us to "pray without ceasing" (1 Thess. 5:17). Surely part of our obedience to these commands includes prayer in our private worship of God. The Lord Jesus taught us to pray in private when he said, "But you, when you pray, go into your inner room, close your door and pray to your Father who is in secret, and your Father who sees *what is done* in secret will reward you" (Matt. 6:6). Jesus also modeled frequent private prayer:

After He had sent the crowds away, He went up on the mountain by Himself to pray; and when it was evening, He was there alone. (Matt. 14:23)

In the early morning, while it was still dark, Jesus got up, left *the house*, and went away to a secluded place, and was praying there. (Mark 1:35)

After bidding them farewell, He left for the mountain to pray. (Mark 6:46)

And it happened that while He was praying alone. . . . (Luke 9:18)

Since prayer ascended from the public worship of the New Testament church (Acts 2:42) and since we should include in private worship every element of public worship that we can legitimately practice apart from other believers, certainly then we should pray in our private worship of God.

As in a public worship service, prayer is appropriate at any point throughout private worship. To *begin* your time of worship by asking the Lord to illuminate your understanding of his word is both a biblical and historic practice. For thousands of years believers worldwide have prayed Psalm 119:18 whenever they spread the Scriptures before them: "Open my eyes, that I may behold / wonderful things from Your law."

But to pray *during* the intake of Scripture is a valuable way of absorbing and applying the text and a way of conversing with God about what he is saying through these words or how he would have you put them into practice. Today, for example, I read Psalm 95:3–8 and then prayed the words that I placed in italic type:

> For the Lord is a great God
> And a great King above all gods,
> *Amen, Lord, you are a great God. There is none like you.*
> In whose hand are the depths of the earth,
> The peaks of the mountains are His also.
> The sea is His, for it was He who made it,
> And His hands formed the dry land.
> *Everything belongs to you, Lord. You made it all.*
> Come, let us worship and bow down,
> Let us kneel before the Lord our Maker.
> *I do worship you, Lord. You made me.*

For He is our God,

And we are the people of His pasture and the sheep of His hand.

Oh, God, you are my God. And I pray for all my family to be your
people, your sheep.

Today, if you would hear His voice,

Do not harden your hearts.

Lord, I do want to hear your voice today. I do not want to harden
my heart. I pray for myself and for Caffy and Laurelen
that we would have tender hearts toward you today.

Some passages lend themselves to such prayerful reading more easily than others. Frequently you might read an entire chapter and pray no more than "Lord, please keep me from ever sinning like the person in this story." But whatever the text, do not just read it—respond to it.

Most likely *after* prayerful Bible intake and meditation, worship regulated by Scripture surely involves some time devoted exclusively to prayer. In order to "pray without ceasing" (1 Thess. 5:17), we should find ourselves praying while driving, working around the home, and doing all our daily activities. This is good, solid Christianity. But at these moments the primary activity is driving, working, and so on, and praying is supplemental. Private worship, however, calls for a time when prayer is your primary activity.

I'm convinced that most Christians, despite their desire to do so, find it hard to sustain undivided attention on God in prayer for more than a few minutes—and consider themselves second-rate Christians as a result. But the cause of this, as I said earlier, is the habit of prayer that most fall into, that is, saying the same old things about the same old things. Breaking this pattern by sheer resolve takes an inordinate amount of concentration, a good deal of creative thought (praying differently about routine matters), and the time to do it as well.

By the Lord's grace we do not have to pray under such grinding, God-forgetting pressure to find fresh ways of expressing our prayers and of "keeping alert in it" (Col. 4:2). By praying through a passage of Scripture—especially through one of the psalms—we speak the words that God has already inspired for us to say.

How is praying through a section of Scripture different from the prayerful reading of it described above? In prayerful reading the primary activity is reading; in praying through Scripture the primary activity is prayer. In

306

the example of prayerful reading from Psalm 95, I read, "For He is our God, / and we are the people of His pasture and the sheep of His hand"; and I simply prayed, "Oh, God, you are my God. And I pray for all my family to be your people, your sheep." Then I continued reading, occasionally pausing to pray briefly. If I were going through the same chapter with the primary purpose of praying through it, I would probably pause after reading this verse and pray at greater length than in the example. I might pray much more extensively for my family as "the sheep of His hand." The words "we are the people of His pasture" might prompt me to pray for my local church also. Perhaps I would think to pray for some unconverted friends to become the people and sheep of God. In summary, during the prayerful reading of Scripture I will spend more time reading than praying, but when praying through that same section I will spend more time praying than reading.

To pray through a passage of Scripture is not the only way to pray, for Psalm 62:8 entreats us freely to "pour out your heart before Him." While we would be foolish to think that our own words in prayer could improve on words inspired from heaven, there are times when we are so hurt, so burdened, or so obsessed with a matter that all we can do is cast ourselves at the Lord's feet and pour out our hearts to him. But on most days, using inspired words as our own prayers can give us a freshness and depth in prayer that human ingenuity and effort cannot produce.

How can there be any worship—including private worship—without prayer? When worship blazes in our hearts, prayer is the flame that ascends from the fire.

Worshipful Song

In one way or another, worship begins with a revelation of God. But it is more than just encountering a revelation of God. Worship is incomplete without a response to God revealed. One of the God-ordained responses to him is prayer, and another is worshipful song.

That private worship should be characterized by worshipful song may be the most unanticipated part of this chapter to you. Once again, we are commanded (and privileged!) to sing to the Lord, as we read in Psalm 96:1–2a: "Sing to the Lord a new song; / sing to the Lord, all the earth. / Sing to the Lord, bless His name" (see also 1 Chron. 16:9, 23; Pss. 13:6; 33:3; 68:4, 32; 98:1; 105:2; 147:7; 149:1; Isa. 42:10; Jer. 20:13). Why would anyone think that all such worshipful singing is never meant for private worship?

And again, worship regulated by Scripture requires singing in public worship, for in two places in the new covenant (Eph. 5:19; Col. 3:16) we are told that in the presence of "one another" we should be "singing and making melody with your heart to the Lord" through the use of "psalms and hymns and spiritual songs." And since we are capable of singing and making melody with our hearts to the Lord by ourselves as well as in the presence of other Christians, we may conclude that the regulative principle of worship instructs us not only to absorb the Scriptures and pray in private worship, but also to sing psalms, hymns, and spiritual songs.

Singing psalms, hymns, and spiritual songs characterizes those filled with the Spirit (Eph. 5:18) and those in whom the word of Christ richly dwells (Col. 3:16). If ever there is a time when we would hope to be filled with the Spirit and when the word of Christ is richly dwelling in us, it should be in our public and private worship. Whether in God-saturated congregational worship or in a time of solitary intimacy with the Lord, to sing to him expresses our love and adoration, our reaffirmation of his living truth, not to mention our submission to his command to sing. Singing the psalms or the edifying songs of godly Christians helps us to focus on God and teaches us about the things of God in memorable, poetic ways. Singing to him helps us to articulate our own deep feelings to the Lord and enables us to convey things to him in more beautiful and expressive ways than we otherwise would. Engaging the heart and voice in worshipful song brings our emotions and bodies into the enjoyment of God, not just our minds.

In some situations it may be impractical to sing aloud in private worship, but unless there is a compelling reason to sing in a whisper or only in your mind, why not sing aloud? It is almost impossible to envision public worship without openly singing our praise to God; what makes private worship so different?

This means you will probably want to keep a songbook next to your Bible in the place where you have private worship. (Ask at your church how to get a copy of the songbook used there, or at your Christian book resource for a wider variety.) If you play an instrument, use it to accompany your worshipful song to the Lord if you find that it helps.

Sometimes you may want to sing the Scriptures spontaneously instead of using published music. Say, for example, you are reading Psalm 68 and come to verse 4: "Sing to God, sing praises to His name; / lift up *a song* for Him who rides through the deserts, / whose name is the Lord, and exult before

Him." You might want to do as I—though neither a musician nor a composer —often do in a passage such as this and sing these words in a simple, impromptu tune improvised moment by moment. Rather than singing spontaneously with only some of the words and themes of the text, you might try singing them all just as you find them, in a way similar to chanting.

If you are not accustomed to singing in private worship, I hope you will begin to experience there the riches of the truth of Psalm 147:1: "It is good to sing praises to our God."

The Essential Intangibles of Private Worship

Knowing and practicing the activities of worship that God has ordained is indispensable, but there is more to worship than just doing the right things. Apparently even the Pharisees said and did many right things in worship, but Jesus condemned them: "You hypocrites, rightly did Isaiah prophesy of you: 'This people honors Me with their lips, but their heart is far away from Me. But in vain do they worship Me, teaching as doctrines the precepts of men' " (Matt. 15:7–9).

Jesus warns us that it is possible to engage in what we call worship, only for God to reject it as worship "in vain." How is it that we can worship the true God in vain? Jesus gives two causes. First, God turns away from worship when the worshiper's "heart is far away" from him. Second, he refuses worship when the teaching or doctrines about worship are "the precepts of men," not the precepts of God. While the latter problem is addressed by the regulative principle of worship (in that it seeks only for God's precepts for worship), the former reminds us that for our worship to be acceptable to God we must be equally concerned about the heart, about the intangibles of worship, not just its forms and activities.

Jesus teaches the same balanced emphasis in one of the most important texts on worship in all Scripture. In John 4:24 he proclaimed: "God is spirit, and those who worship Him must worship in spirit and truth." What does it mean to worship in truth? It means to worship according to the truth of Scripture. In other words and as repeatedly emphasized, we should go to God-revealed truth—the Bible—to learn how God wants us to worship him publicly and privately. And in the Bible we learn not only of the God-ordained activities of worship, but also of the spiritual qualities required to keep our worship from being in vain. That leads us to the other half of John

4:24, where we are taught to "worship in spirit," and a brief look at four biblical intangibles needed in private worship.

Worship in Spirit

For starters, no one can worship in spirit unless they are indwelled by the Spirit of God whom the Lord has given to those who repent and believe in Jesus Christ for salvation. As the Apostle Paul emphasizes in 1 Corinthians 12:3: "No one can say, 'Jesus is Lord,' except by the Holy Spirit." Oh, like the Pharisees they may be able to say the right words in worship. They may even be able to speak the phrase *Jesus is Lord* in prayer or song, but not as a true and sincere expression of their relationship to him.

But those who do have the Holy Spirit and are now capable of worshiping in spirit do not worship in spirit if they do not worship in holiness. "Worship the Lord in holy array," says Psalm 29:2. The holy array that God required of the Old Testament priests was that they dress in a very particular way and prepare themselves in minute detail before presenting their sacrifices. Likewise the priests who come before the Lord today—that is, all believers in Christ (1 Peter 2:9)—must also come in holy array. First and foremost, our holy array is the holiness of Christ. God receives our worship based upon Jesus' having already offered to him the perfect sacrifice—himself—on our behalf. And all our subsequent worship of the Lord is received, not because we are now so sincere, but because the blood of the high priest Jesus has made it acceptable to God. That does not, however, mean that our ongoing sin, though already forgiven, has no effect on our worship. As the writer of Psalm 66:18 put it: "If I regard wickedness in my heart, / the Lord will not hear." So any Christian who attempts private worship and yet refuses to deal with known sin does not worship in spirit, but in vain.

One other point here: while worship in spirit is more than worshiping sincerely, it is not less than worshiping sincerely. The Lord looks on more than the heart; that is, what we do in worship also matters, but he does look closely at our hearts. One of the best-loved Puritan writers, Stephen Charnock, said, "How can we imagine God can delight in the mere service of the body, any more than we can delight in converse with a carcass? Without the heart it is no worship; it is a stage play; an acting a part. . . . If we lack sincerity; a statue upon a tomb, with eyes and hands lifted up, offers as good and true a service."[21] Regardless of what we say with our lips or do with our bodies in our private worship, God turns away if our heart is far away.

310

Worship in Edifying Ways

One of the reasons the Apostle Paul wrote the letter of 1 Corinthians was to correct the disorderly worship services in the church at Corinth. He was writing specifically about worship in 14:26 when he said: "Let all things be done for edification." The worship difficulties of the Corinthians were not only about including the biblical elements of worship, but also with the ways the biblical elements were being practiced. For example, they were right to observe the Lord's Supper in worship, but their practice of it led to division within the church, not to building it up. Paul wanted them (and us) to see that when the elements of worship that God prescribed are experienced and expressed in the right way, the worshiper will be edified.

What's true here for the church in public worship is also true for the individual Christian in private worship. The most effective means of strengthening our souls are the means that God has given for our souls to commune with him. But as with the church as a whole, it is also possible for the Christian worshiping alone to engage in those elements of worship in ways that do not edify. To return to the illustration of prayer, all believers want to pray because "God has sent forth the Spirit of His Son into our hearts, crying, 'Abba! Father!' " (Gal. 4:6). But this supernatural heavenward orientation of prayer can be expressed in ways that sooner or later become tedious, prayerless praying. The biblical worship element of prayer is present, but it is not edifying. It brings no joy, no encouragement, no spiritual strength, and no closeness to God. Yet the problem may be nothing more than methodology. The same can be said for our approaches to getting into Scripture or singing to the Lord. Whenever the biblical elements of worship become boring there is a problem, and it is almost always with either the heart or the method.

This struggle for freshness in private worship is a common problem. Longtime Scottish pastor Maurice Roberts observes: "To keep up the power of godliness in the soul is about the most difficult thing the Christian can do."[22] So when your private worship is not as edifying as it ought to be, sometimes the solution is simply to do the same things a different way. Use a different method of meditation, choose a different songbook, read from another translation of the Bible. Nothing in the Bible says that your way of ordering private worship, your place, your Bible reading plan, your time, and so on always has to be the same or like anyone else's. Your private worship practices should promote edification, not calcification.

Worship in Reverence

A pair of essential intangibles for worship is found in Hebrews 12:28–29: "Therefore, since we receive a kingdom which cannot be shaken, let us show gratitude, by which we may offer to God an acceptable service with reverence and awe; for our God is a consuming fire." The New International Version renders the central part, "Let us be thankful, and so worship God acceptably with *reverence* and *awe*" (emphasis added).

Worshiping God with reverence involves viewing the time of worship as more than mere duty or a formality, but an actual meeting with God himself. When I'm reverent in worship I'm mindful of his holiness and justice, remembering that "our God is a consuming fire." I worship in the sobering knowledge that this consuming fire of a God takes no pleasure in a mouth that honors him while the heart and the mind are far away.

To worship in reverence means that I humbly recognize my unworthiness before God apart from the goodness of Jesus that he has graciously credited to me. Reverence for God makes me serious minded in private worship. This does not mean that I'm grim or joyless; quite the contrary, but it does mean I'm not frivolous. I'm not meeting with a comedian or a clown. Since I am a child of my heavenly Father, I can be at home in his loving, accepting presence. But I never forget that I am meeting with God — my maker, my judge, my king.

Worship in Awe

God accepts our worship, according to Hebrews 12:28, when we offer it "with reverence and awe." While worship in reverence should be our response to God's holiness and justice, worship in awe should be our reaction to his grace, glory, and power. The better I comprehend that "our God is a consuming fire," the more I am in awe of God. For the grace of this consuming fire spared me even as his fiery wrath consumed others for sinning the same sins as I. The radiant glory of this consuming fire dazzles angels without ceasing. The infinite power of this never-ending fire illuminates heaven forever. When I remember who it is that I worship, worship is *awful*, that is, as the word originally meant, full of awe.

Private worship, therefore, should put us in awe of God. That is not to say that our worship is anemic unless it culminates in inexpressible visions of wonder. But we should come away from it with a new sense of the greatness of God. By meditation on and appreciation of some truth of Scripture, by the sense of intimacy in prayer, by the exhilaration of expression in worshipful song, something should refresh our vision of who our God is and what he is like. After all, it is God we are encountering in worship, and if we avail ourselves of the means of experiencing him we should be impressed.

The purpose for evaluating our private worship by these intangibles is to make sure that we are not offering to God only the husk, not just the carcass of worship. Perhaps they could all be summarized in this comment by Roberts: "The way to measure whether we are lively or else formal in our devotions is to face up to the question: are we *seeking* God in them or not?"[23]

Barriers to Private Worship Confronted

He is startled by the clock radio, and yet it takes a few minutes before he can barely raise his head from the pillow, because it has been yet another night of much too little sleep. Because of his chronic need for rest, he had set the alarm for the latest possible moment, and so he feels the pressure of time almost from the moment he staggers from the bed. He leans wearily against the sink with a warm, wet rag on his skin as he tries to wake up, hardly believing that it is morning again already. "I have to get to bed sooner at night," he resolves for the thousandth time, hoping that life will somehow magically change to make it possible. If he takes time for any breakfast at all he gulps it down, finishing most of it while standing in the kitchen or moving about doing other things. He glances repeatedly at the time — sometimes twice during the same minute — confirming each mention of it on the radio. He finishes dressing in a hurry, rushes a toothbrush over his teeth, scurries out the door, and takes a deep breath as he starts his daily marathon. That night, a lot later than he had hoped, he realizes again how much he's left undone as he falls into bed and loses consciousness almost immediately. Another day without time alone with God. Does this sound familiar?

The world, the flesh, and the devil will construct barrier after barrier to keep us from meaningful private worship. In addition to those already addressed, I want to confront three in particular.

The Desire Barrier

There are many people who, if they were honest with themselves and God, would have to say that they really have no desire for private worship.

I suppose every Christian goes through springs, summers, autumns, and winters, various cycles of ups and downs in their attitudes toward private worship. But the person in whom it is always winter in their desires for private worship is a person with a cold, dead soul. When there are no longings month after month, year after year, for regular communion with God, obviously there is no life from God or life with God. In Galatians 4:6 the Bible explicitly describes the desires for communion with God on the part of those who are children of God, who have his Holy Spirit: "Because you are sons, God has sent forth the Spirit of His Son into our hearts, crying, 'Abba! Father!' " Without such a heart cry to draw near to God, there is no Spirit of God in the heart. And without the presence of the Spirit of God, there is no relationship with God.

So if you seldom think about engaging in private worship with God and if you do not often grieve over the absence of regular communion with God, you are in great danger. And the danger to which I alert you is not that you can content yourself with some sort of subpar Christianity that feels no need for Bible intake, prayer, and worshipful song, but rather the peril that you are not a Christian at all. May your lack of longing for the means of intimacy with God shock you and startle you into the pursuit of God through Jesus Christ. Ask him to have mercy on you, to open your eyes, and to give you the desires that evidence a spiritual heartbeat.

The Routine Barrier

Another barrier to private worship is the rigidity of daily routines. Daily routines are hard to change, regardless of the benefits of changing or the costs of not changing. Even when we can see and feel in our bodies the chronic need for more sleep or for exercise or for changing our diet, it is hard to permanently alter the routines that affect those things. So if we find it nearly impossible to change our routines even when we can physically touch and see the need, how much more difficult is it to redirect our routines for less perceptible needs like the health of our souls?

I knew for years that I should take the initiative to begin regular family worship in our home. I often felt guilty about not having it and was convinced that God would bless us if we would start. But it was so hard to change the customs of our family life to make the time for it. However, the only way to intervene into the routine, whether for family worship or private worship, is to do so intentionally. A place for private worship will not magically

314

open up in your schedule. Acknowledge the difficulty that everyone has when changing daily life patterns and by the grace of God deliberately begin private worship as a new and regular practice.

The Time Barrier

The biggest obstacle in my own struggle with faithfulness in private worship is the time barrier. Time pressures also seem to be the primary problem for everyone who aspires to more meaningful time alone with the Lord. This is true for Christian singles, who are often misperceived as having great blocks of free time each week, and for moms of young children who never seem to have a minute to themselves, and for everyone in between. I have been preached at, scolded, reminded, and shamed in regard to making time for private worship, and as a minister and a specialist in the area of spiritual formation I have probably done a bit of that to others. And despite my decades of a fairly consistent devotional life, the older I grow I find that more and more discipline is required to chisel out time for solitary worship.

But there is no escaping that essentially the practice of private worship is about making time for God. Sometimes I hate to admit it, but Jesus also had a hectic schedule, as Nancy DeMoss points out:

> We can feel much like Jesus must have felt — pressured and without reprieve. How did Jesus deal with this problem? The same way we should: by spending time alone with God. We're told that "very early in the morning, while it was still dark, Jesus got up, left the house, and went off to a solitary place, where He prayed" (Mk. 1:35).[24]

Very early in the morning may not work for you, though many discover that if those hours are lost as an opportunity for private worship they are never regained. And there are seasons in life — especially for mothers of very little ones — when thoughts of a consistent time or anything more than a couple of minutes sounds unrealistic even with the most iron-willed resolve. But resolve we must, doing what we can to follow hard after the greatest priority in life — God. My wife, Caffy, and I have a friend who's now a godly grandmother but who once had three children in diapers simultaneously. Unable to devote the kinds of time she was used to spending with God before she had children, she accepted her circumstances as from the Lord, sought to experience him in the mundane details of her day, and did what

315

she could. Many days it was little more than a verse read from the open Bible she kept on the kitchen counter or on the changing table in the nursery. But she maintained a disciplined daily commitment in spite of such meager spiritual meals, and when those days and seasons of her life permitted more time in private worship, her routines were already in place.

Many Christians yearn to simplify their lives and believe that, if by simplifying they could just get some breathing room, then they would have time for private worship. Let's set such thinking right side up. The first step in simplifying is to clear a space in your life to be alone with God. If you gave away everything you owned and did not have a thing on your to-do list, but you had no closeness to Jesus, your life would still be a mess. Private worship is a part of the life that every child of God dreams of—a life spent with God. Come home to that life. Come home every day to Jesus, the home of your soul.

The Vision of a Lifetime of Private Worship

It is amazing how much progress one can make by moving forward just a little at a time. Author Ernest Hemingway wrote only about two pages a day. That does not sound like much, but over a lifetime he produced nine novels and some seventy short stories. I once read an interview with another famous writer who was admired for his enormous productivity. "Write every day for forty years," he responded, "and you'll produce a lot of books too."

Closeness to God, growth in Christlikeness, and knowledge of the Bible generally come in small daily increments as well. And as with growth of the body, growth of the soul is not noticed every day, every week, or even for months. But over time the consistent private worship of God will become one of the most powerful and transformational experiences of your life.

What change do you need to make? Why not begin now? The simple secret to so much of your spiritual future lies hidden in your daily routine.

13

A CALL TO
FAMILY WORSHIP

J. LIGON DUNCAN III AND
TERRY L. JOHNSON

There has been a recent miniboom of interest in the renewal of family religion and family worship in the evangelical community. Perhaps fueled by (a) the sense of cultural assault upon the family, (b) the strong current emphasis on parental involvement in childhood education, and (c) in some quarters a recapturing of a covenantal vision of church and family life, many are open to and desirous of learning what the family as a unit ought to be doing together in the way of daily worshiping of God in the reading, singing and praying of Scripture. And not only is there a new impetus, but many helpful resources are now available that were nonexistent just a few years ago.[1]

None too soon. The family itself is an endangered species in our culture, and the Christian family is under the severest of strains: the pace of life, the worldliness and materialism of church and society, the self-destructive freedoms in which we love to indulge, the capacity for temptations to access us even in the safety of our homes through satellite television and the internet, men's loss of the sense of responsibility to take up the duty for spiritual leadership as fathers in the home, the culture of divorce, the culture of day care, and more. Furthermore, there are those who so undervalue the traditional family that they are seeking to redefine it, while at the same time some suggest that a day will come when biotechnology, community, and government programs will pave the way for the obsolescence of the traditional family.

God has never underestimated the importance of the family. After all, like marriage, he invented it. The family is the original society from which every other society emerges. This is seen in creation itself as unfolded in the early chapters of Genesis. Redemptive history and the covenant of grace both indicate the essential role of family in God's program. Founded by a divine directive and regulated by divine ordinances, it is the normal school in which faith in God and obedience to his law are taught. Its suitability for this function is seen in its unique features: (1) it is small and close: no bureaucratic barriers impede the recognition of need and the application of discipline, no administrative distance prevents the identification of patterns or allows for idealistic assessments and solutions; (2) authority is displayed, but its harshness is tempered with parental affection; (3) ideally two parents, two parties, complement one another and are vested with joint authority; and (4) mutual accountability and divine, transcendent authority are illustrated in every relationship.

In the family, God illustrates the fundamental principles of his universal moral government, but family life also reflects the principles of grace. The principle of representation is manifest in paternal spiritual headship, the principle of mediation in suffering and toil is seen in maternal child-birthing and child-rearing, and the mighty power of love is ideally manifest not only in the parental relations but in their wise and firm, but warm and gracious parenting.

So, the family is a special kind of household, ideally consisting of husband and wife and desirably children. It is the oldest and most basic of God's institutions for humankind. It is designed by God to be a spiritual entity and to provide for the training up of children into mature adult character. Moses spoke of the very process of its perpetuation in Genesis 2:23–24: "The man said, 'This is now bone of my bones, and flesh of my flesh; she shall be called Woman, because she was taken out of Man.' For this reason a man shall leave his father and his mother, and be joined to his wife; and they shall become one flesh." The reference to leaving and cleaving points to the formation of a new family unit out of the union of husband and wife. This does not mean that singleness, single-parenthood, or childlessness must always bear reproach, but it does mean that single-parent families and childless marriages are the exception to the rule.

318

The family has a built-in, divinely given authority structure. The husband is spiritual head of the home, and the parents are leaders to the children. This headship and leadership is to express itself in ministry, not tyranny, and thus must be loving and selfless. In the wake of the fall, this basic creational order was reaffirmed (Gen. 3:16). One of Abraham's fundamental responsibilities in the covenant was to "command his children and his household after him to keep the way of the Lord by doing righteousness and justice" (18:19). Even pagan cultures have an appreciation of the divine, natural family order (Esth. 1:20, 22). The family order of creation and the role distinctions that flow from it were confirmed in the new covenant, and Paul called Christians to live deliberately in their light:

> But I want you to understand that Christ is the head of every man, and the man is the head of a woman, and God is the head of Christ. (1 Cor. 11:3)

> Man . . . is the image and glory of God; but the woman is the glory of man. (1 Cor. 11:7)

> Wives, *be subject* to your own husbands, as to the Lord. (Eph. 5:22)

> Wives, be subject to your husbands, as is fitting in the Lord. (Col. 3:18)

> He [an overseer or elder] *must be* one who manages his own household well, keeping his children under control with all dignity (but if a man does not know how to manage his own household, how will he take care of the church of God?). (1 Tim. 3:4–5)

Peter joined Paul in these affirmations and directives: "In the same way, you wives, be submissive to your own husbands. . . . Just as Sarah obeyed Abraham, calling him lord, and you have become her children if you do what is right without being frightened by any fear" (1 Peter 3:1, 6). Egalitarianism of all sorts (whether it involves the abdication of husbandly, paternal, or parental responsibility and authority) undermines family religion and the cultivation of godliness in the home, and only the biblical view (often today called "complementarian") can sustain a truly Christian discipleship.

Just how seriously God takes the family can be seen by looking at his law. Four of the ten commandments are directly related to the family. The fourth commandment requires the head of the household to lead the family in Sabbath-keeping. The fifth commandment requires children to respect and submit to their parents. The seventh commandment protects the family from sexual infidelity (whether it is expressed in a spouse's being unfaithful to the family itself or in someone else's endangering the family core by intrusion). The tenth commandment protects the family from those who would, in virtue of their coveting, take its necessary property or disrupt its relations. God is clearly concerned to throw around the family every moral/legal protection he can find.

Why? Because the family is God's divinely appointed "small-group" discipleship program. The family is the first place that God appointed for teaching and learning about God and godliness. Children are to be instructed (Gen. 18:18–19; Deut. 4:9; 6:6–8; 11:18–21; Prov. 22:6; Eph. 6:4), guided in the way of life (Prov. 1:8; 6:20), and disciplined both directively and correctively (13:24; 19:18; 22:15; 23:13–14; 29:15, 17). Family worship is important (Ex. 12:3; Josh. 24:15), and in the New Testament the household was the basic unit of Christian commitment (Acts 11:14; 16:15, 31–33; 1 Cor. 1:16). Indeed, a man's performance as spiritual head of his family was a major factor in assessing his fitness for church office (1 Tim. 3:4–5, 12; Titus 1:6). Nothing can replace or substitute for the family's failings in these functions.

Our goal in evangelical churches ought to be (1) for every family unit to become a discipleship group; (2) for every husband and father to become an active, self-denying, spiritual leader in his home; (3) for our congregations to have as many families functioning as "family-based growth groups" as there are families; and (4) for family religion to be the fountain of healthy, robust, corporate worship, as well as worship in all of life.

Covenantal Responsibilities of Parents

As Christian parents we can do significant things to promote the spiritual health and growth of our covenant children. In Deuteronomy 6:4–9, Moses said:

> Hear, O Israel! The Lord is our God, the Lord is one! You shall love the Lord your God with all your heart and with all your soul and with all your might. These words, which I am commanding you today, shall be on your heart. You shall teach them diligently to your sons and shall talk of them when you sit in your house and when you walk by the way and when you lie down and

when you rise up. You shall bind them as a sign on your hand and they shall be as frontals on your forehead. You shall write them on the doorposts of your house and on your gates.

These words remind us of two things. First, though salvation is of God and though the Spirit works when and how and with whom he wishes, Christian parents have covenantal responsibilities toward their children that God is pleased to use as means of those covenant children's spiritual birth and growth. Second, it is in the natural rhythm and activity of life that parents teach most and best. It is not primarily through church or paraministry youth programs but rather through parental life infused with Christ, grace, and Scripture—and normal opportunities looked for and taken—that we principally edify our children. Among those means and opportunities are the following.

First, we ought to give serious consideration to the spiritual condition and spiritual needs of our children. Do we care more for their bodies than for their souls? Do we think about how they look, whether they are physically healthy, what their career ought to be, whether they are running with the "first and best," how popular they are—and neglect a concern to see Christ formed in them, to see them growing in grace, to see them walking in faith, to see them denying themselves and taking up the cross?

Second, we ought to use baptisms as an occasion to call our children to faith. Whether we are credobaptist or paedobaptist, baptisms provide us with a unique opportunity to talk with our own children about what it means to be united to Christ. The Westminster Larger Catechism says:

> Baptism is a sacrament of the New Testament, wherein Christ has ordained the washing with water in the name of the Father, and of the Son, and of the Holy Spirit, to be a sign and seal of ingrafting into himself, of remission of sins by his blood, and regeneration by his Spirit; of adoption, and resurrection unto everlasting life; and whereby the parties baptized are solemnly admitted into the visible church, and enter into an open and professed engagement to be wholly and only the Lord's. (Q. 165)

I cannot see anything in that statement that credobaptists and paedobaptists would not agree on, but what a rich spiritual discussion could start in a conversation with our children back home after the administration of baptism during a church service!

Third, we ought to instruct our children in the great issues of salvation. We should talk with them about the content of sermons. We should ask them about Scriptures that they have memorized in Sunday school. We should aim to see how far they understand and to know and learn their souls.

Fourth, we ought to correct and restrain our children from that which is prejudicial to their spiritual vitality. There should be a sweet but firm display of parental authority in the home. We ought not to indulge them or to allow them to trample us. They should "fear you with delight." Challenge straying teenagers. Do not be cute with them about their sin.

Fifth, we ought to challenge our children to embrace the promises of God and to embrace Christ by faith. We should exhort them in the things of the Lord (1 Chron. 28:9; 1 John 3:23). Plunder the Scriptures for charges and challenges, for exhortations and spiritual commands for your children. A godly mother, just a week away from her death, asked her spiritually straying son to read to her Jesus' words from John 14:2: "I go to prepare a place for you." She afterward assured her son of her firm hope that Jesus had indeed prepared her a place and then said to him: "I want to ask you a question: Will you meet me there?" What a powerful way to bring home the truth of the ultimate life-and-death matters of trust in Christ and our eternal destiny.

Sixth, we ought to be disciples ourselves. We must love God if we want our children to love God. We must be disciples if we want our children to be disciples (Ps. 34:1, 4, 11). Along with this, we must remember that we are examples (for good or ill) in our life, priorities, and choices. Our children will see what is important to us. Is God important to us? his worship? the Lord's Day? the Bible? the Christian life? Or is our life taken up with trivialities, focused only on secular labor without a distinctively Christian worldview and lifeview and the pursuit of pleasure or just escape from pain? Our children will see what is really important to us, and it will either contradict or confirm our words about Christ and Christianity to them.

Seventh, we ought to pray for our children. We should pray for their salvation, for their spiritual growth, for their future spouses—and pray with them, as well as for them.

Promoting Family Religion

When all is said and done though, some of the profoundest things we can repeatedly do to promote a heart for God in our children are also the simplest things.

First, sit together at church. Go to church every week (even on vacation), fifty-two weeks a year, year after year, and sit together. That is it. I guarantee it will have a profoundly beneficial spiritual impact. The family ought to be in corporate worship faithfully and in it together. Children can get with their friends after the services, but in church, the family ought to be prime. Do not underestimate the power of the ordinary means of grace in the life of the family.

Second, work to have a Lord's Day. Live as if Sunday is the Lord's, not yours. View it as the "market day of the soul." Do not let the day become cluttered up. Avoid unnecessary labor and travel. Anticipate it with enthusiasm rather than bemoaning it. Make going to church the high point of the week. Let your children know you love it. Do special things with them on that day that you do no other (e.g., Dad: cook them breakfast, wake them in a special way, spend relational time with them in the afternoon, read them spiritual books and stories, make ice cream sundaes for them after the evening service, and the like).

Third, attend evening worship. If we believe the whole day is the Lord's Day, then it ought to be framed with worship. Morning and evening worship in the Reformed tradition is the single most powerful and effective total congregational discipleship program in the history of Christianity. I have never known a family that was faithful in Sunday evening attendance in an evangelical church that, when the great crises of life came, did not weather the storm and walk in faith and persevere.

Fourth, memorize the catechisms. It is a proven method. It is simple. It is content rich. It teaches our children the language of Zion, as well as the precious doctrines of the Bible. It increases memory ability and capacity for thinking.

Fifth, worship together as a family at home. Praise, pray, and read the Bible together as a family at home. Why should we do family worship? (1) Because we are stewards to God of our children, whom he has graciously given to us. Psalm 127:3 tells us how we are to view them: "Behold, children are a gift of the Lord." How will we account to him of the soul-care that we are to give these precious trusts? (2) Because God has commanded us to train our children up in the Lord in the home. As we have already seen in Deuteronomy 6:7, God says, "You shall teach them diligently to your sons and shall talk of them when you sit in your house and when you walk by the way and when you lie down and when you rise up." (3) Because the home is the seedbed of piety and religion for the church (1 Tim. 3:4–5, 12).

The Nature and Content of Family Worship

What should be in family worship? There is no reason to make it complicated, and you really need nothing more than a Bible and a good hymnbook to lead in it. "Song, scripture, supplication," says Jerry Marcellino—that is what should be in family worship.[2] That is, the three basic components of family worship are singing, Scripture reading, and prayer, led by the father or head of the household.

"Let those refuse to sing who never knew our God" go the lyrics of one stirring old hymn (Isaac Watts's "Come, We That Love the Lord"). An old proverb says, "As we sing, so we believe." So singing is an important component of both family and corporate worship. Do not let this intimidate you if you are not musical. Sing children's songs with the young and favorite hymns with older children (but do not underestimate how young children can pick up hymns, even hard ones—my two-year-old sings "Angels we have heard on high," with its tricky Latin refrain, flawlessly and on pitch!). If you cannot sing, get a tape to help lead your children in singing. Do not forget to sing psalms with them too.

God's word written is at the heart of all Christian worship: private, family, or corporate. Follow a Bible reading plan (many good ones are available, such as Robert Murray M'Cheyne's, kept in print by the Banner of Truth Trust). But do not hesitate to utilize solid Bible story books for the very young. Venture into some Scripture memory work. Test your children's knowledge of Bible facts (they may surprise you). But above all, be committed to reading God's word aloud to them.

"Prayer is an offering up of our desires unto God, for things agreeable to his will, in the name of Christ, with confession of our sins, and thankful acknowledgment of his mercies" (Westminster Shorter Catechism A. 98), so make sure your family prayer reflects that well-rounded balance of adoration of God, confession of sin, thanksgiving for God's favor, and intercession for ourselves and others. Use Scripture as your guide to prayer, and lead your family to the throne of grace.

A whole host of practical questions and problems come to mind once we determine to begin family worship. How long should it last? It should be regularly brief, as little as ten minutes when the children are very young. Gradually, it will run a little longer as they grow older and conversations strike up. Do not kill it by trying to go too long. Pace yourself. Regularity and repetition is the key. When should we do family worship? When it works — morning/breakfast, suppertime, or bedtime are the three most common times. What about the obstacles to starting and continuing family worship? Fair question. There are many:

- ✧ *A late start*: you have already been married for many years or a parent for many years, and you have never done it before. If this is your situation, be prepared for it to begin with all the ease of pulling teeth without anesthesia. Pray for the grace of perseverance, and do not begrudge your family the jarring sense of change.
- ✧ *An unsupportive wife*: your wife does not think it is important or is critical of what you are trying to do or is uncooperative. Woo her to the habit. Indulge her all you can. Refuse to speak sharply to her about her lack of support. Explain it to her. Enlist the prayers and encouragement of your pastors and elders, but make every effort not to shame her outside the family circle.
- ✧ *A lazy father*: your husband is indolent and unconcerned, but you really desire family worship. Pray for him in your private devotions. Ask God to change his heart and to make you the most attractive and nonaggressive advocate for the importance of family worship he will ever meet. Talk to him kindly and respectfully. Explain your desires. Make it easy for him to do. Offer to help him choose passages, hymns, and Scripture prayers. Do not nag. Encourage him to get involved in a male Christian discipleship friendship with a pastor or elder who will help him take up his fatherly and husbandly role. Place a Bible and a hymnal within easy reach of the family dinner table.
- ✧ *A resistant audience*: your children are older, unused to the practice, and resistant to it. They hate it, complain about it every day, discourage you no end. Keep it short, explain why you are doing it, and do it anyway.
- ✧ *An uncooperative schedule*: your schedule is crazy, husband traveling, kids piled up with activities. Meet consistently and flexibly. Let the wife lead while you are away, but take an interest in planning

325

for it and in talking about it when the husband is back. Call home long distance and do a conference call at family worship time.

There are dozens of potential hindrances: lack of discipline, lack of sense of the importance of family worship, lack of experience of family worship in one's own upbringing, and more. But above all, the enemy is idealism. You have this picture of a Puritan family sitting around the table attentively and reverently reading the whole book of 1 Chronicles at a sitting, singing half the Psalter from memory, and praying for ninety minutes, and then you look around your table and your wife is rolling her eyes, your two-year-old is throwing leftover spaghetti around the kitchen, your eight-year-old is making faces at her sister, and your teenager would rather do calculus. Do not let the gap between the ideal and the reality stop you! Those inattentive children will grow up and thank you for persevering, and the memories of a father who loved them enough to make that kind of an effort will etch a permanent affection in their hearts.

We have seen at least five pillars for family religion in this chapter: corporate worship, morning and evening, together as a family; Lord's Day observance; catechism; spiritual conversation in the normal course of family life and parental example; and family worship. The following is an eloquent and personal plea for this vision by Terry Johnson, the coauthor of this chapter.[3]

Family-Based Renewal of Congregational Christianity[4]

When I was a young boy, I walked to my public elementary school every school day for seven years. After school, I rode my bike to the ball park for my Little League games. Every Sunday we walked a few blocks to church. The recreation park was a little further away than the ball park and a little closer than the school. Scout hall was behind the school, so we also rode our bikes or walked to Boy Scout meetings. Life was simple for us kids and our parents. In the suburbs of Los Angeles, the epitome of the commuter city, we lived life within a one-mile radius of our home. We even walked to the doctor's office.

Most people used to live this way. Before the automobile, everything had to be within walking distance, or at least horse-and-buggy distance. Communities had to develop accordingly. Each neighborhood had its local grocer, clothier, druggist, school, church, and so on. People knew their neighbors, because they could not be avoided. One was constantly rubbing shoulders with them as one worked, worshiped, played, ate, and lived in the same area.

I like our cars. I can hardly imagine life without them. But as I was driving to school, work, the store, and a ball game the other day, I kept wondering, Is this really a better way of life? Our city, Savannah, Georgia, like every other community in America, now sprawls. We have big malls, big parks, big hospitals, big medical practices, nice roads in every direction, and nice air conditioned cars in which to drive. But is this a more humanly satisfying way to live?

While driving through town one evening, I noted the remarkable differences between poor and middle-class neighborhoods. The poor neighborhoods are older, more rundown, and yet abuzz with life. Some folks are sitting out on their porches, rocking and talking. Others are walking on the sidewalks. Still others are congregating on a street corner or at a storefront. What do you see in the middle-class neighborhoods? Nothing. Not a soul. Why not? Air-conditioning. In poor neighborhoods the deprived have no air-conditioning, but do have community. Affluent neighborhoods have air-conditioning, but consequently everyone stays inside, and minimal human interaction takes place. Who then is truly deprived? From air-conditioned offices to air-conditioned cars to air-conditioned houses, the socially impoverished move about, while the economically impoverished, though sweltering, enjoy a rich community experience.

We are technologically superior to previous generations. But are we losing too much in the process? First we walked, then galloped, then rode on rails together. Now we drive, largely with windows up, and go home to hermetically sealed homes, coming out only to take out the trash or grab the newspaper. Once we entertained ourselves at home by reading books aloud. In the 1920s families gathered around the radio. In the 1950s, they gathered around the television. Now there is a television in each room. Computers make it only worse. Once the home was a castle, a place of refuge for the family. When behind its doors, the family conducted its affairs without interruption and without outside influence. Now one can hardly eat a meal or conduct family worship without the phone ringing. Sacrosanct family time is violated daily. Friends and strangers alike barge right into the middle of the family's most private and intimate moments via technology.

327

Again my question is, Is this progress? When does life slow down enough so that we can talk? When do we enjoy our neighborhoods? Where do we experience community? In the last hundred years we have gone from life on a porch with family and neighbors to life in isolation in front of a cathode tube. Is the quality of life improving? Is ours a richer human experience? Frankly, I do not believe it anymore. Call it romanticism. Call it naïveté. Call me a Luddite. We have wonderful toys today. But they have cost us too much. Growing prosperity and technological advancement do not necessarily or automatically mark human progress.

I labor this point because I believe the church has largely failed to recognize the death of family and community or to compensate for it. Rather than reaffirm traditional practices that build family life and stimulate community, it tends to baptize secular trends that do the opposite. The small neighborhood church gives way to the large commuter church. The friendly country parson is replaced by the suburban CEO/pastor. Older practices such as the family altar and the family pew receive token attention, while new programs are devised that divide families and segregate the ages. In many ways we become too clever for our own good. We are just as guilty of "chronological snobbery," as C. S. Lewis calls it, as the rest of society. Tried and proven ways of transmitting the heart and soul of the Christian faith to others are abandoned in favor of exciting, entertaining, novel, but ineffectual alternatives. We pride ourselves in being modern. We look down our noses at previous generations. We have a love affair with the novel and the new. Educational, political, social, and religious fads sweep over us again and again, first possessing the field and all right-thinking people and then, in a matter of months, fleeing to the curiosity shelf in our cultural museums, replaced by yet another untested novelty. The time has come to admit our error and pause to look back, before we again look ahead.

What we hope to demonstrate in the pages ahead is that by returning to the practices of previous generations we may be able to revitalize the family and the church of today. The "ancient paths" of Sunday worship, Sabbath observance, family worship, and catechizing are where spiritual vitality for the future will be found.

The Family Pew

What then is the first key to a Christian family's spiritual health? Though you may not have anticipated our answer, the key is not new. It is not novel.

It will not reveal long-hidden mysteries, disclose any secret formulas, provide any new techniques, or require lengthy or costly counseling.

What is it? The first and primary key to your family's spiritual health is a commitment to the weekly public worship services of the church. The most important single commitment you must make to ensure your family's spiritual well-being is to regular, consistent attendance at public worship.

Sound farfetched? I will say it even stronger. I have yet to meet a person for whom it could not be said that all of his or her problems—personal, marital, familial, or vocational—would not be solved by such a commitment. I do not believe that the person for whom this is not true exists. By saying so, I do not minimize the seriousness of the problems that people face. Rather, I maximize our confidence in the power of the gospel. So I will say it again: we do not know of anyone of whom it could not be said, if only he or she were in worship week in and week out, fifty-two weeks a year, year after year, that his or her problems would be basically solved.

That public worship is not generally recognized as playing this central role in spiritual development demonstrates the degree to which modern individualism has rotted the core out of our commitment to Christ. How is it, after all, that we receive the benefits of the death of Christ? How is his grace communicated to us? Does it just drop out of heaven? Or are there means? Yes, there are means. What are they? The Shorter Catechism identifies the primary means as follows:

Q. 88. What are the outward and ordinary means whereby Christ communicates to us the benefits of redemption?

A. The outward and ordinary means whereby Christ communicates to us the benefits of redemption are his ordinances, especially the word, sacraments, and prayer; all which are made effectual to the elect for salvation.

The three primary means are the word ("especially the preaching of the word," says the Shorter Catechism Q. 89), the sacraments, and prayer. Now ask yourself, where are these three primary means normally operative? Where is the word preached? Where are the sacraments administered? And as for prayer, yes, one can pray in one's closet, but do not forget the special promise of Jesus about prayers offered where "two or three have gathered together in My name"—no doubt, given the context of church discipline in Matthew 18, a reference to organized public worship (18:15–20). Jesus

329

said, "Again I say to you, that if two of you agree on earth about anything that they may ask, it shall be done for them by My Father who is in heaven" (18:19). There is a unique efficacy in such public prayers.

When we gather in public worship, we are ushered into the presence of Christ. He is among us (Matt. 18:20). We do in worship what we were created to do—offer to God intelligent praise. We become more truly human at that point than at any other of human existence. Just as a boy is more aware of his identity as a son in the presence of his father, or as a husband is more aware of his identity as provider and protector in the presence of his wife, so we are most aware of who we are and what we were created to do as human beings at that point at which we bow in worship before our Creator and Redeemer. We are humbled as we offer to him our praise and adoration. We are cleansed as we confess our sins. We are built up, torn down, and rebuilt again as we submit to instruction by his word (Eph. 4:11–16). We are fed and united to the whole body of Christ by the sacraments. Through the bread and cup we enjoy *koinōnia* with Christ and one another (1 Cor. 10:16). We access his strength through "all prayer and petition" (Eph. 6:18) and are thereby enabled to fight the spiritual battles of life.

The public worship services of the church are our lifeline. There we are both purged and fed. There we make soul-saving contact with Christ through his word, sacraments, prayer, and the fellowship of his people. That contact, over the long haul, will change us. It will make us into the kind of people who are able to solve our own problems with the strength that the gospel provides.

The opposite view, that we can prosper spiritually on our own—apart from the public ordinances of the church and the public gatherings of the saints—is foolhardy. No, it is worse than that. It is worldliness—worldly individualism, worldly pride, worldly self-sufficiency.

The metaphor of the church as a body is employed by the New Testament to represent both our union with Christ and mutual dependence: "The eye cannot say to the hand, 'I have no need of you' " (1 Cor. 12:21). We need each other: "We, who are many, are one body in Christ, and individually members one of another" (Rom. 12:5). We need each other's gifts (Eph. 4:11–16; 1 Cor. 12–14; Rom. 12). We need each other's graces (as in the many "one anothers" found throughout the New Testament: love one another, be kind to one another, bear one another's burdens, etc.). We need each other's fellowship. So we are warned, "Let us consider how to stimulate one another to love and good deeds, not forsaking our own assembling together." The writer to the Hebrews sees the public assembly as the primary place in which the mutual stimulation to "love and good deeds" takes place: "Not forsaking our own assembling together, as is the habit of some, but encouraging *one another*; and all the more as you see the day drawing near" (Heb. 10:24–25).

How does this commitment to public worship relate to the family's spiritual well being? The effect upon parents is clear enough. Spiritually nourished parents make for better families. But the family pew has more in mind than sanctifying parents. When your children are brought with you into public worship, they too are sanctified. Your children, from their earliest years, will be ushered along with you into the presence of God. They will be brought under the means of grace and will experience the fellowship of God's people week after week as they mature through childhood. Beyond this, they will sit by you Sunday after Sunday, watching you publicly humble yourself before God and submit to his word. Among their earliest and warmest memories will be those of holding their parents' hands during church, sitting close to their sides, following along in the hymnal, placing money in the offering plate, and bowing their heads in prayer. Do not underestimate the cumulative effect of this witness upon covenant children. It is considerable, even incalculable.

The key to your own and your family's spiritual health is remarkably simple. Though there is considerable hype to the contrary, it involves no pilgrimages to sacred places. It requires no week-long or weekend retreats, seminars, or special programs. It depends on no special techniques or novel methodologies. You will not have to spend yet another night out. You will not need to add more meetings to an already frantic schedule. The key is to be found in the regular, ordinary, weekly worship services of the church.

The Lord's Day

Let's explore this further. As we have noted, many well-meaning but misinformed leaders in the Christian world would have you running hither, thither, and yon to find the magic formula for spiritual growth. They would have you out every night attending meetings for prayer, study, and fellowship. They thrust before you countless tapes, study books, and methods, techniques, seminars, retreats, and programs, each promising to provide the key to your spiritual well-being and happiness. Our response is—It is not that complicated. Whatever is of fundamental importance for the Christian life has been known in every era and is reproducible in every culture. If a thing is true and necessary, it can be understood and practiced in a primitive, grass-hut civilization, an igloo, and modern America. This is not to say that the toys of modernity cannot help. We make profitable use of tapes, videos, telephones, fax machines, and computers. We access the modern means of transportation. But we should not lose sight of the greater reality that all that we need to thrive spiritually may be found down the block at our local evangelical church through its regular ministry and worship. In its failure to recognize this, the church today is little better than the world in unnecessarily contributing to the frenetic pace of modern life.

What can we do? Slow down. Stay home. Quit running mindlessly all over town. Limit yourself. And do this: Commit yourself to the Lord's Day in the Lord's house, and little else outside of the home will be necessary for the cultivation of a thriving spiritual life. The Puritans referred to the Lord's Day as "the market day of the soul." Six days a week one buys and sells for the sake of one's body. Sunday however we are to "trade" in spiritual commodities for the sake of our souls. All secular affairs are to be set aside. All Christians, "after a due preparing of their hearts, and ordering of their common affairs beforehand," are to "not only observe an holy rest all the day from their own works, words, and thoughts, about their worldly employments and recreations," but also are to be engaged "the whole time in the public and private exercises of his worship, and in the duties of necessity and mercy" (Westminster Confession of Faith 21.8). The key to consistent attendance at public worship (of which we have spoken above as the key to your spiritual well-being) is a commitment to observing the Christian Sabbath. Or to state it negatively, you will never be able to become consistent about attending public worship until you are convinced that Sunday is not just the Lord's morning, but the Lord's Day.

When the writers of the Westminster Confession created a single chapter entitled "Of Religious Worship and the Sabbath Day," they knew what they were doing. We are the first generation of American Protestants to have forgotten the benefits of the Sabbath command. Prior to the middle of this century, all American Protestant denominations, whether Presbyterian, Methodist, Baptist, or Episcopalian, were sabbatarian. This was true for over 350 years, dating from the establishment of the Jamestown colony in 1607 until the mid-1960s. For generations it was understood that the Sabbath was made for humans, for human benefit (Mark 2:27–28). But once again we have become too clever for our own good. We have crammed our schedules full of activity seven days a week. We have lost our Sabbath rest in the process. What have we given up? Hughes Old writes: "Any attempt at recovering a Reformed spirituality would do well carefully to study the best of the Puritan literature on the observance of the Lord's Day."[5] How is this so? What is the point?

Essentially it comes down to this. If you are not convinced that the whole of Sunday is the Lord's and not yours, you will not be consistent. You will inevitably allow other matters to interfere. Things will come up. But, if you are convinced that Sunday is the market day of the soul, then it changes everything. The question of the Sunday services is settled—you will be there morning and evening. That the issue is dead, so to speak, has a wonderfully therapeutic effect. It is like the divorce laws in the pre–no-fault days. Because it was tough to get out of marriage, one tended to work it out and in the process find marital happiness. Eliminating options helps. Because Sunday worship is an inflexible given, everything else has to accommodate it. The fourth commandment tends thereby to cast its influence over the rest of the week. Life has to be organized around one's Sunday obligations. Shopping, travel, business, yard work, housework, recreation—all must be finished by Saturday evening. Sunday must be cleared of all secular obligations. The blessed consequence is not only that one is free to worship twice on the Lord's Day, but one also enjoys guilt-free, refreshing rest from the concerns and labors of life. I find myself regularly falling asleep about three o' clock in the afternoon with chills of gratitude and pleasure for the rest of the Christian Sabbath. Amazingly, even for preachers for whom Sunday is the busiest day of the week, it is also the most restful.

One can understand why the prophets sometimes speak of the abandonment of the whole of Old Testament religion as "profaning the Sabbath" (Ezek. 20:21; 22:8; 23:38). There is a subtlety to Sabbath observance. Because it excludes secular activity, its "holy rest" comes to dominate all of life. The family's week must be organized around its inactivity. Consequently, it can function as a plumb line, a litmus test for measuring your commitment to God. Will you submit to the lordship of Christ in this tangible way, this way that forces you to organize your life, to prepare, to complete your secular affairs, and to devote half of "your" weekend to the things of God? Will you desist "from your *own* ways, / from seeking your *own* pleasure, / and speaking *your own* word" (Isa. 58:13)? If you will, you will find time for all the things that really count—time for your soul, time for rest, time for the family, and time throughout the week for everything else.

Family Worship

Now we come to the heart of our concern. During the nineteenth century, as Sunday schools began to be introduced in North America, resistance was encountered in a number of traditional Presbyterian churches. Their argument? That as the Sunday school was established, it would result in parental neglect of their responsibility for the spiritual training of their children. Were they right? Cause and effect would be difficult to determine. But if they were, it would be an example of the law of unintended consequences that is typical of the modern world. Our intentions are wonderful. We mean to improve life by the creation of labor-saving devices, the development of new methods, and the provision of supplementary resources. But are we careful to examine the net effect of our innovations? Do they, in the long run, really help? If the consequence of the proliferation of Christian meetings has been the neglect of daily family worship, then the net spiritual effect of those meetings has been negative.

Let us assume for a moment that we all understand that the Bible commands that we conduct daily worship in homes. This was certainly the conviction of previous generations. For example, the Westminster Confession of Faith teaches that worship is to be conducted "in private families daily" (21.6), and the Church of Scotland included in its editions of the Westminster Standards a Directory for Family Worship, its General Assembly even mandating disciplinary action against heads of households who neglected "this necessary duty." Indeed, many of our Reformed ancestors believed in and practiced family worship *twice* daily (following the pattern of the morning and evening sacrifice). Family worship, they all assumed, was vital to the spiritual development of both parents and children.

But today, one does not hear much about family worship. No, instead we seem to have replaced it with small-group activities. These are the key, we hear again and again, to spiritual growth. Everyone needs to be in a small group. Or, it might be said, everyone needs to be in a discipleship group. Perhaps even, one needs to be involved in both. Maybe one needs to be involved in both, plus the church's prayer meeting, plus visitation, plus the choir, plus committee meetings, and so on. You see my point already, I assume. Protestantism has become all but silent on the issue of family worship, a near-universal practice in the recent past, and replaced it with meetings that take us out of the home and away from the family. Not only have we given up a proven method of transmitting the faith to the next generation, one that has a built-in format for Bible study, prayer, and singing, but we have done so for alternatives that add to our already hectic pace of life and take us away from our spouses, children, and neighbors.

I like small-group Bible studies. I will get more involved with them at a later stage in life, when my children are not so young and my wife and I are able to attend them together. But in the meantime we have a discipleship group, and if you are a parent with children at home, so do you. Every day little eyes are watching. Sooner than we realize, they become aware of discrepancies between what we say and what we do. The family, in this respect, is the truest of all proving grounds for authentic Christianity. Parents either practice what they preach or become the surest means yet devised by humans or the devil of sending their children to hell. Daily family worship forces the issues of Christian piety before the family every twenty-four hours. It forces parents into the roles of preachers, evangelists, worship leaders, intercessors, and pastors. Who is adequate for this? No one, or course. He who would attempt to be so must necessarily be forced to his knees. Children growing up with the daily experience of seeing their parents humbled in worship, focusing on spiritual things, submitting to the authority of the word, catechizing and otherwise instructing their children will not easily turn from Christ. Our children should grow up with the voices of their fathers pleading for their souls in prayer ringing in their ears, leading to their salvation, or else haunting them for the rest of their lives.

If your children are in your home for eighteen years, you have 5,630 occasions (figuring a six-day week) for family worship. If you learn a new psalm or hymn each month, they will be exposed to 216 in those eighteen years. If you read a chapter a day, you will complete the Bible four-and-a-half times in eighteen years. Every day (if you follow our format) they will affirm a creed or recite the law. Every day they will confess their sins and plead for mercy. Every day they will intercede on behalf of others. Think in terms of the long view. What is the cumulative impact of just fifteen minutes of this each day, day after day, week after week, month after month, year after year, for eighteen years? At the rate of six days a week (excluding Sunday), one spends an hour-and-a-half each week in family worship (about the length of a home Bible study), 78

335

hours a year (about the length of the meeting hours of seven weekend retreats), 1,404 hours over the course of eighteen years (about the length of the assembly hours of forty week-long summer camps). When you establish your priorities, think in terms of the cumulative effect of this upon your children. Think of the cumulative effect of this upon *you*, after forty or sixty or eighty years of daily family worship—all this without having to drive anywhere.

Catechism

Finally, we commend the catechizing of children, a grand old Protestant tradition that regrettably has fallen on hard times. Few catechize their children any more. For some, the word itself sounds archaic or like something the Catholics used to do. In actual fact, it is an ancient practice reaching all the way back to the earliest centuries of the church. It was revived in the sixteenth century by the Protestant Reformers so successfully that even the Roman Catholics began to mimic them. Catechisms were written by Luther, Calvin, Bullinger, and nearly all the major Reformers. In keeping with this tradition, the Westminster Assembly produced two catechisms, the Shorter Catechism for children and the Larger Catechism for adults. The former has been the most popular and widely used in the English language since the mid-seventeenth century.

Should you catechize your children? Yes, you should, and for a number of reasons:

1. It is a tried and proven method of religious instruction. For generations Protestants have successfully transmitted the content of the Christian faith to their children through catechisms. This was taken so seriously in Puritan New England that a child could be removed from the parents' custody if they failed to catechize him or her! Admission to the Communion table in Scotland for generations was preceded by the successful recitation of the Shorter Catechism. It was not uncommon in nineteenth-century Presbyterian homes in America that the Shorter Catechism would be completed during a child's sixth year. According to John Leith, seventeen thousand Presbyterian youth memorized the Shorter Catechism and had their names published in the *Christian Observer* in 1928, the year in which he achieved that feat. Education pedagogues come and go. Here is a method that works.

2. It is simple. It does not require additional resources. Any parent can catechize any child using no more than a small booklet. (In the process, the parent may learn more than the child!) But since the Bible places the responsibility of Christian education squarely upon Christian parents (Deut. 6:4–9; Eph. 6:1–4), here is a method easily adopted by parents.

3. It is content rich. The old catechisms are rich reservoirs of theological, devotional, and practical content. Fully 40 percent of the Shorter Catechism is concerned with ethics (the law of God) and nearly 10 percent with prayer. God, people, sin, Christ, faith, repentance, and so on are all given succinct, accurate definitions. Children nurtured on the catechism will be formidable theologians in an age of irrationalism and general mindlessness.

4. Memory is a faculty that should be developed. One might liken memory to a muscle—it grows when exercised and shrinks when neglected. J. A. Motyer, former principal of Trinity College in Bristol and lecturer in Old Testament and Hebrew, once said that he noticed a significant change in the capacity of his students to learn Hebrew declensions. What was typically learned upon first hearing by students in the 1930s and 1940s was the labor of a week in the 1970s and 1980s. Obviously, it is a great asset in life to have what we call a "good memory." What has often not been understood is that having such is more a matter of work than nature.

5. Memorizing logical, structured, conceptual material like the Shorter Catechism actually contributes to mental development. J. S. Mill, no friend of orthodox Christianity, claimed in his famous essay *On Liberty* that the Scots become mental philosophers of the first order through their study of the Bible and the Shorter Catechism. Douglas Kelly, noting the work of Scottish theologian T. F. Torrance, states that "children brought up on the Catechism have a greater capacity for conceptual thinking (as opposed to merely pictorial thinking) than those who never memorized it." It provides matter (theological matter!) for building the mental framework within which rational thought can take place. While not superior to the memorization of Scripture, this does explain why the catechisms are to be memorized alongside of Scripture.

Anglo-Catholic essayist J. A. Froude, who spoke of "the Scottish peasant as the most remarkable man in Europe," traced the dignity, intellect, and character of the typical Scottish peasant up to that time "as largely flowing from the memorization of the Shorter Catechism."[6] Let educational fads come and go. Concentrate on a method that has stood the test of time.

A Simpler Life

Now pull together the various threads. Instead of spiritual concerns contributing to an already frantic pace of life, the family should commit itself to the time-proven, biblically based means of spiritual nurture—public worship and family worship. In these settings great psalms and hymns are sung, children are catechized, sins are confessed, and the Scriptures are read and taught. Instead of running all over town, children and parents heading out in every direction, commitments are focused upon the Lord's Day services and daily worship at home. Life is simplified! Not only will we be using means that are more fruitful than the modern alternatives, and more likely to result in the salvation and sanctification of covenant children and parents alike, but the pace of life will slow, allowing more rather than less time for families to be together. Public worship, family worship, the Lord's Day, and catechizing are the ancient paths in which we will find rest for our souls.

14

WORSHIP IN ALL OF LIFE

WILLIAM EDGAR

It has become a truism to speak of the globalization of world culture. Mc-Donalds, the worldwide web, the Visa card, rap music, cell phones—all these represent icons of the network that has become our common experience around the world. Inevitably, such globalization affects the church. Jubilee 2000 saw thousands of people from every corner of the globe coming to Rome. Recently a group of Turkish Christians visited South Korea. They were so impressed with the vibrant churches they saw that they decided to plant Presbyterian churches in Turkey using Reformed theology and the synodical form of government. In China, while house-churches are illegal, hundreds of Chinese scholars trained in Europe are free to teach the Christian worldview in official universities because it is respectable to hold that, pragmatically, faith in Christ is effective for the social good. In Harlem, various African believers formed churches, but have brought their tribal rivalries with them into the new world.

This global setting offers enormous opportunities for the gospel. But there are enormous challenges and threats as well. The growing interdependence of people around the world means that churches are interdependent as well. On one level this is no doubt a good thing, reflecting the injunction that we work together "until we all reach unity in the faith" (Eph. 4:13). Yet it also means the bad habits of strong and powerful churches will be shared with the more vulnerable churches. For example, the tendency of American churches to believe that money is the main force in enabling ministries to succeed is being imported to many different assemblies around the world, even in poor places where wealth is not easily generated. The so-called health-and-wealth gospel has made a substantial impact on the continent of Africa and is wreaking havoc in the churches.

But here we want to concentrate on a particular problem. Another typically Western tendency often exported around the world is impatience. Specifically, we are impatient with the slow pace of change. We long for the gospel to make an impact, to see change in the surrounding cultures, but it does not seem to be happening, at least, at the rate we would like. Perhaps Americans are the least patient of all peoples.

Three Misguided Strategies

These are frustrating times for evangelical Christians in North America. Despite the enormous boost they received when *Newsweek* declared 1976 to be the "year of the evangelical" and the promise during the ensuing years of an increasing evangelical presence in politics, the results, nearly three decades later, are disappointing at best. Sociologist Dale McConkey comments that evangelicals are still largely in the socioeconomic margins, even adding that they will likely remain in their tribes: "All of these [profiles mentioned] place evangelicals at arms length from the strongest forces of modernity, making it more likely that evangelicals will be able to barricade their traditionalist worldview away from the corrosive forces of modernity."[1] Why so little impact? What should be done? What can be done, if evangelicals are to be faithful to their calling?

Three deeply mistaken strategies are often used in a situation such as ours. The first is rationalized aggression. Confounded by the lack of progress and stymied by the apparent inertia of many colleagues, some Christians resort to baptized violence. From attempts to destroy abortion clinics at one extreme to the practice of uncivil methods of discourse at the other extreme (i.e., a softer form of aggression), love that "endures all things" (1 Cor. 13:7 Revised Standard Version) is pushed aside in order to accomplish social goals more forcefully. Unfortunately, such tactics are not only in violation of Jesus' order to Peter to put away the sword (John 18:11), but they are usually counterproductive. Vaclav Havel, the visionary leader of the Velvet Revolution, faced serious criticism once he was established as president of free Czechoslovakia (as it was then known). After the heady years of the overthrow of Communism, now the people longed to move faster into the new freedom. Havel replied that he too was disappointed, yet in order to bring more progress they dare not sink to using the same methods as their former oppressors. It would be like the child trying to make the flower grow faster by tugging at its stem. Instead, the flower is ripped up.

A second approach is quite different. It is the way of resignation. Paul Weyrich, in his now famous *Open Letter* to his constituency, went public, saying evangelicals had been operating on the false premise that a majority of Americans agreed with their basically conservative values. Because they do not, we should all rethink our position on social and political involvement. With the oft-quoted statement, "I believe we probably have lost the culture war," Weyrich called evangelicals to withdraw from public institutions and instead practice holiness.[2] While understandable, this view is quite hopeless, literally, for it is based on two mistaken assumptions. The first is, as Weyrich puts it, that Christians need to find agreement in the surrounding culture before they can truly act as agents for its transformation. Is it biblical to strive for a consensus, hoping that a minority can become the prevailing voice, so that our country may be called "Christian America"? No, the Bible does not call New Testament Christians to work for a consensus where there are winners over losers. Rather, it calls believers to strive to live a godly life. This means a public policy where leaders all seek a truly representative republic, one where every religious group has the right to build its institutions without penalty for what they may believe. This is not because all religions are somehow true or, even less, saying the same thing. This is because we are in the time of God's patience, not in the time of Joshua's armies.

The second assumption is that there are only two options: driving for dominance or fleeing for purity.[3] But is this biblical? The Scriptures call believers in every culture, no matter how apparently friendly or unfriendly to the gospel, to live in the tension of operating within the system without succumbing to it (John 17:13–19). Followers of Christ are called to strive for justice and peace in every setting. There may be occasions when withdrawal is an acceptable *temporary* move. But usually the opposite is the case. It is when we face temptation and take the risks that go with it that we

341

become authentic. Paul tells us to "test everything" (1 Thess. 5:21). The author of Hebrews describes the mature as those "who by constant use have trained themselves to distinguish good from evil" (Heb. 5:14). In fact, withdrawal is usually a shameful accommodation to a social trend that represents the very essence of worldliness.[4] Cultural analysts tell us that America is "going indoors." We do not go to the bank teller or the ticket vendor anymore, but do it all online, from the comfort of our home. Should we really be imitating this worldly pattern of retreat into isolation?

A third stratagem is related: the approach of evangelism only. By this is meant that while cultural activity is perhaps allowable, it is beside the point. Winning souls is the most obedient endeavor in which to engage during the end times. Some say that evangelism is the highest Christian vocation. All other activity is in a support role. A world-class evangelical musician likes to say, "I do not give away my strategy to the enemy." He further explains that when he plays in concerts, he is hoping the music will draw people in the audience to him as a person. Then, in conversation with them afterward, he can give them a tape containing his testimony. But, again, while no one would deny the value of evangelism, it is never a question of either/or in Scripture. The church is called to make disciples of the nations and also to teach them to "obey *everything* I have commanded you" (Matt. 28:20 [emphasis added]). There is much in the Christian life that does not directly relate to evangelism and yet, like playing an instrument well, does not need to be justified by the real work of evangelism. Indeed, evangelism is rarely discussed as an individual calling in the New Testament. Although every believer should "be prepared to give an answer to everyone who asks" (1 Peter 3:15), only a few are specifically qualified as evangelists (Eph. 4:11).

A Better Way

If none of these tactics is appropriate, then what are evangelical Christians to do? Romans 12–16 gives us the answer. The Letter to the Romans is one of the greatest masterpieces of religious writing of all times. No wonder it has been the dynamic for so many crucial turning points in the history of the church. Augustine was brought to faith by reading Romans 13. Martin Luther was delivered from his sense of guilt before a holy God when he understood Romans 3:21–24, where Paul describes the free gift of "alien righteousness." John Wesley felt his "heart strangely warmed" on reading

Luther's preface to his commentary on Romans at the Aldersgate Street society meeting. Robert Haldane's lectures on Romans to the students of Geneva led to the great French revivals of the nineteenth century. Karl Barth's reading of Romans led him to proclaim the return of God's sovereignty in a way that, as he put it, was like a man climbing a dark tower who grasps a rope for guidance, only to find that it rings a bell and awakens the whole countryside. Francis Schaeffer's lectures on Romans from the café in Lausanne established the fundamental doctrinal foundation that led to the wider impact of l'Abri. The force of this letter has no explanation other than the power of its primary author, the one who inspired all of Scripture, but who spoke with particular impact here.

Romans 12–16 contains invaluable truth in answer to the question of how to affect the surrounding culture without falling into the three misguided approaches mentioned. As the word *therefore* indicates, this chapter comes at a transition. Typical of Paul's letters, the first eleven chapters have been foundational. Now he turns to the application. Not that the first part is without application, nor that the second has no foundations. But the first part carefully lays the ground for the universal guilt of humankind, the free gift of God's grace, and the way to live in God's grace until the end of history. Even chapters 9–11 are foundational, because they explain how God is still faithful to his promise, despite the unbelief of his chosen people, the Jews. How is it, Paul asks, God can call them and yet they be unresponsive? He answers with the doctrine of election. They have not been forgotten, but not all Jews are elect. Their unbelief opens a way for the Gentiles to come to faith. But the Jews still may return, and thus both Jew and Gentile can be saved. This plan is so marvelous that Paul ends with a doxology of wonder and praise for the depth and riches of God's wise plan (11:33–36).

On the strength of all this, one could wonder what is left to say. But there are five more chapters! And Paul is quite urgent about it: "I appeal to you," he tells them (Revised Standard Version). What could possibly be so urgent, after all that he has already affirmed?

Worship! Yes, what Paul has to tell his readers, after this matchless buildup, is that they must worship God. This is the culmination of everything he has set down. More precisely, he tells them to offer their bodies as "living sacrifices" (12:1). The Old Testament flavor is apparent here. Like the animal sacrifices of the old covenant, this one must be holy and pleasing to God. No blemished lamb for the Lord God. But unlike the ancient sacrifices, there is no bloodshed in view. It is the human body, regenerate, redeemed from sin, that we are to present "as those who have been brought from death to life" (6:13). Why this stress on the body? It is argued that Paul uses the body here as a symbol for the whole person. Our body is the vehicle for the self. And, of course, there is no reason to limit what he is saying to the physical self. But neither is there good reason to go beyond his words. The body is to be sanctified. Paul often alludes to the physical body, both in this letter and elsewhere (Rom. 6:6, 12; 8:10; 1 Cor. 5:3; 6:13; 2 Cor 5:6; etc.). Unlike Plato, the biblical view is not embarrassed by the physical self. It is part of God's image. Though life in the body has become a curse (Rom. 7:24), redemption is incomplete without the physical resurrection (8:23; Phil 3:21).

Worship with the body is Paul's first and foremost injunction. In view of the many abuses of the body in the surrounding culture, one can well appreciate his emphasis. In our own day we are rapidly slouching toward pure hedonism, the degeneration of the self into permissive decadence. Holiness for the apostle is not withdrawal, but it is sacrifice. We are told here to give up what we want for our gratification, to say no to our appetites, and present ourselves to God. Our entire lives should be an offering to the Lord. The Decalogue tells us to have "no other gods before [God]" (Ex. 20:3). All of life is to be a calling *coram deo,* a covenant walk with the Lord. So much would change if we were to take this seriously and lift ourselves up to God in perpetual sacrifice, for "no one whose hope is in [God] / will ever be put to shame" (Ps. 25:3). This is not evangelism only—far from it. Rather, Paul is calling us to everything that is holy and pleasing to God. He will soon spell out what this means and set forth many areas of life in need of obedience to God. But here he tells us the basic, most fundamental principle, to worship God with our bodies.

He further qualifies this worship as spiritual. The Greek word he uses, *logikēn,* is unusual. It means spiritual in the sense of "rational" (the Authorized Version has "your reasonable service"). This is no doubt, first, because our worship is meant to be voluntary, conscious, intelligent, and not mechanical. The body may be physical, but it is not autonomous, guided purely by instinct. Second, however, the term probably means something like "systematic." The word *logikēn* is related to the term *logos,* from which we derive "argument" or "account." The idea is that worshiping God must be controlled by our worldview. No area of life falls outside of a rational, systematic understanding. While we may not have all the elements of a biblical worldview firmly in hand, we should nevertheless strive toward owning a full-orbed worldview and life view that "take[s] captive every thought to make it obedient to Christ" (2 Cor. 10:5). This is not intellectualism—far from it. And it is the opposite of pietism or of a kind of quietist spirituality that "lets go and lets God." While God is the dynamic and the Holy Spirit is the primary agent of sanctification, to the point that we cannot ever rationally control or even understand the process, there is also a human agency without which no progress can be made. "Work out your salvation," Paul tells his Philippian readers, though "with fear and trembling, for it is God who works in you to will and to act according to his good purpose" (Phil. 2:12–13).

A Wide-Ranging Prohibition

Two aspects coexist in this radical worship. The first is negative: "Do not conform any longer to the pattern of this world," is Paul's next injunction. Christian faith denies the world, the flesh, and the devil. Why does the apostle begin with the negative? In his writings he does not always begin with an interdiction, but he often does. In Ephesians 4–5 he gives a series of requirements that begin with a prohibition: "You must no longer live as the Gentiles do" (4:17); "each of you must put off falsehood" (4:25); "he who has been stealing must steal no longer" (4:28); "do not let unwholesome talk come out of your mouths" (4:29); "there must not be even a hint of sexual immorality" (5:3); and so it goes. Each of these, to be sure, is immediately followed by the positive command that represents the amends. To take but one example, after telling the thief to stop stealing, he continues: "But [he] must work, doing something useful with his own hands, that he may have something to share with those in need" (4:28). But why not simply state the positive and let the negative be assumed?

The reason is the way in which the order of salvation (*ordo salutis*) is built upon the history of salvation (*historia salutis*). Jesus was humiliated, suffered, died, and then raised up to glory. He fulfilled the requirements that humankind failed to enact. In our Christian lives, then, we show forth the virtues of the one who brought us from darkness into God's marvelous light. Again, throughout the text of Ephesians, Paul reminds his readers that they were once children of darkness, living like the Gentiles, but now they have been taught Christ and have put off the old self and put on the new. The Decalogue reflects the same principle. Of the ten, no fewer than eight of the commandments begin with a negative. As children of darkness by nature, we need to be told what not to do first, and then we may go on to the positive. This does not mean law must always precede gospel. In fact, the gospel is always first, and any meaningful application of the law cannot be made without respecting the entire context of the work of salvation. The Decalogue begins with the premise that God brought the people out of Egypt's bondage and into a place where they could worship God in freedom. Still, we need to rehearse the order: because of who you are in Christ, by God's mercy, desist from this practice and then begin another discipline.

In Romans 12:2 Paul prohibits conformity to worldly patterns. The phrase literally says, "Do not scheme together according to this age." Just as worship is systematic, so is worldliness. We are being delivered from our entire era's deep structures. A particular age has a shape or a culture. Everything in life comes in patterns, whether it be trends in the social world, political structures, or personal habits of the heart. C. S. Lewis says somewhere that he could tell what kind of person you are by whether you began the day reading the newspaper or the Bible. Becoming disentangled with the world is more than following a list of rules. It means radically changing one's behavior patterns. Often that means looking into the deep fabric in the surrounding culture. David Inge famously remarks: "If you marry the spirit of the age you will soon find yourself a widower."[5] Marriage is a good analogy, here. This present evil age is not manifest simply with a few clearly perceived idols. Avoiding the world's seductions is not simply a matter of rejecting certain temptations to sin. Rather, since the attachment is like a conjugal alliance, the remedy is divorce! And following divorce, we must continue to avoid any compromise, any ambiguous relational patterns.

J. B. Philips translates this verse, "Don't let the world around you squeeze you into its mold." The world could squeeze us like a boa constrictor, until we suffocate, unless we refuse to conform. Christians often are not aware of the subtlety with which conformity beckons. A modern parable makes the point humorously, if forcefully. Petrov was a prisoner in a work camp, a part of the gulag system under the old Soviets. Each day, he went to work in a designated area and then returned through a checkpoint to his barracks. One evening he returned to his barracks with a wheelbarrow containing a large sack. At the checkpoint, the guard stopped him and asked what he was stealing from the work site in that sack. Petrov protested that he was not stealing a thing and that the bag contained only sawdust. The guard opened it up, and sure enough, it contained only sawdust. The next evening, the procedure was repeated. The guard stopped the inmate with his wheelbarrow and sack, but again all he could find was sawdust. This routine happened again several evenings in a row, until finally the exasperated guard told Petrov he knew that he was stealing something, but could not decide what it was, but he promised not to denounce him if he would only confess. "Wheelbarrows, sir, I am stealing wheelbarrows," the clever prisoner admitted.

It is often the same in the Christian life. We think we are resisting the world because we refuse to be taken in by the content of the world's ways. Yet we are nevertheless seduced by the form, the container that shapes the content. We may reject a secular ideology, for example, or a secular philosophy. But we accept the terms of secularization by privatizing our faith and assuming it has no incidence on government, workplace, school. We may reject any attempt to embezzle church funds, but we nevertheless run the church like a corporation. We switch television channels when there is foul language, but we keep the medium itself alive, forgetting it often tends to reduce almost any program to entertainment. We withdraw our children from the school system, only to seclude them in the worldly atmosphere of our own subculture.

An Intensive Command

In the same sentence, though, Paul runs to the positive: "But," he says, "be transformed." Notice that the opposite of nonconformity is not "be different" or, worse, "be yourself." Rather, it is the constant process of renewal that characterizes the Christian life. This age and its patterns are going to disappear. They are ephemeral, temporary. In them we wither and stagnate. But Christian renewal is permanent, solid, everlasting. In it we progress and grow. The concept of metamorphosis is the same that Paul elucidates in 2 Corinthians 3:18 when he describes believers as those who gaze upon the face of Christ and therefore "are being transformed into his likeness with ever-increasing glory" (3:18). John Murray's commentary on Romans 12:2 is eloquent:

347

Sanctification is a process of revolutionary change in that which is the centre of consciousness. This sounds a fundamental note in the biblical ethic. It is the thought of progression and strikes at the stagnation, complacency, pride of achievement so often characterizing Christians. It is not the beggarly notion of second blessing that the apostle propounds but that of constant renewal, of metamorphosis in the seat of consciousness.[6]

The change is nothing less than radical. Again, the notion of worldview expresses the radicalness. But we should take care not to limit ourselves to merely an outlook. The optic metaphor in the term *worldview* can be misleading. It fails fully to carry the dynamic aspect of our vision. We are not limited to having the right ideas, even the right doctrines, in Paul's command. We are told to change, to be converted.

We may sense a problem here. We are uncomfortable with being told to be changed by the renewing of our minds, as though we could possibly effect such a transformation ourselves. On the surface, it sounds as though Paul were telling us to "get it together," to "pull up our bootstraps." Surprisingly, in a way, he is saying just that. He is telling us to be changed and to renew our minds. This is no different from any command in Scripture. We are told by our Lord to "be perfect, therefore, as your heavenly Father is perfect" (Matt. 5:48). We can no more achieve this by our own merits than we can accomplish any of the biblical commands. Only God can effect such a change. And yet he does so, not by violating human agency, but by engaging it. In the same way that our worship is rational, here it is voluntary. The great difference between self-generated transformation and biblical conversion is that God is the one ultimately at work to effect the change. The underlying presupposition here in Paul's text is that we do all of this by faith. How can we know that? Simply because of the opening words: "in view of God's mercy." This is a world away from the self-help pabulum of the Oprah Winfrey Show or the New Age bromides of Deepak Chopra. The only way we can be transformed is by operating, in all areas of life, under the grace of God, who gives to all who believe in him unconditionally.

Again, Phillips puts it nicely: "Don't let the world around you squeeze you into its mold, but let God remold your minds from within." Paul is gospel driven. The gospel is God's mercy for undeserving sinners. But the gospel effects change. That change is no less caused by the God of all mercies than initial salvation. And it is comprehensive.

In telling us to have our minds renewed, Paul is not courting intellectualism. The Greek word for mind (*nous*) is not a technical term for the
logical self. Rather, it includes all faculties of perception, the feelings, and
the capacity to make judgments. In Ephesians 4:23, Paul tells us we have
been made new, "in the attitude [spirit] of our minds." From the context
we can tell he is being quite broad, since he likens this to having "put on
the new self" (4:24). Here, in Romans 12:2, he is no doubt telling us to be
renewed in our essential, spiritual selves. Our logic would certainly be a
part of this mind, but so would our acumen, our discernment, our understanding, in short, our worldview.

In the second part of Romans 12:2, Paul tells us what this is going to look
like. It is in order to test or approve God's will. We ought to be careful here
to discern exactly what Paul has in mind. He is not saying that we should
suddenly become the arbiters of God's will. We are mere creatures, and it
is nothing short of sabotage to imagine we can in any sense become judges
of the law. James compares this kind of attitude to slander. In his argument,
he puts it this way:

> Brothers, do not slander one another. Anyone who speaks against his brother
> or judges him speaks against the law and judges it. When you judge the law,
> you are not keeping it, but sitting in judgment on it. There is only one Law-
> giver and Judge, the one who is able to save and destroy. But you—who are
> you to judge your neighbor? (James 4:11–12)

What Paul means, rather, is that we should learn by experience what God's
will might be. God's will never fails. It applies to every situation.

God's will is the very definition of what is good, pleasing, and perfect.
The good is the will of God. The pleasing is the will of God. The perfect
is the will of God. The will of God is nothing less than his character, shaped
into laws for our conduct. We can never change that. It is the *summum
bonum*. But we can discover his will in its marvelous breadth and beauty.
His commands are never burdensome (1 John 5:3). But they need to be
practiced in order fully to demonstrate their liberating character. It is interesting to note that the word translated "approve" (*dokimazō*) in Romans
12:2 is the same word used earlier in 1:28, when Paul describes the human
depravity that deserves God's displeasure: "Furthermore, since they did not
think it worthwhile to retain [*dokimazō*] the knowledge of God, he gave

them over to a depraved mind, to do what ought not to be done." The failure of humanity to recognize the goodness and perfection of God's will deserves God's judgment. And that judgment takes the form of relegating that humanity to desperate life-styles.

Upon the approval of God's will—that is where everything is based and where everything is determined. And so it is that only those who are under God's mercy, the beneficiaries of his alien righteousness, can effectively approve God's will. Another way of putting it is this: Developing a fully biblical worldview in which we are constantly showing forth the virtues of God's character, as revealed in his law, that is where all things are decided. Once again, we have the clearest possible teaching that all of life is meant to be worship. There is no area falling outside of the will of God.

Now, of course, this opens up the whole question of discerning God's will. It is one thing to affirm in theory that everything is included in God's will, it is quite another to demonstrate what this means. Reformed Christians are rightly criticized for waxing eloquent on the theory of worldviews but coming up short on concrete examples. It may not always be easy to find out what God's will might be for certain questions. What does his law say about stem-cell research, about musical rhythms, about teaching mathematics? The answer to these kinds of issues is not always evident. And yet in principle there must be answers, or we could not be transformed and renewed. Is there a biblical approach to science? To marketing, the arts, or politics? Where should we begin?

An Extensive Command

What sorts of issues will be at the top of the agenda for the church in Rome as it renews its mind? The subsequent lines tell us. Paul's first concern is for the life within the church community. He is anxious that no one in the body assume that his or her gifts be considered higher or more important than those of any one else (Rom. 12:3–8). Yet he reminds his readers right away that theirs is a global outlook. He wants them to be aware of the worldwide fellowship of the saints, some in affliction and need, but all of them family (12:9–16). Relations to outsiders are crucial as well. So Paul moves right to the question of persecution. He is anxious that believers not take justice into their own hands, but always defer to God's judgment. He asks them to do everything possible to ensure a peaceful coexistence with

350

their neighbors. In fact, he tells his readers, in a counterintuitive way, that if they treat their enemies with the kindness of the gospel, rather than with the justice of vengeance, they will accomplish great things for the advancement of the kingdom (12:17–21).

These are matters directly flowing out of the worldview the apostle is setting forth. Not that it is easy or immediately apparent how the worldview should apply. For example, how would a balanced, biblical doctrine of calling be developed from the verses on the gifts (12:3–8)? Some things are obvious. The fundamental equality, the equal worth of each gift, rather than a hierarchy, can be derived directly from these verses. In chapter 14, Paul speaks further about treatment of fellow believers whose conscience is more tender. Indeed, he cares a great deal about the protection of those weaker believers from self-betrayal. That much is quite clearly established. But what about the larger issues surrounding calling? Are there not governing offices in the church? What about the missionary calling to evangelize the world? And what about the legitimate vocations in the world, such as professions, citizenship, family life, and so many others? And what about cultural transformation? Many agree with H. Richard Niebuhr's option, "Christ the transformer of culture," which happens to be that of Augustine and Calvin.[7] But there are many critics of this view. When Paul says, "Do not be overcome by evil, but overcome evil by good" (12:21), how active is that overcoming meant to be?

It is important to work through these texts and see how the apostle argues. He is not presenting an abstract theory of calling. Many of us have benefited from Abraham Kuyper's notion of sphere sovereignty. In it the church is independent, but in dialectical relation to other domains, such as school, state, and family. If this is Paul's view, he does not arrive at it by means of social theory. Yet, he assumes certain social structures in which it is perfectly legitimate for Christians to participate. He assumes them, because he tells his readers how to treat them, how to live in relation to them. In this way his message is quite universal, for he does not presuppose an ideal social order before a Christian vocation may be lived out. But his assumption sends an important message. Social change will occur in the present regime, but within the existing structures. Paul never calls for a revolution that changes the structures of society. This is partly because he respects the propriety of the order that God laid down at the creation of the world. But even when those structures are not altogether good ones or when we may not live in the best of circumstances, Paul still does not encourage abrupt change. He tells the Corinthians not to change jobs or to seek release from marriage (1 Cor. 7:17–40). This is not for reasons of social conservatism, but because of the greater priority of the kingdom of God. Indeed, change will occur when the church is faithful to its calling in every realm of life. Thus, even within these earthly structures, significant change may occur. For example, in a marriage where only one spouse is a believer, the unbelieving spouse is sanctified and the children are holy (7:14).

Indeed, the apostle clearly sets down kingdom injunctions for believers according to their situation. Toward church neighbors he tells them to employ spiritual gifts with zeal. The devotion of Christian love is in an eschatological setting: "joyful in hope, patient in affliction, faithful in prayer" (Rom. 12:12). Hospitality, living in harmony, refusing elitism—these characterize life in the body of Christ. Toward outside neighbors Paul's commands take a different shape. With them we must learn the patience of a persecuted people. Resisting vigilante justice, Christians should bless their enemies, and "overcome evil with good" (12:21). Submitting to governing authorities is right, because they are established by God himself (13:1–5). This is counterintuitive for believers, who will inherit the earth (Matt. 5:5) and even judge the world (1 Cor. 6:2), that is, until we realize that the creation structures are still in place. Marriage, procreation, labor, worship, and indeed government—these are still fundamental to the ordering of God's world today. Magistrates are thus "God's servants" (Rom. 13:6), and though they may not be believers, they are to be honored because their task includes doing good for believers and citizens and punishing evil. Paul could never say this of the church. He would never say that the church is an agent of wrath and "does not bear the sword for nothing" (13:4).

Notice how positive Paul is about governing authorities. Though not the church, they are established by God, and their task is to promote the social good as well as to judge against evil. True, he tells believers to obey not only for fear of punishment but for conscience's sake (13:5). But even here the issue is not merely pragmatic, but based on the ultimate criterion of divine institution (13:2). This approach gives comfort to the Reformed view of "Christ the transformer of culture." Many Christians today disagree. Stanley Hauerwas, for example, takes exception to the Reformed idea of transforming society through social involvement. This is because he is opposed to a worldview that seeks to secure a more just society by participating in politics. The only political involvement we may have is "because we recognize that our politics inherently involves compromise and accommodation." Thus, for him, the church is the primary sphere of activity. To be sure, in the church we "gain the experience to negotiate and make positive contributions to whatever society in which we find ourselves."[8] But any change in society must be indirect. Hauerwas is unable with enthusiasm to invite Christians to consider a life in politics as a fully valid calling. Furthermore, the church for him becomes a sort of pilot plant that models the virtues and ethical norms for the rest of society. The idea of each sphere carrying its own set of norms and being mutually complimentary is foreign to him.

Based on our understanding of Paul's argument in Romans 12–13, we would have to disagree. To be sure, the church is called to holiness. Paul can intersperse injunctions to obey governors with behavioral norms for the body of Christ. The entire fourteenth chapter is devoted to discussing the strong and the weak of conscience. In a way that seems to comfort Hauerwas's approach, Paul relates the life of the church to missions. At 15:7 Paul makes the link between mutual toleration in the church and the plan of God for the nations. He recalls the argument from chapters 9–11 about Jews and Gentiles, and then appeals to the "priestly duty" of his own missionary work (15:16). But Paul is not so much saying that the church will convert the world as he is saying that God is extending his kingdom throughout the world, of which the church and its life are a primary component.

Think Globally

In his brilliant comments on Paul's missionary theology, Herman Ridderbos notes that the evangelistic consciousness of the church is expressed at several levels. For example, the church is deeply involved in Paul's own efforts. Moreover the church is to be ready with the equipment of the gospel of peace (Eph. 6:15). It is an essential part of the church's nature that it give testimony, directly and indirectly, to those on the outside. Its inner dynamic, however, is an understanding of God's great work of redemption, both extensively and intensively, now and until history comes to an end:

> And the deepest motives for this, just as for the work of the apostle himself, lie in the consciousness that the church is *included* in the great world-encompassing work of God in Jesus Christ. It is not the church itself that is

the ultimate object, not its number and prestige, but the revelation of the full eschatological salvation in Christ, of whom the church is the *plērōma*, that is to say, the bearer of the glory of Christ (Eph. 1:23; 4:13, 16).[9]

At this level, then, we are looking at questions beyond evangelism and even missions. We are looking at the fullest possible picture of God's work in the world. We are seeing an eschatologically comprehensive approach to cosmic history.

This is why the apostle can so freely use language from the Old Testament, even while he is profoundly aware of the special characteristics of the present time. From his quotations of Job, the Psalms, the Prophets, and the Pentateuch to his use of the Decalogue, there seems to be no dichotomy in the instruction given between the old and new administrations. That is because both are administrations of grace, and both require obedience to the law of God. It is true that in the New Testament era the configuration of spheres is different from Mosaic times. But the fundamental principles are the same. The movement known as theonomy errs in compressing the two administrations and thus confusing the two different contexts for the exercise of God's law. But it correctly reminds us that God's law is very much in force even in the Christian dispensation.

So, is there a Christian view of the arts, a biblical approach to politics, education, commerce, entertainment, and so on? The answer must be affirmative, or we will find ourselves claiming that God's law has gaps in it and that we cannot truly "test and approve what God's will is" in every situation. Making the connections requires patiently drawing implications from God's law and applying them in every sphere of life. There is far more data to draw from than we might imagine. When we are free to navigate in the Old and the New Testaments together, we will be surprised at how much there is. Sometimes the information will be direct, clearly spelled out. At other times it will be indirect, requiring wisdom and insight. God gives his wisdom freely and ungrudgingly to all who ask in faith (James 1:5).

But there is one condition for success in developing a biblical worldview that is truly comprehensive. And that is to heed the fundamental call to worship. This is truly worship for all of life. Historian Arnold Toynbee is said to have been struck by the notion that civilization can survive only when it is undergirded by a strong religious drive. He noticed that in Western civilization, more often than not, it was the presence of Christians that

354

lay behind the most remarkable developments, from the arts to medicine, democracy, a higher standard of living, and so forth. He wondered exactly what the connection might be. In one of his books he describes a dream he had had years before the book materialized. In the dream, he walked into Ampleforth in Yorkshire and looked up at the altar. Above it he saw a cross, and he went and clung to it. Then he heard a voice saying *amplexus expecta* (embrace and hope). He suddenly understood the connection. Great change occurs in lives and in cultures not when people prescribe elaborate programs for change. Rather, they occur when believers humble themselves before the crucified, risen Christ and cling to him, expecting change. In his dream, Toynbee preached this message to the congregation. The key is the attitude. Change will occur, but in *his* way and in *his* time. Not that believers are passive. Quite the contrary. They are fully engaged. But only as worshiping creatures, sacrificing all to the Savior whom God did not spare, but gave up for us, giving us, along with him, all things besides (Rom. 8:32).

Act Locally

When we read that all of this is "in view of God's mercy," we realize that we have only begun to grasp where that can take us. But there are many practical directions we can move in, building on the past and looking to the future. We said at the beginning that our world is increasingly globalized. How, then, can we function as a church, rooted in the local setting, but yet aware of our worldwide reach? One answer is to never neglect the local communitarian character of the church. It is tempting for church leaders to move around, following the trend toward increasing mobility. The average American family moves every four years. Pastors should consider very carefully the wisdom of staying in one parish for many, many years. It is patent that Dr. Boice's life-long commitment to Tenth Presbyterian Church and to living right in the city of Philadelphia was a visible testimony to the stability of his relationship to Jesus Christ in a chaotic world. Not only leaders, but families and singles should ponder very carefully before they decide to move. What will the impact be on the children? On the local church? Is a job promotion always the only option?

This does not mean the church should be tribal. It always has the great responsibility of connecting to the surrounding culture and even to the surrounding world. In the recent crisis of the destruction of the World Trade

Center, many churches in New York became engaged in giving critical aid to victims. Some of it was financial, and churches around the world responded by sending love-gifts to specific New York ministries. But it also consisted in providing counseling for those who were traumatized. We had the sobering privilege of attending the worship service at Redeemer Presbyterian Church on the Sunday following the terrorist attacks. Of course, it was packed with people, and the church had to multiply the number of services throughout the day just to accommodate the demand. The bulletins were pared down to a simple page. The music was a mixture of lamentation and resolution. The sermon was a powerful application of John 11, where Jesus faced the death of his friend Lazarus with grief and anger. He neither blamed the victim nor indulged in a good-guy-bad-guy narrative. He furiously conquered death by becoming its victim. Thus, the unspeakable evil of this attack—and all other manifestation of depravity—will one day vanish as in a bad dream.

Local churches can do a great deal, despite globalization. They can instruct their members on proper Christian involvement in politics, science, the arts, agriculture, family life, careers of all kinds—in short, in every sphere of life. One remarkable African American church in a major city endeavors to focus on training men in leadership. This is not due to chauvinism, but because of its conviction that the significant loss of male involvement in black American families and local churches has reached crisis proportions. Going back to slavery, when so many families were simply broken up, which was then compounded in the earlier part of the twentieth century by the false promise of prosperity in northern cities, when men left their local settings to find work in places like Chicago and Detroit, men were often isolated from communities that could call them to account. This church works especially with younger African American males, trying to reach them early, before they fall into the same patterns of isolation as their forefathers. They create ministries requiring male leaders to function as visionaries, they visit families to encourage men to nurture their wives and children, they set up mentoring programs where young men can be guided by older, more experienced males.

None of this means that specialized parachurch groups cannot also have significant roles to play in encouraging believers to participate in every sphere. The Arts Center Group in London and the *Parvis des arts* in Marseille are but two in the growing numbers of fellowships dedicated to promoting a Christian aesthetic in the artistic realm. Part of their work is simply to instruct Christians in a full-orbed, biblical worldview. Part of it is to put Christians from various fields—be it visual art, poetry, theater, and so on—into contact with one another. Publications, shows, employment opportunities—all of these form aspects of their ministry.

Christians around the world need to return to this Pauline balance of worship for all of life. In this way, when they resist the American temptation to impatience, they can begin to see true change—long term, no doubt, but substantial nevertheless. We are blessed at the seminary where I teach to have a strong group of Chinese students. Hearing their stories is both fascinating and revealing. One can hardly find examples of more devoted believers, whose faith has been hammered out on the anvil of persecution. At the same time, many of them report that the theology of the house-church movement is often pietistic, unable to "test and approve what God's will is" in every sphere of life. Politicians are simply enemies of the gospel. Culture is a distraction. Science is for technicians, the arts for the sensuous. And so many of our students are studying Reformed theology, with a few of them developing a specifically biblical approach to politics and culture, an approach that will enable them to return one day, in God's providence, to their homeland and be the kind of salt and light in society that their master calls them to be.

And so, if we are to recognize ourselves as worshiping creatures, sacrificing all to the Savior whom God gave up for us, we may see great change. For truly, we have a God who is anxious to give us, along with Christ, all things besides. If only we could grasp this. What a difference it would make!

15

WORSHIP AND THE EMOTIONS

W. ROBERT GODFREY

Early in the 1920s Aimee Semple McPherson, the influential Pentecostal evangelist, held a service in Denver. Her recent biographer Edith Blumhofer records how Sister McPherson led the song before the sermon:

> She asked everyone aged fifty to sixty to raise their hands, then those sixty to seventy, seventy to eighty, and eighty to ninety. While the rest of the audience listened, she led each group in singing a stanza of "My Faith Looks up to Thee." By the time the octogenarians sang softly "When ends life's transient dream; when death's cold, sullen stream shall o'er me roll," an eerie hush had fallen over the thousands who stood vulnerably before Sister, ready to yield to her control.[1]

Here was brilliant orchestration of emotion.

McPherson was a forerunner of the carefully crafted use of emotion that has moved in our time from its largely Pentecostal origins to many other churches. Whether with shouting, dancing, and clapping or with praise bands, praise songs, and drama, McPherson led the way. She understood the power of emotions and the power of music particularly. Again Blumhofer summarizes:

358

> Whenever Sister arrived for meetings, she used music to set the mood, express a message, convey emotions, unite the crowd, and offer worship. She often used thirty minutes of music — with bands, choirs, and ensembles — to warm the crowd for her entrance at Angelus Temple. . . . She had an instinct for timing and knew how to rouse or calm the crowd with music. Sister used simple choruses with effect for both social and religious purposes. . . . They built anticipation, covered unacceptable noise or behavior, and provided background as people greeted one another. . . . In every service, Sister took special care with the selection of the opening hymn: she wanted it "bright and bouncy."[2]

McPherson believed that emotions must be much more free, intense, and prominent than in traditional worship and she put those beliefs into practice.

Such convictions and practices relative to the emotions spread widely and are an essential part of the reason for so many changes in worship in the last thirty years. Pentecostals, building on the revivalism from which they sprang, claim that open expression of strong emotions is more truly human and more truly biblical than more traditional forms of worship. Older worship, they say, is more the product of the cold climates and cultures of Europe than of the biblical revelation, being more intellectual and Hellenic, than Hebraic. Today many outside Pentecostal circles accept this contention. Sometimes in the name of expressing different ethnic and cultural traits, sometimes to fit into a culture where rock-and-roll and the importance of self-expression are powerful, always in the name of evangelism and connecting with contemporary life, the new emotional worship has spread like wildfire.

Is this new worship, however, really more biblical? Many chapters in this volume address some of the outward forms of the new worship and hold them up to biblical evaluation. In this chapter we want to turn to the emotions or affections in worship from the heart. How should we express emotion in worship? Is traditional Reformed worship too much a denial of emotions? Should the affections be given a more free and prominent place in Christian worship?

To begin we must note that Reformed worship has always seen itself as a proper and genuine expression of human emotion. Emotion has always been a part of Reformed experience and worship. Of the affections in general, John Calvin declares:

For truly, that abundant sweetness which God has stored up for those who fear him cannot be known without at the same time powerfully moving us. And once anyone has been moved by it, it utterly ravishes him and draws him to itself. Therefore, it is no wonder if a perverse and wicked heart never experiences that emotion by which, borne up to heaven itself, we are admitted to the most hidden treasures of God and to the most hallowed precincts of his Kingdom."[3]

Of worship and the affections in particular Calvin writes: "But as the chief and most essential part of this harmony [of praise] proceeds from a sincere and pure affection of heart, none will ever, in a right manner, celebrate the glory of God except the man who worships him under the influence of holy fear."[4] He insists: "It is not sufficient to utter the praises of God with our tongues, if they do not proceed from the heart."[5] Near the beginning of his *Institutes of the Christian Religion* Calvin connects faith, affections, and worship: "Here indeed is pure and real religion: faith so joined with an earnest fear of God that this fear also embraces willing reverence, and carries with it such legitimate worship as is prescribed in the law."[6]

We must see then at the outset that the Reformed heritage is just as concerned with the proper inward engagement of the heart and affections of the believer in worship as it is with the proper outward forms of worship. English Puritan Richard Sibbes aptly summarizes the conviction of all Reformed Christians: "Outward worship without inward is but the carcase of worship."[7]

Emotions and the Heart

To understand the proper role of the emotions in true worship, we first must look at the theology of the affections in human experience. Reformed theology generally follows the traditional theological anthropology derived from Aristotle, which sees intellect, will, and affections in the soul of the person. These three elements of the soul reflect the image of God in humans, so that humans know in a way analogous to God's knowing; will in a way analogous to God's willing; and feel in a way analogous to the Bible's description of God's feeling—whether in love or wrath, in delight or jealousy. For example, the Canons of Dort use this traditional anthropology to present both the created and fallen state of humans:

Man was originally formed after the image of God. His understanding was adorned with a true and saving knowledge of his Creator, and of spiritual things; his heart and will were upright, all his affections pure, and the whole man was holy. But revolting from God by the instigation of the devil and by his own free will, he forfeited these excellent gifts; and in the place thereof became involved in blindness of mind, horrible darkness, vanity, and perverseness of judgment; became wicked, rebellious, and obdurate in heart and will, and impure in his affections.[8]

While Reformed dogmaticians do make use of this threefold distinction, more of the focus is on the intellect and the will. Calvin is a typical example: "The human soul consists of two faculties, understanding and will."[9] In Calvin and other Reformed theologians, the emotions tend to be subsumed under the will as an expression of the heart. The precise definitions and interrelationships of the intellect, will, heart, and affections as presented by various theologians need not detain us. Rather we will say with Calvin, "But I leave it to the philosophers to discuss these faculties in their subtle way. For the upbuilding of godliness a simple definition will be enough for us."[10] The simple truth is that all of these human faculties come together in what the Bible calls the heart. The heart is the point at which intellect, will, and affections come together. The heart is the religious center of the individual. As the Book of Proverbs declares, "Above all else, guard your heart, / for it is the wellspring of life" (4:23). Making the same point about the heart, Hebrews warns, "See to it, brothers, that none of you has a sinful, unbelieving heart that turns away from the living God" (Heb. 3:12).

This teaching on the heart echoes throughout Reformed theology. Calvin writes: "For it [the Christian life] is a doctrine not of the tongue but of life. It is not apprehended by the understanding and memory alone, as other disciplines are, but it is received only when it possesses the whole soul, and finds a seat and resting place in the inmost affection of the heart."[11] Jonathan Edwards similarly states: "True religion is evermore a powerful thing; and the power of it appears, in the first place, in the inward exercises of it in the heart, where is the principal and original seat of it."[12] J. C. Ryle rightly observes: "The reason, the understanding, the conscience, the affections, are all second in importance to the heart."[13] They are secondary to the heart because it is in the heart that they come together and come to expression.

Reformed writers have not, therefore, often focused on the affections in isolation from other faculties of the soul. This paucity, however, is not evidence of a lack of interest in the affections. Most of the time Reformed authors discuss the affections in their integral relationship with the other faculties of the soul rather than single them out for separate attention.[14]

The most notable exception to that general practice is the detailed discussion by Edwards in his important *Treatise on Religious Affections*. This work was Edwards's response to critics of the Great Awakening, who maintained that the awakening was not a genuine work of God because it was characterized by excessive emotion. On the surface Edwards appears to agree with the critics by declaring that the affections are the heart of true religion: "Hence the proposition or doctrine, that I would raise from these words is this, . . . *True religion, in great part, consists in holy affections.*"[15] He elaborates this point: "The Holy Scriptures do everywhere place religion very much in the affections; such as fear, hope, love, hatred, desire, joy, sorrow, gratitude, compassion and zeal."[16]

In reality Edwards does not agree with his critics. Rather he cleverly redefines the affections, integrating them into a much more holistic anthropology:

God has indued the soul with two faculties: one is that by which it is capable of perception and speculation, or by which it discerns and views and judges of things; which is called the understanding. The other faculty is that by which the soul does not merely perceive and view things, but is some way inclined with respect to the things it views or considers; either is inclined to 'em, or is disinclined, and averse from 'em; or is the faculty by which the soul does not behold things, as an indifferent unaffected spectator, but either as liking or disliking, pleased or displeased, approving or rejecting. This faculty is called by various names: it is sometimes called the *inclination*: and, as it has respect to the actions that are determined and governed by it, is called the *will*: and the *mind*, with regard to the exercises of this faculty, is often called the *heart*.

. . . There are some exercises of pleasedness or displeasedness, inclination or disinclination, wherein the soul is carried but a little beyond a state of perfect indifference. And there are other degrees above this, wherein approbation or dislike, pleasedness or aversion, are stronger; wherein we may rise higher and higher, till the soul comes to act vigorously and sensibly. . . . And it is to be noted, that they are these more vigorous and sensible exercises of this faculty, that are called the affections.[17]

Edwards thus defines the affections not as a separate faculty of the soul but as "the more vigorous and sensible exercises of the inclination and will of the soul."[18] The affections then are seen as the will at work in a vigorous manner. By this definition of affections he successfully shows how true emotions are an essential part of true religion without religion becoming emotionalism.

Emotions and Faith

Notably absent from Edwards's discussion of the affections, however, is a clear role for faith in relation to the affections. He does make clear that faith is foundational in the Christian life: "There is no promise of the covenant of grace [that] belongs to any man, till he has first believed in Christ; for 'tis by faith alone that we become interested in Christ, and the promises of the new covenant made in him."[19] He also recognizes that the affections were the effect and evidence of faith: "Nor does it at all diminish the honor and importance of faith, that the exercises and effects of faith in practice, should be esteemed the chief signs of it; any more than it lessens the importance of life, that action and motion are esteemed the chief signs of that."[20] The problem, however, in Edwards's treatise is the failure to develop in any detail this positive role of faith in the Christian life, including worship, and to show the proper relationship between faith and the affections. He seems much more concerned to warn his readers about the dangers of antinomianism resulting from a misuse of the doctrine of justification by faith alone.[21]

We need to be clear about the role of faith not only in justification, but in every aspect of living the Christian life. The foundation of all Christian living, as well as of justification, is faith's looking away from the self to Christ and his promises. There is a time and place for introspection to see if the fruits of true faith are present in a Christian, but the examination of such fruit must not lead us away from the centrality of faith itself.

For a proper understanding of the affections therefore in the Christian life generally and especially in worship, faith must be kept central. Paul writes, "In him [Christ] and through faith in him we may approach God with freedom and confidence" (Eph. 3:12). Christ and faith in Christ open the way to fellowship with God, and that fellowship is characterized by affections that include confidence in our acceptance and a sense of freedom from condemnation in God's presence.

Here Calvin is a great help and good guide for us in developing this biblical point: "Now we shall possess a right definition of faith if we call it a firm and certain knowledge of God's benevolence toward us, founded upon the truth of the freely given promise in Christ, both revealed to our minds and sealed upon our hearts through the Holy Spirit."[22] Notice that Calvin here relates faith to both the intellect and the human will and defines faith in relation to its object: the promises of Christ.

For Calvin, this faith is always especially related to the will or the heart. He writes that it is characterized by "that firm and steadfast constancy of heart which is the chief part of faith."[23] Faith "is more of the heart than of the brain, and more of the disposition than of the understanding."[24] He elaborates this point eloquently over and over again:

> Our mind has such an inclination to vanity that it can never cleave fast to the truth of God; and it has such a dullness that it is always blind to the light of God's truth. Accordingly, without the illumination of the Holy Spirit, the Word can do nothing. From this, also, it is clear that faith is much higher than human understanding. And it will not be enough for the mind to be illumined by the Spirit of God unless the heart is also strengthened and supported by his power. . . . In both ways, therefore, faith is a singular gift of God, both in that the mind of man is purged so as to be able to taste the truth of God and in that his heart is established therein.[25]

Again he writes:

> It now remains to pour into the heart itself what the mind has absorbed. For the Word of God is not received by faith if it flits about in the top of the brain, but when it takes root in the depth of the heart that it may be an invincible defense to withstand and drive off all the stratagems of temptation. But if it is true that the mind's real understanding is illumination by the Spirit of God, then in such confirmation of the heart his power is much more clearly manifested, to the extent that the heart's distrust is greater than the mind's blindness. It is harder for the heart to be furnished with assurance than for the mind to be endowed with thought. The Spirit accordingly serves as a seal, to seal up in our hearts those very promises the certainty of which it has previously impressed upon our minds; and takes the place of a guarantee to confirm and establish them.[26]

This faith is foundational for all Calvin's thinking about Christian life and worship. It is the source of all virtue and affection in the Christian. For example, Calvin writes on love: "It is faith alone that first engenders love in us."[27] On repentance he maintains: "Now it ought to be a fact beyond controversy that repentance not only constantly follows faith, but is also born of faith. . . . There are some, however, who suppose that repentance precedes faith, rather than flows from it, or is produced by it as fruit from a tree. Such persons have never known the power of repentance, and are moved to feel this way by an unduly slight argument."[28]

In Francis Turretin, scholastic theologian of seventeenth-century Geneva, we can see Calvin's conviction about the centrality of faith continued among the Reformed. Turretin refers to faith as "a universal virtue":

So great is the necessity of faith in the matter of salvation that as Christ alone is the cause of salvation, so faith alone is the means and way to Christ. . . . Thus it is in some measure deservedly a universal virtue, which either formally includes or consequently and necessarily draws after it all the duties of the believer. Hence according to its various acts and relations [*schēseis*], it is compared rightly now to the eye (in respect of the knowledge of Christ), then to feet (in respect of approach and refuge), then to hands and mouth (in respect of reception and application).[29]

Emotions Responding to the Word

The centrality of faith in worship will help us keep the Lord Jesus Christ at the heart of our worship. Jesus must always be central in our worship because he is always the object of our faith and the true inspiration of faith's genuine affections. When we grasp this clearly, we can see how the affections function in worship as the response of faith and as the expression of faith.

Worship as our meeting with God essentially consists of two parts: God's speaking to us and our speaking to God. God speaks in Bible readings, sermons, sacraments, and benedictions. Faith listens eagerly for the word of God. As Calvin writes: "We must be reminded that there is a permanent relationship between faith and the Word."[30] Faith knows that it is nourished by that word: "The same Word is the basis whereby faith is supported and sustained; if it turns away from the Word, it falls. . . . Now, therefore, we

365

hold faith to be a knowledge of God's will toward us, perceived from his Word."[31]

As God speaks in worship, the people of God respond with faith, which manifests itself in various affections, depending on the character of God's speech and the spiritual condition of the worshiper. The call to worship should be heard with joy, the reading of the law with sorrow, the assurance of pardon with gladness. All worshipers, and especially those wrestling with specific sins or problems, may be more intensely affected at one time than another. The Holy Spirit applies the word to the faithful with different intensity at different times.

The worshiping community speaks to God in prayers, songs, and confessions of faith. When we speak to God in answer to his speaking to us, our faith is expressing itself in the forms God has given it and ought to be affected: eager in prayer, joyful in praise, sincere in confession. The Book of Psalms is full of such communication with God. Consider Psalm 63:1–5:

> O God, you are my God,
>   earnestly I seek you;
> my soul thirsts for you,
>   my body longs for you,
> in a dry and weary land
>   where there is no water.
> I have seen you in the sanctuary
>   and beheld your power and your glory.
> Because your love is better than life,
>   my lips will glorify you.
> I will praise you as long as I live,
>   and in your name I will lift up my hands.
> My soul will be satisfied as with the richest of foods;
>   with singing lips my mouth will praise you.

Here is praise of God rich in the language of the intellect, the will, and the affections. Here is an expression of the way in which the heart through faith is to be engaged in worship.

If our central aim in worship is to seek Christ by faith through the forms he instituted and promised to bless, then we have a basis on which to expect deep and lasting affections to result. Such emotions will be true and fruitful as the response and result of our worship. When our faith and our worship look away from themselves to Christ, then the sweet and true affections of our faith will be felt. Then we will recognize that the affections reinforce the worship that we offer out of faith. But when emotions are the center of concern and the object of the worshiping experience, only impure and fleeting emotions will result.

True affections, springing from faith, can be the work of only the Holy Spirit in our hearts. As English Puritan Stephen Charnock writes:

> Spiritual worship is done by the influence and with the assistance of the Spirit of God. . . . Our worship is then spiritual when the fire that kindles our affections comes down from heaven, as that fire upon the altar wherewith the sacrifices were consumed. . . . Without an actual influence, we cannot act from spiritual motives, nor for spiritual ends, nor in a spiritual manner. . . . To render our worship spiritual, we should, before every engagement in it, implore the actual presence of the Spirit, without which we are not able to send forth one spiritual breath or groan; but must be wind-bound, like a ship without a gale, and our worship be no better than carnal.[32]

The Spirit cannot be manipulated. He is sovereign in the blessing that he bestows on worshipers and in the degree of it. But he is to be expected and found in the forms that he appointed for worship.

We must remember the promise of the Father to send his Spirit to bless the forms of worship instituted by his Son. Worship in the Spirit is always worship according to truth (John 4:24). Christ's institutions of the sermon and the sacraments as means of grace will always bless his faith-filled people (Acts 2:42; Rom. 10:14; 1 Cor 10:16; 11:24, 29; 1 Peter 3:21). God will always receive with joy the prayers and praise of the faithful, for God sits enthroned on the praises of Israel.

Emotions Restrained by the Word

While Reformed theology recognizes a necessary and legitimate function for the affections in worship, it also recognizes potential dangers in the affections. As the mind can be deceived and the will corrupted, so the affections can be impure. The problem of affections that are improper or misused is not just a problem of the unregenerate, but continues among believers as well. David was incited by impure affections to desire what he ought not have. Peter was controlled by a fear that he ought not to have felt. Paul had to warn the enthusiastic Corinthians to do everything "decently and in order" (1 Cor. 14:40 Authorized Version). So the Reformed churches believe that the emotions themselves must not be trusted as an accurate guide to truth, virtue, or the presence of the Holy Spirit. Rather the emotions must be properly channeled and directed. They must be governed by the sanctified intellect and will of the Christian. They must be the effect of true faith.

When emotions are misused, there is a constant danger of manipulation. It is easy for effective leaders to move people, especially trusting and expectant people, to feel what they want them to feel. Easily the church becomes a theater where feeling and catharsis take the place of true faith.

Nineteenth-century revivalist Charles Finney recognized the importance of the emotions in the work he did, and he gave a clear theological explanation for the purely natural ways in which he controlled emotions. In his *Lectures on Revivals* he writes: "Almost all the religion in the world has been produced by revivals. God has found it necessary to take advantage of the excitability there is in mankind, to produce powerful excitements among them, before he can lead them to obey."[33] Emotional excitement is essential to revival: "There must be excitement sufficient to wake up the dormant moral powers, and roll back the tide of degradation and sin."[34] Finney frankly recognizes that this emotion was not at all supernatural. It was entirely natural, at the disposal of the preacher and listener: "There is nothing in religion beyond the ordinary powers of nature. It consists entirely in the *right exercise* of the powers of nature."[35] Indeed for Finney, "a revival is as naturally a result of the use of the appropriate means as a crop is of the use of its appropriate means."[36]

In Finney, emotion or excitement became the essential focus of revival or worship and was linked to a Pelagian or Semipelagian understanding of the human will. Finney saw clearly that to excite and move the free will something new would always be needed. He dealt with the problem by saying that since the millennium was coming soon, the need for ever-new excitement would not be a long-term problem. But as Finney was wrong about the nearness of the millennium, so has the burden of finding new excitements remained a constant challenge for his heirs. The restlessness in some charismatic circles to find where the Spirit is moving anew reflects that outlook.

An accomplished leader in the tradition of Finney can easily manipulate emotions in worship, particularly through preaching and music. An effective preacher can create emotions ranging from reverence to sorrow, from joy to a tangible sense of power. An effective musician can move the emotions through the words, melody, and instrumentation of music. Especially in the Pentecostal tradition, music has been very self-consciously used to move worshipers. Grant Wacker, a sympathetic historian of Pentecostalism, comments on this phenomenon in early Pentecostalism:

> And then there was congregational singing, one of the most notable and remarked on features of Pentecostal worship. . . . Music offered leaders a ready means for managing the intensity of the service. They could ratchet up the tempo until worshipers broke into ecstatic praise, or tone it down when things seemed to be getting out of hand. Either way, music gave leaders a tool for regularizing the expression of emotion.[37]

What Wacker sees as true of early Pentecostalism is even truer with the Contemporary Christian Music phenomenon. Praise songs, which originated in charismatic circles and spread widely in other Protestant churches, seem often to express rather spontaneous waves of emotion. But their use is carefully planned with an eye to the emotional effect on the worshiper. In such a session of singing one can predict exactly when the hands will be raised and when other emotional responses will be exhibited.

Many argue for these praise songs as a key way to connect with contemporary culture and to revitalize emotional involvement in Christian worship. Charles H. Kraft, professor of anthropology and intercultural communication at Fuller Theological Seminary, offers a theological rationale for these songs: "True worship . . . usually takes a lot of singing to create an atmosphere of praise and worship." This experience of worship is created significantly by the music of praise songs: "And it is the new music, sung with eyes closed for 10, 15, or 20 minutes at a time that makes that experience possible." Kraft praises these songs for breaking the excessively intellectual character of much worship: "Our worship services revolve around an informational sermon preceded by a token number of informational hymns." These hymns reinforce the unemotional character of traditional worship: "We sing hymns so chock-full of rational content and information that they are unmemorizable." Kraft calls on Christians: "Let's stop being

369

enslaved to the present rationalistic, intellect-centered approach to church that characterizes much of evangelicalism."[38]

Kraft's rationale for the new music stands at marked contrast to the idea of praise found in the book of praises, the Psalter. In the psalms (and many great hymns), praise focuses on God, his character, and particularly his great acts in history. Praise also expresses the problems and hopes of individuals and of the believing community before God. It is not some kind of transcendence that the psalm singer seeks, but faithfulness in knowing, celebrating, and serving God. This faithfulness by individuals and congregations takes place through thought and in time and history. The Christian does not seek escape from time, history, and thought, but fulfillment in time, history, and thought. The contrast between praise songs and psalm singing is not at root a contrast of different styles of music, but a contrast of different theologies of music. In much contemporary Christian music, emotion is the object of the song. The emotions engendered by the music become a new sacramental connection to God. In historic psalm singing, emotions are the effect of the heart's engagement with God through the words that he gave us to sing.

It is surely ironic that those who criticize the traditional forms of worship for their lack of spontaneity and of the Spirit often become the most careful planners of emotion. They seem to see no inconsistency between the Spirit and their careful planning and staging of worship, yet argue that carefully planned liturgies and sermons of traditional worship must be dead to the Spirit. They are skeptical that the Spirit will be present in the forms of worship that he revealed in the Bible, but are confident that he will be present in their human inventions. They seem never to fear that they are offering strange fire on the altar of God (Lev. 10:1) or that they might be following Israel's sincere and emotional worship offered to the golden calf (Ex. 32). We all need to heed Robert Dabney's eloquent warning about the danger of allowing emotion to be the judge of true religion and worship: "Blinded men are ever prone to imagine that they have religious feelings because they have sensuous animal feelings in accidental juxtaposition with religious places, words or sights. This is the pernicious mistake which has sealed up millions of self-deceived souls for hell."[39]

Conclusion

A Reformed approach to worship is as much concerned with the heart in worship as with the form of worship. It insists that all true Christians will worship not only with mind and will according to the ordinances of God, but also with godly affections. Faith as it hears the word of Christ responds with affections and expresses itself in prayer and praise affectionately. While recognizing the ease with which the emotions can be manipulated and abused, Reformed Christianity seeks to express the full range of proper affections in worship. As Charnock writes so eloquently:

God is a Spirit infinitely happy, therefore we must approach to Him with cheerfulness; He is a Spirit of infinite majesty, therefore we must come before him with reverence; He is a Spirit infinitely high, therefore we must offer up our sacrifices with the deepest humility; He is a Spirit infinitely holy, therefore we must address Him with purity; He is a Spirit infinitely glorious, we must therefore acknowledge His excellency in all that we do, and in our measures contribute to His glory, by having the highest aims in His worship; He is a spirit infinitely provoked by us, therefore we must offer up our worship in the name of a pacifying Mediator and Intercessor.[40]

371

Part 4

WORSHIP, HISTORY, AND CULTURE

*I*n this final section several important issues are in urgent need of being addressed. In an age of post-modern indifference to the past (history, tradition), with what C. S. Lewis called "chronological snobbery," it is time once more to examine the historical roots of Reformed worship. Only arrogance argues that we begin afresh without regard for the hard-fought opinions of the church through the ages. In part, traditions need to be identified that have distinguished one branch of the church from another, but are not necessarily of first importance. They can be laid aside without violation of principle. But other things are done out of the deepest respect for what the Bible says about worship, and these need to be identified and their supporting arguments examined and either reaffirmed or denied.

Nick Needham examines in summary form the historical roots of worship, giving attention to those aspects of public worship that emerge in various traditions.

Hughes Oliphant Old takes up the crucial area of liturgy. Everyone has a liturgy, even those traditions who think they do not! It may be a minimalist (Directory of Public Worship) liturgy, but it is still a liturgy. In a carefully researched and argued chapter, Old examines the writings of John Calvin and concludes that he "would have found the high-church movement out and out ceremonialism. He would not have been very patient with its artiness, its romanticism, its luxury. He would have been no more at home in the refined emotionalism of Ivy League chapels than in the brute emotionalism of American revival tents." One of the deservedly honored scholars in the history of worship, Old does not mince his words. His essay is worth careful reading and rereading.

Someone has to address the "worship wars" in a book devoted to worship! Michael Horton does so, touching on the issues of postmodernity (does it exist?) and modernity (that it does and has some crucial characteristics). Horton argues that "there is nothing new under the sun," that idolatry—whatever its precise form—is essentially the same in every age, a worship of self rather than God. It is, to go back once more to Calvin, the same old song: the human mind is "a perpetual factory of idols." It is the worship of God, the true God, in the way he has commanded— or it is idolatry, pure and simple!

16

WORSHIP
THROUGH THE AGES

NICK R. NEEDHAM

If we ask, "How should we worship God?" a healthy Christian and Protestant instinct will be to respond with another question: "What does the Bible say?" Rightly understood, this is a necessary and indeed a sufficient response. We must not, however, presume that we alone know what the Bible says on this or any other issue. Wisdom and humility conspire to lead us to a broader attitude and to ask: "What have Christians down through the ages understood the Bible to say about how we should worship God?" Unless we wish to make a virtue of solipsism, any serious consideration of worship must take into account the history of worship, as a sort of running commentary on Scripture, a commentary embodied in practice and preserved in literary monuments, especially liturgies. Accordingly, what I propose to do in this essay is offer a sketch of that history.

First, though, I must deliver an apologia. The reader will by no means find this a comprehensive account. Limitations of space forbid any such thing. There are glaring omissions here that anyone will be able to spot. All I attempt is an introductory outline of the main features of the main traditions that will be of interest primarily to a distinctively Reformed readership. I have therefore omitted consideration of a number of traditions that certainly deserve their own treatments but that constraints of space and purpose reluctantly lead me to neglect here.

Further, I propose here to focus attention on *how* the church has worshiped through the ages—the practice rather than the theory. I will not ignore the theory entirely, but a focus on practice has two benefits. It brings home to us more immediately and vividly the phenomena of worship in the actual experience of the church. And a good way of learning theory is by looking at practice. As we expose ourselves to the worship structures and practices of historic Christianity, we may find ourselves discerning underlying patterns and principles. We may then take the trouble to articulate the meaning and basis of our perception, which will be a fruitful exercise; but in any case, we often perceive that something is good or bad before we can express the rationale for our perception. Surveying the historic forms of worship will give us the opportunity to form our perceptions.

Bearing this in mind, then, let us consider something of the history of Christian worship.

Worship in the Patristic Age

What was a Christian service of worship like in the postapostolic period? We are fortunate to have a good description of a normal Christian gathering for worship in the writings of second-century theologian Justin Martyr:

> On the day called Sunday there is a meeting of all believers who live in the town or the country, and the memoirs of the apostles, or the writings of the prophets, are read for as long as time will permit. When the reader has finished, the president in a sermon urges and invites the people to base their lives on these noble things. Then we all stand up and offer prayers. When our prayer is concluded, bread and wine and water are brought; and the president offers up prayers and thanksgivings to the best of his ability, and the people assent with Amen. Then follows the distribution of the things over which thanks have been offered, and the partaking of them by all; and the deacons take them to those who are absent. And those who are prosperous, and willing, give what each thinks fit; and what is collected is deposited with the president, who succors the orphans and widows and those who, through sickness or any other cause, are in want, and those who are in bonds and the strangers sojourning among us, and in a word takes care of all who are in need. We hold our common assembly on Sunday because it is the first day, on which God put to flight darkness and chaos and made the

world; and on the same day, Jesus Christ our Savior rose from the dead. (*Apology* 1.67)

The president of the assembly, who expounded the Scriptures and oversaw Holy Communion, was the senior presiding elder—or the bishop, as church organization developed in the second century. In another place, Justin gives a more detailed account of the Lord's Supper or Eucharist (from Greek *eucharisteō*, to give thanks):

Then bread and a cup of wine mixed with water are brought to the president of the brothers. He takes them and offers up praise and glory to the Father of the universe, through the name of the Son and of the Holy Spirit. He gives thanks at considerable length for our being counted worthy to receive these things from his [Jesus'] hands. When he has finished the prayers and thanksgivings, all the people present express their joyful agreement by saying Amen. ("Amen" means "Let it be so" in Hebrew.) . . . Then those whom we call deacons give to each of those present the bread and the wine mixed with water over which the thanksgiving was pronounced, and carry away a portion to those who are absent.

We call this food "eucharist," which no-one is allowed to share unless he believes that the things we teach are true, and has been washed with the washing that is for the forgiveness of sins and a second birth, and is living as Christ has commanded. For we do not receive them as common bread and common drink. But as Jesus Christ our Savior became flesh by the word of God, and clothed himself in our flesh and blood to save us, so also we have been taught that the food which is blessed by the word of prayer handed down from Christ, by which our blood and flesh are nourished as the food becomes part of ourselves, is the flesh and blood of the same Jesus who became flesh. For the apostles, in the memoirs composed by themselves called "Gospels," have delivered to us what was commanded to them: that Jesus took bread, and when he had given thanks said, "Do this in remembrance of me, this is my body"; and in a similar way, after taking the cup and giving thanks, he said, "This is my blood," and gave it only to them. (*Apology* 1.65–66)

From Justin's account, we learn that the main ingredients of Christian worship in the second century were (1) the reading and expounding of Scripture, (2) prayer, and (3) the celebration of the Lord's Supper. Indeed, compared with many churches today, the Lord's Supper held a remarkably high place in early Christian worship. The local church celebrated it every Sunday, and it formed a large part of the service. Singing, which for many modern Christians is such a central part of worship, was not so important in the early church; in fact, Justin does not mention it here at all. However, we know from other accounts that singing and chanting were a widespread practice in the worship of the early Christians. In the second century, the most common form of singing and chanting was "responsive." This means that one person (a Scripture reader or a clergyman) would sing or chant a passage, usually from a psalm, and the congregation would then make a response—either a single word, such as "Alleluia," or a chorus. There was also solo singing and full congregational singing, although the latter did not really become popular until the fourth century.

What the early Christians chanted and sang in public worship were the psalms of the Old Testament and some of the poetic parts of the New Testament (e.g., the virgin Mary's praise of God in Luke 1:46–55). It was probably not until the fourth century that the singing of noncanonical hymns began to become common.[1] No musical instruments accompanied the chanting and singing; Christians did not use instruments in their worship in the second century or indeed for many centuries afterward. The early church looked on musical instruments as being part of Jewish or pagan worship, but not part of the apostolic tradition of Christian worship.[2]

We should also note that standing throughout worship was the traditional practice in the early church period and for centuries afterward. The Western church introduced pews only in the fourteenth century—quite a late development. The Eastern church never introduced pews into Eastern church buildings. People who were tired during early church worship could sit around the edges of the building ("the weak go to the wall"), but everyone had to stand to pray; the early Christians considered standing the only proper posture for public spoken prayer. Early Christian art also shows us that when praying, Christians spread out their arms with upturned palms and kept their eyes open, looking upward to heaven.

As Justin's account shows us, early Christian worship was (generally speaking) simple in form and fixed in structure. The pattern that Justin describes would not have varied greatly in any church throughout the Roman Empire. An important point that does not come out so clearly from Justin is that the service of worship was divided into two distinct parts. The first part, known as "the service of the word" (singing, reading, and sermon), was open to baptized believers, those who were receiving instruction in the Christian faith, and probably also those who were simply curious about Christianity. The second part, the prayers and the Eucharist (the Lord's Supper), was for only those who had been baptized; the rest had to leave. From descriptions and instructions in the writings of the early church fathers, we can say that a fairly typical service of worship in the second or third century lasted about three hours and was structured something like this:

Part 1: Service of the Word

1. Opening greeting and response: Usually the bishop said, "The Lord be with you"; and the congregation responded, "And with your spirit."
2. Scripture reading: Old Testament.[3]
3. Psalm or hymn.
4. Scripture reading: New Testament. The first New Testament reading was from any book between Acts and Revelation, normally an epistle.
5. Psalm or hymn.
6. Scripture reading: New Testament. The second New Testament reading was from one of the four gospels.[4]
7. Sermon: The bishop preached in a sitting posture.[5]
8. Dismissal of all but baptized believers.

Part 2: Eucharist

1. Prayers: The prayer leader (in the West, the bishop; in the East, the senior deacon) announced a topic for prayer. The congregation prayed silently for a time. Then the leader, with an audible prayer, summed up the congregation's petitions on that topic. The leader then announced another topic; the congregation prayed silently; then the leader summed up again with audible prayer. And so on, for quite a lengthy time.[6]
2. Holy Communion: (a) Greeting by the bishop, response by the congregation, and the "kiss of peace" (the men kissed men, the women kissed women). (b) The offertory: each church member brought a small loaf and a flask of wine to Communion; the deacons took these gifts and spread them out on the Lord's Table. The flasks of

379

wine were all emptied into one large silver cup. (c) The bishop and congregation engaged in a dialogue with each other (see the example from Hippolytus recorded below), and the bishop then led the congregation in prayer. (d) The bishop and deacons broke the loaves. (e) The bishop and deacons distributed the bread and offered the cup to the congregation. Something would be said to each person as he or she received the bread and wine—for example, in the Roman church, the deacon said, "The bread of heaven in Christ Jesus"; the church member replied, "Amen." Communion was always received in a standing posture. Church members took home the bread and wine that had not been consumed and used them on weekdays for the celebration of Communion in the home.

3. Benediction: A phrase such as "depart in peace" was spoken by a deacon.

For many modern Christians, two aspects of this early church worship will stand out as quite striking. (1) The first is that the early church did not allow unbelievers to be present when the congregation prayed. This was because, in early church thinking, the congregation at prayer was participating by the Holy Spirit in the glorified Christ's own heavenly ministry of prayer. This was something in which unbelievers could not share, for they lacked the Spirit. (2) The second is the way that all church members brought their own bread and wine to be used in Communion. Early Christians attached great significance to this provision of the Communion bread and wine by every church member: it was the whole church offering itself to God, as together all its members presented to him the fruits of his creation. When the deacons placed the loaves and wine on the Lord's Table, they were (in a symbolic sense) laying the congregation itself on the table through its gifts, thus consecrating the people to Christ. As early church father Augustine told his people at Communion, "There you are, on the table; there you are, in the cup."

The use of liturgy—fixed, written prayers and exhortations to be read out by the bishop and congregation—is found from a very early date in Christian worship. The oldest known example of a church liturgy for Holy Communion occurs in the writings of Hippolytus (died 236). Hippolytus's *Church Order* contains the Communion liturgy from the church in Rome. After the offertory (described above), the following dialogue and prayer were recited by the bishop and congregation:

bishop: The Lord be with you.

congregation: And with your spirit.

bishop: Lift up your hearts.

congregation: We lift them to the Lord.

bishop: Let us give thanks to the Lord.

congregation: It is fitting and right.

bishop: We thank you, O God, through your beloved servant Jesus Christ, whom in these last times you have sent to us as Savior, Redeemer, and Messenger of your counsel, the Logos who comes from you, through whom you have made all things, whom you were pleased to send from heaven into the womb of the virgin, and in her body he became flesh, and was revealed as your Son, born of the Holy Spirit and the virgin. To fulfill your will and prepare a holy people for you, he stretched out his hands when he suffered, so that he might release from suffering those who have believed in you.

And when he delivered himself willingly to suffering, to loose the bonds of death and break the chains of the devil, to tread down hell and enlighten the righteous, to set up the boundary stone and manifest the resurrection, he took a loaf, gave thanks and said, "Take, eat, this is My body which is given for you." In the same way he took the cup and said, "This is my blood which is poured out for you. Whenever you do this, you remember me."

Remembering, therefore, his death and resurrection, we offer to you the loaf and the cup, and give thanks to you that you have counted us worthy to stand before you and serve you as priests.[7] And we pray to you, that you will send down your Holy Spirit on this offering of the church.[8] Unite it, and grant to all the saints who partake of it that we may be filled with the Holy Spirit and strengthened in our faith in the truth, so that we may praise and glorify you through your servant Jesus Christ, through whom be glory and honor to you in your church, now and forever. Amen.

Hippolytus wrote in the early third century, but since he was recording the established tradition in the Roman church, this Communion liturgy certainly goes back to the second century. In the first few centuries of Christian worship, each individual church tended to have its own liturgy; it was much later that liturgy became standardized, so that all churches in the West eventually followed the Roman church's liturgy and all in the East followed that of Constantinople. It is also important to realize that in the early centuries, liturgy did not rule out free prayer by the bishop (i.e., praying his own prayers not written in the liturgy); there was a mixture of both elements. Again, it was only later that liturgy became all important to the exclusion of free prayer.

Christian worship revolved around Sunday, or the Lord's Day as the early church called it—the day on which the Lord Jesus had risen from the dead. However, this weekly pattern of worship was allied to a yearly pattern that revolved around Easter. Easter was the Christian equivalent of the Jewish Passover. Christ had died at the same time that the Passover lamb was sacrificed; so Christians celebrated their Savior's death at Easter, when Jews were celebrating the Passover. The churches of Asia Minor observed Easter on the precise day of Passover, Nisan 14 in the Hebrew calendar, which was not necessarily a Sunday. But the churches of Palestine, Alexandria, and Rome always observed Easter on the Sunday that fell just after Nisan 14. This caused a serious controversy in the second century, the Quartodeciman controversy (from the Latin word for "fourteenth"), but at the Council of Nicea in the fourth century the custom of Palestine, Alexandria, and Rome triumphed.

Finally, one worship custom that was integral to church life in these early centuries was the *agapē* feast. Tertullian described it thus:

> Our feast explains itself by its name. The Greeks call it *agapē*, that is, love. Whatever it may cost, our expenditure in the name of godliness is gain, since with the good things of the feast we benefit the needy. We do not behave as you pagans do in your feasts, where parasites strive for the glory of satisfying their sensual dispositions, selling themselves to all kinds of shameful treatment for a belly-feast. With us, imitating God himself, a special respect is shown to the poor. If the purpose of our feast is good, in the light of that goodness consider its further rules. As it is an act of religious worship, it permits no vice or impurity. Those who partake, before reclining, first taste the sweetness of prayer to God. They eat only so much as satisfies the demands of hunger; they drink only so much as is suitable for temperate persons. They say it is enough, as those who remember that even during the night they must worship God. They talk as those who know that the Lord is one of those listening. After they have washed their hands, and the lights have been brought in, each person is asked to stand up and sing, to the best of his ability, a hymn to God, either taken from the holy Scriptures or one of his own composing. This proves how sober our drinking is! As the feast began with prayer, so with

prayer it is closed. We go from the feast, not like troops of mischief-makers, nor bands of vagrants, nor to rush forth into licentious deeds, but to have as much care of our modesty and chastity as if we had come from a school of virtue rather than a banquet. (*Apology* 39)

The *agapē* was originally integrated with the Eucharist (see 1 Cor. 11:20–34) but was separated into a distinct event at a very early stage. It endured as part of normal Christian life and worship into the fifth century, when it began to fade into disuse; between the sixth and eighth centuries, it vanished altogether.

The worship of the patristic church was not static. It underwent important developments, especially in the fourth century. Up until now, virtually all churches throughout the empire conducted their worship in the same language, Greek. However, in the fourth century, the West increasingly used Latin, until by about 350 it had replaced Greek as the preferred language of Western worship. This reflected the cultural drifting apart of the Eastern and Western halves of the empire, and it contributed powerfully to the process by which Eastern and Western Christianity went different ways theologically and spiritually. Also, within the East many Syrian churches began to use Syriac in worship, and many Egyptian churches began to use Coptic. This paved the way for Syrian and Egyptian Christians to form their own independent national churches in the fifth and sixth centuries, separate from the mainstream of Eastern Byzantine Christianity.

There was also an increasing emphasis in fourth-century worship on liturgy. As we have seen, liturgies had been in use in Christian worship from the earliest times, but there was now less and less room for the bishop, who led the worship, to vary from the set pattern. Again, in the earlier centuries the different main churches had their own liturgies; but now, in the East the liturgies of Basil of Caesarea and of the church in Constantinople came to dominate. Basil revised the liturgy of the church in Caesarea, which is still used in Eastern Orthodoxy today during Lent and Christmas. The rest of the time, Eastern Orthodoxy employs the shorter Constantinople liturgy, known as the liturgy of John Chrysostom. Churches throughout the West increasingly conformed their liturgies to either the one used in Rome or (usually) the Gallican liturgy of the French churches.

Other aspects of worship also underwent change in the fourth century, for example, the way Christians celebrated Easter. In previous centuries, only Easter Sunday was really important; but the fourth century saw the development of the forty days of Lent and the entire Easter week, with Good Friday becoming as significant as Easter Sunday. The celebration of Christmas on December 25 also became an established practice in the fourth century. It is first mentioned in Western worship in the year 336. The date was the pagan festival of the birth of the sun, taken over and Christianized by the church. The customs of the old Roman festival of the Saturnalia on December 17–21, when candles were lit, parties held, and gifts exchanged, also became attached to Christmas.[9]

Fourth-century worship also witnessed a powerful trend toward a greater use of ritual and ceremony. We find the clearest example of this in the church of Jerusalem during the leadership of Cyril (310–86), bishop from 350. It is in Cyril's Jerusalem church that we first hear of clergy wearing special vestments, the use of incense, the carrying of lights (lamps, candles, tapers), and other ceremonies.

Along with the growth of ritual and ceremony in fourth-century worship went the expansion of the cult of saints and relics. Christians attached an ever greater importance to the dead bodies of those who were considered outstandingly holy in their lifetimes, especially martyrs. Chapels, shrines, and sometimes churches were built over the tombs of saints. Believers increasingly prized relics of saints, for example, a piece of clothing or even a bone. The full-blooded doctrine developed (it had been present in seed-form since earliest times) that the dead saints, now in heaven, could help struggling believers on earth by their prayers. After all, "the effectual fervent prayer of a righteous man avail[s] much" (James 5:16 Authorized Version); surely a saint's prayers would be even more effective now that he or she was in heaven? So Christians practiced—not praying *to* the saints—but asking the saints in heaven to pray *for* them. This was called invocation or invoking the saints (from Latin *invocare*, to call upon). In popular piety, it often drifted into a custom of actually praying *to* the saints, which was little different from the way that pagans prayed to their various gods. People considered certain saints to be especially good at meeting particular needs: one could bring about a cure for childlessness, another could protect travelers, another could reveal the future, and so on.

Most of the great church leaders of the time positively encouraged this cult of the saints and relics. Others, however, did not like what was going on. A French presbyter named Vigilantius protested when he saw Christians lapsing into pagan customs and practices: "Disguised as religion, we almost see the ceremonies of the pagans being introduced into the churches. People light rows of candles in broad daylight, and in all places they kiss and adore the dust of a dead body, contained in a little pot and wrapped up in a precious cloth" (quoted by Jerome, *Against Vigilantius* 4).

It was also during the fourth century that believers began to adorn churches with pictures of Christ and the saints (including holy men and women from the Bible itself and from the history of the Christian church). Christians in the East called these pictures icons, the Greek word for "image." Prior to the fourth century, Christian icons were hardly ever used to decorate churches, although Christians certainly used them in other contexts. For example, Tertullian spoke disapprovingly of cups that depicted Christ as a good shepherd carrying a sheep. Clement of Alexandria mentioned signet rings with which Christians attached their personal seal to a letter; these rings impressed a Christian symbol into the sealing wax—a fish (Christ), a dove (the Holy Spirit), an anchor (faith—Heb. 6:19), a loaf of bread (Holy Communion). The fish was a favorite icon symbolizing Christ. The Greek word for fish was *ichthys* since each letter in the word could be assigned to a name of Jesus: *iēsous* (Jesus), *christos* (Christ), *theos* (God), *huios* (Son), and *sōtēr* (Savior). Fourth-century church historian Eusebius of Caesarea, although himself personally opposed to icons, mentioned their widespread existence: "The features of the apostles Paul and Peter, and indeed of Christ himself, have been preserved in colored portraits which I have examined" (*History of the Church* 7.18).

Christian icons were particularly used in Rome on and around the tombs of believers. These tombs were located in secret underground passages known as catacombs and date back to the first century a.d. Early Christian art in the Roman catacombs often depicted biblical scenes: favorite scenes from the Old Testament were Noah's ark, Abraham sacrificing Isaac, Jonah in the fish, Daniel in the lion's den, and Shadrach, Meshach and Abednego in the fiery furnace; best-loved scenes from the New Testament were Christ being baptized, the Samaritan woman at the well, Peter walking on the water, and the raising of Lazarus. The first church we know about that had pictures like these painted on its walls is a third-century church in Dura (in present-day Iraq).

It was only in the fourth century, however, that the adorning of churches with icons became common practice. In part, this was because it was only in the fourth century that church buildings themselves became common; before the conversion of Constantine, when the threat of persecution continually hung over Christians, most assemblies of believers met in private houses. But when the fear of government persecution vanished in Constantine's reign, Christians could afford to be much more open and public in expressing their faith; and so the construction of special buildings for worship and the adorning of these buildings with Christian art went hand in hand. Even so, some fourth-century fathers, notably Epiphanius of Salamis, were violently opposed to this use of icons in churches. Epiphanius once saw a picture of Christ woven into a curtain in a church in Palestine and was so angry that he tore it down and complained to the bishop of Jerusalem.

But Epiphanius was fighting a losing battle. Other great fathers of the fourth century, like Ambrose of Milan and Augustine of Hippo, defended the adorning of church buildings with religious icons. They became extremely popular; most churches soon displayed images of Christ and the saints in the form of paintings, tapestries, mosaics, and sculptures. Bibles, too, increasingly contained religious illustrations, which were often very beautiful. However, Epiphanius's hostility to icons never entirely died out in the church, and it blazed up again in the Eastern church with devastating ferocity in the great iconoclastic controversy of the eighth and ninth centuries.

Western Catholic Worship in the Middle Ages

One of the gravest problems affecting the life of the Western church after the collapse of the Roman Empire in the West in the fifth century was a widespread decline in the level of education among the clergy. The culture, knowledge, and literacy of any society's clergy tend to reflect the general standards in society at large; and these standards fell seriously in Western Europe in the aftermath of the great Germanic invasions of the 400s, with the disruption and devastation they inflicted on the fabric of Western civilization. The Carolingian renaissance in the eighth and ninth centuries did something to improve this state of affairs, but the overall picture remained bleak.

The most obvious evidence of this loss of education in church life was that most clergy now limited themselves to carrying out liturgical and sacramental functions—celebrating Holy Communion, hearing confessions, baptizing infants, burying the dead. They no longer preached sermons. Western Catholics thus became accustomed to a form of worship in which many things were done but hardly anything was explained. The continued use of Latin, which became the language of a tiny educated elite, meant that even the spoken parts of the service became a mystery to the new Germanic inhabitants of the old Roman West.[10]

During the Carolingian renaissance, the Western liturgy itself was finally standardized. Up until now, Western churches followed two different liturgies, the Roman and the Gallican (French). The Gallican liturgy, the more popular of the two, went something like this:

Part 1: Service of the Word

1. Greeting by priest: "The Lord be with you"; response by people: "And with your spirit."
2. *Kyrie eleison:* "Lord, have mercy" (chanted).
3. Hymn: *Benedictus dominus* (Luke 1:68–79) or *Gloria in excelsis* (Glory to God in the highest).
4. Collect (set prayer for the day).
5. Old Testament reading.
6. New Testament reading: epistle.
7. Hymn: *Benedictus es* (blessed are you, O Lord—the prayer of Azariah from the Septuagint version of Daniel) or *Benedicite* (bless the Lord—the song of the three children from the Septuagint version of Daniel).
8. Bringing in of the gospel book while *Gloria tibi, domine* (glory to you, O Lord) is sung.
9. Gospel reading.
10. Chants: *Trisagion* (holy God, holy and mighty, holy and immortal, have mercy on us) or *Kyrie eleison*.
11. Sermon.
12. Litany (responsive liturgical prayers), led by deacon.
13. Dismissal of all but baptized believers.

Part 2: Eucharist

1. Offertory: preparation of bread and wine, wine mixed with water, while a psalm is sung.

2. Litany of the faithful.
3. Reading of diptychs (official list of the names of those for whom prayer is offered) and prayer for those named in the diptychs.
4. Kiss of peace and prayer for peace.
5. Dialogue between priest and people:

> priest: The Lord be with you.
> people: And with your spirit.
> priest: Lift up your hearts.
> people: We lift them to the Lord.
> priest: Let us give thanks to the Lord.
> people: It is fitting and right to do so.

6. Prayer of consecration of the bread and wine.
7. Singing of the *Sanctus* (Isa. 6:3).
8. Breaking of bread into nine pieces in the shape of a cross; a piece of bread mixed into the wine.
9. The Lord's Prayer.
10. Act of Communion (while Ps. 34 is sung).
11. Prayer of thanksgiving.
12. Deacon dismisses the people.

Charlemagne, the first Holy Roman emperor (emperor from 771 to 814), desired that all churches in his empire worship according to the same liturgy; and so great was his zeal for all things Roman that he ordered Alcuin to prepare a new scholarly edition of the Roman liturgy for use throughout the Holy Roman Empire. Alcuin added some prayers from the Gallican liturgy to the Roman liturgy, but his liturgical reform meant that Western Christendom now followed one standard form of worship derived largely from the Roman church. The early medieval Roman liturgy was at first much simpler than the Gallican. After the reforms of Gregory the Great (pope from 590 to 604), it would have gone something like this:

Part 1: Service of the Word

1. *Kyrie eleison* (Lord, have mercy) chanted three times. Gregory the Great changed the middle chant to *Christe eleison* (Christ, have mercy).

2. Greeting by priest: "The Lord be with you"; response by people: "And with your spirit."
3. Collect (set prayer for the day).
4. Antiphonal chant.
5. New Testament reading: epistle.
6. Singing of psalm.
7. Gospel reading.
8. Sermon.
9. Dismissal of all but baptized believers.

Part 2: Eucharist

1. Offertory: preparation of bread and wine, wine mixed with water, while a psalm is sung.
2. Dialogue between priest and people:

> priest: The Lord be with you.
> people: And with your spirit.
> priest: Lift up your hearts.
> people: We lift them to the Lord.
> priest: Let us give thanks to the Lord.
> people: It is fitting and right to do so.

3. Prayer of consecration of the bread and wine.
4. Singing of the *Sanctus* (Isa. 6:3).
5. Reading of diptychs and prayer for those named in the diptychs.
6. The Lord's Prayer.
7. Kiss of peace.
8. Breaking of bread; a piece of bread mixed into the wine.
9. Act of Communion: first the priest, while *Agnus dei* (O Lamb of God who takes away the sin of the world, have mercy upon us) is sung; then the people, while a psalm is sung.
10. Prayer of thanksgiving.
11. Deacon dismisses the people.

The center of Western worship was the Eucharist or Holy Communion. Of course, ever since the apostolic fathers, Holy Communion had been at the heart of all Christian worship; but the new Western name for Communion, "Mass," was accompanied by some important changes in practice too ("Mass" comes from the closing words of the Western Latin liturgy: *ite, missa est* [go, the congregation is dismissed]). The most outstanding difference between the Eucharist in the early church and in the Western medieval church was the role played by the laity. In the age of the early church fathers, all Christians took part in Communion every Sunday; but from the fifth century onward, lay Communion became less and less frequent in the West, so that only clergy and monks took part on a regular basis. By the sixth century, the Western church required laypeople to receive Communion only three times a year: Christmas, Easter, and Pentecost. Even this was soon cut down to once a year at Easter. Yet parish priests continued to celebrate Communion every Sunday, in accordance with early church tradition; the priest, however, now ate the bread and drank the wine by himself, while the laity simply watched.[11]

The reasons behind this huge shift in the way the Eucharist was celebrated in the West were twofold. First, the tremendous feelings of reverence, dread, and fear that became attached to Holy Communion deterred ordinary laypeople—especially the new Germanic converts—from taking part. They felt unworthy and afraid to approach the awesome mystery of Christ's sacrifice as it was once again made present and effective in the Eucharist for the remission of the sins of the living and the dead. These feelings of awe toward Holy Communion were deepened still further by the increasing strength of belief that the bread and wine were miraculously and entirely converted into Christ's very flesh and blood.

Second, the clergy themselves, especially the best educated and most spiritually minded, discouraged the majority of laypeople from taking part frequently in Communion. Strangely, it was not actually the church's intention to inhibit lay Communion; indeed, priests exhorted their congregations to take part more often. However, they also insisted that in order to take part, people had to be serious, committed Christians who lived in obedience to God's commands. The most devout of the clergy were only too aware that many of the Germanic peoples had embraced Christianity in a very loose and shallow way, simply following the religious loyalties of their leader. By stressing that only true Christians with a genuine repentance and love for God could take part meaningfully in Communion, the clergy often set the moral and spiritual standard so high that it deterred even the most sincere believers from taking part.

Another important development in Western worship that took place in the eighth century was the distinction between High Mass and Low Mass. High Mass was a simplification of the traditional Communion liturgy; it is sometimes called "sung Mass" because it included singing (in contrast to Low Mass). All the clergy and laity of a congregation participated in the liturgical part of High Mass, and most parish churches celebrated it every Sunday. In Low Mass, only the priest performed; there was no singing, and the priest spoke the liturgy in a very quiet voice (hence Low Mass is also called "said Mass"). The laity did not take part in any way; they merely watched and carried out their own private devotions. The parish priest celebrated Low Mass every day. Spiritually minded laypeople would attend Low Mass on weekdays, praying and meditating in silence while the priest ate and drank the bread and wine on his own.

This taking of the bread alone by the laity, while only the priest drank the wine, was quite a late development in the Western church. It became widespread only in the thirteenth century, around the time that the doctrine of transubstantiation was officially defined, and it seems to have grown out of a fear (by both the laity themselves and the theologians) that the blood of the Savior would be dishonored if any of the wine were spilt. Similar fears led to the use of a special wafer instead of ordinary bread: the wafer did not crumble, so no transubstantiated bits of Christ's body could fall on the floor and be trodden on. Giving only the bread to the laity was a purely Western Catholic practice. The Eastern Orthodox Church continued to serve both the bread and the wine to the laity and also used real bread.

As eucharistic theology and piety evolved in the medieval period, the distinction between the Mass as a sacrament and as a sacrifice became quite crucial. Thomas Aquinas explains this with his customary clarity: "This sacrament is at the same time both a sacrifice and a sacrament. It has the nature of a sacrifice to the extent that it is *offered,* but it has the nature of a sacrament to the extent that it is *eaten.* Therefore, it has the effect of a sacrament in the one who eats it, but the effect of a sacrifice in the one who offers it, or in those for whom it is offered" (*Summa theologiae* part 3, Q. 79 art. 5 [emphasis added]).

In other words, the Mass had a twofold aspect. When people ate the wafer, it was a sacrament, feeding the believer by means of Christ's very flesh and blood. But in fact, as we have seen, a Western medieval congregation hardly ever ate the wafer at a celebration of Mass; normally, they just watched the priest celebrating it. Indeed, by Aquinas's time, the

391

Catholic Mass had become a spiritual "spectator sport." People fought to get the best seat in church, so that they could see the wafer being held up by the priest for their adoration; the wafer was placed in a special device called a "monstrance." At church festivals like Corpus Christi (body of Christ) in June, there was a great religious procession in which the priest carried the wafer through the streets in a golden monstrance.[12] So for ordinary Catholics, their normal act of worship at Mass was looking at the wafer, rather than eating it. So much was this the case that the Fourth Lateran Council in 1215 had to insist that Catholics must actually eat the wafer at least once a year.

So when Aquinas distinguished between Mass as a sacrament and Mass as a sacrifice, his point was that even when the congregation did not eat the wafer, the Mass still had value because the priest was offering a sacrifice. The Mass (so to speak) "tapped into" and took hold of Christ's once-for-all sacrifice on the cross, making that past sacrifice present in all its power. The result was that the Mass washed away the sins of those for whom it was offered. This enabled Aquinas to explain theologically how a priest could offer Mass as a sacrifice both for the living and the dead—for those still on earth and for souls in purgatory. In the case of souls in purgatory, offering masses for them would apply Christ's sacrifice to them, thus helping to pay off their debt of sin and hastening their progress to heaven.[13]

The medieval period also witnessed the introduction of musical instruments into Western worship. We first hear of a musical instrument being used in Western worship in the eighth century, for in the year 757 the Frankish king Pepin presented an organ to the church of Saint Corneille in Compiègne, north of Paris.[14] From the eighth century onward, we also occasionally find the harp, violin, and cither depicted in some Western musical manuscripts. In the period 900–1100, organs became common features of the great Western abbeys and cathedral churches.

At first, the organ was used simply to give the right note for the monks and choirs (like a tuning fork). Soon, however, new developments in Western church singing gave strong impetus to more complex use of the organ and other instruments in worship. Up until now, the established style of singing had been Gregorian chant, which was "unison plainsong"—that is, all the singers sang the same words, to the same tune, at the same time. But in our period a new style called "part-singing" (or "polyphony") began to become popular. In part-singing, different singers sang the same words to a slightly variant tune; more complicated forms of part-singing involved singing different words at the same time. To help the singers sing their own parts, abbeys and cathedrals used an organ to accompany the words of one singer or group of singers, adding other instruments (e.g., pipes and cornets) to accompany the words of other singers.

This period did not actually lead to widespread use of instruments in ordinary parish churches and thus in normal Western Catholic worship. Even in the great abbeys and cathedrals, the organ's use was limited to important church festivals. Churches did not begin to employ the organ in the celebration of ordinary masses until the twelfth century. Some historical sources speak of an "organ controversy" in the thirteenth century, which resulted in the Catholic Church's declaring against the use of organs. Thomas Aquinas, the greatest Western theologian of the thirteenth century, seems to confirm this, for Aquinas simply repeated the early church fathers' condemnation of all musical instruments in Christian worship:

> The Church does not use musical instruments such as the harp or lyre when praising God, in case she should seem to fall back into Judaism. . . . As Aristotle says, "We must not introduce flutes into teaching, nor any artificial instrument such as the harp, nor anything of the kind, but only such things as make people morally good." For musical instruments usually move the soul more to pleasure than create inner moral goodness. But in the Old Testament, they used instruments of this kind, both because the people were more coarse and carnal, so that they needed to be aroused by such instruments and with worldly promises, and also because these bodily instruments were symbolic of something. (*Summa theologiae* part 2.2, Q. 91 art. 2)

In fact, it was not until after Aquinas, in the fourteenth and fifteenth centuries, that the playing of musical instruments became a widespread, regular, and accepted feature of ordinary Western worship. The first great church organist known to history was the Italian Francesco Landino (died 1390), of the church of Saint Lorenzo in Florence.

Eastern Worship in the Middle Ages

Since most of the readers of this book will probably be Protestants, this is a good place to say something about the pattern of worship that developed in the Eastern church. This form of worship has changed very little and still characterizes Eastern Orthodoxy today. It is in many ways quite different from Western worship, both Protestant *and* Roman Catholic.

Eastern Orthodox church buildings have no pews, no pulpit, and no organ (or any other musical instrument). There are no religious statues, but covering the walls is an abundance of flat two-dimensional images of Christ, biblical characters, and Orthodox saints. These pictures are known as icons. The icons often have olive-oil lamps burning beneath them. The idea behind the icons is that the worship of the congregation on earth is a joining and sharing in the worship of the glorified church in heaven; the icons are a window into that heavenly worship, revealing the presence of the saints and angels. It is in company with them, and with the help of their prayers, that believers on earth approach and worship the Trinity.

An Orthodox church interior is divided in half by a step (or set of steps) and an icon-screen known as the iconostasis (icon-stand), which is covered in icons. The icon-screen separates the Communion table from the rest of the church. Historians are not sure when this separation first arose; there is some evidence to suggest that it dates back to the early fifth century. At first the icon-screen was a simple plain screen. In the ninth century, after the iconoclastic controversy, the screen began to be adorned with some icons; the almost total covering of the screen with icons (as in Orthodox churches today) was a later development—perhaps as late as the fourteenth or fifteenth century.

The icon-screen has three doors, signifying the Trinity; the middle door is a set of double doors called the "holy doors." On the left of the holy doors is an icon of the virgin Mary, on their right an icon of Christ. These central doors then lead through to a room that Westerners call a sanctuary, but Orthodoxy calls the whole room the "altar." The altar is always at the east end of the church and represents heaven. Normally, clergy alone are allowed to enter the altar. It contains a draped square block from which the priest celebrates the Eucharist; this draped block is what Roman Catholics call the altar, but Orthodox call it the holy table or sometimes the throne of God. Atop the holy table are a crucifix, two candles, and a copy of the gospels. Behind the holy table lies a seat for the bishop and benches for lesser clergy. The holy table is always positioned over relics of Orthodox saints, and Orthodox churches often house other relics.

Those leading Orthodox worship give the Bible readings, sermon, and prayers from the steps before the icon-screen. Portable lecterns (*analogia*) are positioned wherever necessary for the Bibles and liturgical books to rest on; some icons will also be on *analogia*. An Orthodox congregation will stand throughout most of the service, including Holy Communion, when they receive the bread and wine. An Orthodox priest serves Communion from a special spoon, so that people receive the bread and wine at the same time, the bread soaked in the wine. This method of serving Communion seems to have had its origins in Syria, perhaps as early as the late fourth century; however, the practice of drinking from the cup lasted in some parts of Byzantium until the ninth or tenth century. The bread is ordinary leavened bread, baked in flat round cakes about four centimeters thick, stamped with a cross and the Greek letters IC XC NI KA (Jesus Christ conquers). The Communion wine is mixed with hot water. In some parts of the Orthodox world today, for example, Greece, it is still the custom (dating from earliest patristic times) for the worshipers themselves to supply the Communion bread and wine. The East never went down the later Western path of withholding the wine from the laity. At the end of a Communion service, those parts of the bread that were not consecrated for eucharistic use are handed out to all worshipers, including non-Orthodox; this bread is called the *antidoron* (instead of the gift). The same custom prevailed until recently in French-speaking Catholic churches.

In an Orthodox service, Eastern worshipers, unlike their Protestant and Roman Catholic counterparts, do not all do the same thing or watch or listen to the same thing at the same time. (The idea that the entire congregation must all be doing the same thing at the same time is largely Western in origin.) Each Eastern worshiper is free — within limits — to participate in the worship in his or her own way. Various worshipers will therefore go from one part of the church to another in order to call upon Christ or different saints at different icons; they will make the sign of the cross or bow or kneel down at different parts of the service, according to their own feelings of devotion. At some points in the service, the priest will "cense" the icons and congregation, that is, he will spread incense about from a special container (a censer). The theology behind censing icons is that incense is being offered to God for his presence and work in the saints; the worshipers are censed because human beings themselves are the true icon (image) of God.

Some parts of an Orthodox service are sung—by the people, a choir, or a reader alone (it varies from one Orthodox region to another); in almost all Orthodox churches, no musical instruments accompany the singing.[15] Much traditional Orthodox singing follows the pattern of antiphony, which employs two singers (or chanters) or two choirs. In Orthodox antiphonal singing, one chanter will sing the first part of a hymn or prayer, and then the second will complete it.

Because Eastern Orthodoxy has been so conservative in its attitude to worship, it is possible to see in most Orthodox churches today the same basic pattern of worship that was practiced in the Byzantine Empire a thousand years ago.

Worship in the Reformation Traditions

The Protestant Reformation of the sixteenth century was just as much a reformation of worship as it was a reformation of soteriology. While Luther, Zwingli, and Calvin were of course deeply concerned about justification by faith, they were equally concerned that the worship of justified believers should embody the gospel. This led to the development of two new and vibrant traditions in Christian worship: the Lutheran and Reformed traditions.

The Lutheran Reform movement made very swift progress throughout Germany in the years just after the Diet of Worms, especially in the towns and cities. The impact on popular worship was almost immediate. Luther's followers preached the gospel of justification by faith alone in Christ alone; as people placed their religious confidence directly in Christ for salvation, the virgin Mary and the saints ceased to have any place in worship as objects of religious invocation or veneration through icons. Crucially, Lutherans began conducting their worship in German instead of Latin. One of the most basic thrusts of the Reformation was to make worship an act of the whole congregation. Theologically, this congregational model of worship was undergirded by the doctrine of the priesthood of all believers: the whole Christian congregation is a priestly body, and therefore its worship must be corporate and congregational in nature, rather than a performance by a professional worshiper (the priest in the medieval sense) watched by a passive people. Clearly, worship could not be a congregational act if Latin was the language in which worship was conducted, for the vast majority of ordinary Christians could not understand Latin. It was therefore in the liturgical sphere that the Reformation produced its most revolutionary popular impact, as ancient ecclesiastical Latin was replaced in one Protestant land after another by the native tongue of the people. Once again worship could be the united act of a Christian people rather than a passive listening to priestly Latin.

The same concern for the congregational dimensions of worship inspired the Reformers to encourage vocal participation by the people. In this regard we probably think immediately of the congregational singing of psalms and hymns, which was certainly an integral part of the new Reformed worship. However, it also included congregational singing (or chanting or reciting) of the Lord's Prayer, the Apostles' or Nicene Creed, and the Ten Commandments and perhaps a general confession of sin (the details varied from one Protestant region to another). Prayer books were a radical Protestant invention to enable the people to take part collectively in a form of worship that was both corporate and vocal. Further, the Protestant insistence on congregational participation in worship motivated the reintroduction of weekly celebrations of the Lord's Supper, as against the later medieval practice in which laypeople took Communion only once a year. The participatory dynamic was also the driving force behind the Protestant practice of giving the Communion wine as well as the bread to the laity.

In most matters, Luther himself took a very conservative attitude to forms of worship, keeping to traditional Catholic practice except where it clearly contradicted Scripture. He therefore translated the medieval Catholic liturgy into German, for the reasons outlined above, but did not change it very much; the main alteration was in the liturgy for the Mass, where Luther did write a new order of worship that expressed a Lutheran understanding of the Lord's Supper. He retained the system of the church lectionary. He also gave a high place to Holy Communion in worship, building it into the normal Sunday morning service of German Lutheran congregations.

In 1526 Luther's new complete worship-book was finally published for use in Lutheran congregations. The normal Sunday morning service was set out as follows:

1. Hymn or psalm.
2. *Kyrie eleison.*
3. Set prayer (written down in the liturgy).
4. Scripture reading chanted from the set passage for the day: Acts to Revelation.
5. Hymn sung by choir.

397

6. Scripture reading chanted from the set passage for the day: the gospels.
7. The Apostles' Creed, sung by the whole congregation.
8. Sermon.
9. The Lord's Prayer in a long paraphrase.
10. Exhortation (leading into Holy Communion).
11. The words of institution, chanted by the minister.
12. Consecration and distribution of the bread, while a hymn is sung.
13. Blessing and distribution of the cup, while a hymn is sung.
14. Set prayer (written down in the liturgy).
15. The benediction: the Aaronic blessing (Num. 6:24–26).

This pattern of worship was basically the same as in medieval Catholicism, except in three areas: (a) the Lutheran service was in German, not Latin; (b) Luther's new Communion liturgy replaced the medieval Catholic liturgy of the Mass; and (c) Luther exalted preaching to a central position in worship. On other matters such as altars, candles, priestly robes, and so on, Luther did not really care whether they were kept or abolished. The Lutheran churches of northern Germany and Scandinavia retained them; the Lutheran churches of southern Germany did away with them.

Also central to the Lutheran reformation of worship were the Lutheran hymns, some of them (words and tunes) written by Luther himself. These had the greatest impact of all in nourishing Lutheran belief and spirituality. The first Lutheran hymnbook was published in 1524. Luther replaced the medieval Catholic practice of a choir singing in Latin by what became the normal Protestant practice of the whole congregation singing in its native tongue. Popular melodies were used to make the singing easier, and the hymns were full of strong Lutheran doctrinal content. More than any other Protestant church, the Lutherans were marked out by their love of church music and hymn-singing.[16]

Zwingli's outlook produced in Switzerland a much more obvious, visible break with the traditional worship of the Middle Ages than occurred in Lutheran Germany. Luther said that traditional Catholic worship should be left as it was unless Scripture positively demanded that it be changed. Zwingli said that nothing should be done in worship unless God actually authorized it in the New Testament—the regulative principle of worship, as it came to be called. Acting on this principle, the Zurich Reformer secured the removal from Zurich's churches of all religious pictures, statues, crucifixes, candles, altars, and relics and the abolition of the organ, choir, priestly robes, and religious processions. None of these things, Zwingli argued, were authorized by the New Testament. He also introduced the exclusive use of the native language in worship (a Swiss dialect of German) and a Communion service in which the laity received the wine; the liturgy enshrined a Protestant understanding of the Lord's Supper. In the Zurich Communion service, the laity received the bread and wine sitting in their pews—a common Protestant practice today, but first pioneered by Zwingli.

Zwingli retained the liturgical form of worship, with set prayers and the congregational recitation of the Apostles' Creed. He did not, however, simply translate the medieval Catholic liturgy into the native tongue as Luther did. Zwingli's was more of a genuinely new Protestant liturgy, which made use of, but did not copy, the old Catholic liturgy. Singing was not a part of worship in Zwinglian Zurich; instead, the congregation simply read out the psalms and the patristic-era hymn *Gloria in excelsis* antiphonally, with half the congregation reading one line, the other half reading the next line, and so on (Zwingli seems to have divided the lines between men and women, which implies that they were seated on different sides of the church building). This abolition of singing in Zurich was not because Zwingli hated music; in fact, none of the Reformers were so musically gifted as Zwingli.[17] It was simply that Zwingli opposed musical instruments in worship and felt that his congregation would understand the psalms better by reading them out together rather than singing them.

The normal Sunday morning worship in Zwinglian Zurich was essentially a preaching service, consisting of Bible readings, prayers, and a sermon. Zwingli was unique among the Reformers in not regarding the Lord's Supper as integral to Sunday worship; he was happy that it should be celebrated four times a year: Christmas, Easter, Pentecost and a local Zurich festival on September 11. This infrequency of the Zwinglian supper may be related to Zwingli's low view of what actually happened in the supper, since for most of his reforming career he saw it as little more than an act of pious commemoration. Again, in this, Zwingli was virtually alone among the Reformers; Luther famously opposed him on this issue, and after Zwingli's death, Martin Bucer, John Calvin, and Peter Martyr guided the Reformed churches into a much higher doctrine of Holy Communion.

Zwingli's Communion service was rather more elaborate than the normal Sunday preaching service to which it was appended. It was structured like this:

1. Set prayer (written down in the liturgy).
2. Scripture reading: the New Testament letters.
3. *Gloria in excelsis,* recited antiphonally by congregation.
4. Scripture reading: from the gospels.
5. The Apostles' Creed, recited antiphonally by congregation.
6. Exhortation (leading into Holy Communion).
7. The Lord's Prayer, recited by congregation.
8. Set prayer.
9. Words of institution.
10. Consecration and distribution of the bread and wine.
11. A psalm, recited antiphonally by congregation.
12. Set prayer.
13. Benediction.

The distinctively Reformed perspective on worship was pioneered by Zwingli, but it was really Bucer and Calvin who gave it its decisive shape. We may take Calvin as our case study. His approach to the reform of worship in Strasbourg and Geneva was similar to, yet different from, that of Zwingli in Zurich. Calvin too believed that nothing should be done in Christian worship unless the New Testament authorized it (the regulative principle). So he followed Zwingli in rejecting most of the ritual of medieval Catholic worship—images, candles, priestly robes, and so on. However, Calvin and Bucer were rather more positive than Zwingli in seeking a constructive reformation of worship, based not only on the teaching of Scripture, but also on the worship practices of the patristic era. It was not exactly "patristic fundamentalism," but Reformed worship in the sixteenth century did engage in a profound dialogue with the early church and fostered a genuine repristination of patristic forms, albeit always beneath the ultimate critical norm of Scripture.[18]

In one important practical area, Calvin differed hugely from Zwingli: he was positively committed to congregational singing, rather than merely reciting Scripture as the worshipers of Zurich did. In 1539, when he was in Strasbourg, Calvin published a French songbook that contained seventeen psalms, the *Nunc dimittis* (Simeon's song in Luke 2:29–32), the Ten Commandments, and the Apostles' Creed set to music. The singing of the Ten Commandments was a normal part of Sunday worship in Calvin's Strasbourg congregation, and worshipers always sang the Apostles' Creed during the Lord's Supper and the *Nunc dimittis* at its conclusion. Calvin's 1542 Genevan liturgy contained thirty-nine psalms, the *Nunc dimittis*, and musical versions of the Ten Commandments, the Lord's Prayer, and the Apostles' Creed. However, especially in his second period in Geneva (1541–64), Calvin gave pride of place to the psalms in public worship. He expressed his view in the preface to the 1542 Genevan liturgy:

> Now, what Augustine says is true, namely, that no one can sing anything worthy of God which he has not received from Him. Therefore, even after we have carefully searched everywhere, we shall not find better or more appropriate songs to this end than the songs of David, inspired by the Holy Spirit. And for this reason, when we sing them, we are assured that God puts the words in our mouth, as if He Himself were singing through us to exalt His glory.[19]

Since Calvin agreed with Zwingli (and the early church fathers) in strongly opposing the use of musical instruments in worship, Reformed Geneva sang the psalms without any instrumental accompaniment; this became the pattern in all the Reformed churches, in contrast to the Lutheran churches, which retained the use of the organ.[20]

Calvin's encouragement lay behind the complete translation of the psalms into French by the poets Clément Marot (1497–1544) and Theodore Beza (1519–1605). Marot's first Genevan psalter of 1543 contained forty-nine French psalms, the *Nunc dimittis*, the *Ave Maria* (based on Luke 1:28, 42); musical versions of the Ten Commandments, the Apostles' Creed, and the Lord's Prayer; and two graces to be sung at mealtimes. Marot died the following year, but Beza completed the French translation of the psalms in 1562. This final version contained all 150 psalms, the *Nunc dimittis*, and the Ten Commandments set to music and was used throughout the French-speaking Protestant world. The French psalms were sung to simple but lively tunes, sometimes based on popular melodies. The greatest French Reformed composers were Louis Bourgeois (c. 1510–61) and Claude Goudimel (1510–72). Bourgeois edited Calvin's Genevan psalters between 1545 and 1557 (and possibly earlier), writing many of the tunes, which mu-

401

sical scholars have considered the best in the collection. Goudimel produced a brilliant musical edition of the psalms in 1565 for singing in the home; he died a martyr for his Protestant faith during the Massacre of Saint Bartholomew's Day. French Reformed believers fell passionately in love with psalm singing, and so did their brothers and sisters in all the Reformed churches, as the psalms were translated into German, Dutch, and English.

Based on Bucer's German service, the complete form of worship in Calvin's Strasbourg congregation was structured as follows:

1. Scripture sentence: Psalm 124:8.
2. Opening set prayer: confession of sin (written down in the liturgy).
3. Scriptural words of pardon.
4. Words of absolution.[21]
5. The Ten Commandments sung, with *Kyrie eleison* (Lord, have mercy) after each commandment (the first four commandments were sung first, followed by a prayer for instruction in God's law and the grace to obey it; then the other six commandments were sung).
6. Prayer for illumination (an example was supplied in the liturgy, but the minister could pray his own prayer).
7. Scripture reading.
8. Sermon.
9. Collection (offering).
10. Set prayers of intercession, followed by long paraphrase of the Lord's Prayer (all written down in the liturgy).
11. The Apostles' Creed or a psalm sung.
12. Benediction: the Aaronic blessing (Num. 6:24–26).

Contrary to Calvin's wishes, the magistrates of Strasbourg permitted the French congregation to celebrate the Lord's Supper only once a month. Calvin differed from both Luther and Zwingli in his conception of the Eucharist: Christ is present, Calvin argued, not locally in the bread and wine (as Luther said) nor in his divine nature alone (as Zwingli said), but in the power of the Holy Spirit. As the mouths of believers received the bread and wine, the Spirit fed their souls with the glorified human life of the ascended Christ. Naturally, holding so positive a view of the believer's communion with Christ in the Lord's Supper, Calvin argued that the supper was an integral part of normal Sunday worship. He wanted it to be celebrated with great frequency—"at least once a week."[22] Calvin was never able to get his way on this in either Strasbourg or Geneva, owing mostly to opposition from the city magistrates, who did not want the awesome power of excommunication to receive the high profile that weekly Communion would inevitably give it. However, Calvin's clearly expressed ideal was that the Lord's Supper should be celebrated whenever the local church gathered for worship.

On Communion Sundays, after the sermon, collection, and prayers on intercession, Calvin's Strasbourg service continued like this:

1. The Apostles' Creed sung by the congregation, while the minister prepares the bread and wine.
2. Prayer of consecration.
3. The Lord's Prayer.
4. Words of institution.
5. Exhortation to congregation.
6. Communion, while a psalm is sung.
7. Set prayer.
8. The *Nunc dimittis* sung.
9. Benediction: the Aaronic blessing (Num. 6:24–26).[23]

Calvin was more restricted in Geneva than he had been in Strasbourg as a reformer of worship. The Geneva liturgy, therefore, does not embody Calvin's ideal; he had to compromise with the magistrates and with popular practice. However, it is still worth exploring the Geneva liturgy, because of its unique influence as the form of worship practiced in the international headquarters of Reformed Protestantism. It was set out like this:

1. Scripture sentence: Psalm 124:8.
2. Opening set prayer: confession of sin (written down in the liturgy).
3. Psalm.
4. Prayer for illumination (an example was supplied in the liturgy, but the minister could pray his own prayer).
5. Scripture reading.
6. Sermon.
7. Set prayers of intercession, followed by long paraphrase of the Lord's Prayer (all written down in the liturgy).

8. The Apostles' Creed recited.
9. Psalm.
10. Benediction: the Aaronic blessing (Num. 6:24–26).

On Communion Sundays, after the sermon and prayers of intercession, the service continued like this:

1. The Apostles' Creed sung by the congregation, while the minister prepares the bread and wine.
2. Words of institution.
3. Exhortation to congregation.
4. Prayer of consecration.
5. Communion, while a psalm or other Scripture passage is read out.
6. Set prayer.
7. Benediction: the Aaronic blessing (Num. 6:24–26).

The Geneva liturgy was basically a stripped-down version of the fuller Strasbourg liturgy. Missing from Geneva were the scriptural words of pardon, the declaration of absolution by the minister, the Lord's Prayer, the singing of the Ten Commandments and the *Nunc dimittis,* and the collection.

Calvin kept the church calendar (the "Christian year") in a simplified form: Christmas, Good Friday, Easter, Ascension Day, and Pentecost were all observed in Reformed Geneva.

Worship in the Puritan Tradition

One of the great experiments in reforming Reformed worship itself was enacted within the English-speaking world in the mid-seventeenth century by the Westminster Assembly. The assembly tried to embody the aspirations of English Puritans and Scottish Presbyterians in contrast to the worship tradition of Anglicanism in England and Episcopalianism in Scotland.[24] The result was the Directory of Public Worship. Rather than being a prescriptive liturgy, the directory was a set of ground rules that the Westminster divines believed ought to be observed in any service of worship, although they left it up to individual ministers to put specific content into each component. Nevertheless, the directory is very clear about what those components are and the order in which they should occur:

1. Call to worship.
2. Prayer of adoration and supplication.
3. Psalm.
4. Old Testament reading.
5. Psalm.
6. New Testament reading.
7. Prayer of confession and general intercession.
8. Sermon.
9. Prayer of thanksgiving and special intercession.
10. The Lord's Prayer.[25]
11. Psalm.
12. Benediction.

When the Lord's Supper was observed after the Lord's Prayer, the directory set out the following order of service:

1. Offertory: the bread and wine placed on the table, perhaps as a psalm is sung.
2. Invitation.
3. Consecration of bread and wine.
4. Words of institution.
5. Exhortation.
6. Prayer.
7. Communion.
8. Exhortation.
9. Prayer.
10. Psalm.
11. Benediction.

In many ways the Westminster Directory stands in line with Calvin's Geneva liturgy. The chief differences are the nonprovision of set prayers for the minister and the absence of the Apostles' Creed. These omissions derive largely from the independent branch of English Puritanism, which exercised an influence out of all proportion to its numerical strength owing to the massive stature of its leaders, spiritual giants like Thomas Goodwin and John Owen. Puritanism was not monolithic in its approach to worship or to anything else, and there was a discernible trend in the independent "left wing" of Puritanism toward a less liturgical, more spontaneous form of worship. Independents objected to the mandated use of any nonscriptural form, such as a noncanonical set prayer or even the Apostles' or Nicene Creed, as a human imposition on the free Spirit-directed conscience of the Christian. The tendency is perhaps best exemplified in Owen, often regarded as the greatest of the seventeenth-century Puritan divines. Owen disapproved so vigorously of set prayer, which he feared would quench the Spirit, that he even argued stoutly against the use of the Lord's Prayer (it was an essentially Old Testament prayer, he insisted, unsuitable for Christians living in the light of the postresurrection era). In fact, the Lord's Prayer is prescribed in the Westminster Directory, but it soon fell out of use in Puritan worship.[26]

Another aspect of this antiparticipatory dynamic in Puritan worship, which swiftly came to dominate the landscape, was a rejection of vocal sharing by the congregation in the service (apart from singing the worship songs). So we find that at the Savoy conference in 1661, where Presbyterians and Episcopalians argued about a future order of service in the Church of England, the Presbyterians maintained that "the minister being appointed for the people in all public services appertaining to God . . . the people's part in public prayer [is] to be only silence and reverence to attend thereunto and to declare their consent in the close by saying Amen."[27] Accordingly the Presbyterians ruled out all congregational responses, including the responsive reading of the psalms.

If the left-wing independent attitude to worship came to prevail among English Nonconformists, this was probably in large measure a psychological reaction against the vindictive and bloody persecution to which they were subjected by liturgy-loving Anglicans after 1662. When freedom came in 1689, a new mindset evolved among the heirs of the Puritans, which (unsurprisingly) equated liturgy with the perceived unspirituality of a persecuting Episcopal state-church.[28]

The same stream of thinking found its way into the ranks of the Scottish Covenanters. The pioneers of the movement had argued against Episcopalians for the freedom of extemporary prayer, but they soon found they were having to argue against their own radicals for the freedom to use set prayers! During the "killing times" of 1660–89, the use of the Lord's Prayer, the Apostles' Creed, and the doxology (the threefold glory to the Trinity, traditionally sung at the end of every psalm) came to be associated in many Presbyterian minds with the detested Episcopal regime that so brutally persecuted Presbyterians. These liturgical elements were quite understandably dropped by most Presbyterians in the post-1690 church, although a few retained them.[29] Perhaps more surprisingly, the public reading of Scripture fell into strikingly wide disuse among Scottish Presbyterians: the Bible was expounded (often very richly and at great length) but not actually read out as a distinct act. The Church of Scotland General Assembly in 1856 set out to correct this abuse, enjoining on all ministers the observance of the Westminster Directory's instruction to read out a chapter of the Old and of the New Testament in every service.

The Puritan movement ultimately opened up a certain divide between the Continental and Anglo-Saxon Reformed traditions, at least for a time, since the Continental Reformed never abandoned their historic liturgical forms. Noncanonical set prayers, the Lord's Prayer, and the Apostles' Creed continued to be part of the staple of Continental Reformed worship. The permanent strengths of Puritan worship were its sense of reverence and anticipation, its conscious prayerful reliance on the Holy Spirit to bless every ordinance, its eucharistic consciousness,[30] and its perhaps unrivaled sermonic power—Puritan preaching remains one of the brightest glories of pulpit history for its saturation in Scripture and searching application to the human heart.

More Recent Trends in Worship

In Protestant Christendom today, worship is less monolithic than at any time in our previous history. Cultural pluralism has no doubt had a hand in promoting the idea of a free-choice marketplace of worship styles, just as it has contributed to a free-choice marketplace of theologies (even within evangelicalism, where it sometimes seems that nothing is actually true any more, but that everyone has an insight). However, if we could pick out one theme that has been particularly insistent in the evolution of Protestant worship since the eighteenth century, it would have to be subjectivity. By this I mean the tendency to construct and evaluate worship in terms of the human subject—human experiences, feelings, and responses—rather than in terms of the divine object, God, the blessed self-revealing Trinity, and his will, word, and activity. This subjectivity takes various forms, but they all share in common the view that worship is essentially something we experience, rather than something we offer, and that the quality of that experience is the measure of effective worship.

407

This is probably contentious territory, but it seems to me that the evangelical awakenings of the eighteenth century gave the first powerful impetus toward this subjectivity in worship. David Wells comments that the revivals had an unintended net effect of replacing the passion for truth by the passion for souls. We can see something of this even in a genius like Jonathan Edwards, who very much gives the impression in his revival writings that the function of a worship service is the conversion of sinners.[31] We can understand the forces at work that inspired our ancestors to think in this way, but it already marks a fateful step on the subjectivist journey. Worship structures are now in danger of being judged by the pragmatic criterion, "How good are they in producing conversions?" From here to the most modern user-friendly, seeker-sensitive service is no long road.

Once the criterion of effect is adopted, the corporate worship life of God's people quickly becomes a kind of laboratory. Leaders experiment endlessly with what will produce the desired effect—endlessly, because the collective mood and spirit of a people change, so that today's successful method becomes tomorrow's worn-out museum piece. And even the effect that is desired changes. Is it conversion? Is it the intellectual edification of believers? Is it a blissed-out state of ecstasy? A breathless fluidity has consequently been introduced into many congregations' worship forms, so that you may be worshiping God quite differently today than you were ten years ago. And no one can tell what the next ten years will bring. Worship, classically understood as our participation in the eternal pattern of the heavenly sanctuary, instead comes to mirror the kaleidoscopic flux of time and fashion.

At first, the subjectivity trend within Protestantism mainly brought about a new exaltation of preaching. Everything else tended to be regarded as mere preliminaries: the all-important thing was to have the "preaching experience," to be intellectually and emotionally stimulated by the sermon. What William Maxwell says of English Presbyterians and Congregationalists can be applied to the generality of non-Episcopal, non-Lutheran Protestants in the English-speaking world: "During the eighteenth and nineteenth centuries, worship in England among Presbyterians and Congregationalists alike sank to a low level. The structure was meagre, the prayers lengthy and didactic, with the sermon as the principal act of public worship."[32]

Thomas Binney, the great nineteenth-century Congregationalist minister and hymn writer (author of "Eternal Light! Eternal Light!"), records a dismal picture of Nonconformist worship, as attested by an anonymous friend who was a famous preacher:

> Some of my people live at a distance, and are often late; I am exposed to the constant intrusion of strangers who do not know when service begins, or are willing to be just in time for the sermon; and there is always, as everywhere, a large proportion of "hearers" who regularly attend without any idea, or any serious purpose, of worshipping at all. For the first half hour after the service has commenced, and even longer, I am annoyed and disturbed by people coming in and walking up the aisles (without shame!)—by the opening of doors, the slamming of seats, the ruffle of feet—to say nothing of other noises still more ignoble! Prayer and song, which I pant to enjoy, are thus often interfered with by irritating distractions. . . . Even at the end of the entire service preceding the sermon, people come in and press forward as if everything was just beginning![33]

"As if everything was just beginning. . . ." Here we see the preaching-experience model of worship wreaking its worst havoc in evangelical life. The congregation has become an audience, the minister has become an orator, and everything else in the service can be safely ignored or even treated with casual contempt. Liturgy, creed, Scripture lections, confession, intercessory prayers, psalms and hymns, Eucharist—all have either been dropped or emptied of existential engagement. The only thing that really matters is to be uplifted through the sermon. Subjectivity has won its first victory.[34]

However, at least in this first wave of subjectivity, a powerful channel for truth was still open in the sermon. The second wave, in its long-term effects, eventually shattered even this bridgehead. First Pentecostalism, which attained global significance through the Azusa Street revival of 1906–13, and then the charismatic movement, which was Pentecostalism jumping ship into the mainline denominations in the 1950s and 1960s,[35] set in motion a powerful trend to relocate the uplifting experience of the worshiping subject from the sermon to various (alleged) manifestations of the Holy Spirit: tongues, prophecies, healings, slayings in the Spirit, and so forth. One account of the Azusa Street revival describes "public weeping, shouting, dancing, leaping, lying in a heap on the rostrum before the congregation: falling backward across steps, constant speaking in tongues often simultaneously, tongues which usually no one understood and which mostly were not interpreted."[36] From here to the Toronto Blessing may be ninety years in time but it is no distance in concept. Subjectivity has won its second victory. Worship is now all too often perceived, orchestrated, and evaluated according to its capacity to produce these or similar effects, which—unlike the earlier preaching-experience model—bypass the mind. The spirituality of the altered state of consciousness has found a home in Christian worship.

Through an alliance between the widespread influence of the charismatic movement and modern secular culture's media-dominated conditioning of people into audiences hungry for physical and emotional stimulation and self-fulfillment, tendencies have been encouraged in our worship that have had—and continue to have—very visible results. Perhaps we can glance at some of those results by considering the legacy of John Wimber, founder of the Vineyard Movement, whose influence on contemporary evangelicalism has extended far outside his own denomination.[37] Prior to his conversion, Wimber was a jazz musician, manager of the "Righteous Brothers" music group. He carried over into Vineyard worship the relaxed, informal atmosphere and musical style that he had soaked up in the jazz world. Worship bands, subjective songs, and sensuous syncopated tunes became the liturgical order of the day. Wimber was a major factor in popularizing this style of worship among the wider evangelical community. Indeed, this whole ethos (in full-blooded or diluted form) has now become so common in evangelical churches that it can almost be called the norm. What we see in the Wimberite worship style is the same kind of shift from truth-oriented objectivity to feeling-oriented subjectivity, which also pervaded Wimber's theology, in which he famously called for a paradigm shift from a Western logical, rational, cause-and-effect mindset to an Eastern perception of reality in terms of experience, intuition, and the inexplicable (the supernatural, the miraculous—and/or the psychic, the magical).

This fed into another crucial aspect of Wimber's liturgical legacy: his redefinition of the concept of ministry. In the older Protestant tradition, ministry meant the ministry of the word—supremely, as mediated in preaching. The Holy Spirit was understood as working in people through the instrumentality of the word. In Wimber's outlook, with his emphasis on the immediate work of the Spirit, perceptions changed radically. Ministry was no longer seen as primarily grounded in the objective word of God in Scripture; the focus was shifted to the Spirit's physical action on people, channeled through prayers, laying on of hands, and various deliverance methods.

410

Here was the fruit in worship-practice of Wimber's two famous principles: "God is above his word" and "God is not limited by his word." In churches that have bought Wimber's package, ministry now tends to be seen in terms of music, song, dance, words of knowledge, and other activities that appeal chiefly to immediate feeling. But the crown of honor goes to a "ministry time" where those in need come to the front, are prayed for, have hands laid on them, and are sometimes the recipients of more involved techniques.

The end product? The place of the Holy Spirit is no longer God's eternal word, nor is the Lord's Table, but this new institution of ministry time. And correspondingly, therefore, the signs of the Spirit's activity are no longer conviction of sin, repentance, spiritual illumination, quickening, and edification in Christ, but people falling over, feeling physical sensations, undergoing emotional euphoria, and eventually (because nonsense will finally take over when truth is sidelined) hysterical laughter and animal noises. How do we know the Holy Spirit was truly at work in our gathering? Because Jane could not stop laughing, and Fred cock-a-doodled. Where does Scripture sanction this? Nowhere, because God is above his word and not limited by his word. Subjectivity has triumphed.

None of this, of course, is to suggest that Wimberism is the only appearance worn by modern subjectivity in worship. I include it here simply as a concrete and popular example of this trend in extreme and therefore obvious form. Nor is it to suggest that all evangelical churches have swum with the stream or to the same degree. The so-called worship wars reveal the extent of alarm felt by many in the Reformed and Puritan traditions. However, comparison of the worship forms that characterized the patristic, medieval, and Reformational eras and those that seem predominant in large swathes of the evangelical world today shows the quantum leap into subjectivity that has been taken in much modern worship, even within the Reformed camp. Reformed Christians, who have traditionally claimed a particular concern for shaping the church's worship according to the regulative principle of Scripture (and in the light of patristic practice), should take special note, unless they wish to destroy their historical identity.

Sometimes it is said with respect to history that those who do not know it are doomed to relive it. In the present context of liturgical history, there may be a case for saying instead that those who do not know it are doomed to squander their inheritance. May the Lord of the church give us humility and wisdom.

411

17

CALVIN'S THEOLOGY
OF WORSHIP

HUGHES OLIPHANT OLD

The word *liturgy* was not a very important part of Calvin's theological vocabulary.[1] In fact, it was a word rarely used by the theologians of his day.[2]
The learned theologian was aware of the word that the Greeks used for the
Mass, but the word had not really passed into the Latin theological vocabulary the way it has passed into our theological vocabulary.[3] If, of course,
Calvin had thought that the word meant "the people's work," as some would
have us believe, he would not have thought the word had much to commend itself. All that would imply a much-too-Pelagian understanding of
worship for any of the early Reformed theologians, let alone Calvin.[4] Calvin
understood the word to mean public service, that is, service performed for
the benefit of the community or state, although the word could, as Calvin
points out, refer to the public service of worship.[5]

What word then did Calvin use to speak of what we usually mean by
liturgy? A brief study of Calvin's vocabulary yields some interesting results.
One searches in vain the title pages and prefaces of the liturgical books of
Geneva to find Calvin's word for liturgy. The *Genevan Psalter* bears the title
Form of Prayers.[6] That is hardly the term we are looking for, although perhaps here as in other places the service of worship seems to be referred to
simply as "prayers."[7]

412

One might expect the word *service* to be the equivalent term. In the French version of the *Institutes* and in the French version of his commentaries Calvin does speak of "le service de Dieu," "le service ceremonial," or "la forme de servir Dieu."[8] While it is clear that such terms denote the liturgy, one does not get the impression that *le service*, without further designation, has become a term for the liturgy. In Calvin's Latin texts, however, the use of the word *service* is quite different. In the first place one finds the word used less frequently. Both in his use of the Latin noun *servitus* and in his use of the verb *servire*, Calvin understands something much more inclusive than what we mean by the liturgical service. The service of God implies both the moral and the liturgical. In Calvin's discussion of idolatry he takes up the distinction that his opponents would like to make between *douleia* and *latreia*. *Douleia*, he tells us, is *servitus*, and "no one doubts," the Reformer says, "that it is greater to be enslaved than to honor."[9]

In the preface to the *Genevan Psalter* of 1542, Calvin speaks of attending the service of worship as "frequentant les assemblees . . . pour honnorer et servir Dieu."[10] This more dynamic sort of reference to the liturgy is frequently found in Calvin's writings. In the same way, to worship is sometimes referred to as to honor or reverence God.[11] Such phrases make us aware that Calvin is concerned with much more than the external observance of rites. Much of Calvin's reforming concern was to emphasize the inward aspect of worship. He was concerned that Christian worship—the prayers, the preaching, and the celebration of the sacraments—be "a living movement proceeding from the Holy Spirit."[12]

Another word that might come into question as the equivalent of our word *liturgy* is the Latin word *caerimonia*. Calvin speaks of the ceremonies of the Old Testament law, the papal ceremonies, and also the ceremonies that are according to Scripture. The word is not purely negative. It does seem to put the emphasis on things that are done rather than said, liturgical acts rather than liturgical texts. Today the word *liturgy*, particularly as it is understood in Catholic circles, means much more than Calvin's "ceremonies."[13]

Calvin uses the word *ritus* as a synonym for the word *caerimonia*, although he uses the word much less frequently. In Classical Latin both words refer to external observances and the manner in which they are performed. While *ritus* may be used to speak of any custom or traditional usage, *caerimonia* denotes a religious custom or observance. This explains why Calvin spoke more frequently of ceremonies than he did of rites.[14]

The one word that Calvin uses more than any other to speak of worship is the word *cultus*. It seems to be the closest word he uses for our word *liturgy*. The word comes from the Latin verb *colere* (to cultivate, care for, reverence, worship). Cicero defines the word as "the truest, the most pure, most holy, the most pious worship of the gods is that we honor them always with pure, sincere and innocent heart and voice.[15] *Cultus* could be used by the Scholastic theologians in much the same way, although its use was limited by a very precise definition.[16]

Certainly the way Calvin understood the word is not conveyed by the English word *cult*. The Latin word *cultus*, however, was a good choice for Calvin because it referred to both the inner religious affections and the outward religious observances. It speaks of both the objective and subjective aspects of worship. It could refer to both public worship and private devotions. In other words, it has a broader meaning than the word *liturgy*, which more properly designates the public service of worship. The word was good Ciceronian Latin, and this certainly commended it to Calvin. Calvin's attraction to the word undoubtedly stems from its implication that with the outward performance of religious rites there must be a corresponding devotion to the heart and holiness of life.

Calvin understands *cultus* as the proper translation of *latreia*.[17] This was not the way Jerome translated the word in the Vulgate, which probably explains why it was not an important word in the vocabulary of the Scholastic theologians. Jerome most often used the word *obsequium* to translate the Greek in such key passages as Romans 12:1, which speaks of the "logical" or "reasonable" or "spiritual" worship of Christians.[18] To translate *proskynein* in John 4:24 concerning the worship that is in spirit and truth, Jerome used *adorare*. If Jerome did not use the word in some of these key passages, there was one ancient Christian writer who did — Lactantius.

Lactantius had a tremendous influence on those Reformers who, like Calvin, were educated by the Christian humanists. Lactantius's use of the Latin language was considered exemplary in the early sixteenth century. It must be admitted that while Lactantius was widely respected for his use of language, he was not particularly regarded as a theologian. Calvin, for instance, does not even mention him on his list of the leading theologians of the ancient church.[19] A brief look at his use of the word *cultus* may help to explain Calvin's preference for the word.

Lactantius was an early Christian writer who used the best Ciceronian

414

Latin. He was born about 240 and, therefore, experienced the persecutions that the church suffered before the conversion of Emperor Constantine. Having been appointed professor of rhetoric at Nicomedia by Emperor Diocletian, he was dismissed because of his conversion to the Christian faith about the year 300. His major work, the *Divinae institutiones*, was written before the Edict of Milan and therefore reflects the spirit of the ante-Nicene church.[20] Lactantius won a considerable reputation for his learning. In later years Constantine entrusted him with the education of his son. He was regarded even then as the Christian Cicero. The *Divinae institutiones* is addressed to the literati of the empire. Discussed at length are the religious philosophy of classical antiquity and above all the work of Cicero, that great epitome of Romanitas. The *Divinae institutiones* might almost be considered a Christian response to Cicero's *De natura deorum*. In this classic of apologetic literature Lactantius uses a number of words for worship. *Veneratio* and *adoratio* are among the most frequent, especially when speaking of the worship of the pagan gods.[21]

When Lactantius wants to speak of the true worship of the one God, however, his preferred word is *cultus*.[22] A good part of the ante-Nicene polemic against the religion of ancient Greece and Rome was directed against idolatry. Lactantius makes much of the futility of venerating and adoring statues. He exposes the vanity of performing religious rites without the maintaining of justice and the moral virtues. After attacking the superstitions, sacrifices, and idolatry of paganism, Lactantius turns his attention to the nature of true worship. At this point he introduces book six of his work and gives it the title *De vero cultu* (Concerning true worship). As Lactantius understands it, true worship is the hymn of praise that comes from the mouth of a just and virtuous man.[23] As Lactantius uses the word *cultus*, it means true worship that comes from a pure heart.

It is not at all surprising that Calvin should avail himself of this same word. He wanted to get beyond the Scholastic debate over *ex opere operantis* and *ex opere operatio* and recover the concern of the earlier fathers that there must be an integrity between devotions and devotion, between the outward performing of religious rites and the inward disposition of the heart.[24] On the other hand, Calvin found nothing attractive in the errors of the Donatists. Surely the validity of worship does not depend on the sincerity or even the moral purity of those who lead it, much less those who participate in it. Nevertheless, for the Reformer of Geneva the worship to

415

which God calls his people could never be separated from purity of life and the doing of justice. Undoubtedly Calvin chose to use the word *cultus* to speak of the service of worship because it expressed both a broader and a deeper concept of worship than the terminology that was more current in his day.

The Law of Moses and the Worship of the Church

Perhaps one of the best ways to get at the heart of Calvin's concept of worship or, if you prefer, his concept of liturgy is to study his interpretation of the first tablet of the law. The *Institutes* contains a chapter devoted to commenting on the law. Surely a complete study of Calvin's theology of worship will also deal with his chapters on the sacraments, his chapter on prayer, the *Genevan Psalter*, and other documents. This study, however, deals with Calvin's theology of worship as found in his teaching on the meaning of the first four commandments.

In the *Institutes* Calvin tells us that the first part of the Decalogue pertains "to those duties of religion which particularly concern the worship of his majesty."[25] To be sure the law of Moses needs to be studied in the light of its fulfillment in Christ. Nevertheless, as Calvin understands it, "the public worship that God once prescribed is still in force."[26] The fundamentals, the foundations of true worship, are for Calvin first laid down in the law. The worship found in the law of Moses foreshadows the worship that is in spirit and truth found in the gospel. As Calvin explains in his commentary on John 4:20–23, with the coming of Christ the external ceremonies of the law are abolished: "The worship given under the Law was in its substance spiritual, but in regard to its form, it was in some way carnal and worldly."[27] Under the law, too, God was truly served by that inner faith that engenders genuine prayer and true thanksgiving, by the purity of conscience, the renouncing of self in obedience to God that is the true offering, the true sacrifice: "But there were diverse additions under the Law, so that in a way the truth was covered, or enveloped by many shadows and figures; but now there is nothing to hide or obscure I readily confess that today we still have certain external exercises of piety, which is necessary because of our human weaknesses, but the measure and sobriety of these are such that the simple truth of Christ is in no way obscured."[28] When Calvin studied the Ten Commandments, he was concerned with discovering the nature of that basic worship common to the faithful under both covenants. In the law, Calvin tells us, God calls both Jew and Christian "to reverence his divinity, and specifies wherein such reverence lies and consists."[29]

Surely one of the things that characterizes Calvin's approach to worship is his deep appreciation of God's revelation of himself to Israel. This appreciation of the Old Testament and its relevance to the Christian is in no way unique to Calvin. He inherited it from his older colleagues Oecolampadius, Capito, Zwingli, and Bucer. They had been pioneers in the recovery of Biblical Hebrew.[30] Calvin shared this deep appreciation of Hebrew with Bullinger, who, in his working out of covenant theology, put such an emphasis on the unity of the old and new covenants.[31] Certainly Calvin was encouraged by Augustine in this as in much of the rest of his theology.

This positive approach to the Old Testament is one aspect of Calvin's thought that distinguishes him from Luther on one hand and the Anabaptists on the other. Luther was more inclined to emphasize the distinction between law and grace, putting the two in a dialectic. The Anabaptists were more inclined to see the distinction in terms of a dialectic between law and spirit. For Calvin, and the whole school of Upper Rhineland Reformers so influenced by Christian humanism, the recovery of Biblical Hebrew was formative. It was that recovery of Biblical Hebrew that inspired the new appreciation of the Old Testament. It is not at all surprising that that school of Reformers should be very critical of the liturgical use of images and very interested in the recovery of the Lord's Day. To study Calvin's liturgical theology as in his commentary on the first tablet of the law is, therefore, to bring into focus some of the unique aspects of Reformed liturgical tradition.

The First Commandment

When Calvin formulates the first commandment in a positive form, he puts it this way: God "commands us to worship and adore him with true zealous godliness."[32] One might have expected Calvin to have developed the commandment in a more doctrinal way. For example, he might have said the first commandment teaches us to *believe* in one God. Surely that is what one might expect of a leader of the Protestant Reformation who was so preeminently a theologian. There are, alas, those who imagine that Calvin was little interested in worship, giving much more attention to doctrinal

417

formulations, questions of social ethics, and ecclesiastical structure. Here
we read that the first thing the law teaches us is to *worship* God and God
alone.[33] Let us consider this a bit more deeply. Could anyone really be surprised that Calvin gave such an important place to worship? We all know
what an important place Calvin's theology gave to the affirmation that humans are created to glorify God. What then would follow more naturally
than that the Reformer of Geneva should find written in the first commandment that worship is the first business of life, the ultimate vocation of
the human race! For Calvin, it is in worship that all our other activities find
their meaning. The law sets down for us this first of all duties: "To contemplate, fear, and worship his majesty; to participate in his blessings; to
seek his help at all times; to recognize, and by praises to celebrate, the greatness of his works—as the only goal of all the activities of life."[34]

For Calvin, the worship of strange gods is always a danger even for Christians.[35] The true God is to be worshiped with all our hearts, all our minds,
and all our souls. The gods of fortune and fertility, culture and nationalism,
are not even to be named among us. Calvin would have a hard time with
those who today like to make worship an occasion to display their ethnic or
national culture or to promote political solidarity, social awareness, peace
of mind, financial success, self-realization, or family togetherness. "You shall
have no other gods before me" (Ex. 20:3) teaches us to make worship theocentric rather than anthropocentric. There will undoubtedly be those who
will find Calvin's great concern for the glory of God disturbing. They will
find little value in his emphasis on the transcendent. For Calvin, nevertheless, true worship is above all to glorify, honor, and reverence God: "Then
let us beware of wicked superstition, by which our minds, turning aside
from the true God, are drawn away hither and thither to various gods. . . .
We are to drive away all invented gods and are not to render asunder the
worship that the one God claims for himself."[36] Finding the first commandment to mean that we are to worship God and God alone, Calvin effectively brings into question many of our contemporary motivations and
justifications for worship.

In a society where we are all too inclined to promote worship because it
makes us feel good, Calvin underlines that worship is a sacred duty.[37] The
duty of worship is taught us by revelation and also by reason. Reason even
without divine illumination teaches us that worship is appropriate to the
human condition. It is only in a beclouded way that the natural person rec-

418

ognizes the duty of worship. We are not able to offer true worship to God unless we are instructed by God's word.[38] But from the very beginning we were created to worship God. When we are "confronted by his majesty," we can do nothing else but worship him.[39] For the natural person, this duty of worship may be recognized only grudgingly, but for the godly it is a delight. To those who worship an unknown god, it is a dreadful fear, but to those who have heard the gospel in faith it is a holy fear: "Because it acknowledges him as Lord and Father, the pious mind also deems it meet and right to observe his authority in all things, reverence his majesty, take care to advance his glory, and obey his commandments. . . . Besides, this mind . . . , because it loves and reveres God as Father, worships and adores him as Lord."[40] Under the law one may perform the duty in fear of retribution, but under the gospel it is done in thankfulness because one is assured of one's salvation. We worship God because it is a sacred duty: "God, as he is our Creator, has toward us by right the place of Father and Lord; for this reason we owe to him glory, reverence, love, and fear."[41]

In the *Institutes* Calvin elaborates his concept of worship: "Even though there are innumerable things that we owe to God, yet they may be conveniently grouped in four headings: (1) adoration . . . , (2) trust, (3) invocation, (4) thanksgiving."[42] Let us look at each element in turn. For the sake of clarity I will use the rich Latin words that Calvin used.

Adoratio

Adoratio is defined as "the veneration and worship that each of us, in submitting to his greatness, renders to him."[43] That the ministry of praise was extremely important to Calvin hardly needs to be urged. It is evident from the great attention he gave to providing the church with metrical psalmody. For the Reformer of Geneva, adoration was the natural reaction of the creature when confronted by the majesty of God. This experience of awe in the presence of God is the context in which both our worship and our theology take place. Worship is primarily doxological. What Calvin is concerned about here is not so much that the worship of the church should include praise along with prayer, preaching, and sacraments, but that all these things should be done in adoration. For example, Calvin, if I understand him correctly, would be very much concerned that preaching be doxological. That is, it should be done out of a fresh sense of the majesty of God. Sermons should be both preached and heard with a sense of the holiness of the God who addresses us in Scripture. Just as the prophets preached with a holy zeal for the sacredness of the word that had been given them and as Peter urged that one who preached do so "as one who utters oracles of God . . . that in everything God may be glorified" (1 Peter 4:11), so in the preaching of the church in his day Calvin would urge that preaching be an act of adoration.

Fiducia

Fiducia "is the assurance of reposing in him that arises from the recognition of his attributes, when—attributing to him all wisdom, righteousness, might, truth, and goodness—we judge that we are blessed only by communion with him."[44] True worship is not so much an attempt to achieve communion with God as it presupposes communion with God. "Reposing in him" is the essence, the heart, and center of communion with God. We repose in him when we recognize his attributes. True knowledge of God enables trust. It enables both faith and faithfulness. It assures us that we have every reason to trust God and to put our lives into his hands. True worship must be the product of this kind of trusting. To use again the example of preaching, the preaching and hearing of the word of God must be from faith to faith. It must witness to faith in order to engender faith. Preaching must be faithful in order to produce faithfulness. When the word of God is preached and heard in faith, it bears fruit. It bears fruit because it is preached in confidence and heard in confidence, the kind of confidence that follows the word because one knows from whom the word comes, the kind of confidence that does what the word says. Sound teaching is essential to true worship. To this principle Reformed worship has always been faithful. The didactic aspect of worship has been affirmed repeatedly by our liturgical tradition, and indeed it should be steadfastly maintained. True knowledge of God is essential to the true worship of God. While for the age of Romanticism didactic preaching and doxological preaching were antithetical, for Calvin they were complimentary. The celebration of the sacrament of Communion is another place in the worship of the church where it becomes particularly obvious that worship is a trusting abiding in the presence of God. The forms of praise, prayer, reading, and preaching the Scriptures and the celebration of the Lord's Supper are the ways in which we experience this trust and assurance. Central to all these acts of worship is this trust, this assurance, for all these acts are acts of communion with God.

420

Invocatio

Invocatio is turning to God in time of need. It should be remembered that *invocatio* is the Latin translation of Greek *epiklēsis*. Literally *invocatio* means to call upon. It is "resorting to his faithfulness and help as our only support."[45] It is essential to the human nature that we are constantly in need. Again and again we must call upon God for help. In the *Genevan Psalter* we find that the service of worship regularly began with the invocation "our help is in the name of the Lord, / who made heaven and earth" (Ps. 124:8).[46] The service of worship then continued with the confession of sin. As great as the importance of praise and thanksgiving is to Calvin, the Reformer would not have agreed that praise and thanksgiving are somehow a higher form of prayer than confession and supplication. We glorify God when we call upon him in time of need. The confession of sin is, as Calvin understands it, a prayer of praise.

Not only must worship be doxological, it must be epicletic as well. *Epiklēsis* occupies an essential part of the liturgy of Geneva. The service as a whole begins with an *epiklēsis*, the preaching begins with an *epiklēsis*, and the prayers begin with an *epiklēsis*. There is a baptismal *epiklēsis* and a Communion *epiklēsis*. The point of an *epiklēsis* is that we realize that our liturgical doing must be Spirit-filled. It must be inspired and empowered by a divine doing within us. Worship is not magic! It is "valid" not because of what we have done, but because of what God's Spirit does with it and through it.[47]

Something else here needs to be brought out. The worship that God requires of us is not so focused on the glory of God that it is oblivious to our need, because our need is for him, and God having created us for himself is glorified in our turning to him in time of need. He is glorified when he is praised as our help and our savior. The glory of God is open to human need. God is served by our supplications because God is *philanthropos* (philanthropic), to use that favorite phrase of the Greek liturgy. God is served by our supplications for his blessing because it is his will to bless us. In true worship God is glorified and the faithful are edified. The prayer of thanksgiving of the *Genevan Psalter* prays "that we might live out our life in the exaltation of your glory and the edification of our neighbor."[48] It is clear that the two are closely related. As the Apostle Paul put it, when Christians suffer need or affliction, it is that we might rely not on ourselves but on God. When we do this, we rediscover our true selves. Human beings are by nature creatures in need. That

421

we need God and that we need each other is not accidental to our nature but essential to our nature. The right relationship between humans and God is reestablished when we relate to him in our need. The glory of God is revealed when he is discovered as the one who supplies our need: "You also must help us by prayer, so that many will give thanks on our behalf for the blessing granted us in answer to many prayers" (2 Cor. 1:11).

That worship should edify or build up the faithful was a favorite theme of Calvin's. Communion is a spiritual food for the faithful, so that those who hunger and thirst after righteousness might be filled. It is a medicine for those who are spiritually sick.[49] So, too, the preaching of the word nourishes and builds up the faith of the church. It is perhaps the genius of Calvin's concept of worship, just as it is the genius of ethical monotheism, that the serving of God and the serving of the neighbor are inseparably bound together. The two are properly ordered when the worship of God is the first of the commandments and the service of the neighbor is like unto it.

Gratiarum Actio

Gratiarum actio "is that gratitude with which we ascribe praise to him for all good things."[50] Worship is first doxological and finally eucharistic. It is when we have experienced the fulfillment of praise, the joy of Communion, and the answer to our prayer that we render thanksgiving to God for these his blessings. There is a real distinction between thanksgiving and the praise and adoration that is our first response on being confronted with the majesty of God. When we are first confronted with his majesty we respond with awe and wonder; but when we have experienced his grace, then we know the God to whom we render thanks. Calvin sees thanksgiving as not only being directed to God, but as having significance to humans as well. Thanksgiving to God is witness to the neighbor at the same time. Calvin puts it this way: "To recognize by hymns, and to celebrate by witnessing to the greatness of his works" (my translation).[51] Here Calvin catches the true sense of the Hebrew word *yādâ*. Thanksgiving is the public recognition of having received God's help in a time of need. True thanksgiving accepts the obligation of service to God that having received his benefits entails. Here we see that the true worship of God, which is always theocentric, nevertheless edifies the neighbor. True thanksgiving is also a witness. It is precisely in its being theocentric that it is most philanthropic. The praises that celebrate his mighty acts, the witness to his salvation, the cele-

422

bration of his works, the confession of his truth, and dedication to this service are the end of the experience that begins with adoration. When we have come to this point, then thanksgiving to God is the completion of human existence.[52]

When Calvin defines worship in terms of adoration, trust, invocation, and thanksgiving, he is not going over into some sort of subjectivism or spiritualism. Calvin saw this sort of thing happening among the Anabaptists. He was aware of these tendencies in Carlstadt, Schwenckfeld, and others, and he had no intention of following their direction. For Calvin, the maintaining of the ministry of praise, the preaching of the word, the service of prayer, and the celebration of the sacraments are all essential to the life of the Christian as well as to the life of the church as a whole. For Calvin, there is never any thought of some kind of purely spiritual worship. To attempt to do this would be to ignore the finite, physical nature of humans.[53] Such purely spiritual worship is impossible to creatures whom God has not seen fit to create as purely spiritual beings. Calvin charges those who attempt to create a purely spiritual worship with attempting to be wiser than God.[54] God established outward forms of worship (i.e., the ceremonies established in his word) in such a way that they fit our human nature. It is a matter of the divine accommodation to the human capacity. With Calvin the concept of accommodation is important. It is important to his doctrine of holy Scripture and it is important to his doctrine of worship.[55] That Calvin understands worship in terms of the divine accommodation should not be understood as a disparagement of worship any more than his understanding of Scripture in terms of the divine accommodation is in any way a disparagement of either the written or preached word. True worship is not something aside from the singing of hymns, the saying of the creed, and the sharing of Communion done in the regular worship of the church. The outward forms are the exercises of true worship.[56] It is in the exercising of praise, invocation, and thanksgiving that the church is edified or built up. True worship takes place through and by means of the outward rites and ceremonies of worship. We are to sing psalms, hymns, and spiritual songs with grace, making melody in our hearts as well as with our tongues.[57] In the *Catechism of Geneva* we read that no one should think himself so spiritual that he can neglect the preaching in public assemblies of worship.[58] Christ established preaching along with the prayers and sacraments as part of the public order of his church. These are, to be sure, outward and external forms, but because God has appointed them for that purpose they convey God's blessings. It is not, of course, because of any power that they have in themselves, but because the Holy Spirit makes them effective to this end.[59]

That at this point Calvin puts the emphasis on adoration, trust, invocation, and thanksgiving comes not from any thought that the liturgical forms are irrelevant or dispensable, but because he is concerned that the liturgical forms come alive. He is all too familiar with lifeless and dead worship. He is all too familiar with services that are simply done for the sake of doing them. Much of his concern for liturgical reform is that the liturgical act spring from true religious affections, that they become not just human works, but works of the Holy Spirit.[60] For Calvin, as for many of his fellow Reformers, one of the first concerns of his liturgical reform was to unite liturgical form and religious affection. It was to bring about a balance between the objective and the subjective aspects of worship.

This comes out with particular clarity in Calvin's commentary on the first commandment. Calvin gives particular attention to the final phrase of the commandment: "You shall have no other gods *before my face*."[61] In the *Catechism of Geneva* Calvin says concerning this phrase: "This means that it is not only by an external profession of faith that God wishes to be confessed, but just as important is the true devotion of the heart."[62] We find the same thing insisted upon in the *Institutes*. The glory of God's divinity is to be celebrated, not only in outward confession, but in the secret recesses of our hearts where God's eyes alone see our true inclination.[63] It should be carefully observed at this point, however, that for Calvin the subjective aspect of worship is not just a matter of inner feeling but much more a matter of inner purity; it is a matter of the pure conscience. True worship is the work of the Holy Spirit. It is the work of the Holy Spirit sanctifying us, crying out from within us, manifesting his glory in our human flesh, making us a holy priesthood. It is not just the outward washing of water, to paraphrase the words of 1 Peter, but the answer of a pure conscience.[64] True worship occurs when the outward forms are observed by those who have been justified by faith and are being sanctified by grace.

The Second Commandment

The protest against the liturgical use of images goes back to the very roots of the High Rhenish Reformation.[65] Calvin inherited this concern from Bucer,

424

Zwingli, and Oecolampadius. The historic position of Reformed Protestantism on the use of pictures and sculpture in worship is basic to a Reformed
understanding of worship. It is one of those concerns that distinguishes the
High Rhenish Reformation from the North German, or Lutheran, Reformation. This reformatory concern had great popular support in the free cities
of South Germany. The Anabaptists, much to the disgust of Zwingli, Bucer,
and Oecolampadius, were able to organize a number of iconoclastic riots,
which is probably explained by the widespread resentment of the poor toward
the great amount of money that was spent on gilded altar pieces and poly-
chrome statuary.[66] The premillenarianism of these iconoclastic riots offended
the Reformers.[67] They would have removed the *Kirchenzierden* in a more
peaceful and orderly fashion, but nevertheless, they were bent on removing
the images from their churches just the same.[68] Calvin had theological reasons for ridding the churches of statues and pictures. Without an appreciation of Calvin's position on this matter, one could hardly perceive the full
scope of Calvin's theology of worship. Let us look at how this objection appeared in his commentary on the second commandment.

First, let us notice that in this commandment Calvin finds the principal
that Christian worship should be according to God's word. The positive formulation of the command would probably be something like this: Let us
worship God as he has directed us in his word. We read in the *Institutes*,
"Now he declares more openly what sort of God he is, and with what kind
of worship he should be honored. . . . The purpose of this commandment,
then, is that he does not will that his lawful worship be profaned by superstitious rites."[69] For Calvin, there is a big difference between the forms of
worship that God established and the rites that humans invented. Calvin
understands the second commandment much as it is interpreted by the
story of the golden calf.[70] The sacrilege of Aaron consisted in his inventing
from his own imagination religious rites to serve the Lord at the bottom of
the mountain, when at the top of the mountain God was giving Moses other
religious rites. It is the old controversy between revealed religion and natural religion. To use a current phrase, Calvin sees idolatry as being an "alternate approach" to worship. This alternate approach flows logically from
natural religion. One might comment that for modern philosophical humanism, just as for the classical humanism of Greece, art occupies the central position that God's self-revelation in Scripture occupies for the Christian.
Today art is for many a form of self-revelation. For the Italian Renaissance,

art was beginning to play this same role. It is interesting to note that those Reformers who were most exposed to Italian humanism were most concerned with the question of the limits of the use of art in Christian worship. Calvin alludes to the famous saying of Hilary of Poitiers that God himself is the only sufficient witness to himself: "For He whom we can know only through His own utterance is a fitting witness concerning Himself."[71] Calvin draws attention to the commentary of Deuteronomy 4:12 on the second commandment: "You heard the sound of words, but saw no form."[72] Calvin obviously thought of the argument that surely God can reveal himself to the eye as well as to the ear. The Deuteronomist, Calvin argues, is aware of the same line of argument: "To sum up, he wholly calls us back and withdraws us from petty carnal observances, which our stupid minds, crassly conceiving of God, are wont to devise. And then he makes us conform to his lawful worship."[73]

For Calvin, the worship that is according to Scripture is not conceived of in a literalistic way. This became clear to the earliest High Rhenish Reformers—Zwingli, Bucer, and, above all, Oecolampadius—in their controversy with the Anabaptists over infant baptism.[74] They did not imagine, any more than did Luther, that Scripture laid down all the liturgical forms of Christian worship. As Calvin and the High Rhenish Reformers understood it, Scripture clearly institutes the preaching of the gospel, the sacraments of baptism and the Lord's Supper. Scripture also clearly teaches us how to pray and to give alms, but leaves it to the church to work out the details of how these are to be ordered. The church's ordering of such things is, nevertheless, to be worked out according to Scripture, that is, according to basic biblical principles. How the church works such things out should be consistent with the gospel that the church proclaims and with the cardinal theological tenets and the basic doctrines of the church.

To be sure, there are matters that are "indifferent" in the public worship of the church.[75] Calvin's use of prayer forms is an example of how he understood this. He did not hesitate to use the prayer forms written by Bucer for the church of Strasbourg. Calvin knew the prayer of confession and the prayer of intercession used in the *Genevan Psalter* to have been written by Bucer, but he knew that the prayers had been carefully composed in accordance with biblical teachings on prayer. The general confession was modeled on the prayer of confession in Daniel 9, much of its language having been inspired by Psalm 25. The prayer of intercession was written following 1 Timothy 2:1–8 and other New Testament admonitions to prayer.[76] These prayer forms were not written out word for word from Scripture, but they were nevertheless according to Scripture.

For Calvin, it was important that Christian worship be more than a mere human work. He understood that when our celebrations of worship are performed according to God's command, in obedience to his command, then they are divine works. When our worship is made alive by his Spirit working in our hearts, then our worship is the work of God's Spirit. Such worship is truly spiritual worship. For Calvin, spiritual worship is above all worship that is in obedience to God's revealed will: "And then he makes us conform to his lawful worship, that is, a spiritual worship established by himself."[77] In his commentary on John, Calvin says that worship in spirit and truth "is a matter of the spirit, because it is nothing other than an inner faith which expresses itself in prayer; it is purity of conscience and the renouncing of ourselves to the end of dedicating ourselves to the obedient service of God."[78]

Opposed to spiritual worship is superstitious worship. Superstitious worship is motivated not by the Spirit but by dread of God, by an unholy fear of God and an anxiety about his will toward us. The worship of an "unknown God" is superstitious worship that tries to appease a shadowy, dark divinity seen from the standpoint of the guilt of those who have not kept his commandments rather than from the standpoint of grace, the standpoint of the thousand generations of those who know him and keep his commandments. Surely to understand fully Calvin's notion of superstition one must read the discussion of the word by Lactantius. There we find that superstitious worship is the performing of rites invented by human beings in honor of gods that were invented by human beings. Superstition according to Lactantius is human-made religion.[79]

The Christian is not to use works of art as an aid to worship because, in the first place, God has not given this to us as a form of worship. God has not asked us to serve him by making images and then venerating these images. It is not a service because it has not been asked of us. The true servant performs the service that is asked of him or her. This ought to be sufficient reason not to use images in worship. But as Calvin understands it, God has forbidden the use of images in worship. That being the case, there should be no question but that we are not serving God by the liturgical use of art.

As Calvin sees it, God had good reason to forbid the making of images for liturgical purposes.

Calvin's thought on the Christian understanding of the second commandment is greatly elucidated by his commentary on Acts 17, where the Apostle Paul preaches against the idolatry of the Athenians: "God cannot be represented by a picture or sculpture, since He has intended His likeness to appear in us."[80] Here is, to be sure, the key to understanding the biblical prohibition of the liturgical use of images—whether in the New Testament or the Old Testament. Calvin rightly understood that image making is just as inconsistent with the Christian gospel as with the Mosaic law. That is abundantly clear from the Apostle Paul's sermon in Athens. When the pagans made images of God, they in fact made images of themselves and worshiped them in the place of God. As the Apostle Paul put it, they worshiped the creature rather than the Creator. The Christian no less than the Jew is called not to make images of God, but to be the image of God.

To be sure, sculpture and painting are gifts of God, and they have their legitimate use.[81] As Calvin understands it, the images of gold and silver, wood and stone, are not only contrary to his law but deceiving: "God is worshipped wrongly and irreverently, and His truth is turned into a lie as often as His majesty is represented by some visible form. . . . Yet it was not for nothing that the prophets always made the objection . . . that Paul is now making, that God is not made like wood and stone, or gold, when an image is made to Him out of dead and corruptible matter."[82] Calvin is well aware of the argument of the Byzantine theologians that with the incarnation God has taken on human flesh and, therefore, that physical icons of him are possible. Calvin points out that the argument of the apostle clearly ignores such an approach, adopting the prophetic argument in all its rigor. God is not material, and therefore we detract from his glory when we represent him by material forms. It is abundantly clear at this point that Calvin's opposition to the liturgical use of images is just as firmly grounded on the New Testament as it is on the Old Testament. Calvin has shown that the Apostle Paul was just as opposed to the use of pictures and statues in worship as the prophets were. He has shown the continuity of the Old Testament and the New Testament.

428

The Third Commandment

The third commandment, "you shall not take the name of the Lord your God in vain," teaches us reverence and respect for that which is sacred. As Calvin puts it in the *Institutes:* "The purpose of this commandment is: God wills that we hallow the majesty of his name, . . . that we should be zealous and careful to honor his name with godly reverence. Therefore we ought to be so disposed in mind and speech that we neither think nor say anything concerning God and his mysteries, without reverence and much soberness."[83]

Calvin immediately connects the third commandment with the first petition of the Lord's Prayer: "Hallowed be thy name." One recognizes here once again Calvin's strong sense of the doxological in Christian worship. For Calvin, worship is a lifting up of our hearts on high; it is the celebration on earth of the majesty that is in heaven; it is the manifesting among us of the glory that is above:[84] "Whatever our mind conceives of God, whatever our tongue utters, should savor of his excellence, match the loftiness of his sacred name, and lastly, serve to glorify his greatness."[85]

In his commentary on the law of Moses, Calvin draws on those parts of the ceremonial law that treat the offering of votive sacrifices in order to explain the third commandment. This part of the ceremonial law should teach Christians to guard their tongues in religious matters, to speak carefully and reverently. One should never use the name of God in a light or trifling manner.[86] The Reformer tells us that there is a synecdoche involved in the formulation of this commandment. The commandment does not deal only with the use of the tetragramaton, but as Jesus teaches us in the Sermon on the Mount, with anything by which God makes himself known.[87] The commandment teaches us to handle the things of God in all sobriety and solemnity or, to use Calvin's own words, with "reverence and much soberness."[88]

One can hardly imagine Calvin trying to develop a "secular liturgy" or some sort of liturgy suited to the needs of Hebrew slaves in Egypt, a comfortable liturgy that could be celebrated in Egypt without making the pilgrimage into the wilderness. Worship in the tradition of Calvin has always been simple, but this simplicity has always been with solemnity. It is something of a paradox, perhaps, but for Calvin this solemn simplicity is the witness to the transcendent glory. The simplicity is a way of focusing on the eternal. Reformed worship has, at its best, always aimed at a simple directness as a sort of discipline. One might even call it an ascetic discipline. This discipline of simplicity helps to clarify the witness. But even further, the transcendent glory is manifested in this world by righteousness, by simplicity of heart, and by purity of life. This same paradox is found in Calvin's insistence on one hand that worship be in the vernacular and on the other hand that it be doxological.[89] For Calvin, there is a clear distinction between the sacred and the profane. We serve the sacredness of God's name when our lives reflect his holiness. We profane his name when our lives turn truth into falsehood.[90] Sin in the life of the worshipers profanes the worship. The worship of God's people is sacred when the people are a holy people. Worship in spirit and truth is what God seeks. For Calvin, there is no more urgent liturgical reform than this: that God's name be hallowed by holy living. The name of God is set apart to sacred use and yet everything that we do is to be done in the name of Christ.[91] "Hallowed be thy name" is logically followed by "thy will be done, on earth as it is in heaven." It is the sacred vocation of Christians to manifest the glory that is above in all that we do here below.[92]

Calvin's liturgical texts give ample evidence of his concern for the honoring of God's name. The order of service begins, "Our help is in the name of the Lord" (Ps. 124:8).[93] The service is concluded by sealing the congregation in God's name. This benediction repeats God's name three times: "The Lord bless you and keep you: / The Lord make his face to shine upon you, and be gracious to you: / The Lord lift up his countenance upon you, and give you peace" (Num. 6:24–26).[94] The service of worship begins and ends in the name. In fact, the service of worship is sometimes simply referred to as meeting together in his name: "quand nous convenons en son Nom." Finally and most remarkable of all is this one fact. All the way through the liturgical text printed in the *Genevan Psalter*, one finds the name of Jesus printed entirely in capital letters. The theology behind this we leave to be drawn out by others, but one remark can be made. How clearly we discern Calvin's concern for the christocentric approach to the law of Moses. For Calvin, as for the Apostle Paul, the name of Jesus is that name which is above every name. The law commanded the honoring of God's name, and in honoring the name of Christ that commandment is truly fulfilled.

The Fourth Commandment

For the High Rhenish Reformers the Christian calendar had a priority

430

on the list of liturgical reforms. As they saw it, the Sabbath was one of those biblical signs that was obscured by a thick overlay of human traditions. The feast days, the seasons of fasting, the saints' days, and the manner in which they were celebrated was a matter of great concern. Zwingli opposed the observance of Lent as early as 1522.[95] Oecolampadius, while providing for the observance of Christmas, Easter, and Pentecost, gave renewed emphasis to the observance of the Lord's Day.[96] Bucer recognized the recovery of the Lord's Day as major concern for reform in his *Grund und Ursach* in 1524.[97] Some of the Strasbourg Anabaptists advocated a return to Saturday observance, and Capito wrote an elaborate defense of Sunday worship.[98] The reform of the Christian calendar was widely discussed in the early sixteenth century. Luther developed one approach. Jacques Lefèvre d'Étaples (i.e., Jacobus Faber) proposed still another approach. By the time Calvin resumed his work at Geneva in 1541, there was almost a consensus in Reformed circles that the main emphasis of the Christian calendar should be the weekly celebration of the Lord's Day but that in addition the "evangelical holy days"—Christmas, Good Friday, Easter, Ascension, and Pentecost—should be celebrated each year. The observance of the liturgical seasons, particularly Lent, was carefully avoided. Essentially what happened was this: the Reformed churches developed a calendar that emphasized the weekly observance of the Lord's Day rather than the liturgical seasons. Calvin's interpretation of the fourth commandment must be seen against the background of this very simple church calendar.

What Calvin has to say on this subject seems to be extremely restrained. This is particularly the case when one considers the rich elaboration of the theme of the Lord's Day among his followers. His interpretation of the fourth commandment leaves a number of unanswered questions. We would, for instance, like to know exactly in what sense he considered the Lord's Day to be the Christian Sabbath. In his commentary on the harmony of the law he arranges the laws for celebrating the annual feasts of Passover, Pentecost, and Tabernacles as interpretations of the commandment to observe the Sabbath. Does this imply that he favored a Christian celebration of Easter, Pentecost, and perhaps even Christmas? Why does he make so little of the occurrence of the resurrection on the first day of the week?[99] As much as we find incomplete in Calvin's thought on this subject, we do find some important aspects of his theology of worship brought into clear focus in his interpretation of the fourth commandment.

Calvin makes three points concerning the Sabbath commandment. "First, under the repose of the seventh day the heavenly Lawgiver meant to represent to the people of Israel spiritual rest, in which believers ought to lay aside their own works to allow God to work in them."[100] Calvin recognized the Sabbath as an important biblical sign. He recalls how the Sabbath is frequently called a sign in various Old Testament passages. He does not elaborate this at any great length, choosing only a limited number of traditional Sabbath themes to develop. First he takes the theme of rest. The Reformer builds on the teaching of Augustine set down in one of his polemical writings against the Pelagians that the Sabbath is a sign of spiritual rest. One can hardly resist seeing in this an apologetic for justification by faith. Surely the Protestant emphasis on Sabbath rest is a significant corollary to the Augustinian soteriology of the Reformers. The Sabbath reminds us that we are not saved by our own works, but by God's mighty acts of salvation. For Calvin, the Sabbath is a day of rest, but even more a day of worship. The main reason for keeping the Sabbath rest was that one might devote oneself to worship. One is freed from one's work in order that one might be open to God's work.[101] In Calvin's commentary on Luke 4:16 we read that the true keeping of the Sabbath is the meditation on God's works. Christians are to observe this commandment in the same way as the Jews in this one respect: we are to assemble to hear the word, for public prayer, and for other religious exercises. In such observances the Christian Lord's Day succeeds the Jewish Sabbath.[102] The day is kept by remembering God's works. It is the day of *anamnēsis*, of remembering what God has done and of remembering what God has promised to do: "It would seem, therefore, that the Lord through the seventh day has sketched for his people the coming perfection of his Sabbath in the Last Day."[103] Here we gain an important insight into how Calvin understood the eschatological dimension of Christian worship. Worship opens us up to the future. Christian worship remembers God's mighty acts of redemption in the past, proclaims God's covenant promises, and looks forward to their fulfillment at the last day. In our doing this we allow God to work in us, fulfilling in us his promises.

The Reformer continues: "Secondly, he meant that there was to be a stated day for them to assemble to hear the law and perform the rites, or at least to devote it particularly to meditation upon his works, and thus through this remembrance to be trained in piety."[104] Calvin is aware of those passages of the New Testament that tell us that the feasts and Sabbaths of the law are but shadows of things to come and that in the coming of Christ they are fulfilled. The Reformer of Geneva, like the Apostle Paul, is concerned that there be no superstitious observance of days. Yet, Calvin reminds us that there is much value in setting aside special times and days for worship. The church has done this as a matter of order and Christian discipline. It is the church, as Calvin sees it, that established Sunday as the day for hearing the word, for the administration of the sacraments and for public prayers.[105] Calvin doubtlessly has in mind that the church made this decision in apostolic times.[106] He evidently did not feel that the Lord's Day was the fulfillment of the Sabbath in the same way that baptism was the fulfillment of circumcision. On the other hand the Reformer does speak of the Lord's Day succeeding the Jewish Sabbath.[107] When Calvin addresses himself to the question of why we celebrate worship on Sunday rather than Saturday, he tells us, "Because it was expedient to overthrow superstition, the day sacred to the Jews was set aside; because it was necessary to maintain decorum, order, and peace in the church, another was appointed for that purpose."[108]

The Reformer goes on: "Thirdly, he resolved to give a day of rest to servants."[109] Here Calvin draws heavily on the Deuteronomic interpretation of the fourth commandment, which, both in its unique formulation of the law in chapter 5 and its development in chapter 23, draws out the concern for servants, the poor, and the overburdened. Besides this, Calvin mentions how the Apostle Paul appointed the collection for the poor of Jerusalem for the first day of the week.[110] Worship for Calvin clearly has a diaconal aspect. Here again we find Calvin following Bucer, who developed this dimension of public worship by making the collection of alms a regular part of worship. Bucer interpreted Acts 2:42 to mean that the public worship of the church should consist in four parts: the teaching of the apostles, the giving of alms, the celebration of the Lord's Supper, and public prayer. Calvin follows Bucer in this.[111] To be sure Calvin did not develop this aspect of worship to the extent that Bucer developed it in Strasbourg or Oecolampadius in Basel; nevertheless, Calvin did understand that the giving of alms was an aspect of the fourth commandment that had continual validity. His words concerning the practice of the Apostle Paul are noteworthy: "Indeed, in the churches founded by him, the Sabbath was retained for this purpose. For he prescribes that day to the Corinthians for gathering contributions to help the Jerusalem brethren."[112] Here again we see how Calvin's theocentric approach to worship has philanthropic results. God is truly served when we share with the poor. This is, as Jesus taught so amply, a service that glorifies God. It is part of worship that is according to Scripture.

What is of most interest for us in Calvin's commentary on the fourth commandment is its development of the theme of *anamnēsis* (memorial). Calvin, Hebraist that he was, had an appreciation for the rich meaning of the Hebrew word *zākar*.[113] Celebrations of Christian worship, preaching, giving of alms, prayers, and sacraments are all to be observed as memorials to Christ. The heart of this commandment—which speaks to both Old Testament Jew and New Testament Christian—is that we are to worship God by celebrating or remembering God's works of creation and redemption. For the Christian, we are to "do this . . . in remembrance of me" (cf. 1 Cor. 11:25). We are to celebrate God's acts of redemption in Christ. The point is not the observance of the day, but the celebration of the memorial. The essence of the commandment as Calvin understands its Christian interpretation is not to be found in the word *Sabbath*, but in the word *remember*. The Christian fulfills the commandment by remembering, by celebrating, our redemption in Christ.

Conclusion

For the various liturgical movements of recent years, the austere figure of John Calvin has often been a stone for stumbling. And not without justice. The Reformer of Geneva would hardly have matched the decor of the gothic revival. Surely Calvin would have found the high-church movement out and out ceremonialism. He would not have been very patient with its artiness, its romanticism, its luxury. He would have been no more at home in the refined emotionalism of Ivy League chapels than in the brute emotionalism of American revival tents. Ralph Adams Cram and Gregory Dix did well to find Calvin a scandal. When in the 1960s the liturgical movement went modern, no one cared what Calvin might have thought about worship. The banal banners, the liturgical prancing and dancing, the holy hugging called forth by the American branch of the house of Aaron ignored Calvin completely. It is just as well. But now that there is nothing new about folk masses and the novelty of guitars has worn off, the question of how to worship is still being asked. There is still a liturgical movement, a hungering and thirsting for true worship. Millions of starving people who used to turn on P.T.L. are still waiting.

For those who would get beyond the theatrics of "worship experiences," the sober theologian of Geneva has much to say. To be sure, he provided French Protestantism with several collections of psalms and hymns to be used in their services of worship, but much more important to him was that praise be a living work of the Holy Spirit in the hearts of his people. Even more, that in the singing of these psalms God be truly praised. Calvin published liturgical texts for the celebration of the Lord's Supper, but he was much more concerned that those who celebrated those rites entered into genuine communion, that our redemption in Christ be remembered in spirit and in truth. Calvin wrote about the problem of prayer in the vernacular and about the problem of the invocation of the saints. They were the liturgical issues of his day. He published forms of prayer for his congregation. He developed the gift of extempore prayer in the daily prayer services of Geneva, but he knew that prayer was much more than a form of prayer or an ability to extemporize public prayer. Prayer was for him the principal exercise of religion. Learning to pray was a lifelong discipline that went hand in hand with sanctification. For him the reform of the prayer life of the church was in the first instance a matter of deepening the faith of the church. For Calvin, there was no liturgical reform without teaching people to pray. The liturgist of today who would listen to Calvin must be prepared to go beyond questions of liturgical rites and forms. These formal problems must be solved, to be sure, but deeper spiritual problems must be solved at the same time. For Calvin, worship is the sanctifying work of God's Spirit in the hearts of his people. Those who would hear Calvin today must be concerned to discover in our doing of liturgical rites the working of the Holy Spirit. They must aspire above all to glorify God in spirit and in truth. They must pass on through the questions of liturgy to the question of worship.

18

CHALLENGES AND OPPORTUNITIES FOR MINISTRY TODAY

MICHAEL S. HORTON

"Seinfeld," the popular sit-com, styles itself as "the show about nothing." Unlike its predecessors—the ones we grew up on—like "The Andy Griffith Show" or even "All in the Family," "Seinfeld" is the epitome of the Beatles' "Nowhere Man":

> Living in his nowhere land,
> making all his nowhere plans for nobody.
> Doesn't have a point of view,
> knows not where he's going to.
> Isn't he a bit like you and me?

Indeed.

The sad thing is that I like "Seinfeld." I identify with his lead character and his hapless castaways on the island of Manhattan. Even more rootless are the folks on "Friends." Do they ever grow up? Are they ever serious? Do they ever commit themselves to people or to beliefs or to institutions in ways that require great sacrifice on their part? Sure, they want community, but when it is their turn to contribute, they find some way of reasserting their autonomy. All this is familiar to me. It is not just a phenomenon I greet with a shaking head and wagging finger as it is reported to me. I am a product of my generation, a child of postmodernism. Or am I?

When Moses came down to a congregation engaged in idolatrous revelry around the golden calf and demanded of his assistant pastor why he allowed this, Aaron feebly replied, "You know how the people are." We know how the people are. If ever we knew how the people are, it is today. Gallup, Barna, and a host of other data-gathering services join with the corporate world in monitoring our habits in the interest of consumer profiling. And like Aaron, those of us in ministry or serving on worship committees find ourselves justifying our accommodations in terms of simply citing the latest trends.

It will be the burden of this chapter to accomplish three goals: first, to give a broad map explaining where I think we are in this particular historical moment; second, to pose the question as to whether we really are products of our culture; and, third, to propose a way forward on the basis of the "new creation" that has dawned in our Redeemer's death and resurrection.

Where We Are

It is the new big thing, and those who do not keep up will be left behind. Of course, we are talking about postmodernism, the latest in a series of modern projects. In fact, it will be our burden in this essay to challenge some of the apparently widespread assumptions in Christian circles concerning the nature of postmodernism and to press the question: Are we taking postmodernism too seriously, whether we are among those who regard it as the end of civilization as we know it or belong to its circle of admirers.

Everything seems to have "post" as a prefix these days. In evangelical theological circles we hear it all the time: postdenominational, postcritical, postliberal, postevangelical, postconservative. But is this "post" fever really something brand new or is it a radicalized version of the same old thing?

G. E. Lessing, scion of the Enlightenment (hence, of modernity), summarizes the secularized eschatology of the age in the title of his book: *The Education of the Human Race*. The past, with its traditions and authorities, was out; the present and the future, with their irrepressible yearning for autonomy and freedom, were in. "Dare to think for yourself!" was Immanuel Kant's cry, and he had a lot of fans cheering him on. The idea was that history is moving from primitive, lower forms of civilization to a sophistication

437

that would finally lead to utopia, the perfect society that had been denied to those living under the old regime. The avant-garde rallied around such slogans as Ezra Pound's "Make it new!" The modernist movement in art in the early part of the twentieth century called for radical demolition of any remains of the past. Centuries-old city buildings and rambling streets were razed to be replaced by utopian planning: modern skyscrapers, wide boulevards radiating from glass-and-concrete centers, and orderly suburbs. Progress became the watchword of modernity, and Pelagianism (confidence in human nature) was the theology behind it. There are no longer any boundaries to transgress. Or, as pioneer psychologist John Lofton explains it, multiple personalities used to be a disorder, but is now pretty much recognized as the normal state of existence for many people today. Is this modern? Postmodern? Hard to say.

No doubt, modernity did achieve some worthy goals. Who wants to return to feudalism, slavery, or the days when women could not even vote? As goofy as the rhetoric of tolerance has become in some respects, surely it is better than state-sanctioned intolerance. Modern democracy is probably better than feudalism. Of course, there will always be different assessments of modernity, even in the church, but there should be room to recognize God's providential hand even in this epoch of history. A lot of high earthly ideals and aspirations were met, even if they were sometimes motivated by rank forms of self-assertion against the authority of God and his Christ.

But then the wheels came off. The exact date is not known, although many guesses are hazarded. Perhaps postmodernism is best associated with the third stage of capitalism: its global phase, or with "the death of the author," "the death of God," "the death of self," "incredulity toward metanarrative," "writing," "erring," or any number of synonyms for nihilism.

Regardless of where we date it or how we define it, most people agree that modernity has certain clearly defined characteristics. It is recognized by its commitment to progress, human ability apart from divine grace or revelation, independence from particular creeds and the institutional church in whatever form, a "perfect society" blueprint, and the rationalization of all aspects of life. We may not know exactly when the wheels came off, but everybody is pretty sure they have. There was a time not so long ago when the cynical lyrics of the musical artist Sting would have been considered heresy, but today they reflect the attitude of the person on the street:

You may say I lost my faith in science and progress.
You could say I lost my belief in the holy church.
You could say I lost my sense of direction.

In other words, Madonna comes to refer to a nihilistic entertainer, and America is glued to "the show about nothing."

But is the postmodern mood simply the flip side of modernity? In other words, why would people be so disillusioned with science and progress, for instance, if they had never made these into idols?

And what about this theme of progress? While self-described postmodernists berate the modern notion of progress, the very term itself betrays a devotion to it. Just as the Renaissance thinkers successfully dubbed everything before them the "Dark Ages," many postmodernists imitated modernity's obsession with the idea of the new, latest, and greatest epoch in world history. Many Christian writers, especially church-growth gurus, advocate faith in progress, technology, pragmatism, consumerism, and many other distinctive traits of modernity while appropriating the label *postmodern*. There is often a fatalism about this: we are no longer in the era of stable, traditional culture with corresponding values. Everything is up in the air. It is crazy. Everything is on the move. Change is what life is all about: this is the rhetoric of a fairly crude modernity masquerading as postmodernism. Reading some church-growth experts, one comes away with a sense of this fatalism just mentioned: This is just the way things are today. No further discussion. The sociological "is" determines the theological "ought," instead of being challenged by the latter. The question must be raised as to whether the contemporary churches are to exist passively in this evil age or draw a countercultural identity from the word of God. That brings us to the next point.

Fate or Fantasy?

Even if there are significant reasons to believe that there has been a paradigm shift in Western culture, and there probably are, why do so many pastors and other church leaders treat it as so definitive? Ironically, in the name of reaching Christianity's postmodern "cultured despisers," evangelical apologetics and mission often become about the most *modern* enterprises on the market. To the extent that we do not surrender to the grand narra-

439

tive of Jesus Christ in promise and fulfillment, we become enamored with the grand narrative of modernity/postmodernity, with its aimless, plotless, "erring"—and its lifeless gods of technology, entertainment, sex, power, consumerism, and what John Seabrook marvelously describes as "the culture of marketing and the marketing of culture."[1] As if this story can compete with the greatest story ever told?

I cannot help but observe the similarity between the practical denial of the sufficiency of Scripture (the grand narrative proclaimed by the gospel) in our day and in the medieval church. "But may not images be permitted in the churches as teaching aids for the unlearned?" the Heidelberg Catechism asks. "No, we should not try to be wiser than God. He wants his people instructed by the living preaching of his word" (Q. 98). Contrast this "swim against the tide" attitude with the following thoroughly unheroic fatalism from another pastor: "Evangelical churches have thrived on careful exposition of the Scriptures, and lengthy sermons. But we are approaching the place where there is no intellectual content left in the sermon. So we will be driven to the power of liturgy and the communication of the gospel through the arts."[2] Why answer a dearth of intellectual content in the sermons by turning to golden calves? Is this really an inexorable, ineluctable destiny? Why not answer the problem of shallow sermons by suggesting substantive ones? Is this all that we can expect from today's preachers, so we had just better find a different medium? The power of liturgy is itself none other than the power of the word as it cascades from the pulpit into everything else, from the call to worship to the benediction. If liturgy possesses its own independent power and the arts may now be our only hope in reaching an idolatrous culture, one wonders whether evangelism and outreach have become euphemisms for apostasy.

Clouding our judgment at times is the fog of fatalism: "You know how the people are." What if President Bush responded to the September 11 terrorist attacks with such passivity? Imagine his advisors consulting restraint. "It is difficult to accept, I know," they tell the President. "We are so used to doing things a certain way. Freedom, democracy, and all that. But we just live in a different world now. We do not live in the same 'Leave It to Beaver' world. We just have to get used to the fact that we live in a world where terrorism is a major force." Instead, Mr. Bush invoked American principles and backed them up with action. The difference between leaders and followers is that the latter accept the world the way it is and leaders make the world a different place. The gospel introduces a new force into the "powers and principalities" that dominate—or pretend to dominate—our lives. There is every reason for a believer to say no to the reign of sin and death, no to the world, the flesh, and the devil, to resist the seductions of our shallow and fading culture. Jesus Christ is alive and holds the keys of death and hell. He has sent his Spirit into our hearts, making us who were not a people the very people of God. Instead of submitting to the powers of this present evil age, we need to become resistance fighters, confident not in ourselves but in the reality of the kingdom of God that is even now coming down out of heaven like a bride adorned for her husband.

To suggest that the Bible is not inherently relevant or that its message is not already practical to modern/postmodern people is a serious challenge to the conviction that the gospel "is the power of God for the salvation of everyone who believes" (Rom. 1:16). It is to suggest, at least implicitly, that the real needs of people today do not correspond to the needs of people in ancient times. We need to "translate"—that is, *transpose* a Christianity that is the answer to sin and the need for reconciliation with God into a religion that is therapeutically useful for human ends. Never mind God's precious reminder in Romans 10 that his word is as near us as the preaching that we hear. It is nothing that we have to bring down or pull up, but is always already ready and active.

In the process, are we losing the reached instead of reaching the lost? In other words, are our "translations" really accommodations that empty the faith of its inner resources to the point where we have actually made those under our care more secularized despite a superficial enthusiasm for things spiritual? Doubtless, evangelicalism has been used by God to bring many to a saving knowledge of Christ. But what of its success over generations? When every generation is the quintessential, most important, epochal event of our age, can we ever achieve a unity across time and place? In a world driven by niche marketing, is the church capable of serving as a transgenerational underground?

A leading mainline theologian told me that his adult children took him to their evangelical church, a vibrant megachurch marketing itself as an outreach to "our postmodern world." Returning home, they asked him what he thought. "Was it not 'alive' and 'relevant'?" they asked. Pausing to collect his thoughts, the father replied, "In all my years in mainline Protestantism, the target of all the just barbs against its sentimental liberalism, I have never seen such a studied avoidance of anything specifically Christian." Stanley Hauerwas makes this point in striking terms. "We accepted the politics of translation," he says, "believing that neither we nor our non-Christian and half-Christian neighbors could be expected to submit to the discipline of Christian speech."[3] This is precisely the assumption, he rightly contends, that must be challenged.

An advertisement keeps popping up for a new paraphrase of the Bible. It is a full-page color photograph of a young woman who appears to be sophisticated and well educated—with a hint of cynicism. "Pastor," the caption reads, "if you want to reach me, you better watch your language." The inside copy elaborates: "Distracted by deadlines and bills, this is the only time she takes to nurture her spiritual life. You can't afford to lose her attention when you reference Bible passages that are too lofty and obscure." We take such advertising copy almost like tomorrow's sunrise, as a given. If this woman is at all representative of how a lot of people in our churches think and live, then surely we ought to follow this ad's advice.

But why cannot a good pastor respond, "No, this is not about making things comfortable for you. If you are baptized, then this speech that the Bible uses is your language. You have to make an effort to understand it, to live in its world, and to breathe its air. If you are too distracted by deadlines and bills to take any time outside of this one hour a week for your faith, then you will pardon me for not losing the rest of my congregation to the world just for you." In our fear of losing a customer, we lose our nerve—and in the process, lose our opportunity to really reach people with the message that can stop them in their tracks and sweep them into the in-breaking of the age to come in Jesus Christ, by the power of the Holy Spirit. When will we learn what so many of our forebears knew from experience: that the success of the Christian gospel lies precisely in its offense. The moment we undo that paradox, we simply become part of "this present evil age" and its rebellious plot.

C. Peter Wagner argues, "Traditional church models no longer work in our fast-changing world. A commitment to reaching the lost is driving new apostolic churches to find new ways to fulfill the Great Commission."[4] In this outlook, "our fast-changing world"—what the Bible knows as "this fading age"—becomes the norm, and church models are viewed in thoroughly relativistic terms, as if God had left the twenty-first century church to find "new ways to fulfill the Great Commission" than word and sacrament. Near the beginning of the twentieth century, writer and social commentator Walter Lippmann wrote: "The philosophy which inspires the whole process is based on the theory, which is no doubt correct, that a great population under modern conditions is not held by sustained convictions and traditions, but that it wants and must have one thrill after another."[5] Steinar Kavale writes more recently: "Fascination may take the place of reflection; seduction may replace argumentation."[6] When Lippmann wrote, it was called "the modern age"; now Kavale calls it "postmodernism," but either way it is the same cultural captivity.

One piece of good news is that despite the baby boomer generation's fascination with itself, the coming generations exhibit a renewed interest in roots, the very thing that our age, whatever one wants to call it, treats with hostility when its values of autonomy are called into question. A host of recent studies confirms that the ecclesiastical ideology of "mission to postmodern culture" works least among the people who are supposed to be the most impressed: the so-called Gen-Xers and younger. Even aside from the all-important challenge of biblical fidelity, not even the demographics support the hype that almost tyrannically controls contemporary approaches to mission and worship.

The obsession with the modern/postmodern typology not only fuels an uncritical embrace of everything currently marketed as important and interesting. It is problematic because it also fosters an antimodern despair that cripples our witness on the more conservative side of the fence. Sweeping generalizations concerning postmodern relativism and the paradigm shift from rationality to irrationality may not only be technically inaccurate in specifics; they can create an almost nostalgic longing for "the good old days" that were dominated by some other offspring of "the spirit of this age." Why not abandon this obsession altogether and recognize that the real contrast is between the "age of the Spirit" that dawned with the resurrection of Christ from the dead and "the spirit of the age" that has throughout history dominated the nations in their rage against the Lord and his Anointed One? Whether we are talking about the businesswoman Lydia, whose heart the Spirit opened as Paul preached Christ, or today's businesswoman in the ad referred to above, the real divide is between the kingdom of Christ and the kingdoms of this world.

Between the Times: A Different Typology

In scholarship, the debate over the nature of postmodernism and its relation to modernity results in so much lost energies and meager results that the whole business has been largely abandoned. And yet, in the church this typology seems so definitive in driving the rhetoric of relevance. What if, instead of adopting the division of history into modern and postmodern, we followed the New Testament distinction between "this present evil age" and "the age to come," the reality of life "in the flesh" versus "life in the Spirit"? Jesus frequently referred to this contrast, as did Paul even more emphatically. Whatever the generation presently in ascendancy, its inhabitants are defined either as belonging to either "this passing age" or "the age to come." In this typology, "That is postmodern" no longer becomes a get-out-of-jail-free card, a justification for all sorts of deviance from historic Christian norms in the name of evangelism, mission, and outreach to the postmodern culture. The person standing with Lydia belongs in a real sense neither to ancient Rome nor to contemporary America, but to "the city with foundations, whose architect and builder is God" (Heb. 11:10). "May our eyes and our preaching be just as terrible" as the truth itself, Hauerwas reminds us. "Indeed, may we preach so truthfully that people will call us terrorists. If you preach that way you will never again have to worry about whether a sermon is 'meaningful.' "[7]

God promised that by his Spirit working through word and sacrament he will slay us and raise us up to newness of life; if "the age to come" is breaking into even "this present evil age" through the preaching of the cross, we really are in the presence of the big idea that has the power to rescript us, taking us "nowhere" people—"aliens and strangers"—and giving us a place around the Lamb's table with Abraham, Isaac, and Jacob. And if not everybody likes us (perhaps our greatest insecurity these days), that might confirm that we are on the right track again.

One word needs to be said to the traditionalist side of the tracks, however. One of the reasons that there is so much craving for a new word from heaven, miraculous spectacles, and new forms of worship that offer dramatic entertainment is that we have lost a sense of the weightiness of God and the unfolding drama of redemption in our own conservative churches. Even where the doctrine is held with unfeigned conviction, our churches are often sterile environments, signaling just about anything but a drama in progress. Perhaps a lecture, but a drama? The service is almost reduced to the sermon, as if everything else were mere window dressing. As a result, the service often seems thrown together and repeated endlessly. Then the sermon itself is often reduced to information and exhortation. When people are looking for an alternative story to make sense of their lives, to give them a plot and a character worth playing, we should be joyfully announcing the greatest story ever told.

The whole service should be a covenant-renewal ceremony in which the people of God, summoned by God himself, gather at the foot of Mount Zion to be judged and justified, taking their place in the drama in progress. To the extent that little thought goes into the liturgy, the music, the preaching, and the sacraments — to that extent the people will become bored with God's ordained means of word and sacrament. It is to be hoped that more of our theologically solid pastors will think more about drama, not less, but with God's drama and not our "soaps" as the paradigm. For in the worship service, God is staging the drama of redemption, taking *lo-ammi* (not-my-people) — "nowhere man" — and rescripting them as the people of the living God. This happens not through our works, but as God himself works through the means he has chosen. As he enacts the drama of which he is the playwright and central character, we find that we are no longer passive prisoners of contemporary culture, but are new creatures in Christ.

Instead of modern and postmodern, our categories are "this passing evil age" and "the age to come." According to God's word, the age to come has already broken into this evil age in the resurrection of Christ. He is the firstfruit of the full harvest; and by his Holy Spirit whom he has sent, through the preaching of the word, baptism, and the Lord's Supper, he is even now making all things new. That is an infinitely more interesting metanarrative than either modernity or postmodernity. "You know how the people are." Indeed, but that is why they must be crucified with Christ and raised with him in newness of life. "But this is where the people are." Unquestionably, but for that very reason we must ignore their felt needs and make them aware of the real needs that Madison Avenue never inculcates in them and, in fact, seeks to suppress. Enough of boring conservatism and self-willed novelty! Let us become truly radical and make a lasting break with the idols of our time. Let us allow ourselves once again to be exposed to the drama of redemption.

So which is it? Is postmodernism the big new thing or the same old thing? For mission, at least, it just does not matter. Whatever it is, it belongs to the fading dreams that cannot compare to the solid joys of Zion. Deep down, God's people know that the song of myself must give way to the song of Moses:

445

I will sing to the Lord,
      for he is highly exalted.
The horse and its rider
      he has hurled into the sea.
The Lord is my strength and song;
      he has become my salvation.
He is my God, and I will praise him,
      my father's God, and I will exalt him. (Ex. 15:1–2)

AFTERWORD

ERIC J. ALEXANDER

By the death of Jim Boice, many of us lost a personal friend, a theological mentor, a true *pastor pastorum,* a wise and thoughtful counselor, and one of the most agreeable companions we had known.

Perhaps the largest number of people who met him did so through his books. He had written over sixty of them before he died. It is therefore particularly fitting that we seek to celebrate his life and influence through this book written in his honor.

I have often thought that even more remarkable than the number of volumes that left his pen was the dedication that each bore. Have you noticed? Without any exception of which I am aware, they are all dedicated in some suitable form to the name and glory and honor of God. For example, the commentary on Philippians is dedicated "to him who began a good work in us, and who will carry it to completion until the day of Jesus Christ." The exposition of Romans 9–11 is dedicated "to him from whom, through whom and for whom are all things." *Making God's Word Plain* (the history of Tenth Presbyterian Church from 1829 to 1979) is dedicated "to him who loves us and has freed us from our sins by his blood, and has made us to be a kingdom and priests to serve his God and Father." And so it went on.

Now this was not merely a habit that, once begun, could not easily be

447

stopped. In fact, it was a studied practice that divulged more of the secret of James Boice's life than almost anything else. "For the glory of God alone" was to him not just a theological slogan: it was the mainspring of his entire being. Apart from this, you just could not understand the man.

Whether in preaching from the pulpit, broadcasting on "The Bible Study Hour," pastoring God's people, planning conferences, studying, or writing, the unifying motive that guided and integrated all his activity was a passion for the glory of God. There is therefore a certain inevitability about the thought that this book you now hold in your hands should end with the words that encapsulate the distinctives of James Montgomery Boice's life:

Soli deo gloria.

NOTES

James Montgomery Boice and the Huguenot Fellowship

1. Richard A. Muller, *The Study of Theology: From Biblical Interpretation to Contemporary Formulation* (Grand Rapids: Zondervan, 1991), 155.

Introduction

1. The magazine was published by Tenth Presbyterian Church and is available through the Alliance of Confessing Evangelicals (*www.alliancenet.org*). See also William S. Barker's essay on Dr. Boice's ministry in Philip Graham Ryken, ed., *Tenth Presbyterian Church of Philadelphia: 175 Years of Thinking and Acting Biblically* (Phillipsburg, N.J.: P&R Publishing, 2004).
2. The account of this conversation and many other biographical details given here are adapted from Linda M. Boice, "A Life in Ministry," in *The Life of Dr. James Montgomery Boice, 1938–2000* (Philadelphia: Tenth Presbyterian Church, 2001).
3. *Stony Brook* (Dec. 1970): 11.
4. James Montgomery Boice, *Whatever Happened to the Gospel of Grace? Recovering the Doctrines That Shook the World* (Wheaton, Ill.: Crossway, 2001), 69–70.
5. Unpublished transcript of anniversary addess, 1979.
6. John R. W. Stott, *Christ the Controversialist: A Study in Some Essentials of Evangelical Religion* (London: Tyndale, 1970), 160.

449

7. James Montgomery Boice, *The Gospel of John*, vol. 1: *The Coming of the Light: John 1–4* (1985; repr. Grand Rapids: Baker, 1999), 296–97.

8. See Boice, *Whatever Happened to the Gospel of Grace?* 176–78.

9. The complete text of the Cambridge Declaration may be found on the website of the Alliance of Confessing Evangelicals (*www.alliancenet.org*).

10. James Montgomery Boice, "Children's Sermons," *Modern Reformation* (Nov./Dec. 1999): 52.

11. James Montgomery Boice, *Psalms: An Expositional Commentary* (Grand Rapids: Baker, 1998), 3.x.

12. James M. Boice and Paul S. Jones, *Hymns for a Modern Reformation* (Philadelphia: Tenth Presbyterian Church, 2000). Copies of the hymnal and companion CD are available through the Alliance of Confessing Evangelicals (*www.alliancenet.org*).

Chapter 1
Does God Care How We Worship?

1. James Montgomery Boice, *Whatever Happened to the Gospel of Grace? Recovering the Doctrines That Shook the World* (Wheaton, Ill.: Crossway, 2001), 178–80.

2. John Calvin, *The Necessity of Reforming the Church* (repr. Audubon, N.J.: Old Paths, 1994), 7.

3. David Peterson, *Engaging with God: A Biblical Theology of Worship* (Grand Rapids: Eerdmans, 1992), 20 (emphasis added).

4. Hughes Oliphant Old, *Worship That Is Reformed according to Scripture* (Atlanta: John Knox, 1984), 171.

5. Boice, *Whatever Happened to the Gospel of Grace?* 188.

6. This kind of criticism can be found in R. J. Gore's *Covenantal Worship: Reconsidering the Puritan Regulative Principle* (Phillipsburg, N.J.: P&R Publishing, 2002) and perhaps implicitly in Tim Keller's comments in "Reformed Worship in the Global City," in *Worship by the Book* (ed. D. A. Carson; Grand Rapids: Zondervan, 2002), 193–99.

7. John Frame makes this kind of an argument (though not as radically as others, it should be said) in *Worship in Spirit and Truth* (Phillipsburg, N.J.: P&R Publishing, 1996), esp. xii–xiii, 44–45.

8. Nahum M. Sarna, *The JPS Torah Commentary: Exodus* (Philadelphia: Jewish Publication Society, 1991), 110 [my addition in brackets].

9. Neil Postman, *Amusing Ourselves to Death* (New York: Penguin, 1985), 8–9 [my addition in brackets].

10. Terry Johnson, *Reformed Worship: Worship That Is according to Scripture* (Greenville, S.C.: Reformed Academic Press, 2000), 24 (emphasis original).

11. See Sarna, *Exodus*, 110.

12. R. Alan Cole, *Exodus: An Introduction and Commentary* (Leicester: IVP, 1973), 156.

13. Sarna, *Exodus*, 110.

14. Cole, *Exodus*, 215.

15. Ibid., 212.
16. Terence E. Fretheim, *Exodus* (Interpretation; Louisville: John Knox, 1991), 280–81.
17. Sarna, *Exodus*, 204.
18. John Currid, *Exodus* (Darlington, England: Evangelical Press, 2001), 2:268.
19. R. P. Martin says, "In some way veneration must have been paid to the angels as part of the cultic apparatus of this religion"; *Colossians and Philemon* (New Century Bible Commentary; Grand Rapids: Eerdmans, 1973), 94. I am well aware of the herculean efforts of modern Reformed critics of the regulative principle to make this passage inapplicable to corporate worship, but Paul's contextual discussion is fatal to their design. What has Paul just been talking about? Baptism! The whole section contains allusions to the practice of public worship.
20. Robert Webber, for instance, makes this charge frequently. This is typical of the diet: "For centuries the focus of Protestant thought about worship has been on worship as a cerebral act"; Robert Webber, "Reaffirming the Arts," *Worship Leader* 8.6 (Nov./Dec. 1999): 10.
21. For instance, Phillip Jensen and Tony Payne, "Church/Campus Connections," in *Telling the Truth: Evangelizing Postmoderns* (ed. D. A. Carson; Grand Rapids: Eerdmans, 2000), 202–3.

Chapter 2
Foundations for Biblically Directed Worship

1. I have been greatly stimulated in my thinking throughout this section by T. David Gordon's "Nine Lines of Argument in Favor of the Regulative Principle of Worship," which originated as class lectures in his ecclesiology courses at Gordon-Conwell Theological Seminary and circulates in various places on the internet. His language can be detected occasionally in mine.
2. R. P. Martin, *The Worship of God: Some Theological, Pastoral, and Practical Reflections* (Grand Rapids: Eerdmans, 1982), 6.
3. Robert L. Dabney, *Lectures in Systematic Theology* (Grand Rapids: Baker, 1985), 183.
4. Quoted in Gordon, "Nine Lines of Argument."
5. Ibid.
6. Hughes Oliphant Old, *Worship That Is Reformed according to Scripture* (Atlanta: John Knox, 1984), 170–71.
7. John Piper, *Brothers, We Are Not Professionals: A Plea to Pastors for Radical Ministry* (Nashville: Broadman & Holman, 2002), 236.
8. D. A. Carson, "Worship under the Word," in *Worship by the Book* (ed. D. A. Carson; Grand Rapids: Zondervan, 2002), 26.
9. I borrow from and pattern this language after the powerful observation of Pat Morley: "*There is a God we want, and there is a God who is — and they are not the same God. The turning point of our lives is when we stop seeking the God we want and start seeking the God who is*"; *The Rest of Your Life* (Nashville: Nelson, 1992), 120 (emphasis original).

10. There are good reasons to believe that the Westminster Assembly did not intend by this term to restrict the sung praise of the congregation to the Old Testament Psalter.

11. As each of these components of biblical worship will be elaborated in subsequent chapters, we offer here only a quick digest of their substance.

12. James Durham, *The Blessed Death of Those Who Die in the Lord* (repr., Morgan, Pa.: Soli Deo Gloria, 2003).

13. J. C. Ryle, *Light from Old Times* (London: Chas. J. Thynne & Jarves, 1924), 7–8.

14. Old, *Worship*, 59–60. See also idem, *The Reading and Preaching of the Scriptures in the Worship of the Christian Church* (Grand Rapids: Eerdmans, 1998), esp. vols. 1–2.

15. Terry Johnson, *Reformed Worship: Worship That Is according to Scripture* (Greenville, S.C.: Reformed Academic Press, 2000), 35.

16. Ibid., 36–37. The books referred to are Matthew Henry, *Method for Prayer* (ed. J. Ligon Duncan III; Greenville, S.C.: Reformed Academic Press/Tain: Christian Focus, 1994); Isaac Watts, *A Guide to Prayer* (repr. Edinburgh: Banner of Truth, 2001); and Hughes Oliphant Old, *Leading in Prayer* (Grand Rapids: Eerdmans, 1995).

17. Johnson, *Reformed Worship*, 36–37.

18. A representative example of this tendency is found in Jeffrey J. Meyers, *The Lord's Service* (St. Louis: Providence Presbyterian Church, 1999).

19. Old, *Worship*, 176–77.

Chapter 3
The Regulative Principle

1. James Montgomery Boice, "Reformation in Doctrine, Worship, and Life," in *Here We Stand! A Call from Confessing Evangelicals* (ed. James Montgomery Boice and Benjamin E. Sasse; Grand Rapids: Baker, 1996), 190. The words are also found in Boice's *Gospel of John: An Expositional Commentary* (Grand Rapids: Zondervan, 1985), 256.

2. "Nearly all the wisdom we possess, that is to say, true and sound wisdom, consists of two parts: the knowledge of God and of ourselves"; John Calvin, *Institutes of the Christian Religion* (2 vols.; ed. John T. McNeill; trans. Ford Lewis Battles; Philadelphia: Westminster, 1960), 1:35 §1.1.1.

3. Marva Dawn, *Reaching Out without Dumbing Down: A Theology of Worship for the Turn-of-the-Century Culture* (Grand Rapids: Eerdmans, 1995); idem, *A Royal Waste of Time: The Splendor of Worshipping God and Being Church for the World* (Grand Rapids: Eerdmans, 1999).

4. David Wells, *No Place for Truth; or, Whatever Happened to Evangelical Theology?* (Grand Rapids: Eerdmans, 1993).

5. Stott gave this as a title to his study of the Sermon on the Mount: *Christian Counter-Culture: The Message of the Sermon on the Mount* (Leicester: IVP, 1978).

6. Dawn, *Reaching Out without Dumbing Down*, 9.

7. John Piper, *The Supremacy of God in Missions* (Grand Rapids: Baker, 1993), 11.

8. Boice, "Reformation in Doctrine, Worship, and Life," 183. Stott's remark is taken from *Christ the Controversialist: A Study in Some Essentials of Evangelical Religion* (London: Tyndale, 1970), 160.

9. John Calvin, *The Necessity of Reforming the Church* (1554; repr. Audubon, N.J.: Old Paths, 1994), 4. Of course, citing Calvin at this point raises the question of the relationship of the sixteenth-century Reformer with the seventeenth-century Puritans. The thesis that the Puritans out-Calvined Calvin is an old chestnut by now, but the issue arises here too. Those who draw a wedge between Calvin and, say, the Westminster Confession see a paradigm shift taking place rather than organic growth. The regulative principle is a case in point. For this thesis, see Ralph Jackson Gore, "The Pursuit of Plainness: Rethinking the Puritan Regulative Principle of Worship" (Ph.D. thesis, Westminster Theological Seminary, 1988); idem, "Renewing the Puritan Regulative Principle of Worship," *Presbyterion* 20 (Spring 1994): 41–50; 21 (Spring 1995): 29–47.

10. Calvin, *Necessity of Reforming the Church*, 7. Cf. *Institutes* 1:383 §2.8.17, where Calvin insists that "lawful worship" is what God instituted "by himself." Other significant documents that evidence Calvin's views of public worship are his sermons on Deuteronomy and the Pastoral Epistles. Calvin's liturgical forms found expression in two works: a booklet entitled *La forme des prières et chantz ecclésiastiques, avec la manière d'administrer les sacremens, et consacrer le marriage, selon la coutume de l'églis ancienne* published in Geneva in 1542 (but with no mention of Calvin as author) and a slightly different edition that appeared in Strasbourg in 1545 and bearing a very lengthy title that began with the interesting words *La manyère*. For detailed information on their contents, see W. de Greef, *The Writings of John Calvin: An Introductory Guide* (trans. Lyle D. Bierma; Grand Rapids: Baker, 1989), 126–31; William D. Maxwell, *A History of Christian Worship* (1936; repr. Grand Rapids: Baker, 1982), 112–19; Bard Thompson, ed., *Liturgies of the Western Church* (Cleveland/New York: Meridian, 1961), 197–210.

11. Elmer Towns, *Putting an End to Worship Wars* (Nashville: Broadman & Holman, 1997), 3.

12. Cf. John F. MacArthur Jr., "How Shall We Then Worship?" in *The Coming Evangelical Crisis* (ed. John H. Armstrong; Chicago: Moody, 1996), 175–87.

13. Boice finds it "inconceivable" that a worship service could have little "significant prayer," adding that many services now have no substantial reading of the word, sermons in which there is "very little serious teaching of the Bible," no confession of sin. Hymns, he adds, are "on the way out," something that he finds "the saddest feature of contemporary worship"; Boice, "Reformation in Doctrine, Worship, and Life," 186–87.

14. Gore, "Renewing the Puritan Regulative Principle" (1994), 41–42.

15. Lewis's statement reads, "Nothing is more characteristically juvenile than contempt for juvenility . . . youth's characteristic chronological snobbery"; *An Experiment in Criticism* (Cambridge: Cambridge University Press, 1961), 73.

16. Cf. J. I. Packer, " 'Sola scriptura' in History and Today," in *Collected Shorter Writings of J. I. Packer*, vol. 4: *Honoring the People of God* (Carlisle, Cumbria: Paternoster, 1999), 121–40.

17. Edmund P. Clowney, *The Church* (Leicester: IVP, 1995), 122; cf. idem, "Distinctive

Emphases in Presbyterian Church Polity," in *Pressing toward the Mark: Essays Commemorating Fifty Years of the Orthodox Presbyterian Church* (ed. Charles G. Dennison and Richard Gamble; Philadelphia: Committee for the Historian of the Orthodox Presbyterian Church, 1986), 99–110.

18. Calvin, *Institutes*, 1:108 §1.11.8.

19. Cited in Horton Davies, *Worship and Theology in England* (Grand Rapids: Eerdmans, 1996), 1:257 (emphasis added).

20. James Bannerman, *The Church of Christ* (1869; repr. Edinburgh: Banner of Truth, 1974), 1:340.

21. See J. I. Packer, "The Puritan Approach to Worship," in Packer's *Among God's Giants: The Puritan Vision of the Christian Life* (Eastborne: Kingsway, 1991), 327; Horton Davies, *The Worship of the English Puritans* (1948; repr. Morgan, Pa.: Soli Deo Gloria, 1997), 48.

22. Every advocate of the so-called Continental Sabbath needs to be locked up in the Geneva of the mid-1540s for a year and then released to see if they still hold the same opinion!

23. Gore, "Renewing the Puritan Regulative Principle" (1995), 46.

24. Ibid., 44.

25. Packer, "Puritan Approach to Worship," 326.

26. Ibid., 325.

27. John Calvin, "Form of Administering the Sacraments, Composed for the Use of the Church at Geneva," in *Tracts and Treatises of the Doctrine and Worship of the Church* (Edinburgh: Calvin Tract Society, 1849; repr. Grand Rapids: Eerdmans, 1958), 2:118. It may be objected that Calvin's words relate to the issue of the sacraments in particular, an issue much in debate at the time, and not to worship in general, but his exhortation to Charles V seems to disprove this.

28. See his discussion on liturgy in "A Discourse concerning Liturgies, and Their Imposition," in *The Works of John Owen* (repr. London: Banner of Truth, 1966), 15:2–55.

29. See Alexander F. Mitchell, *The Westminster Assembly: Its History and Standards* (1883; repr. Edmonton: Still Waters Revival Books, 1992), 212–45; W. Spear, "Covenanted Uniformity in Religion: The Influence of the Scots Commissioners on the Ecclesiology of the Westminster Assembly" (Ph.D. diss., Pittsburgh University, 1976).

30. Reformational understanding differs on the understanding of *occasional* and *necessary* elements in public worship. The sacraments, for example, are an element of worship, but they need not be observed at every service. It is a misnomer to introduce the issue of weekly Communion here, since even those who advocate that the Lord's Supper should be observed every week do not suggest that it should be observed at *both* morning *and* evening services. That is, they do allow for services of worship where the Lord's Supper is *not* observed.

31. Ernest C. Reisinger and D. Matthew Allen, *Worship: The Regulative Principle and the Biblical Practice of Accommodation* (Cape Coral, Fla.: Founders Press, 2001).

32. Hughes Oliphant Old, *Worship That Is Reformed according to Scripture* (Atlanta: John Knox, 1984), 158.

33. See J. I. Packer, *Aspects of Authority: In Our Message, in Our Preaching and Counseling, in Our Decision-Making* (Orthos Papers 9; Cornhill, London: Proclamation Trust, n.d.), 3.

34. The original text of the Westminster Confession of Faith has "if." Most modern editions recognize that this word should be "in."

35. Quoted in Bannerman, *Church of Christ*, 1:337.

36. John Frame, *Worship in Spirit and Truth* (Phillipsburg, N.J.: P&R Publishing, 1996). See also Robert A. Morey, *Worship Is All of Life* (Camp Hill, Pa.: Christian Publications, 1984).

37. John M. Frame, *Contemporary Worship Music: A Biblical Defense* (Phillipsburg, N.J.: P&R Publishing, 1997). Much of the ensuing discussion about this book took place via the internet. Indeed, a collection of email exchanges between John Frame and Darryl Hart, moderated by Andrew Webb, was later collated and published as *The Regulative Principle of Worship: Scripture, Tradition, and Culture; A Debate Featuring Dr. D. G. Hart and Professor John Frame* (ed. Charles B. Biggs; Philadelphia: Westminster Campus Bookstore, n.d.). Darryl Hart also wrote a lengthy review of Frame's book; see "It May Be Refreshing, But Is It Reformed?" *Calvin Theological Journal* 32 (1997): 423–31. In the same year, another review, not just of Frame's particular interpretation of the regulative principle but his historiographic methodology, came from Richard Muller of Calvin Theological Seminary: "Historiography in the Service of Theology and Worship: Toward Dialogue with John Frame," *Westminster Theological Journal* 59 (1997): 301–10. Muller's article was part of a forum in which another theological-social critic of our time, David Wells, also contributed an equally negative assessment of Frame's methodology: "On Being Framed," *Westminster Theological Journal* 59 (1997): 293–300. Frame added a postscript to the forum: "Reply to Richard Muller and David Wells," *Westminster Theological Journal* 59 (1997): 311–18. The articles by Muller and Wells were in response to one contributed by John Frame himself: "In Defense of Something Close to Biblicism: Reflections on *sola scriptura* and History in Theological Method," *Westminster Theological Journal* 59 (1997): 269–92. Terry Johnson summarizes and repudiates Frame's arguments in his timely book *Reformed Worship: Worship That Is according to Scripture* (Greenville, S.C.: Reformed Academic Press, 2000). Frame also added to his position in two articles: "A Fresh Look at the Regulative Principle" (unpublished) and "Some Questions about the Regulative Principle," *Westminster Theological Journal* 54 (1992): 357–66. See the rejoinder by T. David Gordon, "Some Answers about the Regulative Principle," *Westminster Theological Journal* 55 (1993): 321–29.

38. Frame, "Fresh Look at the Regulative Principle." He admits that many Reformed thinkers would be unsatisfied with this assertion.

39. Clowney, *Church*, 125–26.

40. Johnson, *Reformed Worship*, 6.

41. Ibid., 4 n. 4 (emphasis original).

42. Steve Schlissel, "All I Really Need to Know about Worship (I Don't Learn from the Regulative Principle," *Chalcedon Report* 1 (March 1999): 23–26; 2 (May 1999): 31–34.

These articles first appeared in Schlissel's newsletter *Messiah's Mandate*. Several responses were forthcoming, including Brian M. Schwertley, "A Brief Critique of Steven M. Schlissel's Articles against the Regulative Principle of Worship," at *http://www.all-of-grace.org/pub/schwertley/schlissel.html*. To be frank, some of the internet exchanges are unworthy of serious response. It is in the nature of this medium to be embryonic in its thinking, making abortive judgments that have not stood the test of serious scrutiny. A similar critique can be found in Joe Morecraft III, *How God Wants Us to Worship Him: An Exposition and Defense of the Regulative Principle of Worship* (Cumming, Ga.: Triumphant, 2001), 91–104. The most cogent response comes from G. I. Williamson, "A Critique of Steve Schlissel's 'All I Need to Know About Worship, I Don't Learn from the Regulative Principle,'" *Blue Banner* 9.1–3 (2000). (These articles are also available on the following web site: *http://www.fpcr.org/blue_banner_articles/schlissel.htm*.

43. Schlissel, "All I Really Need to Know about Worship," 34. For a more coherent presentation of this argument, see Peter J. Leithart, "Synagogue or Temple? Models for the Christian Worship," *Westminster Theological Journal* 63 (2002): 119–33.

44. Gore, "Pursuit of Plainness"; idem, *Covenantal Worship: Reconsidering the Puritan Regulative Principle* (Phillipsburg, N.J.: P&R Publishing, 2002).

45. Douglas Bannerman, for example, wrote extensively on the synagogue in *The Scripture Doctrine of the Church Historically and Exegetically Considered* (1887; repr. Grand Rapids: Baker, 1976), 123–62.

46. The exact feast referred to in John 5:1 is disputed. D. A. Carson, for example, suggests that the Purim view depends on too many speculative connections to be considered plausible. See *The Gospel according to John* (Grand Rapids: Eerdmans, 1991), 241.

47. See James Jordan, *The Sociology of the Church* (Tyler, Tex.: Geneva Ministries, 1986), 62.

48. R. J. Rushdooney, *The Institutes of Biblical Law* (N.P.: Craig, 1973), 763.

49. See S. Safrai, "The Synagogue and Its Worship," in *Society and Religion in the Second Temple Period* (ed. Michael Avi-Yonah and Zvi Baras; World History of the Jewish People 8; Jerusalem: Massada, 1977), 65–98.

50. The point is noted by Monte Wilson in "Church-o-Rama or Corporate Worship," in *The Compromised Church* (ed. John H. Armstrong; Wheaton, Ill.: Crossway, 1998), 74; Reisinger and Allen, *Worship*, 52–53. Curiously, Reisinger and Allen admit later in the same volume that the regulative principle is "the only theological basis for Baptist distinctives of believer's baptism and baptism by immersion" (77).

51. I refer to it as "exclusive believer's baptism" for fear that it is often overlooked that paedobaptists also practice believer's baptism in the case of those who profess faith having never been baptized.

52. The literature here is vast, but as a representative sampling, see Michael Bushell's somewhat acerbic *Songs of Zion: A Contemporary Case for Exclusive Psalmody* (Pittsburgh: Crown & Covenant, 1977); John Murray and William Young, "Minority Report of the Committee on Song in the Public Worship of God," in the Minutes of the Orthodox Presbyterian Church, 14th General Assembly (1947); J. L. Girardeau, *In-*

strumental Music in the Public Worship of the Church (Richmond: Whittet & Shepperson, 1888); The Voice of the Reformed Presbyterian Church on the Psalmody of the Church and Instrumental Music in the Worship of God (Londonderry: Standard Steam Printing Office for a Committee of Synod, 1873).

53. C. S. Lewis, Letters to Malcolm: Chiefly on Prayer (New York: Harcourt, Brace & World, 1963), 4, quoted in Boice, "Reformation in Doctrine, Worship, and Life," 190.

Chapter 4
Corporate Worship

1. The terms psalm, hymn, and song are used in the headings of the Book of Psalms and could designate the Old Testament Psalter. In this context, however, these words describe the new songs of the new covenant. They come from the wisdom of the Spirit in the church.

2. Lawrence C. Roff, Let Us Sing: Worshiping God with Our Music (Norcross, Ga.: Great Commission, 1991); David Peterson, "Worship in the New Testament," in Worship: Adoration and Action (ed. D. A. Carson; Grand Rapids: Baker/Carlisle, UK: Paternoster, 1993), 51–91.

3. Peterson, "Worship in the New Testament."

4. William D. Maxwell argues for the importance of the weekly Qadesh as the setting of the Lord's Supper; see An Outline of Christian Worship: Its Development and Its Forms (London: Oxford University Press, 1949), 5–7.

5. The translation could be "you come together in assembly."

6. With many translations, the English Standard Version (quoted here) fails to acknowledge that Greek verbs of hearing take the genitive as the direct object. The translation should omit "of."

Chapter 5
Expository Preaching

1. John R. W. Stott, Between Two Worlds: The Art of Preaching in the Twentieth Century (Grand Rapids: Eerdmans, 1982), 15.

2. Michael Green, "Editor's Preface," in ibid., 7.

3. Philip Reiff, The Triumph of the Therapeutic: Uses of Faith after Freud (New York: Harper & Row, 1968).

4. George Barna, "The Pulpit Meister: Preaching to the New Majority," Preaching 12 (Jan./Feb. 1997): 12.

5. David F. Wells, No Place for Truth; or, Whatever Happened to Evangelical Theology? (Grand Rapids: Eerdmans, 1993), 173.

6. David Tracy, The Analogical Imagination (New York: Crossroad, 1981).

7. T. H. L. Parker, Calvin's Preaching (Louisville: Westminster/John Knox, 1992), 79.

8. Haddon Robinson, "The Heresy of Application: An Interview with Haddon Robinson," *Leadership* 18 (Fall 1997): 20–27.

9. John MacArthur, *Rediscovering Expository Preaching* (Chicago: Moody, 1992), 343.

10. Richard Sennett, *Authority* (New York: Norton, 1980), 15.

11. Willard Gaylin and Bruce Jennings, *The Perversion of Autonomy* (New York: Free Press, 1996), 10.

12. Fred B. Craddock, *As One without Authority* (Nashville: Abingdon, 1971).

13. Ibid., 13.

14. Ibid., 14.

15. Ibid., 16.

16. D. M. Lloyd-Jones, *Authority* (Edinburgh: Banner of Truth, 1957), 10.

17. Charles H. Spurgeon, *Lectures to My Students* (London: Passmore & Alabaster, 1881), 23–24.

18. Paul Althaus, *The Theology of Martin Luther* (trans. Robert C. Schultz; Philadelphia: Fortress, 1966), 5.

19. Ibid.

20. Gardiner Spring, *The Power of the Pulpit* (1848; repr. Edinburgh: Banner of Truth, 1986), 69–70.

21. Ibid., 70.

22. Cited in John H. Leith, "Calvin's Doctrine of the Proclamation of the Word and Its Significance for Today," in *John Calvin and the Church: A Prism of Reform* (ed. Timothy F. George; Louisville: Westminster/John Knox, 1990), 222.

23. Martin Luther, sermon on John 4:9–10 preached on September 11, 1540, cited in *What Luther Says* (ed. Ewald M. Plass; St. Louis: Concordia, 1959), 1125.

24. Hughes Oliphant Old, *The Reading and Preaching of the Scriptures in the Worship of the Christian Church*, vol. 4: *The Age of the Reformation* (Grand Rapids: Eerdmans, 2002), 39.

25. Hughes Oliphant Old, *The Reading and Preaching of the Scriptures in the Worship of the Christian Church*, vol. 1: *The Biblical Period* (Grand Rapids: Eerdmans, 1998), 189.

26. James Montgomery Boice, "Exposition Not Entertainment," *Leadership* 14 (Spring 1993): 27.

27. James Montgomery Boice, "The Great Need for Great Preaching," *Christianity Today* (Dec. 20, 1974), 7 (291).

Chapter 6

Evangelistic Expository Preaching

1. Graeme Goldsworthy, *Preaching the Whole Bible as Christian Scripture* (Grand Rapids: Eerdmans, 2000), 95–96.

2. William Perkins, *The Art of Prophesying* (1606; repr. Edinburgh: Banner of Truth, 1996), 62.

3. John Piper, *The Supremacy of God in Preaching* (Grand Rapids: Baker, 1990), 27.

4. While one could point to many books on preaching, let me suggest three: Edmund P. Clowney, *Preaching and Biblical Theology* (Grand Rapids: Eerdmans, 1961; repr. Phillipsburg, N.J.: P&R Publishing, 1979); Graeme Goldsworthy, *Preaching the Whole Bible as Christian Scripture* (Grand Rapids: Eerdmans, 2000); and John Piper, *The Supremacy of God in Preaching* (Grand Rapids: Baker, 1990).

Chapter 7
Reading and Praying the Bible in Corporate Worship

1. This quotation is actually found in the "The Form of Presbyterial Church-Government" under the heading "Pastors," a document crafted by the Westminster Assembly of divines and approved by the General Assembly in February 1645. It is available in many editions of the works of the Westminster Assembly, one particularly helpful version of which is *The Subordinate Standards and Authoritative Documents of the Free Church of Scotland* (Edinburgh: Free Church of Scotland, 1973), 172 (emphasis added).

2. John Currid, *A Study Commentary on Exodus* (Darlington, England: Evangelical Press, 2001), 2:277.

3. Hughes Oliphant Old, *The Reading and Preaching of the Scriptures in the Worship of the Christian Church* (Grand Rapids: Eerdmans, 1998). This multivolume series constitutes Old's *magnum opus* and should be the starting point for any intelligent discussion of this matter.

4. Directory for Public Worship: "Of Public Reading of the Holy Scriptures," in *Subordinate Standards and Authoritative Documents*, 138–39.

5. *The Book of Church Order of the Presbyterian Church in America* (6th ed.; Atlanta: Committee for Christian Education and Publication, 2001), 50–51.

6. This section of the chapter is by Terry Johnson; all first-person references and accounts of personal impressions and experiences come from and refer to that coauthor.

7. Bard Thompson, *Liturgies of the Western Church* (Philadelphia: Fortress, 1961), 159–224, 287–307.

8. Ibid., 311–405.

9. Hughes Oliphant Old, *Worship That Is Reformed according to Scripture* (Atlanta: John Knox, 1984), 102.

10. Matthew Henry, *A Method for Prayer* (ed. J. Ligon Duncan III; Greenville, S.C.: Reformed Academic Press, 1994), xii.

11. Ibid., xv (emphasis added).

12. Hughes Oliphant Old, *Themes and Variations for a Christian Doxology* (Grand Rapids: Eerdmans, 1992), 12.

13. Samuel Miller, *Thoughts on Public Prayer* (1849; repr. Harrisonburg, Va.: Sprinkle, 1985).

14. William Perkins, *The Art of Prophesying* (1606; repr. Edinburgh: Banner of Truth, 1996); Philip Doddridge, *Lectures on Preaching* (London: Baynes, n.d.); Robert Dabney, *Sacred Rhetoric; or, Course of Lectures on Preaching* (1870; repr. Edinburgh: Banner of Truth, 1979); R. W. Dale, *Nine Lectures on Preaching* (London: Hodder & Stoughton, n.d.); Henry Ward Beecher, *Yale Lectures on Preaching* (New York: Fords, Howard & Hulbert, 1893); J. A. Broadus, *On the Preparation and Delivery of Sermons* (rev. ed.; 1870; repr. Nashville: Broadman, 1944); J. H. Jowett, *The Preacher: His Life and Work* (New York: Doran, 1912).

15. Perkins, *Art of Prophesying*, 77.

16. Patrick Fairbairn, *Pastoral Theology: A Treatise on the Office and Duties of the Christian Pastor* (1875; repr. Audubon, N.J.: Old Paths, 1992); Thomas Murphy, *Pastoral Theology: The Pastor and the Various Duties of His Office* (1877; repr. Audubon, N.J.: Old Paths, 1996); Ebenezer Porter, *Lectures on Homiletics and Preaching, and on Public Prayer; Together with Sermons and Letters* (New York: Flagg, Gould & Newman, 1834); W. G. T. Shedd, *Homiletics and Pastoral Theology* (1867; repr. Edinburgh: Banner of Truth, 1965); C. H. Spurgeon, *An All-Around Ministry: Addresses to Ministers and Students* (1900; repr. Edinburgh: Banner of Truth, 1965).

17. An edited version of Watts's *Guide to Prayer* was reprinted by Epworth in 1948.

18. Andrew Blackwood, *The Fine Art of Worship* (Nashville: Abingdon, 1939); idem, *Leading in Public Prayer* (Nashville: Abingdon, 1957).

19. Thomas C. Oden, *Pastoral Theology: Essentials of Ministry* (San Francisco: Harper & Row, 1983), 97.

20. James D. Berkley, ed., *Leadership Handbooks of Practical Theology*, vol. 1: *Word and Worship* (Grand Rapids: Baker, 1992).

21. D. Martin Lloyd-Jones, *Preaching and Preachers* (Grand Rapids: Zondervan, 1971); Samuel T. Logan Jr., ed., *The Preacher and Preaching: Revising the Art in the Twentieth Century* (Phillipsburg, N.J.: P&R Publishing, 1986); Jay E. Adams, *Preaching with Purpose* (Phillipsburg, N.J.: P&R Publishing, 1982); William Still, *The Work of the Pastor* (Aberdeen: Didasko, 1976); John R. Stott, *Between Two Worlds: The Art of Preaching in the Twentieth Century* (Grand Rapids: Eerdmans, 1982); Haddon W. Robinson, *Biblical Preaching* (Grand Rapids: Baker, 1980).

22. William H. Willimon, *Preaching and Leading Worship* (Philadelphia: Westminster, 1984).

23. Ibid., 48.

24. Jean-Jacques von Allmen, *Worship: Its Theology and Practice* (London: Lutterworth, 1965); William D. Maxwell, *An Outline of Christian Worship: Its Developments and Forms* (1936; repr. London: Oxford University Press, 1952); Robert Rayburn, *O Come Let Us Worship* (Grand Rapids: Baker, 1980); Donald Macleod, *Presbyterian Worship: Its Meaning and Method* (Richmond: John Knox, 1967); James Hastings Nichols, *Corporate Worship in the Reformed Tradition* (Philadelphia: Westminster, 1968).

25. Jay Adams, *Shepherding God's Flock* (3 vols.; Phillipsburg, N.J.: Presbyterian & Reformed, 1974–75; 1-vol. repr. in 1980).

26. Harvey M. Conn (ed.), *Practical Theology and the Ministry of the Church, 1952–1984: Essays in Honor of Edmund P. Clowney* (Phillipsburg, N.J.: P&R, 1990).

27. Ibid., 133.

28. John MacArthur et al., *Rediscovering Pastoral Ministry* (Dallas: Word, 1995).

29. Paul D. Robbins, "Comments from the Editor," *Leadership* 1 (Winter 1980): 3.

30. John Killinger, "The Place of Public Prayer," *Leadership* 15 (Spring 1994): 58–65. He recommends that ministers "employ biblical words and phrases" (62).

31. J. G. Miller, "The Bible in Public Prayer," *Banner of Truth* 214 (July 1981): 9–11, 20. He cites the support of Calvin, Lloyd-Jones, the Westminster Directory, Augustine, and Bonhoeffer and says, "For freshness of utterance, for breadth of comprehension, for elevation of thought, for intimacy of rapport, there is no prayer like that which forms itself in words or thought of Scripture, chastely used and reverently offered" (11). Excerpts from Newton, Spurgeon, and Samuel Miller were also printed.

32. Dinsdale Young, "Spurgeon's Pulpit Prayers," *Banner of Truth* 343 (April 1992): 25–27. He writes, "His wonderful knowledge of Scripture made his prayers so fresh and edifying. No man can pray with high effect unless he is steeped in Scripture. Mr. Spurgeon lived and moved and had his being in the Word of God. He knew its remoter reaches, its nooks and crannies. Its spirit had entered into his spirit; and when he prayed, the Spirit of God brought all manner of precious oracles to his mind" (25).

33. John R. deWitt, "Praying in Public Worship," *Banner of Truth* 364 (Jan. 1994): 9–12; Robert Sheehan, "Isaac Watts: A Guide to Prayer," *Banner of Truth* 369 (June 1994): 8–14; David Evans, "Pulpit Prayer: An Area of Concern," *Banner of Truth* 370 (July 1994): 25–27. The articles by deWitt and Evans are excellent, and both express concern for the use of Scripture in prayer. "Indispensable to learning how to pray from the pulpit is a thorough knowledge of the Scriptures," says the former (11).

34. William S. Barker, "Prayers: Carefully Written or Spontaneous?" *Reformed Worship* 1 (Fall 1986): 11–13; Edith Bajema, "Pray It Write," *Reformed Worship* 31 (March 1994): 3–5.

35. For example, Norman Steen, "Let Us Pray," *Reformed Journal* 15 (March 1990): 24–26. See also Thomas Pettinga's article, taken up mainly with the question of to whom we are to address our prayers: "When You Pray . . . ," *Reformed Worship* 31 (March 1994): 6–8.

36. Hughes Oliphant Old, *The Patristic Roots of Reformed Worship* (Zurich: Theologischer Verlag, 1970).

37. Old, *Worship*; idem, *Themes and Variations*; idem, *Leading in Prayer* (Grand Rapids: Eerdmans, 1995).

38. Old, *Leading in Prayer*, 3.

39. Ibid., 7 (emphasis added).

40. Originally entitled "Evangelicals on the Durham Trail," Hart's essay appeared as "Post-Modern Evangelical Worship," *Calvin Theological Journal* 30 (1995): 451–59.

41. Old, *Leading in Prayer*, 5.

42. Henry, *Method for Prayer*, xiv.

43. Fairbairn, *Pastoral Theology*, 317.

44. Dabney, *Sacred Rhetoric*, 358.
45. Miller, *Thoughts on Public Prayer*, 217.
46. Murphy, *Pastoral Theology*, 213.
47. Broadus, *Preparation and Delivery of Sermons*, 368–69.
48. See Terry Johnson, *Leading in Worship* (Oak Ridge, Tenn.: Covenant Foundation, 1996), 10 n. 15, 34 n. 4, 52–54.
49. Miller, *Thoughts on Public Prayer*, 277.
50. Ibid., 277–78.
51. Richard L. Pratt, *Pray with Your Eyes Open* (Phillipsburg, N.J.: P&R Publishing, 1987); W. Graham Scroggie, *Paul's Prison Prayers* (1921; repr. Grand Rapids: Kregel, 1981); Donald Cogan, *Prayers of the New Testament* (New York: Harper & Row, 1967); and Herbert Lockyer, *All the Prayers of the Bible* (Grand Rapids: Zondervan, 1959). Thankfully, while books treating public prayers have neglected the use of Scripture language, the books on private prayer have not. Pratt's is especially good in this respect.
52. Willimon, *Preaching and Leading Worship*, 44.
53. Fairbairn, *Pastoral Theology*, 318.
54. Shedd, *Homiletics and Pastoral Theology*, 271.
55. Ibid.
56. Dabney, *Sacred Rhetoric*, 346–47, 360.
57. Ibid., 360; see also Miller, *Thoughts on Public Prayer*, 288–89.
58. Rayburn, *O Come Let Us Worship*, 199.
59. Miller, *Thoughts on Public Prayer*, 187.
60. Shedd, *Homiletics and Pastoral Theology*, 272–73.
61. Dabney, *Sacred Rhetoric*, 348.
62. Ibid., 355.
63. Shedd, *Homiletics and Pastoral Theology*, 273.
64. Murphy, *Pastoral Theology*, 211–12.
65. Shedd, *Homiletics and Pastoral Theology*, 273.
66. Dabney, *Sacred Rhetoric*, 349.
67. Spurgeon, *Lectures to My Students*, 57.
68. Ibid., 58.
69. Johnson, *Leading in Worship*, 10 n. 15, 34 n. 4, 52–54.

Chapter 8

Baptism

1. Edmund Clowney, *The Church* (Downers Grove, Ill.: InterVarsity, 1995), 278.
2. James Montgomery Boice, *Foundations of the Christian Faith* (Downers Grove, Ill.: InterVarsity, 1986), 598–600.
3. Erroll Hulse, *The Testimony of Baptism* (Haywards Heath Sussex: Carey, 1982), 108.
4. Don Whitney, *Spiritual Disciplines within the Church* (Chicago: Moody, 1996), 138.
5. Meredith G. Kline, *By Oath Consigned* (Grand Rapids: Eerdmans, 1968), 56.

6. Ibid., esp. 55–56, 65–73.

7. John Calvin, *Institutes of the Christian Religion* (2 vols.; ed. John T. McNeill; trans. Ford Lewis Battles; Philadelphia: Westminster, 1960), 2:1313–14 §4.15.13.

8. Ibid., 2:1314 §4.15.14.

9. James Montgomery Boice, *Romans* (Grand Rapids: Baker, 1991), 4:457–58.

10. Calvin, *Institutes*, 2:1277 §4.14.2.

11. *The Book of Church Order of the Presbyterian Church in America* (5th ed.; Atlanta: Office of the Stated Clerk of the General Assembly of the Presbyterian Church in America, 1998), 8–5.

12. Interview with Jim Gilmore, "No Experience Necessary," *Leadership* 22 (Summer 2001): 31.

13. James Emery White, "Gateway Country," *Leadership* 22 (Summer 2001): 35–39, quotation at 37.

14. Joseph Campbell, *Myths to Live By* (New York: Bantam, 1972), 98–99 (final ellipsis dots in original).

15. Paul R. Gilchrist, ed., *PCA Digest Position Papers, 1973–1993* (Atlanta: Presbyterian Church in America, 1993), 78–97.

Chapter 9

The Lord's Supper

1. Benjamin B. Warfield, "The Fundamental Significance of the Lord's Supper," in *Shorter Writings of B. B. Warfield* (Nutley, N.J.: P&R Publishing, 1970), 1:332.

2. Ibid., 333.

3. Hughes Oliphant Old, *Worship That Is Reformed according to Scripture* (Atlanta: John Knox, 1984), 106.

4. Charles Hodge, *Systematic Theology* (repr. Grand Rapids: Eerdmans, 1993), 3:622.

5. Louis Berkhof, *Systematic Theology* (Grand Rapids: Eerdmans, 1939), 650.

6. Warfield, "Fundamental Significance of the Lord's Supper," 334.

7. Berkhof, *Systematic Theology*, 650.

8. Old, *Worship*, 108.

9. John Murray, *Collected Writings of John Murray* (Carlisle, Pa.: Banner of Truth, 1977), 2.377.

10. Berkhof, *Systematic Theology*, 651.

11. Hodge, *Systematic Theology*, 3.628.

12. John Calvin, *Institutes of the Christian Religion* (2 vols.; ed. John T. McNeill; trans. Ford Lewis Battles; Philadelphia: Westminster, 1960), 2:1364–65 §4.17.5.

13. Berkhof, *Systematic Theology*, 652.

14. David B. Currie, *Born Fundamentalist, Born Again Catholic* (San Francisco: Ignatius, 1996), 40.

15. *Catechism of the Catholic Church* (New York: Doubleday, 1995), 1413.

16. Berkhof, *Systematic Theology*, 652.

17. R. L. Dabney, *Systematic Theology* (repr. Carlisle, Pa.: Banner of Truth, 1985), 804–5.

18. Ibid.

19. Calvin, *Institutes*, 2:1382 §4.17.19.

20. Berkhof, *Systematic Theology*, 653.

21. Hodge, *Systematic Theology*, 3:837–38.

22. Old, *Worship*, 134.

23. Berkhof, *Systematic Theology*, 655.

24. *Catechism of the Catholic Church*, 1366–67.

25. Ibid., 1415.

26. Hodge, *Systematic Theology*, 3:499–500.

27. A. A. Hodge, *The Confession of Faith* (repr. Carlisle, Pa.: Banner of Truth, 1958), 362–63.

28. Dabney, *Systematic Theology*, 811.

29. Francis Turretin, *Institutes of Elenctic Theology* (3 vols.; ed. James T. Dennison Jr.; trans. George M. Giger; Phillipsburg, N.J.: P&R Publishing, 1992, 1994, 1997), 3:518 §19.28.

30. Berkhof, *Systematic Theology*, 618–19.

31. Hodge, *Systematic Theology*, 3:516.

32. W. Robert Godfrey, "Calvin on the Eucharist," *Modern Reformation* 6.3 (May/June 1997): 50.

33. Murray, *Collected Writings*, 3:275.

34. Ibid., 2:381.

35. Calvin, *Institutes*, 2:1422. §4.17.44.

36. Berkhof, *Systematic Theology*, 656.

37. Michael S. Horton, "Mysteries of God and Means of Grace," *Modern Reformation* 6.3 (May/June 1997): 13.

38. Calvin, *Institutes*, 2:1418–19 §4.17.41–42.

39. Ibid., 2:1420 §4.17.42.

40. Ibid., 2:1422 §4.17.44.

41. Ibid., 2:1424 §4.17.46.

Chapter 10
Hymnody in a Post-Hymnody World

1. Donald P. Hustad, *True Worship: Reclaiming the Wonder and Majesty* (Wheaton, Ill.: Shaw, 1998), 101.

2. Hughes Oliphant Old, *Worship That Is Reformed according to Scripture* (Atlanta: John Knox, 1984), 39.

3. We shall not distinguish between psalm, hymn, and spiritual song (an idea that is explored by theologians and other authors). A case can be made that these three names identify (a) different types of canonical psalms or (b) different types of musico-poetic

forms (like psalms, hymns, and choruses; or psalms, canticles, and odes; or canonical psalms, inspired hymns, and extemporaneous songs). See also note 4. Of interest, at least, is the distinction that the Greek words *adō* and *psallō* provide for "singing" and "making melody in your hearts." Col. 3:16 uses only *adō*; both verbs are used in Eph. 5:19; and the noun *psalmos* also appears in both passages. *Adō* means "to produce music with the voice." So, Paul in Ephesians is saying "speaking to yourselves in *psalmos* and hymns and spiritual songs, *adō* and *psallō* in/with your hearts to the Lord." The preposition before *psalmos* can be translated "in" or "with." This music is not necessarily silent (as in "humming to oneself"), but could mean "with one's whole being." Since *psallō* is related to a word for playing a plucked, string instrument (like a harp) and since Paul chooses to use both *adō* and *psallō*, one could infer that both voices and instruments in worship find support here.

4. See the pamphlet by Anthony Cowley and Randy W. Harris, "A Diagram Defense of Psalmody" (Elkins Park, Pa.: Covenanter Reformation, 1993). The authors also argue that "psalms, hymns, and songs" are all modified by the adjective *pneumatikais* (spiritual), which suggests that these songs are given directly by the Holy Spirit or, in other words, can refer only to inspired psalms.

5. Wesley W. Isenberg, "Hymnody: New Testament," in *Key Words in Church Music* (ed. Carl Schalk; St. Louis: Concordia, 1978), 181.

6. Hughes Oliphant Old, "The Psalms of Praise in the Worship of the New Testament Church," *Interpretation* 39 (1985): 32.

7. Old, *Worship*, 44.

8. Ralph P. Martin, "Hymns in the New Testament: An Evolving Pattern of Worship Responses," *Ex auditu* 8 (1992): 34–42. (These are two lines from the *Te deum laudamus*, not the complete text.)

9. Horton Davies, *The Worship of the English Puritans* (Morgan, Pa.: Soli Deo Gloria, 1997), 176.

10. Isaac Watts, "The Psalms of David Imitated in the Language of the New Testament and Applied to the Christian State and Worship," quoted in Davies, *Worship of the English Puritans*, 178.

11. See Hughes Oliphant Old, *Themes and Variations for a Christian Doxology* (Grand Rapids: Eerdmans, 1992). Old believes that doxology is the theology of worship and that the Old Testament sounds five musical themes that are fully developed in the New Testament: epiclectic, kerygmatic, wisdom, prophetic, and covenantal doxology.

12. James Montgomery Boice, *Romans: An Expositional Commentary*, vol. 3: *God and History* (Grand Rapids: Baker, 1993), 1410, 1466.

13. Old, *Worship*, 32.

14. Paul Westermeyer, *Te Deum: The Church and Music* (Minneapolis: Augsburg Fortress, 1998), 141.

15. Calvin's preference for exclusive psalmody was just that, a preference, to which he appealed not to Scripture but to John Chrysostom and Augustine for defense (see Old's chapter "The Ministry of Praise" in *Worship*). However, lest one come to believe that no significant music of the Renaissance or Baroque church was produced in Reformed

countries, it should be noted that an important group of French composers was involved in this activity. These composers imported monophonic chants from the *Genevan Psalter* to create polyphonic and other harmonized settings of the psalms, which were then widely published and sung in France and other francophone countries. Clément Marot wrote some of the finest of the metrical psalm texts, and Calvin secured the assistance of some excellent composers, among them Louis Bourgeois, Claude Goudimel, Claudin Le Jeune, and others.

16. Quoted from *Liturgy and Hymns* (ed. and trans. Ulrich S. Leupold; Luther's Works: American Edition 53; Philadelphia: Fortress, 1965), 321–24.

17. Luther's foreword to the first edition of Johann Walter's hymnal: *Wittenberg Geystliches gesangk Buchleyn* (1524).

18. Leonard R. Payton, *Reforming Our Worship Music* (Wheaton, Ill.: Crossway, 1999), 21.

19. Roland H. Bainton, *Here I Stand: A Life of Martin Luther* (Nashville: Abingdon, 1977), 269.

20. James Montgomery Boice, "The Worship of the Elders—Rev. 4:9–11," sermon 14 in a series of 17 sermons on Revelation, preached at Tenth Presbyterian Church (Spring 2000), 1–2.

21. James Montgomery Boice and Paul Steven Jones, *Hymns for a Modern Reformation* (Philadelphia: Tenth Presbyterian Church, 2000), 24, with quotations from James Montgomery Boice, *Ephesians: An Expositional Commentary* (rev. ed.; Grand Rapids: Baker, 1997), 54, 57, 68, 74.

22. James Montgomery Boice, "Soli Deo Gloria—Rev. 1:5–7," sermon 3 in a series of 17 sermons on Revelation, preached at Tenth Presbyterian Church (Spring 2000), 12.

23. Martin Luther, "Preface to the Burial Hymns (1542)," in *Liturgy and Hymns* (ed. and trans. Ulrich S. Leupold; Luther's Works: American Edition 53; Philadelphia: Fortress, 1965), 328 (emphasis original).

24. Westermeyer, *Te Deum*, 144–46.

25. Luther's foreword to Walter's *Wittenberg Geystliches gesangk Buchleyn* (1524).

26. James Montgomery Boice, *Psalms: An Expositional Commentary* (Grand Rapids: Baker, 1994), 1:79.

27. Davies, *Worship of the English Puritans*, 179.

28. Psalms 78, 105, and 136 come to mind. This was a form of instruction as well as worship, particularly tied in with the Wisdom literature of the Old Testament. The Jewish feast of Passover and other high holy days also featured the use of songs in the celebration of deliverance and as reminder of God's works. In addition, the 288 Levites set apart because of their special musical abilities were teachers of the other 3,712, who in turn taught their own sons and daughters.

29. Quoted from *Selected Pauline Epistles I* (ed. and trans. Jaroslav Pelikan; Luther's Works: American Edition 28; Philadelphia: Fortress, 1955–86), 213. See also Carl F. Schalk, *Luther on Music: Paradigms of Praise* (St. Louis: Concordia, 1988), 39.

30. Luther's foreword to Walter's *Wittenberg Geystliches gesangk Buchleyn* (1524).

31. Quoted from *Selected Psalms III* (ed. and trans. Jaroslav Pelikan; Luther's Works: American Edition 14; Philadelphia: Fortress, 1955–86), 81 (emphasis original).

32. The rhyme scheme that Boice fashioned for this hymn interlocks, with the B rhyme in each six-line stanza (AAB-AAB) becoming the A rhyme of the following stanza. For example, "plan" and "man" of stanza 1 lead to "began," "plan," "man," and "can" in stanza 2. This is consistent through all four strophes, resulting in a chain-link poetic form that mirrors the interlocking doctrines of the *ordo salutis* (salvation order) found in Rom. 8:28–31.

33. The New International Version uses the personal pronoun *my* before *mind* and *spirit*; this word, however, is not in the Greek, as it is in 14:14. Paul distinguishes between his own spirit and the Holy Spirit in 5:4, for example.

34. Watts, "Psalms of David," quoted in Davies, *Worship of the English Puritans,* 177.

35. Hughes Oliphant Old, *Leading in Prayer: A Workbook for Worship* (Grand Rapids: Eerdmans, 1995), 321.

36. Many modern hymnals are now published with a companion volume that provides information about the author, composer, text, or tune. John Julian's two-volume *Dictionary of Hymnody* (New York: Dover, 1957) is essential in any church musician's library, as are books of hymn stories. It is also helpful for ministers and music directors to own a collection of twenty to thirty hymnals spanning one's own and other denominations as reference and resource material.

Chapter 11

Restoring Psalm Singing to Our Worship

1. The wording of the New American Standard Bible is slightly modified for phrasing.

2. *Trinity Psalter* and *Trinity Psalter Music Edition* (Pittsburgh: Crown & Covenant, 1994, 2000); "Psalms of the Trinity Psalter" 1 and 2 (Savannah, Ga.: IPC, 1999, 2002).

3. James Montgomery Boice, "Reformation in Doctrine, Worship, and Life," in *Here We Stand! A Call from Confessing Evangelicals* (ed. James Montgomery Boice and Benjamin E. Sasse; Grand Rapids: Baker, 1996), 187.

4. James Montgomery Boice, *Whatever Happened to the Gospel of Grace? Recovering the Doctrines That Shook the World* (Wheaton, Ill.: Crossway, 2001), 181 (emphasis added).

5. Dietrich Bonhoeffer, *The Psalms: Prayer Book of the Bible* (Oxford: Oxford University Press, 1982).

6. Paul Westermeyer, *Te Deum: The Church and Music* (Minneapolis: Fortress, 1998), 24.

7. Matthew Henry, *An Exposition of the Old and New Testament* (Philadelphia: Tavar & Hogan, 1829), 3:196.

8. Quoted in Michael Bushell, *The Songs of Zion: A Contemporary Case for Exclusive Psalmody* (Pittsburgh: Crown & Covenant, 1980), 18.

9. Quoted in John McNaugher, *The Psalms in Worship* (1907; repr. Edmonton, Canada: Still Water Revival Books, 1992), 489.

10. Quoted in Bushell, *Songs of Zion,* 23.

11. Henry, *Exposition of the Old and New Testament.* Given this christological completeness of the Psalms, one wonders about the claim of Isaac Watts that he was seeking to "Christianize" the Psalms in his *Psalms of David Imitated.*

12. Quoted in Bushell, *Songs of Zion*, 18.
13. "Preface to the Psalter" (1528); cf. Bushell, *Songs of Zion*, 17.
14. John Calvin, *Commentary on the Book of Psalms* (trans. James Anderson; Edinburgh: Calvin Translation Society, 1845), 1.xxviii.
15. Quoted in Bushell, *Songs of Zion*, 166.
16. Hughes Oliphant Old, "The Psalms as Christian Prayer: A Preface to the Liturgical Use of the Psalter" (unpublished, 1978).
17. Since the work of Herman Gunkel, modern scholars (e.g., Mowinckel, Noth, Weiser, von Rad, A. R. Johnson, G. W. Anderson) have emphasized the cult or public worship as the setting of the Psalms.
18. Hughes Oliphant Old, *Worship That Is Reformed according to Scripture* (Atlanta: John Knox, 1984), 44.
19. William L. Holladay, *The Psalms through Three Thousand Years: Prayerbook of a Cloud of Witnesses* (Minneapolis: Fortress, 1993), 115.
20. R. E. O. White, "Psalms," in *Evangelical Commentary on the Bible* (ed. Walter A. Elwell; Grand Rapids: Baker, 1989), 373.
21. Holladay, *Psalms through Three Thousand Years*, 162–65, notes that 1 Clement (ca. 96) has forty-nine citations from thirty-two psalms; Barnabas (ca. 130) has twelve citations from ten psalms; Didache (second century) has three citations from three psalms; Ignatius of Antioch (ca. 98–117) and Polycarp (fl. ca. 175–ca. 195) make virtually no reference to the Psalms, but Justin Martyr's writings (ca. 150) are loaded with citations from the Psalms (e.g., *Dialogue with Trypho* has forty-seven references from twenty-four psalms), as are those of Irenaeus (ca. 70–155/160).
22. Quoted in McNaugher, *Psalms in Worship*, 550.
23. Quoted in J. G. Davies, *The New Westminster Dictionary of Liturgy and Worship* (Philadelphia: Westminster, 1986), 451.
24. Quoted in McNaugher, *Psalms in Worship*, 550.
25. Quoted in ibid., 504.
26. Quoted in ibid., 166, 504.
27. Quoted in ibid., 170.
28. Quoted in ibid., 550.
29. Mary Berry, in *The New Westminster Dictionary of Liturgy and Worship* (ed. J. G. Davies; Philadelphia: Westminster, 1986), 450.
30. J. A. Motyer, "The Psalms," in *The New Bible Commentary* (rev. ed.; ed. D. Guthrie, J. A. Motyer, et al.; Grand Rapids: Eerdmans, 1970), 446.
31. J. D. Douglas et al., *The New Bible Dictionary* (Leicester: Inter-Varsity, 1962), 1059.
32. Westermeyer, *Te Deum*, 25.
33. C. S. Lewis, *Reflections on the Psalms* (London: Bles, 1958), 2. "The Psalms were written to be sung, not just read. To sing them is to honor God's intention in giving them to us"; Lawrence C. Roff, *Let Us Sing: Worshiping God with Our Music* (Norcross, Ga.: Great Commission, 1991), 65.
34. McNaugher, *Psalms in Worship*, 40.
35. Ibid., 40.

36. Carson Holloway, *All Shook Up: Music, Passion, and Politics* (Dallas: Spence, 2001), 6.
37. Quoted in ibid., 24.
38. Quoted in ibid., 3.
39. The following quotations are taken from Calvin's "Preface to the Psalter" (1543); see *Les Pseaumes mis en rime françoise par Clément Marot et Théodore de Béze; Mis en musique a quatre parties par Claude Goudimel; Par les héritiers de Francois Jacqui* (1565; facsimile repr. ed. Pierre Pidoux and Konrad Ameln under the auspices of La société des concerts de la cathédrale de lausanne; Kassel: Baeroenreiter-Verlag, 1935 (information taken from the Blue Banner website: *http://www.fpcr.org/blue%5Fbaner%5Farticles/calvinps.htm*).
40. Secular observers do not fail to see the connections. In addition to Holloway's *All Shook Up*, see Allan Bloom, *The Closing of the American Mind* (New York: Simon & Schuster, 1987); and Robert Pattison, *The Triumph of Vulgarity: Rock Music in the Mirror of Romanticism* (New York: Oxford University Press, 1987).
41. Among those who raise concerns are John Blanchard, Peter Anderson, and Derek Cleave, *Pop Goes the Gospel: Rock in the Church* (Darlington, England: Evangelical Press, 1989); Calvin Johansson, *Discipling Music Ministry: Twenty-first Century Directions* (Peabody, Mass.: Hendrickson, 1992); John Makujina, *Measuring the Music: Another Look at the Contemporary Christian Music Debate* (Salem, Ohio: Schmul, 2000); and Kenneth A. Myers, *All God's Children and Blue Suede Shoes* (Wheaton, Ill.: Crossway, 1987).
42. I attempt to develop this theme in *Reformed Worship: Worship That Is according to Scripture* (Greenville, S.C.: Reformed Academic Press, 2000), 32–38.
43. John D. Witvliet, "The Spirituality of the Psalter: Metrical Psalms in Liturgy and Life in Calvin's Geneva," *Calvin Theological Journal* 32 (1997): 296.
44. Old, "Psalms as Christian Prayer."
45. The Presbyterian Church of America at its 21st General Assembly (1993) recommended "that congregations be encouraged to sing at least one Psalm at each of their services."
46. John D. Witvliet, "On Durable Music, the Ten Commandments, and Palm-Passion Sunday," *Reformed Worship* 58 (Dec. 2000): 43.
47. Quoted in Westermeyer, *Te Deum*, 89.
48. Quoted in ibid., 88.
49. Witvliet, "On Durable Music," 43.
50. *The Hymnal for Worship and Celebration* (Waco: Word, 1986) has two; *The Worshiping Church: A Hymnal* (Carol Stream, Ill.: Hope, 1990) has nine.
51. Leonard R. Payton, *Reforming Our Worship Music* (Wheaton, Ill.: Crossway, 1999), 36.
52. Quoted in Millar Patrick, *Four Centuries of Scottish Psalmody* (London: Oxford University Press, 1949), 213–14.
53. Ibid., 225.
54. Ibid., 226. Patrick sites for support even modernist Old Testament theologian W. Robertson Smith who said, "As the Old Testament Church left for our guidance a perfect

model of a childlike faith and devotion . . . it is essential that this model should be kept in all its simplicity. Every artificial touch, every trace of modern taste must be avoided. . . . A translation of the psalms for devotional use must be, above all things, simple, even naïve" (226).

55. Witvliet, "Spirituality of the Psalter," 284.

56. The article entitled "Chants" in *The Dictionary of Worship and Liturgy* (ed. J. D. Davis; Philadelphia: Westminster Press, 1986) reads like an essay on why chanting never caught on in any popular sense. Restoration chants "tend to discourage congregational participation." Nineteenth-century chant was "extremely haphazard." Today, in spite of efforts at simplification, "most congregations still find themselves at a disadvantage in singing prose psalms" (159). The article on "Psalmody" concurs, stating that most of the chanting heard today is "expertly rendered by specialist choirs" (451).

57. A similar discussion may arise as rapping inevitably works its way into evangelical worship services. Is rapping singing? This is not to say that chanting is medieval rap. Rap has the advantage of rhyme. Chant has the advantage of textual coherence. But both are sufficiently unlike ordinary singing to have earned different labels, hence "rap" or "chant."

58. Louis F. Benson, "John Calvin and the Psalmody of the Reformed Churches," *Journal of the Presbyterian Historical Society* 5 (1909): 1–21, 55–87, 107–18.

59. Ibid., 57.

60. Ibid., 67.

61. Ibid., 69.

62. Ibid., 71. There were fifteen editions of the *Genevan Psalter* in 1563, eleven in 1564, and thirteen in 1565—for a total of sixty-four editions in the first four years of publication. Witvliet cites with approval the description of the rapidly selling psalter as "the most gigantic enterprise ever undertaken in publishing until then" ("Spirituality of the Psalter," 274).

63. Frank A. James III, "Calvin the Evangelist" in *RTS: Reformed Quarterly* (Fall 2001): 8; W. Sanford Reid, ed., *John Calvin: His Influence in the Western World* (Grand Rapids: Zondervan, 1982), 77.

64. Witvliet, "Spirituality of the Psalter," 296.

65. Cited in ibid., 297.

66. Ibid., 296.

67. Benson, "John Calvin and the Psalmody," 77–78. All of the following quotations by Benson are from p. 73.

68. All quotations in this and the next paragraph are from Patrick, *Four Centuries of Scottish Psalmody,* 115–16.

69. Boice, "Reformation in Doctrine, Worship, and Life," 187.

Chapter 12
Private Worship

1. David Clarkson, *The Works of David Clarkson* (London: Nichol, 1864; repr. Edinburgh: Banner of Truth, 1988), 3:187–209.

2. Donald S. Whitney, *Spiritual Disciplines for the Christian Life* (Colorado Springs: NavPress, 1991), 86–86, 90; idem, *Spiritual Disciplines within the Church* (Chicago: Moody, 1996), 75–87.

3. Geoffrey Thomas, "Worship in Spirit," *Banner of Truth* 287 (Aug./Sept. 1987): 8.

4. A. W. Tozer, "You Can't Elect to Worship God on Just One Day of the Week," in *The Tozer Pulpit* (Camp Hill, Pa.: Christian Publications, 1994), 1:51.

5. Matthew Henry, *Commentary on the Whole Bible* (Old Tappan, N.J.: Revell, n.d.), 1:427.

6. Ewald M. Plass, comp., *What Luther Says* (St. Louis: Concordia, 1959), 1083.

7. Lewis Bayly, *The Practice of Piety* (London: Hamilton, Adams, 1842; repr. Morgan, Pa.: Soli Deo Gloria, 1995), 102.

8. Iain Murray, *Jonathan Edwards: A New Biography* (Edinburgh: Banner of Truth, 1987), 142.

9. Jonathan Edwards, *The Works of Jonathan Edwards* (gen. ed. Perry Miller), vol. 2: *Religious Affections* (ed. John E. Smith; New Haven, Conn.: Yale University Press, 1959), 374, 376.

10. George Müller, *Spiritual Secrets of George Müller* (ed. Roger Steer; Wheaton, Ill.: Shaw, 1985), 62–63.

11. C. H. Spurgeon, *C. H. Spurgeon's Autobiography* (comp. Susie Spurgeon and J. W. Harrald; London: Passmore & Alabaster, 1897; repr. Pasadena, Tex.: Pilgrim, 1992), 1:161.

12. C. H. Spurgeon, "A Pressed Man Yielding to Christ," in *Metropolitan Tabernacle Pulpit* (London: Passmore & Alabaster, 1901; repr. Pasadena, Tex.: Pilgrim, 1977), 46:142.

13. Sally Magnusson, *The Flying Scotsman* (New York: Quartet, 1981), 104, 138.

14. Iain Murray, *D. Martyn Lloyd-Jones: The Fight of Faith, 1939–1981* (Edinburgh: Banner of Truth, 1990), 763.

15. John White, "Private Devotions: Why?" *Decision* (January 1980): 5.

16. Murray, *Jonathan Edwards*, 143.

17. I explain most of these at greater length in my *Spiritual Disciplines for the Christian Life*, chaps. 3–4.

18. For more see my *Spiritual Disciplines for the Christian Life*, chap. 11: "Journaling . . . for the Purpose of Godliness."

19. Murray, *Jonathan Edwards*, 100.

20. Roger Steer, ed., *The George Müller Treasury* (Westchester, Ill.: Crossway, 1987), 66.

21. Stephen Charnock, *The Existence and Attributes of God* (repr. Grand Rapids: Baker, 1979), 1:225–26.

22. Maurice Roberts, "On Seeking God," *Banner of Truth* 441 (June 2000): 2.

23. Ibid., 3.

24. Nancy DeMoss, "Stop! I Want to Get Off," *Spirit of Revival* 31.1 (Aug. 2000): 9.

Chapter 13

A Call to Family Worship

1. Excellent helps on the subject of family worship are Jerry Marcellino, *Rediscovering the Lost Treasure of Family Worship* (Laurel, Miss.: Audubon Press, 1996); Terry Johnson, *Family Worship Book* (Ross-shire, UK: Christian Focus, 1998); and Douglas F. Kelly, "Family Worship: Biblical, Reformed, and Viable for Today," in *Worship in the Presence of God* (ed. David Lachman and Frank J. Smith; Greenville, S.C.: Greenville Seminary Press, 1992), 103–29. A number of classic works have been reprinted: Cotton Mather, *A Family Well-Ordered* (Morgan, Pa.: Soli Deo Gloria, 2001); J. W. Alexander, *Thoughts on Family Worship* (Harrisonburg, Va.: Sprinkle, 1981); and B. M. Palmer, *Family in Its Civil and Churchly Aspects* (Harrisonburg, Va.: Sprinkle, 1981). See also Kerry Ptacek, *Family Worship* (Greenville, S.C.: Southern Presbyterian Press, 1994) for an annotated version of the old Westminster Directory of Worship.
2. Marcellino, *Rediscovering the Lost Treasure of Family Worship*, 11–12.
3. See Johnson, *Family Worship Book*, especially the superb historical resources that he provides, including the great Thomas Manton's famous letter to the readers of the Westminster Confession and catechisms and the Westminster Directory for Family Worship.
4. In the following section we are not promoting congregationalism as a form of government, though what we advocate by the phrase "congregational Christianity" should draw complete agreement from those committed to that church order. Rather, we mean, precisely, that Jesus' intention was for his disciples to be nurtured in the context of a healthy local church. This is, explicitly, at least part of what the Great Commission means by "baptizing and teaching" the disciples that are made among the nations. Jesus is saying, in effect, "nurture these converts by word and sacrament into growing disciples in the context of a mutually accountable local gathering of believers." Personal Christianity is to grow in the nursery of congregational Christianity. So when we speak of the renewal of congregational Christianity, we are acknowledging that our individualized Western Christianity needs to be "recongregationalized."
5. Hughes Oliphant Old, *Worship That Is Reformed according to Scripture* (Atlanta: John Knox Press, 1984), 37.
6. See Douglas F. Kelly, "The Westminster Shorter Catechism," in *To Glorify and Enjoy God: A Commemoration of the 350th Anniversary of the Westminster Assembly* (ed. John L. Carson and David W. Hall; Edinburgh: Banner of Truth, 1994), 101–26, esp. 123–25, for his comments, referenced here and above, on the impact of memorization of the catechism.

Chapter 14

Worship in All of Life

1. Dale McConkey, "Whither Hunter's Culture War? Shifts in Evangelical Morality, 1988–1998," *Sociology of Religion* 62.2 (Summer 2001): 168–69.

2. Paul M. Weyrich, "A Moral Minority?" *Free Congress Foundation* (Feb. 16, 1999): 1.

3. This view is well described in the *Public Justice Report* 22.2 (1999): 11.

4. This is contrary to the received wisdom that identifies withdrawal as otherworldly. See Dick Keyes, *Chameleon Christianity: Moving Beyond Safety and Conformity* (Grand Rapids: Baker, 1999), 15–22.

5. David Inge, quoted in Peter L. Berger, *A Rumor of Angels* (New York: Anchor Books, 1990), 25.

6. John Murray, *The Epistle to the Romans* (New International Commentary on the New Testament; Grand Rapids: Eerdmans, 1965), 2:114.

7. H. Richard Niebuhr, *Christ and Culture* (New York: Harper & Row, 1951), 190–229.

8. Stanley Hauerwas, "The Church and Liberal Democracy: The Moral Limits of a Secular Polity," in Hauerwas's *Community of Character: Toward a Constructive Christian Social Ethic* (Notre Dame: University of Notre Dame Press, 1981), 73–74.

9. Herman Ridderbos, *Paul: An Outline of His Theology* (trans. John R. De Witt; Grand Rapids: Eerdmans, 1975), 435 (emphasis added).

Chapter 15

Worship and the Emotions

1. Edith Blumhofer, *Aimee Semple McPherson: Everybody's Sister* (Grand Rapids: Eerdmans, 1993), 229.

2. Ibid., 227–28.

3. John Calvin, *Institutes of the Christian Religion* (2 vols.; ed. John T. McNeill; trans. Ford Lewis Battles; Philadelphia: Westminster, 1960), 1:589 §3.2.41.

4. John Calvin, *Commentary on the Book of Psalms* (Grand Rapids: Baker, 1979), 1.380.

5. Ibid., 1:126.

6. Calvin, *Institutes*, 1:43 §1.2.2.

7. Richard Sibbes, *Works of Richard Sibbes* (repr. Edinburgh: Banner of Truth, 1977), 5:71.

8. Canons of Dort 3-4.1. We can see a similar use of this anthropology in Francis Turretin, *Institutes of Elenctic Theology* (3 vols.; ed. James T. Dennison Jr.; trans. George M. Giger; Phillipsburg, N.J.: P&R Publishing, 1992, 1994, 1997), 2:547 §15.6.6: "The question is not, whether grace is resistible in respect of the intellect or affections; for the Arminians confess that the intellect of man is irresistibly enlightened, and his affections irresistibly excited, and affected with the sense of grace. But it is treated of the will alone, which they maintain is always moved resistibly, so that its assent remains always free."

9. Calvin, *Institutes*, 1:194 §1.15.7.

10. Ibid., 1:193 §1.15.6.

11. Ibid., 1:688 §3.6.4.

12. Jonathan Edwards, *The Works of Jonathan Edwards* (gen. ed. Perry Miller), vol. 2: *Religious Affections* (ed. John E. Smith; New Haven, Conn.: Yale University Press, 1959), 100.

13. J. C. Ryle, *Old Paths* (repr. London: Clarke, 1972), 341.

14. Puritan William Bridge provides one example of writing specifically on the affections in his brief work "Affections Rightly Placed," in *The Works of the Reverend William Bridge* (repr. Beaver Falls, Pa.: Soli Deo Gloria, 1989), 5:61. He presents the affections as the product of the heart: "Where our heart is, there our affections will be, for affections are the issues of the heart." He also relates the affections to certain actions of the intellect and will: "Every act of the understanding and will is not an affection. But when the soul of man doth sensibly move, or is sensibly carried out unto good or evil, then it is said to be affected."

15. Edwards, *Religious Affections*, 95 (emphasis added).

16. Ibid., 102.

17. Ibid., 96–97 (emphasis original).

18. Ibid., 96.

19. Ibid., 222.

20. Ibid., 458.

21. See, e.g., ibid., 175–81.

22. Calvin, *Institutes*, 1:551 §3.2.7.

23. Ibid., 1:581 §3.2.33.

24. Ibid., 1:552 §3.2.8.

25. Ibid., 1:580–81 §3.2.33.

26. Ibid., 1:583–84 §3.2.36.

27. Ibid., 1:589 §3.2.41.

28. Ibid., 1:593 §3.3.1.

29. Turretin, *Institutes of Elenctic Theology*, 2:559 §15.7.2. After discussing various essential acts of faith, Turretin relates those acts to the intellect and will: they "have their seat partly in the intellect, partly in the will: in the intellect, the act of knowledge and assent which, although required in faith, do not as yet constitute its formal act (which properly consists in persuasion, which belongs to the intellect); in the will, refuge and reception or adhesion" (2:564 §15.8.12).

30. Calvin, *Institutes*, 1:548 §3.2.6.

31. Ibid., 1:549 §3.2.6.

32. Quoted in Leslie A. Rawlinson, "Worship in Liturgy and Form," in *Anglican and Puritan Thinking* (by Hywel R. Jones et al.; London: Westminster Conference, 1977), 86.

33. Charles G. Finney, *Lectures on Revivals* (Old Tappan, N.J.: Fleming H. Revell, n.d.), 1–2.

34. Ibid., 4.

35. Ibid.

36. Ibid., 5.

37. Grant Wacker, *Heaven Below: Early Pentecostals and American Culture* (Cambridge: Harvard University Press, 2001), 109.

38. Charles H. Kraft, "The Hymnal Is Not Enough," *Christianity Today* (April 7, 1989): 8.

39. Quoted in Ernest Trice Thompson, *Presbyterians in the South* (Richmond: John Knox, 1973), 2:430.
40. Quoted in Rawlinson, "Worship in Liturgy and Form," 86.

Chapter 16
Worship through the Ages

1. However, one of the greatest patristic hymns, the *Gloria in excelsis*, dates from the second or third century.
2. In a writing traditionally ascribed to Justin Martyr, but probably by Theodoret of Cyrrhus, an eminent church father who lived in the early fifth century, we find the following typical statement: "Question: If songs were invented by unbelievers with a purpose of deceiving (Gen. 4:21), and were appointed under the Jewish law because of the childishness of their minds, why do Christians who have received the perfect teachings of grace (which are quite contrary to pagan and Jewish customs) still sing in the churches, like the Jews who were children under the law? Answer: Simple singing is not childish. What is childish is singing with lifeless organs, dancing, cymbals, etc. Therefore we Christians put aside the use of such instruments and other things fit for children, and we retain only simple singing."
3. A deacon gave the readings. In larger congregations, the deacon chanted the Scripture passage rather than simply read it—a practice probably derived from Jewish synagogue worship.
4. This pattern of three readings—Old Testament, epistle, and gospel—goes back to the earliest times. From the third century, lectionaries were drawn up that specified exactly which passages of Scripture should be read on each Sunday of the year.
5. Sitting was the accepted posture for preaching and teaching in the early church. See Matthew 5:1–2; Luke 4:20–21; 5:3; John 8:2; Acts 16:13.
6. This system of prayer is known as "bidding prayers."
7. This is a reference to the entire congregation as priests.
8. This is a reference to the gifts of bread and wine brought by the whole church to Communion and laid on the Lord's Table.
9. In the East, January 6 was for some time the preferred date for celebrating Christ's birth, but in 379 Gregory of Nazianzus introduced the Western date in Constantinople when he was bishop there. Still, it was not until 431 that Egypt accepted December 25 as the date of Christmas; Palestinian Christians did not accept it until the sixth century; and the Armenian church celebrates Christmas on January 6 to this day.
10. It is more accurate to say that most Western medieval clergy did not preach their *own* sermons; but this did not necessarily mean they preached nothing at all. For this was the period in which homilies achieved great prominence in the church's worship. A homily was a sermon written by someone else and read out to the congregation by the priest. The practice had already sprung up by the fifth century, but in the eighth and ninth centuries it became a normal and widespread factor in preaching. Collections

of homilies were based on the church lectionary, the fixed system of Bible readings for each Sunday in the year.

11. The only place in the West that resisted this development, and where lay Communion continued to be frequent until the later Middle Ages, was Rome itself. Weekly lay Communion continued to be the normal practice in the East.

12. Pope Urban IV (1261–64) established the Corpus Christi festival in 1264 in honor of a Communion wafer that allegedly shed blood in Bolsena, near Rome.

13. Rich people often left legacies in their wills to pay for priests to say masses for their departed souls in order to secure for them a swifter release from purgatory. Masses for the dead were called requiem masses, from the Latin prayer *requiem in pace* (may he rest in peace).

14. Some historians think that the organ may have been introduced into Western worship slightly earlier, in Rome itself, by Pope Vitalian (pope from 657 to 672).

15. In the nineteenth century, a few Greek Orthodox congregations in Western Europe introduced organs. In the twentieth century, some Greek Orthodox congregations in America also installed organs. This is exceptional in Eastern Orthodoxy, and traditional Orthodox strongly condemn it as a betrayal of the ancient apostolic practice.

16. Apart from Luther, important Lutheran hymn writers include Melanchthon, Lazarus Spengler (1479–1534), Paul Speratus (1484–1551), Johann Walter (1496–1570), who also composed music, and Elizabeth Cruciger, wife of Wittenberg theologian Caspar Cruciger.

17. Zwingli loved music so much that his Roman Catholic foes sneered at him as "the guitar player" and "the evangelist-on-the-flute."

18. For a masterly survey of the evidence, see Hughes Oliphant Old, *The Patristic Roots of Reformed Worship* (Zurich: Theologischer Verlag, 1970). Arguably the Anglican Reformers, aided by Bucer during the reign of Edward VI (Bucer spent the last portion of his life in England), constructed the most self-consciously patristic form of worship, albeit with some hefty doses of medievalism.

19. People often think that Calvin wished Christians to sing only psalms in worship. This is not true, as we have seen; he was quite happy that other suitable things should be used: the *Nunc dimittis*, the Ten Commandments, the Apostles' Creed. But he clearly thought that nothing could surpass psalms for spiritual beauty in the church's public praise.

20. This Reformed opposition to musical instruments was a classic example of repristinating patristic forms.

21. We find a striking feature of Calvin's Strasbourg liturgy in the words of absolution spoken by the minister after the confession of sin. This was an important element in Calvin's conception of worship. It consisted of a declaration by the minister that the sins of the penitent congregation had been forgiven by God for Christ's sake. This *declaration* by the minister that *God* had forgiven his people was quite different from the Roman Catholic idea of absolution, in which the priest actually (allegedly) conferred forgiveness on the sinner. The declaration of absolution in Calvin's Strasbourg liturgy was adopted by the English Reformers and placed in the Anglican Book of Common Prayer.

Calvin was quite upset when he could not persuade the Genevan church to adopt a formula for absolution in its liturgy and wrote a letter expressing the thinking behind his concept of Protestant absolution: "We must all acknowledge it to be very useful that after the general confession, some striking promise of Scripture should follow, by which sinners might be raised to hopes of pardon and reconciliation. I would have introduced this practice [in Geneva] from the beginning, but some feared that its novelty might give offence. I was too quick to yield to them, so that the absolution was omitted. Now it is no longer opportune to make any change, because the majority of our people begin to get up [off their knees] before we come to the end of the confession" (Charles Baird, *A Chapter on Liturgies* [London: Knight & son, 1856], 22).

22. Calvin, *Institutes*, 2:1421 §4.17.43.
23. Modern Calvinists in the Reformed tradition as it derives from England and Scotland may be surprised to see the strongly liturgical nature of Calvin's Strasbourg order of worship and the high place that the French Reformer gave to the Ten Commandments, the Apostles' Creed, and the Lord's Prayer. This highlights the derivation of much present-day Reformed worship in the English-speaking world more from seventeenth-century Puritanism than from Calvin.
24. Not that Anglicanism was un-Reformed. The Book of Common Prayer, both theologically and structurally, is a Reformed liturgy. But it failed to satisfy the English-speaking Reformed community as a whole. The so-called Anglican and Puritan schools were, in reality, somewhat ill-defined regions of opinion that could crudely be characterized as "reasonably satisfied with the forms of worship and government of the Church of England as a Reformed Church" (Anglican) and "not satisfied but earnestly desiring still further reformation" (Puritan).
25. The Directory of Public Worship says, "And because the prayer which Christ taught his disciples is not only a pattern of prayer, but itself a most comprehensive prayer, we recommend it also to be used in the prayers of the church."
26. Richard Baxter, however, in his Reformed Liturgy of 1661, retains the congregational reciting of the Lord's Prayer.
27. Francis Proctor and Walter H. Frere, *A New History of the Book of Common Prayer* (London: Macmillan, 1908), 172. Some also perceive here a Puritan tendency toward dichotomizing the outward and the inward, as though the inward alone were truly or fully spiritual. Consequently the less distraction by way of physical activity, the more spiritual our worship can be. If this is a correct diagnosis, one can see how it would have led the Presbyterians at the Savoy conference to wish to reduce the congregation to virtual silence and passivity!
28. Puritanism also did away with the observance of the church year, contrary to the Continental Reformed tradition.
29. Duncan Forrester and Douglas Murray, *Studies in the History of Worship in Scotland* (Edinburgh: T. & T. Clark, 1984), 52–62.
30. It may come as a surprise to see this listed; but consider the following from John Owen: "It is a common received notion among Christians, and it is true, that there is a peculiar communion with Christ in this ordinance, which we have in no other ordinance;

that there is a peculiar acting of faith in this ordinance which is in no other ordinance. This is the faith of the whole Church of Christ, and has been so in all ages. This is the greatest mystery of all the practicals of our Christian religion, a way of receiving Christ by eating and drinking, something peculiar that is not in prayer, that is not in the hearing of the Word, nor in any other part of divine worship whatsoever; a peculiar participation of Christ, a peculiar acting of faith towards Christ" (*Sacramental Discourses,* in *The Works of John Owen* [repr. London: Banner of Truth, 1966], 9.620). When in the nineteenth century John W. Nevin wanted to demonstrate the non-Zwinglian nature of Puritan sacramentalism, he cited this passage from Owen (in Nevin's own *The Mystical Presence*). Owen was really doing no more than unfolding the Westminster Confession's teaching that the sacraments are "effectual means of salvation" (Larger Catechism Q. 161).

31. "But the conviction and conversion of sinners is the obtaining the end of religious means. . . . If God is pleased to convince the consciences of persons, so that they can't avoid great outward manifestations, even to interrupting and breaking off those public means they were attending, I don't think this is confusion, or an unhappy interruption, any more than if a company should meet on the field to pray for rain, and should be broken off from their exercise by a plentiful shower. Would to God that all the public assemblies in the land were broken off from their public exercises with such confusion as this the next Sabbath day!" (Jonathan Edwards, *The Works of Jonathan Edwards* (gen. ed. Perry Miller), vol. 4: *The Great Awakening* (ed. C. C. Goen; New Haven, Conn.: Yale University Press, 1972), 267. Edwards slipped up badly here: his argument would require the cessation of all public worship if all members of the community were converted!

32. William D. Maxwell, *An Outline of Christian Worship* (London: Oxford University Press, 1949), 140.

33. Thomas Binney, *Are Dissenters to Have a Liturgy?* in *A Chapter on Liturgies,* by Charles Baird (London: Knight & son, 1856), 317–18.

34. An even more devastating record of nineteenth-century Reformed Nonconformist worship is found in the writings of William Hale White ("Mark Rutherford"), who, however, was speaking from a depth of disillusionment that may have somewhat jaundiced his perceptions: "Each service consisted of a hymn, reading the Bible, another hymn, a prayer, the sermon, a third hymn, and a short final prayer. The reading of the Bible was unaccompanied with any observations or explanations. . . . The first, or long prayer, as it was called, was a horrible hypocrisy, and it was a sore tax on the preacher to get through it. Anything more totally unlike the model recommended to us in the New Testament cannot well be imagined. It generally began with a confession that we were all sinners, but no individual sins were ever confessed, and then ensued a kind of dialogue with God, very much resembling the speeches in the House of Commons from the movers and seconders of addresses to the Crown at the opening of Parliament. . . . Nobody ever listened to this performance. I was a good child on the whole, but I am sure I did not; and if the chapel were now in existence, there might be traced on the flap of the pew in which we sat, many curious designs due to these dreary performances.

478

The sermon was not much better. It generally consisted of a text, which was a mere peg for a discourse, that was pretty much the same from January to December. The minister invariably began with the fall of man; propounded the scheme of redemption, and ended in depicting in the morning the blessedness of the saints and in the evening the doom of the lost. There was a tradition that in the morning there should be 'experience,' that is to say, comfort for the elect, and that the evening should be appropriated to their less fortunate brethren." See William Hale White, *The Autobiography of Mark Rutherford* (14th ed.; London: N.P., n.d.), 6–7.

35. For evidence see the two appendices in William Goode, *Charismatic Confusion* (Plas Gwyn: K&M, 2000).

36. G. H. Lang, *The Earlier History of the Tongues Movement* (Burnham-on-Sea: M. Lang, 1958), 10.

37. For some assessments of John Wimber, see *UKFocus* (December 1997); Phillip Jensen, *John Wimber—Friend or Foe?* (London: St. Matthias, 1990);

> *http://www.gospelcom.net/apologeticsindex/sva-tb01.html*
> *http://www.rapidnet.com/~jbeard/bdm/exposes/wimber*
> *http://www.banner.org.uk/tb/vnyd1.html*
> *http://www.deceptioninthechurch.com/jwimber.html*

Chapter 17
Calvin's Theology of Worship

1. This paper was written at the request of Ford Lewis Battles, distinguished Calvin scholar and translator of the *Institutes*. It was read at the 1981 Calvin Colloquium held at Calvin College in Grand Rapids, Michigan. Due to the death of Professor Battles it was never published.

2. Even if Calvin himself did not use the Latin word *liturgia*, his rite for the French church of Strasbourg was the first Western rite to be called a liturgy. In 1551 his successor, Valerand Poullain, published a Latin translation of the liturgical texts of the French church of Strasbourg: *Liturgia sacra, sue ritus ministerii in ecclesia peregrinorum profugorum propter euangelium Christi Argentinae* (Strasbourg: Stephan Mierdmann, 1551). Liturgical scholars overlook this fact, tracing the first Western use of the word to the work of Catholic theologian Georg Cassander: *Liturgica de ritu et ordine dominicae coenae quam celebrationem graeci liturgiam latini missam appellarunt* (Antwerp, 1558) and *Liturgiae sive missae sanctorum patrum-Jacobi apostoli et fratis domini-Basilii magni . . . Ioannis Chrysostomi* (ed. Johannes a Sancto Andrea; Paris: Morel, 1560). In these titles the word is applied to the rites of the Greek church. Reformed theologians have employed the word ever since. Richard Baxter entitled his Presbyterian version of the Book of Common Prayer *The Reformation of the Liturgy* or, more commonly, *The Reformed Liturgy* (1661; repr. Edinburgh: Banner of Truth, 1974). It is not really until Mabillon's celebrated *De liturgica gallicana* (1685) that the word became part of the theological vocabulary. Up until that time Western Latin authors usually spoke of the

"offices of the church." Isidore of Seville (ca. 600) entitled his book on the worship services of the church *De ecclesiasticus officiis*. Rupert of Deutz used the title *Liber de divinis officis*. Other similar works were given titles such as *De ritibus ecclesiae* or *De sacris ritibus*.

3. Much has been written on the meaning of the word *liturgy*. For a concise history of the attempt of the modern liturgical movement to define the word, see A. B. Martimore, *L'église en prière, introduction à la liturgie* (New York: Desclee, 1961). For bibliography on the subject, see John Harold Miller, "Liturgy," in *New Catholic Encyclopedia* (Washington, D.C.: Catholic University of America Press, 1967), 8:928–37. For a more developed insight, see Bernard Capelle, *Travaux liturgiques de doctrine de d'histoire* (Louvain: Centre liturgique, 1955), 1:11–118.

4. For a study of the word as used in the Septuagint and in the New Testament, see Hermann Strathmann and Rudolf Meyer's study of the *leitourgeō* word group in *Theological Dictionary of the New Testament* (ed. Gerhard Kittel; trans. Geoffrey W. Bromiley; Grand Rapids: Eerdmans, 1967), 4:215–31. Both the noun *leitourgia* and the verb *leitourgeō* translate various forms of *'ābad* and *shārath*. They refer to the service performed in fulfillment of their office by both priests and Levites (Ex. 29:30; Num. 4:24; 16:9; 1 Chron. 9:13). In Classical Greek *leitourgia* was the service rendered to the state by the wealthier citizens at their own expense (i.e., it was public work — not people's work).

5. For Calvin's understanding of the Greek word *leitourgia*, see his commentaries on Luke 1:23; Acts 13:2; and Rom. 15:27. Calvin is obviously aware of its meaning in both Classical Greek and Septuagint Greek.

6. John Calvin, *La forme des prières et chantz ecclesiastiques*, in Calvin's *Opera selecta* (ed. Petrus Barth and Gulielmus Niesel; Munich: Kaiser, 1926–62), 2:11.

7. John Calvin, *Le catechisme de l'église de Geneve*, in *Bekenntneisschriften und Kirchenordnungen der nach Gottes Work reformierten Kirche* (3d ed.; ed. Wilhelm Niesel; Zollikon: Evangelischer Verlag, 1938). The Latin edition, *Catechismus ecclesiae Genevensis*, is in Calvin's *Opera selecta* 2:59–157.

8. The French version of the *Institutes* is quoted from John Calvin, *Institution de la religion chrétienne* (5 vols.; ed. Jean-Daniel Benoît; Paris: Vrin, 1957–63). The Latin text is quoted from Calvin's *Opera selecta*, vols. 3–5. The English translation, unless otherwise noted, is taken from John Calvin, *Institutes of the Christian Religion* (2 vols.; ed. John T. McNeill; trans. Ford Lewis Battles; Philadelphia: Westminster, 1960). References to the *Institutes* in English will include the volume and page number in the Battles edition and the book/chapter/section number to aid readers of other editions. Unless otherwise noted, references to Calvin's commentaries are made simply to the passage of Scripture under discussion rather than to a particular edition or translation. The three French phases just quoted are from *Institutes* 1:348–50 §2.7.1 and the commentary on Job 4:21–24.

9. Calvin, *Institutes*, 1:118–19 §1.12.2.
10. Calvin, *Opera selecta*, 2:12.
11. Calvin, *Catechisme de l'église de Geneve*, Q. 124.
12. "Mais est un mouvement vif, procedant du saint Esprit"; Calvin, *Opera selecta*, 2:13.

13. On the attempt to define the word *liturgy* in Catholic circles, see Miller, "Liturgy." For a good working definition, see F. L. Cross and E. A. Livingstone, eds., *The Oxford Dictionary of the Christian Church* (3d ed.; Oxford: Oxford University Press, 1997), 988: "The prescribed services of the Church . . . as contrasted with private devotion . . . and as a title of the Eucharist."

14. For Calvin's use of the words *rite* and *ceremony*, see the following passages: "Non absque fastidio audire sustinent tam multiplices ritus: neque solum mirantur cur Deus veterem populum fatigaverit tanta ceremoniarum congerie" (*Institutes* §2.7.1); "dum ubique magna est in ceremoniis ostentatio, rara autem cordis, synceritas" (§2.7.1); "Porro ut pietatis exercitia sint ceremoniae, ad Christum recta nos decucant necesse est" (§4.10.29); "legitimum colendi Dei ritum" (§4.10.9); "sacrificia aliique ritus ex Lege Mosaica" (§4.14.20); "Ceremonias omnes et externos ritus omniaque pietatis exercita" (§4.19.3); "quod superstitiosis ritibus legitimum sui cultum non vult profanari" (§2.8.17); "Eius modi attestationem, ubi rite peragitur, speciem esse cultus divini" (§2.8.23). These quotations show that both words can be used to refer to both true worship and false worship, Jewish observances, Roman observances, and observances according to Scripture.

15. "Cultus autem deorum est optimus idemque castissimus atque sanctissimus plenissimusque pietatis ut eos semper pura integra incorrupta et mente et voce veneremur"; Cicero, *De natura deorum* (ed. H. Rackham; Cambridge: Harvard University Press, 1951), 2:xviii.

16. For an example of the way that *cultus* was used by the Scholastic theologians, see Thomas Aquinas, *Summa theologica* (Madrid: La editorial católica, 1962), 2:91, 93. For the Scholastic definition of *cultus*, see "Culte," in *Dictionnaire de théologie catholique* (ed. A. Vacant, E. Mangenot, and E. Amann; Paris: Letouzey & Ané, 1923-75), 3:2404-27.

17. Calvin, *Institutes*, 1:118-19 §1.12.2.

18. See *Dictionnaire de théologie catholique* 3:2404-27 and I. Wordsworth and H. I. White, eds., *Nouum testamentum latine secundum editionum sancti Hieronymi* (Oxford/ London: British and Foreign Bible Society, 1957), 387.

19. Hughes Oliphant Old, *The Patristic Roots of Reformed Worship* (Zurich: Theologischer Verlag, 1975), 146-49.

20. For the text of Lactantius, *Divinae institutiones*, see *Lucii Caecili Firmiani Lactantii opera omnia* in *Patrologiae cursus completus, series latina* (ed. J. P. Migne; Paris: Migne, 1844), vol. 6. On the significance of Lactantius to the Christian humanists, cf. Fritz Büsser, "Zwingli und Laktanz," *Zwingliana* 2 (1971): 375-99. Cf. further Franz Fessler, *Benutzung der philosophischen Schriften Ciceros durch Laktanz* (Leipzig/Berlin: Teubner, 1913); and Old, *Patristic Roots of Reformed Worship*, 175, et passim.

21. "Illis qui partim profuerunt, suam venerationem esse tribuendam" (Lactantius, *Divinae institutiones* 1.19 [Migne, *Patrologia latina* 6.214]); "qui aes, aut lapidem quae sunt terrena, veneratur" (ibid., 2.1 [6.258]); "statuam adorare . . . adorant ergo insensibillia" (ibid., 2.2 [6.261]).

22. Ibid., 2.2; 6.1 (6.258, 633).

23. Ibid., 6.25 (6.729-31).

481

24. Calvin, *Institutes*, 1:1302–3 §4.14.26; cf. note 27 below. On Calvin's objection to the *ex opere operatus*, see note 47 below.

25. Ibid., 1:376–77 §2.8.11.

26. Ibid., 1:367 §2.8.1.

27. "Le service de la Loi en sa substance a ete spirituel; mais quant à la forme, il etait en quelque sorte charnel et terrien"; John Calvin, *Evangile selon saint Jean*, in Calvin's *Commentaires de Jean Calvin sur le nouveau testament* (ed. Michel Revillaud; Geneva: Labor et fides, 1968), 2:113–14.

28. "Mais il y avait diverses additions sous la Loi, en sorte que l'esprit et la verite etaient comme couverts et enveloppes de beaucoup d'ombres et de figures; maintenant il ny a rien de cache ne d'obscur. . . . Je confesse bien que nous avons encour aujourd'hui quelques exercices externes de piete, dont notre rudesse et notre embecillite ont nec-essairement besoin; maid la measure et la sobriete en sont telles, que la verite nue du Christ n'en est point obscuricie"; ibid., 114.

29. Calvin, *Institutes*, 1:367 §2.8.1.

30. On the recovery of Biblical Hebrew by the Rhenish Christian humanists, cf. Lewis W. Spitz, *The Religious Renaissance of the German Humanists* (Cambridge: Harvard University Press, 1963), esp. 61–62; Ernst Staehelin, *Das theologische Lebenswerk Johannes Oekolampads* (Leipzig: Heinsius Nachfolger, 1939), 55–56, 189–90, 396–97; Johannes Müller, *Martin Bucers Hermeneutik* (Gütersloh: Mohn, 1965), 200–201; Friedhelm Kruger, *Bucer und Erasmus: Eine Untersuchung zum Einfluss des Erasmus auf die Theologie Martin Bucers* (Wiesbaden: Steiner, 1970), 71–72; Gottfried W. Locher, *Die zwinglische Reformation im Rahmen der europäischen Kirchengeschichte* (Göttingen/Zurich: Vandenhoeck & Ruprecht, 1979), 162; Beate Stierle, *Capito als Humanist* (Gütersloh: Mohn, 1974); and Old, *Patristic Roots of Reformed Worship*, 109, 122, 124–25, 135, 145–46.

31. Ernst Koch, *Die Theologie der Confessio Helvetica Posterior* (Neukirchen: Verlag des Erziehungsverein, 1968), 387–408; Jack Warren Cottrell, "Covenant and Baptism in the Theology of Huldreich Zwingli" (doctoral diss., Princeton Theological Seminary, 1971), which covers the theology of the covenant according to Bullinger.

32. Calvin, *Institutes*, 1:382 §2.8.16.

33. The same theme is brought powerfully to our attention in Calvin's commentary on the harmony of the last four books of Moses, where the ceremonial law is organized under the heading of the first commandment in such a way that the laws concerning worship are treated as the interpretation and elaboration of the first commandment.

34. Calvin, *Institutes*, 1:382 §2.8.16.

35. Calvin, *Catechisme de l'église de Geneve*, Q. 140.

36. Calvin, *Institutes*, 1:382–83 §2.8.16.

37. Ibid., 1:369 §2.8.2.

38. Ibid., 1:367 §2.8.1.

39. Ibid.

40. Ibid., 1:42–43 §1.2.2.

41. Ibid., 1:369 §2.8.2.

42. Ibid., 1:382 §2.8.16.

43. Ibid.

44. Ibid.

45. Ibid. The Latin text reads, "Invocatio, sit mentis nostrae, quoties urget ulla necessitas, in eius fidem atque opem receptus, tanquam ad unicum praesidium"; Calvin, *Opera selecta* 3.357. The French text reads, "Invocation, est le recours que notre ame a luy, comme a son espoir unique, quand elle est pressee de quelque necessite"; Calvin, *Institution de la religion chrétienne* (ed. Benoît), 2:149.

46. Calvin, *Opera selecta*, 2:18.

47. It is in the recognition of the epicletic nature of Christian worship that Calvin is able to get around the Scholastic debate of *ex opere operantis* and *ex opere operato* (Calvin, *Institutes*, 2:1302–3 §4.14.26). The point that Calvin makes is this: it is not from our liturgical doing, but from God's doing that worship has its effect.

48. Calvin, *Opera selecta*, 2:49.

49. Ibid., 2:47.

50. Calvin, *Institutes*, 1:382 §2.8.16.

51. Ibid. The Latin text reads as follows: "Ad recognoscendum laudisque confessione celebrandam operum magnificentiam" (Calvin, *Opera selecta*, 3:358). Battles translates this well: "To recognize, and by praises to celebrate, the greatness of his works;" see ibid., 1:382 n. 24.

52. Ibid.

53. Calvin, commentary on John 4:20–24.

54. Calvin, *Opera selecta*, 2:13.

55. Jack B. Rogers and Donald D. McKim, *The Authority and Interpretation of the Bible: An Historical Approach* (San Francisco: Harper & Row, 1979), 98–99.

56. Calvin, commentary on Ps. 22:22–24. Commenting on the text "in the midst of the congregation I will praise thee," Calvin says that the purpose of public thanksgiving is that the faithful might encourage each other. This is called an exercise because the act of thanksgiving on the part of one member of the congregation encourages others to give thanks. It is an exercise because the expression of thanksgiving builds up and increases thanksgiving. Calvin's contemporary, Ignatius of Loyola, calls his devotional guide *The Spiritual Exercises*.

57. Calvin, commentary on Col. 3:16.

58. Calvin, *Catechisme de l'église de Geneve*, Q. 306.

59. Ibid., QQ. 300–312.

60. Calvin, *Opera selecta*, 2:13.

61. Calvin, *Institutes*, 1:381–83 §2.8.16. The Revised Standard Version translates "before me" rather than "before my face." For the history of the interpretation of this phrase, see Brevard S. Childs, *The Book of Exodus: A Critical, Theological Commentary* (Old Testament Library; Philadelphia: Westminster, 1974), 402–3.

62. "Il signifie, que non seulement par confession exterieure, il veult estre advoue Dieu: mais ausse en pure verite et affection de cueur"; Calvin, *Catechisme de l'église de Geneve*, Q. 142.

63. Calvin, *Institutes*, 1:383 §2.8.16.

64. Ibid., 2:1300 §4.14.24.

65. The importance of the question of the use of images in worship is indicated by the Second Zurich Disputation's being held in 1523 to specifically discuss "images and the Mass"; Locher, *Die zwinglische Reformation*, 130–31. See also Martin Bucer, *Grund und Ursach auss gotlicher schrifft der neuwerungen an dem nachtmal des herren. . . . Feyrtagen, bildern und gesang in her gemain Christi, wann die zusammenkempt* (Strasbourg: Kopfel, 1524); modern edition in Martin Bucer, *Martin Bucers deutsche Schriften* (ed. Robert Stupperich; Gütersloh: Mohn, 1960), 1:194–278. Bucer devotes a chapter to the question of why the images have been removed from the churches. Likewise the Tetrapolitan Confession devotes an article to the subject (Bucer, *Bucers deutsche Schriften*, 3:150–60; Old, *Patristic Roots of Reformed Worship*, 33–34, 46, 59–60, 66, 69 n. 2, 85, 121, 125, 132, 187).

66. For Strasbourg, see Bucer, *Grund und Ursach* in *Bucers deutsche Schriften*, 1:271–72. For Zurich, see Oskar Farner, *Huldrych Zwingli* (Zurich: Zwingli Verlag, 1943–60), 3:424–51, 483–500.

67. On the iconoclastic strain in the Anabaptist movement, see George H. Williams, *The Radical Reformation* (Philadelphia: Westminster, 1962), 89–101, et passim.

68. Opposition to the use of images is a constant feature of the earliest Reformed confessional statements, e.g., Ten Theses of Bern (1528), Tetrapolitan Confession (1530), First Confession of Basel (1534), Lausanne Articles (1536), First Helvetic Confession (1536). For an English translation of these documents, see Arthur C. Cochrane, *Reformed Confessions of the Sixteenth Century* (Philadelphia: Westminster, 1966).

69. Calvin, *Institutes*, 1:383 §2.8.17.

70. Calvin, commentary on Ex. 32:4.

71. Calvin, *Institutes*, 1:100 n. 2 §1.11.1.

72. Ibid., 1:100–101 §1.11.2.

73. Ibid., 1:383 §2.8.17.

74. This is particularly clear in the three writings of Oecolampadius against the Anabaptists: (1) *Ein gesprech ettlicher predicanten zu Basel, gehalten met etlichen bekennern des widertouffs* (Basel, 1525); (2) *Antwort auff Balthasar Huomeiers buchlein wider die der Predicanten gesprach zuo Basel, von dem Kindertauff* (Basel, 1527); and (3) *Underrichtung von dem Widertauff, von der Oberkeit und von dem Eyd*, auff Carlins N. Widertauffers Artickel (Basel, 1527).

75. Calvin, *Institutes* §4.

76. Old, *Patristic Roots of Reformed Worship*, 223–24.

77. Calvin, *Institutes*, 1:383 §2.8.17.

78. "Le service de Dieu git en esprit, parce que ce nest rien d'autre qu'une foi interieure de coeur, qui engendre l'invocation; et puis une puret de conscience et un renouncement de nous-memes, afin qu etant deies à la obeissance de Dieu"; Calvin, *Evangile selon sainte Jean*, 113.

79. Lactantius, *Divinae institutiones* 1.8, 15, 18.

80. Quoted from John Calvin, *The Acts of the Apostles* (trans. John W. Fraser; Calvin's New Testament Commentaries 7; Grand Rapids: Eerdmans, 1973), 2:121–22.

81. Calvin, *Institutes*, 1:112 §1.11.12. See further, Marta Grau, *Calvins Stellung zur Kunst* (Würzburg: F. Staudenraus, 1917); Karl A. Plank, "Of Unity and Distinction: An Exploration of the Theology of John Calvin with Respect to the Christian Stance toward Art," *Calvin Theological Journal* 13 (1978): 16–37; Charles Garside, *The Origins of Calvin's Theology of Music, 1536–1543* (Philadelphia: American Philosophical Society, 1979). Also helpful is Charles Garside, *Zwingli and the Arts* (New Haven: Yale University Press, 1966).

82. Calvin, commentary on Acts 17:29 (trans. Fraser, 2:122).

83. Calvin, *Institutes*, 1:388 §2.8.22. Cf. Calvin, *Catechisme de l'église de Geneve*, QQ. 162–63.

84. Calvin, *Catechisme de l'église de Geneve*, QQ. 265, 267.

85. Calvin, *Institutes*, 1:388 §2.8.22.

86. Calvin, commentary on Num. 30:1.

87. Calvin, commentary on Ex. 20:7.

88. Calvin, *Institutes*, 1:388 §2.8.22.

89. Calvin, *Opera selecta*, 2:13.

90. Calvin, *Institutes*, 1:390 §2.8.24.

91. Calvin, commentary on Col. 3:17.

92. Calvin, *Catechisme de l'église de Geneve*, QQ. 268–72.

93. Likewise *Les ordonnances ecclesiastiques* begin with "au nom de dieu"; Niesel, *Bekenntnisschriften und Kirchenordnungen*, 43.

94. For the significance of the Davidic invocation and the Aaronic benediction in the 1542 Genevan Psalter, cf. Old, *Patristic Roots of Reformed Worship*, 219–20, 330–31.

95. Farner, *Zwingli*, 3:237–52; Locher, *Die zwinglische Reformation*, 96–98.

96. For the ideas of Oecolampadius on the reform of the church calendar, see my "The Homiletics of John Oecolampadius and the Sermons of the Greek Fathers," in *Communio Sanctorum: Mélanges Offerts à Jean-Jacques von Allmen* (by Boris Bobrinskoy et al.; Geneva: Labor et fides, 1982), 239–50.

97. Bucer, *Grund und Ursach* in *Bucers deutsche Schriften*, 1:262–68.

98. The two documents that contain Capito's answer are found in Manfred Krebs and Hans Georg Rott, eds., *Quellen zur Geschichte der Taufer*, vol. 7: *Elsass*, part 1: *Stadt Strassburg, 1522–1532* (Gütersloh: Mohn, 1959), 363–93.

99. See Calvin's commentaries on Matt. 28:1; John 20:1; and Acts 20:5–7.

100. Calvin, *Institutes*, 1:395 §2.8.28.

101. Calvin, commentary on Matt. 12:1–8.

102. Calvin, commentary on Luke 4:16.

103. Calvin, *Institutes*, 1:396 §2.8.30.

104. Ibid., 1:395 §2.8.28.

105. Ibid., 1:399–401 §2.8.34.

106. Calvin, commentary on Acts 20:7.

107. Calvin, commentary on Luke 4:16.

108. Calvin, *Institutes*, 1:399 §2.8.33.

109. Ibid., 1:395 §2.8.28.

110. Ibid., 1:398 §2.8.32.

111. Calvin, commentary on Acts 2:42.

112. Calvin, *Institutes*, 1:399 §2.8.33. It was, to be sure, the *first* day of the week that the Apostle Paul set aside for collecting alms (1 Cor. 16:2). Calvin, nevertheless, says, "Siquidem in ecclesiis ab eo institutes sabbathum in hunc usum retinebatur. Illum enim diem praescribit Corinthiis, quo symbola ad sublevandos Hierosolymitanos fratres colligatur"; Calvin, *Opera selecta*, 3:375. Here Calvin clearly calls the first day of the week the Sabbath. This may be a slip on his part, but it may also indicate a certain ambiguity in his thought.

113. Cf. Brevard S. Childs, *Memory and Tradition in Israel* (London: SCM, 1962); and Johannes Behm, *anamnēsis* in *Theological Dictionary of the New Testament* (ed. Gerhard Kittel; trans. Geoffrey W. Bromiley; Grand Rapids: Eerdmans, 1964), 1:348–49.

Chapter 18

Challenges and Opportunities for Ministry Today

1. John Seabrook, *Nobrow: The Culture of Marketing, the Marketing of Culture* (New York: Knopf, 2000).

2. David Lyle Jeffrey, quoted in Richelle Wiseman, "Riding the Tidal Wave," *Faith Today* (Sept./Oct. 1999): 23 (emphasis added).

3. Stanley Hauerwas, "Preaching as though We Had Enemies," *First Things* 53 (May 1995): 46.

4. C. Peter Wagner, "Another New Wineskin," *Next* 5.1 (Jan.–March 1999): 3.

5. Walter Lippmann, quoted in Neal Gabler, *Life the Movie: How Entertainment Conquered Reality* (New York: Knopf, 1998), 78.

6. Steiner Kavale, "Themes and Definitions," in *The Truth about the Truth*, ed. Walter Truest Anderson (New York: G. P. Putnam's Sons, 1995), 25.

7. Hauerwas, "Preaching as though We Had Enemies," 49.

CONTRIBUTORS

Eric J. Alexander (M.A., B.D., University of Glasgow) served for fifteen years as a minister in Ayrshire and for twenty years as senior minister of St. George's-Tron Parish Church, Glasgow, from which he retired in 1998. Since then he has taught at seminaries in Europe and North America, including Regent College Vancouver, The Master's Seminary, Beeson Divinity School, and Westminster Theological Seminary. In addition, he has spoken at the Philadelphia Conference on Reformation Theology for the past twenty years.

D. Marion Clark (M.Div., Gordon-Conwell Theological Seminary) is the sixth pastor of Faith Presbyterian Church in Gainesville, Florida. He previously served as the executive minister of Tenth Presbyterian Church in Philadelphia for seven years.

Edmund P. Clowney (Th.B., Westminster Theological Seminary; S.T.M., Yale Divinity School; D.D., Wheaton College) was president of Westminster Theological Seminary for thirty years, where he was also professor of practical theology. He is a recognized authority on ecclesiology, worship, and biblical theology and is author of several popular books. He has served

487

as theologian in residence and minister of teaching at Trinity Presbyterian Church in Charlottesville, Virginia, and at Christ the King in Houston, Texas.

Mark E. Dever (M.Div., Gordon-Conwell Theological Seminary; Th.D., Southern Baptist Theological Seminary; Ph.D., Cambridge University, as J. B. Lightfoot scholar) is senior pastor of Capitol Hill Baptist Church in Washington, D.C., and has taught for the faculty of divinity at Cambridge University. He is also the senior fellow for the Center for Church Reform in Washington and speaks internationally at pastors' conferences and campus ministries. He is author of *Nine Marks of a Healthy Church*.

J. Ligon Duncan III (M.Div., M.A., Covenant Theological Seminary; Ph.D., University of Edinburgh) is the senior minister of the historic First Presbyterian Church in Jackson, Mississippi, and was formerly the John R. Richardson professor of systematic theology at Reformed Theological Seminary. He serves on the Council on Biblical Manhood and Womanhood and the Alliance of Confessing Evangelicals.

William Edgar (M.Div., Westminster Theological Seminary; D.Th., University of Geneva) is professor of apologetics at Westminster Theological Seminary. He previously served as a professor of the Faculté Libre de Théologie Réformée in Aix-en-Provence, France. He is author of *The Face of Truth: Lifting the Veil* and *Reasons of the Heart: Recovering Christian Persuasion*, as well as articles on cultural apologetics, the music of Brahms, and African-American aesthetics. He is also a part-time professional jazz pianist.

W. Robert Godfrey (M.A., Ph.D., Stanford University; M.Div., Gordon-Conwell Theological Seminary) is president of Westminster Theological Seminary in California, where he is also professor of church history. Godfrey is author of *Reformation Sketches: Insights into Luther, Calvin, and the Confessions* and contributor to *John Calvin: His Influence on the Western World*, *Reformed Theology in America*, and *Scripture and Truth*. He is a frequent speaker at Christian conferences.

Michael S. Horton (M.A.R., Westminster Theological Seminary in California; Ph.D., Wycliff Hall, Oxford University, and the University of Coventry) is associate professor of apologetics and historical theology at Westminster Seminary in California, president of the Alliance of Confessing Evangelicals, and editor of *Modern Reformation*. He also cohosts the "White Horse Inn," a nationally syndicated radio talk show. Among his many published works are *Covenant and Eschatology* and *A Better Way*.

Terry L. Johnson (M.Div., Gordon-Conwell Theological Seminary, as a Byington scholar for David F. Wells; diploma in higher education under J. I. Packer, Trinity College in Bristol, England) is senior pastor of the historic Independent Presbyterian Church in Savannah, Georgia. A leader in the study of worship in Reformed circles, Johnson is author of the *Trinity Psalter, When Grace Comes Home, Leading in Worship,* and *The Family Worship Book*.

Paul S. Jones (M.M., D.M., Indiana University) is organist and music director at Tenth Presbyterian Church in Philadelphia, where he conducts the church choir and the chamber players and oversees the music program. He served on the faculty of Philadelphia Biblical University for eight years. He also is director of music and worship for the Alliance of Confessing Evangelicals.

R. Albert Mohler Jr. (M.Div., Ph.D., Southern Seminary) is president of the Southern Baptist Theological Seminary and has distinguished himself by his role in the restructuring of America's largest Protestant denomination. His leadership in the evangelical world has been recognized by *Time* magazine, *Christianity Today,* and other leading publications. He is a frequent guest on nationally televised news programs, including CNN's *Larry King Live,* and is quoted frequently in *The New York Times, The Washington Post,* and other major newspapers. His commentaries appear regularly in Religion News Service and *World* magazine.

Nick R. Needham (B.D., Ph.D., University of Edinburgh) is a Baptist minister in Scotland and teaches at the Highland Theological College. He is author of two books on Scottish church history and, more recently, *2,000 Years of Christ's Power,* part 1: *The Age of the Early Church Fathers,* and part 2: *The Middle Ages*—the first two of a projected five-volume series covering the history of the Christian church—as well as *The Triumph of Grace.* Needham has also taught in Africa.

Hughes Oliphant Old (B.D., Princeton Theological Seminary; D.theol., Université de Neuchâtel) is a member of the Center for Theological Inquiry in Princeton, New Jersey, and a former pastor. He is the author of a magisterial multivolume history of preaching, *The Reading and Preaching of the Scriptures in the Worship of the Christian Church*, and of *Worship: Reformed according to Scripture, The Shaping of the Reformed Baptismal Rite in the Sixteenth Century, Themes and Variations for a Christian Doxology*, and *Leading in Prayer*.

Richard D. Phillips (M.Div., Westminster Theological Seminary) is the senior minister of First Presbyterian Church of Coral Springs in Margate, Florida. Phillips is director of the Philadelphia Conference on Reformation Theology and executive director of Reformation Societies International. His numerous books include *Turning Back the Darkness: The Biblical Pattern of Reformation* and *Faith Victorious*.

Philip Graham Ryken (M.Div., Westminster Theological Seminary; D.Phil., University of Oxford) is senior minister of Tenth Presbyterian Church in Philadelphia. He serves on the council of the Alliance of Confessing Evangelicals. His published work includes *The Heart of the Cross* (with James Montgomery Boice), *Jeremiah and Lamentations*, *The Doctrines of Grace* (with Boice), *The Message of Salvation*, and *My Father's World*.

R. C. Sproul (B.D., Pittsburgh Theological Seminary; Drs., Free University of Amsterdam) is founder and chairman of Ligonier Ministries in Orlando, Florida. Sproul is also the senior minister of preaching at Saint Andrew's Chapel in Sanford, Florida. He can be heard around the country on his daily radio program, *Renewing Your Mind*, and has authored more than fifty books, including *Saved from What?* and *When Worlds Collide*.

Derek W. H. Thomas (M.Div., Reformed Theological Seminary; Ph.D., University of Wales, Lampeter) is the John E. Richards professor of practical and systematic theology at Reformed Theological Seminary in Jackson, Mississippi. He teaches both systematic and pastoral theology and is minister of teaching at First Presbyterian Church in Jackson. Originally from Wales, Thomas pastored for eighteen years in Belfast, Ireland. He has written numerous books and commentaries and served as editor of *Evangelical Presbyterian*.

Donald S. Whitney (M.Div., Southwestern Baptist Theological Seminary; D.Min., Trinity Evangelical Divinity School) is associate professor of spiritual formation at Midwestern Baptist Theological Seminary in Kansas City, Missouri. He previously was pastor of Glenfield Baptist Church in Glen Ellyn, Illinois, for almost fifteen years. He is the author of *Spiritual Disciplines for the Christian Life, How Can I Be Sure I'm a Christian? Spiritual Disciplines within the Church*, and *Ten Questions to Diagnose Your Spiritual Health*.

Biographical Summary for James Montgomery Boice

Born

Pittsburgh, Pennsylvania, July 7, 1938

Died

Philadelphia, Pennsylvania, June 15, 2000

Family

Wife	Linda Ann McNamara Boice, born January 24, 1937
Children	Elizabeth Anne Dawson, born August 5, 1964
	Heather Louise, born March 7, 1970
	Jennifer Sue, born February 27, 1972

Education

1956	Diploma, The Stony Brook School
1960	A.B., Harvard University
1963	B.D., Princeton Theological Seminary

| 1966 | D.Theol., University of Basel, Switzerland |
| 1982 | D.D., The Theological Seminary of the Reformed Episcopal Church |

Career

1966–68	Assistant Editor, *Christianity Today*
1968–00	Senior Minister, Tenth Presbyterian Church, Philadelphia, Pennsylvania
1969–00	Speaker, The Bible Study Hour
1974–00	Chairman, The Philadelphia Conference on Reformed Theology
1977–88	Chairman, The International Council on Biblical Inerrancy
1985–89	Editor, *Eternity* magazine
1985–00	President, Evangelical Ministries, Inc., Philadelphia (until 1997), then the Alliance of Confessing Evangelicals

Service

1970–82	Board of Trustees, The Stony Brook School
1978–00	Board of Trustees, The Huguenot Fellowship
1985–00	Board of Trustees, Bible Study Fellowship

Books

1970	*Witness and Revelation in the Gospel of John* (Zondervan)
1971	*Philippians: An Expositional Commentary* (Zondervan)
1972	*The Sermon on the Mount* (Zondervan)
1973	*How to Live the Christian Life* (Moody; originally, *How to Live It Up*, Zondervan)
1974	*Ordinary Men Called by God* (Victor; originally, *How God Can Use Nobodies*)
1974	*The Last and Future World* (Zondervan)
1975–79	*The Gospel of John: An Expositional Commentary* (5 vols., Zondervan; issued in 1 vol., 1985; 5 vols., Baker 1999)
1976	*Galatians* in the Expositor's Bible Commentary (Zondervan)
1977	*Can You Run Away from God?* (Victor)
1977	*Does Inerrancy Matter?* (Tyndale)
1977	*Our Sovereign God*, editor (Baker)

494

1978	*The Foundation of Biblical Authority*, editor (Zondervan)
1979	*The Epistles of John: An Expositional Commentary* (Zondervan)
1979	*Making God's Word Plain*, editor (Tenth Presbyterian Church)
1980	*Our Savior God: Studies on Man, Christ and the Atonement*, editor (Baker)
1982–87	*Genesis: An Expositional Commentary* (3 vols., Zondervan)
1983	*The Parables of Jesus* (Moody)
1983	*The Christ of Christmas* (Moody)
1983–86	*The Minor Prophets: An Expositional Commentary* (2 vols., Zondervan)
1984	*Standing on the Rock* (Tyndale); reissued 1994 (Baker)
1985	*The Christ of the Open Tomb* (Moody)
1986	*Foundations of the Christian Faith* (4 vols. in 1, InterVarsity Press; original vols. issued, 1978–81)
1986	*Christ's Call to Discipleship* (Moody)
1988	*Transforming Our World: A Call to Action*, editor (Multnomah)
1988, 98	*Ephesians: An Expositional Commentary* (Baker)
1989	*Daniel: An Expositional Commentary* (Zondervan)
1989	*Joshua: We Will Serve the Lord* (Revell)
1990	*Nehemiah: Learning to Lead* (Revell)
1992–94	*Romans* (4 vols., Baker)
1992	*The King Has Come* (Christian Focus Publications)
1993	*Amazing Grace* (Tyndale)
1993	*Mind Renewal in a Mindless Age* (Baker)
1994–98	*Psalms* (3 vols., Baker)
1994	*Sure I Believe, So What!* (Christian Focus Publications)
1995	*Hearing God When You Hurt* (Baker)
1996	*Two Cities, Two Loves* (InterVarsity)
1996	*Here We Stand: A Call from Confessing Evangelicals*, editor with Benjamin E. Sasse (Baker)
1997	*Living by the Book* (Baker)
1997	*Acts: An Expositional Commentary* (Baker)
1999	*The Heart of the Cross*, with Philip Graham Ryken (Crossway)
1999	*What Makes a Church Evangelical?*
2000	*Hymns for a Modern Reformation*, with Paul S. Jones

2001   *Matthew: An Expositional Commentary* (2 vols., Baker)

2001   *Whatever Happened to the Gospel of Grace?* (Crossway)

2002   *The Doctrines of Grace*, with Philip Graham Ryken (Crossway)

2002   *Jesus on Trial*, with Philip Graham Ryken (Crossway)

Chapters

1985   "The Future of Reformed Theology" in David F. Wells, editor, *Reformed Theology in America: A History of Its Modern Development* (Eerdmans)

1986   "The Preacher and Scholarship" in Samuel T. Logan, editor, *The Preacher and Preaching: Reviving the Art in the Twentieth Century* (Presbyterian and Reformed)

1992   "A Better Way: The Power of Word and Spirit" in Michael Scott Horton, editor, *Power Religion: The Selling Out of the Evangelical Church?* (Moody)

1994   "The Sovereignty of God" in John D. Carson and David W. Hall, editors, *To Glorify and Enjoy God: A Commemoration of the 350th Anniversary of the Westminster Assembly* (Banner of Truth Trust)

Index of Scripture

497

INDEX OF
SUBJECTS AND NAMES